Pharmaceutical Public Policy

Pharmaceutical Public Policy

Thomas R. Fulda, MA

Alan Lyles, ScD, MPH, RPh

Henry A. Rosenberg Professor of Government, Business, and Nonprofit Partnerships, University of Baltimore
Fellow, National Academy of Public Administration
Docent, University of Helsinki

Albert I. Wertheimer, PhD, MBA

Professor of Pharmaceutical Economics, Department of Pharmacy Practice
Temple University School of Pharmacy, Philadelphia, PA

CRC Press
Taylor & Francis Group
Boca Raton London New York

CRC Press is an imprint of the
Taylor & Francis Group, an **informa** business
A PRODUCTIVITY PRESS BOOK

CRC Press
Taylor & Francis Group
6000 Broken Sound Parkway NW, Suite 300
Boca Raton, FL 33487-2742

Printed at CPI on sustainably sourced paper
Version Date: 20160229

International Standard Book Number-13: 978-1-4987-4850-6 (Hardback)

Visit the Taylor & Francis Web site at
http://www.taylorandfrancis.com

and the CRC Press Web site at
http://www.crcpress.com

Contents

Foreword

As the most common health-care intervention, prescription drug use shares the most important characteristics of the health-care system in the United States. When everything works well, it makes possible a breathtakingly successful application of science to the prevention and cure of human suffering. But everything often does not work well, and medication use—like the rest of health care—also suffers from shortcomings that cause avoidable harms and expenditures that are hard to sustain. Pharmaceutical policy (actually, myriad policies in the public, private, individual, and societal dimensions) represents our collective attempts to apply the best available knowledge in order to maximize all the good that medications can do, while limiting their inherent risks and making their costs affordable to patients and health-care systems.

This is no easy task. On the positive side, drugs for managing blood pressure, high cholesterol, atrial fibrillation, and osteoporosis have led to dramatic reductions in the rates of cardiovascular disease and hip fracture, to cite only a few examples. Breakthroughs in other fields, including oncology and infectious diseases, have likewise created important new clinical opportunities with substantial public health implications. In approving new products, a constant tension exists between getting new drugs to patients quickly and knowing enough to ensure that they work well and are "safe enough." Policies for approval and early access are evolving rapidly, and the sanctity of the conventional randomized controlled trial as the only gold standard for efficacy is being questioned as never before.

Any molecule that influences physiological processes profoundly enough to cure or prevent illness can also produce unexpected effects that cause harm. The Vioxx debacle, in which a very widely used drug remained on the market for five years without widespread recognition that it nearly doubled the risk of myocardial infarction or stroke, has spurred renewed attention to new methodological approaches and regulatory strategies to optimize the nation's approach to getting this benefit–risk balance right.

Just as the thalidomide disaster of the early 1960s led to important policy advances (most notably including giving the Food and Drug Administration the right to require that a prescription drug be shown to work before it can be marketed), so has the Vioxx experience led to new insights into the possibilities of harnessing the "big data" of typical health-care utilization to yield earlier evidence of drug risks. Growing interest in comparative effectiveness is likely to generate similar progress in using such observational data to understand which medications have the best effectiveness–safety relationships and the best economic value.

The economics of medication use have likewise begun to undergo a sea change of their own. The expiration of patents for many so-called blockbuster drugs has led to their replacement by more affordable generics. This has helped contain the cost of managing most primary care conditions, although extremely high costs have now shifted to medications—including the biologicals—for less common conditions. This has in turn led to renewed debate on why many new medications cost so much, and consideration of where the breakthrough discoveries that make pharmaceutical innovation possible are most likely to come from—publicly funded research in academic settings or the companies that bring such discoveries to market and hold the patents on the resulting products.

With an ever-growing armamentarium of powerful and complex therapies available to prescribers, concern has grown about how well or poorly such clinical decisions are made. A robust debate has begun over what influences prescribers, leading to renewed interest in how best to get decision makers the most current, evidence-based, and unbiased information to guide their drug choices. Many health-care systems have initiated programs of "academic detailing," in which prescribers are educated about the properties of commonly used medications by specially trained pharmacists or nurses who visit with them in their offices to "market" the evidence, much as drug company sales representatives market their employers' products. Such approaches hold the promise of more accurate clinical decision making and more contained drug expenditures.

Each of these areas, and many others, are rife with interesting policy choices at a number of levels in the health-care system. As biomedical science progresses at an accelerating rate, more and more medications are becoming available with impressive power, potential risks, and often astonishing prices. Pharmaceutical policy will play a growing role in seeking to balance the needs and interests of myriad participants in the health-care system to help maximize those benefits, control the risks, and keep costs manageable for patients and the organizations that provide their care.

Jerry Avorn, MD
Professor of Medicine, Harvard Medical School
Chief, Division of Pharmacoepidemiology and Pharmacoeconomics
Brigham and Women's Hospital
Boston, Massachusetts

Preface

In 2013, the United States spent $(USD)2.9 trillion on health care. As a percentage of gross domestic product (GDP), these expenditures have increased from 7.0% of GDP in 1970 to 17.4% of GDP in 2013.[*] Expenditures are still increasing, but for the last five years the rate of increase has slowed down. Prescription drugs accounted for 11% of total health-care expenditures. Interest in prescription drugs has remained high because expenditures for drugs obtained on an outpatient basis have risen faster than expenditures for hospitals and physician services and because until relatively recently much of the expenditures for drugs were paid for out of pocket. In 1970, 82% of prescription drugs were paid for out of pocket, but by 2013, out-of-pocket expenditures for prescription drugs had dropped to 16.9%. As out-of-pocket spending has decreased the role of two government programs, Medicare and Medicaid have increased. As of 2013, Medicare reimbursed for approximately 27.5% of outpatient drug expenditures and Medicaid for 7.8% of such expenditures, with private health insurance responsible for 43% of prescription drug expenditures.[†]

Policy can be defined "as a plan or course of action…intended to influence action."[‡] Policies can be developed, implemented, and used by individuals, professional organizations, and corporate bodies such as pharmaceutical companies and health insurance companies, as well as by governments. Policies usually result from the identification of problems that individuals or groups identify as needing solutions. In this book, we pay special attention to policies developed by the federal and state governments because the government has become an increasingly important factor in providing and paying for health care. Government policies are usually set forth as laws and regulations. Three policy issues have been of concern in health care and with regard to prescription drugs for quite a while: access to care, quality of care, and the cost of care.

If the focus were only on what governments do, examining health policy would be less complex than it is. Each of the stakeholders in the health-care arena has goals and objectives that sometimes align among stakeholders but frequently conflict. Governments want to ensure that drugs that come to market are safe and effective and are available at reasonable costs. Pharmaceutical manufacturers seek to develop drugs that will ameliorate or cure important diseases and bring in enough profit to satisfy stockholders and to fund research and development. Individuals want good health. Providers of care want safe and effective drugs to treat the diseases and conditions

---

* National Center for Health Statistics. Health, United States, 2014. Table 102 Gross domestic product, national health expenditures, per capita amounts, percent distribution, and average annual percent change: United States, selected years 1960–2013. http://www.cdc.gov/nchs/data/hus/hus14.pdf.

† Center for Medicare and Medicaid Services. Office of the Actuary, National Health Statistics Group. Table 16 Retail Prescription Drugs Expenditures; Levels, Percent Change, and Percent Distribution, by Source of Funds: Selected Calendar Years 1960–2013. http://www.cms.gov/Research-Statistics-Data-and-Systems/Statistics-Trends-and-Reports/NationalHealthExpendData/NationalHealthAccountsHistorical.html.

‡ *Webster's New College Dictionary*, 3rd edn. 2008. Houghton Mifflin Harcourt, Boston, MA.

their patients bring to them, and they want adequate reimbursement for their services and professional respect. Employers, their insurance companies, and pharmaceutical benefit managers want to control the cost of care to limit insurance rate increases. Patients want access to safe and effective drugs that will cure or ameliorate the diseases or conditions that afflict them, and they want them at a reasonable cost.

Finally, what makes pharmaceutical public policy challenging is the complex political process that attempts to satisfy the frequently competing goals and objectives of all the players in a way that addresses the policy question at issue and leaves enough participants somewhat satisfied that progress has been made in solving the policy problem brought forward for resolution.

Thomas R. Fulda

Editors

Thomas R. Fulda was a federal civil servant for 30 years and held positions at the Social Security Administration and the Health Care Financing Administration. He conducted research on prescription drug pricing, participated in the development and implementation of the Federal Maximum Allowable Cost Program, participated in the planning for the implementation of the prescription drug provisions of the Medicare Catastrophic Coverage Act of 1988, and was responsible for the implementation of the Medicaid Drug Utilization Review provisions of the Omnibus Budget Reconciliation Act of 1990. He also worked at the U.S. Pharmacopeial Convention (Director of Drug Utilization Review), where he managed an expert scientific panel developing drug utilization review criteria. Fulda earned a Health Care Financing Administration Administrator's Citation, received a Secretary's Award for Exceptional Achievement for his work, and, in 1995, was named an honorary pharmacist by the American Pharmaceutical Association.

Alan Lyles is the Henry A. Rosenberg Professor of government, business, and nonprofit partnerships at the University of Baltimore's College of Public Affairs, Baltimore, Maryland, and a fellow in the National Academy of Public Administration, Washington, DC. His professional interests focus on access to pharmaceuticals (policy, benefits, and evidence) and the role(s) of public–private arrangements. Professor Lyles serves on the editorial advisory panel of the *International Pharmacy Journal* and on the editorial advisory board of the *Generics and Biosimilar Initiative Journal's International*. In 2006, he was visiting chair of pharmacoeconomics, and in 2007 and 2011 he was a Fulbright specialist at the University of Helsinki. He was a student of Shifu Ryan Velivlis and is a life member of the United States Kuo Shu Federation.

Albert I. Wertheimer has had extensive active involvement in the pharmaceutical field for more than 40 years and has held numerous leadership positions. He is author or coauthor of 35 books and more than 400 journal articles. Dr. Wertheimer has guided more than 100 PhD and MS students. He has had experience in the private sector at a pharmaceutical company and with a pharmaceutical benefit management (PBM) firm, in addition to his experience in the academic world. He is a popular lecturer and consultant, having worked in nearly 75 countries.

Contributors

Tony Amos
Health Economics and Outcomes Research
The Janssen Pharmaceutical Companies of Johnson & Johnson
Titusville, New Jersey

Jill Augustine
College of Pharmacy
The University of Arizona
Tucson, Arizona

Brian K. Bruen
Department of Health Policy
George Washington University
Washington, DC

Perry Cohen
The Pharmacy Group
Glastonbury, Connecticut

Curtis W. Copeland
Congressional Research Service
Fairfax, Virginia

Qian Ding
College of Pharmacy
Ferris State University
Big Rapids, Michigan

Gregory Dolin
Center for Medicine and Law
University of Baltimore
Baltimore, Maryland

Tewodros Eguale
Massachusetts College of Pharmacy and Health Sciences
Boston, Massachusetts

Linda Elam
Department of Health Care Finance
Government of the District of Columbia
Washington, DC

Bill G. Felkey
Harrison School of Pharmacy
Auburn University
Auburn, Alabama

Thomas R. Fulda (Retired)
Health Care Financing Administration
Wilmington, North Carolina

Louis P. Garrison, Jr.
Department of Pharmacy
University of Washington
Seattle, Washington

Anna Gu
School of Pharmacy
St. Johns University
Queens, New York

Jianfei J. Guo
Pharmacy Practice and Administrative Science
James L. Winkle College of Pharmacy
Cincinnati, Ohio

W. Mike Heath
Heath Health Care Consulting, Inc.
Martinez, Georgia

Valerie Heitshusen
Analyst on Congress and the Legislative Process
Congressional Research Service
Washington, DC

Jack Hoadley
Health Policy Institute
Georgetown University
Washington, DC

Brian J. Isetts
College of Pharmacy
University of Minnesota
Minneapolis, Minnesota

Meghan M. Kelly
College of Pharmacy
University of Minnesota
Minneapolis, Minnesota

Christina M.L. Kelton
Department of Finance
and
The James L. Winkle College of Pharmacy
and
Carl H. Lindner College of Business
University of Cincinnati
Cincinnati, Ohio

Duane M. Kirking
College of Pharmacy
and
School of Public Health
University of Michigan
Ann Arbor, Michigan

Jillian Clare Kohler
Munk School of Global Affairs
and
Dalla Lana School of Public Health
University of Toronto
Toronto, Ontario, Canada

David H. Kreling
School of Pharmacy
University of Wisconsin–Madison
Madison, Wisconsin

Earle "Buddy" Lingle
School of Pharmacy
High Point University
High Point, North Carolina

Earlene Lipowski
Department of Pharmaceutical Outcomes and Policy
University of Florida
Gainesville, Florida

Ruth Lopert
Center for Pharmaceutical Management
Management Sciences for Health
Arlington, Virginia
and
Department of Health Policy
George Washington University
Washington, DC

Eva Lydick (Retired)
Laguna Woods, California

Alan Lyles
College of Public Affairs
University of Baltimore
Baltimore, Maryland

Louis A. Morris
LAMA Associates
Dix Hills, New York

David Nau
Pharmacy Quality Solutions, Inc.
Lexington, Kentucky

Rajesh Nayak
Department of Pharmacy Administration and Allied Health Sciences
St. Johns University
Queens, New York

Dhamil Patel
Pharbest Pharmaceuticals
Jamaica, New York

Robert E. Pittman (Retired)
U.S. Public Health Service
Rockville, Maryland

Laura T. Pizzi
Jefferson School of Pharmacy
Thomas Jefferson University
Philadelphia, Pennsylvania

Marsha Raebel
Institute for Health Research
Kaiser Permanente
Denver, Colorado

Gordon Schiff
Center for Patient Safety Research and Practice
Brigham and Women's Hospital
Boston, Massachusetts

Julie A. Schmittdiel
Division of Research
Kaiser Permanente
Oakland, California

Jon C. Schommer
College of Pharmacy
University of Minnesota
Minneapolis, Minnesota

Steven H. Sheingold
Division of Health Financing Policy
U.S. Department of Health and Human Services
Washington, DC

John Spain
Medical Service Corps
U.S. Army
Columbia, Maryland

Vaiyapuri Subramaniam
Pharmacy Benefits Management Services
U.S. Department of Veterans Affairs
Silver Spring, Maryland

Michael A. Valentino
Pharmacy Benefits Management Services
U.S. Department of Veterans Affairs
Washington, DC

Albert I. Wertheimer
School of Pharmacy
Temple University
Philadelphia, Pennsylvania

Mary Claire Wohletz
Director of Medicaid Clinical Programs
Prime Therapeutics
Minneapolis, Minnesota

William N. Yates
Medical Affairs
Columbia, South Carolina

Pierre L. Yong
Division of Hospitals and Medication Measurement
Centers for Medicare & Medicaid Services
Baltimore, Maryland

Chapter 1

Policy Process

Alan Lyles

Contents

Introduction

The policy process is not a mechanical sequence of steps that start with a goal and end with a rational, planned optimal outcome. Instead, it depends on formal processes, institutional legacies, and idiosyncrasies of national history and identity.

Compared to other high-income nations, the United States has a greater reliance on the medical marketplace, individualism, and limited federal government for pharmaceutical policy concerns. The institutional legacies of U.S. federalism, laws, and regulations put boundaries on pharmaceutical public policy, more often reacting to crises rather than being proactive to prevent them. Basic policy processes reflect strong stakeholder interests that influence (1) what are considered legitimate issues for public policy and (2) political support for possible policy actions. These conditions plus the numerous autonomous and semiautonomous sources of power make pharmaceutical public policy difficult to achieve without broad support and compromise.

This chapter introduces (1) U.S. federalism relevant to public policy, pharmaceutical market, (2) market failures as opportunities for public policy, (3) major stakeholders in the policy process, and (4) examples of unexpected or unforeseen outcome developments with major policy initiatives.

Background

Policy and Government

Pharmaceutical public policy is guided by responses to four fundamental questions:

1. Are health care and access to medical products and services rights or privileges?
2. Are costs for pharmaceuticals and health-care investments or expenses?
3. How should health-care responsibilities be divided among individuals and public, and private sectors?
4. When government action is required, should it be by the federal or by the state and local governments?

Of course, the answers to these questions are value judgments, not the outputs of calculations. They are based on moral and political philosophies concerning appropriate roles for individuals, private sector, and public authorities.

In the U.S. *de facto* health system, separation of powers between branches of the federal government assures incremental rather than revolutionary policy changes and, usually, a substantial lag between issue identification and policy action(s). Adding to the complexity, the U.S. Constitution reserves authority over health for the states. National initiatives that are called health-care reform concern not a centralized health policy but the limited federal role for financing and use of other authorities as they apply to health.

Authority structures in the U.S. health care are fragmented, with numerous relatively autonomous sources of power that pose enduring resistance to change. Multiple payment systems, consisting of public and private payers with a dizzying menu of alternative payment mechanisms, make a large-scale policy and change improbable without broad support and compromise. Many stakeholders have an interest in things as they are, but even those receptive to change may be averse to uncertain risks posed by policy changes.

National health policies, once achieved, may influence but have limited direct application beyond the nation's borders. The division of public versus private responsibilities for health-care expenditures and outcomes from those expenditures in eight nations demonstrates these differences (Table 1.1). The contrasts are even stronger if low- to moderate-income countries are included.

Among these eight nations, national productivity consumed by health expenditures varies more than threefold (5.4%–17.0% of gross domestic product [GDP]) and the extent of government payments for health care almost by a factor of 2 (47.0%–84.0%), yet years of life expectancy at birth (75–84) show less variation. Price differences, patterns of health services utilization, lifestyle, public versus private sector roles, and national incomes illustrate (1) health outcomes are not a direct result of expenditures—the highest *per capita* expenditure has not produced the longest life spans—and (2) greater reliance on the marketplace and private expenditures does not necessarily result in greater efficiency. For example, the nation with the highest public sector role (United Kingdom at 84.0%) has a per capita expenditure of 3235 (PPP, int. $) and is among the lowest for health care as a component of total government expenditures (16.2%).

Policy incentives and market conditions influence the availability of medicines in general and of specific pharmaceuticals. Let us examine the coverage and payment evolution for an innovative pharmaceutical in the United States and in the United Kingdom. Differences in federalism, parliamentary versus fragmented authorities (United States), and legislative preference for private sector versus public solutions can result in starkly opposite decisions.

Sofosbuvir, an oral product to treat hepatitis C viral infections, received a Food and Drug Administration (FDA) marketing approval on December 6, 2013,[1] and was launched as a 12-week $(USD)84,000 product.[2] The U.S. FDA, as a matter of law, cannot consider cost or economics when making market authorization decisions. Rather than having an official central government price determination, numerous U.S. payer negotiations occur postmarketing.

The costs and potential benefits of Gilead Sciences' sofosbuvir are substantial, but the benefits accrue to a small segment of the population, while the costs are spread through higher insurance coverage costs for all. In the United States, reconciling the difference between those who bear the costs and those who receive the benefits occurs postmarketing and piecemeal, sometimes in insurance or program benefit coverage decisions and sometimes in cost-sharing arrangements. According to CVS Caremark, a pharmaceutical benefit management company, expenses associated with sofosbuvir "could add $(USD)200 to $(USD)300 per year to every insured American's health insurance premium for each of the next five years."[3]

By December 2014, when a market competitor was approved—AbbVie's Viekira Pak[4]—a competition for market share ensued. On December 22, Express Scripts announced that as a result of price negotiations, it would replace Gilead Sciences with AbbVie's Viekira Pak for most patients.[5] By January 6, 2015, CVS gave preferential formulary and benefit coverage to Gilead's product.[6] Shortly afterward, AbbVie came to an agreed discount for Viekira Pak with AIDS drug programs, saying "the task force had previously tried to negotiate with Gilead on the price of Sovaldi, and Gilead had declined to negotiate."[7]

Postmarketing product competition was beginning to do what FDA could not.

In the United Kingdom, the process and the outcome are different. Draft guidance by the National Institute for Health and Care Excellence (NICE) declined to cover sofosbuvir for adult chronic hepatitis C carriers. Instead, Professor Carole Langson, director of the NICE Center for Health Technology Evaluation, reported that "the Committee… [has] requested further information from the manufacturer [and included specific model assumptions to be used in the analyses] before it can decide whether sofosbuvir is a cost-effective use of NHS [National Health Service] resources."[8]

Table 1.1 International Contrasts in Expected Years of Life at Birth (2013) and Public/Private Sector Funds in National Health Expenditures (2012)

National Health Accounts (2012)								
	United States	*Canada*	*China*	*Finland*	*France*	*Germany*	*Japan*	*United Kingdom*
Life expectancy at birth (years; 2013)	79	82	75	81	82	81	84	81
Per capita (PPP int. $)	8845	4610	578	3497	4213	4635	3632	3235
Health expenditures as % of GDP	17.0	10.9	5.4	9.1	11.6	11.3	10.3	9.3
Government expenditures on health as % of total health expenditures	47.0	70.1	56.0	75.0	77.4	76.7	82.1	84.0
Private expenditures on health as % of total health expenditures	53.0	29.9	44.0	25.0	22.6	23.3	17.9	16.0
General government expenditures on health as % of total government expenditures	20.0	18.5	12.5	12.0	15.8	19.3	20.0	16.2
Social Security expenditure on health as % of general government expenditure on health	87.3	1.9	67.9	19.1	95.1	88.8	87.0	0

Source: World Health Organization, *World Health Statistics 2015*, WHO, Geneva, Switzerland, http://apps.who.int/iris/bitstream/10665/170250/1/9789240694439_eng.pdf?ua=1&ua=1. Accessed January 12, 2016.

In an interim action to be reviewed by March 3, 2015, NHS England authorized therapy for an estimated 500 patients "with significant risk of death or irreversible damage within the next 12 months."[9]

U.S. Federalism

U.S. federalism and its institutional legacies shape pharmaceutical policy processes.

The core political values embodied in the U.S. Constitution, its amendments, subsequent federal legislation, and the Supreme Court case law include (1) individual liberty (balancing majority rule with minority rights), (2) popular sovereignty (aka representative democracy), (3) pluralism, (4) checks and balances on power (often focused on institutional separation of powers), (5) federalism as dual sovereignty, (6) constitutional democracy (aka "rule of law, not men"), and (7) judicial independence. While there are other values, they are less immediately relevant to the public policy process.

U.S. federalism has a strong history of state autonomy in matters concerning health, welfare, and education. It arose because the U.S. Constitution was written more than 4 years after the end of the American colonies' revolution. The essentially autonomous, independent states had to agree to concede authorities to the new federal government and, just as in the EU today, there was a great reluctance to do that. Consequently, there was an emphasis on protecting state authorities to the extent possible. The Tenth Amendment to the U.S. Constitution reserves certain authorities to the states, including health. Federal government responsibilities are more concerned with interstate commerce and regulatory authorities derived from that, financing mechanisms, and limited federal preemption of state authority.

Checks on power permeate the U.S. federal government's constitutional structures. Concerns about the volatility of public sentiments and risks of too much power in government officials led the drafters of the Constitution to design a system that constrains the legislature, judiciary, and president through the checks and balances of divided power.

Separation of power among the branches of government is an institutional check and, within the legislative branch, constitutional and "by tradition" divisions of authority work to further reduce aggregated power. Taken together, this means that advancing policy through legislation will, most of the time, require compromise and building coalitions.

This trade-off of efficiency for smaller and incremental change was deliberate. It is intended to avoid radical, dislocating political shifts that might occur from temporarily inflamed popular passions. Major change can occur, but policy development and its implementation require a persistent majority coalition to achieve it.

As federal government authorities increased, having competent, accountable, and apolitical public administrators became essential for performing these functions. The main legislation in shifting from a personnel system based solely on political connections (the spoils system) to one based on competency span more than a half century. The landmark achievements are (1) establishing a merit system of employment (Pendleton Civil Service Reform Act of 1883),[10] (2) prohibiting political activities of executive branch employees while on duty (Hatch Act of 1939 and Hatch Act Reform Amendments of 1993), and (3) increased agency/bureaucratic accountability (Administrative Procedures Act of 1946).

Under Presidents Kennedy and Johnson, creative federalism (1961–1970) expanded the tools, functions, and agencies to achieve policy ends, particularly President Johnson's *Great Society* programs. In 1965, Titles XVIII (Medicare, a federal program funded by employee and employer taxes) and XIX (Medicaid, a federal–state matching funds program) were amended to the

Social Security Act of 1935. Medicare expanded access to health care for the aged, blind, and disabled, and, for those states who accepted the accompanying regulations, Medicaid provided federal matching funds to states for certain categories of qualified poor. Demonstrating the very real autonomy states retain in the health sector, Arizona was the only state not participating in Medicaid by 1972.[11] However, Arizona's alternative Medicaid model was approved in 1982, and, with the Arizona Health Care Cost Containment System, all states have a Medicaid or a qualifying Medicaid equivalent.[12]

Growth in the federal government's role and attendant health-care costs, coupled with a stagnant economy in the 1970s, produced a political and economic backlash: first as demands for greater efficiency in federal programs and subsequently as cost reductions. Starting President Richard Nixon's campaigns and terms in office, this New Federalism emphasized the role of states rather than the federal government in social welfare and health. It resulted in President Ronald Reagan's block grant program. Under the Omnibus Budget Reconciliation Act of 1981,[13] block grants bundled funding for multiple programs, reduced aggregate federal funding, and provided this lesser amount to the states. Devolution of these responsibilities and discretionary authorities to the states permitted the states rather than the federal government to determine program priorities and apportion funds among its local program needs. In theory, states know better what their priorities are and can make informed trade-offs consistent with them.

Market for Pharmaceuticals

Cost, access, quality, safety, and innovation are the leading concerns for pharmaceutical public policy.

Market-focused public policies have made the U.S. pharmaceutical market the largest in the world, with over one-third of global pharmaceutical spending in 2014.[14] From 2004 to 2014, the number of newly approved molecular entities launched in the United States each year ranged from as low as 18 in 2007 to as high as 41 in 2014.[15] Innovation, often defined as a newly marketed pharmaceutical, is a distinguishing feature of the U.S. pharmaceutical industry. Sole-sourced new products, however, come with a price premium that may influence product access and use.

The U.S. health care is costly, in part, because prevention receives little financial reward and has less organized and powerful supporters, although it may have the greatest influence on total health-care costs and long-term outcomes. Other factors that produce higher costs include (1) an aging population, (2) early diffusion of pharmaceutical innovations to medical practices, (3) greater intensity of health services utilization, (4) increased specialty medical and pharmacy care, and (5) price escalation.

Age-adjusted prescription medication use within the past 30 days increased for both males and females from 1988–1994 to 2009–2012 (from 39.1% to 47.3%, Table 1.4). Intensity of pharmacotherapy (using five or more drugs within the past 30 days) also grew (from 4.0% to 10.1%). These increases occurred to all age groups, but polypharmacy grew disproportionately in persons 65 and older—changing from 13.8% to 39.1% reporting use of five or more prescription drugs within the past 30 days.

Employment-based health insurance is common in the United States, representing a stakeholder with strong incentives to the health-care costs of their employees. But the effectiveness of private initiatives is blunted due to the byzantine structure of divided authorities and perverse financial incentives to provide more costly and specialized care. Over time, national health expenditures have increased faster than the economy as a whole and consumed a larger share of GDP, from 5.0% in 1960 to 17.2% in 2012 (Table 1.2). These absolute and relative increases create

Table 1.2 U.S. National and Per Capita Health Expenditures, Selected Years 1960–2013[a]

	2013[b]	*2012*	*2000*	*1990*	*1980*	*1970*	*1960*
Total $(USD B)	2919	2793	1377	724	256	75	27
Per capita $(USD)	9255	8915	4878	2855	1110	356	147
GDP (%)	17.4	17.2	13.4	12.1	8.9	7.0	5.0

[a] Center for Medicare and Medicaid Services. Office of the Actuary, National Health Statistics Group. Table 1.1. http://www.cms.gov/Research-Statistics-Data-and-Systems/Statistics-Trends-and-Reports/NationalHealthExpendData/Downloads/tables.pdf. Accessed June 23, 2015.

[b] National Center for Health Statistics. Health, United States, 2014. Table 102 Gross domestic product, national health expenditures, per capita amounts, percent distribution, and average annual percent change: United States, selected years 1960–2013. Table 109 National health expenditures and percent distribution, by sponsor: United States, selected years 1987–2013. http://www.cdc.gov/nchs/hus.htm. Accessed January 12, 2016.

Table 1.3 U.S. National Health Expenditures by Type of Sponsor (%), Selected Years 1987–2013[a]

	2013	*2010*	*2009*	*2000*	*1995*	*1990*	*1987*
Private	56.5	55.6	56.5	64.5	62.5	67.4	68.2
Public	43.4	44.4	43.5	35.3	37.5	32.6	31.8
Federal	25.9	28.2	27.2	19.0	21.2	17.3	16.6
State and local	17.4	16.3	16.3	16.3[b]	16.3	15.3	15.2

[a] National Center for Health Statistics. Health, United States, 2014. Table 102 Gross domestic product, national health expenditures, per capita amounts, percent distribution, and average annual percent change: United States, selected years 1960–2013. Table 109 National health expenditures and percent distribution, by sponsor: United States, selected years 1987–2013. http://www.cdc.gov/nchs/hus.htm. Accessed January 12, 2016.

[b] Reported as 16.5, edited.

public policy pressures ("do something"), yet they also represent consequences of prior policy choices (that means "undo something").

Whereas the private sector paid 68.2% of national health expenditures in 1987 (Table 1.3), public programs grew from 31.8% to nearly half (43.4%) of a much larger total expenditure by 2013. The relative mix of federal versus state and local also changed—with the federal share increasing by ~1/2 (from 16.6% to 25.9%). Although it appears that the "state and local" share had small growth (from 15.2% to 17.4%), this is relative to the total dollars spent. Total dollars spent also increased, presenting one of the state governments' most pressing fiscal challenges: meeting their payment obligations.

Innovation and medical advances make detection, diagnosis, and treatment more involved than they were previously and require more specialized personnel, technologies, and payment incentives. While arguments have been made for private sector efficiency and innovation, "a focus on blockbuster… drugs squeezes out research into potential treatments that are more affordable"[16] (Table 1.4).

Table 1.4 Prescription Drug Use in the Past 30 Days: United States, Selected Years 1988–2012

	2009–2012	*1999–2002*	*1988–1994*
At least *one* (1) prescription drug			
All persons, age adjusted	47.3	45.2	39.1
Male	42.7	39.8	32.7
Female	51.8	50.3	45.0
Under 18 years of age	23.5	23.8	20.5
18–44	38.1	35.9	31.3
45–64	67.2	64.1	54.8
65 and over	89.8	84.7	73.6
Five (5) or more prescription drugs			
All persons, age adjusted	10.1	7.5	4.0
Male	9.3	6.1	2.9
Female	10.8	8.7	4.9
Under 18 years of age	0.8	0.8[a]	[a]
18–44	3.3	2.3	1.2
45–64	16.3	13.3	7.4
65 and over	39.1	27.1	13.8

Source: National Center for Health Statistics, Health, United States, 2014: With Special Feature on Adults Aged 55–64. Table 85 Prescription Drug Use in the Past 30 days, by sex, age, race and Hispanic origin: United States, selected years 1988–1994 through 2009–2012, Hyattsville, MD, 2015, http://www.cdc.gov/nchs/data/hus/hus14.pdf. Accessed January 12, 2016.

[a] Unreliable.

Public policy and health-care market changes during 1950–1965 dramatically altered the public's exposure to financial risk due to health-care needs through a combination of employer-based health insurance, government programs, Medicare, and/or Medicaid. The accumulated changes resulted in a "protected public" whose interests are separate from the uninsured. The protected majority has health insurance and is resistant to universal insurance policy initiatives that might place their coverage at risk or diminish what they already have.[17] A November 2014 Gallup Poll reported that nationally 66% of adults were satisfied and 33% of adults were dissatisfied with the health-care system. When these respondents were reported by having/not having insurance, the ratings were quite different: of those who had health insurance, 70% were satisfied, whereas of those without health insurance, only 37% were satisfied.[18]

The nearly immediate consequence of the Medicare Modernization Act of 2003, which resulted in the prescription drug Part D benefit in 2006, can be seen in the sharp drop from 2005 to 2013

Table 1.5 U.S. Retail Prescription Drug Expenditures, Selected Years 1960–2013

	Out of Pocket	Private Health Insurance	Medicare	Medicaid	Other Health Insurance Programs	Other Third-Party Payers
2013	16.9	43.5	27.5	7.8	3.3	0.9
2010	18.0	46.4	23.0	7.8	3.4	1.3
2005	25.1	49.8	1.9	17.7	3.6	1.9
2000	27.8	50.5	1.7	16.3	1.7	1.9
1990	56.8	27.0	0.5	12.6	0.2	3.0
1980	71.3	15.0	0.0	11.7	0.2	1.8
1970	82.4	8.8	0.0	7.6	0.1	1.1
1960	96.0	1.3	0.0	0.0	0.1	2.5

Source: Center for Medicare and Medicaid Services, Office of the Actuary, National Health Statistics Group, Table16 Retail Prescription Drugs Expenditures; Levels, Percent Change, and Percent Distribution, by source of funds: Selected calendar years 1960–2013, http://www.cms.gov/Research-Statistics-Data-and-Systems/Statistics-Trends-and-Reports/NationalHealthExpendData/NationalHealthAccountsHistorical.html. Accessed June 23, 2015.

in out-of-pocket payments for retail drug expenditures (from 25.1% to 16.9%), in Medicaid (from 17.7% to 7.8%), and in private health insurance (from 49.8% to 43.5%), but a rise for Medicare (from 1.9% to 27.5%) (Table 1.5).

Market Failures

A free market is an idealized abstraction that is invoked to support deregulation. It assumes (1) many buyers and sellers, (2) perfect competition in which the forces of supply and demand result in an equilibrium price if unhindered by government intervention, (3) complete information available to buyers (which also assumes their ability to understand and determine the validity and significance of the information), (4) low or no barriers to entry or exit from the market, and (5) interchangeability of market goods, i.e., competition. Clearly, this does not describe the pharmaceutical market, so workable policies cannot be based on this abstraction; rather, they should be grounded in what actually occurs.

Focus on this one dimension of the market, deregulation, without examining the evidence, ignores perverse second and third order consequences. It could be argued that a free market actually requires some level and variety of government oversight to keep it functional, or else predatory behaviors will quash innovation and emerging or potential competitors. In the absence of a level playing field provided by regulation, patients will continue to experience the consequences of information asymmetry, lack of price transparency, and diminished competition among potential suppliers.

At the retail level, price transparency and negotiation are critical but availability is limited. Despite substantial public expenditures, pharmaceutical costs continue to pose a barrier to access and adherence to pharmacotherapeutic regimens. Access to prescription drugs is improved by having health insurance, appropriate and adequate coverage, and the ability to meet one's own cost-sharing (or full payment) responsibilities. Whereas 4.8% of persons reported "reduced access to prescription drugs during the past 12 months due to cost" in 1997, by 2013 this rose to 6.4% (Table 1.6). The differences in reported barriers to access to medicines by poverty level are large. In 2013, 18.3% of those below the poverty line reported reduced access due to cost, but 2.8% for those at or above 400% of the poverty line. There is a reduced access to prescription medicine, because its cost also varied as to whether a person had health insurance (from 3.7% in 1997 to 5.8% in 2013) or not (from 18.0% in 1997 to 20.7% in 2013). Since implementation of the Patient Protection and Affordable Care Act, the percentage of people without insurance dropped to 11.9% as of March 2015—the lowest since Gallup began reporting uninsured percentages in 2008.[19]

Demand for health-care products and services in the past relied on the physician as a "learned intermediary" whose professional ethics place the patient's interests above her or his own interests (Agency Model). Couple that with third-party payments and price insensitivity and failures of agency (actions of self-interest) result. At a health system level, firms or other stakeholders engage in "rent-seeking behavior"—lobbying to change the rules of the market (1) to impose barriers to entry and (2) to assure economic success without actual competition (or with less than robust competition). These actions, if successful, may produce market failures.

Table 1.6 Reduced Access to Prescription Drugs During the Past 12 Months Due to Cost, by Selected Characteristics: United States, Selected Years 1997–2013

(%)	*2013*	*2010*	*2003*	*1997*
Total	6.4	8.3	6.3	4.8
Male	6.9	8.8	6.3	5.1
Female	10.6	13.5	9.8	7.4
Poverty Level (%)				
<100	18.3	21.5	17.3	14.8
100–199	14.4	18.4	15.3	11.6
200–300	8.4	11.4	7.6	5.5
≥400	2.8	3.9	2.7	1.7
Insured	5.8	7.3	4.8	3.7
Private	4.4	6.0	3.6	2.9
Medicaid	11.5	13.5	13.2	11.1
Uninsured	20.7	25.7	21.7	18.0

Source: National Center for Health Statistics, Health, United States, 2014: With Special Feature on Adults Aged 55–64, Table 69 Delay or nonreceipt of needed medical care, nonreceipt of needed prescription drugs, or nonreceipt of needed dental care during the past 12 months due to cost, by selected characteristics: United States, selected years 1997–2013, http://www.cdc.gov/nchs/data/hus/hus14.pdf. Accessed June 23, 2015.

Market failures may be a stimulus to change: some industries that are now regulated utilities, such as electrical power, were once market-based goods and services. Alternatively, change may produce market failures. The health insurance industry, where the dominant players are now for profit (often publicly traded firms), was once populated mostly by not-for-profit firms.

Examples of market failures include (1) incomplete, unavailable, or missing information that is necessary to make informed choices among alternatives, (2) predatory pricing, (3) consolidation resulting in lessened competition, (4) shortages of both substitutable and nonsubstitutable products, and (5) unmet treatment needs for conditions in groups considered too small to justify investments in research and development for cures.

Two of the most common public approaches to resolving market failures and their attendant-reduced access to medical products and services are "money or mandates"—that is, pay for services or make their availability mandatory.[20] As of 2012, the Council for Affordable Health Insurance had identified 2262 state health insurance mandates, ranging from 13 in Idaho to 70 in Rhode Island and Virginia.[21] These state-level market corrections are, however, being revised due to provisions in the Patient Protection and Affordable Care Act, which specify mandatory preventive services and a package of 10 essential health benefits.[22]

Policy Process

Public policy has been described as a Garbage Can Model[23]: issues, approaches, and outcomes have elements of randomness.

Examples of typical large pharmaceutical public policy issues include stimulating innovation, determining the extent of intellectual property (IP) protection, access to pharmaceuticals (equity), encouraging research and development of medicines for uncommon conditions, and access to unproven therapies for terminal patients who have exhausted all other options (the "right to try").[24] State-level policies may consider issues such as "provider status" for pharmacists and regulation of compounding pharmacies while balancing federal and state authorities due to federal preemption concerning manufacturers.

In the beginning, there are policy entrepreneurs who often identify policy problems, find champions, guide policy development, and assist in crafting solutions. The specific pressures, coalition(s), feasible options, and determining factors shift across economic cycles and political sentiments. Policy entrepreneurs aggregate these sometimes tangentially related policy problems as they seek to create solutions that will attract sufficient coalition(s) to pass legislation and/or influence regulations. ("Allow for the Unexpected" section discusses the substantial influence that unexpected events can have on policy.)

On specific issues, stakeholders' interests may align, producing interest group collaborations or networks. The larger, more organized, and permanent stakeholders in the process include patients, providers, payers, and industry. Investors and governments can also be influential stakeholders and exert demands for (or against) the policy. When shared, their interests can advance policy initiatives. When not shared, their interests create friction and a potential barrier to providing access, containing cost, and/or assuring quality of pharmaceutical products and services. Over the past half century, policy actions to regulate or stimulate the discovery and use of pharmaceuticals that contain costs or employ price controls have been bipartisan, initiated by Republican and Democratic administrations. More recently, periods of such bipartisan achievement have become the exception and it is common for conflicting interests to stall policy initiatives.

Initiatives suitable for policy interventions cover a wide spectrum: (i) Which policies provide adequate incentives to induce companies to perform the research and development necessary for discovery of breakthrough drugs and manufacturing at scale? (ii) Are tax incentives aligned with regulatory requirements? (iii) Do all members of the society benefit from pharmaceutical discoveries? (iv) How ought the results of research be made available to patients? (v) Does it matter for IP rights if research is performed in government laboratories or in universities but under governmental grants and contracts?

Stakeholders

Interest groups proliferate in health care. Individually and in coalitions, these groups represent formidable forces. Pluralism, the political value that recognizes the legitimacy of diversity, is fundamental to the American constitutional government. The greater the diversity of interests and opinions, according to the theory, the less opportunity for consolidated power and dominance by a majority. James Madison acknowledged "measures are too often decided, not according to the rules of justice and the rights of the minor party, but by the superior force of an interested and overbearing majority" and argued for "the greater security afforded by a greater variety of parties, against the event of any one party being able to outnumber and oppress the rest."[25]

Influencing policies not only requires more than organizing supporters but also requires an understanding of how the legislative, executive, regulatory processes and private sector businesses actually work. Even when individual interests would benefit from influencing the content of health policies, the logistics of the process reduces the likelihood of participation and, if they participate individually rather than collectively, their influence.

Public choice theory offers a rationale why interested individuals and groups decide whether to become involved in the policy process and remain active in the process and their likelihood of success if they do. A rational decision-maker, weighing the costs and expected benefits of the time and resources required to keep them actively informed about emerging policy issues, may choose not to invest their efforts in doing so. The number of issues directly relevant to an individual is likely to be just a few among the many that arise, and individual inputs relative to the roles played by more organized or larger stakeholders may be too dilute to make a difference. That is, they are likely not to prevail in those few matters of importance to them despite expending a considerable time and effort to identify and to stay informed on the issues that may affect their interests. Conversely, other groups of stakeholders, such as providers or industry, have a smaller number of priority policy issues that justify their continuing investment of time and resources to influence the results. Relative to the resources these organized stakeholders have and the significance of the outcomes for them, the costs of continuing participation in the policy process may not be great and could be seen as a "cost of doing business."

Nonetheless, identifying the interests of the unorganized public is used to support or sway policymakers. Polling research methodologies and technology have made public opinion a constant consideration in modern public policy. Reporting it has become more organized, whether it is the uninsureds' perceptions of the insurance exchanges under the Affordable Care Act[26] to public support for increased regulation of the pharmaceutical industry[27] or favorable/unfavorable views of health-care reform associated with political party affiliation.[28] Information on public support or opposition is regularly available, providing opportunities for stakeholders to craft messages to shape public opinion and/or providing a mechanism to organize individuals into a collective force in policy. Lobbying is one way of using this information.

The U.S. Senate defines lobbying as "the practice of trying to persuade legislators to propose, pass, or defeat legislation or to change existing laws. A lobbyist may work for a group, organization, or industry and presents information on legislative proposals to support his or her clients' interests."[29] Lobbying provides a focus for conveying stakeholder interests via the power of organization and funding.

If public opinion polls are anonymous one-way communication to researchers who then distill their findings for policymakers, social media makes public opinions interactive and immediate. From manufacturers' tweets to PatientsLikeMe (@patientslikeme on Twitter, 26,100 followers[30]), barriers between patients and other stakeholders are dropping. Recognizing the importance of social media, the FDA's Center for Drug Evaluation and Research has organized a separate web page of guidance for industry: using social media.[31]

Players

One of the ways individuals may seek to have their views heard and opinions influence outcomes is to organize into associations, harnessing their collective power to represent their shared interests. Lobbying is entrenched in the policy process, as a practical information necessity due to the number of issues that legislators consider, and for the mutual advantages that it presents. The health care and pharmaceutical industry represented some of the largest sponsors of lobbying activities during 1998–2015 (Table 1.7), collectively spending more than $(USD)1.1 billion during that period. But from a regulatory perspective, attempts to define, legislate, and control lobbying seem destined to produce greater creativity in the transfer of resources than to control it.

The main stakeholders who influence and are influenced by pharmaceutical public policy include patients, providers, payers, industry, and coalitions of interest groups. All may use the services of lobbyists.

Patients

Patients may organize into condition or issue affinity groups to advance their policy agenda, e.g., the National Alliance for the Mentally Ill: "the nation's largest grassroots mental health organization dedicated to building better lives for the millions of Americans affected by mental illness."[32]

Table 1.7 Spending on Lobbying, 1998–2015: Four of the Top Seven Sources Are from the Health-Care Industry (Ranked by Total Expenditure)

Lobbying Client	*Total ($[USD])*
# 2 American Medical Association	326,122,500
# 5 American Hospital Association	280,630,905
# 6 Pharmaceutical Research and Manufacturers of America	272,551,420
# 7 Blue Cross/Blue Shield	254,276,770
Total	1,133,581,595

Source: Center for Responsive Politics, Top Spenders, http://www.opensecrets.org/lobby/top.php?showYear=a&indexType=s. Accessed June 26, 2015.

However, patients and their advocacy groups are not homogeneous—they share some basic concerns such as access and quality but may have other interests that separate them from acting as a bloc. The "protected public" (those with insurance coverage) and the uninsured are patient categories, but their health-care experiences and interests are substantially different. For the insured, having third-party payments also implies more than one "customer" is involved in interactions, and those third-party payers represent another distinct stakeholder group. (See the "1988–1989 The Medicare Catastrophic Coverage Act" and "The Power of Public Opinion" sections.)

Providers

Providers include physicians, hospitals, nurses, pharmacists, and other allied health professionals too numerous to list. They have recognized, powerful associations, such as the American Medical Association (AMA), the American Hospital Association, the American Pharmacists Association, and the American Nurses Association. Their organized influence is potent. For example, opposition by organized medicine kept health care out of the Social Security Act of 1935, because President Roosevelt was concerned that including it would draw the AMA's opposition and defeat the entire Social Security legislation.[33]

As a practical matter, other than the most limited issues, divergence of interests may make providers collectively a "thousand points of no"—effectively negating each other. President Clinton's Task Force on National Health Reform, which included more than 500 members,[34] found compromise and agreement painstakingly difficult with discussions more divergent than convergent.

Payers

Payers have related but incompletely aligned interests. They want value for payments, that is, controlling costs while assuring the appropriateness and quality of the care provided. How they go about achieving these goals depends on their time horizon and stakeholders (particularly for publicly traded firms).

As payers, self-insured employers potentially have a long(er)-term view of expenditures as investments in the health of their workforce. Additionally, the Employee Retirement and Income Security Act of 1974 preempts state mandate requirements for self-insured employers, altering their interests relative to employers who purchase commercial insurance for their employees. Insurers, however, may have a more limited, enrollment cycle time horizon for their strategic concerns and design products to be profitable yet financially competitive. The recent increase in high deductible health insurance, in which annual deductibles may be in thousands of dollars, constrains premium growth by shifting more first dollar (and other) costs to the insured. The longer-term consequences of this approach have yet to be assessed.

Associations such as Blue Cross/Blue Shield, the National Council of Self-Insurers,[35] America's Health Insurance Plans (AHIP—a combination of the previous Health Insurance Association of America and the American Association of Health Plans), and the National Business Group on Health (NBGH) provide well-financed political representation of member interests. During 1998–2015, the Blue Cross/Blue Shield alone spent $(USD)254,276,770 on lobbying. AHIP's approaches are direct advocacy and organizing issue-specific advocacy coalitions, such as the Coalition for Medicare Choices and End the Insurance Tax.[36]

The NBGH, representing 392 large employers who employ 55 million workers,[37] is the largest employer health policy advocacy group. Its policy agenda includes improving employee health and productivity, increasing transparency of health-care information, reducing health-care costs and increasing the affordability of health benefits, preserving and strengthening the Employee Retirement Income Security Act (ERISA), promoting flexibility in health benefits design, reducing the cost and complexity of health benefits administration, and maintaining favorable tax treatment for health benefits.[38]

Industry

Although the pharmaceutical industry may share some public policy goals, it consists of corporations whose mission and business models also have substantial differences. Publicly traded and other for-profit companies have similar positions on taxes, tariffs, and trade policies. But their positions may be systematically divergent regarding data exclusivity, public investments in research, IP, and even FDA Guidance(s). For example, research and discovery–based firms, generic manufacturers, and biological, over-the-counter, and/or device companies will likely have different policy priorities and different positions.

Several large associations are discussed in the following:

The Pharmaceutical Research and Manufacturers of America consists of the leading commercial biopharmaceutical research and manufacturing companies. It focuses on policies that concern research, discovery, patent, and IP protection.[39]

The Biotechnology Industry Organization[40] consists of nearly 1400 "biotechnology companies, academic institutions, state biotechnology centers, and related organizations across the United States and in more than 30 other nations" with a focus on policies that concern research and innovations. Recent developments in biological products, biosimilars, and pricing for each assure that this will be an active area of policy elaboration.

The Generic Pharmaceutical Association is a relatively recent entity formed in 2000 through a merger of three associations (the Generic Pharmaceutical Industry Association, the National Association of Pharmaceutical Manufacturers, and the National Pharmaceutical Alliance).[41] It consists of "manufacturers and distributors of generic prescription drugs, manufacturers of bulk active pharmaceutical chemicals, and suppliers of other goods and services to the generic industry."[41] Member interests concern market access and policies governing patents, international tariffs and trade, and manufacturing regulations, among others.

Policy Evolution: From Identifying Issues to Implementing Policies

Pharmaceutical policies form a *de facto* but incomplete system—one that emerged from contested interests and accidents of history rather than one designed to be efficient and effective in achieving specific outcomes. These policies reflect national values, though the dominant priority shifts over time between cost cutting and increased access. They are influenced by new technologies and by arcane rules by which legislative policy is implemented through regulations and subsequently interpreted by the courts.

Policy Evolves

Although it is not a fully linear process, presenting the policy process as occurring in stages can be useful for organizing and clarifying the material (Table 1.8).

Table 1.8 Policy Making Process: From Identifying Issues to Implementation and Reactions

1. Identification
2. Development ("ripening")
3. Policy agenda
4. Policy solutions/alternatives: legislation and regulation
5. Implementation
6. Reactions: monitoring, evaluation, and adjustment to unintended consequences

Issue Identification

Policy concerns have multiple sources, including unintended consequences of prior policies, changed circumstances, new technologies, economic changes, research findings, and specific key policymaker interests (perhaps due to personal or family experiences).

Issues may be identified by regulatory agencies, the press, politicians, and/or interest groups. For example, pharmaceutical shortages have become a policy issue through news accounts, professional reports, and regulatory reporting requirements. Their existence, persistence, and increasing trend invite policy solutions as existing market and regulation activities seem unable to solve the problem.

Development ("The Ripening Influence of Time"[42])

Some policy issues achieve prominence only gradually, while others rise and disappear. Unless precipitated by a crisis, once an issue is on a policy agenda, there is seldom an immediate consensus among key stakeholders and legislators that it even is a policy-appropriate issue. And, if so, which of many actions are appropriate to address it?

Increasingly, think tanks and not-for-profit organizations identify issues and maintain an output of policy position papers, conferences, books, and commentators. When it comes to policy, evidence does not settle issues as much as it becomes a series of contests with regard to the validity of differing reports, studies, and/or "think tank" products. However, as Mark Kleiman observed, "If you have to read the report to know the conclusion, it's a real think tank. If you know the conclusion as soon as you know the topic and where it was written, you're dealing with a phony."[43]

Given contested stakeholder opinions, differences in relative political power, sophistication, and specific interests, it is no surprise that approaches to solutions tend to evolve before there is action.

Policy Agenda

Policy entrepreneurs[44] are a crucial force for moving an issue from general discussion to an active policy agenda. These advocates have ideas, access, and motivation to advance particular issues and approaches.

For example, toward the end of President Clinton's second term, he raised the issue of expanding Medicare to cover prescription drugs, a critical gap in Medicare at that time.[45] The issue was only viable for discussion then because of improvements in the federal deficit. Citing a surplus of $(USD)99 billion, the president (a Democrat) argued that it would be fiscally feasible and politically popular. Although there was a change in the political party occupying the White House after the 2000 presidential election, Medicare expansion to include prescription drugs continued to be pursued. Passage of the Medicare Modernization Act of 2003, which contained this benefit, occurred under President George W. Bush (a Republican). Between the idea and the legislation, proposals evolved with shifting coverage, fiscal approaches, and relative roles for the public and private sectors. This particular policy change, however, would not have happened without President Bush and the then majority of the Republican Party's full and forceful support. (For a more detailed discussion of the legislative evolution of the MMA, see John Iglehart's article, "A Pure Power Play."[46])

Policy Alternatives: Legislation and Regulatory Solutions

> There is nothing more difficult to take in hand, more perilous to conduct,
> or more uncertain in its success,
> than to take the lead in the introduction of a new order of things.
>
> **Niccolo Machiavelli**[47]

Incremental change is more common as the risks of unintended effects (and opponents) of new policies increase with the scale of change required, and opposition is typically greater than support. Developing policy solutions depends on the process, players, and incremental steps. The urgent and the politically feasible may be more influential in determining policy than evidence-based position papers.

Separation of powers, independent stakeholders with relatively autonomous power (such as congressional committee chairs), and shifting coalitions block all but the most determined and necessary legislation. Even then, whether these conditions will influence or lead to enactment of different policies or not is uncertain. Increasing threats of filibuster make "... it... all but impossible [for Congress] to pass legislation these days."[48] Few federal legislative initiatives result in new laws; most die in chamber. An estimated 5% of the bills currently active in the U.S. Congress may become law.[49]

A law states what will or will not be done and what should or should not occur; however, it is the regulations that determine who should do or not do what specifically and how that performance will be determined. Regulations and regulatory changes clarify the intent behind legislative compromises needed to pass legislation; they are more frequent and more responsive than legislative change is. Concerned with the growing size and scope of the federal government from the 1930s through World War II and the relatively autonomous authority of federal agencies, the Congress enacted the Administrative Procedures Act of 1946. The Act provides guidance on federal agencies' accountability in the process of developing and issuing regulations.[50] It requires that agencies (1) provide public notice of intent to seek a regulatory solution (published in the *Federal Register*); (2) invite public comment either at a hearing at a specific time and place, or through letters; and (3) provide an appeals process for those who dispute a regulation.

Implementation

Implementation requires both regulations and appropriations (which are not necessarily assured). Implementation can facilitate or effectively euthanize new policies by the adequacy or inadequacy of staff, budget, actual authorities, and organizational reporting relationships.

Resistance to an intended policy can alter planned implementation. In January 2014, for example, the administration announced a planned change in Medicare Part D drug coverage that could have limited plan choices under Medicare and relaxed requirements in six "protected classes." These drug classes were (1) immunosuppressant, (2) antidepressant, (3) antipsychotic, (4) anticonvulsant, (5) antiretroviral, and (6) antineoplastic drugs.[51] This proposal elicited "withering criticism from the industry, patient advocacy groups, and lawmakers" about the possible reduced access to critical medicines and resulted in the proposed change not being implemented.[52]

Review

Over the long term, aspects of policies that have perverse consequences or that fail to achieve their objectives are usually reversed or otherwise nullified, while the remainder are tweaked or improved.

In addition to appeals of federal regulations through the Administrative Procedures Act, judicial review applies to legislation at the state and federal levels. For example, the Affordable Care Act assumed that all states would expand their Medicaid program and receive federal subsidies to enroll additional low-income persons. However, the Supreme Court of the United States made several recent rulings that profoundly affect the Patient Protection and Affordable Care Act of 2010. First, it ruled that the provision for Medicaid expansion to cover additional categories of individuals not otherwise eligible for Medicaid was optional and that states could opt out without the "coercive" penalty that the law provided of eliminating all federal Medicaid matching funds.[53] With expansion of Medicaid left to individual state discretion, some declined to expand even with the promise of federal subsidies.

Allow for the Unexpected

The emergence of policy issues, their debate, and framing are relatively direct and formal, but equally important indirect and/or informal factors make it an uncertain progression. Several examples follow.

A Changing Landscape

Employee Retirement Income Security Act of 1974

Once a policy is implemented, the circumstances that led to it may change or unexpected developments may cause the policy to have perverse or unintended effects.

Employers who self-insured for health-care expenses in the early 1970s were either nonexistent or a vanishingly small part of the health insurance market. The ERISA of 1974[54] was not concerned with health care when it passed—the focus was protecting employment-based pensions. However, self-insured employers' health insurance policies for their employees, under the terms of

ERISA, would be exempt from state health insurance coverage mandates and requirements, a fact that would assume significance decades later.

The health-care market changed dramatically during the 1980s as self-insurance by employers became a widely used means to manage their growing health benefits costs and bypass state mandates. The ERISA's federal preemption of state health insurance law, which was unintended and unforeseen at the time the legislation was enacted, continues to be in force and has developed such a potent constituency of supporters that it is unlikely to be changed.

Unexpected Events

1974: The Curtain on National Health Care Reform

Timing and randomness of events can influence the policy development in unexpected ways.

In 1974, a large-scale national health reform seemed imminent. Senator Ted Kennedy (D-MA) had devoted his elected political life to achieving this goal. Representative Wilbur Mills (R-AR-2), chair of the powerful House Ways and Means Committee and a policy entrepreneur behind the Social Security Amendments of 1965 that established Medicare and Medicaid, had become a supporter. Labor was withholding support in anticipation of getting a more complete package; AMA and the National Federation of Independent Business were opposed, but compromise was slowly becoming feasible.

Major legislation and policy change seemed to be converging.

Then, on October 7, 1974, intoxicated Rep. Wilbur Mills was stopped by the police and found to have an exotic dancer in the car with him. The muted scandal ignited subsequent events, leading to Rep. Mills' resignation as chair of the House Ways and Means Committee on December 10, 1974. The resulting leadership gap and growing economic austerity ended the possibilities for a large-scale health-care reform.[55]

Power of Public Opinion

1988–1989: The Medicare Catastrophic Coverage Act

Medicare had a short-lived prescription drug benefit prior to the inclusion of prescription drugs as Part D in the Medicare Modernization Act of 2003.

The Medicare Catastrophic Coverage Act (MCCA), passed in July 1988, contained a prescription drug benefit to protect beneficiaries against catastrophic costs, but not against the costs of routine pharmacotherapy. This program feature assured that in any year, only a minority of Medicare enrollees would experience a direct benefit from the coverage under the Act. Furthermore, in a shift from prior policy approaches, payment for this expansion of Medicare had to be fully funded by the elderly themselves (intragenerational) rather than spread across the entire population (intergenerational). In addition, the enrollees' payments were determined by means testing (i.e., payments for those with lower incomes would be subsidized by those with higher earnings). There was confusion among the elderly about what the benefit included, who would pay, and who would be subsidized.[56] A grassroots campaign against the MCCA strengthened opposition, resulting in its repeal in November 1989.[57]

Experience with the MCCA provided policy lessons that inform subsequent legislation: (1) Intragenerational funding is politically volatile—many retirees were satisfied with their health insurance; few were willing to subsidize other elderly's costs and these opponents were active politically. (2) To generate support, benefits should be directly experienced by a large political base.

(3) For those supporting new policies, information campaigns must start early and must be clear and continuous to create and to maintain support, even postimplementation.[58]

Back by Popular Demand

2000–2002: The Case Study of Alosetron

Irritable bowel syndrome (IBS) is a socially and professionally limiting condition, associated with unexpected bowel functions.

Alosetron, a 5-HT_3 antagonist for diarrhea-predominant IBS, received a U.S. marketing authorization in February 2000.[59] By November 2000, however, reported patient deaths and other harms led the manufacturer to withdraw alosetron from the market. An FDA briefing document from April 23, 2002, noted "both GSK and FDA [subsequently] received an unprecedented number of communications from physicians, IBS patients and IBS patient advocacy groups requesting that the withdrawal of LOTRONEX be reconsidered."[60]

In June 2002, FDA reauthorized marketing alosetron subject to a risk evaluation and mitigation program.[61] Moynihan, noting substantial industry payments under the Prescription Drug User Fee Act, questioned whether the FDA's reversal on marketing alosetron was a genuine case of patient rights compelling a change in policy or if, instead, it represented regulatory capture—actions in which a regulatory agency acts in the interests of its industry more than those of the public at large.[59]

A review of 48,544 patients' experiences with alosetron since its reintroduction in 2002 through March 2013 noted one death and two intestinal surgeries. This compares with 11 deaths in 2000, prior to the revised dosing recommendations for the remarketed alosetron and its current program for risk mitigation.[62]

These few, brief examples demonstrate how dynamic and uncertain the policy process can be—requiring the best evidence and some degree of luck prior to its passage, monitoring, and evaluation after and subject to the influence of organized interest groups throughout.

Summary

Beyond basic philosophical differences regarding legitimate roles for the public and private sectors, advocacy and the consequences of pharmaceutical public policy positions must be assessed against national values as well as national accounts.

For the foreseeable future, pharmaceutical public policy will (1) remain more reactive than proactive, (2) have prominent roles for the private sector, (3) have increasingly organized stakeholder–interest group participation, and (4) engage patients and the public at large more directly through social media and emerging technologies.

Additional Resources

Blumenthal D and Morone JA. 2009. *The Heart of Power: Health and Politics in the Oval Office*. University of California Press, Berkeley, CA.

Carpenter D. 2010. *Reputation and Power: Organizational Image and Pharmaceutical Regulation at the FDA*. Princeton University Press, Princeton, NJ.

Engel J. 2006. *Poor People's Medicine: Medicaid and American Charity Care Since 1965*. Duke University Press, Durham, NC.
Hilts P. 2003. *Protecting America's Health*. Alfred A. Knopf, New York.
Kessler D. 2001. *A Question of Intent: A Great American Battle with a Deadly Industry*. Public Affairs, New York.
Reid TR. 2009. *The Healing of America: A Global Quest for Better, Cheaper, and Fairer Health Care*. The Penguin Press, New York.
Starr P. 1982. *The Social Transformation of American Medicine*. Basic Books, New York.
Starr P. 2011. *Remedy and Reaction*. Yale University Press, New Haven, CT.

References

1. United States Food and Drug Administration. Approval of Sovaldi (sofosbuvir) tablets for the treatment of chronic hepatitis C. December 6, 2013. http://www.fda.gov/forpatients/illness/hepatitisbc/ucm377920.htm. Accessed December 5, 2015.
2. Armstrong D. At $84,000 Gilead hepatitis C drug sets off payer revolt. *Bloomberg News*. January 27, 2014. http://www.bloomberg.com/news/articles/2014-01-27/at-84-000-gilead-hepatitis-c-drug-sets-off-payer-revolt.
3. Brennan TA and Shrank W. New expensive treatments for hepatitis C infection. *JAMA*. August 13, 2014;312(6):593–594. http://jama.jamanetwork.com/article.aspx?articleid=1890401&resultClick=1.
4. AbbVie. AbbVie Receives U.S. FDA Approval of VIEKIRA PAK™ (Ombitasvir/Paritaprevir/Ritonavir Tablets; Dasabuvir Tablets) for the Treatment of Chronic Genotype 1 Hepatitis C. December 29, 2014. http://abbvie.mediaroom.com/2014-12-19-AbbVie-Receives-U-S-FDA-Approval-of-VIEKIRA-PAK-Ombitasvir-Paritaprevir-Ritonavir-Tablets-Dasabuvir-Tablets-for-the-Treatment-of-Chronic-Genotype-1-Hepatitis-C. Accessed December 5, 2015.
5. Humer C. Express scripts drops Gilead hep C drugs for cheaper AbbVie rival. Reuters. December 22, 2104. http://www.reuters.com/article/2014/12/22/us-express-scripts-abbvie-hepatitisc-idUSKBN0K007620141222. Accessed December 5, 2015.
6. Walker J. CVS gives preferred status to Gilead's hepatitis C drugs: AbbVie's Viekira Pak will be available if a patient receives medical exception or prior authorization. January 5, 2015. http://www.wsj.com/articles/cvs-gives-preferred-status-to-gilead-hepatitis-c-drugs-1420478490. Accessed December 5, 2015.
7. Armstrong D. AbbVie strikes hepatitis C discount deal with AIDS drug programs. *Bloomberg News*. January 16, 2015. http://www.bloomberg.com/news/articles/2015-01-16/abbvie-strikes-hepatitis-c-discount-deal-with-aids-drug-programs.
8. NICE. (Press Release Archive) NICE consults on draft guidance on the drug sofosbuvir (Sovaldi) for treating hepatitis C. June 16, 2014. https://www.nice.org.uk/News/Press-and-Media/nice-consults-on-draft-guidance-on-the-drug-sofosbuvir-sovaldi-for-treating-hepatitis-c. Accessed December 5, 2015.
9. NHS England. NHS England agrees funding for life-saving hepatitis C drug. April 16, 2014. https://www.nice.org.uk/news/press-and-media/nice-consults-on-draft-guidance-on-the-drug-sofosbuvir-sovaldi-for-treating-hepatitis-c. Accessed December 5, 2015.
10. Hoogenboom A. 1961. *Outlawing the Spoils: A History of the Civil Service Reform Movement 1865–1883*. University of Illinois Press, Urbana, IL.
11. Kaiser Family Foundation. Medicaid: A timeline of key developments 1965–2009. 2008. http://kaiserfamilyfoundation.files.wordpress.com/2008/04/5-02-13-medicaid-timeline.pdf. Accessed December 5, 2015.
12. Orient JM. The Arizona health care cost containment system: A prepayment model for a national health service? *Western Journal of Medicine* 1986;145(1):114–119. http://www.ncbi.nlm.nih.gov/pmc/articles/PMC1306848/.
13. Omnibus Budget Reconciliation Act of 1981. P.L. 97-35. http://history.nih.gov/research/downloads/PL97-35.pdf. Accessed December 5, 2015.

14. IMS Institute for Healthcare Informatics. Global outlook for medicines through 2018. November 2014, p. 1. http://www.imshealth.com/en/thought-leadership/ims-institute/reports/global-outlook-for-medicines-through-2018. Accessed December 5, 2015.
15. U.S. Food and Drug Administration. Novel New Drugs 2014 Summary, p. 3. http://www.fda.gov/downloads/Drugs/DevelopmentApprovalProcess/DrugInnovation/UCM430299.pdf. Accessed December 5, 2015.
16. Bernstein J. MIA in the war on cancer: Where are the low cost treatments? *ProPublica*. April 23, 2014. http://www.propublica.org/article/where-are-the-low-cost-cancer-treatments. Accessed December 5, 2015.
17. Starr P. 2011. *Remedy and Reaction*. Yale University Press, New Haven, CT.
18. Riffkin R. Americans satisfied with how health system works for them. *Gallup*. November 10, 2014. http://www.gallup.com/poll/179294/americans-satisfied-health-system-works.aspx. Accessed December 5, 2015.
19. Gallup. *Well-Being*: In U.S., uninsured rate dips to 11.4%. July 10, 2015. http://www.gallup.com/poll/184064/uninsured-rate-second-quarter.aspx. Accessed December 5, 2015.
20. Weiner J. A conversation with Jonathan P. Weiner, DrPH: Information technology required. *Managed Care*. June 2013. http://www.managedcaremag.com/archives/2013/6/conversation-jonathan-p-weiner-drph-information-technology-required.
21. Council for Affordable Health Insurance. CAHI Identifies 2,262 State Health Insurance Mandates. February 28, 2012. http://www.cahi.org/article.asp?id=1038. Accessed December 5, 2015.
22. Iglehart JK. Defining essential health benefits—The view from the IOM committee. *New England Journal of Medicine* 2011;365(16):1461–1463.
23. Kingdon JW. 1995. *Agendas, Alternatives, and Public Policies*, 2nd edn. Harper Collins, New York.
24. Dennis B and Cha AE. "Right to Try" laws spur debate over dying patients' access to experimental drugs. *Washington Post*. May 16, 2014. http://www.washingtonpost.com/national/health-science/right-to-try-laws-spur-debate-over-dying-patients-access-to-experimental-drugs/2014/05/16/820e08c8-dcfa-11e3-b745-87d39690c5c0_story.html.
25. Madison J. Federalist No. 10: The same subject continued: The union as a safeguard against domestic faction and insurrection. 1787. http://thomas.loc.gov/home/histdox/fed_10.html. Accessed December 5, 2015.
26. Gallup. *Well-Being*. U.S. Uninsured still rate exchange experience negatively. January 2, 2014. http://www.gallup.com/poll/166712/uninsured-rate-exchange-experience-negatively.aspx. Accessed December 5, 2015.
27. Harris. Americans Less Likely to Say 18 of 19 Industries are Honest and Trustworthy This Year: More than one-third of Americans want to see oil, pharma, tobacco and health insurance companies more regulated. December 12, 2013. http://www.theharrispoll.com/politics/Americans_Less_Likely_to_Say_18_of_19_Industries_are_Honest_and_Trustworthy_This_Year.html. Accessed December 5, 2015.
28. Kaiser Family Foundation. Kaiser Health Tracking Poll: March 26, 2014. http://kff.org/health-reform/poll-finding/kaiser-health-tracking-poll-march-2014/. Accessed December 5, 2015.
29. United States Senate. Lobbying. n.d. http://www.senate.gov/reference/reference_index_subjects/Lobbying_vrd.htm. Accessed December 5, 2015.
30. Twitter. @patientslikeme. https://twitter.com/hashtag/patientslikeme. Accessed December 5, 2015.
31. U.S. Food and Drug Administration. For industry: Using social media. http://www.fda.gov/AboutFDA/CentersOffices/OfficeofMedicalProductsandTobacco/CDER/ucm397791.htm. Page Last Updated October 29, 2014. Last accessed December 5, 2015.
32. National Alliance for the Mentally Ill. http://www.nami.org/. Accessed December 5, 2015.
33. Starr P. 1982. *The Social Transformation of American Medicine*. Basic Books, New York.
34. Hamburg RS and Ballin SD. Politics of the demise of healthcare reform. *Circulation* 1995;91:8–9. doi: 10.1161/01.CIR.91.1.8. http://circ.ahajournals.org/content/91/1/8.full.
35. National Council of Self-Insurers. http://www.natcouncil.com/. Accessed December 5, 2015.
36. America's Health Insurance Plans. https://www.ahip.org/Advocacy-Coalitions/. Accessed December 5, 2015.

37. Fiat Chrysler Automobiles. National Business Group on Health Awards Chrysler Group Sixth Consecutive Gold Medal for Promoting Healthy Employee Lifestyles. June 25, 2014. http://media.fcanorthamerica.com/newsrelease.do;jsessionid=A34E4124B260A94D1176530029818D17?&id=15729&mid=2. Accessed December 5, 2015.
38. The National Business Group on Health. Public Policy. https://www.businessgrouphealth.org/resources/public_policy/index.cfm. Accessed December 5, 2015.
39. Pharmaceutical Research and Manufacturers of America. www.phrma.org. Accessed December 5, 2015.
40. Biotechnology Industry Organization. http://www.bio.org/. Accessed December 5, 2015.
41. Generic Pharmaceutical Association. http://www.gphaonline.org/about/the-gpha-association. Accessed December 5, 2015.
42. Anon., Public Policy. A new discussion of public policy platform on labor problems. 1905;12(1):1. http://books.google.com/books?id=CtIpAAAAYAAJ&pg=PA1&lpg=PA1&dq=public+policy+issue+ripening&source=bl&ots=p8SUa6He8J&sig=eSNxLStnJs-hycvirvHiS_oGhlE&hl=en&sa=X&ei=39a7U7eoFZapsATgqIDICQ&ved=0CGsQ6AEwCQ#v=onepage&q=public%20policy%20issue%20ripening&f=false.
43. Kleinman M. On "think tanks." February 21, 2006. http://www.samefacts.com/2006/02/wayward-press/on-think-tanks/. Accessed December 5, 2015.
44. Kingdon JW. 1993. How do issues get on public policy agendas? In Wilson WJ (Ed.), *Sociology and the Public Agenda*. SAGE Publications, Thousand Oaks, CA.
45. Claiborne W. Medicare drug plan applauded. *Washington Post*. July 1, 1999, p. A10. http://www.washingtonpost.com/wp-srv/politics/special/medicare/stories/clinton070199.htm.
46. Iglehart JK. The new medicare prescription-drug benefit—A pure power play. *New England Journal of Medicine* 2004;350(8):826–833.
47. Machiavelli N. 1532. The Prince.
48. Politi J and McGregor R. Congress stalemate gives Pfizer deal an easy ride. *Financial Times*. May 8, 2014, p. 15.
49. GovTrack.us. Tracking the United States Congress. www.govtrack.us. Accessed December 5, 2015.
50. Administrative Procedures Act (5 U.S.C. Subchapter II). http://www.archives.gov/federal-register/laws/administrative-procedure/. Accessed December 5, 2015.
51. U.S. Department of Health and Human Services. Centers for Medicare and Medicaid Services. Medicare prescription drug benefit manual: Chapter 6—Part D drugs and formulary requirements. February 19, 2010. https://www.cms.gov/Medicare/Prescription-Drug-Coverage/PrescriptionDrugCovContra/downloads/Chapter6.pdf. Accessed December 5, 2015.
52. Norman B. Medicare drug changes put on hold after criticism. *Politico*. March 10, 2014. http://www.politico.com/story/2014/03/medicare-drug-changes-obamacare-104486.html. Accessed December 5, 2015.
53. Mariner WK, Glantz LH, and Annas GJ. Reframing federalism—The Affordable Care Act (and Broccoli) in the Supreme Court. *New England Journal of Medicine* 2012;367(12):1154–1158.
54. United States Department of Labor. The Employee Retirement Income Security Act (ERISA). 2013. www.dol.gov/compliance/laws/comp-erisa.htm. Accessed December 5, 2015.
55. Campbell M. One night in the tidal basin: How a stripper doomed health care reform in 1974. *Blue Hog Report*. November 21, 2013. http://www.bluehogreport.com/2013/11/21/one-night-in-the-tidal-basin-how-a-stripper-doomed-health-care-reform-in-1974/.
56. Rice T, Desmond K, and Gabel J. The medicare catastrophic coverage act: A post-mortem. *Health Affairs* 1990;9(3):75–87.
57. Daily S and Worthington R. Seniors' Wrath Stings Lobby: Protest Over Catastrophic-Care Law Targets AARP. *Chicago Tribune*. September 3, 1989. http://articles.chicagotribune.com/1989-09-03/news/8901100068_1_catastrophic-law-modern-maturity-magazine-medicare-catastrophic-coverage-act.
58. Moon M. 2006. *Medicare: A Policy Primer*. The Urban Institute Press, Washington, DC.
59. Moynihan R. Alosetron: A case study in regulatory capture, or a victory for patients' rights? *BMJ* 2002;325:592–595.

60. U.S. Food and Drug Administration. Briefing document for the Joint Gastrointestinal Drugs Advisory Committee and Drug Safety Risk Management Subcommittee. April 23, 2002. http://www.fda.gov/ohrms/dockets/ac/02/briefing/3848B1_01_GSK%20Briefing%20Pkg.pdf. Accessed December 5, 2015.
61. U.S. Food and Drug Administration. Approved Risk Evaluation and Mitigation Strategies (REMS). May 2015. http://www.fda.gov/downloads/Drugs/DrugSafety/PostmarketDrugSafetyInformationforPatientsandProviders/UCM446436.pdf. Accessed December 5, 2015.
62. Thompson CA. FDA's Advisers Recommend Updating Alosetron's REMS. July 24, 2013. http://www.ashp.org/menu/News/PharmacyNews/NewsArticle.aspx?id=3930#sthash.uLIOyD91.dpuf. Accessed December 5, 2015.
63. World Health Organization. *World Health Statistics 2015*. WHO, Geneva, Switzerland. http://apps.who.int/iris/bitstream/10665/170250/1/9789240694439_eng.pdf?ua=1&ua=1.
64. Center for Medicare and Medicaid Services. Office of the Actuary, National Health Statistics Group. Table 1.1. https://www.cms.gov/research-statistics-data-and-systems/statistics-trends-and-reports/nationalhealthexpenddata/nhe-fact-sheet.html. Accessed December 5, 2015.
65. National Center for Health Statistics. Health, United States, 2014: With Special Feature on Adults Aged 55–64. Table 85 Prescription Drug Use in the Past 30 days, by sex, age, race and Hispanic origin: United States, selected years 1988–1994 through 2009–2012. Hyattsville, MD. 2015. http://www.cdc.gov/nchs/data/hus/hus14.pdf. Accessed December 5, 2015.
66. Center for Responsive Politics. Top spenders. http://www.opensecrets.org/lobby/top.php?showYear=a&indexType=s.

Chapter 2

Federal Legislative Process

Valerie Heitshusen

Content

Editor's Introduction

Otto von Bismarck, who became the first chancellor of modern Germany in 1871, once famously said that "laws are like sausage, it is better to not see them being made." The legislative process is not pretty but it is important. It is through this process that policy problems are identified, salient solutions are brought forward, and compromises are worked out, which can allow proposed pieces of legislation to be signed by the president of the United States to become law.

As you will see when you read the nonpartisan Congressional Research Service (CRS) report "Introduction to the Legislative Process in the U.S. Congress" authored by Valerie Heitshusen which appears following the legislative process is very complex. This complexity is not an accident. The framers of our Constitution were men of property who feared "mob rule by those who had no property."[1] As a result, "they attempted to keep popular passions from taking over by sharply restricting popular control of government."[1] They did this by dividing power among the three branches of government (executive, legislative, and judicial). "Article 1 of the U.S. Constitution grants all legislative power to a bicameral Congress."[1] A compromise sought to balance the effect of popular majorities with the interest of the states. As a result, the House of Representatives is composed of 435 members elected from the population-based districts every 2 years. The Senate is composed of two members from each state elected for 6 years. In addition, under the concept of checks and balances, the U.S. Constitution prevents any of the branches of the government from acting independently. The Congress writes the laws, but they do not go into effect unless signed by the president or a presidential veto is overridden by two-thirds of votes in both houses of the Congress.

Given the conservative biases of the founders, it should be no surprise that the legislative process of the Congress includes a number of decision points where proposals can die. The process by which a bill can become a law is not predictable and often varies from one bill to another.

The sequential steps in the legislative process described in the CRS report may or may not be followed uniformly, but the overall process is consistent.

Bills may be referred to one or more committees, but may not be considered by the committee(s) to which they are referred because of lack of adequate support. After the committee consideration, which may include testimony and modification of the language of the bill, a bill may or may not be approved for consideration on the floor of the House or Senate. If it is slated for floor action, the bill may not get a sufficient number of votes to pass in the chamber in which it is being considered. Even if a bill passes both houses of the Congress, it cannot be sent to the president until a conference committee reconciles the differences between the two bills to produce a single bill with identical language. The difficulties in getting legislation through this process are reflected in the statistics with regard to how many bills are introduced in each Congress versus how many become law. The number of bills introduced in the 111th Congress (January 2009–December 2010) indicates that 11,193 bills were introduced but only 385 became law. In the 112th Congress (January 2011–2013), 10,866 bills were introduced and 284 became law.*

Two important pieces of health legislation, the Medicare Prescription Drug Improvement and Modernization Act of 2003 and the Affordable Care Act of 2010, are discussed in Chapters 22 and 25. John K. Iglehart, in an excellent article titled "The New Medicare Prescription Drug Benefit: A Pure Power Play,"[2] describes some of the unusual procedures involved in securing a majority to pass the Medicare Prescription Drug Improvement and Modernization Act of 2003. The Republicans accepted democratic priorities that included enactment of a guaranteed benefit that would apply to all Medicare beneficiaries. Passage by the House of Representatives of a bill by a one-vote majority followed a day of intense political maneuvering by then House Speaker Dennis Hastert, Vice President Chaney, and Secretary Thompson of Health and Human Services. The conference committee, to resolve differences between the House and Senate versions of the bill, included only two Democrats and excluded Senator Daschle who was then the Senate Minority Leader. The final passage in the House occurred only after the longest roll call vote in House history, which lasted for 2 h and 51 min, during which sufficient votes were found to secure victory.

References

1. Aldrich JH, Miller GJ, Ostrom CW, Rohde D. *American Government: People, Institutions and Policies.* Houghton Mifflin Co., Boston, MA, 1986.
2. Iglehart JK. The new medicare prescription drug benefit—A power play. *N Engl J Med*, February 19, 2004;350:826–833.

* Govtrack.us.

Chapter 3

Role of Federal Regulations and How They Are Developed

Curtis W. Copeland*

Contents

Introduction

In studies of federal policy making, much of the attention is directed at the process by which the Congress enacts legislation. On average, the Congress enacts about 200 public laws each year, but many of these laws are not substantive, broadly applicable pieces of legislation. For example, dozens

* This chapter is drawn largely from a report written by the author when he was with the Congressional Research Service. See CRS Report RL 32397 "Federal Rulemaking: The Role of the Office of Information and Regulatory Affairs" by Curtis W. Copeland, June 9, 2009, available at http://fas.org/sgp/crs/misc/RL32397.pdf. In addition, CRS Report RL 32240 "CRS Report for Congress Prepared for Members and Committees of Congress The Federal Rulemaking Process: An Overview" by Maeve Carey June 17, 2013, available at https://www.fas.org/sgp/crs/misc/RL32240.pdf.

of the public laws each year involve naming or renaming a post office, a courthouse, or some other public facility. Other than appropriations acts, only 50–100 public laws are typically enacted each year that most would consider substantive and broadly applicable.

Meanwhile, in that same "typical" year, federal agencies issue more than 3000 final rules on topics ranging from the timing of bridge openings to the permissible levels of arsenic and other contaminants in drinking water. Of these, about 1000 rules are considered "substantive" in nature, and about 80 of those substantive rules are considered "major" rules (e.g., expected to have at least a $(USD)100 million annual effect on the economy). Some examples are as follows:

- In March 2009, the Department of Defense (DOD) published a rule seeking to ensure that pharmaceuticals, provided by network retail pharmacies under the TRICARE Retail Pharmacy Program to eligible covered beneficiaries, are subject to certain pricing standards.[1] DOD said the rule would reduce its spending on pharmaceuticals by more than $(USD)100 million per year.
- In April 2010, the Centers for Medicare and Medicaid Services (CMS) within the Department of Health and Human Services (HHS) published a rulemaking changes to the regulations governing the Medicare Advantage Program (Part C) and Prescription Drug Benefit Program (Part D).[2] CMS estimated that the total cost of this rule in calendar year 2010 would be about $(USD)260.3 million and that the rule would have a total net savings of $(USD)341.7 million over the 6-year period 2010–2015.
- In September 2011, CMS published a rule finalizing revisions to the Medicare Part C, Part D, and section 1876 cost plans.[3] The rule also revised the regulations governing prescription drug pricing, coverage, and payment processes in the Part D program and requirements governing the marketing of Part C and Part D plans. CMS expected aggregate net savings to the federal government of approximately $(USD)520 million for fiscal years (FYs) 2010 through 2015.
- In September 2013, the Food and Drug Administration (FDA) within HHS published a rule generally requiring that the label of medical devices include a unique device identifier.[4] FDA said the rule would permit better identification of device-related adverse events, with domestic costs over 10 years between $(USD)642 million and $(USD)738 million.

Agency rulemaking is where the broad mandates from the Congress are made specific and implemented. Congressional mandates may not be very specific because the Congress lacks the expertise needed to determine a particular course of action, but more often because it is unable to reach agreement on anything other than general goals—leaving the details to regulatory agencies. Therefore, the Congress may enact legislation requiring that the air and water be clean, that workplaces be safe, and that drugs be effective, but it is the regulatory agencies that determine how clean, how safe, and how effective they are. Final rules may also tell regulated entities and the beneficiaries of the rules who must take action, when, and the processes that they must go through to satisfy the requirements. Regulation, like taxing and spending, is one of the basic tools of a government used to implement the public policy. It is where the policy making "rubber hits the road."

The terms "rule" or "regulation" are often used interchangeably in discussions of the federal regulatory process. The Administrative Procedure Act (APA) of 1946 defines a rule as "the whole or part of an agency statement of general or particular applicability and future effect designed to implement, interpret, or prescribe law or policy."* The procedures that federal agencies are required to follow in writing regulations are called the rulemaking process.

* 5 U.S.C. §551(4). The APA itself is 5 U.S.C. §§551 et seq.

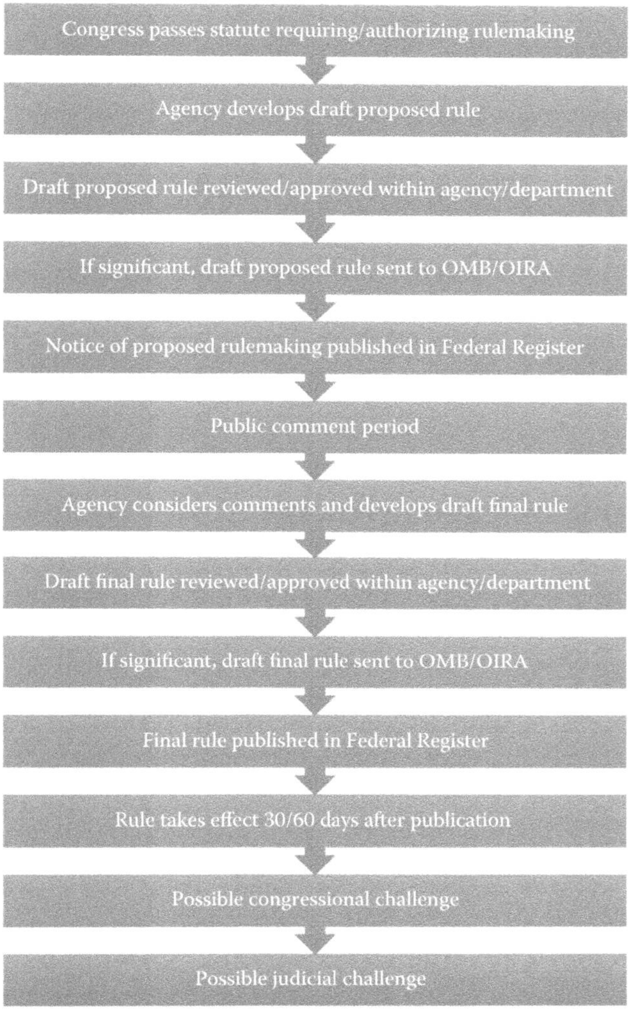

Figure 3.1 The federal rulemaking process.

As shown in Figure 3.1, the federal rulemaking process begins when legislation is enacted either authorizing or requiring an agency to develop and issue a rule. An initiating event (e.g., a recommendation from an outside body, a catastrophic accident, or a personal tragedy) can prompt either legislation or regulation (when a regulatory action has already been authorized by an earlier statute). The figure also illustrates that other parties may also be involved in the rulemaking, including the Office of Information and Regulatory Affairs (OIRA) within the Office of Management and Budget (OMB) and the public through the comment process.

It is important to note that the process depicted in Figure 3.1 does not apply to all agencies or all rules. For example, as discussed in detail later in this chapter, OIRA reviews the substance of draft rules to be issued by Cabinet departments like DOD and HHS and independent agencies like the Environmental Protection Agency, but OIRA does not review draft rules from independent regulatory agencies like the Securities and Exchange Commission and the Federal

Communications Commission that were established by the Congress to be independent of the president.* Even for covered agencies, OIRA only reviews rules that are considered "significant." Also, not all rules are published as proposals for public comment, while some rules may be published for comment more than once.

Implicit within the steps depicted in Figure 3.1 is an elaborate set of procedures and requirements that Congress and various presidents have developed during the past 60–70 years to guide the federal rulemaking process. Some of these rulemaking requirements apply to virtually all federal agencies, some apply only to certain types of agencies, and others are agency specific. Collectively, these rulemaking provisions are voluminous and require a wide range of procedural, consultative, and analytical actions on the part of rulemaking agencies. Those who would like to influence the public policies that are established through regulations would do well to understand the rulemaking process created by these statutory and executive order requirements.

Statutory Rulemaking Requirements

Statutory rulemaking requirements can be generally categorized into two groups—those that are specific to an individual agency or program and those that are more crosscutting in nature and therefore apply to a wider range of agencies or programs. Agency- or program-specific rulemaking requirements may be in authorizing or appropriating statutes and can have a significant or even determinative effect on an agency's rules and rulemaking procedures. As noted previously, these statutes sometimes specifically delineate what the agency's rules should require and may also impose specific procedural requirements on their rulemaking processes (e.g., the conduct of public hearings, the publication of a notice of proposed rulemaking [NPRM] by a particular date, or the coordination of rulemaking with another agency).

In other cases, however, statutes may give rulemaking agencies substantial discretion in how rules are developed and what they require. For example, the Patient Protection and Affordable Care Act (PPACA, P.L. 111–148) contained a number of provisions giving federal agencies broad authority to issue the regulations they deemed "necessary" or "appropriate."†

The following discussion of statutory rulemaking requirements focuses solely on the crosscutting requirements that are applicable to more than one agency. The discussion provides descriptions of some of the major rulemaking-related statutes and is not intended to be a catalog of all such requirements. Some of these rulemaking requirements have been in place for nearly 80 years, but most have been implemented during the past 35 years.

---

* As used in this chapter, the term "independent regulatory agencies" refers to agencies established to be independent of the president, including the SEC, the FCC, and the Consumer Product Safety Commission. The term "independent agencies" refers to agencies that are independent of Cabinet departments but not independent regulatory agencies (e.g., EPA). For a more detailed discussion of types of agencies, see David E. Lewis and Jennifer L. Selin, Sourcebook of United States Executive Agencies, First Edition, December 2012, prepared for the Administrative Conference of the United States, available at http://www.acus.gov/sites/default/files/documents/Sourcebook-2012-Final_12-Dec_Online.pdf.

† For example, Subsection 1401(g) of the act ("Refundable Tax Credit Providing Premium Assistance for Coverage Under a Qualified Health Plan") states that the Secretary of HHS "shall prescribe such regulations as may be necessary to carry out the provisions of this section."

Federal Register Act

The Federal Register Act became a law in July 1935 (44 U.S.C. Chapter 15) and established a uniform system for handling agency regulations by requiring (1) the filing of documents with the Office of the Federal Register, (2) the placement of documents on public inspection, (3) the publication of the documents in the *Federal Register*, and (4) (after a 1937 amendment) the permanent codification of rules in the *Code of Federal Regulations*. The publication of a rule in the *Federal Register* provides official notice of its existence and contents. The *Federal Register* is published each business day and is now available electronically.*

Administrative Procedure Act

The most long-standing and broadly applicable federal rulemaking requirements are in the APA of 1946 (5 U.S.C. §551 et seq.). The APA was written to bring regularity and predictability to agency decision-making, and it provides for both formal and informal rulemaking. Formal rulemaking is used in ratemaking proceedings and in certain other cases when rules are required by statute to be made "on the record" after an opportunity for a trial-type agency hearing.† However, few statutes require such on-the-record hearings.

Informal rulemaking, also known as "notice and comment" rulemaking, is used much more frequently. In informal rulemaking, the APA generally requires that virtually all agencies (Cabinet departments and independent agencies as well as independent regulatory agencies) publish an NPRM in the *Federal Register*.‡ The notice must contain (1) a statement of the time, place, and nature of public rulemaking proceedings, (2) reference to the legal authority under which the rule is proposed, and (3) either the terms or substance of the proposed rule or a description of the subjects and issues involved. After giving "interested persons" an opportunity to comment on the proposed rule and after considering the public comments, the agency may then publish the final rule, incorporating a general statement of its basis and purpose. Although the APA does not specify the length of this public comment period, agencies commonly allow at least 30 days.§ Public comments and other supporting materials (e.g., hearing records or agency regulatory studies) are placed in a rulemaking "docket" that must be available for public inspection. Finally, the APA states that the final rule cannot become effective until at least 30 days after its publication unless (1) the rule grants or recognizes an exemption or relieves a restriction, (2) the rule is an interpretative rule or a statement of policy, or (3) the agency determines that the rule should take effect sooner for good cause and publishes that determination with the rule.

---

* See https://www.federalregister.gov/. Other documents that are generally published in the Federal Register include presidential proclamations and executive orders, notices, and documents that the President or Congress requires to be published.

† United States v. Florida East Coast Railway, 410 U.S. 224 (1973).

‡ Some agencies begin the rulemaking process by publishing an "advance notice of proposed rulemaking" in which the agency notifies the public that it is considering an area for rulemaking and often requests comments on the appropriate scope or topics of the rule. The APA does not require the use of advance notices, but some other statutes require it for particular types of rules. Similarly, agencies may issue a "supplemental notice of proposed rulemaking" after an NPRM is issued if they wish to obtain public comment on new factual proposals before issuing a final rule.

§ Executive Order 12866, discussed in detail later in this chapter, suggests (but does not require) that agencies allow the public at least 60 days to comment for "significant" rules.

The final rule cannot adopt a provision if the NPRM did not clearly provide notice to the public that the agency was considering adopting it. If challenged in court under the APA, an agency rulemaking can be held unlawful or set aside if it is found to be "arbitrary, capricious, an abuse of discretion, or otherwise not in accordance with the law."* The court can also "compel agency action unlawfully withheld or unreasonably delayed." Amendment or revocation of an existing rule generally requires the responsible agency to issue a new rule through the APA process.

However, the APA also states that the notice and comment procedures generally do not apply when an agency finds, for "good cause," that those procedures are "impracticable, unnecessary, or contrary to the public interest." When agencies use the good cause exception, the act requires that they explicitly say so and provide a rationale for the exception's use when the rule is published in the *Federal Register*. The APA also provides explicit exceptions to the NPRM requirements for certain categories of regulatory actions, such as rules dealing with military or foreign affairs, agency management or personnel, or public property, loans, grants, benefits, or contracts. Further, the APA says that the NPRM requirements do not apply to interpretative rules, general statements of policy, or rules of agency organization, procedure, or practice. However, these rules do have to be published in the *Federal Register*.† A federal agency's invocation of the good cause exception (or other exceptions to notice and comment procedures) is subject to judicial review. After having reviewed the totality of circumstances, the courts can and sometimes do determine that an agency's reliance on the good cause exception was not authorized under the APA.[5]

Paperwork Reduction Act

The Paperwork Reduction Act (PRA) (44 U.S.C. §§3501–3520) was originally enacted in 1980. One of the purposes of the PRA is to minimize the paperwork burden for individuals, small businesses, and others resulting from the collection of information by or for the federal government. The act generally defines a "collection of information" as the obtaining or disclosure of facts or opinions by or for an agency by 10 or more nonfederal persons. Many information collections, recordkeeping requirements, and third-party disclosures are contained in or are authorized by regulations as monitoring or enforcement tools. In fact, these paperwork requirements are the essence of many agencies' regulatory provisions. The PRA requires all agencies (including independent regulatory agencies) to justify any collection of information from the public by establishing the need and intended use of the information, estimating the burden that the collection will impose on respondents, and showing that the collection is the least burdensome way to gather the information.

The PRA established OIRA within OMB to provide central agency leadership and oversight of government-wide efforts to reduce unnecessary paperwork burden and improve the management of information resources. Agencies must receive OIRA's approval (signified by an OMB

* The APA judicial review provisions are codified at 5 U.S.C 701–706.

† In August 1998, the General Accounting Office (GAO, now the Government Accountability Office) reported that about half of the 4658 final rules published in the Federal Register during 1997 were published without NPRMs. See GAO/GGD-98-126. In December 2012, GAO reported that about 35% of major rules and about 44% of non-major rules had no NPRM. See GAO-13-21. The agencies most frequently cited the "good cause" exception.

control number displayed on the information collection) for each collection request before it is implemented, and those approvals must be renewed at least every 3 years. Failure to obtain OIRA's approval for an active collection or the lapse of that approval represents a violation of the act and triggers the PRA's public protection provision.* Under that provision, no one can be penalized for failing to comply with a collection of information subject to the act if the collection does not display a valid OMB control number. OIRA can disapprove any collection of information if it believes the collection is inconsistent with the requirements of the PRA. For any collection of information that is not contained in a proposed rule, OIRA staff have up to 60 days under the statute to review the proposed collection and ensure, among other things, that the collection is statutorily authorized and necessary and that the agency's paperwork burden estimate (most commonly measured in terms of "burden hours") is reasonable.†

The PRA was amended in 1995 and gave significant new responsibilities to OIRA and executive branch agencies. One of the key features of the PRA of 1995 was the requirement that OIRA, in consultation with agency heads, set annual government-wide goals for the reduction of information collection burdens. It also required OIRA to establish agency burden reduction goals each year representing "the maximum practicable opportunity in each agency." At the end of FY 1995 (just before the PRA of 1995 took effect), federal agencies estimated that their information collections imposed about 7 billion burden hours on the public. As of December 2013, the agencies' estimated paperwork burden from more than 9000 approved information collections at nearly 10.4 billion h.‡ The agencies frequently contend that they are often unable to reduce paperwork requirements without changes in the underlying statutes that require the information to be collected.

Regulatory Flexibility Act

The Regulatory Flexibility Act (RFA) of 1980 (5 U.S.C. §§601–612) requires federal agencies (including independent regulatory agencies) to prepare a "regulatory flexibility analysis" assessing the impact of their forthcoming proposed and final regulations on "small entities," which the act defines as including small businesses, small governmental jurisdictions, and certain small not-for-profit organizations. The RFA requires the analysis to describe, among other things, (1) the reasons why the regulatory action is being considered; (2) the small entities to which the proposed rule will apply and, where feasible, an estimate of their number; (3) the projected reporting, recordkeeping, and other compliance requirements of the proposed rule; and (4) any significant alternatives to the rule that would accomplish the statutory objectives while minimizing the impact on small entities.

However, these analytical requirements are not triggered if the head of the issuing agency certifies that the proposed rule would not have a "significant economic impact on a substantial number of small entities." The RFA does not define "significant economic impact" or "substantial number of small entities," thereby giving federal agencies substantial discretion regarding when

---

* 44 U.S.C. §3512.

† An agency's annual paperwork burden-hour estimate is a function of (1) the frequency of the information collection, (2) the estimated number of respondents, and (3) amount of time that the agency estimates it takes each respondent to complete the collection. For example, if an agency estimates that an information collection conducted twice each year will take each of the estimated 10,000 respondents 10 h to complete each time, the total annual burden hour estimate for the collection is 200,000 burden hours ($2 \times 10{,}000 \times 10$).

‡ See http://www.reginfo.gov/public/do/PRAMain for the current inventory of approved information collections.

the act's analytical requirements are initiated. Also, the RFA's analytical requirements do not apply to final rules for which the agency does not publish a proposed rule.*

The RFA also contains several other notable provisions. For example, Section 602 requires each federal agency to publish a "regulatory flexibility agenda" in the *Federal Register* each October and April listing regulations that the agency expects to propose or promulgate, which are likely to have a significant economic impact on a substantial number of small entities.† Section 610 of the act requires agencies to review those rules that have or will have a significant impact within 10 years of their promulgation to determine whether they should be continued without change or should be amended or rescinded to minimize their impact on small entities. Section 612 of the RFA requires the chief counsel of the Small Business Administration's (SBA) Office of Advocacy to monitor and report at least annually on agencies' compliance with the act. SBA's primary method of monitoring agencies' compliance is to review and comment on the proposed regulations when they are published for notice and comment in the *Federal Register.*

Congressional Review Act

The statutory provision known as the Congressional Review Act (CRA) (5 U.S.C. §§801–808) was enacted in March 1996 and established expedited procedures by which the Congress may disapprove agencies' rules by enacting a joint resolution of disapproval. Under the CRA, before any final rule can become effective, it must be filed with each house of the Congress and General Accounting Office (GAO). The act also requires federal agencies to submit to GAO and make available to each house of the Congress a copy of any cost–benefit analysis prepared for the rule and a report on the agency's actions related to the RFA and any other relevant act or executive order. The definition of a "rule" under the CRA is very broad, and the act applies to rules issued by Cabinet departments and independent agencies as well as independent regulatory agencies.

If OIRA considers the issuing agency's rule to be "major," the agency generally must delay the rule's effective date by 60 days after the date of publication in the *Federal Register* or submission to the Congress and GAO, whichever is later.‡ Within 15 calendar days of receiving a major rule, GAO is required to provide the Congress with a report on the rule assessing the issuing agency's

* GAO has examined the implementation of the RFA several times within the past 20 years, and a recurring theme in GAO's reports is a lack of clarity in the act and a resulting variability in the act's implementation. For example, in 2001, GAO testified that the promise of the RFA may never be realized until Congress or some other entity defines what a "significant economic impact" and a "substantial number of small entities" mean in a rulemaking setting. See U.S. General Accounting Office, Regulatory Flexibility Act: Key Terms Still Need to Be Clarified, GAO-01-669T, April 24, 2001.

† This requirement, as well as a similar requirement in Executive Order 12866, is generally met via entries in the Unified Agenda of Federal Regulatory and Deregulatory Actions. The Unified Agenda is published twice each year in the Federal Register by the Regulatory Information Service Center, and provides uniform reporting of data on regulatory activities under development throughout the federal government.

‡ The CRA defines "major" rules as "any rule that the Administrator of the Office of Information and Regulatory Affairs of the Office of Management and Budget finds has resulted in or is likely to result in—(A) an annual effect on the economy of $(USD)100,000,000 or more; (B) a major increase in costs or prices for consumers, individual industries, Federal, State, or local government agencies, or geographic regions; or (C) significant adverse effects on competition, employment, investment, productivity, innovation, or on the foreign-based enterprises in domestic and export markets."

compliance with the procedural steps required by the various acts and executive orders applicable to the rulemaking process. Although the CRA establishes these special requirements for major rules, the CRA procedures for disapproving regulations apply to all rules, whether or not they are declared to be major.

Within 60 days after the Congress receives an agency's rule, excluding periods when the Congress is in recess or adjournment, a member of the Congress can introduce a resolution of disapproval that, if adopted by both houses and enacted into law, can nullify the rule, even if it has already gone into effect. Congressional disapproval under the CRA also prevents the agency from proposing to issue a "substantially similar" rule without a subsequent statutory authorization, but this provision is not intended to vitiate altogether the agency's power to establish regulations in the area in question.

The CRA provides that Senate action on a disapproval resolution under the act must occur within 60 days of session after the regulation is submitted, and it makes available during that period an expedited procedure intended to ensure that the Senate can take up and vote on the measure before the period expires. The act establishes no such expedited procedure for the house. If the Congress adjourns less than 60 days of the session after a rule is submitted, a new 60-day period for disapproval under the act begins on the 15th legislative day of the next session. If either house of the Congress rejects a disapproval resolution, the rule can take effect immediately (or as provided by other governing law or rule).

Federal agencies have submitted more than 60,000 rules to GAO (and presumably, the Congress) since the CRA took effect in March 1996, including more than 1200 major rules. However, only one rule has been overturned through CRA's procedures—OSHA's ergonomics standard in March 2001 (P.L. 107-5). Many reasons have been suggested for why the CRA has not been used more often, but chief among them may be the fact that, if the president vetoes a resolution of disapproval (which is likely if the underlying rule is developed during his administration), then enactment of the resolution would require approval of a two-thirds majority in both houses of the Congress to override the veto. The rejection of the ergonomics rule was the result of a specific set of circumstances created by a transition in party control of the presidency. The majority party in both houses of the Congress was the same as the party of the incoming president (George W. Bush). The new Congress convened in 2001 and adopted a resolution disapproving the rule published under the outgoing president (William J. Clinton), which George W. Bush signed into law. The Congress may be most able to use the CRA to disapprove rules in similar, transition-related circumstances.

The Congress can also stop agency rulemaking or regulatory enforcement through provisions added to the agency appropriations legislation. There appear to be four types of such appropriations provisions: (1) restrictions on the finalization of particular proposed rules, (2) restrictions on regulatory activity within certain areas, (3) implementation or enforcement restrictions, and (4) conditional restrictions (e.g., preventing implementation of a rule until certain actions are taken). Some of these kinds of provisions have been included in appropriations bills for many years in a row. The reasons behind these restrictions vary, with some appearing to be based on economic considerations, some requiring or preventing the implementation of rules issued at the end of a presidential administration, and some included for various other reasons. Such provisions are generally applicable only for the period of time and the agencies covered by the relevant appropriations bill, but (depending on how they are worded) can be more broadly applicable. Also, to the extent that agencies have independent sources of funding (e.g., user fees) or implement their regulations through state or local governments, some of the limitations may not be as restrictive as they seem.

Other Statutory Rulemaking Requirements

A variety of other statutory requirements have been enacted establishing requirements on the federal rulemaking process, but each of them has certain limitations. Some examples are as follows:

- Title II of the Unfunded Mandates Reform Act (UMRA, 2 U.S.C. §§1532–1538) was enacted in 1995 and requires Cabinet departments and independent agencies (but not independent regulatory agencies) to, among other things, (1) prepare a written statement containing specific descriptions and estimates of costs and benefits for any proposed rule or any final rule for which a proposed rule was published that includes any federal mandate that may result in the expenditure of $(USD)100 million or more in any year by state, local, or tribal governments, in the aggregate, or the private sector (Section 202) and (2) identify and consider a reasonable number of regulatory alternatives and select the least costly, most cost-effective, or least burdensome alternative (or explain why that alternative was not selected) for each rule for which a written statement is prepared (Section 205). However, GAO has reported on several occasions that, because of the way the statute was written, UMRA has had little effect on agencies' rulemaking actions. There are at least 14 reasons why a rule may not be considered a covered "mandate" under the act.*
- Section 515 of the Treasury and General Government Appropriations Act for FY 2001 (P.L. 106–554), generally known as the "Data Quality Act" or the "Information Quality Act" (IQA), amended the PRA and directed OMB to issue government-wide guidelines that "provide policy and procedural guidance to Federal agencies for ensuring and maximizing the quality, objectivity, utility, and integrity of information (including statistical information) disseminated by Federal agencies." The IQA also instructed agencies (both Cabinet departments and independent agencies, as well as independent regulatory agencies) to issue their own guidelines not more than 1 year after the issuance of OMB's government-wide guidelines and to establish administrative mechanisms allowing affected persons to seek and obtain correction of information maintained and disseminated by the agency. However, in March 2006, the U.S. Court of Appeals for the Fourth Circuit ruled that the act does not permit judicial review of agency denials of information collection requests.† Two district courts had previously reached a similar conclusion, and the Department of Justice issued a brief stating that the IQA does not permit judicial review.‡

---

* See, for example, testimony of Denise M. Fantone, Director, Strategic Issues, U.S. Government Accountability Office, before the Subcommittee on Technology, Information Policy, Intergovernmental Relations and Procurement Reform, House Committee on Oversight of Government Management, available at http://www.gao.gov/products/GAO-11-385T.

† Salt Institute; Chamber of Commerce of the United States of America v. Michael O. Leavitt, Secretary of Health and Human Services, No. 05-1097, March 6, 2006.

‡ 24 In re: Operation of the Missouri River Sys. Litig., No. 03-MD-1555 at 49 (D. Minn, June 21, 2004) (order granting motions for summary judgment); and Salt Institute and the Chamber of Commerce of the United States of America v. Tommy G. Thompson, Secretary, U.S. Department of Health and Human Services, Civil Action No. 04-359, November 15, 2004.

Executive Orders

During the past 40 years, each president has issued executive orders and/or presidential directives designed to guide the federal rulemaking process, often with the goal of reducing regulatory burden. Although independent regulatory agencies are generally not covered by these requirements, they are often encouraged to follow them. By far the most important of the current executive rulemaking requirements is Executive Order (EO) 12866,[6] which describes both the principles and the process by which presidential regulatory review currently takes place. This section also briefly discusses three other executive orders, one that came before EO 12866 and two others that were issued more recently.

Executive Order 12866

Some type of centralized review of agencies' regulations within the Executive Office of the President has been part of the federal rulemaking process for nearly 50 years.[7] Although each of his three predecessors had some type of review process, the most significant development in the evolution of presidential review of rulemaking occurred in 1981, when President Reagan issued EO 12291.* The executive order required federal agencies (other than independent regulatory agencies) to send a copy of each draft proposed and a final rule to OMB before publication in the *Federal Register*. It also required covered agencies to prepare a regulatory impact analysis for each "major" rule (e.g., those with a $(USD)100 million annual impact on the economy). As a result of this order, OIRA's responsibilities were greatly expanded from paperwork reviews under the PRA to examinations of the substance of covered agencies rules—between 2000 and 3000 reviews per year.

On September 30, 1993, President Clinton issued EO 12866 that revoked EO 12291 and established a new process for OIRA's review of rules. Like its predecessor, the new executive order limited OIRA's reviews to proposed and final rules published by agencies other than independent regulatory agencies. However, it also limited OIRA's reviews to the actions identified by the rulemaking agency or OIRA as "significant" regulatory actions, defined as those that were "economically significant" (e.g., those with a $(USD)100 million impact on the economy) or that (1) were inconsistent or interfered with an action taken or planned by another agency; (2) materially altered the budgetary impact of entitlements, grants, user fees, or loan programs; or (3) raised novel legal or policy issues. As a result, the number of rules that OIRA reviewed dropped from between 2000 and 3000 per year to between 500 and 700 per year.

EO 12866 also differs from its predecessors in other respects. For example, the order requires that OIRA generally complete its reviews of proposed and final rules within 90 calendar days (although it allows agencies to request unlimited extensions). It also requires both rulemaking agencies and OIRA to disclose certain information about how the regulatory reviews were conducted. For example, agencies are to identify for the public (1) the substantive changes made to rules between the draft submitted to OIRA for review and the action subsequently announced and (2) the changes made at the suggestion or recommendation of OIRA. OIRA is required to, among other things, provide agencies with a copy of all communications between OIRA personnel and

---

* Executive Order 12291, Federal regulation, Federal Register 46, 13193, February 19, 1981. Although the executive order did not specifically mention OIRA, shortly after its issuance the Reagan Administration decided to integrate OMB's regulatory review responsibilities under the executive order with the responsibilities given to OMB (and ultimately to OIRA) by the PRA.

parties outside of the executive branch and to maintain a public log of all regulatory actions under review and of all of the documents provided to the agencies. OIRA also lists all meetings it has with outside parties while rules are under review.[8]

For each significant draft rule, the executive order requires the issuing agency to provide to OIRA the text of the draft rule, a description of why the rule is needed, and a general assessment of the rule's costs and benefits. For draft rules that are "economically significant," the executive order requires a detailed cost–benefit analysis, including an assessment of the costs and benefits of "potentially effective and reasonably feasible alternatives to the planned regulation."* One of the "principles of regulation" in the order is that agencies shall "propose or adopt a regulation only upon a reasoned determination that the benefits of the intended regulation justify its costs." The order also says that when setting regulatory priorities, "each agency shall consider, to the extent reasonable, the degree and nature of the risks posed by various substances or activities within its jurisdiction." The executive order's "regulatory philosophy" states that unless a statute requires another regulatory approach, "in choosing among alternative regulatory approaches, agencies should select those approaches that maximize net benefits."

During the formal EO 12866 review process, OIRA analyzes the draft rule in light of the principles of the executive order and discusses the rule with the staff and officials at the rulemaking agency. OIRA may also discuss the draft rule with other agencies with whom the interagency coordination will be necessary and may meet or otherwise communicate with interested stakeholders outside of the federal government. At the end of the review, OIRA either concludes that the draft rule is consistent with the principles of the executive order (the majority of the cases) or returns the rule to the agency "for further consideration." In some cases, agencies withdraw their draft rules during OIRA's review. If the draft is a proposed rule, the agency may then publish an NPRM. If the draft is a final rule, the agency may then publish a final rule and allow the rule to take effect. OIRA staff also sometimes review draft rules informally before their formal submission under the executive order—particularly when there is a statutory or legal deadline or when a rule has a large impact on society.

Executive Orders 13563 and 13579

On January 18, 2011, President Obama issued EO 13563 on "Improving Regulation and Regulatory Review."[9] Section 1(b) of the new order states that "This order is supplemental to and reaffirms the principles, structures, and definitions governing contemporary regulatory review that were established in Executive Order 12866 of September 30, 1993." Although similar to the 1993 order in many respects, EO 13563 contains some new provisions. For example, Section 2(b) of the order states that agencies should generally provide

> timely online access to the rulemaking docket on regulations.gov,† including relevant scientific and technical findings, in an open format that can be easily searched and downloaded. For proposed rules, such access shall include, to the extent feasible and

* OMB Circular A-4 provides the office's guidance on how to prepare regulatory analyses under the executive order. For a copy of this guidance, see http://www.whitehouse.gov/omb/circulars/a004/a-4.pdf.

† Regulations.gov is an electronic rulemaking program launched in 2003 to enable citizens to search, view and comment on regulations issued by the U.S. government.

permitted by law, an opportunity for public comment on all pertinent parts of the rulemaking docket, including relevant scientific and technical findings.

Perhaps most notably, Section (b) of the new order requires agencies to initiate retrospective reviews of their existing rules. Specifically, it states that

> Within 120 days of the date of this order, each agency shall develop and submit to the Office of Information and Regulatory Affairs a preliminary plan, consistent with law and its resources and regulatory priorities, under which the agency will periodically review its existing significant regulations to determine whether any such regulations should be modified, streamlined, expanded, or repealed so as to make the agency's regulatory program more effective or less burdensome in achieving the regulatory objectives.

Section 5(a) of EO 12866 had previously required agencies to submit a plan for retrospective reviews to OIRA, so this provision appears to require agencies to update those plans.*

As a follow-up to EO 13563, President Obama issued EO 13579, asking (but not requiring) independent regulatory agencies to follow the key principles of EO 13563 and to produce plans for retrospective analysis of their existing rules.[10]

Other Executive Orders and Directives

Agencies other than independent regulatory agencies must also be aware of an array of other rulemaking requirements contained in executive orders and presidential directives. Some examples are as follows:

- EO 13132 on "federalism" requires covered federal agencies to "have an accountable process to ensure meaningful and timely input by State and local officials in the development of regulatory policies that have federalism implications."[11] The order defines "federalism implications" as "substantial direct effects on the States, on the relationship between the national government and the States, or on the distribution of power and responsibilities among the various levels of government." Federal agencies are prohibited from promulgating any regulation with unfunded federalism implications unless they have (1) consulted with state and local officials early in the development of the proposed rule and (2) prepared a "federalism summary impact statement." However, the order gives agencies substantial discretion regarding its implementation. For example, it does not define what type of regulatory action constitutes "substantial direct effects" and says that the consultation and impact statement requirements apply "to the extent practicable."
- EO 12898 on environmental justice says (among other things) that each agency must develop a strategy that identifies and addresses disproportionately high and adverse human health or environmental effects of its programs, policies, and activities on minority populations and low-income populations.[12] It also says that environmental human health research should include diverse segments of the population in epidemiological and

* Agency retrospective review plans can be viewed at http://exchange.regulations.gov/topic/eo-13563.

clinical studies and that agencies should identify rules that should be revised to meet the objectives of the order.

- EO 13211 on energy impacts requires agencies (to the extent permitted by law) to prepare and submit to OMB a "statement of energy effects" for significant energy actions.[13] The statement, published in the NPRM and the final rule, is to include a detailed statement of "any adverse effects on energy supply, distribution, or use" for the action and reasonable alternatives and their effects.

Conclusion

During the past 70 years, the Congress and various presidents have established numerous requirements governing the regulatory process. The Congress has enacted laws (e.g., the APA, PRA, and RFA) that require some type of procedure, review, and/or analysis of draft rules by the rulemaking agencies themselves or by outside parties. Presidential rulemaking requirements have often focused on the coordination of agencies' regulatory efforts with the president's priorities and attempts to improve the quality of regulations through cost–benefit analysis, risk assessment analysis, and the consideration of specific factors in the rulemaking process (e.g., federalism and environmental justice). Underlying many of these congressional and presidential requirements is an attempt to ensure that certain interests or issues are considered during the rulemaking process and/or to minimize the burden associated with federal regulations.

However, these rulemaking requirements impose burdens of their own on rulemaking agencies and may be a factor in the length of time it takes agencies to issue rules. Federal agencies must be aware of the crosscutting and the program-specific statutory and executive requirements underlying their regulations and must craft rules that are consistent with those requirements—or run the risk of having their rules returned to them by OIRA or rejected by the Congress or the courts. Several of these statutes and orders indicate that their requirements may be integrated with or satisfied by the requirements in other statutes or orders. Some observers believe that integration and consolidation of all these requirements could improve the rulemaking process. In 1993, the Administrative Conference of the United States noted that the simple requirements in the APA for informal rulemaking had been "overlain with an increasing number of constraints," including those imposed by the Congress, presidents, and the courts. The Administrative Conference recommended a "coordinated framework of proposals aimed at promoting efficient and effective rulemaking."[14] Since then, the number of rulemaking requirements has increased.

On the other hand, many of these statutory and executive order provisions provide the agencies substantial discretion regarding when and how the rulemaking requirements are to be applied. For example, because the RFA does not define the term "significant impact on a substantial number of small entities," agencies have a great deal of latitude to determine when a regulatory flexibility analysis is required. Other rulemaking requirements (e.g., UMRA) are written in such a way that they actually apply to only a small number of rules. Because of the inevitability of regulation and its associated burden, efforts to either tighten the existing rulemaking requirements or impose new ones are likely to continue.* A clear understanding of the existing requirements and how they have been implemented may inform any such future efforts.

---

* As of October 2013, a total of 23 bills had been introduced in the 113th Congress to change some aspect of the rulemaking process.

Such an understanding can also assist those wishing to use the rulemaking process to further their policy goals. For example, understanding when federal agencies can properly use the "good cause" exception to the APA's notice and comment procedures can determine whether legal challenges to an agency's action can be filed. Understanding which rules are subject to OIRA's review, and the nature of the office's reviews, provides a venue that others not so informed may miss. Also, those wishing to prevent or delay the implementation of rules by the Congress would do well to know the strengths and weaknesses of CRA resolutions of disapproval versus appropriations restrictions. Regulations are important, which affect every American every day. Therefore, knowledge of how those regulations are put in place is equally important.

Bibliography

Useful websites include the following:

https://www.federalregister.gov/uploads/2011/01/the_rulemaking_process.pdf (Office of the Federal Register, "A Guide to the Rulemaking Process").

http://www.reginfo.gov/public/ (which provides links to upcoming rules identified in the Unified Agenda, rules under review at OIRA pursuant to EO 12866, and information collections under review at OIRA pursuant to the PRA).

http://www.regulations.gov/#!home (which allows the public to identify proposed rules open for comment, submit comments, view the comments of others, and obtain cost-benefit analyses and other supporting documents).

References

1. U.S. Department of Defense, Office of the Secretary, Civilian Health and Medical Program of the Uniformed Services (CHAMPUS)/TRICARE: Inclusion of TRICARE Retail Pharmacy Program in Federal Procurement of Pharmaceuticals, *Federal Register* 74, 11279, March 17, 2009.
2. U.S. Department of Health and Human Services, Centers for Medicare and Medicaid Services, Medicare Program; Policy and Technical Changes to the Medicare Advantage and the Medicare Prescription Drug Benefit Programs, *Federal Register* 75, 19678, April 15, 2010.
3. U.S. Department of Health and Human Services, Centers for Medicare and Medicaid Services, Medicare Program; Medicare Advantage and Prescription Drug Benefit Programs, *Federal Register* 76, 54600, September 1, 2011.
4. U.S. Department of Health and Human Services, Food and Drug Administration, Unique Device Identification System, *Federal Register* 78, 58786, September 24, 2013.
5. For discussions of these court cases, see Ellen R. Jordan, The Administrative Procedure Act's 'Good Cause' Exemption, *Administrative Law Review*, 36, 113–178, Spring 1984; C.J. Lanctot, The good cause exception: Danger to notice and comment requirements under the Administrative Procedure Act, *Georgetown Law Journal*, 68, 765–782, February 1980.
6. Executive Order 12866, Regulatory planning and review, *Federal Register* 58, 51735, October 4, 1993.
7. See J. Tozzi, OIRA's formative years: The historical record of centralized regulatory review preceding OIRA's founding, *Administrative Law Review*, 63, 37–69, 2011 (Special Edition), available at http://www.thecre.com/pdf/20111211_ALR_Tozzi_Final.pdf.
8. Office of Management and Budget. Meeting Records. http://www.whitehouse.gov/omb/oira_meetings/. Accessed December 5, 2015.
9. Executive Order 13563, Improving regulation and regulatory review, *Federal Register* 76, 3821, January 21, 2011.
10. Executive Order 13579, Regulation and Independent Regulatory Agencies, *Federal Register* 76, 41587, July 11, 2011.

11. Executive Order 13132, Federalism, *Federal Register* 64, 43255, August 10, 1999.
12. Executive Order 12898, Federal actions to address environmental justice in minority populations and low-income populations, *Federal Register* 59, 7629, February 16, 1994.
13. Executive Order 13211, Actions concerning regulations that significantly affect energy supply, distribution, or use, *Federal Register* 66, 28355, May 22, 2001.
14. Administrative Conference of the U.S., Improving the environment for agency rulemaking, *Federal Register* 59, 4670, February 1, 1994.

Chapter 4

Access, Quality, and Cost

Julie A. Schmittdiel and Marsha Raebel

Contents

Introduction

The U.S. health-care system is currently one of the most expensive in the world,[1] with Americans spending more on health care as a percentage of national GDP than any other nation.[2] At the same time, evidence suggests that the quality of health care that Americans receive is lower than that in many developed countries, with the United States ranking 31st in life expectancy.[1] Policy makers and researchers have called for improving the value of U.S. health care through pursuing a set of goals known as the "Triple Aim."[1] The Triple Aim calls for simultaneously improving the patient care experience through greater, more equitable *access* to care, improving the *quality* of care provided to the overall population, and decreasing the *costs* of caring for specific population subgroups. The Triple Aim approach is well aligned with the key dimensions of health systems, namely, safety, effectiveness, patient centeredness, timeliness, efficiency, and equity, which were recommended by the Institute of Medicine in its landmark report on "crossing the quality chasm" in health care.[3]

The Triple Aim approach to optimizing access, quality, and costs of care has been discussed as a way toward improving the health-care system as a whole, as well as an approach to improving individual health-care components such as inpatient care delivery.[1] However, little has been written about how the Triple Aim can be used as a framework to improve the care that provides patients with evidence-based pharmacist services and medical products such as pharmaceuticals to treat acute and chronic illnesses. Pharmacists, pharmacies, and pharmaceutical policy-makers not only have a role in improving access, quality, and cost for pharmaceutical products and services but also have a responsibility to contribute to and improve the health-care delivery system overall.[4]

The Triple Aim goals are interdependent[1] and support each other like a "three-legged stool": addressing (or not addressing) any one of the aims will likely impact the others. For example, approaches and metrics for improving access to medications can also improve the health-care quality for patients taking those medications; pursuing insurance drug benefit cost reduction may undermine patient access to medications at the expense of improving costs. Our conceptual model of pharmacy's role in access, quality, and costs for medical products (see Figure 4.1) highlights this interdependence and places many of the key aspects of appropriate care highlighted by the Triple Aim within this framework. We address each aspect of the outlined Triple Aim for pharmacy care in the succeeding texts and set a context for understanding the key issues for improving access, quality, and cost in pharmacy. In addition, we review key health-care policies and innovations that have been designed to address the Triple Aim goals and lay out potential policy directions to improve U.S. pharmacy care and health care overall.

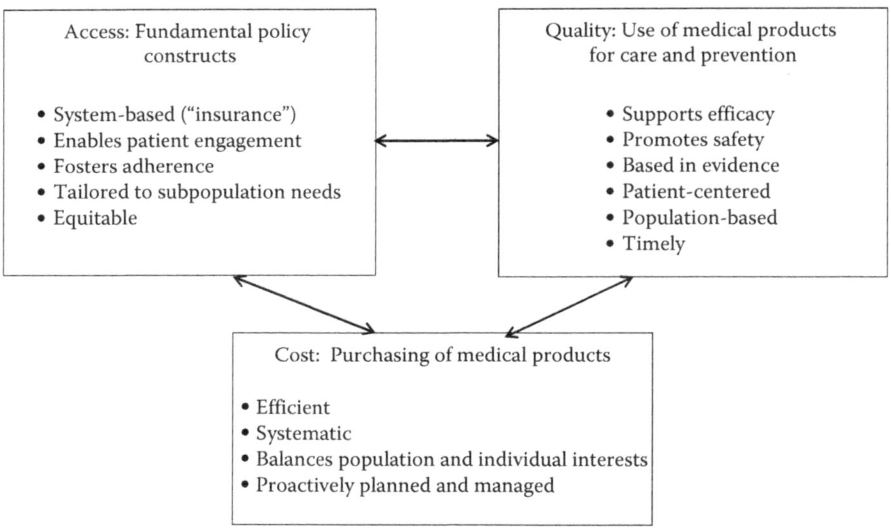

Figure 4.1 Pharmacy policy's roles in access, quality, and cost of medical products (drugs, biologics, vaccines, and medical devices).

Access

Insurance Coverage

A key strategy for improving access to pharmaceuticals is through appropriate insurance coverage for medications and medical devices. Until recently, estimates suggested that up to 46% of Americans under 65 either have no health insurance at all or have inadequate coverage to meet their medical needs.[5] Public policy has played a key role in expanding drug insurance coverage for Americans, such as through the "Medicare Prescription Drug, Improvement, and Modernization Act" of 2003, which introduced the Medicare Prescription Drug Plan (Part D) as an option for Medicare enrollees to obtain prescription drug coverage starting on January 1, 2006. Until this time, seniors who qualified for Medicare did not have access to outpatient drug coverage through the Medicare program. Medicare Part D has improved access to medications for many Americans,[6] and some have suggested that it has also had a positive impact on adherence to medication as well.[7]

When Medicare Part D was introduced, it provided drug coverage through what is known as a "doughnut hole" benefit design[8]: patients had annual drug coverage up to a particular level of overall drug expenses ($[USD]2250 in 2006 in most cases), followed by a gap in drug coverage where patients are responsible for the full cost of their medications up to a certain amount ($[USD]3600 in 2006 in most cases). If this prescription drug cost cap is hit within the year, then "catastrophic" drug coverage begins and drugs are again covered by Part D through the end of the year. While studies on the impact of this coverage gap on adherence and outcomes have had mixed results,[9] some studies suggested the gap in coverage is associated with decreased access to medications.[8]

The passage of the "Patient Protection and Affordable Care Act" (commonly referred to as "ACA") in 2009 began the most sweeping changes in health-care public policy since the Medicare program was instituted in 1965. The ACA legislates numerous changes to the U.S. health-care system, including the requirement that all Americans obtain health-care coverage starting in 2014. The ACA includes changes to Medicare Part D that will phase out the "doughnut hole" by 2020. In addition, the ACA mandates that all health insurance products sold in the United States meet a minimum set of coverage requirements, including some level of prescription drug coverage.[10]

As of this writing, many of the ACA's requirements were just beginning to take effect; it is too early to comment on whether the ACA's intention to improve American's access to medications will be realized. It is important for policy-makers, researchers, and program evaluation experts to carefully measure how the ACA impacts the overall number of Americans with adequate health-care insurance, whether patients receive sufficient insurance coverage for medications, and if there are associated improvements in health-care outcomes.

Pharmacies

For many people, physically accessing a pharmacy is a challenge because no pharmacy is convenient to their home or they cannot easily get to a pharmacy due to issues such as lack of transportation or physical disability. Integrated health-care delivery systems such as Kaiser Permanente have reduced these barriers to pharmacy access by colocating pharmacies in their medical office facilities.[11] If patients are seen for care in the medical office, they have immediate access to a pharmacy.

However, patients may still face transportation and time limitations in reaching their physician's office or in obtaining refills in between office visits.

Mail order pharmacies have largely emerged to facilitate pharmacy access. With mail order pharmacies, prescriptions are typically ordered through a website or by telephone, and the prescription or refill is then mailed to the patient. *Mail order services* are provided by many reputable licensed pharmacies (e.g., independent community, retail chain, health plan, or dedicated mail order pharmacies), and the prescription medications dispensed from these pharmacies are the same as medications dispensed from any reputable "brick and mortar" pharmacy.

Mail order pharmacies are not synonymous with Internet pharmacies. The National Association of Boards of Pharmacy (NABP) found 97% of Internet pharmacies do not comply with state and federal laws or with NABP patient safety and pharmacy practice standards.[12] Unlicensed, unscrupulous Internet pharmacies have provided counterfeit prescription medications to unsuspecting customers and have been implicated in providing prescription medications to patients without the required prescriptions.[13] Subsequently, patient use of Internet pharmacies is not recommended by the NABP. Policy-makers play an important role in designing and enforcing policies to discourage Internet pharmacy use and in providing appropriate oversight and consumer protection for Internet commerce.

Pharmacists

Pharmacists are among the most accessible of health-care providers, and access to a pharmacy is essential for obtaining prescription medications. However, pharmacy access alone is insufficient to enable appropriate medication use. Fundamentally, access to a pharmacist is necessary to confirm dispensing of the correct medication, avoid or manage drug interactions (i.e., with other drugs, diseases, and nutrients), and evaluate and support the patient's understanding of the medication (how to take the medication, reason for use, precautions, contraindications, etc.). While technology is important in each of these medication use activities (e.g., screening for interactions, product bar code checking), technology is no substitute for the clinical knowledge, judgment, and counseling expertise of a trained and licensed pharmacist.

Pharmacists are educated and trained to facilitate optimizing patients' medication use and serve patients by providing medication therapy management (MTM) and other professional services in acute care and ambulatory health-care systems and pharmacies. MTM activities include obtaining medication histories, identifying and collaborating with physicians and other health-care professionals to prevent and resolve medication-related problems, educating patients about proper medication use, identifying and minimizing barriers to medication adherence, providing guidance on nonprescription medications, and documenting and communicating information and recommendations to physicians and other members of the health-care team. These activities are within the pharmacist scope of practice in all practice settings across all 50 states of the United States and are crucial to maintaining patient access to appropriate medications.

Ensuring access to care settings where pharmacists engage in collaborative professional activities that reduce medication-related adverse events and enhance patient safety during transitions in care (e.g., MTM) is a key to optimizing patients' therapeutic outcomes. Pharmacist-managed anticoagulation therapy management services have reduced bleeding complications and lowered clotting frequencies in comparison with anticoagulation therapy managed by physicians.[14,15] Many public and private ambulatory and acute care health-care systems such as the U.S. Department of Veterans Affairs, Group Health Cooperative, and Kaiser Permanente have expanded access to pharmacists and improved patient clinical outcomes by implementing collaborative pharmacy practice models and disease management services for chronic conditions such as diabetes,[16] hypertension,[17] pain management,[18] hyperlipidemia,[17] heart failure,[19] and other diseases.[18] In addition, pharmacists in varied community pharmacy settings provide services such as diabetes care, emergency contraception, and drug information to growing numbers of ambulatory patients.[20,21] These collaborative pharmacy practice models can improve health-care delivery and address some of the demands on health-care system access, and recognition of pharmacists as clinicians is appropriate given the advanced care delivery they provide in many settings. Health policy-makers should support policies that affirm this practice model and further consider ways to optimize the role of pharmacists in delivering a variety of patient-centered care.

Pharmacists also serve consumers by promoting disease prevention and by leading or participating in health promotion and wellness education activities such as smoking cessation counseling within communities and health-care organizations. For example, over 200,000 pharmacists are trained to administer vaccines,[22] and thousands of U.S. independent and chain community pharmacies routinely provide both vaccine information and vaccinations administered by certified pharmacists. Policy-makers should explore policies that enable pharmacies to expand key public health initiatives, such as immunizations and smoking cessation, and ensure that government health-care payment policies appropriately cover their provision.

One of the key goals in improving access to pharmacies and pharmaceuticals is to improve appropriate patient adherence to prescribed medications. When patients with chronic illnesses are adherent to medications, adverse outcomes such as hospitalization rates and mortality can be decreased. However, evidence suggests that ongoing adherence to medications for chronic conditions such as diabetes, hypertension, and hyperlipidemia is low in the general population.[23] The initial uptake of medications when first prescribed is also low, with some studies suggesting at least 25% of patients with chronic illnesses not filling their medications more than once.[24] Efforts to increase pharmacy access through methods such as mail order pharmacy use[25] and increase pharmaceutical access through insurance coverage for needed medications may improve adherence and ultimately improve health-care quality through better outcomes.

Quality

Medical Products

While pharmacies are licensed and regulated through state boards, the Food and Drug Administration (FDA) regulates manufacturers of medical products, including drug, biologics, vaccines, and medical devices. The U.S. FDA has long been responsible for the foundational quality element of pharmacy public policy: ensuring that medical products available in the United States are safe and effective. Unfortunately, much of the legislation that regulates the availability and safety of U.S. medical products came about in response to public health disasters. The Drug Quality and Security Act signed into law in late 2013 is no exception.[26] This legislation was in response to fungal meningitis deaths associated with contaminated steroid injections prepared in unsterile conditions by a large compounding center. It was originally focused primarily toward enhancing federal control over large compounding operations that previously had little oversight from either state boards or the FDA. However, the final law also contains provisions that enhance tracking of all prescription drug products throughout the U.S. supply chain. These provisions further ensure the quality of medications by helping authorities identify stolen or counterfeit drugs. Specifically, manufacturers will be required to add serial numbers to drug packages and to upgrade to electronic codes that facilitate tracking of medications from the drug maker to the dispensing pharmacy.

Pharmacist Professional Services

Pharmacists traditionally are responsible for ensuring quality through the accurate preparation, dispensing, and safe handling of prescription medications and other aspects of medical product procurement, storage, inventory, and handling. For many pharmacists, these critical, technical aspects of pharmaceutical dispensing and management remain important components of their practices. Among other pharmacists, however, medical product handling is not part of their professional responsibilities. For most pharmacists, professional practice now includes checking interactions with medications, counseling patients on the best use of their medications, and other cognitive professional services. A growing number of pharmacists are integrated into health-care teams where they deliver a variety of high-quality direct patient care services under collaborative practice agreements. Such services can include performing patient assessments, prescribing medications (in some settings), ordering, interpreting, and monitoring laboratory tests, formulating clinical assessments and therapeutic plans, coordinating care plans, and providing wellness and preventive services. In these professional practices, pharmacists are functioning as health-care providers.

Recent systematic reviews have confirmed that integrating pharmacists into patient care improves the quality of care through better therapeutic outcomes, reduced hospitalizations, and safer medication use in numerous health-care settings and disease states.[27,28] However, even though pharmacists are increasingly responsible for all aspects of medication use and medication-associated outcomes, pharmacists are not recognized in the U.S. health policy as health-care providers. The absence of enabling legislation and policy reduces the magnitude of potential positive impact that pharmacists can have on the quality of health care for individual patients and for populations. For pharmacists to expand their roles in medication-associated care delivery, they must be recognized as health-care providers in legislation and policy and be compensated through mechanisms commensurate with the services provided.

Pharmacists function in many other professional roles that improve the quality of care for individuals and populations, such as pharmacist-led population management initiatives in patient safety, affordability, or care quality. For example, working in collaboration with physicians in integrated health-care systems, pharmacists can contact patients taking drugs for which the FDA has issued a safety communication and discussed therapeutic alternatives.[17] In another example, many pharmacists are engaged in ensuring that the most cost-effective medications are available to patients through formulary management activities of health systems' Pharmacy and Therapeutics Committees.

A common quality of care role for pharmacists in health plans is to develop and implement initiatives associated with the Health Plan Employer Data and Information Set (HEDIS) metrics,[29] measures that are used to compare multiple quality of processes and outcomes of care across health plans. For example, one HEDIS quality of care initiative targeted women aged 67 or older with a fracture, with the measure being that these women should have either bone mineral density testing or dispensing of an osteoporosis medication within 6 months after the fracture. At Kaiser Permanente Colorado (KPCO), clinical pharmacy specialists intervened among these women, resulting in an improvement of KPCO's performance on this metric to 57% (from 33% at baseline).[29] Several of the HEDIS medication use measures have been developed in conjunction with the Pharmacy Quality Alliance Inc., a consensus-based multistakeholder organization that collaboratively promotes appropriate medication use and develops strategies for measuring and reporting performance information related to the appropriate use of medications.[30]

Quality of the Pharmacist Workforce

The minimum competencies to practice pharmacy in the United States include graduation from an accredited pharmacy program and passing the licensure examination in at least one state. Once a pharmacist is licensed, the license must be renewed periodically, and a condition of renewal is continuing education. In most states, licensees can transfer their license from one state to another. Licensure is a testimony to the American public that the pharmacist has met the entry-level professional qualification to practice pharmacy.

Pharmacists may complete a residency after licensure. Residencies are organized, directed, postgraduate experiential training programs in a defined area of pharmacy practice. Increasingly, specialized pharmacy practice opportunities offered by employers are available only to pharmacists who have completed a residency accredited by the American Society of Health System Pharmacists. Accredited residency training takes place in hospitals, community pharmacies, home care and long-term care facilities, ambulatory care settings, managed care facilities, and other settings. The type and duration (typically 1 or 2 years) of residency depends upon the area of pharmacy practice. Completion of an accredited residency is an evidence of competency in a specialized area of pharmacy practice, because these pharmacists must have become proficient in the set of defined outcomes and training experiences required by the residency program.

Board certification is increasingly important in ensuring a competent, high-quality pharmacist workforce. The Council on Credentialing in Pharmacy (CCP) has published guidelines and principles about post–licensure credentialing of pharmacists in the United States.[31,32] The CCP principles reinforce that differentiated knowledge, skills, and experience of credentialed pharmacists are important to patients and the health-care system and reaffirm the role of board certification and the role of the Board of Pharmacy Specialties in establishing standards and recognizing specialized training, knowledge, and skills.[33] A key principle is that pharmacists in specialized practices should participate in credentialing and privileging processes to ensure they are competent to provide the services and quality of care required by that practice.[34] For example, clinical pharmacists engaged in direct patient care (i.e., pharmacists who directly observe the patient and contribute to the selection modification and monitoring of patient-specific drug therapy, usually within an interprofessional team or collaborative practice) typically have completed a postgraduate residency, are board certified, and have established a collaborative drug therapy management agreement or been granted clinical privileges by the medical staff or credentialing system of the health care in which they practice.[35]

The Triple Aim of better care for individuals, better health for populations, and reduced per capita costs[1] is directly applicable to specialized pharmacist practices (e.g., primary care, oncology specialty practice). Employing pharmacists in specialized roles who have demonstrated competency by meeting the quality requirements associated with residencies and board certification should be the norm. Physicians, payers, institutions, and policy-makers should expect that pharmacists in specialized practices be trained and credentialed to provide high-quality care.[17] Current U.S. health-care system reforms can influence pharmacy policy-makers to require these credentials in specialized practice areas as evidence of competency. To secure the position of pharmacists in direct patient care will require additional government and private sector recognition of pharmacists as health-care providers.

Quality Measurement for Pharmacy Care

Quality measurement standards, such as the HEDIS standard metrics mentioned previously, provide benchmarks for monitoring the quality of health care across U.S. health-care plans and also facilitate direct comparison of health plans by individual consumers and employers/purchasers who select and pay for health insurance for their employees. Many HEDIS metrics monitor quality of pharmacy care, for example, both the antidepressant medication management and the persistence of beta-blocker treatment after a heart attack are measures on the HEDIS scorecard that is applied to commercial, Medicare, and Medicaid plans.[36] Pharmacists play a key role in ensuring that health plans achieve recommended benchmarks of health-care quality by providing the critical pharmacist professional services outlined earlier.

In some cases, performance on pharmacy-related quality metrics is directly tied to financial incentives for health plans. The Medicare STAR program is a major health policy initiative designed by the Center for Medicare & Medicaid Services (CMS)[37] to monitor health-care quality in health plans with Medicare enrollees. The ACA specifically authorized CMS to provide significant monetary and enrollment incentives to health plans that perform well on their Medicare STAR measure. These measures cover a wide range of domains, from clinical outcomes to patient-reported quality of life, and also include a number of measures that are directly linked to pharmacy care such as timely medication review for older adults. CMS introduced a significant pharmaceutical policy innovation in 2012 by including three new metrics to its Medicare STAR portfolio: medication adherence to angiotensin-converting enzyme inhibitors or angiotensin receptor blockers to control hypertension, statins to control LDL-cholesterol, and oral antihyperglycemics to control HbA1c levels. These novel quality measures directly tied patient medication adherence to financial incentives for health plans and emphasized the responsibility of health-care plans to monitor and improve medication adherence in their patients; prior to 2012, most health plans did not systematically measure medication adherence at the population level or publicly report adherence levels. For example, to address these Medicare STAR metrics, at KPCO, medication adherence was estimated for Medicare patients taking oral antihyperglycemic and statin medication. Pharmacists then outreached to patients whose adherence was suboptimal, with subsequent improvement in the adherence metric and the KPCO Medicare STAR rating.[38]

As noted in the "Access" section earlier, greater medication adherence can have a positive impact on patient clinical outcomes, and the Medicare STAR adherence quality metrics reflect the importance of improving medication adherence as a means toward improving health-care quality overall. In providing high-quality professional and clinical services, pharmacists play a key role in helping Medicare patients, and all patients maintain optimal medication adherence, which may then, in turn, be appropriately reflected in that patients' health-care plan quality ratings.

Cost

Costs for pharmaceuticals can be considered from the vantage points of costs to the patient and of costs to the health-care system as a whole. It is important for pharmaceutical policies to address optimizing the cost-effectiveness of pharmaceutical and health care from both perspectives. Currently, prescription drug costs are rising faster than inflation, and prescription drugs are expected to account for up to $(USD)483 billion dollars, or more than 10% of total U.S. health-care expenditures, by 2021.[39,40] Out-of-pocket prescription drug expenditures for patients totaled $(USD)48.8 billion in 2010; while this is less than the out-of-pocket drug expenditures in 2006 (due in part to the introduction of Medicare Part D), these expenses are expected to increase in the coming decade. A significant portion of Medicare expenditures are also accounted for by prescription drug costs: of the $(USD)524 billion spent on Medicare in 2010, more than 10% ($[USD]59.5 billion) was spent on prescription drug costs.

Drug prices in the United States are higher than in many other nations[5]; for example, the prices of many commonly used prescription drugs are more than twice in the United States than they are in the United Kingdom. Many have suggested that part of this higher cost is due to a "premium" charged by U.S.-based pharmaceutical companies to fund research and development for new medications.[41] While some states such as Massachusetts and Maine have proposed importing prescription drugs from other countries such as Canada as a way to control prescription drug costs, importing of drugs is currently banned by the FDA.[41]

One of the main contributors to high prescription drug costs is biologic therapies (or biologics), which are therapies that use living organisms or substances derived from them (either natural or synthetic) to treat diseases.[42] While these breakthrough therapies hold promise for treating illnesses such as cancer,[42] they are very expensive due in part to the sophisticated technologies and manufacturing methods required to produce them.[43] For example, the average annual cost of Herceptin® to treat breast cancer is $(USD)37,000.[44] Currently, biologics are estimated to account for up to 25% of the total drug spending in the United States, and that proportion is increasing yearly. Unlike with more traditional brand-name prescription medications, the pathway for making "generic" versions of biologics, or biosimilar versions of branded biologics, can be challenging because of their increased complexity. As part of the ACA, the Congress enacted the "Biologics Price Competition and Innovation Act," to help establish a clear FDA-managed licensure and regulatory pathway for creating biosimilars to existing brand-name biologics in the marketplace. While it is too early to know the impact of this legislation, many hope biosimilars will help control costs while providing critical therapeutic options for patients with potentially life-threatening diseases.[45] Pharmaceutical policies should continue to address the pricing of these medical products to increase their accessibility to patients who need them, without making the costs prohibitively high to individuals or to the health-care system at large.

Increasing the Cost-Effectiveness of Pharmaceuticals

One of the most important tools for decreasing the costs of pharmacy care is through the appropriate use of generic medications to treat acute and chronic illnesses. The Drug Price Competition and Patent Term Restoration Act (or the Hatch-Waxman Act) of 1984 essentially created the modern generic drug industry,[43–45] which allows for the manufacture and marketing of generic versions of brand-name, patented medications after a specific amount of time. Generic medications are widely considered to be safe, effective, and affordable, and the use of generics has by some estimates saved the U.S. health-care system more than a trillion dollars since 2002.[45] Pharmacists can play a critical role in advancing the use of generics by helping patients make cost-effective drug choices, increasing their awareness of out-of-pocket costs associated with brand-name prescription drugs for which quality generic alternatives exist and helping to monitor and identify physician prescribing patterns to ensure that they maximize the guideline-concordant use of generics. These efforts can have a significant impact on reducing costs for individual patients and for the health-care system as a whole. Pharmaceutical policies should continue to strongly encourage the manufacture and use of generic medications, while also protecting the incentive for pharmaceutical companies to develop and market new medications.

Prescription drug insurance benefit design can also play a role in controlling drug costs while maintaining access and quality. Prescription drug formularies are one example of a benefit design structure that can directly influence the costs associated with delivering prescription medications. Drug formularies, or approved list of medications that a health insurance plan agrees to include in the prescription benefit, fall into five major categories: closed, best available price, reference-based pricing, tiered, and open.[46] With the exception of open formularies, which allow for any medications to be prescribed to patients without incentivizing the use of one over another, formularies are designed to encourage the use of the most cost-effective medications available to treat specific diseases by controlling which drugs are allowed to be prescribed and varying the level of patient-cost sharing for medications depending on whether the medications are generic drugs, covered brand-name drugs, or nonformulary drugs. Formularies are now widely used within U.S. health plans,[46] and when implemented appropriately, they have the potential to control costs while preserving quality.

As discussed in the section on "Quality," pharmacists are increasingly functioning as health-care providers by providing key professional services such as ordering, interpreting, and monitoring laboratory tests, formulating clinical assessments and therapeutic plans, coordinating care plans, and providing wellness and preventive care. Integrating pharmacists into clinical care may be a cost-effective approach to improving clinical outcomes for patients; for example, one study in Kaiser Permanente found that enhanced clinical care for cardiovascular disease (CVD) that integrated pharmacists into care teams was a clinically and cost-effective approach to improving long-term CVD outcomes.[47] Increasing our understanding of the cost–benefits of pharmacist-based clinical care can help to bolster the public policy case for expanding the role of pharmacists and pharmacies in the full spectrum of patient care.

Conclusion

The Triple Aim approach to optimizing access, quality, and costs of care is a constructive framework for improving pharmacy care and maximizing the U.S. health-care system's ability to provide patients with evidence-based pharmaceuticals in a way that is cost-effective and promotes high-quality care. Pharmacists, pharmacies, and pharmaceutical policy-makers can play an important role in improving access, quality, and costs for pharmaceutical products and for health care overall by using the Triple Aim as a cornerstone for creating pharmaceutical public policy initiatives.

References

1. Berwick DM, Nolan TW, Whittington J. The triple aim: Care, health, and cost. *Health Aff (Millwood)*. May–June 2008;27(3):759–769.
2. Organization for Economic Cooperation and Development (OECD). OECD Health Data 2013. How does the United States Compare? 2013. http://www.oecd.org/unitedstates/Briefing-Note-USA-2013.pdf2. Accessed on February 13, 2014.
3. Institute of Medicine (IOM). *Crossing the Quality Chasm: A New Health System for the 21st Century*. National Academies Press, Washington, DC, 2001.
4. Berger JE. The role of the retail pharmacy in the new healthcare environment, 2013. http://www.ajmc.com/publications/ajpb/2013/ajpb_marapr2013/The-Role-of-the-Retail-Pharmacy-in-the-New-Healthcare-Environment. Accessed on February 13, 2014.
5. Collins SR, Robertson R, Garber T, Doty MM. The Commonwealth Fund. *Insuring the Future: Current Trends in Health Coverage and the Effects of Implementing the Affordable Care Act*, April 2013. http://www.commonwealthfund.org/publications/fund-reports/2013/apr/insuring-the-future. Accessed December 5, 2015.

6. Lau DT, Briesacher BA, Touchette DR, Stubbings J, Ng JH. Medicare Part D and quality of prescription medication use in older adults. *Drugs Aging.* October 1, 2011;28(10):797–807.
7. Baik SH, Rollman BL, Reynolds CF, 3rd, Lave JR, Smith KJ, Zhang Y. The effect of the US Medicare Part D coverage gaps on medication use among patients with depression and heart failure. *J Ment Health Policy Econ.* September 2012;15(3):105–118.
8. Schmittdiel JA, Ettner SL, Fung V et al. Medicare Part D coverage gap and diabetes beneficiaries. *Am J Manag Care.* March 2009;15(3):189–193.
9. Raebel MA, Delate T, Ellis JL, Bayliss EA. Effects of reaching the drug benefit threshold on Medicare members' healthcare utilization during the first year of Medicare Part D. *Med Care.* October 2008;46(10):1116–1122.
10. Department of Health and Human Services (HHS). How the health care law benefits you, 2013. http://www.hhs.gov/healthcare/facts/bystate/Making-a-Difference-National.html. Accessed December 5, 2015.
11. Helling DK, Nelson KM, Ramirez JE, Humphries TL. Kaiser Permanente Colorado Region Pharmacy Department: Innovative leader in pharmacy practice. *J Am Pharm Assoc* (2003). January–February 2006;46(1):67–76.
12. Imber S. National boards of pharmacy releases 2013 report, 97% of online pharmacies not recommended, 2013. http://www.safemedicines.org/2013/03/national-boards-of-pharmacy-releases-2013-report-less-than-1-meet-vipps-criteria-518.html. Accessed on January 7, 2014.
13. Imber S. New research highlights risks of unlicensed online pharmacies, 2013. http://www.safemedicines.org/2013/06/new-research-highlights-risks-of-unlicensed-online-pharmacies534.html. Accessed December 5, 2015.
14. Witt DM, Sadler MA, Shanahan RL, Mazzoli G, Tillman DJ. Effect of a centralized clinical pharmacy anticoagulation service on the outcomes of anticoagulation therapy. *Chest.* May 2005;127(5):1515–1522.
15. Witt DM. The Kaiser Permanente Colorado Clinical Pharmacy Anticoagulation Service as a model of modern anticoagulant care. *Thromb Res.* 2008;123:S36–S41.
16. Ip EJ, Shah BM, Yu J, Chan J, Nguyen LT, Bhatt DC. Enhancing diabetes care by adding a pharmacist to the primary care team. *Am J Health Syst Pharm.* May 15, 2013;70(10):877–886.
17. Heilmann RM, Campbell SM, Kroner BA et al. Evolution, current structure, and role of a primary care clinical pharmacy service in an integrated managed care organization. *Ann Pharmacother.* January 2013;47(1):124–131.
18. Council on Credentialing in Pharmacy. *Scope of Contemporary Pharmacy Practice: Roles, Responsibilities, and Functions of Pharmacists and Pharmacy Technicians.* Council on Credentialing in Pharmacy, Washington, DC, February 25, 2009.
19. Milfred-Laforest SK, Chow SL, Didomenico RJ et al. Clinical pharmacy services in heart failure: An opinion paper from the Heart Failure Society of America and American College of Clinical Pharmacy Cardiology Practice and Research Network. *J Card Fail.* May 2013;19(5):354–369.
20. Knapp KRM, Law A, Okamoto M, Chang P. *The Role of Community Pharmacies in Diabetes Care: Eight Case Studies.* California HealthCare Foundation, Oakland, CA, 2005.
21. Center for Disease Control and Prevention (CDC). Clinical diabetes management: Pharmacist's role in diabetes care, 2008. http://www2c.cdc.gov/podcasts/media/pdf/PharmacistsRole.pdf. Accessed on January 7, 2014.
22. Shaffer J. Pharmacy-based immunizations: Getting the word out, 2013. http://www.pharmacist.com/pharmacy-based-immunizations-getting-word-out. Accessed on January 7, 2014.
23. Schmittdiel JA, Uratsu CS, Karter AJ et al. Why don't diabetes patients achieve recommended risk factor targets? Poor adherence versus lack of treatment intensification. *J Gen Intern Med.* May 2008;23(5):588–594.
24. Karter AJ, Parker MM, Moffet HH, Ahmed AT, Schmittdiel JA, Selby JV. New prescription medication gaps: A comprehensive measure of adherence to new prescriptions. *Health Serv Res.* October 2009;44(5 Pt 1):1640–1661.
25. Schmittdiel JA, Karter AJ, Dyer WT, Chan J, Duru OK. Safety and effectiveness of mail order pharmacy use in diabetes. *Am J Manag Care.* November 2013;19(11):882–887.

26. Traynor K. President signs compounding law, 2014. http://www.ashp.org/menu/News/PharmacyNews/NewsArticle.aspx?Id=3995. Accessed December 5, 2015.
27. Chisholm-Burns MA, Kim Lee J, Spivey CA et al. US pharmacists' effect as team members on patient care: Systematic review and meta-analyses. *Med Care.* October 2010;48(10):923–933.
28. Lee JK, Slack MK, Martin J, Ehrman C, Chisholm-Burns M. Geriatric patient care by U.S. pharmacists in healthcare teams: Systematic review and meta-analyses. *J Am Geriatr Soc.* July 2013;61(7):1119–1127.
29. Heilmann RM, Friesleben CR, Billups SJ. Impact of a pharmacist-directed intervention in postmenopausal women after fracture. *Am J Health Syst Pharm.* March 15, 2012;69(6):504–509.
30. Pharmacy Quality Alliance (PQA). Pharmacy Quality Alliance, 2014. http://www.pqaalliance.org/. Accessed on January 24, 2014.
31. Council on Credentialing in Pharmacy. Credentialing pharmacy: A resource paper, 2010. http://pharmacycredentialing.org/Files/CCPWhitePaper2010.pdf. Accessed on January 24, 2014.
32. Council on Credentialing in Pharmacy. Certification programs for pharmacists, 2012. http://www.pharmacycredentialing.org/Files/CertificationPrograms.pdf. Accessed December 5, 2015.
33. Board of Pharmacy Specialties. Board of Pharmacy Specialties, 2014. http://www.bpsweb.org/specialties/specialties.cfm. Accessed December 5, 2015.
34. Council on Credentialing in Pharmacy. Guiding principles for post-licensure credentialing of pharmacists, 2011. http://pharmacycredentialing.org/Files/GuidingPrinciplesPharmacistCredentialing.pdf. Accessed on January 24, 2014.
35. American College of Clinical Pharmacy. Qualifications of pharmacists who provide direct patient care: Perspectives on the need for residency training and board certification. *Pharmacotherapy.* 2013;33:888–891.
36. National Committee for Quality Assurance (NCQA). HEDIS 2014 Summary Measures, 2014. http://www.ncqa.org/Portals/0/HEDISQM/HEDIS2014/List%20of%20HEDIS%202014%20Measures.pdf. Accessed on January 30, 2014.
37. Kaiser Family Foundation. *Reaching for the Stars: Quality Ratings of Medicare Advantage Plans.* Kaiser Family Foundation, Menlo Park, CA, 2011.
38. McGinnis B, Kauffman Y, Olson KL, Witt DM, Raebel MA. Interventions aimed at improving performance on medication adherence metrics. *Int J Clin Pharm.* February 2014;36(1):20–25.
39. Center for Medicare and Medicaid Services (CMS). *National Health Expenditure Projections 2011–2021.* CMS, Baltimore, MD, 2011.
40. America's Health Insurance Plans. USA Today: Prescription drug costs rising at twice the rate of inflation, 2013. http://www.ahipcoverage.com/2013/02/14/usa-today-prescription-drug-costs-rising-at-twice-the-rate-of-inflation/.
41. McArdle M. Maine goes rogue on importing prescription drugs, 2013. http://www.bloombergview.com/articles/2013-10-10/maine-goes-rogue-on-importing-prescription-drugs. Accessed December 5, 2015.
42. National Cancer Institute (NCI) at the National Institute for Health (NIH). Biological therapies for cancer, 2013. http://www.cancer.gov/cancertopics/factsheet/Therapy/biological. Accessed December 5, 2015.
43. Schacht WH, Thomas JR. Follow-On Biologics: The Law and Intellectual Property Issues, Congressional Research Service 7-5700, www.crs.gov, R41483, 2012.
44. Johnson JA. FDA Regulation of Follow-On Biologics, Congressional Research Services 7-5700, www.crs.gov, RL34045, 2010.
45. Generic Pharmaceutical Association. Generic Drug Savings in the US, 2012. Washington, D.C. http://www.gphaonline.org/media/cms/IMSStudyAug2012WEB.pdf. Accessed December 5, 2015.
46. MedPac. *Implementing the Medicare Drug Benefit: Formulary and Plan Transition Issues.* MedPac, Washington, DC, 2004.
47. Yu J, Shah BM, Ip EJ, Chan J. A Markov model of the cost-effectiveness of pharmacist care for diabetes in prevention of cardiovascular diseases: Evidence from Kaiser Permanente Northern California. *J Manag Care Pharm.* March 2013;19(2):102–114.

Chapter 5

Why Is Medication Use Less than Appropriate?

Duane M. Kirking, David Nau, and Jill Augustine

Contents

Introduction

Medications are one of the key tools in the therapeutic management of disease. However, they are not always used in an ideal, or appropriate, manner.[1,2] When medications are not used appropriately, patients may experience adverse events or fail to achieve their therapeutic goals. In turn, these failures result in suboptimal quality of life and wasted resources for our society.

Eight Categories of Drug-Related Problems

Hepler and Strand have used the term "drug-related morbidity" to describe the phenomenon of therapeutic malfunction—the failure of a therapeutic agent to produce the intended therapeutic outcome.[3] This concept encompasses both treatment failure and the production of new medical problems. It has been determined that drug-related problems (DRPs) cause between 5% and 10% of hospital admissions[4–6] and are prevalent in 12% of hospital floors that treat the elderly.[7] The problems accounted for over $(USD)100 billion[8] in unnecessary health-care expenditures. Despite efforts to reduce these figures, drug-related morbidity remains an important public health issue.[4–10]

Drug-related morbidity is often preceded by a DRP.[11] A DRP is an event or circumstance involving drug treatment that actually or potentially interferes with the patient experiencing an optimum outcome of medical care. Strand and colleagues delineated eight categories of DRPs:

1. *Untreated indications*: The patient is in need of a drug that was not prescribed.
2. *Improper drug selection*: The wrong drug is being used.
3. *Subtherapeutic dosage*: Too little of an appropriate drug is being used.
4. *Overdosage*: The patient receives too much of an appropriate drug.
5. *Failure to receive drug*: The patient does not obtain/use the drug that was prescribed.
6. *Adverse drug reaction*: An unintended and potentially harmful effect of a drug.
7. *Drug interactions*: Undesirable consequences of drug–drug or drug–food interactions.
8. *Drug use without indication*: The patient is taking a drug for which he or she has no medical need.[11]

DRPs may arise due to inappropriate prescribing, inappropriate dispensing/administration of the drug, inappropriate behavior by the patient, inappropriate monitoring of the patient, or patient idiosyncrasy. Although idiosyncrasy is inherently unpreventable, most of the other causes of DRPs can be prevented. The following section of this chapter will provide a framework for examining the causes of inappropriate medication use.

Framework for Examining Inappropriate Medication Use

Hepler and Grainger-Rousseau's conceptualization of a pharmaceutical care system offers a good framework for examining the potential sources of DRPs.[12] A pharmaceutical care system begins with a patient seeking care and requires that someone (a health-care professional and/or the patient) recognizes the patient's health problem and assesses the patient's need for medication therapy. Ideally, a therapeutic plan is then developed that may include the prescribing of a medication along with explicit goals and monitoring parameters. The medication is then dispensed to the patient along with advice on its proper use. The patient then receives the medication and participates in the monitoring of his or her progress toward the therapeutic goals. If the goals are not being met or an adverse drug-related event occurs, the therapeutic plan can be modified to resolve the problem. The monitoring and active management of the drug regimen should continue as long as the patient requires the medication.

Hepler's pharmaceutical care system is similar to the drug-use process described by Knapp and colleagues in the 1970s.[13] Hepler's model builds upon the Knapp model by adding the functions of drug monitoring and management to denote the importance of ongoing attention to the patient and drug regimen. Hepler and Grainger-Rousseau suggest that there are three key elements to the proper functioning of a pharmaceutical care system: (1) initiating therapy, (2) monitoring therapy, and (3) managing (i.e., correcting) therapy. Appropriate initiation of therapy requires the recognition and assessment of the patient's signs and symptoms to generate an appropriate diagnosis and therapeutic plan. It also entails the prescribing of a drug that, based upon the knowledge of the prescriber and information available to the prescriber, would be the most appropriate product for the individual patient. Furthermore, the patient must obtain the prescribed medication (most often from a pharmacy that presumably has dispensed the appropriate medication along with appropriate advice to the patient), and the patient must begin using it. Given the numerous steps and people involved in the initiation of drug therapy, it is easy to identify many potential reasons for failures in this process.

Problems with Initiation of Therapy

If patients do not recognize a potential health problem that could be treated with a medication, or do nothing about a recognized problem, then the initiation of drug therapy will not occur. Patients may not recognize a problem because the problem may be asymptomatic or because they lack an understanding of the significance or meaning of symptoms. They may also choose not to seek the advice of a health professional due to fears of what they may be told or because of a distrust of providers. They may also lack access to health care due to an inability to pay for the services or geographic barriers.

Once a patient accesses the health-care system, an evaluation of his or her signs or symptoms should be conducted. However, if the patient is unable to communicate clearly with the provider, an accurate assessment of the problem becomes difficult. The provider may also lack the necessary skills or equipment to accurately diagnose the problem or may not give adequate attention to the patient's problem. If the problem is not correctly diagnosed, it is unlikely that appropriate drug therapy will be prescribed.

Once the diagnosis is made, the clinician then needs to decide whether a drug is warranted for treating the patient. If so, the selection of the drug (along with an appropriate dose, route, duration, and instructions) can be challenging. Given the thousands of drug products that are available and the characteristics of the patient (e.g., age, weight, renal function, cognitive function), the clinician is tasked with selecting the most appropriate therapy for the disease in this patient at this time. The task is made more complex for the prescriber by having to deal with multiple payers who may each specify a different preferred drug for a given condition, as well as by advertisements that lead patients to request specific products, or by conflicting data from clinical trials. Most often, the clinician is working from his or her memory of the numerous products indicated for a particular disease and uses simple decision rules to reduce the complexity and uncertainty inherent in the product selection (e.g., "If the patient is a child with uncomplicated otitis media and no other health problems, I prescribe amoxicillin"). Numerous studies have analyzed how prescribers select drug products, but presentation of the findings of these studies is beyond the space available in this chapter.[14–18] However, a discussion of evidence-based prescribing can be found elsewhere in this book.

Computerized physician order entry (CPOE) systems have become increasingly popular over the last decade. These computer-based systems aid prescribers in selecting medications. The resulting prescriptions are usually printed by computer, thus virtually eliminating the medication errors that occur due to poor or illegible handwriting.

Additional advantages can further reduce the chance for medication errors when CPOE has an automated clinical decision support system (CDSS). These systems improve medication and regimen choice by reviewing patients' electronic health record, medication list, and patient history and then providing helpful hints and suggestions for treatment regimen therapies. The use of a CPOE with CDSS can aid prescribers by reviewing drug allergies, basic dose guidance, and formulary decision support and checking for duplicate therapies and drug–drug interactions (additional information can be found later in this chapter).

Once the prescription for drug therapy is generated, the ambulatory patient generally obtains the medication from a pharmacy. The pharmacist is charged with confirming the appropriateness of the medication for the patient and then dispensing the product, along with instructions on proper use, to the patient or caregiver. The process by which the pharmacist evaluates the appropriateness of the prescribed therapy is referred to as "drug-utilization review,"[19] "medication therapy review,"[20] or "medication therapy management" (MTM).[20] Although the pharmacist should be readily able to detect any obvious problems with the prescription (e.g., a 10-fold overdose of chloral hydrate for an infant), this does not always happen. An individual pharmacist may lack the knowledge of appropriate drug therapy or may not be paying close attention to the prescription in the hurried environment of many community pharmacies. Computerized medication review systems have been developed to assist in identifying potential problems with prescriptions; however, the alerts generated by these systems may not always provide clear guidance on the action to be taken by the pharmacist, and a high volume of low-risk alerts may lead to high-risk alerts being overlooked.[21,22] More information on the benefits and challenges of CPOE are discussed later in this chapter.

Another challenge for the pharmacist is the lack of information regarding the patient's medical condition. The patient's diagnosis and other pertinent clinical information are not often immediately available to the pharmacist, and thus the task of PDUR becomes more challenging. Another chapter provides additional detail on medication review systems.

If the pharmacist has deemed the prescribed therapy to be appropriate, then the correct drug and information need to be provided to the patient or the patient's caregiver. Within hospitals, the product is usually provided by the pharmacy to a nurse who then administers the drug to the patient. However, hospitals may also have medications stocked within a nursing unit, and the pharmacist may be bypassed altogether. This limits the opportunity to double-check the order prior to the drug's administration. Regardless of the setting, there are numerous steps involved with the dispensing and/or administration of a drug product, and often several personnel are involved in processing the drug order before the product reaches the patient. This creates many opportunities for error.

Several tools have been developed in order to limit dispensing and/or administrative errors in hospitals and community pharmacies. One tool that has been adopted is the use of a bar coding system. Within most hospitals, bar codes indentify the patient, the medication, and the nurse or other person administering the medication. Codes are scanned both when retrieving a medication from a medicine cabinet and during administration in order to verify the correct patient, drug, dose, route, and time prior to administration of medication.[23–25] In community pharmacies, bar-coding systems are being utilized to scan prescription labels and medication stock bottles in order to ensure that the appropriate medication is being dispensed. Other technologies developed to reduce dispensing and/or administration errors[26,27] include robots, automated dispensing devices,[28] automated medication administration records,[26] and intravenous (IV) medication safety systems or smart IV pumps.[29] While each technology has weaknesses, each provides the benefit of being another verification tool that reduces the risk of dispensing and administration errors.

There are numerous factors involved in dispensing-related medication errors, and a detailed discussion of the problem is found in Chapters 9, 10, and 21. Errors often result from a combination of human factors and systems failures. Some of the most frequently cited factors include (1) the lack of a consistent dispensing process, or unclear roles within the process, (2) a workload that exceeds the capacity of the personnel and dispensing process, (3) excessive distractions in the dispensing process, (4) unclear handwritten prescriptions, (5) similar drug names that can easily be confused, (6) products or packaging that look identical, (7) lack of training for personnel, and (8) failure to communicate with patients.

Pharmacist–patient communication is important for at least three reasons. First, it provides the pharmacist with information to assess the appropriateness of the prescribed regimen. Second, talking to the patient about the prescribed medication can reveal potential medication errors before the patient receives the medication (e.g., the pharmacist had interpreted the handwritten prescription as being for a cardiovascular drug, but the patient says that she was prescribed the drug for breast cancer). Finally, the pharmacist can provide the patient with information regarding the appropriate use of the medication and can confirm that the patient understands the information.

Unfortunately, verbal communication between a pharmacist and a patient does not always occur. There are several reasons for this. Some pharmacists perceive that patients do not want to talk to them, and thus they do not attempt to initiate a dialogue. However, research has indicated that many patients want more information about their medications.[30] Even when pharmacists do attempt to communicate drug-related information, the patient or caregiver may have difficulty engaging in a productive dialogue if they feel ill or are distracted by a sick child.

One barrier to a productive dialogue exists in patients who have low health literacy. Low or limited health literacy is associated with poor adherence to medication,[31] poor health outcomes, and higher health-care costs.[32,33] Another barrier at effective communication is encountered when attempting to communicate with patients with limited English proficiency.[34] Research has provided evidence that pharmacists are apprehensive about talking with patients when the pharmacist must communicate with patients from whom English is not their native language.[35]

While these present barriers to communication, key legislative changes such as the Medicare Part D (discussed more in Chapter 26) and the 2010 Affordable Care Act (Chapter 25) have provided opportunities for pharmacists to increase communication with patients. These federal laws have increased pharmacist-driven programs with the goal of increased communication between patients and providers as well as improvement in patient health. One program that is being utilized in order to increase communication, improve medication use, and improve patients' health is the MTM.[36,37] As described in more detail in Chapter 17, these programs allow pharmacists to be reimbursed for services that they have been providing for over two decades. However, the process of providing other financial compensation for other pharmacy-related nondispensing services has been slow, although there has been improvement.[36,38]

Perhaps the most important participant in a pharmaceutical care system is the patient. The patient ultimately decides if, and how, she will take the medication. Patients may choose not to fill the prescription or may alter the regimen in ways that are not conducive to optimal outcomes. This may stem from concerns over side effects or addiction, a perceived lack of effectiveness of the drug, or an inability to pay for the medications. Additionally, it may be difficult for some patients to manage a complex drug regimen that involves many medications or complicated directions. Thus, patients may unintentionally miss doses because of the burden involved. More details on patients' use of medication are found in Chapter 8.

Problems in Monitoring and Managing Drug Therapy

The monitoring and management of drug therapy are crucial elements of the pharmaceutical care system since they facilitate the identification of problems with the initial therapeutic plan or problems with the patient's use of the medications. However, these are also the elements of pharmaceutical care, which are most often neglected. The ongoing management of drug therapy may not happen if clinicians or patients fail to monitor the progress toward the therapeutic goals or if they fail to act despite the monitoring data clearly showing the need for change in the plan.

Phillips et al.[39] have used the term "clinical inertia" to describe the "failure of health-care providers to initiate or intensify therapy when indicated." Clinical inertia is due to at least three problems: overestimation of care provided, use of soft reasons to avoid intensification of therapy, and practice organization not being designed for achieving therapeutic goals. Several studies have noted that physicians and other prescribers overestimate their care provided for chronic illnesses, including overestimation of the extent to which they screened for, and monitored, diseases such as diabetes, hypertension, and coronary heart disease.[40–45]

Even when monitoring data indicates that the therapeutic goal is not being achieved, prescribers may use "soft" reasons to justify their decisions not to intensify therapy. For example, if the prescriber perceives that the control of the disease has improved, then he or she may be reluctant to intensify therapy despite the therapeutic target not being achieved.[23] Prescribers may also choose not to intensify therapy if they perceive that the patient would not adhere to the intensified therapy.[46,47] These barriers may stem from concerns over side effects, or a belief that the therapeutic targets proposed in clinical guidelines may not be appropriate for a specific patient, or a lack of prescriber training to "treat to goal."[39]

Many prescribers were not trained to intensify drug therapy until therapeutic targets were achieved.[39] Additionally, many practice sites are not organized to systematically identify patients who are not achieving the therapeutic goal and to prompt action for further monitoring or intensification of therapy. Many practices are organized to focus on the patient's current medical complaint without attention to the ongoing control of chronic disease. For example, a 65-year-old woman with diabetes may present to the physician's practice to discuss menopausal symptoms. The prescriber may discuss menopause but then fails to identify that the patient has not had an assessment of glycemic control for the past 2 years. Although office-based quality improvement initiatives have been developed in recent years to counter this problem, the majority of medical practices are still not engaging in quality improvement efforts toward this aim.[39,48]

Many quality improvement efforts have recognized the important role that nonphysician providers can play in a pharmaceutical care system. Nurses and pharmacists can play a significant role in educating and monitoring patients with chronic illnesses and identifying those patients in need of therapy modification through medication reconciliation and the MTM. Since pharmacists often encounter patients monthly for drug refills, they are in an excellent position to collect objective monitoring information (e.g., blood pressure, hemoglobin A1c) and solicit subjective feedback from patients regarding their experience with the drugs (e.g., side effects, symptom resolution) to identify those patients in need of further evaluation by a physician. Many health systems, particularly the Veterans Health Administration in the United States, have begun to have pharmacists play a significant role in adjusting drug therapy to promote achievement of the therapeutic targets. A recent multistate project demonstrated that community pharmacists who provided enhanced services to diabetic patients helped the patients achieve better health and reduced total health-care expenditures.[49] After the success of the diabetes program, this project expanded to pharmacist-based care in patients with hypertension, dyslipidemia, and asthma and has had similar success at achieving better health outcome and reduced expenditures.[50,51] The profound positive impact of these pharmacist-driven programs had led to the exponential growth of pharmacists-provided services in the community pharmacists and medical care offices.

Problems with Information Flow

A cross-cutting theme regarding the suboptimal use of medications is the poor flow of information throughout the pharmaceutical care system. In order for clinicians to make informed decisions regarding the initiation or modification of drug therapy, they need to have timely access to objective and subjective data regarding the patient. In order for pharmacists to evaluate the appropriateness of a prescribed drug, they need to have information such as the patient's diagnosis, weight, and other medications. Research has found that there is a 70% reduction in adverse drug events (ADEs) in primary care when a CPOE with CDSS is utilized.[52] An additional benefit of CPOE is the opportunity for a prescriber to send the prescription electronically to the patients' pharmacy of choice. This process can streamline the process of dispensing a medication as well as reduce the potential risk of pharmacy transcription and data entry errors. One study found a 50% reduction in the risk of dispensing errors when the prescription was electronically transmitted to the pharmacy compared to the traditional paper-based prescription.[53]

The patient also needs to know the therapeutic goals, how to appropriately use the medication, how to self-monitor for side effects and therapeutic effectiveness, and how and when to contact various clinicians. The availability of this information had been improved through the growth of electronic health records and CPOEs (as discussed earlier). However, limitations still exist with CPOE and CDSSs.

It is important to recognize that information flow, by itself, does not always lead to better decisions or greater achievement of therapeutic goals.[54,55] Electronic-prescribing systems have the potential to decrease several types of medication errors; however, they may also create other types of errors.[54,56] Furthermore, providing pharmacists with more information about the patient does not necessarily lead to better care by pharmacists.[57–59] This is particularly true if the pharmacy's operations are not designed to facilitate interaction between patients and pharmacists. Computerized medication review systems have been developed to assist in identifying potential problems with prescriptions; however, the alerts generated by these systems may not always provide clear guidance on the action to be taken by the pharmacist, and a high volume of low-risk alerts may lead to high-risk alerts being overlooked.[21,22] Nonetheless, increasing the electronic connectivity between providers and with patients reduces barriers that impede the appropriate initiation, monitoring, and management of drug therapy.

How Often Do Problems Occur in the Use of Medications?

Hundreds of studies have been conducted over the past several decades that document a myriad of problems with the use of medications. We selected examples of studies from each of the eight categories of DRPs as defined by Strand and colleagues,[3] as well as from the literature on medication errors. It is important to note that the evidence presented in the category of *adverse drug events* is not limited to reports of idiosyncratic drug reactions and includes reports of both preventable and nonpreventable ADEs.

Adverse Drug Events

A study using the National Ambulatory Medical Care Survey estimated that there were 4.3 million ambulatory visits in the United States during 2001 for the treatment of an ADE.[60] This equates to 15 visits per 1000 population with nearly half of these visits being to a hospital emergency department. The authors of this national study also found that the elderly and women were most likely to receive care for an ADE.

A recent study reported that an ADE occurred at a rate of 15 events for 100 hospital admissions and that 75% were judged to be preventable.[61] A study of pediatric patients found that ADEs and potential ADEs occurred in 2.3% and 10%, respectively, of admitted patients.[62] Yet another study found that ADEs occurred in more than 12% of patients within 3 weeks of discharge from a hospital.[63] The majority of these ADEs were judged to be preventable or ameliorable. Other studies of ADEs have shown similar results.[64] The inconsistency and uncertainty of ADE frequency highlight the challenges of understanding how these errors occur and modifying the complex health system to reduce these errors. Changes to the inpatient medication-use system such as CPOE, clinical decision support programs, and pharmacist involvement with the medical team have been shown to decrease the risk of medication errors and ADEs.[61,65–68]

Untreated Indications

The patient may have a need for drug therapy (a drug indication), but is not receiving a drug for that indication. It has been estimated that less than half of persons who qualify for lipid-modifying therapy are receiving it.[69] The treatment of hypertension is only slightly better with 73% of persons with hypertension receiving drug therapy.[70] Although it is possible that some persons with dyslipidemia and hypertension could achieve control of their disease without a medication, only 20% of patients with coronary heart disease achieve their goal for LDL cholesterol and 34% of hypertensive patients achieve their blood pressure goal.[69,70] Among patients with dyslipidemia and a second chronic disease, only 62% of diabetic patients receive dyslipidemia treatment, which is higher than patients with comorbidity of chronic kidney disease (53% received therapy) and lower than patients with comorbidity of heart failure (69% received therapy).[69] Increases were seen in the use of drug therapy for hypertension and glycemic control in the same population from previous years.[71] Thus, there has been an improvement in the treatment of chronic disease in recent years, although many people still do not receive drug therapy when needed.

Inappropriate Prescribing

Examples of inappropriate prescribing include (1) selecting a drug that will not be effective for treating the patient's condition (i.e., wrong drug), (2) selecting a dose that is too low to be effective, (3) selecting a dose that is too high and potentially harmful, or (4) selecting a drug that is inappropriate based upon the patient's comorbidities or concurrent drug use (drug–disease or drug–drug interactions). Researchers of inappropriate prescribing often combine some of the aforementioned categories when reporting the results of their studies.

A recent trend is to examine the use of potentially inappropriate medication (PIM) in the elderly based upon criteria developed by Beers and colleagues and updated in 2012.[72,73] The Beers criteria focus on drugs that may be inappropriate for use in the elderly due to their propensity to cause ADEs in this population. The elderly are an important population for medication-use studies since they may be more vulnerable to adverse drug-related events and often use many medications. One study found that 58% of elderly patients who were acutely admitted to the hospital had a PIM based on the 2012 Beers criteria. Additionally, they reported that 54% of these admissions were caused by medications that were included on the Beers criteria.[74] Another study reported that patients who were exposed to a PIM as defined by Beers criteria had an 18% elevated risk of unplanned hospitalization compared to patients who had no exposure.[75] Rigler et al. [76] compared the frequency of PIM in three cohorts with the Kansas Medicaid program (nursing home residents, recipients of home and community-based services for the frail elderly, and ambulatory patients). They found that PIM occurred in 38%, 48%, and 21%, respectively, of nursing home residents, frail elderly, and ambulatory patients.

Other criteria have been developed in order to identify PIMs. The Screening Tools of Older Persons' Prescriptions (STOPP)[77,78] and the Screening Tool to Alert doctors to Right Treatment (START)[79] criteria are new assessment tools. The STOPP is used to measure PIMs in the elderly while the START criteria are used to help prescribers with potential prescribing omissions. Gallagher and colleagues found that the use of STOPP/START criteria resulted in a significant and sustained improvement in prescribing appropriateness in reducing PIMs.[80] While the Beers criteria have been used more commonly in research, it is difficult to apply to reducing PIMs in European countries, since several of the medications are rarely prescribed or not available in these countries. Therefore, the STOPP/START criteria are mostly used outside of the United States.[81] However, several studies have found that the STOPP/START criteria have a greater ability to predict adverse drug reactions (ADRs) and prevent PIMs compared to Beers criteria.[77,80,82]

It is not just the elderly who may have inappropriate drugs prescribed. Some hospitalized patients receive antibiotics that are not appropriate for the identified or suspected pathogen.[83] Patients with mental health disorders may also receive drugs that are not appropriate for their diagnoses.[84] For example, some patients with depression receive only tranquilizers, perhaps because a health-care provider failed to recognize that the patient's sleep disorder stemmed from depression.[85]

Even when appropriate drugs are selected, the prescribed dose may be insufficient to achieve the desired therapeutic benefit. A study of the California Medicaid population revealed that two-thirds of patients using antidepressants were receiving a subtherapeutic dose.[86] This trend is also found with other chronic diseases, including diabetes, hypertension, and dyslipidemia. One report found that antihypertensive medications were not intensified, despite the patient having an elevated blood pressure, in 86.9% of patient.[47,87] Pain control medications are also underdosed frequently, particularly in terminally ill patients.[88,89]

Doses that are too high may also be prescribed. One reason for excessive doses is the failure of the prescriber to account for a patient's renal impairment.[90] This is particularly important for drugs with a narrow therapeutic index that are excreted in the urine (e.g., aminoglycosides, digoxin). Many U.S. hospitals have developed pharmacokinetic dosing services to ensure that renally impaired patients receive appropriate doses of medications.[91] Small children, particularly infants, require weight-based dosing of many drugs to ensure that they do not receive overdoses. The drug class most commonly associated with overdoses in nonhospitalized is analgesics followed by sedatives/hypnotics/antipsychotics.[92] Overall, approximately 12.1% of all unintentional overdoses reported to U.S. poison control centers are due to therapeutic errors such as double dosing, wrong medications taken or given, incorrect doses, and medications given or taken too close together.[92]

Failure to Receive Drug

Even if the patient is prescribed an appropriate drug and an appropriate dose is selected, the patient may not receive the drug. The reasons most frequently given for not taking all of their medications were the following: (1) the costs were too high, (2) they didn't think the drugs were helping them, and (3) the drug made them feel worse.[93] Among the elderly who have prescription drug coverage under Medicare Part D, approximately 19% of subjects did not fill a prescription because of cost concerns, 10% cut their dose, and 11% skipped doses of a prescription in order to make their prescription last longer.[94] In this study, the elderly who did not have a Medicare Part D prescription plan were more likely to not take a medication. In Americans with a chronic disease, 46% of adults do not fill a new prescription for fear or experience with a side effect while 25% do not fill because of a lack of perceived need for the medication.[93]

The reasons for suboptimal adherence to medications may depend partly upon the type of drug therapy regimen and may be multifactorial. A study of lipid-lowering therapy identified that only 26% of elderly patients maintained a high level of use of statin drugs over 5 years, with the greatest decline in adherence occurring in the first 6 months of therapy.[95] A similar study noted that only 31% of patients were adherent at 3 years after initiation of therapy with the greatest decline happening in the first 3 months.[96] This study also noted that the short-term effectiveness of the drug therapy was associated with higher adherence in subsequent months. Thus, patients may be more likely to discontinue therapy with statin drugs when they see no improvement in their cholesterol levels and do not feel better. The perceived lack of effectiveness, when coupled with the high cost of statin drugs, may be leading to the high discontinuation rates of these drugs.

Side effects may also contribute to poor adherence with some drug regimens. In particular, antidepressants may produce undesirable side effects such as lethargy and sexual dysfunction with about one-third of depressed patients discontinuing therapy prematurely.[97] Side effects are also noted frequently as a contributing factor in poor adherence to highly active antiretroviral therapy.[98] However, side effects alone do not explain much of the variance in medication nonadherence, and they are most likely weighed against the perceived benefits of the medication when patients decide whether to continue taking a medication.[99,100] Many patients taking antidepressant or antiretroviral drugs discontinue their regimens when their "concerns" about the medications exceed the perceived "necessity" of the medications.[101,102]

Drug Use without Indication

In this category, the patient is taking a drug for which he has no medical need. According to the 2010 National Survey on Drug Use and Health, an estimated 7.0 million Americans are using prescription drugs for nonmedical purposes.[66] This represents 2.7% of the U.S. population over the age of 12. However, an estimated 3.0% of 12–17-year-olds reported past-month prescription drug abuse. The rate of prescription drug abuse among American youth has increased considerably since 1990, but it has decreased in the past 5 years.[103] This reduction may be due to changes in medication drug diversion policies (at outlined in Chapter 10), a decreased willingness of prescribers to prescribe medications such as stimulants, and an increased public awareness of youth substance abuse problems.

Some "nonindicated" drug use stems from overprescribing of drugs by prescribers. For example, the majority of patients with an upper respiratory infection receive antibiotics despite the lack of effectiveness of antibiotics for these conditions.[104,105] It is estimated that 17%–20% of the patients who receive antibiotics lack an indication for the drug.[106,107] The high rate of nonindicated antibiotic utilization may be partly driven by patients' misunderstandings about antibiotic effectiveness for viral infections, providers' desire to satisfy patients' demands, and marketing campaigns for new antibiotics.[108]

Medication Regimen Complexity

While not listed in the Strand and colleagues' categories of DRPs, one issue that is of growing concern among health-care providers is the increasing complexity of a patients' medication regimen (how often or frequently a patient must take a medication). Patients who have chronic diseases and even some infectious diseases (like HIV or tuberculosis) take many different medications at different and multiple times per day depending on their specific medications. The schedule that patients take their medications is commonly referred to as their medication regimen. The regimen details as approximately what time to take a particular medication, like in the morning or at bedtime, but also includes special instructions on how to take that medication. An example is that many osteoporosis-preventing medications should be taken in the morning before any food or drink is consumed, and patients must remain in a sitting or standing position for up to 1 h after consumption. With patients, taking many medications that have special instructions can develop into a complex medication regimen.

Another component of complexity can include having to take multiple trips to the pharmacy to refill medications. This complexity can lead to missed doses, medication interactions, and side effects. Studies have found that adherence to medications decreased as the patient had to take multiple doses per day.[109] Compliance can be as high as 79% for once-per-day dosing to as low as 51% for four-times-daily regimens.[109]

Finally, the development of biologic agents may further increase regimen complexity. Biologic agents are protein drugs that target specific immune cells and function inside the human body. These medications are becoming increasingly popular in the chronic disease of psoriasis, rheumatoid arthritis, and cancer. In general, these medications have a wide range of delivery systems, such as an injection to the muscle every 2 months or monthly IV infusion. The use of these agents has the potential to increase medication complexity because they also have specific drug delivery systems that require detailed medication preparation instructions to be followed. Many different interventions, to reduce medication complexity, have shown to improve overall health outcomes, including fixed-dose combinations or single-pill combination therapy, pill boxes or tools for medication management, and reduction in the number of medication prescribed.

Medication Dispensing/Administration Errors

Although many of the DRPs listed in the preceding sections could result from errors in diagnosis, prescribing, consumption or monitoring of patients, it is also important to examine errors in the dispensing or administration of medications. There has been a considerable variation in the rates of dispensing errors across numerous studies in ambulatory settings. However, a well-conducted study provided a national benchmark rate of 17 errors out of every 1000 prescriptions dispensed (1.7%).[110] Approximately 6.5% of the errors were judged as having the potential for clinically significant consequences for the patient. Given that 4 billion prescriptions are dispensed in the United States each year, an estimated 51 million dispensing errors occur annually.[111]

Medication errors also occur within institutional settings. In 2002, a study of 36 hospitals and skilled-nursing facilities found that 19% of doses were in error with 7% of errors being potentially harmful.[112] The most common types of errors involved giving the drug at the wrong time or omitting a scheduled dose. Given the frail health of many persons in hospitals and nursing homes, these medication administration errors can be particularly devastating.

Although the aforementioned studies derived their estimates of errors via observation of pharmacists or nurses, the public's perception of errors is also important. In 2004, the Kaiser Family Foundation, the United States Agency for Healthcare Research and Quality, and the Harvard School of Public Health conducted a nationwide survey regarding the consumer's view on the nation's quality of care.[113] It was reported that 34% of respondents stated that they or a family member had experienced a medical error at some point, with 21% of all Americans who have reported that their medical errors caused "serious health consequences" like severe pain, long-term disability, or death.[114] A more recent survey of an insured population found that about 18% of respondents had experienced an error by an ambulatory pharmacy at some point in their lives with 6.8% of the subjects experiencing an error within the past year.[115] Despite the personal experiences of the public with medical error, and media attention to this issue, only 6% of the public and 5% of physicians viewed medical errors as one of the nation's most important health issues.[116] Concerns about errors ranked far below concerns about the costs of medical care and prescription drugs.

Conclusion

Why is medication use less than appropriate? Upon reviewing the evidence from this chapter, we conclude that there is a succinct, simple answer to that question: complexity and uncertainty. If only the solutions were as simple as identification of the problems.

The medication-use system is amazingly complex. While we may commonly equate medication use with consumption by the patient, the management of medication use involves physicians, pharmacists, nurses, and other health professionals as well as those involved in the organization and financing of health care. In addition, these persons work in a mélange of physical settings, adding to the complexity. To make such a complex system operate well, there must be sharing of information and other elements of collaboration across providers who may be in separate physical locations. Patient-centered medical homes (PCMHs) may assist in streamlining the complex medical process of treating a patient. PCMHs are models of practice where there is promotion of primary care and use of information technology to improve patient access to care and health outcomes at lower overall health-care costs.[117,118] Early research on these innovative models of care have shown promising experiences for health-care works and patients in terms of better health experiences and reduced staff burnout.[118]

The thousands of different medications that make up our armamentarium and the unique characteristics of individual patients make the selection of medication regimens complicated even in the best system of care. Coupled with this complexity is uncertainty as to how individual patients may respond to a drug and uncertainty generated by conflicting clinical trial results. While the complexity and uncertainty of health care create challenges in initiating and managing drug therapy for an individual patient, the same factors complicate our efforts to build a better medication-use system.

Uncertainty as to the frequency and nature of DRPs and uncertainty about the effectiveness of various system-level interventions complicate our efforts to modify an already complex medication-use system. The complexity of research on DRPs heightens this uncertainty. For example, definitive assessment of the preventability of ADEs is not always possible. One solution to reduce this complexity is through the development of health-care performance measures, as developed by quality standards organizations (e.g., Pharmacy Quality Alliance [PQA], Institute for Safe Medication Practices [ISMP]), pharmaceutical industry, pharmacy benefits managers, academic centers, and governmental organization (e.g., Centers for Medicare & Medicaid Services). These measures provide a uniform definition for medication performance information in high-priority areas. Also, these measures allow health-care providers to collaborate to improve medication safety and appropriateness and provide common definitions that can be used for reporting research results. Furthermore, the extent and nature of drug-related morbidity in the elderly have been obfuscated by the proliferation of studies that examine "potentially inappropriate medications" with varying criteria. Thus, it isn't clear how many elderly patients are experiencing actual drug-related morbidity versus "potential" DRPs.

Also contributing to the uncertainty is the difficulty in detecting and measuring some types of DRPs. For example, the untreated indication is harder to detect than a drug–drug interaction. More broadly, errors of omission (not doing what is needed) may be more difficult to identify than errors of commission (doing something wrong) since there may be no sentinel event, and no easily accessed data, in the case of omissions. Thus, the frequency of untreated indications is less well known than the frequency of drug–drug interactions, and the prevention of untreated indications may be more challenging.

If complexity and uncertainty are the root causes of many DRPs, then quality improvement efforts for the medication-use system should focus on methods to reduce complexity and uncertainty. Hospitals and health systems manage a large amount of data in order to determine improvements in quality and safety initiatives. Information management systems and platforms are needed for health-care organization to be better able to monitor these initiatives as well as track their improvements compared to other organizations. As health care becomes more digitalized (e.g., e-prescribing, electronic health records), information systems will need to be developed so that health systems can confidently conduct analysis of their quality and safety initiatives. These information systems will also need to facilitate evidence-based decision making and to improve both the nature and content of communication between all the participants in health care that will go a long way toward reducing DRPs.

Teamwork, systems thinking, and continuous learning from successes and failures are also essential components in building a safe and effective medication-use system. At the same time, the importance of the individual must not be overlooked. The strong covenantal relationship between the provider and patient can establish an environment that facilitates a truly helpful dialogue. Once we develop a better understanding on how to improve the quality of the medication-use system, we can design payment systems and health-care policies that facilitate the appropriate use of medications.

Explicit recommendations:

1. Heighten awareness of drug-related morbidity and the complexity and uncertainty of DRPs through continued research and dissemination of findings to the public. National Committee for Quality Assurance (NCQA), The Joint Commission (TJC), and other "watchdog" organizations have focused the attention on the quality of care provided to persons enrolled in managed care, long-term care facilities, and hospitals. Certain organizations, such as the ISMP and PQA, focus on the education of health-care providers, health organizations, patients, and consumer advocacy groups about safe practices across all health-care settings.
2. Hold providers and health-systems accountable for inappropriate care and provide incentives for appropriate care. Employers are requesting and using performance indicators for

managed care and hospitals. The fear of losing contracts or having bad publicity may have helped to drive some of the improvements in quality over the past decade. However, the cost-effectiveness of pay-for-performance programs is unclear.

3. Encourage the use of information systems that help to identify patients in need of drug-therapy modifications and encourage the use of error-prevention technologies (e.g., CPOE, bedside bar code systems). Encourage the development of information systems that can be used by health-care providers to analyze large amounts of data and report on the changes in quality and safety initiatives.
4. Encourage multidisciplinary care teams and information systems that allow different health professionals to share medical/drug records. Fostering better communication between health professionals and better communication with the patient are important.
5. Encourage researchers and health-care providers to develop and use new and innovative practices that reduce medication errors and improve safe medication practices. Encourage key stakeholders to promote the use and development of quality and safety standards in order to streamline complex medication-related problem research.
6. Encourage all health-care providers to adopt the principles, standards, and tools for continuous quality improvement.

References

1. Manasse HR. Medication use in an imperfect world: Drug misadventuring as an issue of public policy, part 1. *Am J Hosp Pharm.* 1989;46:929–944.
2. Manasse HR. Medication use in an imperfect world: Drug misadventuring as an issue of public policy, part 2. *Am J Hosp Pharm.* 1989;46:1141–1152.
3. Hepler CD, Strand LM. Opportunities and responsibilities in pharmaceutical care. *Am J Hosp Pharm.* 1990;47:533–543.
4. Salvi F, Marchetti A, D'Angelo F, Boemi M, Lattanzio F, Cherubini A. Adverse drug events as a cause of hospitalization in older adults. *Drug Saf.* 2012;35(Suppl 1):29–45.
5. Beijer HJ, de Blaey CJ. Hospitalizations caused by adverse drug reactions (ADR): A meta-analysis of observational studies. *Pharm World Sci.* 2002;24(2):46–54.
6. Kongkaew C, Noyce PR, Ashcroft DM. Hospital admissions associated with adverse drug reactions: A systematic review of prospective observational studies. *Ann Pharmacother.* 2008;42(7): 1017–1025.
7. Leendertse AJ, Visser D, Egberts ACG, va den Bemt P. The relationship between study characteristics and the prevalence of medication-related hospitalizations. *Drug Saf.* 2010;33(3):233–244.
8. Ernst FR, Grizzle AJ. Drug-related morbidity and mortality: Updating the cost-of-illness model. *J Am Pharm Assoc.* 2001;41:192–199.
9. Bootman JL, Harrison DL, Cox E. The health care cost of drug-related morbidity and mortality in nursing facilities. *Arch Intern Med.* 1997;157:2089–2096.
10. Winterstein AG, Sauer BC, Hepler CD, Poole C. Preventable drug-related hospital admissions. *Ann Pharmacother.* 2002;36:1238–1248.
11. Strand LM, Morley PC, Cipolle RJ, Ramsey R, Lamsam GD. Drug-related problems: Their structure and function. *DICP Ann Pharmacother.* 1990;24:1093–1097.
12. Hepler CD, Grainger-Rousseau T-J. Pharmaceutical care versus traditional drug treatment. Is there a difference? *Drugs.* 1995;49:1–10.
13. Knapp DA, Knapp DE, Brandon BM, West S. Development and application of criteria in drug use review programs. *Am J Hosp Pharm.* 1974;31:648–658.
14. Denig P, Haaijer-Ruskamp FM, Zijsling DH. How physicians choose drugs. *Soc Sci Med.* 1988;27:1381–1386.

15. Denig P. Scope and nature of prescribing decisions made by general practitioners. *Qual Saf Health Care.* 2002;11:137–143.
16. Groves KEM, Flanagan PS, MacKinnon NJ. Why physicians start or stop prescribing a drug: Literature review and formulary implications. *Formulary.* 2002;37:186–194.
17. Schwartz RK, Soumerai SB, Avorn J. Physician motivations for nonscientific drug prescribing. *Soc Sci Med.* 1989;28:577–582.
18. Segal R, Wang F. Influencing physician prescribing. *Pharm Pract Manage Q.* 1999;19:30–50.
19. The United States Pharmacopeial Convention, Inc. Principles of a sound drug formulary system. www.usp.org/hqi/patientSafety/resources/soundFormularyPrinciples.html. Accessed on January 15, 2014.
20. American Pharmacists Association, National Association of Chain Drug Stores Foundation. Medication therapy management in community pharmacy practice: Core elements of an MTM service (version 1.0). *J Am Pharm Assoc.* 2005;45(5):573–579.
21. Chrischilles EA, Fulda TR, Byrns PJ et al. The role of pharmacy computer systems in preventing medication errors. *J Am Pharm Assoc.* 2002;42:439–448.
22. The US Pharmacopeia Drug Utilization Review Advisory Panel. Drug utilization review: Mechanisms to improve its effectiveness and broaden its scope. *J Am Pharm Assoc.* 2000;40:538–545.
23. Dabestani AT, Perry AB. ASHP statement on bar-code-enabled medication administration technology. *Am J Health Syst Pharm.* 2009;66(6):588+.
24. Mims E, Tucker C, Carlson R, Schneider R, Bagby J. Quality-monitoring program for bar-code-assisted medication administration. *Am J Health Syst Pharm.* 2009;66(12):1125–1131.
25. Hassink JJM, Jansen MMPM, Helmons PJ. Effects of bar code-assisted medication administration (BCMA) on frequency, type and severity of medication administration errors: A review of the literature. *Eur J Hosp Pharm Sci Pract.* 2012;19(5):489–494.
26. Franklin BD, O'Grady K, Donyai P, Jacklin A, Barber N. The impact of a closed-loop electronic prescribing and administration system on prescribing errors, administration errors and staff time: A before-and-after study. *Qual Saf Health Care.* 2007;16(4):279–284.
27. Kaushal R, Bates DW. Information technology and medication safety: What is the benefit? *Qual Safe Health Care.* 2002;11(3):261–265.
28. Helmons PJ, Dalton AJ, Daniels CE. Effects of a direct refill program for automated dispensing cabinets on medication-refill errors. *Am J Health Syst Pharm.* 2012;69(19):1659–1664.
29. Rothschild JM, Keohane CA, Cook EF, Orav EJ, Burdick E, Thompson S, Hayes J, Bates DW. A controlled trial of smart infusion pumps to improve medication safety in critically ill patients. *Crit Care Med.* 2005;33:533–540.
30. Kimberlin C, Brushwood D, Allen W et al. Cancer patient and caregiver experiences: Communication and pain management issues. *J Pain Symptom Manage.* 2004;28:566–578.
31. Williams MV, Baker DW, Honig EG, Lee TM, Nowlan A. Inadequate literacy is a barrier to asthma knowledge and self care. *Chest.* 1998;114:1008–1015.
32. Mika VS, Wood PR, Weiss BD et al. Ask Me 3: Improving communication in a Hispanic pediatric outpatient practice. *Am J Health Behav.* 2007;31(Suppl 1):S115–S121.
33. Youmans SL, Schillinger D. Functional health literacy and medication use: The pharmacist's role. *Ann Pharmacother.* 2003;37(11):1726–1729.
34. Bradshaw M, Tomany-Korman S, Flores G. Language barriers to prescriptions for patients with limited English proficiency: A survey of pharmacies. *Pediatrics.* 2007;120(2):e225–e235.
35. Schwappach DL, Massetti CM, Gehring K. Communication barriers in counselling foreign-language patients in public pharmacies: Threats to patient safety? *Int J Clin Pharm.* 2012;34(5):765–772.
36. Ramalho DOD, Brummel AR, Miller DB. Medication therapy management: 10 years of experience in a large integrated health care system. *J Manag Care Pharm.* 2010;16(3):185–195.
37. Zabinski RA, Valley G. 18 Analysis of pharmacist-provided medication therapy management (MTM) services in community pharmacies over 7 years. *J Manag Care Pharm.* 2009;15(1):18–31.
38. Stubbings J, Nutescu E, Durley SF, Bauman JL. Payment for clinical pharmacy services revisited. *Pharmacother J Hum Pharmacol Drug Ther.* 2011;31(1):1–8.
39. Phillips LS, Branch WT, Cook CB et al. Clinical inertia. *Ann Intern Med.* 2001;135:825–834.

40. McBride P, Schrott HG, Plane MB et al. Primary care practice adherence to National Cholesterol Education Program guidelines for patients with coronary heart disease. *Arch Intern Med.* 1998;158:1238–1244.
41. Drass J, Kell S, Osborn M et al. Diabetes care for Medicare beneficiaries. Attitudes and behaviors of primary care physicians. *Diabetes Care.* 1998;21:1282–1287.
42. Khunti K, Wolden ML, Thorsted BL, Andersen M, Davies MJ. Clinical inertia in people with type 2 diabetes a retrospective cohort study of more than 80,000 people. *Diabetes Care.* 2013;36(11):3411–3417.
43. Safford MM, Shewchuk R, Qu H, Williams JH, Estrada CA, Ovalle F, Allison JJ. Reasons for not intensifying medications: Differentiating "clinical inertia" from appropriate care. *J Gen Int Med.* 2007;22(12):1648–1655.
44. Phillips LS, Twombly JG. It's time to overcome clinical inertia. *Ann Intern Med.* 2008;148(10):783–785.
45. Simpson SH, Majumdar SR, Tsuyuki RT et al. Effect of adding pharmacists to primary care teams on blood pressure control in patients with type 2 diabetes: A randomized controlled trial. *Diabetes Care.* 2011;34:20–26.
46. El-Kebbi IM, Ziemer DC, Gallina DL et al. Diabetes in urban African-Americans. XV. Identification of barriers to provider adherence to management protocols. *Diabetes Care.* 1999;22:1617–1620.
47. Huebschmann AG, Mizrahi T, Soenksen A, Beaty BL, Denberg TD. Reducing clinical inertia in hypertension treatment: A pragmatic randomized controlled trial. *J Clin Hypertens.* 2012;14(5):322–329.
48. Institute of Medicine. *Crossing the Quality Chasm.* Washington, DC: National Academy Press, 2001.
49. Garrett DG, Bluml BM. Patient self-management program for diabetes: First-year clinical, humanistic, and economic outcomes. *J Am Pharm Assoc.* 2005;45(2):130–137.
50. Bunting BA, Smith BH, Sutherland SE. The Asheville Project: Clinical and economic outcomes of a community-based long-term medication therapy management program for hypertension and dyslipidemia. *J Am Pharm Assoc.* 2008;48(1):23.
51. Bunting BA, Cranor CW. The Asheville Project: Long-term clinical, humanistic, and economic outcomes of a community-based medication therapy management program for asthma. *J Am Pharm Assoc.* 2006;46(2):133–147.
52. Devine EB, Hansen RN, Wilson-Norton JL et al. The impact of computerized provider order entry on medication errors in a multispecialty group practice. *J Am Med Inform Assoc.* 2010;17(1):78–84.
53. Moniz TT, Seger AC, Keohane CA et al. Addition of electronic prescription transmission to computerized prescriber order entry: Effect on dispensing errors in community pharmacies. *Am J Health Syst Pharm.* 2011;68(2):158–165.
54. Zhan C, Hicks RW, Blanchette CM, Keyes MA, Cousins DD. Potential benefits and problems with computerized prescriber order entry: Analysis of a voluntary medication error-reporting database. *Am J Health Syst Pharm.* 2006;63:353–358.
55. Han YY, Carcillo JA, Venkataraman ST et al. Unexpected increased mortality after implementation of a commercially sold computerized physician order entry system. *Pediatrics.* 2005;116(6):1506–1512.
56. Institute for Safe Medication Practices. It's time for standards to improve safety with electronic communication of medication orders. Available at: http://www.ismp.org/MSAarticles/improve.htm. Last accessed on February 20, 2014.
57. Weinberger M, Murray MD, Marrero DG et al. Effectiveness of pharmacist care for patients with reactive airways disease. *JAMA.* 2002;288:1594–1602.
58. Murray MD, Young J, Hoke S et al. Pharmacist intervention to improve medication adherence in heart failure a randomized trial. *Ann Intern Med.* 2007;146(10):714–725.
59. Roughead EE, Semple SJ, Vitry AI. Pharmaceutical care services: A systematic review of published studies, 1990 to 2003, examining effectiveness in improving patient outcomes. *Int J Pharm Pract.* 2005;13(1):53–70.
60. Zhan C, Arispe I, Kelley E et al. Ambulatory care visits for treating adverse drug effects in the United States, 1995–2001. *Joint Comm J Qual Patient Saf.* 2005;31:372–378.
61. Hug BL, Witkowski DJ, Sox CM, Keohane CA, Seger DL, Yoon C, Matheny ME, Bates DW. Adverse drug event rates in six community hospitals and the potential impact of computerized physician order entry for prevent. *J Gen Intern Med.* 2009;25(1):31–38.

62. Kaushal R, Bates DW, Landrigan C et al. Medication errors and adverse drug events in pediatric inpatients. *JAMA*. 2001;285:2114–2120.
63. Forster AJ, Murff HJ, Peterson JF, Gandhi TK, Bates DW. The incidence and severity of adverse events affecting patients after discharge from the hospital. *Ann Intern Med*. 2003;138:161–167.
64. Lazarou J, Pomeranz BH, Corey PN. Incidence of adverse drug reactions in hospitalized patients: A meta-analysis of prospective studies. *JAMA*. 1998;279:1200–1205.
65. Leape LL, Bates DW, Cullen DJ et al. Systems analysis of adverse drug events. *JAMA*. 1995;274:35–43.
66. Evans RS, Pestotnik SL, Classen DC et al. A computer-assisted management program for antibiotics and other antiinfective agents. *N Engl J Med*. 1998;338:232–238.
67. Leape LL, Cullen DJ, Clapp MD et al. Pharmacist participation on physician rounds and adverse drug events in the intensive care unit. *JAMA*. 1999;282:267–270.
68. Kucukarslan SN, Peters M, Mlynarek M et al. Pharmacists on rounding teams reduce preventable adverse drug events in hospital general medicine units. *Arch Intern Med*. 2003;163:2014–2018.
69. Wong ND, Chuang J, Wong K, Neff D, Marrett E. Residual dyslipidemia among United States adults treated with lipid modifying therapy (data from National Health and Nutrition Examination Survey 2009–2010). *Am J Cardiol*. 2013;112(3):373–379.
70. Egan BM, Zhao Y, Axon RN. US trends in prevalence, awareness, treatment, and control of hypertension, 1988–2008. *JAMA*. 2010;303(20):2043–2050.
71. Ghandehari H, Kamal-Bahl S, Wong ND. Prevalence and extent of dyslipidemia and recommended lipid levels in US adults with and without cardiovascular comorbidities: The National Health and Nutrition Examination Survey 2003–2004. *Am Heart J*. 2008;156(1):112–119.
72. Beers MH, Ouslander JG, Rollingher I et al. Explicit criteria for determining inappropriate medication use in nursing home residents. *Arch Intern Med*. 1991;151:1825–1832.
73. American Geriatrics Society 2012. Beers criteria update expert panel. American Geriatrics Society updated Beers criteria for potentially inappropriate medication use in older adults. *J Am Geriatr Soc*. 2012;60(4):616–631.
74. Matanović SM, Vlahović-Palčevski V. Potentially inappropriate prescribing to the elderly: Comparison of new protocol to Beers criteria with relation to hospitalizations for ADRs. *Eur J Clin Pharmacol*. 2014;70:483–490.
75. Price SD1, Holman CD, Sanfilippo FM, Emery JD. Association between potentially inappropriate medications from the beers criteria and the risk of unplanned hospitalization in elderly patients. *Ann Pharmacother*. January 2014;48(1):6–16.
76. Rigler SK, Jachna CM, Perera S, Shireman TI, Eng ML. Patterns of potentially inappropriate medication use across three cohorts of older Medicaid recipients. *Ann Pharmacother*. 2005;39:1175–1181.
77. Gallagher P, Ryan C, Byrne S, Kennedy J, O'Mahony D. STOPP (Screening Tool of Older Person's Prescriptions) and START (Screening Tool to Alert doctors to Right Treatment). Consensus validation. *Int J Clin Pharmacol Ther*. 2008;46(2):72–83.
78. Gallagher P, Baeyens JP, Topinkova E et al. Inter-rater reliability of STOPP (Screening Tool of Older Persons' Prescriptions) and START (Screening Tool to Alert doctors to Right Treatment) criteria amongst physicians in six European countries. *Age Ageing*. 2009;38(5):603–606.
79. Barry PJ, Gallagher P, Ryan C, O'mahony D. START (screening tool to alert doctors to the right treatment)—An evidence-based screening tool to detect prescribing omissions in elderly patients. *Age Ageing*. 2007;36:632–638.
80. Gallagher PF, O'Connor MN, O'Mahony D. Prevention of potentially inappropriate prescribing for elderly patients: A randomized controlled trial using STOPP/START criteria. *Clin Pharmacol Ther*. 2011;89:845–854.
81. Corsonello A, Onder G, Abbatecola AM, Guffanti EE, Gareri P, Lattanzio F. Explicit criteria for potentially inappropriate medications to reduce the risk of adverse drug reactions in elderly people: From Beers to STOPP/START criteria. *Drug Saf*. 2012;35(Suppl 1):21–28.
82. Hamilton H, Gallagher P, Ryan C, Byrne S, O'Mahony D. Potentially inappropriate medications defined by STOPP criteria and the risk of adverse drug events in older hospitalized patients. *Arch Intern Med*. 2011;171(11):1013–1019.

83. Hecker MT, Aron DC, Patel NP et al. Unnecessary use of antimicrobials in hospitalized patients. *Arch Intern Med.* 2003;163:972–978.
84. Edgell ET, Summers KH, Hylan TR, Ober J, Bootman JL. A framework for drug utilization evaluation in depression: Insights from outcomes research. *Med Care.* 1999;37:AS67–AS76.
85. Wells KB, Katon W, Rogers WH. Use of minor tranquilizers and antidepressant medications by depressed outpatients: Results from the Medical Outcomes Study. *Am J Psychiatr.* 1994;151:694–700.
86. McCombs JS, Nichol MB, Stimmel GL. The cost of antidepressant drug therapy failure: A study of antidepressant use patterns in a Medicaid population. *J Clin Psychiatr.* 1990;51:60–69.
87. Faria C, Wenzel M, Lee KW, Coderre K, Nichols J, Belletti DA. A narrative review of clinical inertia: Focus on hypertension. *J Am Soc Hyperten.* 2009;3(4):267–276.
88. Cleeland CS, Gonin R, Hatfield AK et al. Pain and its treatment in outpatients with metastatic cancer. *N Engl J Med.* 1994;330:592–596.
89. Larue F, Colleau SM, Brasseur L, Cleeland CS. Multicentre study of cancer pain and its treatment in France. *BMJ.* 1995;310:1034–1037.
90. Olyeai A, de Matos A, Bennet W. Prescribing drugs in renal disease. In: Brenner B (ed.). *The Kidney,* 6th edn. Philadelphia, PA: WB Saunders Co.s, 2000, pp. 2606–2653.
91. Pedersen CA, Schneider PJ, Scheckelhoff DJ. ASHP national survey of pharmacy practice in hospital settings: Monitoring and patient education—2003. *Am J Health Syst Pharm.* 2004;61:457–471.
92. Mowry JB, Spyker DA, Cantilena LR, Bailey JE, Ford M. 2012 Annual Report of the American Association of Poison Control Centers' National Poison Data System (NPDS): 30th annual report. *Clin Toxicol.* 2013;51(10):949–1229.
93. McHorney CA, Spain CV. Frequency of and reasons for medication non-fulfillment and non-persistence among American adults with chronic disease in 2008. *Health Expect.* 2011;14(3):307–320.
94. Safran DG, Strollo MK, Guterman S, Li A, Rogers WH, Neuman P. Prescription coverage, use, and spending before and after part D implementation: A national longitudinal panel survey. *J Gen Intern Med.* 2009;25(1):10–17.
95. Benner JS, Glynn RJ, Mogun H et al. Long-term persistence in use of statin therapy in elderly patients. *JAMA.* 2002;288:455–461.
96. Benner JS, Pollack MF, Smith TW et al. Association between short-term effectiveness of statins and long-term adherence to lipid-lowering therapy. *Am J Health Syst Pharm.* 2005;62:1468–1475.
97. Pampallona S, Bollini P. Patient adherence in the treatment of depression. *Br J Psychiatr.* 2002;180:104–109.
98. Samet JH, Libman H, Steger KA et al. Compliance with zidovudine monotherapy in patients infected with Human Immunodeficiency Virus, Type 1: A cross-sectional study in a municipal hospital clinic. *Am J Med.* 1992;92:495–502.
99. Gao X, Nau DP, Rosenbluth A et al. The relationship of disease severity, health beliefs and medication adherence among HIV patients. *AIDS Care.* 2000;12:387–398.
100. Walsh JC, Horne R, Dalton M et al. Reasons for non-adherence to antiretroviral therapy: Patients' perspectives provide evidence of multiple causes. *AIDS Care.* 2001;13:709–720.
101. Aikens JE, Nease DE, Nau DP et al. Adherence to maintenance-phase antidepressant medication as a function of patient beliefs about medication. *Ann Fam Med.* 2005;3:23–30.
102. Horne R, Buick D, Fisher M et al. Doubts about necessity and concerns about adverse effects: Identifying the types of beliefs that are associated with non-adherence to HAART. *Int J STD AIDS.* 2004;15:38–44.
103. United States Department of Health and Human Services. Substance abuse and mental health services administration. 2010 National Survey on Drug Use and Health. Available at: http://oas.samhsa.gov/nhsda.htm. Last accessed on January 15, 2014.
104. Gonzales R, Steiner JF, Sande MA. Antibiotic prescribing for adults with colds, upper respiratory tract infections and bronchitis by ambulatory care physicians. *JAMA.* 1997;278:901–904.
105. Watson RL, Dowell SF, Jayaraman M et al. Antimicrobial use for pediatric upper respiratory infections: Reported practice, actual practice, and parent beliefs. *Pediatrics.* 1999;104:1251–1257.

106. Akkerman AE, Kuyvenhoven MM, van der Wouden JC, Verheij TJM. Analysis of under- and overprescribing of antibiotics in acute otitis media in general practice. *J Antimicrob Chemother.* 2005;56(3):569–574.
107. Jelinski S, Parfrey P, Hutchinson J. Antibiotic utilization in community practices: Guideline concurrence and prescription necessity. *Pharmacoepidemiol Drug Saf.* 2005;14:319–326.
108. Avorn J, Solomon DH. Cultural and economic factors that (mis)shape antibiotic use: The nonpharmacologic basis of therapeutics. *Ann Intern Med.* 2000;133:128–135.
109. Claxton AJ, Cramer J, Pierce C. A systematic review of the associations between dose regimen and medication compliance. *Clin Therapeut.* 2001;23(8):1296–1310.
110. Flynn EA, Barker KN, Carnahan BJ. National observational study of prescription dispensing accuracy and safety in 50 pharmacies. *J Am Pharm Assoc.* 2003;43:191–200.
111. Medication errors observed in 36 health care facilities. *Live Science.* 2002. http://www.livescience.com/23143-prescription-drugs-2011.html. Accessed on February 20, 2014.
112. Barker KN, Flynn EA, Pepper GA et al. Medication errors observed in 36 health care facilities. *Arch Intern Med.* 2002;162:1897–1903.
113. Altman DE, Clancy C, Blendon RJ. Improving patient safety-five years after the IOM report. *New Engl J Med.* 2004;351(20):2041–2043.
114. Kaiser Family Foundation, Agency for Healthcare Research, Harvard School of Public Health. National survey on consumers' experiences with patient safety and quality information. Available at: http://www.kff.org. Last accessed on January 24, 2014.
115. Nau DP, Erickson SR. Medication safety: Patients' experiences, beliefs and behaviors. *J Am Pharm Assoc.* 2005;45:452–457.
116. Blendon RJ, DesRoches CM, Brodie M et al. View of practicing physicians and the public on medical errors. *N Engl J Med.* 2002;347:1933–1940.
117. Berenson RA, Hammons T, Gans DN et al. A house is not a home: Keeping patients at the center of practice redesign. *Health Aff.* 2008;27(5):1219–1230.
118. Reid RJ, Fishman PA, Yu O, Ross TR, Tufano JT, Soman MP, Larson EB. Patient-centered medical home demonstration: A prospective, quasi-experimental, before and after evaluation. *Am J Manag Care.* 2009;15(9):e71–e87.

Chapter 6

Medication Adherence and Health Policy

Meghan M. Kelly and Jon C. Schommer

Contents

Introduction

The subject of medication adherence is a timeworn topic. It seems to have confounded practitioners and policy makers alike because, for all the effort and resources thrown at the subject matter, people are still nonadherent to their prescribed medication regimens. Adherence, in the purest sense, is a simple act of taking a medication as prescribed. Trying to impact adherence can be as simple as getting to know patients and their relationship with their medication. Therefore, the act of measuring adherence as a means to define the quality of pharmacy care should simply reflect how well a clinician or health system has met patients' needs. What has resulted from all this research is a large amount of information about the variety of changes that can affect adherence in only a slight way. Attempting to impact adherence has become a tangled mess, each player in health care working in their own, uncoordinated way to improve adherence. As a quality measure, adherence has not been fully developed to represent all the aspects of adherence these players are trying to impact.

The purpose of this chapter is to provide a foundation necessary to consider the following challenges:

- How do you measure the actions of an individual patient in the context of a population?
- What does an adherence measure actually measure?
- How do we engage the patient in adherence behaviors?
- Can quality pharmacy services be demonstrated by adherence measures?

Why the Focus on Adherence?

How did the health-care world land on adherence as the cause of a crusade? The desperation and urgency accompanying the discussion on how to reign in health-care costs led policy makers and providers to look at a variety of paths to solve this crisis. (*Note*: this crisis still remains unsolved to this day.) What authors Osterberg and Blaschke (2005) found is that up to 50% of all Americans have at least one chronic condition, and the Centers for Disease Control and Prevention estimates 75% of U.S. health-care expenditures are associated with the management of chronic conditions. From this, several premises have been proposed.

First premise: Being able to efficiently manage chronic disease is a high priority. Besides lifestyle changes, the single most effective treatment for conditions such as diabetes, hypertension, and hyperlipidemia is chronic medication therapy, and 187 million Americans take one or more prescription drugs (Kaiser Family Foundation, 2010).

Second premise: Vast amounts of money are being wasted on chronic medication therapy. Of the 187 million patients taking medications, approximately 50% do not take their medications as prescribed (Osterberg and Blaschke, 2005). In one study of patients taking statin medications, the number of patients adhering to medications was 80% at 3 weeks, 56% at 6 months, and only 25% after 5 years (Benner et al., 2002).

Third premise: Nonadherence to medication therapy leads to poor health outcomes. The New England Healthcare Institute (NEHI) estimated in 2007 that a total of $(USD)290 billion was spent on poor outcomes due to medication nonadherence (NEHI, 2007). Nonadherence-related hospitalizations made up a third of that expenditure.

Fourth remise: Money is being wasted in health care for events that could be prevented and/or improved.

Thus, it was concluded that improving medication adherence could result in major cost savings. Pharmacy organizations, the pharmaceutical industry, the insurance industry, and health-care providers began to build numerous programs to impact adherence. However, there are cracks in the foundation upon which this conclusion is based. The literature that was the primary source of this estimation looked at rates of hospitalizations due to adverse drug events. Many of these studies then looked at a subsection of this population and identified the events that were due to adherence. Adherence-related hospitalization was not a primary outcome for many of these studies. The most frequently cited studies in policy research were limited to the extent that they described adherence and generalized the relationship between adherence and economic outcomes (Senst et al., 2001; McDonnell and Jacobs, 2002; Pladevall et al., 2004; Sokol et al., 2005; Chapman et al., 2008). The conclusion that medication nonadherence is a direct source of financial waste is not fully defended in the literature but is widely accepted. This relationship is inferred, and while the logic behind it seems appropriate, does it warrant the effort put forth by so many organizations? Do we understand the true relationship between nonadherence and waste or did adherence become guilty of causing waste by association?

The health-care world marched forward on its attack on nonadherence in its effort to win the war against high health-care costs. Their slogan? C. Everett Koop stated once: "Drugs don't work in patients who don't take them." The logical solution is to get patients to take their drugs. The next steps? To define adherence and then to figure out how we know we are winning in the fight against nonadherence by establishing measurement tools. Notice though that the primary intent at this point was to lower costs and not focused explicitly on improving care or meeting patient needs.

Definitions of Adherence: A Patient Perspective

What is adherence? The WHO defines adherence as "the extent to which a person's behavior—taking medication, following a diet, and/or executing lifestyle changes corresponds with agreed recommendations from a health care provider" (Sabate, 2003). Medication adherence is the behavior that results when a patient sums up all the parts of his or her medication experience.

The medication experience is composed of all the factors that build the relationship a patient has with his or her medication and dictate the interaction between the patient and his or her medication and the action of taking his or her medication. The medication experience is the patient's attitude toward medications, understanding of drug therapy, wants and expectations, concerns, and cultural, ethical, and religious perspectives on medications (Cipolle et al., 2012). All of these pieces play a role in the patient's medication behavior and, as a result, impact adherence. Factors impacting patient adherence can be categorized into patient factors, clinical factors, and health system factors. Patient factors are those that are unique to the patient and range from physical characteristics to health beliefs. It has been shown that demographic characteristics (age, gender, and race) play weak roles in adherence (Sabate, 2003; URAC, 2011). Level of education, language or cultural differences, and level of health literacy can create barriers to understanding the directions of a medication, including timing or number of doses and auxiliary instructions such as to take the medication with food. A patient's cognitive status can change the way a patient is able to manage medications, and a decrease in adherence is common in patients who have a low cognitive status (Balakrishnan, 1998; Gellad et al., 2011). Even in patients whose cognitive status is unaltered, the amount of information that is provided to patients can be overwhelming, and patients must be able to recall, comprehend, and use the information provided to them to make the decisions in taking their medication. Depression plays a role in adherence, and it has been shown that patients with depression may have decreased overall adherence (Balakrishnan, 1998).

Add to the individual patient the clinical factors such as chronic diseases that may or may not make the patient feel sick and can be treated with maybe one, but likely more than one, medication. These medications may make the patient feel better, feel worse, or result in no detectable effects. Characteristics of the condition requiring treatment can impact an individual's adherence behaviors (Gellad et al., 2011). Some of the most common conditions treated are asymptomatic, such as hypertension, or the effects of the medication not felt by the patient, as is the case with lipid-lowering medications. Although the benefits of treating these conditions are communicated to the patient, they are more likely not to perceive the reason for needing medication therapy and therefore be nonadherent. Also, some conditions may be surrounded by social connotations such as implications of blame, responsibility, or implied fault associated with the condition (Sabate, 2003). Coping mechanisms, such as hiding medications from others, may make it more difficult to be adherent to the medication regimen. These patient-specific factors create the basis for addressing the treatment of the condition by health-care providers.

Besides the way the condition makes a patient feel, the patient also will judge the medication, or series of medications, being used to treat the condition in other ways. The medication regimen (which may vary in terms of duration of treatment, frequency of dosing, and number of doses taken) needs to be considered a priority when providing care (Sabate, 2003; URAC, 2011, 2012). Each of these aspects will impact the willingness a patient has to take his or her medication. For example, a patient with a chronic condition who requires treatment with medication for an undefined amount of time may feel helpless in treating such a condition. The idea that there is no end in sight may seem like an insurmountable challenge and the patients give up. The perception that they are unable to maintain this behavior will cause them to simply stop taking their prescribed medications. The number of pills and the complexity of a patient's medication regimen can be overwhelming (Balakrishnan, 1998; Sabate, 2003). The more pills a person takes and the more often they have to take a pill, the more the likelihood that a patient is noncompliant. This is when health-care system factors can provide support in promoting adherent behaviors.

One of the first steps in promoting adherent behaviors is building a positive patient–provider relationship (Sabate, 2003; URAC, 2011, 2012). Patient–provider relationships play an important role in the medication experience and may affect trends in adherence behaviors. Providers must be able to give health information in a clear manner. Communication styles, particularly providers who demonstrate empathy and warmth, can positively impact adherence and patient trust and satisfaction with their provider. It has been shown that relationships featuring shared decision making lead to higher levels of adherence and outcomes (AHRQ, 2012).

Next, the health system should provide resources to both the patient and clinician to help promote adherence (Sabate, 2003; URAC, 2011). Clinicians should be supported to provide patient education programs and to receive training on how to impact adherence. Most importantly, anyone who is going to make an impact on a patient's behavior needs time to engage with their patients. Providers need to be trained and have the ability, resources, and time to provide education to patients. Coordinated care teams improve adherence by ensuring correct and efficient care that meets the need of the patient across all settings of the health-care system (Mackey et al., 2012).

Finally, the health-care system should be designed to help maximize the likelihood of each patient achieving the most out of his or her medication and promoting a positive medication experience. All the effort made to impact a patient's behavior is only worth it if the medication a patient takes is prescribed for an appropriate reason, works when taken correctly, and has not resulted in any harm to the patient. If these aspects of medications have not been addressed, then patients are cleared of blame for not taking their medication. In these instances, they simply cannot see the value or do not believe that taking their medication is worth the financial, physical, or emotional cost. No matter how adherent a patient is, the level of adherence will not stand for any clinical significance unless it is an appropriate, safe, and effective drug. In fact, Cipolle et al. (2012) have demonstrated that many of the problems in achieving goals of therapy are actually related to an inappropriate or unsafe drug and that adherence remains a small proportion of the overall barriers to achieve goals of therapy. Once the factors mediating the patient's medication-taking behaviors have been defined, the behavior itself can be defined and then quantified.

Definitions of Adherence: A Measureable Concept

A behavior can be hard to quantify. In order to do so, a definition of the behavior should be established. The common problems in the discussion of adherence are the variety of adherence definitions, the types of adherence being measured, and the calculations and the sources of data for medication adherence. The WHO definition expands adherence from simply observing medication-taking behavior to a definition that encompasses an entire lifestyle (Sabate, 2003). This is reflective of the fact that adherence is more than just a medication behavior, it is a way of life, and to impact the behavior, it is the responsibility of more than just the pharmacy department. Lifestyle changes are an important aspect of managing chronic conditions and the majority of these conditions are being treated with medication. There are several terms used to describe the behaviors surrounding medication taking and these are described next.

Compliance is defined as the "extent to which the patient follows the health professionals' advice and takes the treatment" (Cushing and Metcalf, 2007). This is one of the most commonly used terms to describe adherence and it is one of the first terms introduced in the discussion of medication adherence (Tilson, 2004). The use of the term compliance is falling out of favor as it denotes an imbalanced relationship between the prescriber and the patient. Historically, this relationship has been described as paternalistic and the term compliance often implies a patient who does not have an active role in medication-taking behaviors (Cushing and Metcalf, 2007; Cramer et al., 2008). Medication taking is a decision that a patient makes every day and therefore a more appropriate term is required to reflect the need to engage a patient in the process of maintaining healthy behaviors. *Adherence* is the term currently used most often in health care to describe a patient's ability and willingness to follow a health-care provider's recommendations (Cushing and Metcalf, 2007). The term adherence denotes a patient's role in maintaining his or her health by making decisions in their health care (Tilson, 2004). In research, adherence can refer to behaviors such as medication-taking behaviors including the patient's ability to follow medication regimens, including the number and frequency of doses, timing of doses, and auxiliary directions such as take with food or take on an empty stomach (Cramer et al., 2008). *Concordance* describes an active process of decision making between the health-care provider and the patient. The patient agrees to follow the prescriber's directions and is allowed to negotiate with the prescriber to develop therapies that may better suit the patient. Concordance is a newer term brought into the adherence discussion in the United Kingdom and has been viewed as an important concept in eliciting adherence within the care delivery process (Cushing and Metcalf, 2007). *Persistence* refers to medication adherence for the prescribed length of treatment (Cramer et al., 2008). For chronic conditions, persistence will likely refer to the length of time the patient is being observed.

Unfortunately in adherence research and policy publications, the terms defined earlier are often simply referred to as "adherence." It becomes unclear what aspect of adherence is being studied and blurs the observed impact of interventions on adherence. There has been an increased focus on maintaining the difference in persistence and adherence in the research community in order to provide more specific and effective interventions (Ho et al., 2009; AHRQ, 2012). Since research has not been consistent or specific about the outcome being studied, finding a measurement tool to measure an outcome becomes difficult. What makes finding a measurement tool even more difficult is the fact that each of these definitions describes a patient's behavior. In other words, how does a clinician measure what is known about the patient in respect to medication-taking behaviors? How do these measures represent the work that is done to get a patient to be an adherent patient?

Sources of Medication Adherence Data

Understanding a patient's adherence is getting to know the patient and what perceptions a patient has about medication. It is a description of what is keeping patients from understanding the need to take their medication. Are they finding it difficult to access their medications? Are there patterns in their medication regimen or in their prescription refills that might indicate barriers to healthy adherent behaviors? Since the factors contributing to adherence are complex, defined in a variety of ways, the ability to measure a patient's adherence is equally complex. There is no single measure of adherence that encompasses all aspects of the behavior and no measure is completely accurate in describing the level of adherence. There are a variety of methods that can provide insight into the different aspects of adherence and range from focusing on the patient as an individual to putting the patient in the context of a larger population. The use of these methods varies on the intent of the researcher or policy program (or how well the researcher wants to know the patient) (Fariman and Motheral, 2000).

Adherence data can be collected in two basic ways: directly or indirectly. Direct observation methods include measuring drug concentrations in the blood or metabolites in the urine. Direct observation is time-consuming, expensive, and impractical. This method is most appropriate when a patient does not achieve clinical goals with drugs such as warfarin or antiepilepsy drugs like valproic acid or phenytoin (Osterberg and Blaschke, 2005; Brown and Bussey, 2011). This method is not practical for assessing overall adherence trends in large patient populations and therefore adherence is most commonly assessed using indirect observation methods.

Indirect observation methods allow clinicians, researchers, and policy makers to collect information on and understand adherence trends. A variety of indirect methods of adherence have been developed in order to assess patient adherence behavior, including medication monitoring, self-report measures, and prescription claims data. The simplest form of medication monitoring is pill counting; however, this does not ensure that the patient has taken the medication or that the medication was taken at the correct time. New technologies, such as the Medication Events Monitoring System (MEMS®), allow electronic monitoring of medication access with a sensor that detects when a pill bottle has been opened. This form of monitoring is considered a gold standard but is too expensive to be used on a large-scale basis (Rittenhouse, 1996).

Self-reported measures are a quick way to measure a patient's level of adherence. Patient diaries and some surveys provide a description of the reasons for nonadherence. Other questionnaires, such as the eight-item Morisky scale (Morisky et al., 2008), the visual analog scale for adherence (Kalichman et al., 2009), and the brief medication questionnaire (Svarstad et al., 1999), provide an assessment of the level of adherence a patient has to his or her medications using a scoring system developed by each method. Surveys and questionnaires are most often administered by clinicians in practice or as a part of adherence research and patient behaviors. This form of data collection can be done fairly simply. However, the analysis of these data can be cumbersome. Most policy makers look toward administrative data to understand trends in a patient's adherence level and behaviors over long periods of time (Fairman and Motheral, 2000).

Sample Adherence Questions—Eight-Item Morisky Scale (Morisky et al., 2008)

Ex. 1. Do you ever forget to take your medicine?

Ex. 2. Sometimes if you feel worse when you take your medicine, do you stop taking it?

Ex. 3. Do you know the long-term benefit of taking your medicine as told to you by your doctor or pharmacist?

Administrative and claims data have become the most common sources of data to measure an individual's level of adherence. Most policy makers commonly rely on these sources in order to make decisions regarding medication adherence. Electronic prescription claims are analyzed and rates of adherence can be estimated. Pharmacy claims data provide information about the patient, including patient demographic details, the drug and quantity dispensed, the refill date, and days' supply. These data are used in a variety of calculations that are categorized into the following: medication possession measures, medication gap measures, medication persistence, and discontinuation measures (Sattler et al., 2013). Figure 6.1 adapted from Sattler et al. (2013) provides a visual guide to the different ways adherence can be calculated.

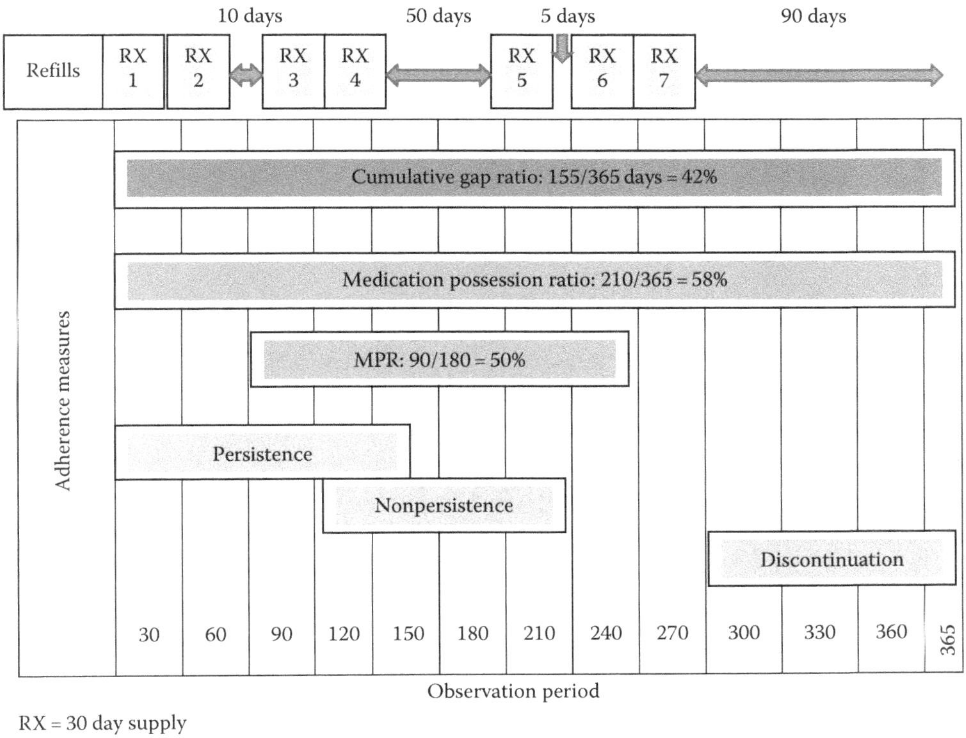

Figure 6.1 Adherence calculations. (Adapted from Sattler, E.L.P. et al., *Drugs Aging*, 30, 383, 2013.)

Medication Possession Measures

The *medication possession ratio* (*MPR*) is the most commonly used calculation in claims-based adherence analysis. There are a variety of MPR calculations that rate the amount of time a patient has a drug within their possession (Sikka et al., 2005; Andrade et al., 2006; Hess et al., 2006; Sattler et al., 2013). The basic concept of the MPR is a sum of the days' supply divided by the total number of days in the observation period:

$$\text{MPR} = \frac{\text{total days' supply in the observation period}}{\text{number of days in the observation period}}$$

Adherence measured by the MPR looks at a single medication over a period of time. The time period being observed begins with the first fill of a medication, or index date, and ends with the last fill of a medication occurring before a predetermined end date. It is possible that the MPR calculated is greater than 100% due to a final fill of a medication occurring immediately before the end of the observation period or due to early refills. Since the time period of an MPR ends with the last fill of a medication, it does not account for discontinuation of a drug.

The *proportion of days covered* (*PDC*) is similar to the MPR in that it looks at the ratio of days covered by medication during an observation period. However, the PDC is more complex because it considers overlapping refills of a single drug or multiple drugs. For a single medication, the PDC will assume that a patient takes all the medication before they start the next fill. In a class of medications, or multiple drugs being observed, the PDC looks at the proportion of days in an observation period covered by at least one medication in the class. For example, a PDC calculation looking at statin adherence will calculate a level of adherence even if the patient switches from one statin to another statin. The observation period in a PDC calculation is a predetermined time period, most commonly a calendar year. The maximum level of adherence when calculated with a PDC is capped at 1.0.

Medication Gap Measures

The *cumulative medication gap* (*CMG*) measure identifies the percent of time a patient is without medication during an observation period. The calculation uses the days' supply of a medication compared to the total days observed. Observing gaps in patient refills assumes that the patient is taking the medication as prescribed. However, sometimes gaps indicate a decrease in dosage.

Persistence and Discontinuation Measures

Persistence and discontinuation measures are often used interchangeably and can be described as whether or not the days' supply of a patient's refills meet or exceed the predetermined threshold. Often researchers will allow a specified grace period for late refills in discontinuation or persistence measures. The result of the measure is a simple deeming of being persistent or nonpersistent. Some researchers will consider an individual to be nonpersistent for gaps greater than 30 days and will define discontinuation as no refill activity for at least a 90-day period.

The majority of these measures are reserved for research purposes, while the PDC is the calculation of choice for adherence-related health policy (Nau, 2013). This is due to its relative ease, unobtrusiveness, and low cost of calculating adherence rates in large populations. It also provides an ability to observe adherence across medication classes. Despite its ease, there are limitations to the PDC particularly with the use of claims data to determine this measure. First, the claims data used to determine medication use often is not available in a timely manner. It does not capture problems in adherence occurring in the present. Second, the calculation is easily impacted by refills that occur outside the time being observed leading to an underestimation of the level of adherence. These challenges can be found in Figure 6.1. In the figure, the measurement period is 365 days and the MPR is 58% (210/365 days). If the measurement period only captured days 60 through 240, the MPR could be computed as 50% (90/180 days) if refill 6 was not yet available in the data. If refill 6 was counted, even if it had not yet been completely used by the patient by day 240, the MPR would be computed as 67% (120/180). In order to have a more accurate adherence calculation, a time frame must be selected that allows for observing variations including such things as medication refills amounting to a 90-day supply in some cases. Finally, the adherence rate does not account for patient factors nor does it provide insight as to the barriers that may be occurring in achieving adherence.

Another challenge to using MPR is under the conditions of automatic refills. In these scenarios, patients may have signed up for automatic refills that are mailed to the person on a regular basis every 30 days. Thus, a person could be 100% adherent according to refill records and the resultant MPR calculation but in fact not be adherent. The person could be storing the refills in their home without ever taking them. Shrank (2011) reported that millions of pounds of prescription medications go unused each year and are stored in "bulging medicine cabinets," which he called "the other side of medication nonadherence." Research by Wieczorkiewicz et al. (2013) showed that almost all respondents to their survey had excess and leftover medications in their homes due to both overprescribing and poor medication adherence.

In the end, all measures are inherently patient focused, patient specific, and intended to focus on the individual. In choosing a measure, one should consider how to understand how a patient acts. An appropriate metaphor would be to consider the following example. Say you wanted to assess a patient's current overall health behavior. The first option to assess the patient's behavior is to ask them a few questions about their lifestyle habits, such as exercise and diet. This may take some time and resources but you end up with a highly individualized description of the patient. The second option is to collect a month's worth of grocery receipts and analyze them. Each method provides a description of the patient and both are prone to interpretation. What would a researcher say about a person who bought six pizzas and a tub of ice cream? In the first method, a patient is allowed to represent their choices and their needs. They could let the researcher know they work out regularly and bought the items for a social event. With the second method, a researcher has to determine the patient's status simply based on the purchase of six pizzas and ice cream that the patient bought and not know how or why they were purchased and if they were consumed. In both instances, the food items are not healthy, but the researcher is not likely to come to the same conclusion on the patient's health status. In adherence, the patterns may both demonstrate nonadherence, but by getting to know the patient, the researcher can decide if the behavior is the product of other factors or if it is actually nonadherence.

Many policy makers choose a measure that is purely quantitative and remove the individual from the calculation to focus on a measure of the overall level of adherence of a population. In other words, the measure no longer represents an individual patient, his or her preferences, or his or her behavior. Rather, it represents a number of patients' behaviors with no way to see the patient as an individual or to know how one should impact the behavior. The patient-centered aspect of adherence is complex, and no satisfying and simple answer has been found in understanding how to improve adherence. In the rush to establish a quality pharmacy measure, policy makers kept the patient out of the adherence discussion.

Adherence as a Measure of Quality Care

The rush to focus immediately on adherence is unsettling. Although the subject of adherence has been a hot topic in health care for several decades, it has only recently become the emphasis of quality measures for health-care payers and providers. Part of this is due to the recent availability of claims data that allowed for population analysis. It is also in part due to the urgent push to find answers to reduce health-care expenditures. Even though adherence has long been studied and no satisfactory solution to nonadherence identified, it took almost no time for it to become a quality measure since it was first identified as a cause for wasteful health-care spending. In 2007, the National Council on Patient Information and Education called for an increased focus on improving medication adherence. In 2009, the National Quality Foundation established measures of medication adherence as indicators of quality pharmacy care. This measure was developed by the Pharmacy Quality Alliance (PQA), and they defined the PDC as the recommended method of calculating a patient's adherence rate (Nau, 2013). PQA is an organization that seeks to identify measures of quality pharmacy care and its members identified adherence as an important component of medication-use quality (www.pqaalliance.org). That same year, URAC, an organization promoting quality and efficiency in health care through accreditation programs, created an accreditation program for pharmacy benefits management and drug therapy management programs (www.urac.org). A key domain measuring quality drug therapy management uses adherence as the marker for quality. In 2012, the Centers for Medicare and Medicaid Services (CMS) adopted three measures assessing adherence to medications treating diabetes, hypertension, and cholesterol.

The measures adopted by CMS are used to assess the quality of services provided by a Medicare Part D plan. The ratings are reported as STAR ratings to the public and are part of a financial incentive program to improve quality care. The ratings are similarly calculated within the respective class of medications. These ratings are titled "Taking Medication as Directed" and are calculated using PQA's methodology (CMS.gov, 2013). A patient is considered adherent when he or she fills enough medication to cover 80% or more of the time observed or a PDC of 80% (0.80). PDCs are calculated using claims data and 80% has been used often as the delimiter of adherence and nonadherence (Osterberg and Blaschke, 2005). Previous studies have identified 80% to be the generally accepted level of adherence needed to achieve outcomes, but clinical success can be defined by a range of levels.

Evidence that links adherence with economic outcomes and clinical outcomes remains inconclusive but is dominated by a positive association. A meta-analysis by DiMatteo et al. (2002) noted that 26% more patients who were adherent experienced improved clinical outcomes compared to nonadherent patients. This is noteworthy, but what of the remaining 74% of patients? According to the logic of Koop's statement, shouldn't the remaining patients also be able to achieve their clinical outcomes? The strength of the relationship between nonadherence and clinical outcomes or health-care expenditures is still unclear. So currently, as organizations pour money into developing adherence programs, monetary gain from pay-for-performance programs might be predictable, but the improvements in patient outcomes are not so certain (Martin et al., 2005).

From working with a patient to assessing a plan's efficacy in providing medication services, it is important to consider the following: How well do these measures capture a patient's behavior?

Deciding on what measurement tool is the most appropriate depends on the goal of the program. If the goal is to impact an individual and to understand a patient's adherence behavior, then the goal is achieved by getting to know the patient and the perceptions a patient has about their medication. Identifying the factors that make it difficult for a patient to access their medications will determine the course of action and necessary care plan to achieve adherence behaviors. The quality of this interaction between the patient and his or her provider, health system, or even health-care payer, is what needs to be measured. This is why the rush to use adherence as a quality measure is unsettling. If the goal is to measure patterns in patients' medication regimens or in their prescription refills, then the current system of adherence measurement is well suited for that purpose. However, care is personal and the insight obtained on the quality of care through claims is rather ambiguous, impersonal, and misleading.

Impacting Medication Adherence

The only meaningful and persistent impact on adherence has come simply from a lot of hard work to interact with the patient and provide integrated care (AHRQ, 2012). Often, adherence interventions get parsed out to the health system who takes care of issues like care coordination (to an unsatisfying extent) and pharmacy insurers who manage coverage, cost, and refill access. Pharmacists, prescribers, case managers, nurses, educators, social workers, and whoever else is in contact with the patient are all trying in their individual way to impact patient adherence. Interventions shown in the following chart range from process-oriented changes, such as refill reminders, to education, to improving the clinical care of the patient.

Much of the research on the effectiveness of the interventions has provided inconclusive results (NEHI, 2007, 2009; AHRQ, 2012). Sustainable change is even harder to demonstrate with many of the adherence interventions. The mixed outcomes of adherence interventions research are due to poorly controlled studies, poorly defined interventions, and an unclear definition of the type of adherence being studied (Cramer et al., 2008; NEHI, 2007). Many of the studies surrounding adherence observe interventions in the context of a single condition rather than on multiple conditions. One of the most common failures in these studies is to control for patient characteristics such as patient beliefs. Finally, many studies find that single interventions are not enough to maintain long-term adherence outcomes and require a combination of interventions to improve long-term outcomes (AHRQ, 2012). Despite this, interventions can provide some benefits and short-term improvements. The interventions most commonly used to impact adherence are the following:

Interventions	
Case management	Behavioral support
Collaborative care	Blister packaging
Education and counseling	Reminder calls
Social support	Self-management
Health coaching	Shared decision making
Decision aids	Risk communication
Virtual clinics	Telemonitoring

These interventions are all focused on making changes at the patient level to improve medication adherence. Considerations when assessing the impact of an intervention include the target of the intervention, the agent delivering the intervention, delivery method, number of components, intensity, and duration. These interventions require a variety of health-care staff to apply the intervention, and this includes pharmacists, nurses, physicians, case managers, disease educators, and even the patient's peers. Delivery methods can range from face-to-face encounters to telephonic encounters or be passively administered such as in the form of mailings. The intensity and frequency of the intervention has been shown to impact adherence outcomes, with high intensity and more frequent contacts with patients leading to positive changes in adherence (AHRQ, 2012). High intensity and high frequency interventions, such as care coordination, are often limited by the high cost associated with them (AHRQ, 2012). Additionally, in order for these adherence interventions to be successful, there needs to be an environment that facilitates these interventions.

Adherence and the State of Health Care

Health care is an extended experiment on how to provide the most efficient care and there are constant tests on how health policy can change adherence. After discussing the factors impacting adherence and the possible interventions, health policy can really focus on two areas to support adherence: facilitating personalized patient care and removing barriers to care.

In 2006, Medicare Part D began to provide drug coverage to millions of seniors. As a part of this coverage, seniors were often subject to a "donut hole" or a period of time where all drugs were paid for out of pocket until the patient reached catastrophic care. At a time when many drugs such as statins were only available as costly brand name products, the coverage gap was a concern for many Medicare Part D members. Adherence to almost all classes was decreased after a member reached this coverage gap (Hsu et al., 2006; Sun et al., 2009; Zhang et al., 2009; Gu et al., 2010).

Around this time, several employer groups sought ways to handle increased health-care costs by shifting some of the financial responsibility and decision making to the patient. The plans offering value-based insurance design aimed to direct patients to effective care through increased co-pays for ineffective drugs and to provide prescriptions at little to no cost for medications are considered effective. When the cost to the patient was increased, the utilization of the drug generally decreased (Goldman et al., 2007; Klepser et al., 2007; Pesa et al., 2012). Although this may steer patients toward certain treatment options, the lesson learned is that patients react to cost.

In considering health insurance and policy, cost and access to medications are significant mediators of patient behavior. As in the case of value-based design, the decrease of utilization of ineffective drugs is the goal. These programs have been the most frequently studied in regard to adherence, and there is a strong evidence to support moderate improvement in adherence levels. However, the impact on long-term adherence rates is not as well supported. In designing these policies, consideration needs to be given to the individual's needs. This leads to the need for patient-specific or patient-centered coordinated care.

A move to support coordinated care is represented by changes in the health-care system to a setting for providers to support patients in maintaining adherent behaviors. This is manifested in the push for accountable care organizations. Accountable care organizations, established as a part of the 2010 Accountable Care Act, aim to improve efficiencies in health-care delivery through capped payment structures. This strategy places the responsibility of achieving health-care goals in the hands of providers and their patients. Payment structures are put in place to encourage and allow practitioners to focus on medication adherence interventions and strategies.

The Chronic Care Model provides a framework for providing care across different care settings (Coleman et al., 2009). The communication that facilitates coordinated care improves the clinical care of a patient and removes barriers to adherence. Of note, care coordination was found to be one of the most successful interventions in improving adherence rates (AHRQ, 2012; Mackey et al., 2012). Other programs focusing on care transitions by providing medication reconciliation, transition care coaches, and hospital discharge counseling all seek to improve coordinated care, but do not necessarily seek to impact medication adherence. This increased focus on care coordination provides an additional opportunity to impact patient adherence.

As part of the Medicare Prescription Drug, Improvement, and Modernization Act (2003), prescription drug plans are required to offer medication therapy management services to ensure effective and efficient use of medications. This service ensures that medications are clinically appropriate, effective, and safe through pharmacist-provided medication therapy management (Cipolle et al., 2012). This service focuses on the patient and their medication needs to develop a uniquely personal care plan. This service also fosters communication regarding patient care across providers to help reduce medication errors and therapy gaps and increase appropriate pharmacy care. Addressing the appropriate use of a medication creates the base on which a patient can develop healthy medication-taking behaviors.

Coordinated care cannot occur without appropriate access to information, and although great improvements have been made in health-care information, there are still plenty of opportunities to improve coordinated care (URAC, 2011). Communication regarding patient care across providers will help reduce medication errors and therapy gaps and increase appropriate pharmacy care.

Conclusions and Suggestions for Further Discussion

Impacting adherence is a process that requires more than just the work of prescription service providers. It can only be impacted when health care is provided to the patient in a way that encompasses all aspects of care in an integrated manner. The industry is still struggling to incorporate medication management into the overall care of a patient. Is it fair to use adherence to measure the quality of one aspect of a patient's care that requires the participation of a team of providers?

As the quality of pharmacy care is being measured, the question of what demonstrates quality care should be asked again. How do we know patients are getting the most out of their medications? How does pharmacy work with other health-care providers to ensure quality services? The value of adherence should be reassessed because adherence behavior is not the goal of the health-care system. The goal is to achieve health. How is adherence a valuable measure of quality care in the eyes of patients and providers?

The state of adherence as an important aspect of quality pharmacy care remains unseen. It still holds a strong focus since it is a measure emphasized by the CMS and it is easy to measure in a population. As more information is gathered on adherence, clinical outcomes, and economic outcomes, the role of adherence may change. Payers of health care may also play a role in determining the place of adherence in outcomes measurements. The amount of money spent by organizations to improve adherence is not quantified, but any major health-care payer and many health-care providers have adherence programs. It is yet to be determined if the return on investment of these programs is positive. The use of adherence as a measure is fairly new, and the full financial impact on health-care payers may lead payers to embrace or reject the measure as more data are gathered.

Finally, the measure will fail because it does not mean anything to the patient. How can a patient attribute the score to their health? Since the whole adherence program is an attempt to change patient behavior, there must be an effort to bring the patient into the conversations. Quality of care is personal and individual; if a patient needs to be involved in creating the change, then the patient must be involved in deciding what quality care is. Forever we will try to pursue a measurement tool that accurately measures a person's attributes. It is a persistent and old challenge. Yet, is the tool that is being used developed and refined enough to punish or reward based on the behaviors of a group?

Being able to measure quality health care is a worthy challenge. All the data are screaming to improve the current health-care system. It is not even a financial issue; it is an ethical issue because patients are hurt when health-care providers and systems keep patients from using their medications to their full potential. They end up hospitalized because they cannot reach their goals or because they have been harmed by inappropriate use. Medications should be the most efficient way to treat patients, and the potential impact of improved medication use makes this issue urgent. Since this is such an urgent and important issue, there needs to be an immense amount of thought and discussion between all those involved in making the necessary changes. It cannot be a quick and easy approach to making changes. Just as adherence interventions rarely result in long-term changes, a quickly developed measure surely cannot support a long-term change. Moving forward, should adherence be referred to as appropriate medication use? How do we measure change that is meaningful and long term? How do we create value for the patients we serve? These are the questions that should drive the discussion about quality pharmacy care. Adherence is important but adherence is meaningless without the input of the patient.

References

Agency for Healthcare Research Quality (AHRQ). (2012). *Closing the Quality Gap Series: Medication Adherence Interventions: Comparative Effectiveness*. Rockville, MD: Agency for Healthcare Research and Quality. Available at: http://effectivehealthcare.ahrq.gov/index.cfm/search-for-guides-reviews-and-reports/?pageaction=displayproduct&productid=1249. Accessed December 5, 2015.

Andrade SE, Kahler KH, Frech F, Chan KA. (2006). Methods for evaluation of medication adherence and persistence using automated databases. *Pharmacoepidemiol Drug Saf*, 15, 565–574.

Balakrishnan R. (1998). Predictors of medication adherence in the elderly. *Clin Ther*, 20(4), 764–771.

Benner JS, Glyn RJ, Mogun H, Neumann PJ, Weinstein MC, Avorn J. (2002). Long-term persistence in use of statin therapy in elderly patients. *JAMA*, 288, 455–461.

Brown MT, Bussey JK. (2011). Medication adherence: WHO cares? *Mayo Clin Proc*, 86, 304–314.

Chapman RH, Petrilla AA, Benner JS, Schwartz JS, Tank SSK. (2008). Predictors of adherence to concomitant antihypertensive and lipid-lowering medications in older adults. *Drugs Aging*, 25, 855–892.

Cipolle RJ, Strand L, Morley P. (2012). *Pharmaceutical Care Practice: The Patient-Centered Approach to Medication Management*, 3rd edn. Chicago, IL: McGraw-Hill.

CMS.gov. Part C and D performance data. Available at: http://www.cms.gov/Medicare/Prescription-Drug-Coverage/PrescriptionDrugCovGenIn/PerformanceData.html. Accessed December 2013.

Coleman K, Austin BT, Brach C, Wagner EH. (2009). Evidence on the chronic care model in the new millennium. *Health Aff*, 28(1), 75–85.

Cramer JA, Roy A, Burrell A, Fairchild CJ, Fuldeore MJ, Ollendorf DA, Wong PK. (2008). Medication compliance and persistence: Terminology and definitions. *Value Health*, 11(1), 44–47.

Cushing A, Metcalfe R. (2007). Optimizing management: From compliance to concordance. *Ther Clin Risk Manag*, 3, 1047–1058.

DiMatteo MR, Giordani PJ, Lepper HS, Croghan TW. (2002). Patient adherence and medical treatment outcomes: A meta-analysis. *Med Care*, 40(9), 794–811.

Fairman K, Motheral B. (2000). Evaluating medication adherence: Which measure is right for your program? *JMCP*, 6(6), 499–504.

Gellad WF, Grenard JL, Marcum ZA. (2011). A systematic review of barriers to medication adherence in the elderly: Looking beyond cost and regimen complexity. *Am J Geriatr Pharmacother*, 9, 11–23.

Goldman DP, Joyce GF, Zheng Y. (2007). Prescription drug cost sharing: Associations with medication and medical utilization and spending and health. *JAMA*, 298(1), 61–69.

Gu Q, Zeng F, Patel BV, Tripoli LC. (2010). Part D coverage gap and adherence to diabetes medications. *Am J Manag Care*, 16(12), 911–918.

Hess LM, Raebel MA, Conner DA, Malone DC. (2006). Measurement of adherence in pharmacy administrative databases: A proposal for standard definitions and preferred measures. *Ann Pharmacother*, 40, 1280–1288.

Ho PM, Bryson CL, Rumsfeld JS. (2009). Medication adherence and its importance in cardiovascular outcomes. *Circulation*, 119, 3028–3035.

Hsu J, Price M, Huang J, Brand R, Fung V, Hui R, Fireman B, Newhouse JP, Selby JV. (2006). Unintended consequences of caps on Medicare drug benefits. *NEJM*, 354, 2349–2359.

Kaiser Family Foundation. (2010). Prescription drug trends, May 2010. Available at: http://kff.org/health-costs/fact-sheet/prescription-drug-trends-fact-sheet-may-2010/. Accessed December 5, 2015.

Kalichman SC, Amaral CM, Swetzes C, Jones M, Macy R, Kalichman MO, Cherry C. (2009). A simple single-item rating scale to measure medication adherence: Further evidence for convergent validity. *J Int Assoc Physicians AIDS Care*, 8, 367–374.

Klepser DG, Heuther JR, Handke LJ, Williams CE. (2007). Effect on drug utilization and expenditures of a cost-share change from copayment to coinsurance. *J Manage Care Pharm*, 13(9), 765–777.

Mackey K, Parchman ML, Leykum LK, Lanham HJ, Noel PH, Zeber JE. (2012). Impact of the chronic care model on medication adherence when patients perceive cost as a barrier. *Prim Care Diabetes*, 6(2), 137–142.

Martin LR, Williams SL, Haskard KB, DiMatteo MR. (2005). The challenge of patient adherence. *Ther Clin Risk Manag*, 1(3), 189–199.

McDonnell PJ, Jacobs MR. (2002). Hospital admissions resulting from preventable adverse drug reactions. *Ann Pharmacother*, 36, 1331–1336.

Medicare Prescription Drug, Improvement, and Modernization Act, Pub. L. no. 108–173, 117 Stat 2066 (2003). http://www.gpo.gov/fdsys/pkg/PLAW-108publ173/pdf/PLAW-108publ173.pdf.

Morisky DE, Ang A, Krousel-Wood M, Ward HJ. (2008). Predictive validity of a medication adherence measure in an outpatient setting. *J Clin Hypertens*, 10, 348–354.

Nau DP. (n.d) Proportion of days covered (PDC) as a preferred method of measuring medication adherence. Pharmacy Quality Alliance (PQA). Available at: http://www.pqaalliance.org/images/uploads/files/PQA%20PDC%20vs%20%20MPR.pdf.

NEHI (2007). *Waste and Inefficiency in the Health Care System—Clinical Care: A Comprehensive Analysis in Support of System-Wide Improvements*. Cambridge, MA: NEHI.

NEHI (New England Healthcare Institute). (2009). Thinking outside the pillbox: A systematic approach to improving patient medication adherence for chronic disease. Available at: http://www.nehi.net/writable/publication_files/file/pa_issue_brief_final.pdf. Accessed December 5, 2015.

Osterberg L, Blaschke T. (2005). Adherence to medication. *NEJM*, 353(5), 487–497.

Pesa JA, Van Den Bos J, Gray T, Hartsig C, McQueen RB, Saseen JJ, Nair KV. (2012). An evaluation of the impact of patient cost sharing for antihypertensive medications on adherence, medication and health care utilization, and expenditures. *Patient Preference Adherence*, 6, 63–72.

Pladevall M, Williams LK, Potts LA, Divine G, Xi H, Elston Lafata J. (2004). Clinical outcomes and adherence to medications measured by claims data in patients with diabetes. *Diabetes Care*, 27(12), 2800–2805.

Rittenhouse BA. (1996). A novel compliance assessment technique: The randomized response interview. *Int J Technol Assess Health Care*, 12, 498–510.

Sabate E, ed. (2003). *Adherence to Long-Term Therapies: Evidence for Action*. Geneva, Switzerland: World Health Organization. Available at: http://www.who.int/chp/knowledge/publications/adherence_introduction.pdf. Accessed December 5, 2015.

Sattler ELP, Lee JS, Perri M. (2013). Medication (re)fill adherence measures derived from pharmacy claims data in older Americans: A review of the literature. *Drugs Aging*, 30, 383–399.

Senst BL, Achusim LE, Genest RP, Cosentino LA, Ford CC, Little JA, Raybon SJ, Bates DW. (2001). Practical approach to determining costs and frequency of adverse drug events in a health care network. *Am J Health Syst Pharm*, 58, 1126–1132.

Shrank WH. (April 28, 2011). Our bulging medicine cabinets—The other side of medication nonadherence. *New Eng J Med*, 364, 1591–1593.

Sikka R, Xia F, Aubert RE. (2005). Estimating medication persistency using administrative claims data. *Am J Manag Care*, 11, 449–457.

Sokol MC, McGuigan KA, Verbrugge RR, Epstein RS. (2005). Impact of medication nonadherence on hospitalization risk and healthcare cost. *Med Care*, 43(6), 521–530.

Sun SX, Lee KY, Aruru M. (2009). Examining Part D beneficiaries' medication use in the doughnut hole. *Am J Pharm Benefits*, 1(1), 19–28.

Svarstad BL, Chewning BA, Sleath BL, Claesson C. (1999). The brief medication questionnaire: A tool for screening patient adherence and barriers to adherence. *Patient Educ Couns*, 37, 113–124.

Tilson HH. (2004). Adherence or compliance? Changes in terminology. *Ann Pharmacother*, 38, 161–162.

URAC (2011). *Supporting Patient Medication Adherence: Ensuring Coordination, Quality and Outcomes.* Washington, DC: URAC.

URAC (October 11, 2012). *Medication Adherence and Medication Reconciliation Workshop*. San Francisco, CA: URAC.

Wieczorkiewicz, SM, Kassamali, Z, Danziger, LH. (2013). Behind closed doors: Medication storage and disposal in the home. *Ann Pharmacother*, 47, 482–489.

Zhang Y, Donohue JM, Newhouse JP, Lave JR. (2009). The effects of the coverage gap on drug spending: A closer look at Medicare Part D. *Health Aff*, 28(2), w317–w325.

Chapter 7

Good Governance and Corruption in the Pharmaceutical System

Jillian Clare Kohler

Contents

Introduction

Through the legal obligations to "respect," "protect," and "fulfill" the right to health, governments have implicit duties to ensure that health services are provided effectively to their populations.[1] The World Health Organization (WHO) estimates that by improving access to existing essential medicines and vaccines, approximately 10 million lives per year can be saved.[2] One of the biggest threats to the right to health is a lack of good governance in the health system, which limits the ability of the health system to fulfill its essential functions and can create opportunities for corruption. Corruption in pharmaceutical systems compromises governments' abilities to provide safe and reliable access to medicines for its populations and its capacity to provide the highest attainable standard of health. If there is a lack of concern for basic governance principles in health-care delivery, health-care resources may have no impact on the intended end user. Poor governance and corruption thus undermine health-care delivery by reducing the availability of resources and access to health care, placing the heaviest burden on the poor and marginalized.[3]

Understanding how corruption can impact health outcomes is a critical public health concern. In the past decade, available research has provided increasing evidence that greater vulnerability to corruption can lead to limiting access to medicines and health services.[4,5] The consequences of corruption within the pharmaceutical system are unfortunately fairly easy to identify. Corrupt practices in the health system can have a threefold impact: (1) an *economic impact* (large amounts of public funds are wasted), (2) a *health impact* (as the waste of public resources reduces the government's capacity to provide good quality services and products, patients may turn to unsafe medical products available on the market instead of seeking health services, leading to poor health outcomes for the population), and (3) a government *image and trust impact* (as inefficiency and lack of transparency reduce public institutions' credibility, this decreases donor's trust in the capacity of the government to deliver on promises and lowers investments in such countries). If quality control regulations are not sufficient or are not implemented or enforced, health and economic consequences result.

It is well known that the global pharmaceutical market is enormously lucrative. Annual global pharmaceutical spending is forecasted to reach $(USD)1.2 trillion by 2016, and annual spending growth will increase from $(USD)30 billion in 2012 to $(USD)70 billion in 2016.[6] Pharmaceutical expenditures are typically one of the top health-care expenditures for governments globally and can reach as high as 50% of the total health spending in some developing countries.[7] Despite this, a significant amount of this money does not reach its intended beneficiaries. As one example, in the area of procurement alone, it is estimated that between 10% and 25% of global spending on public procurement in the health system is lost to corruption.[8] This results in significant financial losses and creates a serious threat to public health, patient safety, and human rights. The scale of corruption also varies: it can be a direct result from state capture, which is often linked with political corruption; it may be petty, for instance, at the implementation level where the public interacts with public officials, such as surplus payment demands from health professionals; or it can be grand (i.e., fraud and procurement abuse).

The presence of corruption in any of the critical decision points in the pharmaceutical system, from manufacture to retail sales, can limit the population's access to quality medicines, thereby reducing the health gains associated with the proper use of pharmaceuticals. In Venezuela, for example, approximately two-thirds of hospital personnel surveyed were aware of theft of medical supplies and medications.[9] Similarly, in Costa Rica, 71% of doctors and 83% of nurses reported that equipment or materials had been stolen in their hospitals.[10] Collectively, these case studies identify how weak governance in the health-care system exacerbates many existing challenges that health systems face and can create new ones for governments and patients. It increases costs, decreases the effectiveness and volume of health-care services, and reduces resources, as some examples.

While corruption in the pharmaceutical system can affect a country's entire population, it is typically the poor that are most susceptible to its detrimental effects. As a result, the global poor are often forced to make suboptimal choices that include purchasing less expensive drugs from unqualified or illegal drug sellers distributing falsified or substandard drugs, not taking needed medicines if they are unavailable in the public health system, or impoverishing themselves by having to purchase expensive drugs in the private health system.[11] Developing countries with already scarce public resources, and oftentimes weak institutions, are particularly vulnerable to the effects of poor governance. In many developing countries, pharmaceuticals account for over half of their health expenditures but end up being unavailable to consumers who need them,[12] mainly due to a lack of good governance practices. For example, a study by Amnesty International on maternal health in Burkina Faso found that corruption by health professionals is one of the primary causes of death of thousands of women during pregnancy. Poor women may not get critical health-care services simply because they are unable to pay informal fees.[13] Further evidence comes from the International Monetary Fund, which demonstrated that corruption has a significant, negative effect on health indicators such as infant and child mortality, even after adjusting for income, female education, health spending, and level of urbanization.[5] Corruption lowers the immunization rate of children; can prevent patient treatment, particularly for the poor; and discourages the use of public health clinics.[14]

According to the WHO, "up to 90% of the population in developing countries purchase medicines through out-of-pocket payments, making medicines the largest family expenditure after food."[12] Where the public health-care system affords coverage of pharmaceuticals, it is the poor who are obviously more dependent on the system than the rich and who suffer the consequences of its mismanagement. It is estimated that, in low- and middle-income countries, more than 70% of all pharmaceutical purchases are paid for out of pocket and that these purchases represent the largest share of household health-care expenditure.[15,16] Governments in these countries still have a responsibility to ensure that even the poorest can obtain quality essential drugs. This means enforcing good governance measures. While corruption is difficult to eradicate, good governance can certainly be used by governments to reduce its manifestation. Broadly speaking, good governance is a sine qua non for ensuring access of the population to essential medicines. Corruption can thrive when good governance is not in place in the pharmaceutical system.

What Is Corruption?

Corruption can be understood as "the abuse of public roles and resources or the use of illegitimate forms of political influence by public or private parties" (p. 62).[17] The issue of corruption and the development of public policy to mitigate the effects of corruption have gained traction within the global development community since the World Bank President James Wolfensohn's 1996 speech on the "cancer of corruption."[18] The World Bank has identified corruption as the single greatest obstacle to economic and social development, while the United Nations (UN) Convention against Corruption, adopted by the UN General Assembly in October 2003 and came into force in 2005, raised the importance of fighting corruption worldwide. In 2009, the UN Secretary General Ban Ki Moon even highlighted the impact of corruption on the Millennium Development Goals (MDGs), stating that corruption can hinder the realization of the MDGs. He publicly stated that corruption can kill development and may very well impede efforts to achieve the MDGs.[19] Despite this increased attention and importance, there are few existing examples of how to incorporate good governance in health system strengthening.[20]

United Nations MDGs Post-2015 Agenda and Good Governance

As we are approaching 2015, development experts and policy makers are now being faced with the task of deciding what goals should succeed the current UN MDGs. A high-level panel summoned by the UN convened in Indonesia in the spring of 2013 to recommend new targets and goals of the post-2015 development agenda. The panel called for a new goal entirely devoted to ensuring good governance and effective institutions with a target to reduce bribery and corruption in order to work toward the eradication of poverty and the reduction of inequality. According to Transparency International, not including good governance in the current MDGs is a contributing to factor to why they may go unmet. This speaks to the growing recognition that good governance and anticorruption policies play a role in achieving various development goals including the improvement of health and the combat against disease.[21]

The capacity of a government to curb corruption in the pharmaceutical system is also dependent on crosscutting political economic factors that fall outside of the health sector. For example, what political mandate does the government have? Is it first of all a government that will take on corruption seriously even at the risk of marginalizing some groups? Is institutional capacity in the country strong enough to underpin specific sectoral anticorruption efforts? Does the agency charged with the enforcement mandate have appropriate capacity and financial resources for undertaking this role? Corruption is a multisectoral issue and a comprehensive approach is necessary if governments are to combat it truly and forcefully. While basic elements of this framework for curbing corruption in the pharmaceutical sector should be present in all countries, some variation will be observed depending on the country's size, the resources available, the structure of the health system, and the importance of the local pharmaceutical industry to the balance of trade and employment. Anticorruption measures, if implemented successfully, have the potential to improve access to medicines, save public money, and improve the credibility of governments and other organizations like the World Bank that are involved in drug delivery programs. Government commitment to mitigating corruption in the sector is therefore vital.

What Is Good Governance?

Good governance can be understood as "the exercise of economic, political, and administrative authority to manage a country's affairs at all levels, comprising the mechanisms, processes, and institutions through which that authority is directed. Good governance is, among other things, participatory, transparent, accountable, and efficient. It promotes the rule of law and equal justice under the law. Good governance ensures that political, social, and economic priorities are based on broad consensus in society and that the voices of the poorest and the most vulnerable are heard in decision making over the allocation of development resources. It requires the involvement of the private system, civil society, and the state and is a prerequisite for sustainable human development."[22] Evidence has shown that good governance can improve key development goals and expose inefficiencies and corrupt practices; a study from Transparency International demonstrated that increasing transparency, accountability, and integrity in 48 countries had a robust correlation to better outcomes in health, education, and water access.[23] Another example is program evaluation efforts by the Inter-American Development Bank (IDB) that conducted an external audit of public hospitals in Bogota, Colombia analyzing the current situation of hospital finances, highlighting problematic areas, creating action plans to resolve issues uncovered, and implementing a monitoring and evaluation process with dissemination of information related to this project through workshops. This external review provided Bogota's Secretariat of Health with evidence that fraud was taking place and, in response, measures were taken to reduce theft and improper

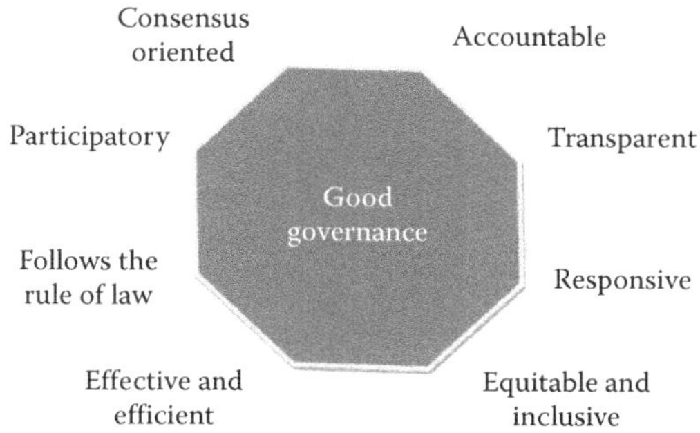

Figure 7.1 Characteristics of good governance. (From UNESCAP [United Nations Economic and Social Commission for Asia and Pacific], What is good governance? UNESCAP, 2012, retrieved from http://www.unescap.org/pdd/prs/ProjectActivities/Ongoing/gg/governance.asp, February 14, 2014.)

billing in the hospital setting.[23] Another clear example of how good governance generates benefits is with pricing transparency. The public posting of medical supplies purchased by public hospitals by the city government of Buenos Aires, Argentina, resulted in price reductions within the first few months of this intervention. Arguably, the mere anticipation of price reporting/transparency helped lower prices (Figure 7.1).

How Weak Governance Creates Opportunities for Corruption in the Pharmaceutical Sector

Weak or no governance in the pharmaceutical system creates opportunities for corruption and results in additional barriers to drug access. The absence of good governance in the pharmaceutical sector results in wasted resources like pharmaceutical products and services, which obstructs access to life-saving and life-enhancing medicines particularly for the poorest and marginalized. Weak or nonexistent rules and regulations, as well as overregulation, lack of accountability, low salaries, and limited offer of services (i.e., more demand than supply), are among the key manifestations of poor governance in the health system.

Despite the growing recognition of the importance of good governance, corruption continues to be reported in national and global health systems across a range of environments and has undermined progress in health service delivery and system strengthening at a time when investments in global health interventions have historically never been higher.[24,25] This includes a diversity of forms of health-related corruption in both the private and public sphere in high-income countries, developed country settings, and multilateral initiatives.[24] Certain aspects of good governance may be mostly relevant to lower- and middle-income countries where governance is deficient in national health systems. This includes governance areas of maintaining regulatory impartiality, ensuring quality and safety of medicines in manufacturing and procurement practices, and preventing undue payoffs for health-care services. Others are highly relevant in high-income countries such as preventing fraud and abuse and preventing illegal marketing practices of pharmaceutical companies. For example, the United States, the largest pharmaceutical market in the world, has experienced record-breaking criminal and civil fines associated with illegal pharmaceutical marketing, including some $(USD)4 billion in recoveries in 2010.[24] Illegal pharmaceutical marketing in the United States has been uncovered by whistle-blowers, likely helped by enabling

U.S. legislation that includes certain protections and incentives, and has revealed practices that led to increased drug costs, biasing or misrepresenting scientific evidence/education, and direct risks to patient safety through illegal off-label promotion.[24,25] This includes a recent settlement against Johnson & Johnson of $(USD)2.2 billion for misleading doctors about the safety of its antipsychotic Risperdal.[26] Furthermore, with increasing prevalence of noncommunicable diseases globally that often require sustained pharmaceutical treatment, coupled with annual global pharmaceutical spending that is forecasted to reach $(USD)1.2 trillion by 2016, the integrity of the global pharmaceutical supply chain is clearly important to the future of global health.[6] Yet, despite this increasing need and rapid market growth, pharmaceutical good governance in individual countries has been markedly uneven globally.

Good governance in the health-care system is instrumental in helping to lessen the likelihood of corruption taking place. Fortunately, there is growing recognition among policy makers that the pharmaceutical system can waste valuable resources allocated to pharmaceutical products and services and denies those most in need of life-saving or life-enhancing medicines. In recent years, a number of studies such as Kohler [4], Vian et al. [27], Lewis and Pettersson [28], Vian [29], Cohen et al. [30], Lewis [3], and Di Tella and Savedoff [10] have examined health and corruption and have begun to provide examples of what strategies work best to enforce good governance and lessen the likelihood of corruption. Global organizations and donor-funded organizations such as the World Bank, the WHO, the Medicines Transparency Alliance and the Global Fund for AIDS, Malaria, and Tuberculosis (Global Fund), UNDP, UNITAID, and the GAVI Alliance have also attempted to develop indicators and indexes to better assist states in improving governance, controlling corruption, assessing the rule of law, and minimizing potential negative impact from these factors in development projects. While this is encouraging news for improving drug access for the global poor, who are the most vulnerable, there is very little documented "hard" evidence on the results of these initiatives, particularly in terms of how they may improve a population's access to essential medicines. To be successful, generally good governance programs addressing corruption must be more focused in their target areas. This often includes assessment of diverse elements of both the public sector and the private sector environment. In order to inform future efforts and establish better causality between good governance initiatives and health outcomes in this sector, careful examination and comparison of existing initiatives attempting to address this issue are essential. This will ensure that future work in pharmaceutical good governance is appropriately informed by evidence and lessons learned, increasing the likelihood of continued success and improvement.

Complexity of the Pharmaceutical System

As the conversation on corruption has progressed, attention has shifted to how it can be prevented, with an emphasis on good governance. In theory, supporting the eight characteristics of good governance should make any system less vulnerable to corruption. However, the pharmaceutical system is highly complex and consists of multiple[31] that make it challenging to govern. There are several core decision points in the supply system, each of which must be recognized and understood so that corruption cannot thrive out of ignorance.[32] For example, there are information gaps at all levels, including between the consumer and the health-care provider in terms of prescription drug choice, the between health-care provider and the manufacturer in terms of therapeutic qualities of the product, and even between the manufacturer and the government.[31] The system also consists of the actions from both public and private stakeholders as drugs make their way through the supply chain. The market is also distorted by patent protection, which allows companies to

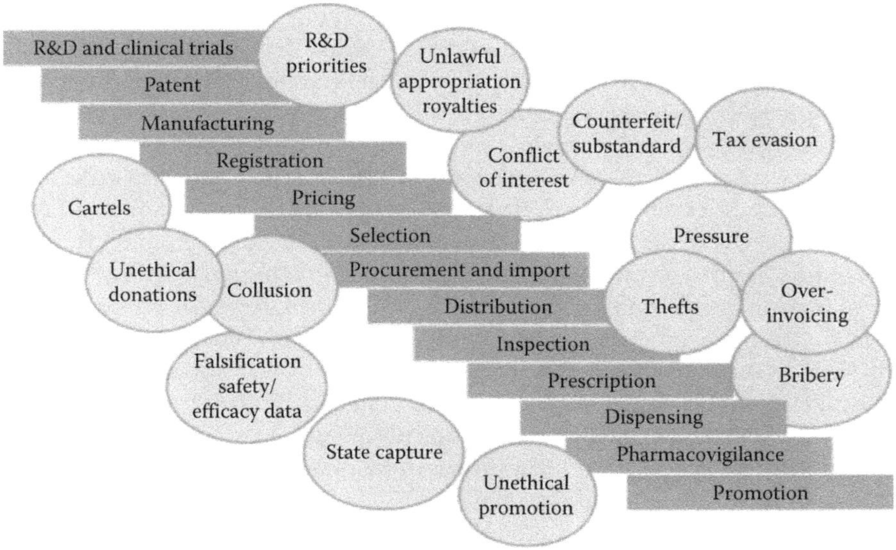

Figure 7.2 Corrupt and unethical practices that occur in the supply chain. (From Baghdadi-Sabeti, G. and Serhan, F., WHO good governance for medicines programme: An innovative approach to prevent corruption in the pharmaceutical sector—Compilation of country case studies and best practices, World Health Organization, Geneva, Switzerland, World Health Report, Background Paper, 25, 2010, retrieved from http://www.who.int/healthsystems/topics/financing/healthreport/25GGM.pdf. Accessed January 12, 2016.)

hold monopolies on product sales. Price competition is prevented until the patents expire; at that point, generics can then compete in the marketplace, which can lead to lower prices of pharmaceuticals. Therefore, by understanding the market, the multiple decision points in the pharmaceutical system and the different stakeholders involved, where and how corruption can occur, can be determined (Figure 7.2) to implement anticorruption strategies to improve transparency and accountability (Figure 7.1). Each core decision point needs to function well so that the system as a whole can offer safe, efficacious, and cost-effective quality medicines.[31]

The pharmaceutical system is susceptible to corruption if good governance is not in place for a number of reasons. First, the sale of pharmaceutical products is lucrative, more so because the final customers (patients and their families) are more vulnerable to opportunism than in many other product markets. This is due to information gaps and often very inelastic demand. Pharmaceutical suppliers typically are "profit maximizers" and will choose to behave in ways that maximize their interests. There is nothing inherently wrong with profit maximization as long as it is not counter to the public interest. However, as scandals such as the Vioxx case illuminate, pharmaceutical suppliers have in the past disregarded public interest for financial gains.[33]

The second reason why the pharmaceutical system is susceptible to corruption is that it is subject to a significant degree of government regulation, such that if there are not appropriate checks in place, government officials may have a monopoly on several core decision points in the pharmaceutical supply chain and also have some discretion in making regulatory decisions. Government intervention is essential in the pharmaceutical system given the imperfect nature of the market and the need to improve the efficiency of resource allocation. Also, regulation is rationalized on the grounds of protecting human life and public health by ensuring that only safe and efficacious medicines are made available in the market. But if there are state capture and poor institutional checks on individual discretion, the public interest may be jeopardized. For instance, governments usually determine what drugs are included on a national essential drugs list or reimbursement list of a public health-care payer. The inclusion of a drug on such a list, particularly a reimbursement list, can mean significant financial income for a drug manufacturer as it guarantees the product a relatively predictable market share. If there is a lack of oversight, regulators may be able to make discretionary decisions about what drugs should be selected based on individual gain and not on the public good.

The third reason why the pharmaceutical system is a "breeding ground" for weak governance is because it is often challenging to govern it. In many countries with weak regulation and enforcement of drug distribution standards, the sale of falsified, unregistered, or expired drugs is very common. Therefore, given the global nature of the pharmaceutical sector, collective action is needed to address the issue of falsified medicines. The WHO estimates that about 25% of drugs consumed in poor countries are falsified or substandard.[34] It is very difficult to control such practices particularly where patients and even health professionals are not able to differentiate between legitimate and falsified drugs. Falsifiers are often very skillful at copying the form, color, trademarks, and packaging of legitimate products. While in many markets patients tend to have more confidence in recognized foreign-produced drugs, the high prices for the legitimate versions of these relative to purchasing power drive many consumers to seek lower cost alternatives, which in many cases are not legal, safe, or reliable. These actions have had significant social costs both in terms of access to drugs, particularly for the poor, and in terms of the quality and safety of the drug supply. In addition, the likelihood of developing resistance to substandard and/or falsified antibiotics is elevated, which can result in huge health costs. It is only when there is blatant sloppiness in copying that patients and health-care providers are able to identify falsified medicines. Government commitment to better governance in the system is vital particularly in low- and middle-income countries, where it is estimated that over 70% of all pharmaceutical purchases are paid for out of pocket[16] and represent the largest household health expenditure.[15]

Governments have a responsibility to create sound institutional structures, processes, and policies and to reinforce outcomes that promote public welfare. Governments have two core responsibilities in the pharmaceutical system. First, they are responsible for regulating the manufacture, distribution, sale, and use of pharmaceutical products, which include regulating all actors involved in the pharmaceutical sector. Second, where governments provide free access to medicines, public purchasers are responsible for the selection, purchase, and logistical management of drugs for use through the public health-care system. Both roles are of equal importance to ensure good governance in the pharmaceutical system and to ensure access to rational drugs for the population. Conversely, changes in government, a lack of cooperation across relevant ministries, and unbalanced representation of stakeholders (for example, low participation from civil society groups) have been found to be challenges in initiatives aimed at introducing good governance in pharmaceutical systems. This dependency on commitment from political leadership makes establishing sustainable programs and policies more difficult, and any future initiatives must recognize that simply changing policies on paper is likely to be insufficient. It further indicates that governance initiatives must be supported with adequate transparency and rules in relation to participation of stakeholders, establishment of formal and accountable cooperation mechanisms among parties, and work plans to address possible programmatic or government changes. Cultural shifts in how good governance is perceived may also be necessary for changes to be effective even if accompanied with needed changes in commitment/leadership.

Closely related to challenges of country ownership and political buy-in is whether initiatives have effectively addressed challenges in the political economy dimensions of pharmaceutical good governance. Are the potential "losers" from good governance initiatives dealt with so that efforts are not undermined? The pharmaceutical system operates as a part of an overarching and much more complex health system, and this is clearly recognized by good governance initiatives. It is unfortunately too common for global institutions to evade the examination of uncomfortable but critical political issues in the health sector, such as state, regulatory, and policy capture as well as the global policy context. The resulting reality is that systemic change takes time, capacity, and broad commitment to implement initiatives and to determine results from them. More focused efforts on specific issues (i.e., drug registration, national formulary inclusion, or public sector generic substitution policies) can result in more rapid changes but may not result in the deeper systemic shifts necessary to improve overall system performance.

Conclusion

The bottom line is that corruption affects the ability of the poor to access essential health services. Good governance approaches and the absence of corruption in both the public and private pharmaceutical sector are crucial in maintaining adequate distribution of essential medicines for populations who lack access, preventing diversion/theft of pharmaceuticals, protecting against illegal pharmaceutical promotion (e.g., illegal off-label promotion), and ensuring that medicines are safe and not falsified.[35,36] Corruption in the pharmaceutical system cannot be taken lightly; in the worst-case scenario, it can lead to death. We need to gain more knowledge about the causes and consequences of corruption in the health system and what interventions work best to minimize it. This chapter has illustrated the complexity of the pharmaceutical sector and the number of critical decision points that exist throughout the entire system, from manufacturing to drug consumption. There is no single "prescription" to entrench the challenges of ensuring good governance in such a complex system: demand is often greater than the supply, there is significant uncertainty in how much of each product is needed, and the complex globalized drug supply chain comprised of both public and private sector actors has the potential for market failure at each step. For this reason, use of the pharmaceutical diagnostic tools can help policy makers learn where the weaknesses lie, determine the effect of these weaknesses on health and economic outcomes, set priorities for action, and then design appropriate anticorruption strategies.

The first step toward stopping corruption in the pharmaceutical sector is to understand its structure, actors, and motivations and be able to identify the key points where corruption can occur. Only then can short-, medium-, and long-term goals be mapped out clearly and appropriate strategies identified. If there is a choice, priority should be given to areas where the identified corruption is a threat to safety and health; tackling corruption that has only economic implications should not come before health concerns.

Policy makers need to determine whether they will turn their first efforts to areas where anticorruption strategies can easily be implemented or instead focus on areas where an end to corruption is likely to produce the highest returns, even if these are the areas that may involve tremendous political negotiations. There is no prescriptive answer. Government preferences will vary depending on resources and commitment and can only be made after a comprehensive diagnostic of the pharmaceutical sector is undertaken. Policy makers will need to make trade-offs. Should they make small gains quickly or try to implement large-scale reform with longer time horizons? Should they opt to save lives in the short term or to build service delivery institutions as a long-term solution? Ideally, there should be some combination of the two approaches. Small measures that are relatively inexpensive to undertake, such as posting pharmaceutical prices on a website, should be undertaken concurrently with larger measures such as investing more resources into a national drug regulatory agency; both will result in pharmaceutical systems that are more robust and less prone to corruption. To be sure, even small measures in themselves can pay off and make good governance socially "contagious."[37]

Therefore, in order to examine the relationship between good governance and outcomes in the pharmaceutical services, there is a clear need for better data collection and agreed upon metrics to support research and evidence-based policy making. Today, there is a growing body of literature and practical policy tools available that are being applied in various country contexts to diagnose or tackle pharmaceutical sector corruption by several organizations, including the World Bank, the Transparency International, and the World Justice Project. These organizations that have attempted to develop indicators and indexes to better assist states in improving governance, controlling corruption, assessing the rule of law, and minimizing potential negative impact from these factors in development projects. However, they are not intended to represent the universe of possible anticorruption strategies but are designed to inspire thinking on the topic and to promote some concrete measures that could yield tangible results in specific areas. Divergent institutional approaches, varying indicators across organizations, and lack of robust research addressing the underlying causal relationship between governance and corruption currently pose challenges to promoting anticorruption activities, especially in the pharmaceutical sector. Building upon previous research that identified the need for political analysis, monitoring, and evaluation, particularly with regard to the measurement of results and the streamlining and uniformity of assessment tools across institutions, there is a need to study global good governance initiatives and their ability to achieve their intended goals, as evidenced by measurable outcomes in the pharmaceutical services.

Acknowledgments

Thanks to the Initiative for Drug Equity and Access, Research Associates Crystal, Moneypenny, Anh Nguyen, and Martha Gabriela Martinez for their research and formatting assistance.

Authors' Notes

This chapter is based on the authors' following previous works:

Kohler, J.C. (2011). Fighting corruption in the health sector: Methods, tools and good practices. United Nations Development Programme. Retrieved from http://www.undp.org/content/undp/en/home/librarypage/democratic-governance/anti-corruption/fighting_corruptioninthehealthsector/. Accessed December 6, 2015.

Kohler, J.C. and Baghdadi-Sabeti, G. (2011). *The World Medicines Situation 2011—Good Governance for the Pharmaceutical Sector*. Geneva, Switzerland: World Health Organization, WHO/EMP/MIE/2011.2.5. http://www.who.int/medicines/areas/policy/world_medicines_situation/WMS_ch20_wGoodGov.pdf. Accessed December 6, 2015.

Kohler, J.C., Mackey, T.K., and Ovtcharenko, N. (2014). Why the MDGs need good governance in pharmaceutical systems to promote global health. *BMC Public Health*, 14(1), 63.

Kohler, J.C. and Ovtcharenko, N. (2013). *Good Governance for Medicines Initiatives: Exploring Lessons Learned*. Bergen, Norway: Chr. Michelsen Institute (U4 Issue, 2013(3)). https://www.google.com/url?sa=t&rct=j&q=&esrc=s&source=web&cd=1&ved=0ahUKEwjX5JPwm8jJAhUCDT4KHWY7AzQQFggdMAA&url=http%3A%2F%2Fwww.u4.no%2Fpublications%2Fgood-governance-for-medicines-initiatives-exploring-lessons-learned%2Fdownloadasset%2F3355&usg=AFQjCNFGw4z6iAxJHEzT46UgvD8vJWFcLw. Accessed December 6, 2015.

References

1. UN (United Nations). (1966). International covenant on economic, social and cultural rights. United Nations Office of High Commissioner on Human Rights, New York City, New York. Retrieved from http://www.ohchr.org/EN/ProfessionalInterest/Pages/CESCR.aspx. Accessed December 6, 2015.
2. WHO. (2004). Equitable access to essential medicines: A framework for collective action. WHO Policy Perspectives on Medicines, No. 8. Retrieved from http://apps.who.int/iris/bitstream/10665/68571/1/WHO_EDM_2004.4_eng.pdf Accessed December 6, 2015.
3. Lewis, M. (2006). *Governance and Corruption in Public Health Care Systems* (No. 78). Washington, DC: Center for Global Development.
4. Kohler, J.C. (2011). Fighting corruption in the health sector: Methods, tools and good practices. United Nations Development Programme, New York City, New York. Retrieved from http://www.undp.org.tt/News/UNODC/Anticorruption%20Methods%20and%20Tools%20in%20Health%20Lo%20Res%20final.pdf Accessed December 6, 2015.
5. Gupta, S., Davoodi, H.R., and Tiongson, E. (2000). Corruption and the provision of health care and education services (No. 2000–2116). International Monetary Fund, Washington, D.C. https://www.imf.org/external/pubs/ft/wp/2000/wp00116.pdf. Accessed December 6, 2015.
6. IMS Institute for Healthcare Informatics. (2012). The global use of medicines: Outlook through 2016. IMS Institute for Healthcare Informatics, Collegeville, PA. Retrieved from http://www. imshealth.com/deployedfiles/ims/Global/Content/Insights/IMS%20Institute%20for%20Healthcare%20Informatics/Global%20Use%20of%20Meds%202011/Medicines_Outlook_Through_2016_Report.pdf.
7. WHO. (2014). Why is good governance relevant to the pharmaceutical public sector? World Health Organization, Geneva, Switzerland. Retrieved from http://www.who.int/medicines/areas/policy/goodgovernance/why/en/. Accessed December 6, 2015.
8. Transparency International. (2006). Curbing corruption in public procurement. Transparency International, Berlin, Germany. Retrieved from http://www.transparency.org/whatwedo/publication/curbing_corruption_in_public_procurement_a_practical_guide. Accessed December 6, 2015.
9. Jaén, M.H. and Paravisini, D. (2001). Wages, capture, and penalties in Venezuela's public hospitals. In Di Tella, R. and Savedoff, W.D. (Eds.), *Diagnosis Corruption: Fraud in Latin America's Public Hospitals*, pp. 57–94. Washington, DC: Latin American Research Network, Inter-American Development Bank.
10. Di Tella, R. and Savedoff, W.D. (2001). Shining light in dark corners. In Di Tella, R. and Savedoff, W.D. (Eds.), *Diagnosis Corruption: Fraud in Latin America's Public Hospitals*, pp. 57–94. Washington, DC: Latin American Research Network, Inter-American Development Bank.
11. Niëns, L.M., Cameron, A., Van de Poel, E., Ewen, M., Brouwer, W.B., and Laing, R. (2010). Quantifying the impoverishing effects of purchasing medicines: A cross-country comparison of the affordability of medicines in the developing world. *PLoS Medicine*, 7(8), e1000333.
12. WHO. (2013). WHO guidelines on country pharmaceutical pricing policies. Geneva, Switzerland: World Health Organization. Retrieved from http://apps.who.int/medicinedocs/en/d/Js21016en/. Accessed December 6, 2015.
13. Amnesty International. (2010). Pregnant women in Burkina Faso dying because of discrimination. Amnesty International, London, U.K. http://www.amnesty.org/en/news-and-updates/report/pregnant-women-burkina-faso-dying-because-discrimination-20100127. Retrieved from March 10, 2014.
14. Azfar, O. and Gurgur, T. (2005). Does corruption affect health and education outcomes in the Philippines? Economics of Governance 9(3):197–244.
15. WHO. (1998). WHO public-private roles in the pharmaceutical sector—Implications for equitable access and rational drug use. Geneva, Switzerland: World Health Organization. Retrieved from http://archives.who.int/tbs/global/whozip27e.pdf. Accessed December 6, 2015.
16. WHO. (2004). The World Medicines Situation. Essential Medicines and Health Products Information Portal. The World Health Organization (WHO). Retrieved from http://apps.who.int/medicinedocs/en/d/Js6160e/2.html. Accessed December 6, 2015.
17. Johnston, M. (1997). Public officials, private interests, and sustainable democracy: When politics and corruption meet. In Elliott, K.A. (Eds.), *Corruption and the Global Economy*, pp. 61–82. Washington, DC: Institute for International Economics.

18. World Bank. (2005). World Bank takes further step in anti-corruption fight: Bank initiates annual report detailing investigations. The World Bank News and Broadcast, Washington, D. C. Retrieved from http://web.worldbank.org/WBSITE/EXTERNAL/NEWS/0,,contentMDK:20368613~menuPK:34463~pagePK:64003015~piPK:64003012~theSitePK:4607,00.html. Accessed December 6, 2015.
19. UN (United Nations). (2009). Secretary-General, in message for International Anti-Corruption Day—Cites convention as strongest way to fight graft, build integrity. United Nations, Secretary-General, SG/SM/12660/OBV/843. Retrieved from http://www.un.org/News/Press/docs/2009/sgsm12660.doc.htm. Accessed December 6, 2015.
20. Brinkerhoff, D.W., Fort, C., and Stratton, S. (2009). Good governance and health: Assessing progress in Rwanda. TWUBAKANE Decentralization and Health Program Rwanda Report. USAID, IntraHealth, RTI International. http://www.intrahealth.org/~intrahea/files/media/good-governance-and-healthassessing-progress-in-rwanda/goodgovandhealth.pdf. Accessed December 6, 2015.
21. Transparency International. (March 25, 2013). The global coalition against corruption. Poverty and Development. Building anti-corruption into the Millennium Development Goals. Retrieved from http://www.transparency.org/news/feature/building_anti_corruption_into_the_millennium_development_goals. Accessed January 12, 2016.
22. UNDP. (1994). Good governance and sustainable human development. A UNDP policy document. UNDP, New York City, New York. Retrieved from http://hdr.undp.org/sites/default/files/reports/255/hdr_1994_en_complete_nostats.pdf. Accessed December 6, 2015.
23. Transparency International. (2010). The anti-corruption catalyst: Realising the MDGs by 2015. Transparency International, Berlin, Germany. Retrieved from http://www.transparency.org/whatwedo/publication/the_anti_corruption_catalyst_realising_the_mdgs_by_2015. Accessed December 6, 2015.
24. Mackey, T.K. and Liang, B.A. (2012). Combating healthcare corruption and fraud with improved global health governance. *BMC International Health and Human Rights*, 12(1), 23.
25. Mackey, T.K. and Liang, B.A. (2013). A United Nations global health panel for global health governance. *Social Science and Medicine*, 76, 12–15.
26. Thomas, K. (2013). J.&J. to pay $2.2 billion in Risperdal settlement. *The New York Times*. p. B1. Retrieved from http://www.nytimes.com/2013/11/05/business/johnson-johnson-to-settle-risperdal-improper-marketing-case.html. Accessed December 6, 2015.
27. Vian, T., Savedoff, W.D., and Mathisen, H. (2012). *Anticorruption in the Health Sector*. Boston, MA: Kumarian Press.
28. Lewis, M. and Pettersson, G. (December 2009). Governance in education: Raising performance. World Bank, World Bank Human Development Network Working Paper.
29. Vian, T. (2008). Review of corruption in the health sector: Theory, methods and interventions. *Health Policy and Planning*, 23(2), 83–94.
30. Cohen, J.C., Mrazek, M.F., and Hawkins, L. (2007). Corruption and pharmaceuticals: Strengthening good governance to improve access. In *The Many Faces of Corruption: Tracking Vulnerabilities at the Sector Level*, Campos JE and Pradhan S (eds.). Washington, DC: World Bank. https://openknowledge.worldbank.org/bitstream/handle/10986/6848/399850REPLACEM101OFFICIAL0USE0ONLY1.pdf?sequence=1. Accessed December 6, 2015.
31. Kohler, J.C. and Ovtcharenko, N. (2013). *Good Governance for Medicines Initiatives: Exploring Lessons Learned*. Bergen, Norway: Chr. Michelsen Institute (U4 Issue, 2013(3)). https://www.google.com/url?sa=t&rct=j&q=&esrc=s&source=web&cd=1&ved=0ahUKEwjX5JPwm8jJAhUCDT4KHWY7AzQQFggdMAA&url=http%3A%2F%2Fwww.u4.no%2Fpublications%2Fgood-governance-for-medicines-initiatives-exploring-lessons-learned%2Fdownloadasset%2F3355&usg=AFQjCNFGw4z6iAxJHEzT46UgvD8vJWFcLw. Accessed December 6, 2015.
32. Cohen, J.C., Cercone, J., and Macaya, R. (2002). *Improving Transparency in Pharmaceutical Systems: Strengthening Critical Decision Points against Corruption*. Washington, DC: World Bank. Mimeo.
33. NBC News. (2004). Report: Vioxx linked to thousands of deaths. *NBC News*. Retrieved from http://www.nbcnews.com/id/6192603/ns/health-arthritis/t/report-vioxx-linked-thousands-deaths/#.VmSwUcqeyOl. Accessed December 6, 2015.

34. WHO. (2003). Substandard and counterfeit medicines. WHO Media Centre, Geneva, Switzerland. Retrieved from http://www.who.int/mediacentre/factsheets/2003/fs275/en/. Accessed December 6, 2015.
35. Mackey, T.K. and Liang, B.A. (2011). The global counterfeit drug trade: Patient safety and public health risks. *Journal of Pharmaceutical Sciences*, 100(11), 4571–4579.
36. Cohen, J. C., Mrazek, M., and Hawkins, L. (2007). Tackling corruption in the pharmaceutical systems worldwide with courage and conviction. *Clinical Pharmacology and Therapeutics*, 81(3), 445–449.
37. Gladwell, M. (2000). *The Tipping Point: How Little Things Can Make a Big Difference*. New York: Little Brown & Company.
38. UNESCAP (United Nations Economic and Social Commission for Asia and Pacific). (2012). What is good governance? UNESCAP, Bangkok, Thailand. http:www.unescap.org/pdd/prs/ProjectActivities/Ongoing/gg/governance.asp. Retrieved from February 14, 2014.
39. Baghdadi-Sabeti, G. and Serhan, F. (2010). WHO good governance for medicines programme: An innovative approach to prevent corruption in the pharmaceutical sector—Compilation of country case studies and best practices. World Health Organization Geneva, Switzerland, World Health Report, Background Paper, 25. Retrieved from http://www.who.int/healthsystems/topics/financing/healthreport/25GGM.pdf. Accessed December 6, 2015.

Chapter 8

U.S. Food and Drug Administration

Gregory Dolin

Contents

Introduction

Starting in the middle of the nineteenth century, the United States transformed from a mostly local, agrarian society to an industrialized national market. With this transformation, the citizens began to rely not on themselves to grow the food that they were going to consume, but on nonlocal corporations that could distribute the food from farms to distant cities. The lengthening of the supply chain increased the likelihood that the food actually reaching consumers was not of the same purity and quality as when it left the farm.[1]

Around the same time, and in keeping with the spirit of "Jacksonian democracy," various medical licensure laws that had been adopted in the late eighteenth to early nineteenth century were being repealed. Because anyone who had a medical school diploma could practice medicine and dispense various potions and remedies, there was much money to be made from either quack remedies or impure and poorly made medications.[2] Concerns about low-quality or adulterated food and medical products led to the enactment of the Federal Pure Food and Drugs Act of 1906—the first federal law meant to protect consumers from any "article of food or drug which is adulterated or misbranded." The 1906 Act directed the Departments of Treasury, Agriculture, and Commerce and Labor to create rules and regulations for examining foodstuffs and drugs and prevent the interstate traffic in any drug that had been adulterated. It did not ban the sale of quack remedies or regulate the availability of medications based on doctor's prescription. The Act's goals were modest—it only prohibited the sale of drugs "recognized in the United States Pharmacopoeia or National Formulary," if the drug as sold "differ[ed] from the [official] standard of strength, quality, or purity," and even then only if such differences were not clearly labeled on the bottle.[3] This legislation, however, was only the beginning.

With the 1906 Act, the federal government dipped its toes in the regulatory waters of the drug market, but significant regulation did not come until two decades later, with the New Deal's creation of a robust regulatory state. In 1938, the Congress enacted the Federal Food, Drug, and Cosmetic Act (FDCA), which empowered the Secretary of Agriculture not only to remove adulterated or misbranded foods and drugs from the market but also to prohibit the introduction of any new products that had not been shown to be safe.[4] These functions were delegated to the Food and Drug Administration (FDA, then an agency within the Department of Agriculture); thus, the FDA approval process was born. Since 1938, the FDA has been moved from the Department of Agriculture to the (now defunct) Federal Security Agency, then to the (later reorganized) Department of Health, Education, and Welfare, and finally to its current home at the Department of Health and Human Services.[5] Through all this time, however, and to the present day, the FDA continued to be governed by the 1938 Act (though, of course, the Act has been amended and enlarged on multiple occasions).

As the name of the FDA's governing statute suggests, it contemplates regulation not just of drugs, but of foodstuffs and cosmetics. Although these are important functions of the FDA, in light of the nature of this book, the present chapter will focus only on the agency's role in regulating drugs, biologics, and medical devices.

Some More History and the FDA's Role

The FDA's role has changed and expanded throughout the years. That change was almost always in response to public concern in the wake of one or another unfortunate event. Initially, the public's concern with the purity of their food and medicine, fanned by the journalism and literary works of muckrakers such as Sinclair Lewis, led to legislation dealing specifically with the issue of purity.[6] Thus, the FDA predecessor's sole function initially was to ensure that the foodstuffs and drugs being sold in the United States not be "adulterated" or mislabeled, i.e., that what was sold did not differ from what a reasonable consumer would have expected. In other words, the original function of the FDA was essentially policing the honesty of information presented to consumers. As long as the drug seller was honest about the contents of the bottle he or she was selling, he or she complied with the federal statutes. It did not matter whether the bottle's contents actually cured any ailment or even if they were causing more harm than good. All that mattered was whether the label reflected the ingredients and their concentration. The market would sort out the rest.[7]

In the 1930s, two major drug calamities spurred the broadening of FDA's authority. During September and October of 1937, a new drug meant to treat streptococcal infections instead killed

100 people in 15 states. What was particularly troubling is that the drug itself (sulfanilamide) has long been used to great effect to treat these infections. What was new was the form of the drug. Whereas previously sulfanilamide was administered in a pill or powder form, in 1937 a new form went on the market—elixir sulfanilamide—which was simply sulfanilamide dissolved in diethylene glycol. The company that produced this mixture tested it for flavor, appearance, and fragrance and found all to be satisfactory. However, this new preparation was never tested for its *safety*. And as it turned out, diethylene glycol (commonly used as an antifreeze) is, in fact, deadly. Thus, instead of providing patients with antibiotics, doctors ended up feeding them deadly poison.[8]

In addition to the elixir sulfanilamide disaster, another series of injuries stemming from the use of dinitrophenol ("DNP") gave an additional push to the new regulations. DNP was widely used in the 1930s as a weight loss drug. As with other drugs, it was never tested for safety, despite the fact that the margin between the safety and toxicity of the drug is incredibly narrow. As a result, thousands of people who took DNP became blind and suffered other injuries. The DNP story was presented to the U.S. Senate when it considered the 1938 Act. Thus, the bad experience with unsafe drugs was the impetus for legislation requiring the drug manufacturers to prove the safety of their wares prior to introducing them to the market.[9]

The next big reform came in 1962, when the Congress enacted the Kefauver–Harris Amendments to the 1938 Act. The stimulus for this legislation was the experience, in the late 1950s and early 1960s, with thalidomide. In 1960, the Merrell Company filed an application with the FDA to use thalidomide as a treatment for nausea in pregnant women (as well as for a variety of other illnesses). While the drug manufacturer had to prove that its drugs were safe, there were no particular restrictions on how the testing was to be done. Taking advantage of this "Wild West" approach to clinical studies, Merrell distributed (for study purposes) 2.5 million pills to about 20,000 individuals prior to submitting its application. Luckily, the FDA's examiner assigned to Merrell's application was suspicious of the testimonials submitted by Merrell's doctors and rejected the application on six separate occasions. By the time of the last rejection, more and more information from Europe (where the drug had been used for years) became available, linking thalidomide with severe birth defects.[10] Merrell eventually withdrew the application, but the entire episode boosted Senator Kefauver's reform efforts. The senator was at the time holding hearings on high cost of drugs, and the thalidomide episode allowed him to broaden his proposed reform. The resulting Kefauver–Harris Amendments for the first time required that clinical studies proving safety be conducted with patients' consent and according to strict guidelines. The new law also imposed a new requirement on drug manufacturers—they would now be forced to show not only that their drug was safe but also that it was *effective* for the purposes claimed. This new requirement was also an outgrowth of the thalidomide fiasco.[11] Merrell promoted thalidomide as a cure for "abdominal pain, alcoholism, anorexia, asthma, cancer, cardiovascular disease, dental procedures, emotional instability, functional bowel distress, kidney disease, marital discord, menopause, nausea and vomiting, nervous exhaustion, nightmares, poor school work, premature ejaculation, and tuberculosis."[12] Needless to say that most of these claims were quite fanciful but, prior to 1962, not illegal. After 1962, a drug manufacturer would have to substantiate his claims with properly conducted clinical studies.

The next major change to FDA's regulatory authority occurred in 1984. Since the enactment of the Kefauver–Harris Amendments, the cost of getting an FDA approval rose significantly. The brand-name drug manufacturers could recoup this cost because they were protected against competition by patents held on new drugs. Thus, when a brand-name manufacturer secured approval to market a new drug, it could be sure that by virtue of its patent right, he would be, at least for some time, the exclusive producer of that drug. This exclusivity allowed the brand-name companies to charge higher prices than they would in a perfectly competitive market, and these higher prices allowed these companies to recoup their investment. (Admittedly, the FDA process imposed significant costs on the patentees as well, because their patent rights, which began with the discovery of the drug, rather than sales of that drug, wasted away while the FDA considered their applications to enter the market.)

Once the patents expired, theoretically, the field would be open to generic companies to provide identical yet cheaper medication. The problem was that the FDA insisted (with some minor exceptions) that any generic wishing to enter the market conducts its own safety and efficacy studies in order to secure the FDA's marketing approval. Given the cost of such studies and the lack of exclusivity protections that were available to pioneering manufacturers, it made little financial sense for generics to engage in the process. As a result, there was little competition in the drug market, and consumers continued to pay high prices long after patents on the drugs expired. In order to address this problem, the Congress enacted the Drug Price Competition and Patent Term Restoration Act of 1984 (commonly known as the Hatch–Waxman Act), which allowed generic companies to enter the market by merely proving that their drugs are bioequivalent to the previously approved brand-name medications and foregoing duplicative safety and efficacy studies. The 1984 Amendments thus created two different types of drug approval processes and allowed for flourishing of generic drug companies.[13]

The final major reform to date to the FDA process is connected to the HIV epidemic of the late 1980s. By that time, the FDA approval process had increased to somewhere between 9 and 13 years. (In comparison, prior to the Kefauver–Harris Amendments, an application would be automatically approved within 60 days of submission unless the FDA affirmatively rejected it. Each resubmission would also be subject to the same 60-day window.) With the AIDS epidemic ravaging the country in the 1980s, the delays in the FDA's approval process were seen as a contributing cause to the death of those stricken with the disease. The FDA responded by enacting some reforms that let certain patients access unapproved drugs that were still in the clinical trials phase. The Congress also joined the action and in 1992 enacted the Prescription Drug User Fee Act, which allowed the FDA to collect fees from drug companies in order to hire more staff to review applications.[14] The Act also created a mechanism for priority review for certain drugs. The Congress then followed up with the FDA Modernization Act of 1997.[15] That Act made it easier to win FDA approval, reduced the number of clinical studies required to prove the effectiveness of a drug, and created a special fast-track process for drugs that treat a "serious medical condition" and "demonstrate the potential to address unmet medical need." In 2012, the Congress enacted the FDA Safety Innovations Act, which added yet another expedited approval mechanism. These changes allowed the FDA to reduce significantly the time to approve drugs for the market. While the overall drug development process, from the lab to the shelf, is still quite long, reaching 10–15 years, on average, the amount of time spent in FDA review has been reduced.[16]

The account mentioned earlier is by no means exhaustive of the FDA's history or the legislation that governs the FDA's drug approval process. It is merely meant to highlight that while the scope of FDA authority and the nature of FDA processes have changed over the last century, the overall goal of consumer protection remained constant. When consumers needed to be protected against unsafe compounds, legislation was enacted to address that issue; when consumers needed protection against the new scourge of AIDS, the rules were changed again to respond to this new challenge while maintaining quality control. Undoubtedly, the FDA's processes will continue to evolve in response to new, future challenges, but it is equally certain that the FDA's overarching purpose of protecting patients will stay the same.

FDA Approval Process for Drugs and Medical Devices

This section will discuss in greater detail the process of obtaining FDA approval for new drugs and medical devices. It is meant only to give an overview of the process. The actual regulations fill thousands of pages in the Code of Federal Regulations and the Federal Register, and it would be quite impossible to do the entire system justice in one chapter. Instead, this section will simply focus on important milestones in the approval process.

Approval of New Chemical Drugs

The process of bringing a drug to the market begins in laboratories of universities and drug companies. Chemists, pharmacologists, biochemists, and other scientists spend countless hours attempting to create new chemical entities to treat various ailments. These initial research activities are not directly subject to FDA regulation, though the FDA does monitor the drug companies' cleanliness and sterility procedures to ensure that whatever drugs do ultimately enter the market are not contaminated. Once a promising chemical entity is created, it is subject to rigorous studies. The first set of testing is conducted on animals.[17] Again, the FDA is not directly involved in this stage of the process, though that is not to say that animal testing is unregulated. Furthermore, because the results of animal testing have to be acceptable to the FDA in order to proceed to the next phase, the testing has to be done in accordance with proper scientific and ethical standards.[18]

Once the drug manufacturer conducts the basic studies on animals and shows that the drug is not overly toxic and has a therapeutic effect in animal subjects, the manufacturer can apply to the FDA for permission to begin human testing. The process is referred to as Investigational New Drug (IND) application. Technically speaking, federal law prohibits shipment of unapproved drugs across state lines for any purpose. Yet in order to conduct broad studies of a new drug, the manufacturer needs to distribute it to a sufficiently wide spectrum of doctors and hospitals for testing on a broad population of relevant patients. In order to do so, the manufacturer needs to seek an exemption from the ban on shipping unapproved drugs. The IND process allows the manufacturer to obtain such an exemption.[19]

Approval of an IND is not by any means automatic. Rather, the manufacturer has to submit the results of animal pharmacology and toxicology studies that show, to the FDA's satisfaction, that the product is reasonably safe for further testing. The manufacturer must also demonstrate that the manufacturing process is consistent and uncontaminated. Finally, the manufacturer must submit a proposed study protocol that is sufficiently detailed to permit the FDA to assess whether the investigation is likely to expose the subjects to unnecessary risks and whether the clinical investigators are sufficiently qualified to conduct the proposed studies. Once the IND is submitted, the manufacturer must wait for at least 30 days before beginning the trial so as to allow the FDA sufficient time to evaluate the application. Should the FDA conclude that the application is in any way inadequate, it can place it on hold until the defects are cured; otherwise, the manufacturer is free to begin clinical testing.[20]

Human clinical testing proceeds in three phases, each involving a larger number of subjects than the preceding one. Phase I typically lasts several months and includes between 20 and 100 healthy subjects and is meant to evaluate drug's toxicity and maximum safe dosage.[21] Once Phase I is completed, Phase II (designed to test drug's effectiveness) can begin. However, the FDA must give its approval for the drug to proceed from Phase I to Phase II. Thus, Phase I trials must show to the FDA's satisfaction that the drug is indeed safe.[22] Whereas Phase I is designed to test the safety, Phase II is focused on efficacy of the proposed treatment.[23] For that reason, participants in

Phase II are individuals afflicted with the disease that the drug is meant to treat. Typically, Phase II lasts about 2 years and involves anywhere between a few dozen and a few hundred participants.[24] Finally, if Phase II results are promising, the drug can move to large-scale Phase III trials. As before, the FDA must approve this progression to the next phase. Prior to approving progression to Phase III, the FDA officials meet with the drug manufacturer to reach an agreed-upon protocol about the large-scale Phase III studies.[25] These studies are complex because they involve different populations, different dosages, and possible interactions with other drugs. Usually, these studies enroll from several hundred to several thousand people.[26] This is the longest and most expensive phase of clinical trials.[27]

Because of the complexity, length, and multiple barriers, most drugs that enter clinical trials do not complete all three phases. Indeed, the overall success rate is 11%, meaning that 89% of all drugs that are tested in humans fail in one of the three stages. (The numbers would be even more staggering if preclinical trial failures were included.) What is more, for some more complex diseases, the numbers are even more disconcerting. Thus, new cancer treatments only succeed about 5% of the time, while new therapies for central nervous system disorders clock in at an 8% success rate. The vast majority of failures occur in Phases II and III. For example, about 45% of all compounds that enter Phase III fail at that stage.[28] This enormous failure rate contributes to the high cost of drug development (over $(USD)1 billion for each newly approved drug, by some estimates).[29]

Once all these studies are completed (over the course of about 7–10 years), the next step of the FDA approval process begins. If the drug successfully navigates all three phases of clinical trials, the manufacturer can submit an application to the FDA for the approval of the drug. This is known as the New Drug Application (NDA). The NDA is a comprehensive document, often containing thousands of pages of data gathered through all stages of clinical and preclinical trials.[30] In addition to the data obtained in clinical trials, the manufacturer is required to submit a proposed label for the drug. The label must contain appropriate instructions, warnings, dosages, potential adverse reactions, contraindications, known drug interactions, and other similar information. Additionally, the label must contain indications for the use of the drug.[31] Thus, the FDA approves drugs for *specific uses*, which are listed on the label.[32] The importance of this caveat will become clear in the following texts. The FDA generally reviews the NDA within 10 months (or 6 months if the application is on an expedited track).[33] The review includes both the drug itself and the proposed label. The NDA can be rejected if the FDA concludes that the drug is either unsafe or nonefficacious or that the label is false, misleading, or otherwise inadequate.[34] Despite the fact that by this point the drug has gone through years of trials and has had millions of dollars spent on it, one in four NDAs fails to gain an FDA approval. The number is higher for oncologic medications, reaching 30%, and women's health, reaching a staggering 42% of post-NDA submission failure. In other words, successfully navigating clinical trials is no guarantee that the new drug will be able to enter the market.[35]

FDA approval of an NDA allows the new drug to enter the market, but it does not end FDA involvement in and oversight of the drug. The manufacturer remains responsible for postmarketing monitoring of the product and for reporting adverse events to the FDA. This is often known as Phase IV trials. These trials are used "to delineate additional information about the drug's risks, benefits, and optimal use [by] studying different doses or schedules of administration …, us[ing] of the drug in other patient populations or other stages of the disease, or us[ing] of the drug over a longer period of time."[36]

Unfortunately, the FDA's capacity to process the information about adverse events is somewhat limited (especially as compared to its ability for processing premarket submissions). By some estimates, the FDA receives over 200,000 reports of adverse events per year. This information is gathered by physicians and other health-care providers and, therefore, is not reported in any systematic way.[37] It is for this reason that it usually takes a major event for the FDA to withdraw a product from the market. (Indeed, even Vioxx, which was subject to perhaps the most prominent postmarketing failure in recent years, was withdrawn not by the order of the FDA, but by voluntary action of Merck.)[38] Postmarketing monitoring is thus the weakest link in the FDA's approval and monitoring processing.

As briefly mentioned earlier, the FDA approves drugs for specific indications and uses. A drug manufacturer is not permitted, absent FDA approval to add additional indications for use to the label. So if drug A was initially approved to treat condition B, the manufacturer is not permitted to add condition C to the label even if studies support the finding that the drug is effective against that condition as well, unless and until the FDA approves such an addition. Nor is the manufacturer permitted to advertise that his drug can be used to treat an "off-label" condition. Theoretically, the manufacturer can submit an application to add new indications to the label. At first glance, doing so seems to make sense; after all, the more indications a drug can be marketed for, the higher the likely sales and profit for the company. In reality, however, the calculation is not that simple. In order to obtain FDA approval to list new indications, the manufacturer has to go through the entire testing protocol again, save for Phase I, as the safety has already been established.[39] The cost of submitting such a "supplemental" application is in millions of dollars,[40] while the approval time may actually exceed the time spent approving the initial application.[41] What is more, the new studies may bring previously unknown problems to the fore[42]—a useful outcome for the patients, but a risky one for the pharmaceutical company. Finally, while the company is conducting these additional studies and the FDA is conducting its review, the clock continues ticking on any patent-based exclusive rights that the company may have on the underlying chemical compound.

While all of the aforementioned play an important role in manufacturers' decisions to submit supplemental applications rarely, the key reason is that prohibitions on label alterations and off-label advertising do not translate to prohibition of off-label *use*. It is the FDA's position that "Congress did not intend FDA to interfere with the practice of medicine. Thus, once a product is approved for marketing for a specific use, FDA generally does not regulate how, and for what uses, physicians prescribe that drug. A licensed physician may prescribe a drug for other uses, or in treatments, regimens, or patient populations, that are not listed in the FDA-approved labeling."[43] Physicians are, therefore, free to prescribe any drug for any indication they deem appropriate, so long as they do not deviate from standards for malpractice liability. Indeed, "off-label" use is prevalent in almost all areas of medical practice.[44] Sometimes the "off-label" use is similar to the FDA-approved use, as is the case with *Actiq* (oral transmucosal fentanyl citrate), which is approved for breakthrough pain in cancer patients, but is often used to treat moderate to severe chronic, nonmalignant pain.[45] Other times though, the prescribed use differs radically from the FDA-approved indication. Thus, Zoloft (sertraline) is often used to treat premature ejaculation while being approved only as an antidepressant.[46] The upshot is that despite the millions of dollars spent on clinical studies and testing for efficacy, many drugs are used for purposes that were never rigorously tested. Furthermore, this "off-label" use makes the already difficult monitoring of adverse postmarketing events even more so.

Generic Drug Approval Process

Prior to 1984, a generic manufacturer had to go through the same premarketing process as the brand-name drug, even if the generic was, in all respects, identical to the previously approved brand-name counterpart. Because of the costs of the process and the diminishing returns in the competitive market, few generics did so. Following the passage of the Hatch–Waxman Act, however, generics have a much easier route to the market. They no longer have to conduct their own clinical and preclinical studies or submit an IND or an NDA. Instead, generic manufacturers have to submit an Abbreviated New Drug Application (ANDA). The ANDA application need not establish safety or efficacy of the proposed drug. Instead, it must scientifically show that the generic is bioequivalent (i.e., performs in the same manner as the innovator drug). There are a number of ways to show bioequivalence, including measuring how fast the generic version dissolves in the blood and comparing that rate to the dissolution rate of a brand-name drug. If such bioequivalence is shown and if the FDA is satisfied with the manufacturing facilities and processes, it will approve the generic to enter the market. Additionally, the generic's label must match the label of the brand-name drug. Should the generic wish to list any additional uses for its formulation, it needs to submit its own NDA for those uses.

There are two issues that can hold up a generic's market entry, and they both deal with statutory market exclusivity that the brand name may enjoy. One type of exclusivity stems from the Patent Act and another from the FDCA. When submitting an ANDA, the generic company must state whether the brand-name drug is covered by a patent. If it is, the generic manufacturer has two choices—it can choose to wait until the patent expires or it can certify that the patent is invalid or would not be infringed by the generic. The latter option (often known as "Paragraph IV certification") often gives rise to patent lawsuits that seek to resolve patent claims prior to the FDA's action on the ANDA. The precise details of such lawsuits are beyond the scope of this chapter, but it is worth noting that such lawsuits often delay generic market entry. On the other hand, patents can be invalidated in litigation, potentially opening the doors for yet more generic manufacturers to enter the market.[47]

The other type of exclusivity that a brand-name drug may enjoy, however, is generally not subject to judicial attack. FDA approval of a pioneering drug comes with a bonus known as the new chemical entity (NCE) exclusivity. If the drug contains an active ingredient that has never previously been approved for other uses, the pioneering brand-name drug gets to enjoy 5 years of exclusive marketing rights. During that period, the FDA will not approve any generic application on the same active ingredient, irrespective of whether such an ingredient is subject to a valid patent (though in most cases they are).[48]

In addition to the NCE and pediatric exclusivity provisions, there are two additional exclusivity periods of which the pioneer drug can avail itself. First, if the drug is meant to treat an "orphan disease" (defined as a "condition that affects less than 200,000 people in the US" or one "for which it is unlikely that US sales of the drug will recoup its development costs"), the brand name can enjoy 7 years of market exclusivity.[49] Finally, if the brand name submits new clinical studies that show the drug's efficacy in different formulations and dosages or for different indications, the brand name is entitled to 3 years of exclusivity.[50] Unlike the NCE or pediatric exclusivity, however, the orphan and new clinical studies exclusivity provisions are much more limited in scope. Whereas NCE exclusivity precludes FDA approval of any drug having the same active ingredient that is subject to NCE exclusivity, the orphan and new clinical studies exclusivity provisions only preclude FDA approval for the specific uses. In other words, the FDA may approve a generic version of an orphan drug (where brand name is not subject to a patent or NCE exclusivity, but is subject to orphan exclusivity) provided that generic's label does not list the orphan condition.[51] The physicians, of course, remain free to prescribe the generic to treat any condition they think appropriate. Indeed, even if physicians prescribe the brand name, pharmacists may, and often must, substitute the generic version, irrespective of the reason for the prescription.[52]

Finally, under a separate provision, all exclusivity periods can be extended by 6 months if the brand-name manufacturer conducts pediatric studies on the safety and efficacy of its drug.[53]

Medical Device Approval Process

The FDA approval of medical devices generally follows the same process as drug approval. There is, however, one fundamental difference. Unlike drugs, which are all subject to the same general approval protocol, all medical devices are classified as a Class I, II, or III device and are categorized by the level of dangers they may present to a consumer, with Class I being the least and Class III the most potentially dangerous.[54] Class III devices are subject to premarket approval, whereas Class I devices are not. Class II devices are subject to "premarket notification," a process in which the FDA evaluates whether the device is similar to an already approved and safe device and, if not, whether it poses sufficient danger to be classified as Category III.[55]

Although Class I is exempt from premarket approval or notification, only those devices that are shown to be safe and effective whenever not adulterated or misbranded qualify for this designation.[56] A classic example of such a device is a home pregnancy test that does not present significant danger to human health and safety even if it "malfunctions." Class III medical devices, on the other hand, have to follow nearly the same process that all drugs have to follow.[57]

Biologics Approval Process

In the last few decades, medical research and medical science have increased the focus on biologic (rather than chemical) treatments of the disease. As a result, since 1997 the FDA has regulated biologic materials in the same general way that it regulates drugs. Prior to marketing any biologic, the manufacturer must submit and have the FDA approve a Biologic License Application (BLA). The manufacturer must show that the biologic is safe, pure, and of proper potency, as well as demonstrates the integrity of the facility and the manufacturing process.[58] Not every biologic material, however, is within the scope of the FDA's regulatory process. The FDA's authority only extends to those products that are classified as such under the Public Health Service Act of 1944.[59] Under that Act,

> the term 'biological product' means a virus, therapeutic serum, toxin, antitoxin, vaccine, blood, blood component or derivative, allergenic product, protein (except any chemically synthesized polypeptide), or analogous product, or arsphenamine or derivative of arsphenamine (or any other trivalent organic arsenic compound), applicable to the prevention, treatment, or cure of a disease or condition of human beings.[60]

However, genetic materials, lipids, etc., as such are not considered to be biologics for the purposes of FDA regulation.[61] Although governed by different statutory and regulatory provisions, "the FDA expects BLAs to contain essentially the same information and data as NDAs."[62]

FDA Controversies and Competing Missions

As is evident from the previous discussion, the FDA's mission is to ensure that drugs and medical devices that enter the market are safe and salutary. The FDA, however, is not tasked with guarding public health as a whole, regulating the medical practices of health-care providers or ensuring access to drugs. The FDA's limited mission is sometimes cause for significant controversy surrounding the agency's actions.

A good example of the FDA's limited mission was the FDA's failed attempt to regulate tobacco in the 1990s. In the early 1990s, the FDA attempted to regulate cigarettes in order to reduce the health consequences associated with smoking. It asserted that cigarettes are drug delivery devices because they deliver a drug—nicotine—to smokers. In response to the FDA's rule that would have limited the promotion, labeling, and accessibility of tobacco products to children and adolescents, the tobacco industry sued. In a seminal case *FDA v. Brown & Williamson*, the Supreme Court struck down the FDA's regulation. In doing so, it concluded that because "the [FDCA]'s core objectives is to ensure that any product regulated by the FDA is 'safe' and 'effective' for its intended use," and because the FDA's own finding show that "tobacco products are unsafe, dangerous, and cause great pain and suffering from illness," the only logical conclusion is that "if tobacco products were 'devices' under the FDCA, the FDA would be required to remove them from the market"—something the FDA had no authority to do. It is worth noting that the Court did not challenge FDA's findings about the dangers of tobacco or its conclusion that the public health might be improved if the distribution of cigarettes were restricted. Nonetheless, the Court concluded that such findings are insufficient to allow the FDA to regulate tobacco.[63] Although in 2009 the Congress gave the FDA explicit authority to regulate tobacco,[64] the import of the *Brown & Williamson* case remains, and it is this: The FDA is powerless to issue regulations simply because they may benefit public health. Instead, the FDA must confine itself to protecting public health only by making sure that food, drugs, cosmetics, medical devices, and biologic products that are on the market are safe and effective for the advertised purposes.

A flip side of this outcome in *Brown & Williamson* can be observed in two cases that dealt with the drugs used to administer the death penalty. In the 1980s, several death row inmates filed suit claiming that the drugs that were used in the lethal injection, "although approved by the FDA for the medical purposes stated on their labels, were not approved for use in human executions … and that, given that the drugs would likely be administered by untrained personnel, it was also likely that the drugs would not induce the quick and painless death intended." The prisoners requested that the FDA intervene and require the drugs to carry a warning label that they are unapproved and unsafe for execution, "to adopt procedures for seizing the drugs from state prisons and to recommend the prosecution of all those in the chain of distribution who knowingly distribute or purchase the drugs with intent to use them for human execution." The FDA declined. The Supreme Court, in a case known as *Heckler v. Chaney*, affirmed concluding that the FDA can (as can most other enforcement agencies) choose whether or not to bring any sort of regulatory or enforcement action. Thus, the FDA's decision not to get involved in monitoring the lethal injection cocktail was to make and not subject it to judicial review, even if all of the claims made by the death row inmates were to be believed.[65]

Thirty years later, however, there arose a sequel to the *Chaney* case. As the supply of one of the drugs used in execution cocktails ran out, and with all domestic manufacturers ceasing production of the drug, several states imported the drug from a small British manufacturer. The FDCA directs the FDA to deny admission of any drug into the country, which is "manufactured, prepared, propagated, compounded, or processed in an establishment not duly registered" with the FDA. The FDA refused to impound the drug, and the death row inmates sued. This time, in a case called *Cook v. FDA*, the courts sided with them. The court's reasoning was simple. The drug in question had to be denied admission into the country not because it was used in executions, but because it was manufactured in an unapproved facility.[66] Though the outcome of *Cook* and *Chaney* were different, the message in both cases is the same—the FDA must enforce the law in a way to protect the general public from unapproved drugs, but does not have the responsibility to preclude the use of approved drugs for unapproved or even nefarious purposes.

Even within the limits of FDA authority, the agency often runs into competing pressures. On one hand, it is charged with making sure that the drugs and medical devices that reach the public are safe and perform as advertised. On the other hand, there is a significant pressure to approve drugs quickly, especially lifesaving ones. The statutory directive and the public's desire for quicker access to what may often be a patient's only medical hope are often at loggerheads. The FDA has often been criticized for dragging its feet in approving new drugs. In the early 1990s, the FDA was roundly criticized as "the leading job killer" in America and its leader was called a "bully and a thug." Ultimately, the Congress enacted a series of reforms meant to speed up drug approval.[67] These reforms, however, have not satisfied all of FDA's critics. In the early 2000s, a group known as Abigail Alliance for Better Access to Developmental Drugs sued the FDA. The alliance argued that terminally ill patients have a right to access "experimental drugs that have passed limited safety trials but have not been proven safe and effective." Although (and as a result of the 1990s era reforms) the FDA has some authority to permit terminally ill patients to access drugs that have not yet been fully approved and are still undergoing clinical trials, the FDA will not grant such permission if there is no "reasonable basis" to conclude that the drug is effective or if granting the request unreasonably risks additional illness or injury.

The courts eventually ruled against the alliance and held that terminally ill patients have no constitutional right to access unapproved drugs.[68] Nonetheless, the case illustrates that the system for drug approval is not without costs that can be measured not just in money, but sometimes in lives.

At the same time the FDA is being castigated for being too slow to approve drugs or too restrictive in letting terminally ill patients access experimental treatments, it is also often criticized for being too lax in approving drugs and monitoring them postapproval. The case of Vioxx presents a good example of such criticism. Politicians, scientists, and even the FDA's own officials rushed to criticize FDA procedures and methods.[69] Interestingly enough, nearly a decade after Merck voluntarily withdrew Vioxx, the FDA's advisory panel recommended against banning it.[70] It seems that in retrospect, experts believed that Vioxx has significant benefits. Yet, if the FDA were to change its approaches as a result of the criticism lobbed at it following the Vioxx fiasco, other drugs that provide significant benefits might never be approved or ordered withdrawn from the market. In short, the pressures on the FDA to approve drugs quickly while simultaneously ensuring near absolute safety put the agency between the proverbial rock and a hard place.

Finally, although the FDA is generally viewed as a scientific agency operating on the basis of cold hard scientific facts, it should be acknowledged that, like other governmental agencies, it is not immune to purely political pressure. The commissioner of the FDA, after all, is nominated by the president subject to Senate confirmation and serves at the pleasure of the president.[71] In this sense, the FDA commissioner is no different from other high ranking political appointees. An example of political pressures at the FDA can be seen in its approval process for the sale of emergency contraceptive pills. A large political fight over approving the sale of these pills over the counter (i.e., without a prescription) erupted in Washington. Democratic senators blocked George W. Bush's choice to lead the FDA over the FDA's refusal to approve such sales. Eventually, Dr. Andrew von Eschenbach was approved, but only after the FDA approved the sale of these pills to consumers older than 17 years of age.[72] A few years later, the FDA was set to approve the removal of age restrictions on the sale of these pills, but was overruled by President Obama's Health and Human Services secretary, Kathleen Sebelius. This action prompted a lawsuit against Secretary Sebelius and a judge ultimately ruled that the FDA must remove the age restriction on the sale of over-the-counter emergency contraception pills.[73] The bottom line is that although the FDA generally bases its decisions on the results of clinical studies alone, it is not immune from, and occasionally succumbs to, political pressure—a result that is entirely unsurprising given that the FDA is headed by a political appointee who, in turn, reports to another political appointee (secretary of Health and Human Services).

Conclusion

The FDA is charged with protecting the American consumer from dangerous and ineffective drugs. Over the course of the last century, its mission expanded from merely ensuring that the drugs are not mislabeled to verifying that they are not dangerous and to ultimately policing their effectiveness. While these goals are admirable, they do not come without significant costs—both in terms of the enormous resources spent in bringing a drug to the market and the potential lives lost as a result of inability of people to access unapproved drugs. At the same time, the FDA's role may be viewed as *too* limited because it does not concern itself with the general protection of public health or regulating off-label use of drugs even when such use is for nonmedicinal purposes. Ultimately, the debate about the proper role of the FDA is a debate about the costs and benefits of its regulatory regime. While it is always possible to make drugs and medical devices safer, doing so will entail significant costs. Conversely, it is possible to reduce the costs and increase the speed of bringing new drugs to the market, but likely at the expense of more detailed safety and efficacy studies. Where the proper balance between these two considerations lies is and will remain a source of constant debate.

Bibliography

Cases

United States Supreme Court:
FDA v. Brown & Williamson Tobacco Corp., 529 U.S. 120 (2000).
Heckler v. Chaney, 470 U.S. 821 (1985).

Circuit Courts of Appeals:
Abigail Alliance for Better Access to Developmental Drugs v. von Eschenbach 495 F.3d 695 (D.C. Cir. 2007).
Cook v. FDA, 733 F.3d 1 (D.C. Cir. 2013).
Sigma-Tau Pharms. v. Schwetz, 288 F.3d 141 (4th Cir. 2002).

United States District Courts:
Tummino v. Hamburg, ___ F.Supp.2d ___, 2013 WL 1348656 (E.D.N.Y. April 5, 2013).

Statutes and Regulations

21 CFR § 312.21(b).
21 C.F.R. § 312.23.
21 C.F.R. § 312.85
21 C.F.R. § 601.2(a).
P. L. No. 59-384, 34 Stat. 768.
Pub. L. No. 75-717, 52 Stat. 1040.
Pub. L. No. 78-410, 58 Stat. 682.

The Orphan Drug Act of 1983, Pub. L. No. 97-414, 96 Stat. 2056.
Pub. L. No. 102-571, 106 Stat. 4491 (1992).
Pub. L. No. 105-115, § 115(a), 111 Stat. 2296.
Family Smoking Prevention and Tobacco Control Act, Pub. L. No. 111-31, 123 Stat. 1776 (2009).
21 U.S.C. § 355a(b).
21 U.S.C. § 360c.
21 U.S.C. § 360c(a)(1)(A) (2012).
21 U.S.C.§ 393(d).
35 U.S.C. §156(c).
42 U.S.C. § 262(i)(1).

Secondary Sources

Abbott, R., Big data and pharmacovigilance: Using health information exchanges to revolutionize drug safety. *Iowa Law Review*, 99, 225 (2013).
Ahmad, S.R., Evolution of the FDA drug approval process, in *Handbook of Pharmaceutical Public Policy*, T.R. Fulda and A.I. Wertheimer (eds.) (2007). The Haworth Press. Binghamton, NY.
Andersen, M.J., Bound guidance: FDA rulemaking for off-label pharmaceutical drug marketing. *Case Western Reserve Law Review*, 60, 531 (2010).
Baswell, K., Time for a change: Why the FDA should require greater disclosure of differences of opinion on the safety and efficacy of approved drugs. *Hofstra Law Review*, 35, 1799 (2007).
Bert Black, Clinical trials—Why they're done, what they tell us, and what they don't tell us, ALI-ABA CLE (August 18–19, 2005).
Brannon, L., Regulating drug promotion on the internet. *Food and Drug Law Journal*, 54, 599 (1999).
Carrier, M.A., A real-world analysis of pharmaceutical settlements: The missing dimension of product hopping. *Florida Law Review*, 62, 1009–1017 (2010).
Clark, M.J. A critical analysis of Pliva, Inc. vs. Mensing. *Indiana Law Review*, 46, 173 (2012).
Devlin, A., Systemic bias in patent law. *DePaul Law Review*, 61, 57 (2011).
Dolin, G., Licensing health care professionals: Has the United States outlived the need for medical licensure? *Georgetown Journal of Law and Public Policy*, 2, 315 (2004).
Dolin, G., Reverse settlements as patent invalidity signals. *Harvard Journal of Law and Technology*, 24, 281 (2011).
Dolin, G., Nonprice competition in "Substitute" Drugs: The FTC's blind spot. *Antitrust Bulletin*, 59 (2014).
Feeney, G.J., Pliva, Inc. vs. Mensing: How generic-drug manufacturers avoided liability for "Failure to Warn" tort claims. *Loyola Law Review*, 58, 251 (2012).
Green, M.D. and Schultz, W.B., Regulatory compliance as a defense to products liability: Tort law deference to FDA regulation of medical devices. *Georgetown Law Journal*, 88, 2119 (2000).
Hall, R.F. and Sobotka, E.S., Inconsistent Government Policies: Why FDA off-label regulation cannot survive first amendment review under greater New Orleans. *Food and Drug Law Journal*, 62, 1 (2007).
Hazaray, N.F., Do the benefits outweigh the risks? The legal, business, and ethical ramifications of pulling a blockbuster drug off the market. *Indiana Health Law Review*, 4, 115 (2007).
Heled, Y., Patents vs. statutory exclusivities in biological pharmaceuticals—Do we really need both? *Michigan Telecommunication and Technology Law Review*, 18, 419 (2012).
Kingham, R., Klasa, G. and Carver, KH. (2013). Key regulatory guidelines for development of biologics in the U.S. and Europe, in *Biological Drug Products: Development and Strategies*, vol. 75, W. Wang and M. Singh (eds.). Wiley Online Library. http://onlinelibrary.wiley.com/doi/10.1002/9780470571224.pse503/abstract.
Kola, I. and Landis, J., Can the pharmaceutical industry reduce attrition rates? *Perspectives*, 3, 711 (2004).
Lykken, S., We really need to talk: Adapting FDA processes to rapid change. *Food and Drug Law Journal*, 68, 357 (2013).

McGrath, S., Only a matter of time: Lessons unlearned at the food and drug administration keep Americans at risk. *Food and Drug Law Journal*, 60, 603 (2005).
Merrill, R.A. The architecture of government regulation of medical products. *Virginia Law Review*, 82, 1753 (1996).
Pagnattaro, M.A., From China to your plate: An analysis of new regulatory efforts and stakeholder responsibility to ensure food safety. *The George Washington International Law Review*, 42, 1 (2010).
Parasidis, E., Patients over politics: Addressing legislative failure in the regulation of medical products. *Wisconsin Law Review*, 929(5): 929–1002 (2011).
Roin, B.N., The case for tailoring patent awards based on time-to-market. *UCLA Law Review*, 61, 672 (2014).
Ruocco, M.V., Brand name or generic? A Case Note on Caraco Pharmaceutical Laboratories v. Novo Nordisck. *Journal of National Association of Administrative Law Judiciary*, 33, 341 (2013).
Schwartz, V.E. et al., Warning: Shifting liability to manufacturers of brand-name medicines when the harm was allegedly caused by generic drugs has severe side effects. *Fordham Law Review*, 81, 1835 (2013).
Shreffler, J.E., Bad medicine: Good-faith FDA approval as a recommended bar to punitive damages in pharmaceutical products liability cases. *North Carolina Law Review*, 84, 737 (2006).
Smirniotopoulos, A., Bad medicine: Prescription drugs, preemption, and the potential for a no-fault fix. *NYU Review of Law and Social Change*, 35, 793 (2011).
Stephens, T. and Brynne, R. *Dark Remedy: The Impact of Thalidomide and Its Revival as a Vital Medicine* (2001). Basic Books. http://www.amazon.com/Dark-Remedy-Thalidomide-Revival-Medicine/dp/0738205907.
Struve, C.T., The FDA and the tort system: Postmarketing surveillance, compensation, and the role of litigation. *Yale Journal of Health Policy, Law and Ethics*, 5, 587 (2005).
Temple, R., Commentary on "The Architecture Of Government Regulation of Medical Products." *Virginia Law Review*, 82, 1877 (1996).
Todd, A.E., No need for more regulation: Payors and their role in balancing the cost and safety considerations of off-label prescriptions. *American Journal of Medicine*, 37, 422 (2011).
Underhill, K., Risk-taking and rulemaking: Addressing risk compensation behavior through FDA regulation of prescription drugs. *Yale Journal of Regulation*, 30, 377 (2013).
Zacher, A., False hope and toxic effects: Proposed changes to the FDA drug approval process would fail to benefit the terminally ill. *Quinnipiac Health Law Journal*, 14, 251 (2010–2011).
Zelenay, J.L., Jr., The prescription drug user fee act: Is a faster food and drug administration always a better food and drug administration? *Food and Drug Law Journal*, 60, 261 (2005).
Note, Reforming the food safety system: What if consolidation isn't enough? *Harvard Law Review*, 120, 1345 (2012). http://cdn.harvardlawreview.org/wp-content/uploads/pdfs/food_safety_system.pdf.

References

1. S. Lykken, We really need to talk: Adapting FDA processes to rapid change. *Food and Drug Law Journal*, 68, 357 (2013).
2. G. Dolin, Licensing health care professionals: Has the United States outlived the need for medical licensure? *Georgetown Journal of Law and Public Policy*, 2, 315 (2004).
3. P. L. No. 59-384, 34 Stat. 768 (1906).
4. Pub. L. No. 75-717, 52 Stat. 1040 (codified as amended at 21 U.S.C. §§301 *et seq.*).
5. Note, Reforming the food safety system: What if consolidation isn't enough? *Harvard Law Review*, 120, 1345 (2012).
6. M.A. Pagnattaro, From China to your plate: An analysis of new regulatory efforts and stakeholder responsibility to ensure food safety. *The George Washington International Law Review*, 42, 1 (2010).
7. S.R. Ahmad, Evolution of the FDA drug approval process, in *Handbook of Pharmaceutical Public Policy*, vol. 25, T.R. Fulda and A.I. Wertheimer (eds.) (2007). The Haworth Press. Binghamton, NY.
8. A. Zacher, False hope and toxic effects: Proposed changes to the FDA drug approval process would fail to benefit the terminally ill. *Quinnipiac Health Law Journal*, 14, 251 (2010–2011).

9. R. Temple, Commentary on "The Architecture Of Government Regulation of Medical Products." *Virginia Law Review*, 82, 1877 (1996).
10. S. McGrath, Only a matter of time: Lessons unlearned at the food and drug administration keep Americans at risk. *Food and Drug Law Journal*, 60, 603 (2005).
11. K. Baswell, Time for a change: Why the FDA should require greater disclosure of differences Of opinion on the safety and efficacy of approved drugs. *Hofstra Law Review*, 35, 1799 (2007).
12. T. Stephens and R. Brynne, *Dark Remedy: The Impact of Thalidomide and Its Revival as a Vital Medicine* (2001). Basic Books. NY, NY. http://www.amazon.com/Dark-Remedy-Thalidomide-Revival-Medicine/dp/0738205907.
13. G. Dolin, Reverse settlements as patent invalidity signals. *Harvard Journal of Law and Technology*, 24, 281 (2011).
14. Pub. L. No. 102-571, 106 Stat. 4491 (1992) (codified as amended in scattered sections of 21 U.S.C.).
15. Pub. L. No. 105-115, § 115(a), 111 Stat. 2296 (codified at 21 U.S.C. § 355(d)).
16. E. Parasidis, Patients over politics: Addressing legislative failure in the regulation of medical products. *Wisconsin Law Review*, 929(5): 929–1002 (2011).
17. B. Black, Clinical trials—Why they're done, what they tell us, and what they don't tell us, ALI-ABA CLE (August 18–19, 2005).
18. V.E. Schwartz et al., Warning: Shifting liability to manufacturers of brand-name medicines when the harm was allegedly caused by generic drugs has severe side effects. *Fordham Law Review*, 81, 1835 (2013).
19. FDA, Investigational new drug (IND) application, FDA, Investigational new drug (IND) application, http://www.fda.gov/drugs/developmentapprovalprocess/howdrugsaredevelopedandapproved/approvalapplications/investigationalnewdrugindapplication/default.htm Last updated October 27, 2014. Last accessed December 6, 2015.
20. 21 C.F.R. § 312.23.
21. M.V. Ruocco, Brand name or generic? A Case Note on Caraco Pharmaceutical Laboratories v. Novo Nordisck. *Journal of National Association of Administrative Law Judiciary*, 33, 341 (2013).
22. R.A. Merrill, The architecture of government regulation of medical products. *Virginia Law Review*, 82, 1753 (1996).
23. K. Underhill, Risk-taking and rulemaking: Addressing risk compensation behavior through FDA regulation of prescription drugs. *Yale Journal of Regulation*, 30, 377 (2013).
24. 21 CFR § 312.21(b).
25. FDA, The FDA's drug review process: Ensuring drugs are safe and effective, http://www.fda.gov/drugs/resourcesforyou/consumers/ucm143534.htm. Last updated November 6, 2014. Last accessed December 6, 2015.
26. J.L. Zelenay, Jr., The prescription drug user fee act: Is a faster food and drug administration always a better food and drug administration? *Food and Drug Law Journal*, 60, 261 (2005).
27. A. Devlin, Systemic bias in patent law. *DePaul Law Review*, 61, 57 (2011).
28. I. Kola and J. Landis, Can the pharmaceutical industry reduce attrition rates? *Perspectives*, 3, 711 (2004).
29. B.N. Roin, The case for tailoring patent awards based on time-to-market. *UCLA Law Review*, 61, 672 (2014).
30. J.E. Shreffler, Bad medicine: Good-faith FDA approval as a recommended bar to punitive damages in pharmaceutical products liability cases. *North Carolina Law Review*, 84, 737 (2006).
31. G.J. Feeney, Pliva, Inc. vs. Mensing: How generic-drug manufacturers avoided liability for "Failure to Warn" tort claims. *Loyola Law Review*, 58, 251 (2012).
32. R.F. Hall and E.S. Sobotka, Inconsistent Government Policies: Why FDA off-label regulation cannot survive first amendment review under greater New Orleans. *Food and Drug Law Journal*, 62, 1 (2007).
33. FDA, Fast track, breakthrough therapy, Accelerated approval and priority review, http://www.fda.gov/forpatients/approvals/fast/ucm20041766.htm Last updated September 14, 2015. Last accessed December 6, 2015.
34. M.J. Clark, A critical analysis of Pliva, Inc. v. Mensing. *Indiana Law Review*, 46, 173 (2012).

35. I. Kola and J. Landis, Can the pharmaceutical industry reduce attrition rates? *Perspectives Nature Reviews Drug Discovery*, 3: 711–716 (August 2004). http://www.nature.com/nrd/journal/v3/n8/abs/nrd1470.html.
36. 21 C.F.R. § 312.85.
37. C.T. Struve, The FDA and the tort system: Postmarketing surveillance, compensation, and the role of litigation. *Yale Journal of Health Policy, Law and Ethics*, 5, 587 (2005).
38. FDA, FDA issues public health advisory on Vioxx as its manufacturer voluntarily withdraws the product (September 30, 2004), http://www.fda.gov/NewsEvents/Newsroom/PressAnnouncements/2004/ucm108361.htm. Accessed December 6, 2015.
39. G. Dolin, Nonprice competition in "Substitute" Drugs: The FTC's blind spot. *Antitrust Bulletin*, 59: 579–591 (2014). http://abx.sagepub.com/content/59/3.author-index.
40. L. Brannon, Regulating drug promotion on the internet. *Food and Drug Law Journal*, 54, 599 (1999).
41. M.J. Andersen, Bound guidance: FDA rulemaking for off-label pharmaceutical drug marketing. *Case Western Reserve Law Review*, 60, 531 (2010).
42. A.E. Todd, No need for more regulation: Payors and their role in balancing the cost and safety considerations of off-label prescriptions. *American Journal of Medicine*, 37, 422 (2011).
43. Michael Friedman, Deputy Comm'r for Operations, FDA, Prepared Statement Before the Subcommittee on Human Resources and Intergovernmental Relations of the House Committee on Government Reform and Oversight (September 12, 1996), http://www.gpo.gov/fdsys/pkg/CHRG-104hhrg44757/pdf/CHRG-104hhrg44757.pdf. Accessed December 6, 2015.
44. R. Abbott, Big data and pharmacovigilance: Using health information exchanges to revolutionize drug safety. *Iowa Law Review*, 99, 225 (2013).
45. J. Carreyrou, Potent product: Narcotic 'Lollipop' becomes big seller despite FDA curbs—Actiq is only for cancer pain but Cephalon pitches it to many types of doctors—Like the Most Delicious Candy. *Wall Street Journal* (November 3, 2006). http://www.wsj.com/articles/SB116252463810112292.
46. C. Adams and K. Ridder, Off-label drug use concern, *San Jose Mercury News* (May 9, 2005).
47. Y. Heled, Patents vs. statutory exclusivities in biological pharmaceuticals—Do we really need both? *Michigan Telecommunication and Technology Law Review*, 8(2): 419–479 (2012). http://repository.law.umich.edu/cgi/viewcontent.cgi?article=1018&context=mttlr.
48. Y. Heled, Patents vs. statutory exclusivities in biological pharmaceuticals—Do we really need both? *Michigan Telecommunication and Technology Law Review*, 18, 419 (2012).
49. The Orphan Drug Act of 1983, Pub. L. No. 97-414, 96 Stat. 2056.
50. 35 U.S.C. §156(c).
51. Sigma-Tau Pharma. v. Schwetz, 288 F.3d 141 (4th Cir. 2002).
52. M.A. Carrier, A real-world analysis of pharmaceutical settlements: The missing dimension of product hopping. *Florida Law Review*, 62, 1009–1017 (2010).
53. 21 U.S.C. § 355a(b).
54. M.D. Green and W.B. Schultz, Regulatory compliance as a defense to products liability: Tort law deference to FDA regulation of medical devices. *Georgetown Law Journal*, 88, 2119 (2000).
55. 21 U.S.C. § 360c.
56. 21 U.S.C. § 360c(a)(1)(A) (2012).
57. A. Smirniotopoulos, Bad medicine: Prescription drugs, preemption, and the potential for a no-fault fix. NYU Review of Law and Social Change, 35, 793 (2011).
58. 21 C.F.R. § 601.2(a) (2005).
59. Pub. L. No. 78-410, 58 Stat. 682 (1944).
60. 42 U.S.C. § 262(i)(1).
61. FDA, What are "Biologics" questions and answers, http://www.fda.gov/AboutFDA/CentersOffices/OfficeofMedicalProductsandTobacco/CBER/ucm133077.htm Last updated August 5, 2015. Last accessed December 6, 2015.
62. R. Kingham et al., Key regulatory guidelines for development of biologics in the U.S. and Europe, in *Biological Drug Products: Development and Strategies*, vol. 75, W. Wang and M. Singh (eds.). Wiley Online Library. http://onlinelibrary.wiley.com/doi/10.1002/9780470571224.pse503/abstract.

63. FDA v. Brown & Williamson Tobacco Corp., 529 U.S. 120 (2000).
64. Family Smoking Prevention and Tobacco Control Act, Pub. L. No. 111-31, 123 Stat. 1776 (2009).
65. Heckler v. Chaney, 470 U.S. 821 (1985).
66. Cook v. FDA, 733 F.3d 1 (D.C. Cir. 2013).
67. Ahmad, *supra*.
68. Abigail Alliance for Better Access to Developmental Drugs v. von Eschenbach 495 F.3d 695 (D.C. Cir. 2007).
69. J. Kelly, Harsh criticism lobbed at FDA in Senate Vioxx Hearing (November 23, 2004), http://www.medscape.com/viewarticle/538021. Accessed December 6, 2015.
70. N.F. Hazaray, Do the benefits outweigh the risks? The legal, business, and ethical ramifications of pulling a blockbuster drug off the market. *Indiana Health Law Review*, 4, 115 (2007).
71. 21 U.S.C.§ 393(d).
72. J.D. Rockoff, FDA Signals Plan B Move, Baltimore Sun (August 1, 2006). https://www.highbeam.com/doc/1G1-148908355.html.
73. Tummino v. Hamburg, ___ F.Supp.2d ___, 2013 WL 1348656 (E.D.N.Y. April 5, 2013).

Chapter 9

Risk Minimization: A New Regulatory Challenge Directive

Louis A. Morris and Eva Lydick

Contents

Historic Perspective

New Era of Risk Management

Drugs are approved only if they are determined to be safe to use for the conditions described in their label. This basic tenet of the Food, Drug, and Cosmetic Act has not changed. What has changed in recent years is the interpretation of the term *safe*. Historically, the Food and Drug Administration (FDA) has interpreted the requirement that a drug must be safe to mean that the benefits of a drug outweigh its risks. The determination was made on a categorical basis, on which the totality of risks was weighted against the totality of benefits when considered for the purposes outlined in the drug product's labeling. If a drug did not meet this criterion, it was not approved or its label was rewritten to narrow the conditions for use. This logic was endemic in the FDA for most of the twentieth century.

Modern concepts of pharmaceutical risk management have changed and are now based on the premise that drug manufacturers, health-care professionals, and patients have a responsibility to minimize the risks of using pharmaceutical products. It is not enough to make drugs minimally safe; they must be as safe as possible over the life cycle of the product's use.[1–7]

In the mid-1970s, historically, the FDA has interpreted the requirement that a drug must be safe to mean that the benefits of a drug outweigh its risks. The determination was made on a categorical basis, where the totality of risks was weighted against the totality of benefits when considered for the purposes outlined in the drug product's labeling. If a drug did not meet this criterion, it was not approved or its label was rewritten to narrow the conditions for use. This logic was endemic in the FDA for most of the twentieth century. On average, two to four drugs over each 5-year period were withdrawn from the marketplace after postmarketing data uncovered new risks.[4] On occasion, the FDA would require some special tool or intervention to improve a product's safety profile and augment the drug labeling directed to physicians in order to improve drug safety. For example, patient package inserts (PPIs) were used to warn women about the risk of birth control pills, and a special distribution system was used to limit the dispensing of Clozaril (clozapine) to patients who undertook blood tests that demonstrated that they were not having a serious adverse reaction. However, starting in the early 1990s, this philosophy started to change, as the FDA began to take a more active role in postmarketing surveillance and began instituting a more aggressive management process to assure greater safety in the use of marketed drugs. No longer dido, the manufacturer and the FDA provide passive oversight and labeling changes to control risks; now, the manufacturer must actively monitor for suspected but unquantified risks and actively manage and minimize known risks.

Evolution of Risk Management

Precursor History

The FDA's new concepts for risk management amount to a cultural shift in the logic of drug approval and the FDA's role. The key events that led to this change can be traced to a series of reports that highlighted the need for improved medical safety. In 1999, the Institute of Medicine (IOM) released a report entitled *To Err is Human* (IOM, 2000).[35] This report reviewed the nature and cause of medication errors, estimating that up to 98,000 people die each year due to these errors. The IOM included both adverse drug reactions and human errors in drug administration in their assessment. The report captured the attention of news reporters and the government. Headlines shouted alarm at the larger number of fatalities caused by medical errors. A government-wide initiative was started to develop methods and institute procedures to reduce medical errors.

For its part, the FDA was already concerned about medical safety and sought to increase its oversight and control of the safe use of marketed drugs. The IOM report provided both impetus and support for an already developing policy of increasingly active intervention. During the 4-year period from 1998 to 2001, at least 10 drugs were withdrawn from the market (see Table 15.1). For each preceding 5-year periods from 1979 to 1998, only two to four drugs were withdrawn.

In recent years, the impact of this new philosophy of risk management has continued with the withdrawal of Vioxx, Bextra, and Palladone and the initiation of risk management programs for nonsteroidal anti-inflammatory drugs (NSAIDs), ED drugs, and SSRIs. Product liability cases for Vioxx and press reports have also demonstrated public concerns for drug safety.

Statements made by FDA officials regarding some of these withdrawals suggested that the FDA no longer believed that passive oversight and relabeling drugs with new warnings were sufficient. Furthermore, the FDA no longer believed that it was sufficient to identify safe conditions of use in the label; health-care professionals and patients had to comply with advocated directions for use for the drug to remain on the market.

As a summary and embodiment of this new philosophy of risk management, FDA staff issued a report to the commissioner that highlighted processes for developing risk management systems and signaled new ideas for measuring risks and intervening to manage risk (U.S. FDA, 1999).[6] Entitled *Managing the Risks from Medical Products Use: Creating a Risk Management Framework*,[46] the FDA report borrowed heavily from risk management philosophies in other fields, such as environmental risk management and airline safety. It emphasized the process of developing risk management plans to control and manage drug safety. It outlined, in detail, FDA's new approach to pharmaceutical risk management.

Advent of RiskMAPs

The risk management revolution at the FDA continues today. Under FDA regulations and the FDA's Modernization Act, the FDA may approve new drugs with new restrictions that intended to assure safe use (Subpart H). These restrictions include limiting distribution to certain facilities or physicians with special training or experience or limiting distribution based on the condition of the performance of specified medical procedures. The regulations specify that the limitations must be commensurate with the specific safety concerns presented by the product. In addition, drugs continue to be approved with restrictions imposed by manufacturers seeking FDA approval.

In 2004, the FDA released a series of draft concept paper guidances that described a new requirement for drug manufacturers. For certain new drug applications, companies needed to develop a risk management action plan (RiskMAP).[5–7]

A RiskMAP is a strategic safety program designed to minimize known product risks while preserving its benefits. RiskMAPs targeted one or more safety goals and used one or more interventions or tools. These tools extended beyond the package insert (PI) and routine postmarketing surveillance. They are categorized into three areas: education and outreach, reminder systems, and performance-linked access systems.

The FDA guidance also describes the conditions stimulating the need for a RiskMAP, the selection of tools, the format for RiskMAPs, and the evaluation processes necessary to develop and monitor the success of a risk minimization plan. The RiskMAP describes the background, research, rationale, and logic necessary to develop and implement the strategy and tactics for the risk management program.

The requirement development of a RiskMAP became superseded by the federal legislation. On September 27, 2007, President George W. Bush signed into law the Food and Drug Administration Amendments Act of 2007 (FDAAA).[8] Among other requirements, the FDAAA gave the FDA the authority to require a "risk evaluation and mitigation strategy" (REMS) for existing or approved new drug products. Many of the principles that were included in the RiskMAP guidance are embodied in the REMS provisions.

Enter REMS

Like a RiskMAP, a REMS could be required by the FDA when the agency believed that REMS was necessary to ensure that the benefits of a drug outweigh its risks. The REMS legislation specified three types of interventions or tools that could be required by the FDA as part of a REMS:

1. A patient communication tool such as a medication guide (MG) or PPI
2. A communication plan to health-care providers such as Dear Healthcare Provider letters
3. Elements to assure safe use (EASU) or a plan to control and limit the distribution of medicines to only qualified prescribers, distribution centers, or patients who meet predefined criteria

MGs and PPIs are leaflets distributed to patients when they obtain prescriptions at the pharmacy. The FDA had required PPIs for a few selected drugs (e.g., oral contraceptives, estrogen products) and manufacturers had voluntarily distributed patient information leaflets for a few drugs to pharmacies for distribution. MGs were not required by the FDAAA (federal legislation had previously given the FDA the authority to require MGs for drugs that posed a serious and significant public health threat in 1996 and the FDA issued regulations for MGs in 1999).[9,10] The FDAAA, however, placed MGs as part of a REMS program. Implementing MGs as part of a REMS placed an additional burden for manufacturers, because all REMS required manufacturers to conduct evaluations of the interventions at 1.5, 3, and 7 years after strategy implementation. Thus, not only did manufacturers have to distribute an MG with their medication, but they also had to evaluate the effectiveness of the tool.

In the mid-2000s, REMS began to be a frequent requirement for drug approval. As of mid-2013, the FDA had required about 200 REMS since 2008.[11] The majority of these REMS required only an MG. In 2011, the FDA took a step back and started to lessen the requirements for REMS. The FDA withdrew the requirement that all drugs needing an MG had to be part of a REMS.

In the guidance,[12] the FDA requires pharmaceutical companies to think through not only how a drug is supposed to be used (indications, contraindications, precautions, warnings, etc.) but also how it may be used or misused by prescribers, dispensers, and patients using the medication. As a matter of best practices, some companies have begun to apply the RiskMAP development process to all drugs, not only to those that will require formal RiskMAPs, to more thoroughly apply the risk minimization process to improve drug safety. The role of the RiskMAP is to minimize risks throughout the life cycle of the drug. For the most part, the plan deals with the control of known or suspected risks, whereas other risk management activities concentrate on the discovery and quantification of suspected risks.

To fulfill the obligations of developing a competent RiskMAP, drafters must seek to influence the behavior of the parties responsible for drug safety, particularly patients, physicians, pharmacists, and allied medical staff. This is not an easy task. It requires understanding of the specific behaviors to be influenced, the environment in which the behaviors take place, the development of a set of strategies to influence behaviors, and an evaluation program to determine the impact (and source of failure) for intended interventions. Therefore, a reasonable RiskMAP must demonstrate that the company understands the system of drug prescribing, dispensing, monitoring, and use for their particular product, the impact (positive and negative) and limits of various tools or combination of tools selected for implementation, how to test tools before implementation and evaluate the implemented RiskMAP with sufficient specificity to understand the impact of the selected interventions, and how to improve outcomes if the original program does not reach reasonable effectiveness targets. In addition, the implemented RiskMAP should not detract from product sales. Developing risk minimization action programs that assure safe use while maintaining sales presents an added difficulty and series of concerns.

To comply with the guidance, drafters need to apply an appropriate analytical framework, along with insights from the original research:

- To conceive a rational approach for controlling risks
- To justify the selection of tools or the development new tools
- To justify why other tools that may be more "potent" (but cause patients or prescribers to reject the medication) are not selected
- To evaluate the tools prior to implementation and the program after implementation
- To plan for quality improvements in the plan as it evolves and to plan for the ultimate withdrawal of the risk management program

The purpose of this chapter is to describe the FDA's RiskMAP requirements and to suggest how to develop a RiskMAP. Not every MG would necessarily be part of a REMS. Depending on the risks involved, the agency would approve some MGs not only under labeling regulations, but, occasionally, also as part of a REMS; the FDA withdrew the evaluation requirement for the existing MG-only REMS. This reduced the number of REMS. As of July 2013, there are 66 REMS for individual drugs and 6 "shared systems" covering 84 drug entities.[11] The FDA lists over 400 drugs with MG requirements.[13]

Have REMS Been Effective?

The evaluation requirements for REMS programs should lead one to expect that we would have a good perspective on whether (or which) REMS programs have met their goals. However, this has not necessarily been the case. The evaluation program requires manufacturers to submit evaluations of REMS program at 1.5, 3, and 7 years after REMS approval. In an issue paper distributed in June 2012, the FDA discussed the results of this evaluation program (FDA, 2012).[14] As of December 31, 2011, the FDA had received and reviewed 144 assessments that contained surveys for 105 individual drugs. A total of 55 of these REMS were of the *MG-only* type, 33 had an MG and a communication plan, and 56 were classified as *other*, which were predominantly REMS with EASU.

According to the issue paper, the patient surveys submitted as part of a REMS assessment had generally shown evidence of limited understanding of some important risk information (in some surveys, patients had less than 50% correct answers to questions about critical risks). Surveys of health-care providers showed that the REMS were meeting their information goals (as defined by a knowledge rate ≥ 80%).

The FDA expressed great concern about the validity of these findings and the quality of the evidence submitted by manufacturers. The adequacy of some of the surveys conducted was questioned. For example, the FDA noted the following:

- Sometimes the sample size achieved appears too low to draw conclusions with confidence.
- The surveyed population did not necessarily reflect the demographics of the target patient population.
- Because convenience samples were commonly used, surveys were likely to be biased in some way.
- The level of difficulty of the questions varied across surveys.
- Question wording and level knowledge tested made the correct answer self-evident.
- Sometimes the wording of a question was open to interpretation, which may explain a low knowledge rate.
- There are no objective standards for an adequate knowledge rate (i.e., the threshold for success) of the REMS educational component.

OIG Review

A systematic review of the FDA's experience evaluating REMS programs was also conducted by the Office of the Inspector General (OIG, 2012).[15] The OIG reviewed approved REMS since program inception in 2008 through 2011 and conducted structured interviews with FDA officials about FDA's efforts to evaluate REMS components. OIG also reviewed 49 sponsors' REMS assessments and FDA's reviews from these assessments. The quality of completeness of the assessments was determined as well as the time frames and conclusion regarding the adequacy of the REMS in meeting specified goals.

The FDA had approved 199 REMS between 2008 and 2011, 99 of which were still required in 2012. The OIG found that nearly half of the sponsor assessments for the 49 REMS did not include all information requested in the assessment plans and 10 were not submitted to the FDA within the required time frames. The FDA had determined that only 7 of the 49 REMS (14%) met all of their goals. However, as discussed earlier, the FDA expressed a strong lack of confidence in the methods used to assess the effectiveness of REMS.

Almost half (23 of 49) of the sponsor assessments did not include all of the information requested in FDA assessment plans. For example, one sponsor did not include the number of pharmacies that were deauthorized to dispense the drug because of noncompliance with the REMS, as requested in the assessment plan. The same sponsor also did not include the amount of the drug shipped to health-care providers compared to actual patient orders, as requested.

FDA review memorandums indicated that the FDA could not determine whether 17 REMS were meeting all of their goals. FDA review memorandums did not contain statements regarding whether the remaining four REMS were meeting all of their goals.

The FDA determined that only 1 of 19 REMS with EASUs was meeting all of its stated goals. In review memorandums, FDA reviewers stated that eight REMS with EASUs were not meeting all goals and that they could not determine whether eight others were meeting all goals.

Where there was sufficient information for the FDA to reach a conclusion about the adequacy of the REMS, the FDA frequently determined that the REMS were insufficient. The FDA most often determined that REMS were not meeting their goals because of deficiencies in patient and prescriber awareness of drug risks. The FDA determined that REMS were not communicating risks sufficiently to patients (in 14 of 21 assessments) and/or prescriber (in 12 of 21 assessments).

Problem with REMS

The general conclusion reached by the FDA was that many REMS successes or failures cannot be determined because of a lack of confidence in outcome measurement validity. For those REMS where outcome measurement validity is accepted, there are often deficiencies in risk communication. Rather than try to improve on these deficiencies, the FDA opted to drop the requirement of having MGs as part of a REMS system, eliminating the need to evaluate whether the MG is communicating sufficiently.

Timing of Evaluation

For its part, drug manufacturers have had difficulty complying with REMS evaluation requirements. Often it is extremely difficult, if not impossible, to find sufficient numbers of patients taking rarely used drugs (REMS are often required for risky drugs that are rarely used). Sponsors and health-care providers have often expressed concerns about the challenges associated with collecting data on the compliance of third parties (e.g., patients, pharmacies, drug distributors). Specifically, concerns about patient confidentiality and the lack of a standardized format for sponsor assessments may contribute to the lack of data in some assessments.

However, there is another structural problem with REMS assessments of MG effects. The way the law is written, a REMS evaluation is required at 1.5, 3, and 7 years after REMS adoption. This evaluation should be focused on whether the REMS is working. However, the intervention being evaluated is measuring whether a document is being remembered. Thus, is a lack of knowledge expressed at the time of evaluation due to initial communication failure by the document or to forgetting the information that was initially presented?

Morris et al.[16] examined the requirement that companies need to wait for 1.5 years before evaluating the effect of a MG on patient knowledge. To investigate this effect, the authors surveyed 400 individuals via the Internet to determine how previous experience with an MG for NSAIDs influenced knowledge. Half of the respondents had received a prescription for an NSAID in the previous 6 months (during that time, an MG was required) and the other half had not received an NSAID prescription. Independently, half was shown the NSAID MG and allowed to read or reread it prior to taking a knowledge test (four experimental cells).

Those who read the MG prior to taking the knowledge test correctly answered about two-thirds of the questions regardless of previous use, regardless of whether they were prescribed the drug previously or if they were naïve in this respect. Those who had used the medicine but did not review the MG prior to the test correctly answered about half of the questions. Those that neither used the medicine nor reviewed the MG correctly answered about one-fourth of the questions. The results indicated that there was an independent contribution of both experience using the medicine and MG readership. Reading the material and immediately answering questions led to a 66% success rate. However, there was a clear benefit to having received the MG in the past as those who received it were twice as likely to answer the questions correctly (50% compared to 25%). Clearly, there was evidence of forgetting (16% detriment comparing those that took the immediate test and those that took the test in a delayed fashion).

It is intriguing to note that comprehension tests for OTC drugs[17] have been viewed by the FDA and regulated industry as highly successful but MG evaluations are viewed as failures. The general process for the testing is similar (people are shown the material and answer questions about it) but there are some key differences that may explain the differences in success. The most important is the timing of the testing. OTC drug labels are tested before they are distributed and MGs are tested one and one-half years after they are distributed to the public. OTC labels are tested so that they can be modified and improved prior to distribution and MGs are tested to determine whether they are working (a success or failure decision). There is often much qualitative work done to refine the OTC label and the OTC comprehension test prior to implementation in a quantitative study, thereby, improving the questionnaire flow and understandability and improving the label so that it emphasized the key objectives measured in the study. For MG, the questionnaire may be qualitatively tested but there is no change to the MG based on this qualitative review. If OTC drug labels do not meet a priori standards for sufficiency, the label is rewritten and retested. In some cases, OTC comprehension tests have been redone if they have failed to achieve recruitment goals (e.g., for hard-to-find populations). For MGs, it appears that the decision has been to drop the testing requirement. This focus on quality improvement for OTC, as opposed to a "pass-fail" focus for MGs, may attribute to the perceived success of comprehension testing.

It is interesting that the European Union (EU) has taken a different approach for the evaluation of patient information. According to the EU 2009 Guidelines,[18] only small numbers of participants are needed to evaluate patient leaflets. The aim of this research is to meet an a priori success criterion in a total of about 20 participants (excluding a pilot test). A satisfactory test outcome is met when the information presented in the package leaflet can be identified or remembered by 90% of test participants and 90% can show that they understand it, which means 16 out of 20 participants are able to identify the information and answer each question correctly and act appropriately. The success criteria need to be achieved with each question. The EU suggests an iterative process for testing. If the success criteria are not met, the information is to be rewritten and tested again using a different group of 10 respondents. The test needs to be repeated (along with appropriate revisions of the material) until the success criteria are met. This iterative testing approach, like OTC comprehension testing, provides a method of improving patient information documents before circulation.

Creeping Burdens and Need for Standardization

Early in REMS initiation, it became clear that there could be considerable confusion when two companies, marketing drugs for identical indications, had different REMS information or distribution limits or strategies. This became evident when Accutane (isotretinoin) became available as a generic drug. Accutane had an extensive risk management program. The evolution of the risk management program used for Accutane also demonstrates how risk management burdens can grow in an effort to develop a system that is highly effective (i.e., nearly perfect) at controlling patient and health-care provider behavior.

Accutane Risk Management Systems

When approved in 1982, patients were required to receive a brochure that warned about the risk of birth defects if the drug was taken during pregnancy. In 1998, the manufacturer (Roche) instituted a Pregnancy Prevention Program, which included warning labels, an informed consent sheet, a kit for prescribers (part of the professional communication system), a tracking study to assess use of kit, and patient survey to access enrollment in the program. The program, although extensive, was seen as inadequate.

In 2001, Roche instituted the System to Manage Accutane-Related Teratogenicity (SMART) program. The SMART program included enhanced education for patients, a physician qualification program, yellow stickers issued by physicians to be delivered to pharmacists authorizing each prescription, two pregnancy tests prior to the first Rx, mandatory pregnancy testing before each Rx, an MG, use of two forms of birth control, a 30-day supply limit for each Rx and no refills, and a program for mandatory registries.

When the FDA started to approve generic isotretinoin, it became clear that generic manufacturers, even if they tried, could not duplicate all of the elements of the Roche SMART program. The FDA called for a modification of the risk management plan. In 2010 (modified in 2012), the FDA asked manufacturers of isotretinoin to adopt a single REMS program. The program was called "iPLEDGE." It covers five separate manufacturers and institutes a single complex system (compose of all three elements or tools) for the distribution of this medication.[19]

The iPLEDGE program is a computer-based program that requires registration of all wholesalers distributing isotretinoin, all health-care professionals prescribing isotretinoin, all pharmacies dispensing isotretinoin, and all male and female patients prescribed isotretinoin. This program is designed to create a verifiable link between the negative pregnancy test and the dispensing of the isotretinoin prescription to the female patient of childbearing potential. The iPLEDGE program requires that all patients meet qualification criteria and monthly program requirements. Before the patient receives an isotretinoin prescription each month, the prescriber must counsel the patient and document in the iPLEDGE system that the patient has been counseled about the risks of isotretinoin.

There are also additional qualification criteria and monthly requirements for female patients of childbearing potential. As part of the ongoing risk management of isotretinoin products, females of childbearing potential must select and commit to use two forms of effective contraception simultaneously for 1 month before, during, and after isotretinoin therapy. Women must have two negative urine or blood (serum) pregnancy tests before receiving the initial isotretinoin prescription. The first pregnancy test is a screening test and can be conducted in the prescriber's office. The second pregnancy test must be done in a certified laboratory. Each month of therapy, the patient must have a negative urine or blood (serum) pregnancy test conducted by a certified laboratory prior to receiving each prescription.

Each month, the prescriber must enter the female patient's pregnancy results and the two forms of contraception she has been using in the iPLEDGE system. The iPLEDGE system verifies that all criteria have been met by the prescriber, patient, and pharmacy prior to granting the pharmacy authorization to fill and dispense isotretinoin. The pharmacist must obtain authorization from the iPLEDGE system via the program website or phone system prior to dispensing each isotretinoin prescription for both male and female patients.

It is not surprising that with such an extensive system, there has been an extensive criticism of iPLEDGE risk management program. The time and expense of compliance with iPLEDGE is significant and may pose a barrier to treatment if doctors do not wish to expend the effort required. For many patients, the iPLEDGE program has caused delays in receiving isotretinoin. Doctors cannot prescribe more than a 30-day supply. A new prescription may not be written for at least 30 days. Pharmacies are also under similar restriction. No more than a 30-day supply may be filled. There is also a 7-day window in which the medication must be picked up at the pharmacy; if the prescription has not been filled within the seventh day by the doctor handing the patient the prescription, it is then voided and cannot be filled. If the original prescription is lost, or a pickup window is missed, the patient must wait 30 days without any medication. Doctors and pharmacists must also verify written prescriptions in an online system before patients may fill the prescription. This sequence of requirements can make it very difficult for patients to receive and take isotretinoin on the prescribed schedule. Many patients are forced to wait several days without medication.

Some patients have complained about the requirements of the iPLEDGE in terms of the burden of the testing requirements and violation of their privacy (a potential breach in patient/doctor confidentiality). Compliance to the program requires a participating physician to reveal many aspects of a patient's sexual history including STDs, when a patient is registered into the program.

This experience with the iPLEDGE system has led the FDA to consider the effects of a program on the burden it produces. However, it has not inhibited efforts to streamline REMS programs. In 2011, the FDA created the REMS Integration Initiative.[20] This was designed to develop consistent requirements on how to apply the statutory criteria to determine when a REMS is required and what type of tool is needed: improved standardization and assessment of REMS and improved integration of REMS into the existing and evolving health-care system. In 2013, the FDA held a series of meeting and a public workshop to gather stakeholder input into its efforts for standardization.

Opioid REMS

This increased integration of REMS requirements is best seen in the development of a risk management program to limit drug abuse. In 2012, the FDA approved a REMS for manufacturers of extended-release (ER) and long-acting (LA) opioid medications.[21] These extensive REMS sought to standardize requirements among manufacturers and products. The REMS program included an MG to be dispensed with each ER/LA opioid analgesic prescription. There is also a patient-counseling sheet for physicians as an outline of what to tell patients about the medicine. There is an extensive training for health-care providers who prescribe ER/LA opioid analgesics. Standards are set to assure that the training is "REMS compliant" (the FDA issued a "blueprint" for the training), including course participant evaluation of appropriate prescribing knowledge. To make prescribers aware of the existence of the REMS and the prescriber training, manufacturers must deliver letters to all DEA-registered prescribers who are registered to prescribe Schedule II and III drugs. Two letters are specified to inform prescribers of the existence and necessity of the training. In addition, manufacturers must inform licensing boards and professional organizations of the REMS and its requirements.

Burden and Overwarning

In addition, sales for drugs with heavy risk management burdens, such as Lotronex, have been linked to reduced prescribing after the initiation of EASU distribution controls. Rather than undertake the effort and considerable time (and possibly increased malpractice liability) to engage in a risk management program, some physicians will choose to avoid prescribing heavily controlled medicines. In 2004, the maker of Lotronex (GSK) attributed decreased sales of the drug to the REMS program.[22]

Other studies have shown that physicians may opt to avoid prescribing indicated drugs if the risk management program is overly burdensome. For example, La Ponte et al.[23] investigated the effects of a risk management program for dofetilide (Tikosyn). Dose-dependent torsades de pointes has been shown to occur with dofetilide (Tikosyn) and sotalol HCl (Betapace AF); thus, there are detailed dosing and monitoring recommendations to minimize this risk, which are included in the product labeling for both drugs. Only dofetilide, however, had a mandated risk management program that restricted distribution of the drug and required prescriber education on the drug. The authors investigated whether this risk management program improved adherence to dosing and monitoring recommendations for dofetilide as compared with sotalol. They reviewed the charts for 47 patients taking dofetilide and 117 patients taking sotalol. They found that the recommended starting dose was prescribed more frequently in the dofetilide group than in the sotalol group, and a higher number of patients in the dofetilide group compared with the sotalol group received the recommended baseline tests. They concluded that better adherence to several dosing and monitoring recommendations in the dofetilide group may be caused by the presence of the risk management program. However, they also concluded that low usage of dofetilide during the study period may signify an unintended, negative consequence of the risk management program.

The finding that drug warning messages (or symbols of drug dangers, such as a REMS) can backfire has been shown with other medicines. Gibbons et al.[24] found that sales of SSRI antidepressants to adolescents decreased dramatically in the United States and Europe after warnings were added about a possible association between antidepressants and suicidal thinking and behavior. It is likely that people who have suicidal thinking and behavior are more likely to be candidates for antidepressant medication. If SSRIs are associated with increased suicide rates, does that mean that it caused the effect or that it did not prevent the effect? Thus, decreasing use may increase suicides. Indeed, the decrease in sales of SSRIs was associated with increases in suicide rates in children and adolescents.

Standardization of Patient Information

Types of Information Distributed to Patients

Although PPIs and MGs have been required for many medicines, the FDA has mostly relied on private sector programs to achieve the goal of educating patients about the prescription drugs they are prescribed. In addition to FDA-required materials, patients may receive another source of prescription drug information called Consumer Medication Information (CMI). CMI, which is not FDA approved, is a private sector initiative to educate patients about their prescription. In addition to requiring MGs for a few prescription drugs, the FDA believed that there was a significant public health need. Public Law (PL) 104-180 established incentives for the private sector to distribute useful prescription drug information.[9] This law set specific distribution and quality goals and time frames for the private sector distribution of written prescription drug information to consumers. The law required that the secretary of the Department of Health and Human Services (HHS) evaluates the private sector progress toward meeting these goals, including that, by 2006, 95% of people receiving new prescriptions would receive "useful" written patient information with their prescriptions. If the goals were not met, the secretary could issue regulations requiring manufactures to implement MG regulations for all drugs.

Distribution and Quality of Information

In December 1996, a collaboration of private sector organizations presented the secretary of HHS an "action plan" to achieve the goals of PL 104-180 (the Keystone Plan).[25] The plan established criteria for "useful" information (quality standards). The FDA has performed a series of evaluations to determine the degree to which private sector programs have met these quantity and quality performance standards.

In 2000, the FDA sought to measure how well the private sector was meeting the interim goals of the action plan. A nationwide study was performed by Svarstad et al.[26] They sent trained shoppers to fill 918 new prescriptions at 306 randomly selected pharmacies in 8 states to evaluate the CMIs received. They filled prescriptions for four study drugs. The study found that the distribution threshold for CMIs (75% at the time) was met, with 87% of prescriptions accompanied by a CMI. However, the CMI quality was poor, with its contents, length, and quality varying greatly. Fewer than half of the materials met acceptable quality standards about how to take the medication, how to receive maximal benefit, and how to interpret benefits. About only a quarter included sufficient information about medication precautions and how to avoid adverse reactions, and fewer than a fifth contained sufficient information about contraindications and what to do in case of a contraindication.

The evaluation was repeated in 2007 by Kimberlin and Winterstein.[27] In this study, shoppers obtained new prescriptions for lisinopril and for metformin at 364 community pharmacies in 41 states. Twenty-two pharmacies (6%) did not provide any written information beyond the directions on the prescription vials. The remaining 94% provided printed CMI for filled prescriptions for lisinopril (n = 343) and metformin (n = 342). These 685 leaflets were rated by a panel to assess the degree to which they met performance standards for content and format. Fourteen percent of lisinopril and 16% of metformin CMI leaflets had very low levels of quality less than 40% meeting quality performance thresholds.

This 2007 study showed that while 94% of consumers received a CMI with new prescriptions, only about 75% of this information met criteria for usefulness. In general, the 2007 study noted continued room for improvement in finding that

1. Adequate information about medication use and monitoring of effectiveness and safety is lacking
2. There was variability in both the amount and format of information
3. Despite progress, CMI continued to fall short of the congressionally mandated goal that 95% of new prescriptions be accompanied by useful CMI by 2006

PMI Initiative

To improve CMI quality, the FDA has initiated a Patient Medication Information (PMI) program.[28] The goal of the PMI program is to standardize the format and content of patient information on prescription drugs. The FDA is testing various new prototypes to develop a single format for all patient/consumer information. The method of distribution or source of the documents is unclear; however, during testimony on December 11, 2013, before the Senate Special Committee on Aging, Janet Woodcock, chief of FDA's drugs division, stated that manufacturers would best be able to develop such standardized information with FDA's guidance and review (manufacturer-produced PMIs are used in the EU, Canada, Japan, Australia, and New Zealand).[29]

Thus, risk management and REMS programs continue to evolve in their nature with trends to standardization. However, basic requirements have not changed and companies and health-care professionals need to prepare to institute risk management programs when specified by the FDA or drug manufacturers. In the next section, we discuss the need and implementation of risk management programs for newly approved medicines.

REMS Requirements

Despite all of the problems people have had with REMS, the idea that informational interventions and distributional controls can be used to improve drug safety remains an important concept that remains intact among regulatory authorities. Some drugs that could greatly benefit some people may be deemed safe only if they are approved with some type of risk management tool. Thus, for drug manufacturers, the need to consider under which circumstances a REMS would be needed and how that REMS should be implemented and evaluated is important. It is also clear that even if a REMS is not needed, manufacturers also must consider if a MG is necessary. If required, the manufacturer would also need to know if it would be a labeling requirement (without the need for evaluation) or whether it would need to be evaluated as part of a REMS.

When Is a REMS RiskMAP Needed?

To determine if a new drug will need a REMS RiskMAP, the company must consider the risks posed by the product in light of its benefits. For drugs for serious or life-threatening illnesses, such as cancer and AIDS, there is a great deal of more tolerance for personal risk than for drugs used for cosmetic purposes, such as for acne or head lice. However, even for serious drugs, when the risk posed may be prevented, a REMS RiskMAP will need to be seriously considered.

The starting point for any REMS RiskMAP is as complete knowledge as possible of the product's safety hazards. Some hazards may be suspected and subjected to continuing postmarketing surveillance. There is always a debate regarding which signals denote real risks and which denote false-positives. Following the precautionary principle, it is likely that even suspected risks will be the subject of some risk intervention, even if it means only notifying prescribers of its possibility. The target product profile or proposed PI is likely to serve as the best source of information about the known or suspected risks of the product and the best basis for risk minimization planning.

The FDA suggests there are three broad considerations for determining if a REMS RiskMAP is needed:

1. The nature of risks versus benefits (risk tolerance issues such as population affected, alternative therapy available, and reversibility of adverse events)
2. Preventability of the adverse event
3. The probability of benefit or success of the risk minimization intervention

Drugs that have serious or life-threatening contraindications, warnings, precautions, or adverse effects are the most likely candidates for a REMS RiskMAP. Patient behaviors that can mitigate risks such as pregnancy prevention, blood tests, overdose/misuse avoidance, awareness, and action related to specific safety signals (e.g., a hypersensitivity reaction, depression, and suicide) make a REMS RiskMAP more appealing. When people other than the patient may be at risk (e.g., a child may use the product inadvertently), a REMS RiskMAP may also be required. The FDA singles out Schedule II drugs, with concerns for misuse, abuse, addiction, diversion, and overdose as likely candidates for a REMS RiskMAP.

Rationale and Justification

The most important aspects of developing a RiskMAP is to understand the risks involved in using the product in question and the factors that might increase or mitigate those risks. The drug development program should provide information on safety and potential adverse reactions of the drug, as well as potential misadventures in using the drug. In addition, clues from similar medications and animal or mutagenicity studies may also indicate potential risks. The sections of the drug label where the risk information is provided may provide a clue as to the overarching goals or objectives for the REMS RiskMAP. Contraindications may be related to patient selection or testing that must occur before the drug is prescribed; precautions may relate to advice about how to use, or not use, the product; and adverse reactions may be related to warning signs that must be monitored by the patient and physician or risk/benefit decisions underlying use of the medication.

Companies must provide a logical rationale for the implementation of a risk management program. The RiskMAP developed must specify this rationale in the background section. Here, the company must enumerate each of the risks to be managed by the program. For each risk, the company must fully characterize the risk severity; the population (or subpopulation) at greatest risks; the extent to which the risk is predictable, preventable, or reversible; and the time course of the risk (if the risk is time limited, continuous, or cumulative).

Content of the Proposed REMS Proposal

The FDA has issued a guidance that delineates the content and format for REMS proposals.[30]

Goals, Objectives, and Tools

The guidance mandates that each plan must specify the overall goals of the risk minimization plan.

All REMS should include a statement of one or more overall goals. A goal is defined as the desired safety-related health outcome or the understanding by patients and/or health-care providers of the serious risks targeted by the use of specified REMS elements. REMS goals should target the achievement of particular health outcomes or knowledge related to known safety risks and should be stated in a way that aims to achieve maximum risk reduction.

The FDA stated that a goal, as the term implies, is a statement of the ideal outcome of a REMS. REMS goals should be associated with pragmatic, specific, and measurable program objectives that result in processes or behaviors leading to achievement of the REMS goals. Objectives can be thought of as intermediate steps to achieving the overall REMS goal. A REMS goal can be associated with more than one objective, depending upon the frequency, type, and severity of the specific risk or risks being minimized. For example, a goal may be the elimination of occurrences of a serious adverse event caused by an interaction of the drug with another drug.

These goals are the desired endpoints for safe product use. For example, if a drug causes birth defects, a reasonable goal would be that no women who are pregnant should be given the drug. A second goal might be that no women should become pregnant while taking the drug. It should be noted that some goals may never be fully met. However, making progress toward meeting the goal, rather than actually achieving the goal, may be an acceptable outcome.

Once the goals have been enumerated, the company can identify a series of objectives for each goal. The objectives should be specific and measurable. They specify the behaviors and processes necessary for the stated goals to be achieved. For example, if the goal is to prevent pregnancy, then an objective may be specified that all women must have a negative pregnancy test performed within 7 days of initiating therapy. Objectives often identify particular people (i.e., patient, pharmacist, physician, allied health professional) responsible for the desired behavior. This aids in the development of a communication plan directed to that individual, which will likely be a core element of the risk management program.

Tools to be Used

Once goals and objectives are specified, the company must select a series of tools designed to intervene and mitigate risks. The FDA specifies three categories of tools. The first category is MG and/or PPI targeted education or outreach. These tools concentrate on the communication of information intended to minimize risk. Generally, information "remedies" are thought to be "weak" interventions in terms of affecting long-term patient behavior. However, they are clearly necessary for patient safety. Patients must be able or recognize and know what to do if a hazardous situation arises (e.g., sign of a drug adverse effect).

The second tool described in the REMS guidance is a communication plan. These tools include a variety of media that carry messages to health-care professionals (e.g., letters, training programs [including continuing education programs, courses, or materials], and public notifications [such as letters to the editor]). In addition, promotional techniques can be used to publicize risk management concerns, including advertisements and sales representatives' distribution of risk minimization information.

Similarly, communications to consumers such as MGs and PPIs may be used. Interestingly, the FDA includes limitation on the use of promotional techniques such as product sampling or direct-to-consumer advertising as a risk minimization tool. However, these latter tools may do more to limit demand for the medication than directly communicate information on how to minimize product risks.

The second category of risk minimization tools is characterized by the FDA as reminder systems. This is a broad category of tools that goes beyond mere information dissemination. Often, they solicit a commitment to engage in the dictates of the risk minimization program. For example, these tools include training or certification programs or physician attestation of capabilities to use the medication safely. They also include patient agreements or acknowledgment forms that seek the patient's commitment to follow dictates for safe drug use. They include specialized product packaging to enhance safety by influencing who may take a medication or providing reminder information at the point of product use. This category also includes distribution channel controls such as limiting the amount of medication in any single prescription or refill of the product and specialized systems or records that limit dispensing unless certain measures have been satisfied (e.g., prescription stickers).

The third category of tools described in the FDA guidance is the "Elements to Assure Safe Use." These are the most controversial aspects of the REMS program. They not only include a variety of interventions that have the ability to control the distribution of marketed drugs but also may inadvertently limit or inhibit distribution to patients who need the medicine. EASU also include training programs for patients and health-care providers.

The guidance describes a number of possible EASUs. For example, health-care providers who prescribe the drug can be limited to those that have particular training or experience, or are specially certified. The REMS could specify that the prescriber attests to their qualifications to prescribe the medicine, or they specify that they have had specific experience or knowledge before the provider is enrolled in a program that allows that provider to prescribe the product.

EASU could limit the locations where a drug is prescribed, such as a certified hospital or pharmacy. Certification could be based on staff training, having certain resources (patient testing apparatus) or stipulating that there is sufficient control to monitor prescribing. This certification may require distribution outlets to agree to limit drug dispensing to certain patients or under certain conditions.

For example, the applicant may be required to ensure that the drug is dispensed only to patients in hospitals that have met certain conditions, that the drug is dispensed only to physicians' offices equipped to treat the potential risks associated with the drug, or that they have certain facilities (e.g., access to medication and equipment necessary to treat a serious allergic reaction).

There also may be behavioral restrictions specified in the EASU. For example, the drug could be limited to be dispensed only to patients with evidence or other documentation of safe-use conditions, such as laboratory test results, or patients meet specified criteria before drug exposure, such as successfully completing an educational program.

System-wide controls can be instituted by a REMS with EASU. Patients may receive the drug only after specified authorization is obtained from a physician and verified by the pharmacy. Examples of authorizations include checking laboratory values and checking for physician qualification (e.g., a program could distribute authorization prescription stickers only to qualified prescribers). Each patient using the drug could be subject to certain monitoring or undergoing prescribed laboratory tests.

Performance-linked access systems are tools intended to limit access to the medication based on the fulfillment of certain criteria. For example, the product may not be made available unless there is an acknowledgment, certification, and enrollment, or appropriate test records are made available. This category of tools would also include limiting prescribing to specially certified health-care practitioners and limiting dispensing to specially certified pharmacies or practitioners or to patients with evidence of fulfilling certain conditions (e.g., negative laboratory test results).

The FDA tool enumeration and characterization is helpful in providing a wide range of options for REMS RiskMAP designers. However, it does not provide a mechanism for determining which tools (or combinations of tools) would be the most appropriate in which circumstances. At this point, there is a good deal of experience with instituting REMS with MGs, communication plans, and EASU. Yet what may work for a particular drug is unclear. Also, the "unintended consequences" of a REMS intervention in terms of limiting access to care and overwarning effects or other "side effects" cannot be fully anticipated. Patients, to be fair, although there have been some evaluations of risk management interventions, have been evaluated (cf., Goldman, 2004).[67] There is an inadequate knowledge base that exists for objectively determining how these tools should be applied. However, there are a broad set of theoretical models that may be applied to characterize the behavioral aspects of product prescribing, dispensing, and utilization. These models may be applied to help determine what mix of tools makes the most sense in terms of influencing safe-use behavior. However, acceptance of the tools must also be considered. It is clear, even at this early stage, that risk management tool implementation may have unintended consequences. Prescribers and dispensers of medicines may find certain tools overly burdensome, offensive, or adverse and may avoid use of the drug because of the risk minimization tools selected. Therefore, the acceptance and the effectiveness of any risk minimization plan must be considered when designing the RiskMAP.

Designing the RiskMAP REMS

Companies must select and justify their choice of tools. In doing so, it behooves a company to develop a conceptual model for how their drugs are going to be used and what "system failures" may lead to product misuse. In addition to relying on a systems analysis, using a behavioral model of product use (i.e., how beliefs, motives, and situational constraints influence how a drug is used) can help a company select a coordinated set of tools and specify core messages that must be communicated or systems that must be implemented to define the elements of their risk management program.

FMEA

A good starting point for developing a model of drug use is to identify the various steps necessary to use a drug properly. Failure mode and effects analysis (FMEA) is a systematic analysis of how failures in any system may occur.[31,32,33b] An FMEA is conducted before the system is implemented. It delineates the steps in a system and identifies potential mistakes that may occur at each step (i.e., potential failure modes). It is a complement to root cause analyses, which are aimed at identifying the source of a system failure once a mistake has occurred. If a drug is already marketed, a root cause analysis should be used to identify problems or concerns based on existing information. If the drug has not been marketed, an FMEA is the best alternative. In addition to listing the steps in using a drug effectively, an effective FMEA identifies corrective actions required to prevent failures and to assure the highest possible system quality.

To undertake an FMEA, the system steps and potential failure modes are identified. Each step may be broken down into subprocesses with each substep in the system being considered as a separate element with the potential for failure. Each of the postulated steps in which a failure might occur is assigned a severity value, a probability that a given effect might occur, and a likelihood value that a user may detect (and correct) the problem. Recommended actions (i.e., tool interventions) are developed to reduce the probability and (most importantly) severity of harm, with priority given to the highest risk.

Although developed as a method to improve product quality, an FMEA can only be as good as the quality of the system description. Specifying steps at too broad a level of specificity can miss important elements. For example, it is often assumed that dispensing errors are due to poor handwriting by physicians. However, a system analysis for a medication error problem found that many physicians clearly wrote the drug name on the prescription and the pharmacist accurately dispensed what the physician had written. The problem was that physicians recalled the incorrect drug name from memory when they wrote the prescription. An FMEA that did not specify the need for the physician to recall the correct drug name from memory would have missed an important source of error.

In addition, to specify the subprocesses, it is necessary to understand the system from the perspective of the individuals performing the tasks involved. It is well established that the relationship between knowledge and behavior is not direct or simple. We often know what we should do, but fail to behave in a fashion consistent with that knowledge. To develop a predictive model, it is necessary to understand (1) the full set of beliefs underlying behavioral intentions, (2) the motivations that support or stand in the way of exhibiting desired behavior, and (3) the environmental conditions that facilitate or place barriers to compliance.

There are a variety of psychological and health behavior models that can be used to organize these influences. Some models may help to improve the processing of the presented information, for example, by improving participants' involvement (personal relevance) or competency (self-efficacy) with the information or advocated behavior. Some models may help to understand the processes underlying the choice among alternative courses of behavior (behavioral decision making). Some models may help to structure advocated behavior into a series of stages, permitting a series of messages that seek to move respondents through a necessary series of stages in order to attain behavioral compliance (stage models or precaution adoption). Some models seek to motivate compliance through emotion (fear appeals or positive affect) or through highlighting desired outcomes (approach or avoidance goals).

Which model to use depends on the particular problem (objective) addressed. If we advocate complex behaviors, such as avoiding drug dependency, it may be necessary to move respondents through a series of stages in order to overcome situational barriers. If we advocate simpler behaviors, such as standing upright when taking tablets, providing a strong, even emotional, rationale for compliance and developing a reminder system might provide the best model to influence behavior. Diagnosing the behavioral problem and selecting (or custom building) the correct behavioral model can provide a clear method for design of the risk management plan.

Because we are dealing with programs that are expected to reach and influence the vast majority of participants, it may be difficult to anticipate the full range of issues influencing the behavior of all of the patients and health-care professionals. Identifying particular at-risk segments can also help to design program interventions targeted at particular failure modes for a specified group of individuals.

Communication Tools: Message, Design, and Distribution

If our main method of influencing behavior is an informational approach, there is still a variety of tools for interventions that may be used to influence patient behavior. For purposes of communication, these tools may be cataloged by the format and media used to communicate the information. In this chapter, the focus will be on communication tools used to deliver information to patients. Here, we focus on patient communication tools with a full knowledge that there are additional tools used to communicate relevant information to physicians, pharmacists, and allied health professionals, as forcing functions that guide or direct behavioral compliance. These forcing functions include programs that certify prescribers, dispensers, or patients. They may also require patients to obtain certain tests prior to refill authorization; other systems may also be developed to help improve patient compliance or avoid noncompliance.

To develop an acceptable patient communication plan (i.e., selecting an optimal set of tools), it is important to consider the communication objectives (COs) and the recommended behaviors necessary for safe use of the medication. The COs are the key messages included in a risk communication document (such as an MG, CMI, or advertising patient brochure) that outlines what patients must know to use the drug safely. The recommended behaviors are actions the patient must undertake to use the medicine properly (such as avoiding contraindicated drugs or monitoring their bodily state for signs of possible side effects).

Table 9.1 Patient Communication Vehicles

Tool	*Distribution*	*Purpose*
Brochure	Physician	General information
Patient package insert	Package or pharmacist	Risk communication
Medication guide or CMI	Package	Risk communication and methods of avoidance
Informed consent	Physician	Acknowledgement of risks
Warning stickers	Package	Risk "signal"
Wallet card	Starter kit	Reminder
Stickers for medication vial	Pharmacist on medication vial	Reminder
Patient agreement or contract	Physician	Behavioral commitment
Decision aid	Physician	Choice of therapy
Video tape or CD	Physician or starter kit	Persuasion or choice of therapy
Recurring interventions (telephone calls)	Telephone	Behavioral maintenance

Obviously, for simpler behaviors, brief communication tools may be indicated. For more complex behaviors, where more explanation is needed, longer forms and multiple interventions may be necessary. Although all tools have a general purpose to inform, various tools have different advantages and disadvantages. Tools may have one or more purposes, with certain tools better suited for different functions. Table 9.1 shows a set of sample tools and their communications function.

Perhaps, even more important than form, the content of the patient communication requires careful planning and an understanding of the target audience. For prescription drugs, the product label (or package insert written for health professionals) summarizes the scientific basis of product approval and lists the conditions under which the drug may be used safely and effectively. Under the Food, Drug, and Cosmetic Act, virtually all communications about the product provided by the manufacturer are characterized as labeling and must be consistent with the PI to avoid misbranding charges. Thus, the PI serves as the basis for the content of all patient communications.

Based on the PI, one can draft a series of COs/communicator goals describing the educational objectives/goals of patient information. By reviewing these objectives and the general purpose of the communication, a tool, or a series of tools, to match the function can be selected. For example, if the purpose of a communication is to help a consumer decide whether to take a medicine or to select an alternative form of therapy, then the communication tool must function as a decision aid that provides the advantages and disadvantages of various therapy alternatives. However, if the function of the communication is to simply remind the patient of a particular behavior to avoid (e.g., not to use if pregnant), then a simple warning message may be placed on the package (perhaps backed up with a symbol that reminds the patient not to use if pregnant).

Moderate-length patient communication tools (e.g., PPIs or MGs) tend to follow a general format that (at least in theory) matches the general "script" (i.e., cognitive or mental model) of how a patient would seek to learn about a new medication. The PMI program discussed earlier may change these headings; however, current MG regulations specify these six topic headers that are required for MGs:

1. What is the most important information I should know?
2. What is the name of the "drug"?
3. Who should not take the "drug"?
4. How should I take the "drug"?
5. What should I avoid while taking the "drug"?
6. What are the possible or reasonably likely side effects of the "drug"?

Under the first heading (the most important information), key risk management messages are provided. This placement and heading provide explicit emphasis to help patients recognize the most important information for them to learn about the medication. It also provides an intellectual scaffold for patients to store additional information about the drug, and it permits reinforcement and redundancy within the document. A variety of graphic (e.g., typeface, bolding) and language devices (e.g., headers, core concepts) can help structure the document to provide signals (i.e., methods to emphasize the importance of certain sections) that improve the communication of essential information to patients or health-care providers.[33a] At the same time, language can be simplified and extraneous information can be deleted (so-called seductive details that provide interesting but nonessential information regarding risk management). This combination of drafting techniques reduces the cognitive load and increases the ease of processing while focusing readers on the most important information.

In addition to content based on the drug product's risks, benefits, and usage directions, additional information can educate patients and stimulate behavioral compliance. However, fully explaining every possible risk in terms of its causation (i.e., physiological pathway), significance (e.g., severity), likelihood (probability of occurrence), and means of control or avoidance would lead to a very long and arduous document. Such a document would be too long and complex for an average reader to use. Rather, explanatory language must be used selectively. It should be based on the readers' existing knowledge and beliefs and communicate information that is consistent with the COs for the document.

Morgan et al.[34] advocate a mental-models approach to risk communication in which the mental schema of product experts is compared to the mental schema of laypersons.[9,10] Communications are drafted to correct misconceptions of laypersons and increase awareness of the less obvious, but important, information. Using a mental-models approach may help us understand which aspects of the developed document are successful and which messages should be emphasized in further interventions. However, such drafting communications based on a mental-models approach must be guided by the COs for that particular product, because experts are likely to have much more complete schema for prescription medication and because much of their knowledge is irrelevant to patients' choices and product use.

Need to Influence Behavior

There is an old expression, "it's easier to sell soap than brotherhood." Selling soap requires both convincing people that one brand is superior to another and controlling the sales environment so that the promoted brand is widely available and well regarded. Selling brotherhood requires a more extensive selling process. For example, we must clearly define what we mean, convince the audience that a problem exists, suggest solutions perceived as acceptable, demonstrate that such solutions can be effective and implemented by the respondent, provide people with information and training necessary for implementing the proposed solution (e.g., use of the product), and convince the respondent that any perceived barriers or negative impacts can be overcome or negated.

This expression is meaningful in its application to prescription drug usage behavior because of the range in complexity in the type of behaviors necessary to comply with safe usage directions. For example, a patient may comply with dosing instructions by simply taking one tablet by mouth each day. Risk avoidance sometimes may be in the form of a fairly simple behavior. For instance, the risk management plan for alendronate (Fosamax) sought to inform patients who are informed to stand upright for one-half hour after ingestion in order to avoid side effects affecting the esophagus.

For other drugs, however, compliance may require a more complex set of behaviors. For example, for certain cholesterol-lowering drugs, patients are told to undertake liver function tests prior to treatment, after 12 weeks of treatment, following any elevation of dose, and periodically (e. g., semiannually) thereafter. Obtaining a liver function test may require complex problem solving for the patient. He or she may need to find a laboratory acceptable to the patient's medical insurance company and may need to fast for 12 h before undertaking the test, depending on what specific tests the physician orders. The patient also may need to make an appointment and travel to the testing facility. Having to repeat this behavior over many years adds to the behavioral complexity as the patient's situation may change and new adaptations may be necessary.

Problem recognition may be an issue for some drugs where patients should look for the warning signs of serious side effects. For example, some people who have taken metformin (Glucophage) for diabetes have developed a serious condition called lactic acidosis. Lactic acidosis is caused by a buildup of lactic acid in the blood and can be fatal. Patients are told to look for signs of lactic acidosis and report them immediately to their physician. Such signs include the following:

Feeling very weak, tired, or uncomfortable
Having an unusual muscle pain
Having trouble breathing
Having an unusual or unexpected stomach discomfort
Feeling cold
Feeling dizzy or lightheaded
Developing suddenly a slow or irregular heartbeat

Because these symptoms also occur frequently in people who are not taking the medication and who do not have lactic acidosis, detecting and interpreting these above signs may be complicated. Patients must determine that (1) they have the indicated symptom, (2) the symptom is caused by a medical problem, and (3) the symptom (or constellation of symptoms) is a sign of lactic acidosis.

The particular set of skills and resources necessary to obtain a liver function test differ considerably from the problem-solving skills necessary to determine whether to ask the doctor about various common symptoms. Interventions to help patients comply with these varying instructions would similarly require a vastly different set of information.

Distribution and Behavioral Control Systems

While much of what we hope to accomplish in managing pharmaceutical risks may be realized through carefully designed communications, information dissemination may not be sufficient to force lead to behavior change. Often, information is viewed as a weak intervention. For information to have an impact, it must be received, read, understood, motivational, persuasive, remembered, and implemented for behavior change to be effective. Furthermore, behavior maintenance means that information must be effective over the long term, often for many years. Although voluntary adaptations are viewed as the most positive method of influencing health behavior, it may also be necessary to institute distribution or behavioral control systems that influence risk avoidance behavior.

A distribution system is necessary for a drug to be delivered to the patient. For all prescription drugs, it is necessary for the physician to order a prescription (in writing or orally) and a pharmacist to dispense the drug. Certain drugs, such as scheduled medicines, also require limits on refills and additional record keeping. For certain risk management programs, there have been additional controls developed to minimize risky behaviors. For example, for Clozaril (clozapine) (where certain blood disorders may result from taking the drug), patients are required to obtain monthly blood tests (weekly, biweekly, and monthly after a year) that show the drug is not having an undesirable effect. Using this method, the risk of blood dyscrasia has minimized, permitting a useful drug to remain on the market.

Another example of a distribution control system is a verification sticker program as used by certain acne drugs (most notably Accutane [isotretinoin]). In this instance, the drug may have important adverse consequences (such as causing birth defects if taken during pregnancy). A woman taking Accutane must have a monthly test to demonstrate that she is not pregnant. The test results are forwarded to a centralized system. The pharmacist must access this system to verify that the patient is not pregnant prior to dispensing the prescription.

Other distribution control systems, such as obtaining a prescription for the medication only from a physician who has been certified to prescribe the medicine or providing medication only to a patient who has been certified to receive the prescription, have been suggested or implemented by various companies. The logic undermining such designs is derived from systems theory, which has been used by various industries (such as the aircraft industry) to design safety into the systems used.

Systems theory relies on a number of design elements to force an individual to behave in a prescribed fashion. According to the systems theory, any activity may be conceived as a system that requires actions to occur for the activity to be accomplished. For example, the issuance of a prescription requires the doctor's diagnosis of an illness (or prescription of a drug to prevent an illness), the choice of a medication (along with dosage and directions), the delivery of the prescription to a patient (or surrogate), the delivery of the prescription to a pharmacy, the review and checking of the prescription by pharmacy staff, the retrieval of the medication from storage, the counting of tablets, the labeling of the vial, the temporary storage of the prescription, and the dispensing of the prescription to the patient (or surrogate). There may (and should) be additional stages in this model, such as counseling of patients by physicians and pharmacists, information collection and retrieval, administrative activities for reimbursement, compliance with various laws and regulations, and additional risk management activities. However, even this simplified system requires many different activities, and mistakes may occur at many different points. To prevent such errors, we may institute various procedures, controls, or design changes. For example, to prevent taking the wrong bottle off the shelf, we may color-code bottles, use bar codes that must be checked, or institute a mandatory checklist of actions to prevent dispensing the wrong medication. There are a number of forcing functions (design features that build in safety, such as having drug names be printed in a certain size, or constitute a certain percentage of the front display panel) and redundancies (such as having the drug name on multiple places on the bottle of medicine) that help design safety. At the heart of systems theory is the logic that such procedures must be followed every time an activity is undertaken, or the resulting action cannot take place.

Evaluation

An important contribution of the FDA guidance on risk management that should not be overlooked is the need to fully evaluate the impact of both the entire risk management program and the individual tools intended to control risks.

As in the drug development program itself, three types of evaluation should be considered. First, in an effort to utilize the best possible tool or set of tools, manufacturers should consider developmental testing. Levels of evaluation should occur. First, the test of individual tools can be pilot tested. For example, using focus groups of potential audience members (people taking the target drug) can be used to discuss the tool and to review early prototypes. For example, in an effort to communicate the risks of opioid overdose to drug users, Morris et al.[35f] conducted focus group interviews with rural drug abusers in three locations. They tested the concept, design, and early drafts of patient information materials. The materials were redesigned based on this feedback to more narrowly focus on the needs, interests, and desired information content as well as adapt the language to meet users' style of communication, perhaps as part of the development process. For example, implementing comprehension tests early (i.e., before the drug is distributed) may aid in the design of impactful communications. Second, a series of interventions may be instituted in a field test in the form of a clinical trial in which various distribution sites are randomized to deliver various combinations of interventions. By comparing the results between the sites, the value of various interventions may be evaluated. However, care must be taken to ensure sufficient power to determine differences among sites and to avoid confounding sites with intervention biases.

Third, the FDA proposed that, as required by legislation, all REMS RiskMAPs must be fully evaluated once implemented. The 1.5-, 3-, and 7-year evaluation process is legally mandated. The FDA proposes alternate ways to evaluate the effects of a REMS RiskMAP depending on the goal of the particular program. If side effect reduction is a goal, analysis of spontaneously reported adverse drug events might be the primary method of evaluation. An evaluation might include analysis using administrative databases or an active surveillance using patient surveys. As every evaluation and method has problems and limitations, it may be necessary to use multiple; the FDA suggests incorporation of two different methods and use of well-defined and validated measures for assessing the effect to improve the reliability.

Ideally, intervention effectiveness should be evaluated based on ability to improve actual health outcomes. For example, if the goal of a REMS is to decrease cases of jaundice, liver disease, and/or liver failures, having a tracking study that enumerates these cases over time would serve as a valid evaluation method. However, these endpoints may be rare and would require following up large numbers of patients for a long period of time. A quicker assessment of the value of the REMS RiskMAP could be obtained by monitoring surrogates (for example, changes in laboratory markers that are known to precede the actual health outcome, as, for example, in the previous case, which are increases in the alanine aminotransferase/aspartate aminotransferase). A less than optimum but useful evaluation could involve ascertainment of process measures (for example, the frequency of testing for liver enzyme elevations). A third evaluation criterion would be testing for comprehension, knowledge, and attitude among patients, prescribers, and pharmacists about the risks and consequences of the drug.

The first type of evaluation for REMS with side effect avoidance goals is often the careful review of spontaneous reports of adverse drug events and changes in number and kind of such reports. However, there are multiple biases that exist in the determination of which events are reported, so this analysis is merely the first step in the evaluation. In the case of Accutane, a decrease in pregnancies after the institution of the SMART program led to the conclusion that the program was ineffective and iPLEDGE was instituted. However, another interpretation is that the institution of SMART led to an increase *reporting* of pregnancies (rather than an increase in pregnancies itself). This could mean that SMART was effective in reducing the actual number of pregnancies; however, the publicity surrounding SMART increased spontaneous reporting and the perception that the program did not work.

A second type of strict risk management program can require all individuals receiving the drug to be followed for appropriateness of treatment and monitoring and/or specific outcomes under conditions of a registry. However, more broadly, the term, *registry*, means only a cohort formed on the basis of all individuals included possessing some attribute in common, for example, exposure to the drug in question. This could be a sample of individuals followed for specific monitoring and/or outcomes such as compliance with laboratory monitoring and/or the effectiveness of that monitoring in preventing one or more clinical adverse events. Although, ideally, one would wish to follow all individuals exposed, in all likelihood, logistics will dictate that only a percentage of these individuals can be followed for the occurrence of health outcomes, surrogates, process measures, or comprehension. A registry is commonly composed of willing individuals who have received the drug or have the underlying disease for which the drug may be prescribed.

Large-linked databases of health-care claims, such as outpatient visits, inpatient visits, pharmacy fills, and laboratory tests and results, have proven valuable both in the assessment of the magnitude of risks and for monitoring the effectiveness of specific interventions to decrease risk. These administrative databases can be used to answer routine queries on the occurrence of contraindicated coprescribing or overdosing, appropriate monitoring, and associations between prescribing of selected drugs and specific events.[1] Note that observed associations do not imply causality, but can add to the understanding of the effectiveness of the REMS RiskMAP.

The third type of evaluation method involves active surveillance. This methodology would be very expensive for rare outcome events, but surveys of health-care practitioners or patients could provide some information about the rate of more common events. In addition, the effectiveness of the REMS RiskMAP into the changing knowledge, attitudes, and practices could be ascertained through such surveys.

When it is not clear which invention(s) would be most effective, it may be worthwhile to use an experimental design comparing different interventions. This interventional design could be followed either through administrative databases or actively with surveys.

Based on the evaluation of the REMS RiskMAP, it may become apparent that the REMS intervention(s) need to be modified to increase their effectiveness. As in Accutane, increasing restrictions can be added to limit the distribution of the drug to (hopefully) only those for whom the medication is medically necessary. Of course, these increasing burdens can backfire and restrict the distribution to whom it would be indicated. On the other hand, evaluations or additional clinical studies that investigate the suspected risks of the medicine can show that existing restrictions are unnecessary. These evaluations can result in decreased burdens. For example, REMS restrictions for Avandia (rosiglitazone) were reduced following the new information regarding the cardiovascular risk of the medicine. Results from the Rosiglitazone

Evaluated for Cardiovascular Outcomes and Regulation of Glycemia in Diabetes clinical trial showed no elevated risk of heart attack or death in patients being treated with Avandia when compared to standard-of-care diabetes drugs. REMS restrictions were instituted in 2007 following a signal of increased risk of heart attacks that was found in a meta-analysis of clinical trials. The Avandia REMS was modified to remove the requirement that health-care professionals, pharmacists, and patients had to enroll in the rosiglitazone REMS program to prescribe, dispense, or receive rosiglitazone medicines (in the REMS program, patients were not able to receive rosiglitazone through their regular pharmacy without enrolling in a restricted distribution program).[36]

Conclusion interventions if not successful. Few interventions implemented in the past have been rigorously evaluated. Those that have been evaluated have too often shown that for all their good intentions, the effect was less than desired. For example, PI requirements for liver enzyme monitoring are not well followed, even in the face of major media coverage of the risks of hepatic failure (Graham et al.).[2] Risk management programs must eventually be able to show that they decrease or mitigate the likelihood of adverse events.

Risk management arose in an era of "safety at any cost." The "risks" of risk management were not considered. We have now come to learn that there are costs to any risk management system (i.e., financial, social, and personal and overall population health). REMS can have great benefits to improving the safe use of drugs, but it may also have harm in restricting access to needed medicines.

The current emphasis on risk management appears to be on standardization. Making a risk management system "workable" and integrating it into existing prescribing, dispensing, and utilization process is a laudable goal. Making sure that patients receive a consistent message also has a merit. However, these goals, which seem prominent in FDA's thinking, are pale in comparison with the goal of improving overall public health. Developing REMS interventions that have a maximized risk/benefit ratio (by gaining the best possible benefits and with the least possible burdens and side effects) would appear to be a more laudable goal. Federal focus on how to achieve this goal seems an important priority.

Regardless of the evaluation study, interventions need to be assessed not only on their effectiveness of preventing serious adverse events but also on their cost and burden on the health-care system. Too rigorous an intervention may result in many additional visits, tests, and other forms of monitoring. This, in turn, may result in increased mistakes due to increased tasks. Increased costs may make the new therapy of less value than other less effective therapies and/or raise patient privacy concerns. Decreased benefits that follow from risk management interventions that are too stringent can result from decreased patient compliance and decreased drug access to patients that would benefit from that particular drug therapy.

Conclusion

In conclusion, risk management is a new and evolving discipline. It is difficult to argue that drugs should not be provided to patients in a manner that minimizes potential hazards. The FDA has advanced the public health by fostering greater attention over the discovery, quantification, and management of risks. However, any policy that results in new activities to control one set of hazards may result in creating new, unexpected hazards. Thus, continuing to evaluate not only the hazards of drugs but also the interventions intended to control these hazards is essential to assure that the benefits of a RiskMAP will, itself, outweigh its risks.

References

1. Chan KA, Davis RL, Gunter MJ et al. *The HMO Research Network in Pharmacoepidemiology*, 4th edn., Strom BL (ed.), John Wiley & Sons, Ltd., 2005, pp. 261–269.
2. Graham DJ, Drinkard CR, Shatin D, Tsong Y, Burgess MJ. Liver enzyme monitoring in patients treated with troglitazone. *JAMA*, 2001, 286, 831–833.
3. Institute of Medicine. *To Err is Human: Building a Safer Health System*. National Academy Press, Washington, DC, 1999.
4. Food and Drug Administration, Morgan MG, Fischhoff B, Bostrom A, Atman CJ. *Risk Communication: A Mental Models Approach*. Cambridge University Press, Cambridge, U.K., 2002. Managing the risks from medical product use creating a risk management framework: Report to the FDA Commissioner from the Task Force on Risk Management. May 1999. Available at: http://www.fda.gov/downloads/safety/safetyofspecificproducts/ucm180520.pdf. Accessed on March 19, 2014.
5. U.S. Food and Drug Administration. Guidance: Premarketing risk assessment. Available at: http://www.fda.gov/downloads/RegulatoryInformation/Guidances/UCM126958.pdf, March 2005. Last accessed December 6, 2015.
6. U.S. Food and Drug Administration. Guidance: Development and use of risk minimization action plans. Available at: http://www.fda.gov/downloads/RegulatoryInformation/Guidances/UCM126830.pdf, March 2005. Last accessed December 6, 2015.
7. U.S. Food and Drug Administration. Guidance: Good pharmacovigilance practices and pharmacoepidemiologic assessment. Available at: http://www.fda.gov/downloads/RegulatoryInformation/Guidances/UCM126834.pdf, March 2005. Last accessed December 6, 2015.
8. Public Law 110-85. Food and Drug Administration Amendments Act of 2007. 2007. Available at: http://www.gpo.gov/fdsys/pkg/PLAW-110publ85/pdf/PLAW-110publ85.pdf. Accessed on March 17, 2014.
9. Public Law 104-180. Agriculture, Rural Development, Food and Drug Administration, and Related Agencies Appropriations Act, 1997. August 6, 1996. TITLE VI. Available at: http://www.talkaboutrx.org/documents/Public_Law_104–180.pdf, Accessed on March 14, 2014.
10. Federal Register of December 1, 1998 (63 FR 66378). Final Rule: "Prescription Drug Product Labeling; Medication Guide Requirements". Effective June 1, 1999. Available at: http://www.gpo.gov/fdsys/pkg/FR-1998–12–01/pdf/98–31627.pdf. Accessed on March 14, 2014.
11. Toigo T. Standardizing and Evaluating Risk Evaluation and Mitigation Strategies (REMS) Public Meeting. July 25–26, 2013. Available at: http://www.fda.gov/downloads/forindustry/userfees/prescriptiondruguserfee/ucm361076.pdf. Accessed on March 14, 2014.
12. U.S. Food and Drug Administration. Guidance: Medication guides—Distribution requirements and inclusion in risk evaluation and mitigation strategies (REMS). November 2011. Available at: http://www.fda.gov/downloads/Drugs/.../Guidances/UCM244570.pdf. Accessed on March 17, 2014.
13. U.S. Food and Drug Administration. Medication guides. Available at: http://www.fda.gov/Drugs/DrugSafety/ucm085729.htm. Last updated November 3, 2015. Last accessed December 6, 2015.
14. U.S. Food and Drug Administration. Risk evaluation and mitigation strategy assessments: Social science methodologies to assess goals related to knowledge. Issue Paper. June 2012. Available at: http://www.fda.gov/downloads/Drugs/NewsEvents/UCM301966.pdf. Accessed on March 17, 2014.
15. Department of Health and Human Services Office of Inspector General. FDA lacks comprehensive data to determine whether risk evaluation and mitigation strategies improve drug safety. February 2013. Available at: https://oig.hhs.gov/oei/reports/oei-04–11–00510.pdf. Accessed on March 14, 2014.
16. Morris LA, Whitcup M, LaMattina K. Failure to communicate: Medication guide or memory? *Drug Information Journal*, 2011, 45, 775–786.
17. U.S. Food and Drug Administration. Guidance for industry label comprehension studies for nonprescription drug products. August 2010. Available at: http://www.fda.gov/downloads/Drugs/GuidanceComplianceRegulatoryInformation/Guidances/UCM143834.pdf. Accessed on March 15, 2014.
18. European Union. Guideline on the readability of the labeling and package leaflet of medicinal products for human use. Revision 1, January 12, 2009. Available at: http://ec.europa.eu/health/files/eudralex/vol-2/c/2009_01_12_readability_guideline_final_en.pdf. Accessed on March 15, 2014.

19. iPLEDGE. About iPLEDGE. (n.d.) Available at: https://www.ipledgeprogram.com/AboutiPLEDGE.aspx. Last accessed December 6, 2015.
20. U.S. Food and Drug Administration. REMS integration initiative. Available at: http://www.fda.gov/ForIndustry/UserFees/PrescriptionDrugUserFee/ucm350852.htm. Last updated December 1, 2015. Last accessed December 6, 2015.
21. U.S. Food and Drug Administration. Extended-release (er) and long-acting (la) opioid analgesics risk evaluation and mitigation strategy (REMS). 2013. Available at: http://www.fda.gov/downloads/drugs/drugsafety/postmarketdrugsafetyinformationforpatientsandproviders/ucm311290.pdf. Accessed on March 15, 2014.
22. Wolfe S. Testimony of Sidney Wolfe M.D., Health Research Group of Public Citizen, to FDA Drug Safety and Risk Management Advisory Committee on the Adequacy of Lotronex (alosetron) REMS. July 10, 2013. Available at: http://www.citizen.org/documents/2141.pdf. Accessed on March 17, 2014.
23. La Ponte N, Chen A, Hammill B, DeLong E, Dramer J, Califf R. Evaluation of the dofetilide risk-management program. *American Heart Journal*, November 2003, 146(5), 894–901.
24. Gibbons Rl, Brown C, Hcur K, Marcus S, Bhaumik D, Erkens J, Herings R, Mann J. Early evidence on the effects of regulators' suicidality warnings on SSRI prescriptions and suicide in children and adolescents. *American Journal of Psychiatry*, 2007, 164, 1356–1363.
25. Keystone Group. Action plan for the provision of useful prescription medicine information. December 1996. Available at: http://www.fda.gov/downloads/aboutfda/centersoffices/officeofmedicalproductsandtobacco/cder/reportsbudgets/ucm163793.pdf. Accessed on March 17, 2014.
26. Svarstad B, Mount J, Tabak E. Expert and consumer evaluation of patient medication leaflets provided in U.S. pharmacies. *Journal of American Pharmacological Association*, 2005, 45, 443–451.
27. Kimberlin C, Winterstein A. Expert and Consumer Evaluation of Consumer Medication Information-2008, Report to the Food and Drug Administration. 2008. Available at: http://www.fda.gov/downloads/AboutFDA/CentersOffices/CDER/ReportsBudgets/UCM163783.pdf. Accessed on March 15, 2014.
28. Pearson B, Araojo R, Hinton D. Essential medication information for patients: Ensuring access. *Therapeutic Innovation and Regulatory Science*, 2014, 48(2), 162–164.
29. Traynor K. FDA Backs Manufacturer-Produced Patient Information. AJHP News. 2014;71(3):176–177. Available at: http://www.ashp.org/menu/News/PharmacyNews/NewsArticle.aspx?id=4004. Last accessed December 6, 2015.
30. Format and Content of Proposed Risk Evaluation and Mitigation Strategies (REMS). REMS assessments, and proposed REMS modifications. September, 2009. Available at: http://www.fda.gov/downloads/Drugs/Guidances/UCM184128.pdf. Accessed on March 17, 2014.
31. Stamatis D. *Failure Mode and Effect Analysis: FMEA from Theory to Execution*. Quality Press, Milwaukee, WI, 2003.
32. U.S. Food and Drug Administration. Guidance for industry safety considerations for product design to minimize medication errors. December 2012. Available at: http://www.fda.gov/downloads/Drugs/GuidanceComplianceRegulatoryInformation/Guidances/UCM331810.pdf. Accessed on March 17, 2014.
33. (a) Morris LA, Aikin KJ. The "pharmacokinetics" of patient communications. *Drug Information Journal*, 2001, 36(2), 509–527; (b) Stamatis DH. *Failure Mode and Effects Analysis*. American Society for Quality, Milwaukee, WI, 1995.
34. Morgan MG, Fischhoff B, Bostrom A, Atman CJ. *Risk Communication: A Mental Models Approach*. Cambridge University Press, Cambridge, U.K., 2002.
35. (a) Morris LA, Aikin K. The "pharmacokinetics" of patient communications. *Drug Information Journal*, 2001, 36(2), 509–527; (b) Stamatis DH. *Failure Mode and Effects Analysis*. American Society for Quality, Milwaukee, WI, 1995; (c) U.S. Food and Drug Administration. Guidance: Premarketing risk assessment. 2005. Available at: http://www.fda.gov/cder/guidance/6357fnl.htm. Accessed on March 2005; (d) U.S. Food and Drug Administration. Guidance: Development and use of risk minimization action plans. 2005. Available at: http://www.fda.gov/ohrms/dockets/ac/05/briefing/2005-4136b1_03_Risk%20Minimization%20Action%20Plans.pdf.

Accessed on March 2005; (e) U.S. Food and Drug Administration. Guidance: Good pharmacovigilance practices and pharmacoepidemiologic assessment. 2005. Available at: http://www.fda.gov/downloads/regulatoryinformation/guidances/ucm126834.pdf. Accessed on March 2005; (f) Morris LA, Sandstrom L, Coplan P. The role of qualitative research in patient comprehension testing for product labels and medication guides. *Journal of Patient Compliance*, 2012, 1(1), 53–56.

36. U.S. Food and Drug Administration. FDA requires removal of certain restrictions on the diabetes drug Avandia. 2013. Available at: http://www.fda.gov/NewsEvents/Newsroom/PressAnnouncements/ucm376516.htm. Accessed on March 16, 2014.

Chapter 10

Drug Shortages

Anna Gu, Dhamil Patel, and Rajesh Nayak

Contents

Introduction

Drug shortage in the United States is defined as "a situation in which the total supply of all clinically interchangeable versions of an FDA-regulated drug is inadequate to meet the current or projected demand at the user level."[1] A term rarely encountered decades ago, it was not until recent years that the magnitude and impact of drug shortage has progressed to critical levels. While the annual list of new drug shortages remained fairly stable prior to 2005, a rapid, steady increase has been observed over the second half of the past decade. In 2010, there were 211 newly reported drug shortages, tripling the amount in 2006, with almost 75% being sterile injectables.[2] The shortage is seen in all health-care practice settings and affects nearly all drug classes, with critical therapeutic areas such as oncology and antimicrobials being affected the most.[2] Largely due to government efforts, the past few years saw a declining trend of new shortages—after the number peaked in 2011 (251 new shortages), it dropped to 117 in 2012.[3] However, since shortage of a particular drug typically persists for an extended period of time, the actual number of shortages (new plus existing) is still higher. More than 300 shortages remained active at the end of 2012.[3] The current chapter discusses the causes and impact of drug shortages, policies, plans and actions undertaken by stakeholders, and proposed actions.

Causes of Drug Shortages

Quality Problems and Raw Material Issues

The causes of drug shortages are complicated and rooted in every phase of a drug's life cycle. A number of factors contribute to the shortage, ranging from shortage of raw materials, corporate affairs (pharmaceutical mergers and acquisitions, decisions based on projected earnings), and regulatory and legislative factors to labor disruption. It is worth noting that approximately 27% of the shortages remain unexplained.[4] Each factor is explained in detail in the following texts.

Recently, the U.S. FDA found that manufacturer quality problems (e.g., impurities, microbial contamination, and chemical instability) were the most common cause of drug shortages, contributing to nearly 46% of all drug shortages in 2011.[5] It is notable that currently, eighty percent of the raw materials comes from foreign markets, which imposes challenges to quality control of the raw materials as practiced in the United States.[6] For example, the market for Chinese active pharmaceutical ingredients (APIs) was reduced by nearly 50% in 2010, partly attributable to concerns over quality issues with Chinese APIs, exemplified by heparin contamination in 2008.[7] The shortages can be especially problematic when a major or sole-source supplier ceases production of raw materials, affecting all of the producers of a finished product.[8]

Corporate Decisions, Mergers, and Acquisition

A number of factors can lead to manufacturer's decision to discontinue the production of certain drugs. These may include discontinuing APIs due to increased capital investment required to meet FDA's quality requirements and compliance guidelines, diminishing demand, and dropping margins and profitability, for liability reasons, to utilize resources elsewhere. For example, GlaxoSmithKline recalled its Lymerix vaccine off the market due to diminishing demand and increasing consumer criticism.[9] Nearly 20% of injectable drug shortages were consequences of product discontinuation. Unfortunately, manufacturers are not obligated to inform FDA about product discontinuation plans unless their product is the only medication to treat a life-threatening condition or debilitating disease. In addition, there is no legal requirement for a firm to continue producing any drug, even one that is deemed medically necessary.[3] Consolidations and mergers among manufacturers can result in decisions to consolidate product lines or decisions to discontinue the manufacture of certain drugs, particularly if companies have two similar products.

Regulatory Issues, Noncompliance with Current Good Manufacturing Practices

Another significant contributor to drug shortages results from regulatory barriers and ambiguities, including the lack of sufficient communications between the FDA and manufacturers. Specific cases include a lengthy period for FDA review of Abbreviated New Drug Applications and supplemental applications, which are necessary steps for a change in source for APIs and change in manufacturing processes. Some manufacturers view the process of completing a New Drug Application to be costly, lengthy, and complicated, and this has been a disincentive for entering the largest pharmaceutical market in the world.

The FDA requires manufacturers to comply with the current good manufacturing practice (cGMP) guidelines. Although the cGMP requirements were established to be flexible in order to allow each manufacturer to use individualized approaches, the cGMP framework has evolved over time. The shortage of immune globulin intravenous pentelate, an injectable drug for enhancing the immune system, resulted from a manufacturer's failure to meet regulatory standards. Arguably, manufacturers that are in compliance and produce the same drug tend to operate close to their production capacity and are often unable to meet greater demand.[10]

Unexpected Increases in Demand and Shift in Clinical Practice

Occasionally, drug shortages stem from an unexpected rise in demand that exceeds production capacity. This may occur when treatment patterns change in response to new clinical guidelines, when a significant disease outbreak occurs, or when a new indication is approved for an existing drug product. A typical example is the rapid disruption of the regular supply chain due to a rare disease outbreak toward the end of the last decade. In 2009, when the H1N1 pandemic came on the scene, FDA amended the original Emergency Use Authorizations for both Tamiflu and Relenza as part of the federal government's responses to the public health emergency.[11] Subsequently, the shortages of Tamiflu were reported everywhere, particularly in pediatric practices.[12]

Natural Disasters

Natural disasters may result in a shortage by affecting the raw materials needed by the sole producer of a drug and impose unexpected impairment to manufacturing facilities. In 1998, Hurricane George caused a major damage in Puerto Rico when several drug shortages occurred as many pharmaceutical manufacturing facilities located on the island were severely disrupted.[12] In 2005, an increase in demand for and a shortage of certain drugs also resulted from hurricanes Katrina and Rita.[13]

Other causes include voluntary recalls from manufacturers, changes in clinical practice patterns, and restricted distribution. The aforementioned reasons are not mutually exclusive, and, in many cases, shortages may result from a combination of factors. The possibilities enumerated earlier may be aggravated by a number of factors. If a drug is a sole product in a therapeutic area, then any dislocation in supply can result in unavailability of the drug. However, even if the drug is not a sole source, but manufactured by a small number of companies, a decrease in supply by one manufacturer can lead to shortages if the other manufacturers are unable to increase production to compensate for the shortfall.

Consequences of Drug Shortages

Impact of Drug Shortages on Health-Care Quality

According to a recent FDA report, of the 127 studied drug shortages between 2010 and 2011, sterile injectables accounted for the majority (80%).[14] The major therapeutic classes of drugs in shortage included oncology drugs (28%), antibiotics (13%), and electrolyte/nutrition drugs (11%).[14] These products are essential for treating most critical health conditions, and shortages in any of them inevitably caused disruptions in patient safety and quality of health care.

In situations where a drug in shortage is the sole treatment option for a life-threatening condition or appropriate alternative agents are difficult to obtain, patients' lives can be immediately placed at risk. Incidences of shortage-related patient deaths have been reported in all health-care practice settings in the past few years, and a number of deaths have been attributed to the shortages.[15] Even when alternative drugs are available, prescription errors due to unfamiliarity with the new regimen, adverse events caused by unexpected drug–drug interactions, and suboptimal treatment outcomes associated with alternative agents can place severe distress to health-care practices. For example, prochlorperazine was used in combination with droperidol to treat chemotherapy-induced nausea and vomiting. After the shortage of prochlorperazine occurred at the University of Pittsburgh Medical Center, promethazine was selected for therapeutic interchange. The adverse events related to the use of promethazine had increased by over 3.3-fold in the subsequent year, due to unexpected drug–drug interactions.[16] A survey conducted by the National Tuberculosis Controllers Association found that in 2012 and 2013, nearly 80% of the tuberculosis (TB) programs reflected difficulties in obtaining isoniazid, one of the four drugs considered to be the core of any first-line treatment for TB. As a result, 68% of the programs delayed treatment and 88% tried alternative regimens.[17] Shortages of drugs for attention deficit hyperactivity disorder have led consumers to seek pricey alternatives that are less effective.[18] According to a recent report, drug shortage has also caused a barrier for patient enrollment in clinical trials. More than 300 NIH-funded clinical trials involve a drug that is in shortage.[19]

Financial Impact of Drug Shortages

The results of drug shortage, particularly the rapid increase in its magnitude, have imposed substantial financial burdens on hospitals and to the health-care system as a whole. To respond to shortages, health-care organizations have taken various approaches, which can divert resources away from routine care. According to a survey conducted by Premier, a hospital buying group, the annual financial impact of drug shortages on Premier alliance members alone exceeds $(USD)78 million. More than $(USD)66 million (or 85%) of the impact is felt by Premier's 2500 hospital members, with the remaining amount within Premier's nonacute care sites.[3]

Gray Market Distributors

The gray market, also known as a parallel market, is a trade of products through supply channels that, while legal, is unintended, unofficial, unauthorized by the original manufacturer. Gray market distributors buy available drug supplies and sell them to providers or end purchasers at markups of several hundred percent. During times of drug shortages, this supply chain diversion may threaten drug integrity in addition to fleecing payers. According to a recent investigation led by Congressman Elijah Cummings,[20] in the event of shortage for some critically needed medications, it is estimated that gray market vendors can raise the product price by more than 80 times a typical contract price. For example, cytarabine, a chemotherapy agent used to treat acute myeloid leukemia and non-Hodgkin lymphoma in children and adults, was typically priced at approximately $(USD)12 per vial but was sold at over $(USD)900 per vial by a distributor from southern Florida. The activities from gray market distributors have been widespread and aggressive. In July and August this year, the Institute for Safe Medication Practices (ISMP) conducted a survey regarding gray market activities and drug shortages, which included health-care providers from 549 hospitals across the nation. Over half (56%) of all participants reported receiving daily solicitations from vendors offering pharmaceutical products no longer available through authorized channels. It is also suggested by more than 10% of respondents that gray market vendors may have also purchased vital medications with impending shortages from hospitals, presumably to sell to other health-care providers at inflated prices.[21] Further investigations revealed deeper rooted issues in the multilayered nature in the gray market. Many distributors reported buying the medications at already highly inflated prices and selling them at a normally increased rate; thus, they considered generated profits were "reasonable."[22]

Responses from the Government, Health-Care Organizations, and Pharmaceutical Markets

Evolution of the FDA's Roles and Activities

Over the past 15 years, the FDA has been gradually empowered with more authorities in mitigating drug shortages. In 1999, a small Drug Shortage Program (DSP) was established under the Center for Drug Evaluation and Research (CDER), the largest of FDA's five centers. The DSP is aimed at resolving all issues related to shortages of the products reviewed by the CDER and releasing information about these drugs to the public. The DSP primarily uses tools of communication, facilitation, and negotiation to formulate and implement effective plans for preventing and managing drug shortages.[23]

DSP maintains a partnership with the American Society of Health-System Pharmacists (ASHP), with the latter regularly sharing available data with the DSP. The DSP assesses the severity and duration of the shortage, as well as determines if the drug is medically necessary, currently defined as "...any drug used to treat or prevent a serious disease or medical condition for which there is no alternative drug, available in adequate supply, that is judged by FDA medical staff to be an adequate substitute."[24] A shortage involving medically necessary products is likely to cause significant disruption in patient care. FDA has established a website for posting information related to shortages of medically necessary products.[23] In addition to posting news on the web page, the DSP staff answers each e-mail inquiry that it receives at its drug shortage e-mail account.

Since 2005, the DSP has implemented more proactive strategies to prevent or resolve shortages. Upon receiving a manufacturer notification of a potential drug shortage, the DSP determines the cause and works with manufacturers and appropriate FDA divisions to develop short-term and long-term management plans. These plans would include helping the company to identify an alternative source for the active ingredients required for manufacturing of the drug, expediting review of an existing manufacturing supplement, or even accelerating an inspection request.[25]

In July 2012, following an executive order in the previous year, President Obama signed into law the Food and Drug Administration Safety and Innovation Act (FDASIA). Among other provisions, Title X of the FDASIA directs the FDA to establish a task force detailing strategies to enhance the agency's response to preventing and mitigating drug shortages.[26] In response to this act, the FDA released "Strategic Plan for Preventing and Mitigating Drug Shortages" (strategic plan) in October 2013. Two principle goals were identified to address drug shortages: improving mitigation response to imminent or existing shortages and implementing strategies for the long-term prevention of shortages by focusing on the root causes of shortages. The strategic plan identified four specific areas that warrant external stakeholder attention: potential financial incentive from payers to encourage high-quality manufacturing that could help prevent the occurrence of shortages; use of data on manufacturer's historical ability to produce quality products in purchasing decisions; opportunities for building redundant manufacturing capacity or increasing inventory levels to lower the risks of shortages; and minimizing gray market activities.[27]

American Society of Health-System Pharmacists

In November 2010, a Drug Shortage Summit was held jointly by the ASHP, the American Society of Anesthesiologists, American Society of Clinical Oncology, and ISMP.[28] Participants included pharmaceutical manufacturers, wholesalers and distributors, the FDA, the University of Utah Drug Information Service, and Premier Inc. The goals were to (1) discuss the causes of drug shortages, (2) examine the impact of drug shortage on health-care quality, (3) identify the need and feasibility for changes in public policy to relieve and eradicate the detrimental impact of drug shortage, and (4) develop an action plan based on the recommendations of stakeholders.

Summit participants provided extensive recommendations to minimize the impact of drug shortages, including improving communication among stakeholders in the pharmaceutical supply chain and health-care providers and removing barriers faced by the FDA and drug manufacturers. With regard to the handling of regulatory and legislative factors that contributed to the shortage of drugs, it was recommended that greater authority should be given to the FDA for requiring manufacturer advance notification of impending market withdrawals. Participants also proposed a revision of FDA's current definition of medically necessary. The FDA will facilitate their communications with manufacturers to relieve shortages with the hope to mitigate patient risk. Furthermore, an approval process for alternative products is subject to acceleration, based on reviewing the potential impact on health-care quality and patient safety.[28]

Preserving Access to Life-Saving Medications Act

In February 2011, Senator Amy Klobuchar introduced a bill, S. 296, the Preserving Access to Life-Saving Medications Act, which would provide FDA with key strategies to prevent drug shortages. These approaches include imposing a minimum of 6 months in advance for manufacturers to report to FDA of an impending market exit or product discontinuation. The legislation also requires FDA to perform expedited reinspections of manufacturers in the case of a drug shortage.[29] The bill granted the FDA authority to impose penalties on noncompliant manufacturers.

Proposed Actions

Strengthen FDA's Roles

Currently, FDA has limited authority in forecasting, preventing, and controlling drug shortages. The DSP, under CDER, one of the five centers within the FDA, receives information about drug shortages mainly from the public e-mail account maintained by DSP.[30] Reporting of shortages to the FDA is not an obligation for manufacturers, except for medically necessary products.[31] Furthermore, the FDA is not granted authority to regulate product discontinuation, a decision usually made by manufacturers. Senator Klobuchar's bill, S. 296, would require all pharmaceutical manufacturers to report to FDA at least 6 months before planned market exit.[32] The legislation also would provide feasibility for FDA to know the reasons for such discontinuations (e.g., whether it is caused by a raw material shortage or lack of projected profits) and work with manufacturers to establish a continuity of operations to address drug shortages. While a 6-month period would leave a considerable leeway for FDA to seek alternative solutions, a prolonged length should be recommended to accommodate additional procedures required for other manufacturers to increase production of drugs in short supply, or for reimportation of such products.

It may also be necessary to consider specific elements for revision of the current definition of medically necessary. For example, what would be the qualification standards for a "serious disease"? Is there a threshold for its prevalence, incidence, and survival period? Would it be feasible for FDA to define a list of "serious diseases" for which any disruption in treatment would cause detrimental impact to the population? A standardized and more precisely defined terminology for the indispensable pharmaceutical products can facilitate the process of empowering the FDA to regulate manufacturers' behavior to ensure continued production of drugs that are deemed medically necessary.

Regulations to Halt Gray Market Activities in Short Supply

Stronger regulatory actions are needed to control and monitor distribution channels for pharmaceutical products. Regulatory engagements will focus on two aspects: a national pedigree law that restricts the distribution of pharmaceutical products to authorized wholesalers (Verified-Accredited Wholesale Distributor) and with enhanced monitoring systems and standardized pricing from distributors that prohibits price gouging, even during drug shortages. Health-care providers can take advantage of the gray market solicitation and gain insight into potential drug shortages, which can lead to optimized planning for the allocation of remaining supplies in the practice setting, as well as the potential exchange of products with other hospitals to avoid utilizing gray market vendors. In the event of an impending shortage, direct ordering from manufacturers should be considered, if a situation warrants. Ultimately, FDA is entitled to greatly enhanced authorities for its pivotal role in the battle against drug shortages. When manufactures know their products will soon be in shortage, FDA should be informed a minimum of 6 months before the shortage occurs. To prevent potential purchases from gray market vendors during the reporting window, regulations should be passed to mandate manufactures to stop deliveries to distributors and wholesalers after the impending shortage is reported to the FDA, and access to products should only be granted to crucial health-care practices (e.g., hospitals, clinics, and pharmacies).

Grant Temporary Authorization to Foreign Markets and Approve Pharmaceutical Products from Western European Countries

Drug purchases over the Internet from foreign countries is not a new term. Although studies have shown that generic drugs in Canada or western Europe were generally more expensive than the same products in the U.S. market, without even taking shipping cost into consideration, temporary regulatory adjustment process to allow larger-scale drug importation from countries with established drug quality management systems (primarily western European countries, Canada, Japan, and Australia) can provide relief to the current crisis of massive drug shortages. In Europe, the majority of drugs are authorized through the European Medicines Agency (EMA), a scientific agency that is roughly parallel to the U.S. FDA. A centralized procedure allows manufacturers to submit a single application to EMA to obtain from the European Commission a centralized (or "community") marketing authorization valid in all EU member states. A more collaborative relationship between FDA and EMA has been cultivated in recent years. Earlier this year, the U.S. FDA and the EMA launched a 3-year pilot program that will allow parallel evaluation of new drug marketing applications that are submitted to both agencies.[33] By establishing regular communication and consultations between the two agencies throughout the process, the programs will provide further opportunities for FDA and EMA reviewers to share full knowledge about the application and harmonize regulatory decisions to the greatest extent possible.

While still far away from a unified market, the United States and western Europe share the commonality in many ways as they pertain to drug approval, regulation, quality inspection, and monitoring. With the amount of foreign-produced drugs approved in the United States increasing steadily over the past decade, the FDA's regulatory actions have expanded across Europe, Asia, and Latin America to ensure the safety of imported products.[34] While criticisms were raised against FDA's delayed approval of foreign pharmaceutical products, asserted as being primarily to protect domestic manufactures, actions have been taken to expedite approval of critically needed drugs from foreign markets,[35] and FDA's approval procedures for foreign drugs are heavily based on clinical trial data coming from overseas sites. Currently, there are no regulatory procedures to grant FDA with sufficient authority to monitor these trials. It is encouraged that sponsors of foreign clinical trials voluntarily consult with the FDA on their trial protocols prior to the submission of Investigational New Drug application to the agency.[36]

Conclusion

The escalating increase in the shortage of drugs has compromised patient quality of care and imposed a tremendous burden on our health-care system. In response to the crisis, health-care and government organizations have taken numerous initiatives, aiming to find rapid solutions. Nevertheless, the battle against drug shortage is likely to be long term and requires joint efforts from all sectors of the health-care system, as well as consumers, pharmaceutical traders, and legal entities. New bills have been proposed to prevent or mitigate supply issues, but it will take efforts in lobbying for their incorporation into law, and their ultimate effect is unclear. Key elements to a successful program for managing drug shortages include a good understanding of the causes for the shortages, a clear channel for international communication and collaboration, execution plans with all parties involved, and proven strategies for involving the entire health-care system.

References

1. Center for Drug Evaluation and Research (CDER) at Food and Drug Administration (FDA). Drug shortage management. September 3, 2014. http://www.fda.gov/downloads/AboutFDA/CentersOffices/CDER/ManualofPoliciesProcedures/ucm079936.pdf. Accessed on August 28, 2013.
2. Vaida AJ. Drug shortages: A patient safety crisis that affects everyone. http://www.npsf.org/. Accessed on January 16, 2014.
3. U. S. Food and Drug Administration (FDA). Strategic plan for preventing and mitigating drug shortages. October 2013. http://www.fda.gov/downloads/Drugs/DrugSafety/DrugShortages/UCM372566.pdf.
4. Tyler LS, Mark SM. Understanding drug & managing shortages. Presented at *37th ASHP Midyear Clinical Meeting*. December 9, 2002. Atlanta, GA. http://www.ashp.org/DocLibrary/Policy/DrugShortages/DShort-abbott-drug.aspx. Accessed on November 12, 2013.
5. ISPE. 2013. Report on the ISPE Drug Shortages Survey. http://ispe.org/. Accessed on December 12, 2013.
6. Silverman E. Why drug shortages cost healthcare providers. 2011. http://www.pharmalot.com/2011/03/what-drug-shortages-cost-healthcare-providers/. Accessed on December 12, 2013.
7. Staton T. China's API exports hurt by quality issues. *FiercePharma*. 2010. http://www.fiercepharma.com/story/chinas-api-exports-hurt-quality-issues/2010-02-22. Accessed on October 10, 2013.
8. Ventola CL. The drug shortage crisis in the United States: Causes, impact, and management strategies. *P&T* 2011; 36(11): 740–757.
9. Neergaard L. Lyme vaccine pulled off market. 2002. http://www.lymepa.org/html/vaccine_pulled_off_the_market.html. Accessed on October 28, 2011.
10. Stone K. Drug shortages. n.d. http://pharma.about.com/od/Manufacturing-and-Technology/i/Drug-Shortages.htm. Accessed on October 22, 2013.
11. FDA. Updated questions and answers: 2009 H1N1 flu virus and emergency use authorization of tamiflu and relenza. 2010. http://www.fda.gov/NewsEvents/PublicHealthFocus/ucm153228.htm. Accessed on December 21, 2013.
12. Stein R. Spot shortages of tamiflu for children are frustrating parents. *The Washington Post*, October 29, 2009. http://www.washingtonpost.com/wp-dyn/content/article/2009/10/28/AR2009102803823.html. Accessed on October 12, 2013.
13. ASHP Expert Panel on Drug Product Shortages. ASHP Guidelines on Managing Drug Shortages in Hospitals and Health Systems. *Am J Health-Syst Pharm*. 2009; 66: 1399–1406. https://www.ashp.org/DocLibrary/Policy/DrugShortages/ASHP_shortage_guide09.pdf.
14. FDA. Executive summary: A review of FDA's approach to medical product shortages. 2011. http://www.fda.gov/AboutFDA/ReportsManualsForms/Reports/ucm277744.htm Accessed on January 15, 2014.
15. Anonymous. CBS news September 23. Drug shortages blamed in at least 15 deaths. http://www.cbsnews.com/stories/2011/09/23/earlyshow/health/main20110587.shtml. Accessed on December 5, 2015.
16. Sheth HS, Verrico MM, Skledar SJ et al. Promethazine adverse events after implementation of a medication shortage interchange. *Ann Pharmacother* 2005; 39(2): 255–261.
17. McBride A, Holle LM, Westerndof C et al. National survey on the effect of oncology drug shortages on cancer care. *Am J Health Syst Pharm* 2013; 70(7): 609–617.
18. Loftus P, Dooren JC. ADHD drug shortages lead to hunt for options. *The Wall Street Journal*, May 10, 2011. Page D1 of the Eastern Edition. http://online.wsj.com/article/SB1000142405274870373080457631344140425l246.html. Accessed December 5, 2015.
19. Dooren JC. Drug shortages threaten cancer research. *The Wall Street Journal*, September 23, 2011. http://online.wsj.com/article_email/SB10001424053111903703604576588852090052670-lMyQjAxMTAxMDIwMzEyNDMyWj.html?mod=wsj_share_email#articleTabs%3Darticle. Accessed on December 5, 2015.
20. Cummings investigates "drug speculation" and "gray market" sales of drugs in critically short supply. http://democrats.oversight.house.gov/index.php?option=com_content&view=article&id=5445&Itemid=107. Accessed on October 16, 2013.

21. Institute for Safe Medication Practices (ISMP). Gray market, black heart: pharmaceutical gray market finds a distributing niche during the drug shortage crisis. 2011. http://www.ismp.org/newsletters/acutecare/showarticle.asp?id=3. Accessed on October 12, 2013.
22. Johnson LA. Congress investigating drug shortages. http://www.dddmag.com/news-Congress-Investigating-Drug-Shortages-10611.aspx. Accessed on December 10, 2013.
23. FDA. Current drug shortages. 2011. http://www.fda.gov/Drugs/DrugSafety/DrugShortages/ucm050792.htm. Accessed on November 15, 2013.
24. Greb E. FDA publishes guidance for the production of medically necessary drugs. 2010. http://pharmtech.findpharma.com/pharmtech/Regulation/FDA-Publishes-Guidance-for-the-Production-of-Medic/ArticleStandard/Article/detail/651533. Accessed on November 5, 2013.
25. Kweder SL, Dill S. Drug shortages: The cycle of quantity and quality. *Clin Pharmacol Therapeu* 2013; 93(3): 245–251.
26. FDA. Food and Drug Administration Safety and Innovation Act (FDASIA). http://www.fda.gov/RegulatoryInformation/Legislation/SignificantAmendmentstotheFDCAct/FDASIA/ucm20027187.htm. Accessed December 5, 2015.
27. FDA: Strategic plan for preventing and mitigating drug shortages. 2013. http://www.fda.gov/Drugs/drugsafety/DrugShortages/default.htm. Accessed on January 16, 2014.
28. American Society of Health System Pharmacists (ASHP). Drug shortages summit summary report. 2010. http://www.ashp.org/drugshortages/summitreport. Accessed on October 22, 2013.
29. Casey Jr RP. (Press release) Casey, Klobuchar introduce bill to address unprecedented prescription drug shortages. 2011. http://www.casey.senate.gov/newsroom/releases/casey-klobuchar-introduce-bill-to-address-unprecedented-prescription-drug-shortages. Accessed November 27, 2015.
30. Jensen CV, Kimzey R, Saliba J. An overview of the FDA's drug shortage program. *P&T* 2005; 30(3): 174–177.
31. U.S. Federal Food, Drugs, and Cosmetic Act, Section 506 c. FD&C Act Chapter V: Drugs and Devices. http://www.fda.gov/RegulatoryInformation/Legislation/FederalFoodDrugandCosmeticActFDCAct/FDCActChapterVDrugsandDevices/. Last updated October 5, 2015. Accessed December 5, 2015.
32. Klobuchar calls for drug shortage notification system. http://minnesota.publicradio.org/display/web/2011/02/12/klobuchar-duluth/. Accessed on October 22, 2013.
33. FDA news release. FDA, EMA announce pilot for parallel assessment of Quality by Design applications. http://www.fda.gov/NewsEvents/Newsroom/PressAnnouncements/ucm247332.htm. Accessed on September 12, 2013.
34. FDA. How does FDA oversee domestic and foreign drug manufacturing? http://www.fda.gov/AboutFDA/Transparency/Basics/ucm194989.htm. Last updated October 19, 2015, last accessed December 5, 2015.
35. Agovino T. FDA, in an expedited review, approves generic AIDs drug combo. 2005. http://lubbockonline.com/stories/012605/upd_075-4806.shtml#.VmMKVcqeyOk. Accessed on December 8, 2013.
36. Gever J. FDA faulted for spotty oversight of data coming from overseas. 2010. http://abcnews.go.com/Health/Wellness/fda-approves-drugs-based-foreign-data-researchers/story?id=10996370. Accessed on October 12, 2013.

Chapter 11

Drug Reimportation into the United States

Albert I. Wertheimer and Qian Ding

Contents

Background

Like citizens in other industrialized countries, Americans are experiencing relatively high levels of growth in prescription drug spending.[1] The United States had the highest level ($[USD]985) of per capita spending on prescription drugs in 2011 among the developed countries in the Organization for Economic Cooperation and Development.[2]

National health spending has increased from $(USD)1.2 trillion in 2000 to $(USD)2.7 trillion in 2011, representing 17.9% of gross domestic product (GDP).[3] As a result, it was estimated that U.S. national health-care expenditures will increase 6.1%, reaching $(USD)3.09 trillion, or 18.3% of GDP, in 2014.[4] Prescription drug spending was $(USD)263 billion, accounting for 10% of personal health-care expenditures in 2011.[3]

The cost of the medication is an important predictor of cost-related nonadherence.[5] In the United States, 53% of the population had private health insurance for their basic coverage and 32% of the population (the elderly, people with low income, or with disabilities) had publicly financed coverage (Medicaid or Medicare), leaving 15% of the population without health coverage in 2011.[2] Due to the economic burden of full pay and/or cost sharing for prescriptions, 24% of the uninsured population and 7% of insured population did not get needed prescription drugs in the past 12 months in 2011, increased from 17% and 4%, respectively, in 2000.[3]

As the prices of prescriptions climb in the United States, some countries such as Canada and some European countries regulate the prices of prescription drugs. The Americans started purchasing these affordable prescription drugs as drug importation or drug reimportation from those countries where the brand-name drugs have a lower price. Consequently, the demand for less-expensive sources or versions of medications has increased the controversial and illegal practice of drug reimportation from other countries such as Canada and Mexico. Although reimportation gives people the opportunity to purchase pharmaceutical products at a significantly lower cost,[6] the U.S. Food and Drug Administration (FDA) has opposed this practice with concerns of safety and effectiveness of the drugs due to the lack of monitoring.

Definition of Reimportation

In order to better appreciate this issue, it is important to understand the definitions of drug importation and drug reimportation.

Drug importation refers to the practice of bringing drugs to the United States for personal or commercial use from a foreign country. Currently, the only types of legally imported drugs are (1) those that are manufactured in foreign FDA-inspected facilities and adhere to FDA approval standards or (2) those that are FDA-approved prescription drugs and manufactured in the United States, sent abroad, and then reimported back into the United States by the manufacturer under proper controls and in compliance with the Federal Food, Drug, and Cosmetic (FD&C) Act.[7]

Therefore, drug reimportation is a special category of drug importation where the imported drugs were originally manufactured in the United States, sold directly to persons or entities in foreign countries, and then brought back into the United States.

History of Reimportation

Between 1995 and 1999, a total of $(USD)13 billion U.S.-made prescription drugs had been reimported for human consumption.[8] Using IMS data, approximately $(USD)700 million of medications were imported to the United States from Canada alone in 2003, via Internet sales and travel to Canada by American consumers.[7] Traditionally, Americans can physically cross the border to buy medications in Canada or Mexico and carry them into the United States through 355 ports of entry, including airports, seaports, or land border. In 2000, FDA's Southwest Import District, with the assistance of other agencies, conducted a survey of prescription drugs being brought by pedestrians into the United States at eight ports of entry along the 2000-mile border with Mexico.

Of the 600 persons interviewed, 63% had prescriptions for antibiotics or pain relievers (59% were U.S. prescriptions and 41% were Mexican).[7] In 2001, a similar survey of prescription drugs being brought into the United States at seven ports of entry along the United States and Mexican border was conducted, and approximately 56% of the 586 interviewees had a prescription for the medicines (61% were U.S. prescriptions and 39% were Mexican).[7]

Nowadays, medications can be imported into the United States through either mail or Internet pharmacies from a variety of countries, including developing countries and developed countries. The majority of the medications were imported from Canada, but medications were also imported from other countries including Japan, India, the Netherlands, Taiwan, Thailand, Belize, Malaysia, the Philippines, Nicaragua, Romania, Cambodia, Uganda, and the United Kingdom.[7] At the beginning of 2004, a new form of storefront pharmacy, for example, Rx Depot Inc., emerged with walk-in business to facilitate consumers in the United States obtain prescription drugs from foreign (mostly Canadian) drugstores and receive 10%–12% commission for each sale they facilitated.[9] Rx Depot received the customer's prescription form either by downloading it from Rx Depot's website or when a patient visited one of the storefront pharmacies that transmitted the prescription to cooperating Canadian pharmacies. After the transmitted prescriptions were rewritten by a Canadian physician, it was filled by a Canadian pharmacy and mailed directly to the customer in the United States. Cross-border Internet pharmacy sales between Canada and the United States grew rapidly from 2000 to 2003 and were $(USD)103 million in 2011.[10] In contrast, a federal judge ordered Rx Depot, to shut down its 85 storefronts in the United States providing access to discounted prescription drugs from Canadian pharmacies over the Internet, which violated laws allowing only manufacturers to import drugs for sale.[11]

Laws and Regulations on Reimportation

Even though states have their own laws that regulate drugs, the FDA maintains primary responsibility at the federal level that oversees the safety and efficacy of prescription drugs. This includes the approval, manufacturing, and distribution of such drugs in the United States under the FD&C Act. Under the FD&C Act passed by the Congress in 1938, unapproved, misbranded, and adulterated drugs are prohibited from importation into the United States.[12]

However, this FD&C Act providing consumer safety by regulating the process of drug sales did not contain any provisions on reimportation of prescription drugs. In both 1984 and 1985, a million counterfeit of G.D. Searle's Ovulen 21 birth control pills were shipped to Miami and New York from Panama and 1800 bottles of Eli Lilly's counterfeit antibiotic Ceclor capsules were imported to Miami and Boston from Singapore as American Goods Returned, which were perpetrated on American drug manufacturers and were declared to customers and granted entry by the FDA.[13]

The 100th Congress (1987) acknowledged such serious potential problems relating to the reimportation of prescription drugs that put the health and safety of American citizens at risk. The existence and operation of a wholesale submarket, commonly known as the "diversion market," prevented effective control over or even routine knowledge of the true sources of prescription drugs in a significant number of cases.[14] Large amounts of counterfeit drugs would be reimported under the cover of free-trade zones—areas specially designated by a growing number of countries to encourage trade, where tariffs are waived and there is minimal regulatory oversight.[15] However, the integrity of the distribution system for prescription drugs was insufficient to prevent the introduction and eventual retail sale of substandard, ineffective, or even counterfeit drugs.

Therefore, the Prescription Drug Marketing Act (PDMA) of 1987 was enacted to prohibit the practice of drug reimportation unless the drug is reimported into the United States by the entity that manufactured the drug in the United States or the drug is required for emergency medical care.[14] The PDMA was modified by the Prescription Drug Amendments of 1992 that prohibits, with certain exceptions, the sale, purchase, or trade of (or the offer to sell, purchase, or trade) prescription drugs that were purchased by hospitals or other health-care entities or donated or supplied at a reduced price to charities.[16]

In 2000, the 106th Congress acknowledged the following facts: (1) The cost of prescription drugs for Americans continued to rise at an alarming rate. (2) Millions of Americans, including Medicare beneficiaries on fixed incomes, face a daily choice between purchasing life-sustaining prescription drugs and paying for other necessities, such as food and housing. (3) Many life-saving prescription drugs are available in countries other than the United States at substantially lower prices, even though such drugs were developed and are approved for use by patients in the United States. (4) Many Americans travel to Canada or other countries to purchase prescription drugs because the medicines that they need are unaffordable in the United States. (5) Americans should be able to purchase medicines at prices that are comparable to prices for such medicines in other countries, but efforts to enable such purchases should not endanger the gold standard for safety and effectiveness that have been established and maintained in the United States.[17]

Due to the preceding findings, the Congress proposed the Medicine Equity and Drug Safety (MEDS) Act (2000) that, if implemented, would have allowed pharmacists or wholesalers to reimport American-made, FDA-approved prescription drugs, previously exported to foreign countries, back into the United States to sell them to Americans at cheaper prices. The MEDS Act would require the pharmacist or wholesaler to provide to the secretary (1) a description of the product, including the name, the amount being imported, and the price paid for the product; (2) information indicating the destination of the product; (3) information indicating the date on which and the place where the product was purchased; (4) the name, address, and telephone number of the importer and the professional license number of the pharmacist or wholesaler; and (5) a certification that the product is approved for marketing in the United States and assurance that all labeling requirements of the FD&C Act are met.[17]

However, both the Department Health and Human Services (HHS) Secretary Donna Shalala, President Clinton's last HHS secretary, and Tommy Thompson, President Bush's first HHS secretary, declined to certify that their implementation of the provision would pose no additional risk to the public's health and safety though it would result in a significant reduction in the cost of covered products to the American consumers.[18] Due to lack of the congressionally required certification by HHS, the MEDS Act was terminated at the end of December 2000.[19] The provisions of drug reimportation Medicare Prescription Drug, Improvement and Modernization Act of 2003 (MMA), similar to MEDS Act, if effective, would have (1) allowed pharmacists and wholesalers to import drugs from Canada and (2) granted individuals a waiver to permit importation of a 90-day supply of any FDA-approved prescription drug imported from Canada from a licensed pharmacy for personal use.[7] Hence, drug reimportation was kept out of the 2003 bill that created Medicare Part D and the 2010 health-care law, though as a senator, President Obama had cosponsored a measure to allow it.[20]

In 1998, FDA developed a guidance of Coverage of Personal Importations in its Regulation Procedures Manual not taking enforcement actions against such importation for some circumstances[21] when (1) the intended use of the drug is unapproved and for a serious condition for which effective treatment may not be available domestically either through commercial or clinical means, (2) there is no known commercialization or promotion to persons residing in the United States by those involved in the distribution of the product at issue, (3) the product is considered not to represent an unreasonable risk, and (4) the individual seeking to import the product affirms in writing that it is for the patient's own use (generally not more than 3 months of supply) and provides the name and address of the doctor licensed in the United States responsible for his or her treatment with the product or provides evidence that the product is for the continuation of a treatment begun in a foreign country. However, it does not change the law or provide a license to individuals to import unapproved drugs into the United States for personal use.

Debates on Drug Reimportation

The political battles regarding legalization of drug reimportation have been continuously escalated since 2005 when David Vitter, senator and a member of Louisiana Republican delegation, proposed several bills, but none of those has finally been approved by the Congress. David Vitter criticized the deal that the White House made with the Pharmaceutical Research and Manufacturers of America (PhRMA) to reject any prescription drug reimportation legislation in order to gain PhRMA's financial support for the Patient Protection and Affordable Care Act of 2010 (Obamacare).[22] On the other hand, PhRMA argued that many policy proposals would have weakened medical innovation and ultimately harmed patients' ability to assess life-saving medicines.[22]

The battle over drug reimportation was reignited as the Wall Street Journal reported that Maine became the first state to pass a law that residents could directly purchase mail-order drugs from pharmacies abroad (October 2013). It was estimated that importing medications from Canada could have saved about $(USD)3 million between 2004 and 2012 for employees' drugs. For example, using the broker CanaRx, a Canadian prescription provider, Portland pays $(USD)200.90 for a 90-day supply of 40 mg tablets of the heartburn drug Nexium with a waiver of any employee co-pay, whereas the city pays $(USD)621.08, with the employee contributing 25% of that ($[USD]155.27) for the same order as negotiated by Portland's health insurer, Aetna Inc.[23] However, 6 months after the state law became effective, Kenneth McCall, the president of the Maine Pharmacy Association, reported that his mail-order medications from Canada had been manufactured in India and the prescriptions had been filled in India, Turkey, and Mauritius on labels.[24]

Drug Price Difference between the United States and Other Developed Countries

In 2004, the Congressional Budget Office concluded that, based on a review of existing literature, prices for brand-name prescription drugs are 35%–55% lower in other industrialized countries than in the United States.[25] A 2013 study examined the prices and spending for brand-name drugs that were under patent protection in Australia, Canada, France, Germany, Switzerland, the United Kingdom, and the United States in 2005, 2007, and 2010.[26] The results found that the prices for brand-name drugs in the United States were 5%–117% higher in all 3 years (except Switzerland and Germany in 2005).

There are several possible explanations for prescription drug price differences between the United States and other developed countries including governmental oversight by means of a review board, third-party purchasers, litigation fees, and research and development (R&D) costs.[27] The main reason for the price differentials is that Canada and most European countries (13 of the 15 countries in Western Europe) directly regulate the prices of prescription drugs.[28] For example, Canada's federal Patented Medicine Prices Review Board ensures that the prices of patented medicines sold in Canada are not excessive.[29]

Although brand-name prescription drugs are more expensive in the United States, a direct comparison of retail prices for 64 generic drugs between the United States and Canada in 2008 found that the average retail prices of generic prescription drugs in the United States were 90% lower than the retail prices in Canada for identical drugs.[30] Among the 64 generic drugs, only 21 generic drugs were more expensive in the United States. For these 21 generic drugs that were more expensive in the United States, prices were an average of 38% higher than those in Canada. For the 43 generic drugs that were more expensive in Canada, prices were an average of 153% higher than those in the United States.

The lowest-price generic prescription drugs were not consistently found in either the United States or Canada.[31] In 1998, one of the leading authors on price differentials, Patricia Danzon, criticized that excluding generic prescription and over-the-counter medications would overstate medication prices in the United States, leading to the appearance that they were much more expensive than other countries, including Japan, Canada, Germany, Sweden, Switzerland, Italy, the United Kingdom, and France.[32] In 2009, Walmart stores announced that customers could get up to a 30-day supply from among 350 generic prescriptions for only $(USD)4 and a 90-day supply for $(USD)10.[33] The generic prescriptions program in Walmart stores brought innovative competition among nationwide stores, such as Target and K-Mart, offering similar discounts for 30- or 90-day supplies.[30]

Another Strategy of Prescription Drug Benefit

Although the MMA provision that would govern drug reimportation was not approved by Congress, a voluntary outpatient prescription drug benefit for seniors and people with disability on Medicare, known as Medicare Part D, was effective in 2006. Medicare Part D coverage allows eligible fee-for-service Medicare recipients to enroll in a prescription drug plan (PDP); it also established the alternative of Medicare Advantage plans, a type of managed care plan that also offered a prescription drug benefit.[34] In 2013, among the 36 million beneficiaries enrolled in Part D plans, about 63% (22.7 million) were in PDPs; the others were enrolled in Medicare Advantage drug plans.[35] Enrollees pay an average monthly premium of $(USD)41.9 in 2014, with a $(USD)310 deductible and 25% coinsurance up to an initial coverage limit of $(USD)2850 in total drug costs, which is followed by a coverage gap where enrollees are responsible for a larger share of their total drug costs than in the initial coverage period, until their total out-of-pocket spending reaches $(USD)4550, known as "donut hole."[35]

Affordable Care Act, effective in 2014, is eliminating this gap in Part D by giving a $(USD)250 rebate to Medicare beneficiaries who reached the prescription drug donut hole in 2010 and providing discounts on covered brand-name drugs and savings on generic drugs in 2011 with gradual increase until 2020 when the donut hole will be closed.[36] Up to 2013 more than 7.3 million seniors and people with disabilities who reached the donut hole in their Medicare Part D plans have saved $(USD)8.9 billion on their prescription drugs, an average of $(USD)1209 per person since the program began.[36]

Advocacy of Drug Reimportation in the United States

Between 2003 and 2006, many states, including Alabama, Massachusetts, Illinois, Maryland, Minnesota, Vermont, Oregon, and Oklahoma, have introduced or proposed programs of drug reimportation.[37] In October 2013, Maine passed the law that Maine residents can directly purchase mail-order drugs from pharmacies abroad.[23]

One driving force supporting drug reimportation, as argued by its advocates, is that they expect that reimportation would translate into real cost savings for patients. For example, it was estimated that Maine's law permitting the importation of medications from Canada would save employers about $(USD)3 million between 2004 and 2012 for employees' drugs.[23] This estimate was similar to that of Minnesota's drug reimportation program, which was estimated to save the state $(USD)1.4 million by the end of 2005.[38] Alabama's program, a voluntary part of the city's health benefit program for city employees and retirees who want to get their drugs from a Canadian pharmacy, was claimed to save its citizens a half-million dollars a year.[37] Illinois estimated in 2003 that if all prescriptions for participants of Illinois' employee and retiree health benefits program were to be filled from Canadian sources, it could save more than $(USD)90 million annually.[39]

In terms of safety, advocates suspected that the FDA's concerns about the safety of Canadian drugs were exaggerated because the Health Products and Food Branch of Health Canada has the equivalent function as FDA on drug regulation.[40] In 2003, a national survey revealed that around 58% of the consumers perceived Canadian drugs to be safe or somewhat safe and 68% thought that the practice of purchasing drugs directly from Canada should be legalized.[41] It was asserted that many brand-name drugs sold in Canada were produced by U.S. manufacturers in FDA-approved facilities and were equally safe as drugs consumed currently by Americans.[39] The Health Products and Food Branch of Health Canada also has equivalent procedures for the drugs that Canadians use to ensure drug safety, including a rigorous drug approval process, importation and marketing procedures, and postmarketing surveillance.[42]

However, since no sufficient safeguards are provided for reimported drug distribution systems by FDA, pharmacies or wholesalers who desire to reimport and distribute prescription medications will need to conduct adequate testing to ensure the safety and purity of the reimported drug products, which would increase the acquisition costs of the reimported medications.[43]

Concerns from the Federal Government

HHS mandated that any drug imported into the United States has the same quality and adheres to the "gold standard" of safety, efficacy, and legitimacy expected from FDA-approved drugs. Currently, the drug distribution system in the United States is a closed system involving manufacturers, wholesalers, and pharmacies that adhere to the "gold standard." Due to insufficient safeguards, legalization of drug reimportation would increase the opportunities for counterfeit and other substandard drugs to enter the current closed distribution system regulated by FDA.[44]

Different countries have different regulations for the safety and efficacy of drugs. Foreign versions of drugs may look identical to FDA-approved versions and may be manufactured in the same facility as the U.S. drugs, but may have different formulation and ingredients or have been manufactured on a different line with different standards and controls to meet the requirements of the respective countries. Advocates argued that Canada has similar standards for monitoring safety and efficacy of licensed drugs. However, Section 37 of the Canadian Food and Drugs Act states that this Act does not apply to any packaged food, drug, cosmetic, or device not manufactured for consumption in Canada and not sold for consumption in Canada.[45]

The FDA acknowledged that drug reimportation would raise safety issues because there are not sufficient financial and technological resources to detect the origin of the drugs, monitor the international websites, control the inventory for imported drugs, oversee the international recalls, and assure the safety and authenticity of drugs imported personally from foreign countries.[46]

Another concern is the impact of reimportation on drug R&D because the high price of brand-name drugs is considered as a stimulation of drug innovation in the future.

Concerns about the Safety of Imported Drugs

The FDA and the Customs and Border Protection conducted two series of "blitz" examinations in 2003 at international mail facilities and courier hubs; over 85% of the imported drug products (1728 of 1982) were found to be unapproved drugs that have potential risks to the patients' health.[47] The risks of the imported drugs are summarized as follows:

- Drugs were "foreign versions" and have not been approved by FDA in the United States.
  - It is considered not safe because the potential side effects of the foreign versions of drugs were not tested on patients in the United States.
  - The drugs were inadequately labeled in foreign languages. Therefore, the instructions of the dosage could be misinterpreted.
  - Some of the drugs were withdrawn from the U.S. market due to safety reasons.
  - More dramatically, some of the drugs were animal drugs that FDA has not approved for human use.
- Drugs that require careful dosing, initial screening, and/or periodic patient monitoring by a medical professional to help assure safe use.
- Drugs were inappropriately packaged and stored during importation.
  - These drugs (including insulin) arrived in the regular mail and at room temperature (insulin loses effectiveness at higher temperatures and is supposed to be shipped overnight to ensure it remains chilled).[48]
- Drugs with dangerous interactions were imported together.
- Illegal controlled substances were among the imports.

Potential Impacts of Reimportation on R&D of New Drugs in the United States

PhRMA and other opponents of reimportation frequently asserted that reimportation may lower prices in the short run but that drug companies would suffer decreased revenues and would respond by cutting R&D, including spending on discovery, development, and launching of new drugs.[34]

It is recognized that continuously supporting new drug launches in the market is one aspect of a superior advantage to maintain sustainable competition among pharmaceutical companies. However, obtaining FDA approval and the rights to market a drug is very expensive and time-consuming with about 10–15 years from choosing a valid target molecule for dedicated clinical trials. A systematic review indicated that the cost of bringing a new drug to market has increased ninefold from $(USD)92 million cash in Hansen's 1979 study to $(USD)884 million cash in Paul's 2010 study.[49] Even with acknowledging the inflammation rate and the differences in methodologies, costs still have substantially increased.

In 2010, the U.S.-based pharmaceutical firms had a total budget of about $(USD)67 billion designated for research, and the National Institutes of Health funded $(USD)31 billion for research in public sector institutions (primarily government labs and universities).[50] When a molecule is first synthesized, the new drug is usually under patent protection in the early development process, preventing the making and selling by other companies for 20 years. When brand-name drugs are under patent, pharmaceutical companies have the authority to set the price that could cover the full cost including R&D and profit until patents expire. Because, during the period of patent protection, the medicine must earn enough revenue to fund the drug development pipeline for other candidates that may become new drugs, about 21% of domestic sales of the new drugs went to domestic R&D, and 16% of the total sales went to total R&D in 2012.[51]

Generic drugs can be sold at lower prices because they do not face the same clinical trial costs as brand-name drugs. Under the Drug Price Competition and Patent Term Restoration Act of 1984, also known as the Hatch-Waxman Act, generic drug companies do not have to repeat expensive clinical trials but instead rely on those from the originators.[52]

From 2004 to 2013, a total of 263 novel new medicines, known as new molecular entities (NMEs), have been approved by the FDA. Although regulatory processes differ widely between FDA and those of regulatory agencies in other countries, almost three-quarters of the NMEs approved in 2013 (20 of 27) were approved first in the United States before any other country.[53] According to IMS data, 62% of sales of new medicines launched during 2007–2011 were on the U.S. market, compared with 18% on the European market.[54] Because U.S. pharmaceutical companies are the current world leader in drug innovation, American consumers benefit greatly by having earlier access to the best and newest treatments[7] but will consequently pay more for brand-name drugs.

The U.S. pharmaceutical sector is not only the world leader in drug discovery and development but also an employee hub for scientists and researchers. It was estimated that U.S. pharmaceutical companies provide more than 810,000 direct jobs and 3.4 million nationwide in total, including indirect and induced jobs in 2013.[51] However, when medications sold by a patent holder to a foreign market at a lower price are imported back to the original country, the producer would face a competition with its own medications offered at a lower price.[55] Legalizing importation drugs to the countries with high-sale prices from the countries with lower-sale prices that are maintained through price controls is considered a threat that would reduce pharmaceutical revenues and adversely affect R&D of new drugs due to reduced profits and cash flow.

HHS estimated that legalized importation could generate a 1% (direct) reduction in drug spending and a 2% (indirect) reduction in pharmaceutical company revenues.[7]

Economic Burden to the Society of Conditions Where Patients Take Counterfeit Drugs

A concern raised by the FDA is increased risks that customers might be exposed to counterfeit drugs. Normally, customers have little ability to differentiate genuine drugs from the unknown level of regulation in other countries from counterfeit drugs. Pursuing the high potential for profit, some of the controlled medications that are exported outside the United States are reimported through illegal channels. Counterfeit drugs, mostly imported through Internet pharmacies in an unregulated environment, are threatening those patients in the United States who seek cheaper, stigmatized, or unauthorized treatments.

The FDA defines counterfeit drugs as drugs with a falsely labeled trademark, trade name, or other identifying mark, imprint, or device without authorization or misrepresenting itself as being manufactured or distributed by a legitimate drug manufacturer, processor, packer, or distributor.[56] The WHO defines a counterfeit drug as one that is deliberately and fraudulently mislabeled with respect to identity and/or source. Counterfeit branded and generic drugs could include products with the correct ingredients or with the wrong ingredients, without active ingredients, with insufficient active ingredients, or with fake packaging.[57] A variety of factors may contribute to the occurrence of counterfeit drugs[58]:

- Lack of legislation—where legislation and regulations do not exist or are inadequate for proper control of medicines, criminals are incented to produce counterfeit medicines.
  - Absent or weak national drug regulatory authority
  - Lack of enforcement of existing legislation
  - Weak penal sanctions
  - Lack of regulation by exporting countries and within free-trade zones
- Corruption and conflicts of interest.
- Inefficient cooperation between stakeholders—as when the cooperation between national Drug Regulatory Authorities (DRAs), police, and customs services and the judiciary in combating the counterfeiting of drugs is ineffective, counterfeiters can escape detection, arrest, and penal sanctions.
- Transactions involving many intermediaries—consequently, the opportunities for intermediation by counterfeiters will be increased.
- Demand exceeding supply—when demand for drugs outstrips supply, counterfeiting may be encouraged for large profits.
- High prices—as an active market force, high price is a by-product of high demand.
- Sophistication in clandestine drug manufacture—the sophisticated equipment and packaging of counterfeit drug products have increased the difficulty of detecting them.

High demand, the potential for high profits, and the lack of enforcement of legislation are always incentives for counterfeiting drugs. The patients who are not able to afford the access to the medications may be exposed to the counterfeit drugs. Although counterfeit drugs were often found in developing countries, counterfeiting has become more and more prevalent in developed countries as well, representing serious challenges and threats to public health. Of 771 reports of counterfeit medicines received by WHO between 1982 and 1999, 13.6% were from the Europe region, and 5.9% originated from the industrialized North America region.[57] In 2009, the European Union (EU) seized 34 million fake tablets in just 2 months, including antibiotics, cancer treatments, and sildenafil citrate (Viagra).[59] At the end of 2010, a global effort to combat the distribution and sale of counterfeit and illegal medicines online culminated in "Operation Pangea III," resulting in the seizure of approximately 1 million illegal and counterfeit medicines valued at approximately $(USD)2.6 million.[60]

Patients may have advanced disease after taking counterfeit drugs. If the medicines contain little or no active ingredients, patients will not have therapeutic benefits with such inactive ingredients. However, delayed effective treatment will then be associated with increased morbidity and mortality. Counterfeit drugs are dangerous in an even worse case, one where the ingredients are toxic or have adverse effects on the patients. Some patients may not respond at all or as quickly as other patients do. But some patients may have an immediate response as a direct consequence that inevitably leads to patient deaths. For example, in 2006, more than 200 patients were killed in Panama by cough syrup using cheap diethylene glycol instead of glycerin.[61] A similar event had happened in the United States about 70 years earlier, leading to the 1938 law of FD&C Act that unapproved, misbranded, and adulterated drugs are prohibited from importation into the United States. During the same year, the WHO created the first global initiative using "Counterfeit Drugs Kill" as its slogan, known as the International Medical Products Anti-Counterfeiting Taskforce consisting of all 193 WHO members on a voluntary basis.[62]

Counterfeit drugs also have a significant economic burden on patients and society. It was estimated that the global counterfeit drugs market was approximately $(USD)75 billion in worldwide sales in 2010.[63] Counterfeit "lifestyle" drugs and those for chronic conditions are more commonly found in industrialized countries.[64] First of all, drug treatment is an expense either to the insurance providers or the patients who were insured. For those who were not insured, the expense of drugs may cost an equivalent payment for a few working hours. If the patients had adverse effects with the counterfeit drugs, they would suffer diminished quality of life and perhaps work productivity loss. Both patients and health-care systems would bear the increased costs due to these unexpected treatments.

Due to these risks of additional disease burdens and economic burdens on patients, counterfeit drugs would damage patients' confidence in the public health-care systems.

Canadian Perspective on U.S. Drug Reimportation

Compared to prescription drug expenditures of $(USD)263 billion ($[USD]985 per capita) in the United States,[3] Canada spent $(USD)32 billion on prescription drugs ($[USD]701 per capita) in 2011.[65]

Is Canadian capacity sufficient to provide a continual supply of medications to meet the demand in the U.S. market if drug reimportation is adopted on a large scale? Canada's health minister, Ujjal Dosanjh, raised this concern repeatedly: "It is difficult for me to conceive of how a small country like Canada could meet the prescription drug needs of approximately 280 million Americans without putting our own supply at serious risk. Canada cannot be the drugstore of the United States."[66]

Canadian drug exporters have experienced increasing economic pressures from both Canadian government officials and big pharmaceutical companies. Canadian officials, worried about the threat of liability lawsuits and the problem of maintaining an adequate, reasonably priced supply of prescription drugs for their own population, are casting an increasingly wary eye on the industry.[66] At the same time, Canadian online and mail-order pharmacies had an even more difficult time finding supplies because major pharmaceutical manufacturers like Pfizer and GlaxoSmithKline warned these Canadian pharmacies that exported brand-name drugs to U.S. customers at lower prices to stop shipping their drugs to U.S. customers, or they would cut off their supplies. The letters told these Canadian pharmacies that they could face U.S. FDA action because the drugs were not approved for sale in the United States.[67,68]

If adequate supplies of drugs are not available for Canadians, Canadian resellers would likely have a significant incentive to sell limited supplies of drugs to the United States at a higher price than they would normally sell to Canadians, which would be expected to cause the price of pharmaceuticals in Canada to increase.[28,39] In order to fulfill the increased demand of U.S. consumers, there is a high possibility that Canadian pharmacists might order drugs from other countries such as India, Thailand, and Africa where the rate of drug counterfeiting might be higher.[6]

Importation Policies of Some Other Developed Countries

Some developed countries allow limited drug importation for personal use. Since a majority of health products consumed in Canada are imported from other countries, Canada also allows drug importation for personal use. The Health Products and Food Inspectorate within Health Canada has a similar responsibility as FDA. All the imported health products for personal and commercial use must meet the requirements under the Food and Drugs Act and its regulations from the Health Products and Food Inspectorate. Any attempt to import health products that are found to have a known risk to public health will be prevented by Health Canada.

Health Canada allows visitors or Canadians who return from abroad to bring medications with them, but under restriction that those medications must be for the individual's own personal use and cannot exceed a limited supply, defined as a single course of treatment or a 90-day supply based on the directions for use, whichever is less, of a health product.[69]

In addition, the imported health products must have one of the following[69]:

- Hospital- or pharmacy-dispensed packaging
- Original retail packaging
- The original label affixed to it that clearly indicates what the health product is and what it contains

The EU is best addressed as a separate category and will be considered in the next section.

Canadians are encouraged to buy health products that have received market authorization from Health Canada from reputable or known suppliers/retailers (via mail, courier, etc.). If the suppliers or retailers are not authorized for market by Health Canada, more restrictions are applied[69]:

- A single course of treatment or a 90-day supply based on the directions for use, whichever is less, of a health product as long as the product does not contain a substance listed in Schedule F of the Food and Drug Regulations

In Japan, an importer of medication (which includes drugs, quasi-drugs that have restricted uses, products that have a mild action on the human body, and a product that is not categorized as a medical device or cosmetic device) for business purposes needs a license from the Minister of Health, Labor, and Welfare under the Pharmaceutical Affairs Law.[70]

A person who imports restricted quantities of medications for personal use only does not need to apply for a license for individual's importing from the Minister of Health, Labor, and Welfare. The quantities are restricted as follows[70]:

1. Drug or quasi-drug: up to 2 months of supply
2. Poisonous drug, powerful drug, or prescription drug: up to 1 month of supply
3. Drug or quasi-drug for external use (excluding poisonous drug, powerful drug, or prescription drug): up to 24 pieces
   a. Cosmetic: up to 24 pieces per item
   b. Medical device (for home use only): 1 set (e.g., electric massager)

The Japanese government strictly prohibits importing narcotics and psychotropics into Japan except in the case for a specific patient along with the prescription of treatment and the permission by the directors of the Regional Bureaus of Health and Welfare under the Narcotics and Psychotropics Control Law before entrance into Japan is permitted.

Parallel Imports in the European Union

As the drug importation debate of the cost and safety issues proceeds in the United States among customers, pharmaceutical industries, and government officials, the EU has more than 3 decades of experience with commercial parallel imports of pharmaceuticals among the original 15-member states of the EU and other members of European Economic Area (EEA). Parallel imports are accepted. However, personal importation of prescription drugs is not allowed in the EU. The term "parallel imports" refers to the legitimately produced goods purchased in one member state and resold legally in another member state, where it is more expensive, without the consent of a trademark, copyright, or patent of the original manufacturer. To ensure the safety of pharmaceutical parallel imports, parallel imported medicinal products can only be distributed under a licensed pharmaceutical distributor in any EU member state after obtaining proper authorization. Qualified parallel imported medical products must meet the following two conditions[71]:

1. The imported product has been granted a marketing authorization in the member state of origin.
2. The imported product is essentially similar to a product that has already received marketing authorization in the member state of destination.

There are also some limitations on the parallel imported products[72]:

- Parallel imports are only permitted inside of the EU (and the EEA).
- Drug manufacturers may block the sale of an imported product if its original packaging has been modified in a way other than what is necessary to permit its sale in the importing country.
- Member states are allowed to prohibit or limit exports to protect the human life and public health.
- Manufacturers can ask national authorities or courts of the member state of destination to protect the right of stop or restrict the exports to the member state.

An article estimated that pharmaceutical companies lose $(USD)3 billion annually on parallel trade in Europe.[73] Parallel trade was estimated to amount to €5000 million (~$[USD]6900 million) in 2011, about 28% of total prescription drug sales in the EU.[54]

The experience of the consequences of parallel trade of pharmaceuticals on safety, costs, and pharmaceutical industry in the United States has detected[72] the following:

- Reports of incidents involving regulatory violations relating to repackaging, relabeling, and consumer inserts and to the use and storage of parallel import medicines.
- A number of complaints about product shortages in exporting countries. Figure 11.1 shows the share of parallel imports in total pharmaceutical sales in 2011 from the European Federation of Pharmaceutical Industries and Associations data. Denmark experiences the greatest influx of parallel imports than other EU countries.

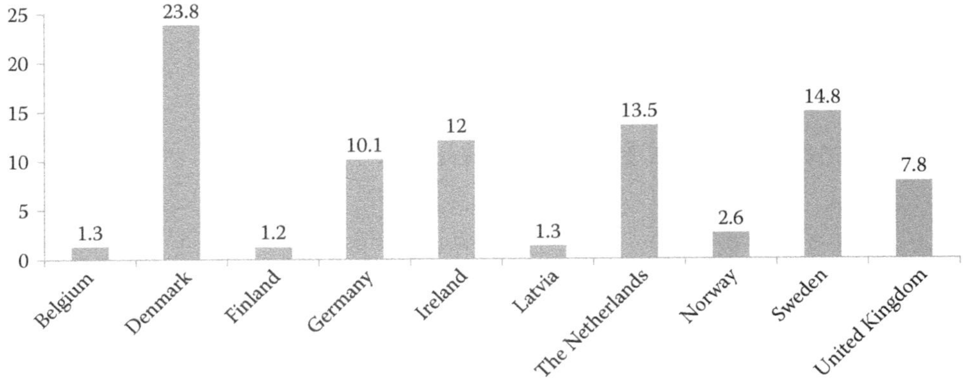

Figure 11.1 Share of parallel imports in pharmacy market sales (%)—2011. (From the European Federation of Pharmaceutical Industries and Associations, the pharmaceutical industry in figures, EFPIA, Brussels, Belgium, 2013, retrieved from http://www.efpia.eu/uploads/Figures_Key_Data_2013.pdf. Accessed January 12, 2016.)

- Although consumers, pharmacies, and statutory health insurance organizations in destination countries theoretically would receive some of the benefit from the lower prices of parallel imported drugs, wholesalers and parallel distributors have the potential to act as profit maximizers—taking advantage of price differences for the same product between low- and high-price countries.
- Significantly reduced manufacturing prices by 12%–19% due to parallel imports.[73] Even though the lowest European prices are 45%–60% of the price for comparable locally sourced products, the parallel imported drugs' prices in the destination country tend to be much closer to the locally sourced product price—roughly 80%–90% of the price, indicating a price arbitrage.

Discussion of Future Prospects

Any business or individual knowingly reimporting prescription drugs in violation of the FD&C Act is subject to a felony offense punishable by up to 10 years in prison or up to $(USD)250,000 in fines, or both.[37] Additionally, businesses that assist or facilitate in the reimportation of prescription drugs may also risk these penalties under the FD&C Act.[37] Since the U.S. government has focused its enforcement resources against business, violations of drug reimportation against individuals have not been heavily enforced. If the FDA regulations were to be strictly enforced (even for small quantities for seniors), drug reimportation would significantly be reduced.

The European parallel import suggests that commercial importation of prescription drugs between countries with similar regulatory standards for drug approval and distribution does not necessarily expose the population as a whole to greatly increased hazards and may conserve payer resources.[72] Some of the safety and efficacy risks would be removed given that there will be greater harmony in the standards. If there were reciprocal regulatory approvals among the U.S. FDA, Ministry of Health, Labor and Welfare in Japan, Canada Health, and the European Medicines Agency, there is an additional confidence that the imported drugs are safe. However, the FDA would also need significant additional resources to provide oversight and enforcement of such responsibilities as identifying the registration of importers and exporters, packaging, and labeling.

Many EU member states, such as the UK's National Institute for Health and Clinical Excellence, have adopted measures to promote the most cost-effective use of prescription drugs and other health technologies. The parallel imported drugs' prices in the destination country are much closer to the locally sourced product price—roughly lower by 10%–20% of the price.[72] Some studies have proposed the term of "uniform pricing" of pharmaceutical products as a means of balancing competing concerns of prices and incentives that one price is set for a particular product across the board.[27] However, it may not be practical for the pharmaceutical industries given that some countries have price control policies. If the drug price gap is narrowed by decreasing the U.S. drug prices closer to international norms or increasing the foreign prices closer to the U.S. drug prices, the need for drug reimportation could be partially eliminated. Considering more than 20% of uninsured people and 7% insured people who did not fill their prescriptions due to cost, if the price of the drugs in the United States could reach the international price norm or reduce the gap to provide affordable drugs, those poor population could have the opportunity to get prescriptions for necessary therapies.

Pharmacies and wholesalers could gain profit from the reimported drug price difference between countries. Customers shop for affordable prices of drugs abroad either because they pay a substantial share of drug costs or they lack prescription drug coverage. If their private or public health insurance paid for the vast majority of drugs, except for a modest co-payment, consumers would not have such a financial incentive to seek lower cost drugs abroad.

To prevent illegal drug reimportation, pharmaceutical companies could consider selling different shape and color tablets and capsules in different countries. For example, a brown JANUVIA® (sitagliptin) tablet sold in the United States by Merck could be blue in the EU and red in Canada. Such a strategy would discourage personal reimportation because customers would see significantly different tablets and may be more reluctant to buy them abroad.

Conclusions

To date, drug reimportation is a continually debated topic in the United States. Although Medicare Part D and generic prescription programs have improved the affordability of drugs for Americans, brand-name drugs are still more expensive than in other developed countries. The number of Americans who seek lower-price brand-name prescriptions through the Internet, mail order, or physically bringing drugs across the border can then be expected to continuously increase. However, drug reimportation is definitely not a long-term solution for the customers in the United States. Whether copying parallel imports as in the EU or Canada's success at restraining prices of patented drugs, a comprehensive solution on drug patent, generic drug programs, transparency of competitive global drug prices, and enforcement of regulations should be considered.

References

1. Gross, D. (2003). *Prescription Drug Prices in Canada*. Washington, DC: AARP Public Policy Institute. Retrieved from http://assets.aarp.org/rgcenter/health/ib62_can_rx.pdf.
2. OECD. (2013). *Health at a Glance 2013: OECD Indicators*. OECD Publishing. Retrieved from http://www.oecd-ilibrary.org/social-issues-migration-health/health-at-a-glance-2013/foreword_health_glance-2013-1-en;jsessionid=4biv35brj51kq.x-oecd-live-02.
3. National Center for Health Statistics. (2014). *Health, United States, 2013: With Special Feature*. Hyattsville, MD: National Center for Health Statistics.

4. Cuckler, G. A., Sisko, A. M., Keehan, S. P., Smith, S. D., Madison, A., Poisal, J. A., and Stone, D. A. (2013). National health expenditure projections, 2012–22: Slow growth until coverage expands and economy improves. *Health Affairs*, 32(10), 1820–1831.
5. Briesacher, B., Gurwitz, J., and Soumerai, S. (2007). Patients at-risk for cost-related medication non-adherence: A review of the literature. *Journal of General Internal Medicine*, 22, 864–871.
6. Bhosle, M. J. and Balkrishnan, R. (2007). Drug reimportation practices in the United States. *Therapeutics and Clinical Risk Management*, 3(1), 41–46.
7. U.S. Department of Health and Human Services (DHHS) Task Force on Drug Importation. http://archive.hhs.gov/importtaskforce/ Last revised December 22, 2004. Last accessed December 5, 2015.
8. Dalzell, M. D. (2000). Prescription drug reimportation. Panacea or problem? *Managed Care*, 9(12), 22–27.
9. U.S. Food and Drug Administration. (October 14, 2005). Oregon: Governor Theodore R. Kulongoski. Retrieved from http://www.fda.gov/Drugs/DrugSafety/ucm179372.htm. Last Updated: 09/10/2009. Last accessed December 5, 2015.
10. Government of Canada. (2014). Pharmaceutical industry profile. Retrieved from https://www.ic.gc.ca/eic/site/lsg-pdsv.nsf/eng/h_hn01703.html. Accessed December 5, 2015.
11. Ukens, C. (2003). Court shuts down Rx depot storefronts. *Drug Topics*, 147, 53.
12. Hubbard, W. K. (July 25, 2002). The importation of drugs into the United States. Retrieved from http://www.fda.gov/newsevents/testimony/ucm115170.htm. Last updated July 24, 2009. Last accessed December 5, 2015.
13. United States 99th Congress. (1986). Dangerous Medicine: The Risk to American Consumers from Prescription Drug Diversion: Report by the Subcommittee on Oversight and Investigations of the Committee on Energy and Commerce, U.S. House of Representatives. Washington, DC: US G.P.O.
14. U.S. Food and Drug Administration. (April 22, 1988). Text of the prescription drug marketing act of 1987. Retrieved from http://www.fda.gov/RegulatoryInformation/Legislation/FederalFoodDrugandCosmeticActFDCAct/SignificantAmendmentstotheFDCAct/PrescriptionDrugMarketingActof1987/ucm201702.htm. Last updated March 1, 2010. Last accessed December 5, 2015.
15. Bogdanich, W. (2007). Counterfeit Drugs' Path Eased by Free Trade Zones. The New York Times. December 17, 2007. Retrieved from http://www.nytimes.com/2007/12/17/world/middleeast/17freezone.html?pagewanted=all&_r=0
16. Department of Health and Human Services. (June 2001). The prescription drug marketing act: Report to congress. Retrieved from http://www.fda.gov/RegulatoryInformation/Legislation/SignificantAmendmentstotheFDCAct/PrescriptionDrugMarketingActof1987/default.htm. Last updated August 19, 2013. Last accessed December 5, 2015.
17. Government Printing Office. (2000). S. 2520 (106th): Medicine equity and drug safety act of 2000. Retrieved from https://www.govtrack.us/congress/bills/106/s2520/text. Accessed December 5, 2015.
18. Department of Health & Human Services. (July 2001). Secretary Thompson determines that safety problems make drug reimportation unfeasible. Retrieved from http://archive.hhs.gov/news/press/2001pres/20010710.html. Accessed December 5, 2015.
19. Vogel, R. and Joish, V. (2001). The potential unintended economic consequences. *Clinical Therapy*, 23, 629–643.
20. Viebeck, E. (May 24, 2012). Senate republicans criticize Obama as drug reimportation amendment fails. Retrieved from http://thehill.com/policy/healthcare/229397-republicans-senators-slam-obama-on-drug-reimportation. Accessed December 5, 2015.
21. U.S. Food and Drug Administration. (2013). Regulatory Procedures Manual—April 2013. (Chapter 9). Retrieved from: http://www.fda.gov/downloads/ICECI/ComplianceManuals/RegulatoryProceduresManual/UCM074300.pdf. Accessed December 5, 2015.
22. Washington DC. (July 11, 2012). Vitter: White House, PhRMA made deals to kill prescription drug reimportation. Retrieved from: http://www.vitter.senate.gov/newsroom/press/vitter-white-house-phrma-made-deals-to-kill-prescription-drug-reimportation. Accessed December 5, 2015.

23. Levitz, J. and Martin, T. W. (October 11, 2013). US news: Maine to allow prescription drug imports first-in-nation law aims to cut costs for employers, workers; Pharmaceutical companies raise concerns about safety. *The Wall Street Journal*, Eastern edition (New York), p. A3.
24. National Association of Boards of Pharmacy. (April 16, 2014). Canadian Drug Seller Fills Maine Prescriptions in India, Alleges Maine Pharmacy Association President. Retrieved from https://www.nabp.net/news/canadian-drug-seller-fills-maine-prescriptions-in-india-alleges-maine-pharmacy-association-president. Accessed December 5, 2015.
25. Baker, C. (2004). *Would Prescription Drug Reimportation Reduce US Drug Spending?* Economic and Budget Issue Brief. Washington, DC: Congressional Budget Office.
26. Kanavos, P., Ferrario, A., Vandoros, S., and Anderson, G. F. (2013). Higher US branded drug prices and spending compared to other countries may stem partly from quick uptake of new drugs. *Health Affairs*, 32(4), 753–761.
27. Drabiak, B. A. (2005). Reimportation of prescription drugs: Long-lasting relief or a short-term analgesic? Retrieved from http://digitalcommons.law.wustl.edu/globalstudies/vol4/iss1/6. Accessed December 5, 2015.
28. Frank, R. G. (2004). Prescription-drug prices. *New England Journal of Medicine*, 351(14), 1375–1377.
29. Patented Medicine Prices Review Board of Canada. (2013). Patented medicine prices review board annual report 2012. Retrieved from http://www.pmprb-cepmb.gc.ca/CMFiles/Publications/Annual%20Reports/2012/2012-Annual-Report_2013-10-17_EN.pdf. Accessed December 5, 2015.
30. Skinner, B. J. and Rovere, M. (2010). Canada's drug price paradox, 2010. Retrieved from https://www.fraserinstitute.org/content/canadas-drug-price-paradox-2010. Accessed December 5, 2015.
31. Gooi, M. and Bell, C. M. (2008). Differences in generic drug prices between the US and Canada. *Applied Health Economics and Health Policy*, 6(1), 19–26.
32. Danzon, P. and Kim, J. (1998). International price comparisons for pharmaceuticals: Measurement and policy issues. *Pharmacoeconomics*, 14, 15–28.
33. Bentonville, A. (February 19, 2009). Walmart's $4 generic prescription drug list added to epocrates' drug reference application. Retrieved from http://news.walmart.com/news-archive/2009/02/19/walmarts-4-generic-prescription-drug-list-added-to-epocrates-drug-reference-application. Accessed December 5, 2015.
34. Lee, B. and Hutt, P. B. (2005). Reimportation: A first step or false step toward transparency in the prescription drug market? Retrieved from http://dash.harvard.edu/bitstream/handle/1/8965568/Lee05.pdf?sequence=1. Accessed December 5, 2015.
35. Kaiser Family Foundation. (November 19, 2013). The medicare prescription drug benefit fact sheet. Retrieved from http://www.kff.org/medicare/fact-sheet/the-medicare-prescription-drug-benefit-fact-sheet/. Accessed December 5, 2015.
36. Centers for Medicare & Medicaid Services. (November 26, 2013). Press release: New data shows affordable care act helped seniors save $8.9 billion on prescription drugs nationwide. Retrieved from http://www.cms.gov/Newsroom/MediaReleaseDatabase/Press-Releases/2013-Press-Releases-Items/2013-11-26.html. Accessed December 5, 2015.
37. Kim, L. (2006). Reimportation of prescription drugs—Legislative, executive judicial and state & local responses. Retrieved from http://dash.harvard.edu/bitstream/handle/1/8852168/KimL06.rtf?sequence=1. Accessed December 5, 2015.
38. Wolfe, W. (2004). State's mail-order drug plan launched. *Minneapolis Star Tribune*, p. 1B.
39. Kamath, R. and McKibbin, S. (2003). *Report on Feasibility of Employees and Retirees Safely and Effectively Purchasing Prescription Drugs from Canadian Pharmacies.* Springfield, IL: Illinois Department of Central Management Services.
40. Choudhry, N. K. and Detsky, A. S. (2005). A perspective on US drug reimportation. *JAMA*, 293(3), 358–362.
41. Stony Brook University. (2003). Health Pulse of America. Retrieved from http://sunysb.edu/surveys/HPANov03_Pharma.htm. Accessed December 5, 2015.
42. Ward, C. (2004). Economic and policy implications of reimportation: A Canadian perspective. *Managed Care*, 13, 17–20.

43. The American Society of Consultant Pharmacists. (2001). Statement on re-importation of prescription drugs. Retrieved from https://www.ascp.com/sites/default/files/ASCP-PA-NewchangesSta01-Reimportation-v2.pdf. Accessed December 5, 2015.
44. Meadows, M. (2002). Imported drugs raise safety concerns. *FDA Consumer Magazine*, 36, 18–23.
45. Canada. Food and Drugs Act. (1985). Food and Drugs Act. Part II, Section 37. Administration and Enforcement. http://www.wipo.int/wipolex/en/text.jsp?file_id=125534.
46. Thompson, C. (2000). FDA admits to lacking control over counterfeit drug imports. *American Journal of Health System Pharmacy*, 57, 1296–1297.
47. U.S. Food and Drug Administration. (2004). Recent FDA/US customs import blitz exams continue to reveal potentially dangerous illegally imported drug shipments. Retrieved from: http://www.fda.gov/NewsEvents/Newsroom/PressAnnouncements/2004/ucm108232.htm. Accessed December 5, 2015.
48. Vogel, R. (2002). Pharmaceutical patents and price controls. *Clinical Therapy*, 24, 1204–1222.
49. Morgan, S., Grootendorst, P., Lexchin, J., Cunningham, C., and Greyson, D. (2011). The cost of drug development: A systematic review. *Health Policy*, 100(1), 4–17.
50. Petrova, E. (2014). Innovation in the pharmaceutical industry: The process of drug discovery and development. In Ding, M., Eliashberg, J., Stremersch, S. (eds.) *Innovation and Marketing in the Pharmaceutical Industry* (pp. 19–81). New York: Springer. http://www.springer.com/us/book/9781461478003.
51. Pharmaceutical Research and Manufacturers of America. (2013). *Biopharmaceutical Research Industry Profile—PhRMA*. Washington, DC: Pharmaceutical Research and Manufacturers of America. Retrieved from http://www.phrma.org/sites/default/files/pdf/PhRMA%20Profile%202013.pdf.
52. U.S. Food and Drug Administration. (2006). Greater access to generic drugs. Retrieved from http://www.fda.gov/drugs/resourcesforyou/consumers/ucm143545.htm. Accessed December 5, 2015.
53. Center for Drug Evaluation and Research. (2014). The Novel New Drugs of 2013. Retrieved from http://www.fda.gov/downloads/drugs/developmentapprovalprocess/druginnovation/ucm381803.pdf. Accessed December 5, 2015.
54. The European Federation of Pharmaceutical Industries and Associations. (2013). *The Pharmaceutical Industry in Figures*. Brussels, Belgium: EFPIA. Retrieved from http://www.efpia.eu/uploads/Figures_Key_Data_2013.pdf.
55. Mantovani, A. and Naghavi, A. (2012). Parallel imports and innovation in an emerging economy: The case of Indian pharmaceuticals. *Health Economics*, 21(11), 1286–1299.
56. U.S. Federal Food, Drug and Cosmetic Act. SEC. 201. [21 USC. 321] 321(g)(2). https://legcounsel.house.gov/Comps/Federal%20Food,%20Drug,%20And%20Cosmetic%20Act.pdf.
57. Wondemagegnehu, E. (1999). *Counterfeit and Substandard Drugs in Myanmar and Viet Nam*. WHO Report. Geneva, Switzerland: World Health Organization.
58. World Health Organization (WHO). (1999). *Counterfeit Drugs: Guidelines for the Development of Measures to Combat Counterfeit Drugs*. Geneva, Switzerland: WHO, pp. 15–17.
59. Editorial of the Lancet. (2012). Counterfeit drugs: A growing global threat. *Lancet*, 379, 685.
60. Interpol. (October 14, 2010). International operation targets online supply of counterfeit and illegal medicines. Retrieved from http://www.interpol.int/News-and-media/News/2010/PR083. Accessed December 5, 2015.
61. Seiter, A. (2009). Health and economic consequences of counterfeit drugs. *Clinical Pharmacology & Therapeutics*, 85(6), 576–578.
62. World Health Organization. (2008). Impact brochure on counterfeit medicines. Retrieved from http://www.who.int/impact/resources/ImpactBrochure.pdf.
63. Mackey, T. K. and Liang, B. A. (2011). The global counterfeit drug trade: Patient safety and public health risks. *Journal of Pharmaceutical Sciences*, 100(11), 4571–4579.
64. Newton, P. N., Green, M. D., Fernández, F. M., Day, N. P., and White, N. J. (2006). Counterfeit anti-infective drugs. *The Lancet Infectious Diseases*, 6(9), 602–613.
65. Canadian Institute for Health Information. (2013). *Drug Expenditure in Canada, 1985 to 2012*. Ottawa, Ontario, Canada: CIHI. Retrieved from https://secure.cihi.ca/free_products/Drug_Expenditure_2013_EN.pdf.

66. Clifford, K. Internet drug exporters feel pressure in Canada. (December 11, 2004). *The New York Times*, p. A1.
67. Bloomberg. (2003). Pfizer Cuts Drug Channel to 50 Canadian Pharmacies (Update1). News on Bloomberg. Retrieved from http://www.bloomberg.com/apps/news?pid=newsarchive&sid=aCvq1haSlI2E.
68. Gately, G. (2003). Drug giant aims to stop sale of Canadian prescriptions in US news on health day. Retrieved from http://consumer.healthday.com/general-health-information-16/prescription-drug-news-551/drug-giant-aims-to-stop-sale-of-canadian-prescriptions-in-u-s-511288.html. Accessed December 5, 2015.
69. Health Canada. (2010). Import and export policy for health products under the Food and Drugs Act and its Regulations (POL-0060). Retrieved from http://www.hc-sc.gc.ca/dhp-mps/compli-conform/import-export/pol-0060_biu-uif-eng.php. Accessed December 5, 2015.
70. Ministry of Health, Labor and Welfare. (2004). Importing or bringing medication into Japan for personal use. Retrieved from http://www.mhlw.go.jp/english/topics/import/index.html. Accessed December 5, 2015.
71. Commission of the European Communities. (2003). Parallel imports of proprietary medicinal products. Retrieved from http://eur-lex.europa.eu/legal-content/EN/TXT/PDF/?uri=CELEX:52003DC0839&from=EN. Accessed December 5, 2015.
72. Kanavos, P., Gross, D., and Taylor, D. (2006). Parallel trading in medicines: Europe's experience and its implications for commercial drug importation in the United States. American Association for Retired Persons (AARP). Retrieved from http://assets.aarp.org/rgcenter/health/2005_07_trade.pdf. Accessed December 5, 2015.
73. Ganslandt, M. and Maskus, K. E. (2004). Parallel imports and the pricing of pharmaceutical products: Evidence from the European Union. *Journal of Health Economics*, 23(5), 1035–1057.

Chapter 12

Competition between Brand-Name and Generic Drugs

Jianfei J. Guo and Christina M.L. Kelton

Contents

Introduction

Government patent law grants to innovators, such as pharmaceutical companies, patents for their discoveries. In turn, the patents allow drug companies to obtain monopoly profits and charge monopoly prices for a period of time. Because bringing a new drug to market has been estimated to cost, on average, over $(USD)800 million,[1] drug companies would not undertake the risks associated with developing new drugs without the opportunity to be rewarded for their efforts. When the innovator company's patent expires, generic companies begin to enter the market, and eventually the market may start to resemble a competitive market. The speed at which the transformation occurs depends on how quickly generic (multiple source) drugs are substituted for branded (single source) medications, and public policy can influence this speed. (While we appreciate that generic companies may brand their products as well, we use the term "branded" in this chapter to refer to the innovator company's brand.) When the market becomes competitive, efficiency of resource allocation is restored as price approaches marginal cost. This chapter is devoted to understanding competition in pharmaceutical markets, as well as public policies that serve either to limit competition or enhance competition in those markets.

Patent is key to the length of time that a firm captures monopoly profits. On the one hand, the government rewards innovation with patents that are "long enough." The Hatch-Waxman Act of 1984 (which added Section 156 to the U.S. Patent Act) permitted patent term extension for up to 5 years for human drug products. The Act restored a portion of the patent term during which the patentee must wait for the Food and Drug Administration's (FDA) review of its drug. The Uruguay Round Agreements Act of 1994 (which amended Section 154 of the Patent Act) extended the patent length for all U.S. patents (including those on pharmaceuticals) from 17 to 20 years. The FDA's Modernization Act of 1997 helped to accelerate the drug review process by reducing or simplifying many of the regulatory obligations imposed on drug manufacturers. The Patent Term Guarantee Authority Act of 1999 required the federal Patent and Trademark Office to compensate firms for delays of over 3 years in processing patents. The Best Pharmaceuticals for Children Act of 2002 gave drug companies a 6-month patent extension if they tested the safety of their drugs in children.

On the other hand, upon patent expiration, the government wants to encourage the entry of generic manufacturers in order to create a competitive market. The Hatch-Waxman Act of 1984 gave the FDA the authority to accept abbreviated new drug applications (ANDAs) for generic entry. Generic manufacturers must demonstrate only bioequivalence to the patented drug in order to be approved by the FDA through the ANDA process. The time period between patent expiration and generic drug entry was shortened from 3 to 4 years before 1984 to 1 to 3 months in the 1990s.[2] The first approved ANDA, in 1984, was for generic disopyramide, marketed as Norpace® and used in the treatment of cardiac arrhythmia. From 1984 to 2000, 8019 ANDAs were submitted to the FDA.[3]

U.S. pharmaceutical companies have been innovative. They increased their research and development (R&D) investment from \$(USD)2 billion in 1980 to \$(USD)8.4 billion in 1990, to \$(USD)26 billion in 2000, and to \$(USD)50.7 billion in 2010.[4] Over the decade of the 1990s, R&D costs rose annually at the rate of 7.4% above inflation.[1] Between 1990 and 2004, the FDA approved a total of 1284 new drug applications.[5]

However, consistently large annual increases in pharmaceutical costs in the 1990s put the current system under tremendous pressure and caused academics and policy makers to revisit the trade-off between innovation encouraged by the patent system and social welfare enhanced by competition. According to a 2002 report prepared by the National Institute for Health Care Management, the explanations for the rising trend in drug expenditures included declining buyer price sensitivity due to better insurance coverage for drugs; an increase in the number of prescription medicines available, especially for chronic conditions; an increase in the diagnosis of diseases in an aging population; and a more aggressive marketing of prescription drugs to doctors and patients.[6] These four factors led to both an increase in the number of prescriptions written (an increase in drug utilization) and an increase in the average price per prescription.

The private sector responded to the rising costs of pharmaceuticals through the use of drug formularies, the emergence of pharmaceutical benefit management companies, and the expansion of mail-order pharmacies. In the public sector, state Medicaid programs adopted preferred drug lists, prior authorization (PA) programs for more expensive drugs, and either required or strongly encouraged substitution of generic drugs. Drug acquisition costs for Medicaid were reduced further by rebates given by the pharmaceutical manufacturers. The Omnibus Budget Reconciliation Act of 1990 required drug manufacturers to rebate a portion of a drug's price back to states and to the federal government. The rebate was 15% of average manufacturer's price (AMP) for brand-name drugs and 11% of AMP for generics.[7] The Patient Protection and Affordable Care Act (PPACA) of 2010 increased federally mandated manufacturer rebate percentages for both generic and brand-name drugs to 17.1% and 23.1% of AMP, respectively.[8] Primarily because of Medicare Part D, which arose from the Medicare Modernization Act of 2003, the Medicare Program spent $(USD)68.2 billion on prescription drugs in 2012.[9] Medicare Part D plans vary considerably in their formularies and cost-sharing requirements, offering the elderly a wide range of options. However, Part D's market-expanding effect has put additional upward pressure on both drug prices and utilization.

Drug Markets in Theory

In some sense, each specific generic compound is its own market; hence, each patented, single-source medication gives its manufacturer a monopoly in that market. Due to the unique characteristics of each medication, no single-source medication is a perfect substitute for any other. Some patients benefit more from some drugs while others benefit more from other drugs. In addition, physicians tend to have their preferred medications. Upon expiration of a branded drug's patent, the monopoly disappears. Companies marketing the same generic entity provide direct competition to the branded drug company, bringing competition to the market, though not necessarily, as discussed in the succeeding text, via a lower price for the branded drug. For drugs in large markets, there may be 25 or more companies competing for sales of a given generic entity. For these markets, the perfectly competitive economic model may be most appropriate as generic firms compete by driving price down to marginal cost. Much of the literature in economics journals in the 1990s focused on drug price trends and how they related to patent expiry and generic entry. The 1984 Hatch-Waxman Act facilitated the entry of generic drug products, and research examined the results of the Act, emphasizing the determinants of entry, the speed of entry, and the resulting change in price and market share for the branded and generic drugs in the market.[2,10–18]

The pharmaceutical sector has also been described as a group of differentiated oligopolies (markets with a few sellers, each offering a product similar to the others).[19] Although a firm may hold a patent for a specific drug, it must often compete in a market consisting of several different drug entities (single and multiple source) that treat the same or similar indications. The Bertrand–Nash model of differentiated oligopoly assumes price competition by branded pharmaceutical companies marketing different chemical entities usable for the same therapeutic purpose. With product differentiation, quantity demanded of a drug depends not only on its own price (inversely) but also directly on the prices of substitute products. A substitutability parameter α determines how closely the drugs substitute for each other. In a duopoly equilibrium presented in Elzinga and Mills,[19] the equilibrium price was shown to be high when substitutability was low, and vice versa. Indeed, direct-to-consumer advertising is an attempt to lower α as well as to increase overall demand for the drug class.

Missing from oligopoly characterizations are purchasers who possess monopsony (single, large buyer) buying power, giving them the ability to negotiate lower drug prices. Pharmacy benefit managers and managed care organizations maintain formularies and encourage the use of generic drugs or older, less expensive branded drugs. Significant buyer power comes specifically from the ability to take advantage of any between-brand competition in a market.[20,21] Indeed, Elzinga and Mills[19] argued that some buyers were able to increase the substitutability parameter α, bringing down prices for themselves. As discussed in the succeeding text, we found that one large hospital buyer was able to obtain substantial discounts on some of the anti-infective medications that it purchased. There is even speculation that effective bargaining by group purchasing organizations, limiting the profitability of suppliers, is partially responsible for the drug-shortage problem, particularly prevalent, at the writing of this book, for injectable drugs primarily used in hospitals.[22]

Finally, even if, using an economic model, we could mimic well the market structure of a pharmaceutical market at a particular point in time, often these markets are quite dynamic. New drugs constantly replace older, less effective medicines. Whole new categories of medicines develop around "blockbusters." For example, the market for angiotensin-converting enzyme (ACE) inhibitors, a subclass of antihypertensive medications, was born in 1981 when captopril (Capoten®) was introduced by Bristol–Myers Squibb (BMS). Captopril was followed by enalapril, lisinopril, and fosinopril, among others. Then in 1995, after many of the ACE inhibitors were available as generics, another antihypertension subclass, angiotensin receptor blockers (ARBs), was born with the introduction of losartan (Cozaar®) by Merck. Again, a number of other products, such as valsartan, irbesartan, and eprosartan, followed. Both drug classes (ACE inhibitors and ARBs) are now available simultaneously and compete with each other.[23]

Similarly, the market for antiulcer gastric medications, which did not exist prior to 1977 when Tagamet® was introduced by SmithKline, is now on its third generation of drugs capable of fighting ulcers. All three generations (histamine H_2-receptor antagonists or H_2RAs, coating agents, and proton-pump inhibitors [PPIs]) are currently available, with the different generations' competing, at least loosely, with each other in some markets.[24]

Competition in Pharmaceutical Markets

Without a single theoretical model of market structure that fits the entire pharmaceutical sector (because oligopoly, monopoly, monopsony, and perfect competition are all applicable for certain aspects of firm behavior), we turn to empirical observations to see how different types of competition affect drug prices and utilization of both branded and generic drugs. In our empirical analyses, we distinguished between innovator, single-source pharmaceutical companies selling brand-name products and generic manufacturers of bioequivalent drugs. We distinguished as well among three different market definitions—wide, narrow, and single generic compound—since drugs can be loose, close, or perfect substitutes for each other, respectively, depending on how the market is defined. With these distinctions, there are various types of competition that occur between the two types of firms and in the different sized markets. We discuss separately some empirical results for each of the following four types of competition:

1. Intermarket ("wide market") competition, which occurs between drugs in different "narrow markets" within the same therapeutic class, for example, between the PPIs and the H_2RAs or between the ACE inhibitors and the ARBs
2. Interbrand ("narrow market") competition, which occurs between drugs in the same narrow market, for example, competition between two different PPIs (Protonix® and Nexium®, for example), H_2RAs (Tagamet and Zantac®), ACE inhibitors (Capoten and Vasotec®), or ARBs (Cozaar and Diovan®)

3. Brand–generic competition, which occurs between a brand-name drug and generic manufacturers of the same generic compound
4. Generic competition, which occurs between generic manufacturers, again of the same generic compound

We have studied these four types of competition in the U.S. Medicaid market for a number of different therapeutic classes: antidepressants,[25] antipsychotics,[26] antiretrovirals,[27] antifungals,[28] statins,[29] benzodiazepines,[30] anithypertensives,[23] and antiulcer gastric medications,[24] among others.

Intermarket Competition

ACE inhibitors are widely used in the treatment of hypertension and work by counteracting systemic vascular resistance and sodium retention. Meanwhile, ARBs, a newer class of antihypertensive medications, affect aldosterone secretion and cause vasodilation through a slightly different mechanism of action from the ACE inhibitors. Although the ARBs are known for their excellent side-effect profiles,[31] they have not been shown to be more effective than ACE inhibitors in terms of blood-pressure reduction or slowing the progression of renal disease or type 2 diabetes.[32] Nevertheless, in 2008, the U.S. Medicaid programs spent $(USD)309.8 million on ACE inhibitors and ARBs, and the latter accounted for 65% of expenditures.[23] Although, in theory, Medicaid programs could have implemented PA and step-up therapy programs for the ARB class, in practice most did not, and those that did not do so in a timely way to capture the most savings.[23] Average (pre-rebate) reimbursement per prescription for an ARB increased from $(USD)38 in 1995 to $(USD)82 in 2008, while the average (again, pre-rebate) spending on an ACE inhibitor prescription decreased from $(USD)37 in 1991 to $(USD)24 in 2008, largely due to generic entry in that class. Overall, average spending on antihypertension prescriptions increased from $(USD)37 to $(USD)45 over the 17 years, representing a percentage increase less than that of the consumer price index over the same period, but certainly not a decline as might be expected from the increased competition from the many new antihyperintensives introduced.[23]

There are three types of antiulcer gastric medications: histamine H_2RAs, coating agents, and PPIs. Both H_2RAs and PPIs reduce the production of acid in the stomach, though are chemically and pharmacologically unrelated drug classes. There was a systematic replacement of older, less expensive H_2RAs by the newer, more expensive PPIs in the Ohio Medicaid market.[24] Average (pre-rebate) reimbursement per prescription for PPIs increased from $(USD)105 in 1997 to $(USD)129 in 2002. Meanwhile, the average per-prescription spending on H_2RAs decreased from $(USD)72 to $(USD)20. The average per-prescription spending on coating agents decreased as well.[24]

As for the situation of ACE inhibitors versus ARBs, direct competition between H_2RAs and PPIs was limited because physicians and patients were essentially free to select a drug from either group barring any formulary or PA restrictions that individual state programs might have had.

Interbrand (Narrow Market) Competition

Just as our research has shown limited competition between drug classes targeting the same indication (as payers have been more willing than might be expected to switch to newer, higher-priced drugs), there seems to be little effect on price or utilization of existing drugs in a drug class of new branded-drug entry. As new branded ACE inhibitors entered the market, there was no evidence that either utilization of or per-prescription reimbursement for branded or generic captopril (or other earlier entrants for that matter) declined. The same phenomenon was found for the ARB class. Moreover, we found no statistically significant effect of new brand entry on either reimbursement for or utilization of other branded drugs among the PPIs.[24] Indeed, the only PPI with decreasing utilization from 1997–2002 was Prilosec®. The utilization of Prevacid®, Protonix, Aciphex®, and Nexium steadily increased. Since a single drug manufacturer, AstraZeneca, supplied both Prilosec and Nexium, the declining share for Prilosec most likely was due to a strategic move by a single company rather than to competition. Moreover, entry of the three new PPIs, Aciphex, Protonix, and Nexium, had no effect on per-prescription reimbursement for Prilosec or Prevacid, the two PPIs sold throughout the period. Nexium and Aciphex were introduced at similarly high prices, and those prices continued to rise. Protonix was introduced at a lower price; its price increased over time as well.[24]

Using more rigorous (time-series intervention) analysis to detect the effect of new entry on Medicaid spending for antidepressants, the entries of Zoloft®, Paxil®, and Celexa® were all found not to have statistically significant effects on Medicaid's spending on Prozac®, the first selective serotonin reuptake inhibitor (SSRI).[33]

Generic Competition to the Branded Drug

Once therapeutically equivalent, generic alternatives to a brand-name pharmaceutical are available, eventually at a significantly lower price than their branded counterpart, most purchasers will select the lower-priced generic substitutes. However, because the savings are so substantial in doing so, public policies are developed to reinforce these natural competitive market forces. Most states in the United States have passed drug product substitution laws that allow pharmacists to dispense a generic drug even when a prescription calls for a brand-name drug. Furthermore, most private insurance companies have tiered co-payment systems for pharmaceuticals. The tiered structures commonly assign generic drugs the lowest co-pay, providing an incentive for patients and providers to choose them.

Because of the strict Medicaid requirements for generic uptake following patent expiration for a branded drug, Medicaid market shares for branded drugs tend to fall precipitously when generic options are available. Following the patent expiration for Prozac in August 2001, the speed of generic uptake across the state Medicaid programs varied somewhat. However, by the end of 2005, no state's uptake percentage was lower than 96%.[34]

Whereas it is clear that the branded drug's market share drops following generic entry, there is no indication that the (pre-rebate) per-prescription reimbursement falls for the branded medication. Indeed, payment per prescription for Prozac continued its upward trend long after generic entry.[34] Per-prescription reimbursement for Capoten and Vasotec continued to rise significantly following entry of generic captopril and enalapril, respectively.[23]

Generic Competition

For the Medicaid market, it is only the fourth type of competition that leads consistently to significantly lower per-prescription spending. The average per-prescription spending on ranitidine by Ohio Medicaid fell from $(USD)60.82, when ranitidine was first marketed in 1997, to $(USD)16.02 in 2002.[24] In a large study of Medicaid spending following generic entry for 83 different drugs that lost their patent between 1992 and 2008, we found that 68 (82%) had lower reimbursement per unit (tablet, capsule, or vial, for example) 3 years post generic entry than before; 15 (18%) cost less than 50% of the original spending on the branded drug. Of the top

10 drugs in terms of annual Medicaid spending the year before generic entry, Medicaid experienced cost relief with respect to all but one. The amount of postentry savings rose with the number of generic competitors as well as time since initial entry. Generic entry brought less relief to Medicaid for injectable drugs than orally or topically administered medications.[35]

In order to be able to take advantage of the cost savings offered by generic drugs, state Medicaid programs must reduce their reimbursement in step with the price decreases experienced by pharmacy wholesalers and retailers. The federal upper limit program sets maximum amounts at which the federal government will participate in Medicaid reimbursement for certain generic drugs. Most individual states, moreover, have their own maximum allowable cost (MAC) program, which can even more aggressively keep reimbursement limits low. Timely updating of the MAC list following patent expiration of a branded drug is important to obtaining maximum available savings.[34]

Although, generally speaking, the availability of generic drugs has offered significant cost savings to buyers, generic drug markets are not immune to anticompetitive forces. In the early 1990s, the Medicaid market for lorazepam, a benzodiazepine, was almost 100% generic with approximately 40 different suppliers competing with each other. Very few branded-drug prescriptions (for Ativan®) were being reimbursed. An alleged conspiracy between Mylan Laboratories and its active-ingredient suppliers in 1997 was associated with an increase in seller concentration in the generic lorazepam market, after which the price of lorazepam increased sharply in 1998 by Mylan and the other market leaders. Because switching from lorazepam to a less expensive benzodiazepine (for example, alprazolam) was difficult for physicians and patients, payers, including Medicaid, were forced to pay substantially more for lorazepam. Although the Federal Trade Commission (FTC) brought suit against Mylan and a settlement was reached in November 2002, the lorazepam market has remained much less competitive with fewer suppliers than before the conspiracy, raising the likelihood of recurrence.[36]

Buyer Power

Pharmaceutical companies face different types of purchasers such as hospitals, clinics, and retail pharmacies. Companies are able to price discriminate across the various purchasers depending on buyers' relative market power, that is, their relative ability to take advantage of the latent competition between pharmaceutical companies. We studied the purchasing behavior of a buyer with significant power in negotiation. The buyer was a nonprofit six-hospital system that served a substantial community base in southwestern Ohio and provided medical services to a large number of uninsured and underinsured individuals. The objective of this buyer was to keep costs to a minimum by negotiating vigorously with its medical vendors. The hospital buyer we studied had a strict formulary, which is updated on a monthly basis. The buyer, along with other health-care providers, had seen its drug costs rise dramatically over the 1990s, although at a rate of 11% between 2000 and 2001 compared to the national average of 18% and Ohio Medicaid's increase of 23% (from $(USD)996 million in 2000 to $(USD)1.23 billion in 2001).[37]

We studied price discounts (percentage discount of the buyer's transaction price from average wholesale price or AWP) across 23 narrow anti-infective markets, in which the buyer had from weak to strong bargaining power depending on the number of competitive options that it had available to it and also depending on a number of other factors such as the amount of overall business conducted with each manufacturer. Out of the 23 markets, 20 were defined based on their six-digit American Hospital Formulary Service classification, while three were markets defined by indication. On average, the buyer received a 46% discount relative to AWP.[38]

For the hospital buyer, unlike for state Medicaid programs, we were able to find statistical evidence of competitive effects for all four types of competition discussed earlier. The study suggested that the addition of one more generic manufacturer led to a 2.44% point increase in the discount received by the buyer on its brand-name or generic purchases of the same generic drug. The addition of one more branded drug to a market based on therapeutic class led to a 0.55% point increase in the discount received by the buyer. The addition of one more branded drug to an indication market (which cut across several therapeutic classes) led to a 0.56% point increase in the discount received by the buyer.[38]

Generic Drug Entry and Patent Settlements in Pharmaceutical Markets

The Hatch-Waxman Act of 1984 essentially allows generic entry immediately after patent expiration. It grants the first successful generic applicant a 180-day marketing exclusivity, after which other generic manufacturers are allowed to enter the market as well. With substantial monopoly profits at stake, however, it is not surprising that brand-name pharmaceutical companies try to maintain their monopolies as long as possible.

Since the passing of the Hatch-Waxman Act, drug companies have raised patent infringement issues through lawsuits involving hundreds of different brand-name drugs, including BuSpar®, Capoten, Cardizem CD®, Cipro®, Claritin®, Lupron®, Neurontin®, Paxil, Pepcid®, Pravachol®, Prilosec, Procardia XL®, Prozac, Vasotec, Xanax®, Zantac, Zocor®, Zoloft, and Zyprexa®.[3] A lawsuit brought against a potential generic competitor triggers an automatic 30-month stay on that company's generic drug approval, potentially delaying significantly the marketing of generic alternatives. In summer 2002, the FTC issued a report on generic entry, after reviewing 20 complex legal cases between brand-name drug companies and first generic drug applicants.[3] The FTC found that the 30-month stay provision was susceptible to manipulation and was being used to create entry barriers for generic companies. Moreover, there was no limit on the number of 30-month stays requested. Indeed, GlaxoSmithKline was able to obtain five 30-month stays for Paxil.[3]

Extending patent life by patenting molecular modifications of the original drug is another common strategy to forestall generic entry. BMS's BuSpar (buspirone) was patented in 1980 and approved by the FDA in September 1986 to treat anxiety. U.S. sales of the drug were $(USD)709 million in 2000, making BuSpar the fifth highest-selling drug for the company in that year. One day prior to the BuSpar patent's expiration in November 2000, BMS received a new patent on extended-release buspirone and requested a delay of any generic buspirone entry; indeed, Mylan Laboratories was about to deliver the first truckload of generic buspirone when it was forced to stop delivery. In late November 2000, Mylan and Watson (approved to market a different dosage form of buspirone) jointly filed a lawsuit to contest the validity of the new BuSpar patent. In March 2001, the generic companies won the lawsuit and were allowed to sell generic buspirone; they captured two-thirds of buspirone sales by June 2001. In October 2001, BMS appealed this decision, which triggered the automatic delay under the Hatch-Waxman Act. Only in February 2002 was the case finally settled without further BuSpar patent extension. BMS had successfully delayed full generic entry for 15 months in the U.S. market.[39]

An alternative to bringing legal action surrounding patent infringement is collusion with the first FDA-approved generic drug company in order to delay generic entry.[40] For example, Hoechst and Andrx entered into an agreement in which Andrx was paid millions of dollars to keep the generic alternative (diltiazem hydrochloride) to Hoechst's Cardizem CD (a calcium channel blocker for the treatment of hypertension) off the market. Because this collusion violated U.S. antitrust law, thirty states filed a class action lawsuit in 2002 against the companies. The final settlement required the two companies to give compensation of $(USD)80 million to consumers (state Medicaid programs and insurance companies) for their overpayment for Cardizem CD from 1998 to 2003.[41]

Similarly, Abbott entered into an agreement with Geneva, in order to deter Geneva from entering the market with a generic version of Abbott's Hytrin® (an alpha-adrenergic blocking agent for treatment of hypertension and prostate cancer). Abbott paid Geneva $(USD)4.5 million per month to delay generic drug entry. When the FTC and the FDA intervened, Geneva was required to waive its right to a 180-day exclusivity period for its generic drug.[3]

Patent Protection in the International Market

Although patent law protects drug company monopolies in the United States for a period of time, international protection should not be taken for granted. Gleevec®, a beta-crystalline form of imatinib mesylate, was approved by the FDA in 2001 to treat chronic myelogenous leukemia and is patent protected from competition in the United States until 2015.

Novartis, the manufacturer of Gleevec, also filed a patent application in India (in 1998) and received an exclusive marketing right in that country in 2003. However, in 2005, the Indian Patent Office rejected the Novartis patent. When Novartis appealed the rejection to the Indian Supreme Court, it lost the case in April 2013, because of insufficient evidence of a difference in therapeutic efficacy between Gleevec and the raw form of imatinib, an older off-patent medication. Indian public health activists were excited by the decision because of its implications for increased availability of inexpensive generics in a developing country. While Novartis set the price of Gleevec at $(USD)2666 per patient per month in India, Indian generic companies were selling their versions at $(USD)177 to $(USD)266 per patient per month.[42]

Biologics and Biosimilars in the Marketplace

Biologic medications, manufactured in or extracted from biological sources, as opposed to chemically synthesized, represent cutting-edge pharmaceutical science. They have had a tremendous impact to date primarily in rheumatology and oncology, but some impact as well in cardiology, dermatology, gastroenterology, and neurology, among other areas of medicine. For some diseases, biologics are the only treatments available. Before 2006 when Myozyme® was approved by the FDA, there was no effective treatment for Pompe disease, a rare autosomal recessive disease caused by an acid alpha-glucosidase gene disorder. Myozyme is an enzyme replacement therapy that uses recombinant DNA technology to produce the enzyme from Chinese hamster ovary cells. In 2010, U.S. Medicaid programs spent $(USD)3.6 million on Myozyme for 360 prescriptions (approximately $(USD)10,000 per prescription).[43] Indeed, most biologics are very expensive. Nevertheless, there are a few hundred biologic drug products and vaccines currently undergoing clinical trials, accounting for a substantial proportion of new drug development. It seems as though the large pharmaceutical companies are willing to collaborate with innovative biotechnology companies on bringing biologics to market.[44]

It is difficult to predict the future role of competition between biologics. In 2009, the Biologics Price Competition and Innovation Act (BPCIA) was passed as part of the PPACA; it created a regulatory pathway for generic biologics to be approved by the FDA through an abbreviated regulatory process. A key aspect of the BPCIA is that generic biologics are classified as being either "biosimilar" or "interchangeable."[45] A biosimilar is a generic that is highly similar to the pioneer product though may have minor differences in clinically inactive components. There are no clinically meaningful differences between the biologic product and the pioneer product in terms of safety, purity, and potency. An interchangeable generic biologic is a medication expected to produce the same clinical result as the branded pioneer drug in terms of safety and efficacy.[45]

Unless the generic drug is determined to be interchangeable, however, it would have to be marketed to physicians as a treatment alternative and would most likely not achieve the same level of substitutability as most small-molecule generic drugs achieve. Hence, if the drug was determined to be only biosimilar, 18 months of exclusivity as allowed by the BPCIA might not be considered as profitable as a 12-year exclusivity period achieved through an approval of a full biologic licensing application. So, although in theory there is a generic pathway for biologics, it remains to be seen how often it will be used.[46] The European Union has had a generic biologics pathway in place since 2004. Since then, however, just a few approved biosimilars have achieved small market shares. Furthermore, these biosimilars have resulted in only modest (25%–30%) price reductions relative to the pioneer brands.[46,47]

Innovation versus Competition

From 1992 to 2002, prescription drug spending in the United States rose precipitously from $(USD)47.0 billion to $(USD)158.2 billion, representing a 236.6% increase. Over that same time period, the out-of-pocket share fell from 50.3% to 25.9% as more people were covered by prescription drug insurance.[9] Although patents expired for many top-selling drugs over the decade, other new branded medications entered the market, and whole new classes of medications come into existence—at patented monopoly prices. As these new drugs were requested by patients and prescribed by their physicians, the share of generics generally decreased. In other words, the innovative new drugs that the patent system encouraged had a more powerful effect on the overall cost of medication than the creation of competitive markets, through generic entry, for older drugs. SSRIs in the U.S. Medicaid program increased their market share among antidepressants from 13% in 1991 to 57% in 2004, while the traditional, primarily generic tricyclic antidepressant market share decreased from 74% in 1991 to 12% in 2004.[25] Overall, the market share for single-source antidepressants increased from 38% in 1991 to 72% in 2001 due to the increasing use of SSRIs.[25] Total expenditure on antipsychotics in the U.S. Medicaid program increased sharply from $(USD)135 million per quarter in 1991 to $(USD)1.25 billion per quarter in 2004 specifically because of the increased use of branded atypical antipsychotics and the decreased use of generic conventional antipsychotics.[26] A more recent example involves oral cancer drugs. Over the period 2002–2004, the conventional breast cancer drug therapy (tamoxifen) was replaced by newer, and considerably more expensive, branded medications like Femara®, Arimidex®, and Taxotere®.[48]

Then, from 2002 to 2012, prescription drug spending rose from $(USD)158.2 billion to $(USD)263.2 billion, a 66.5% increase. During this decade, the share of out-of-pocket spending fell from 25.9% to 17.8%. In 2012, private insurance covered $(USD)117.0 billion; Medicare paid for $(USD)68.2 billion, while Medicaid plus the Children's Health Insurance Program spent over $(USD)20 billion.[9] Although the themes of innovation and competition still characterize the branded drug and generic drug segments of the pharmaceutical sector, respectively, the two forces have been somewhat more balanced in the last decade than during the 1990s. Nevertheless, in 2009, generics represented approximately 66% of all Medicaid prescriptions but only 22% of Medicaid spending.[49]

Conclusions

In its efforts both to encourage new drug innovation and to keep medicines affordable for pharmaceutical payers, the U.S. government has compromised, for new brand-name medications, with a monopoly market structure for a period of time, followed by intense generic competition. The transition from the monopoly to the competitive structure can sometimes be a legal battleground because of the substantial monopoly profits at stake. The legal system handles cases of alleged patent infringement by generic drug companies, which may delay entry of generic alternatives.

Once generic drugs are available, public and private payers encourage the use of generic substitutes through co-pay systems or physician and patient education. While brand–generic and generic competition serve to reduce drug costs after patent expiration, it is much more difficult to harness the power of intermarket and interbrand competition. Only a purchaser with significant buying power, in which a formulary allows, for example, can force loose branded substitutes to compete for a spot on that formulary. Only such a purchaser, moreover, can counteract the rise in drug costs caused by the introduction of new, high-priced medicines by requiring, at least for those patients who tolerate them well, the use of older, less expensive medications.

References

1. DiMasi JA, Hansen RW, Grabowski HG (2003). The price of innovation: New estimates of drug development costs. *Journal of Health Economics* 22: 151–185.
2. Cook A (1998). *How Increased Competition from Generic Drugs Has Affected Prices and Returns in the Pharmaceutical Industry.* Congressional Budget Office Report. Washington, DC: CBO.
3. Federal Trade Commission (July 2002). *Generic Drug Entry Prior to Patent Expiration: An FTC Study.* Washington, DC: FTC.
4. Pharmaceutical Manufacturers of America (July 2013). *2013 Profile Biopharmaceutical Research Industry.* Washington, DC: PhRMA.
5. Center for Drug Evaluation and Research (March 2005). *NDAs Approved in Calendar Years 1990–2004 by Therapeutic Potential and Chemical Type.* Rockville, MD: CDER, U.S. Food and Drug Administration.
6. National Institute for Health Care Management (May 2002). *Prescription Drug Expenditure 2001: Another Year of Escalating Costs.* Washington, DC: NIHCM.
7. Crowley JS, Ashner D, Elam L (December 2003). *Medicaid Outpatient Prescription Drug Benefits: Findings from a National Survey, 2003.* Kaiser Commission on Medicaid and the Uninsured. Washington, DC: The Henry J. Kaiser Family Foundation.
8. Henry J. Kaiser Family Foundation (April 2013). *Summary of the Affordable Care Act.* Washington, DC: KFF.
9. Centers for Medicare & Medicaid Services (2014). *National Health Expenditures by Type of Service and Source of Funds: Calendar Years 1960–2012.* Washington, DC: CMS.
10. Bae JP (1997). Drug patent expirations and speed of generic entry. *Health Services Research* 32: 87–101.

11. Caves RE, Whinston MD, Hurwitz MA (1991). Patent expiration, entry, and competition in the U.S. pharmaceutical industry. *Brookings Papers Microeconomics* 1991: 1–66.
12. Frank RG, Salkever DS (1992). Pricing, patent loss and the market for pharmaceuticals. *Southern Economic Journal* 59: 165–179.
13. Frank RG, Salkever DS (1997). Generic entry and the pricing of pharmaceuticals. *Journal of Economics and Management Strategy* 6: 75–90.
14. Grabowski HG, Vernon JM (1992). Brand loyalty, entry, and price competition in pharmaceuticals after the 1984 drug act. *Journal of Law and Economics* 21: 331–349.
15. Griliches Z, Cockburn I (1994). Generics and new goods in pharmaceutical price indexes. *American Economic Review* 84: 1213–1232.
16. Hudson J (1992). Pricing dynamics in the pharmaceutical industry. *Applied Economics* 24: 103–112.
17. Hurwitz MA, Caves RE (1998). Persuasion or information? Promotion and the shares of brand name and generic pharmaceuticals. *Journal of Law and Economics* 31: 299–320.
18. Scott Morton FM (1999). Entry decisions in the generic pharmaceutical industry. *RAND Journal of Economics* 30: 421–440.
19. Elzinga KG, Mills DE (1997). The distribution and pricing of prescription drugs. *International Journal of the Economics of Business* 4: 287–299.
20. Snyder CM (1996). A dynamic theory of countervailing power. *RAND Journal of Economics* 27: 747–769.
21. Snyder CM (1998). Why do larger buyers pay lower prices? Intense supplier competition. *Economic Letters* 58: 205–209.
22. Conti RM (December 2011). *An Economic Assessment of the Causes and Policy Implications of Current Specialty Drug Shortages*. Remarks to Chairman Baucus, Senator Hatch, and members of the Senate Finance Committee. Washington, D.C.: U.S. Government Printing Office, pp. 77–601.
23. Bian BB, Guo JJ, Kelton CML, Wigle PR (2010). Utilization and expenditure trends of ACE inhibitors and ARBs in the Medicaid program. *Journal of Managed Care Pharmacy* 16: 671–679.
24. Guo JJ, Kelton CML, Pasquale MK, Zimmerman J, Patel A, Heaton PC, Cluxton RJ (2004). Price and market-share competition of anti-ulcer gastric medications in the Ohio Medicaid market. *International Journal of Pharmaceutical Medicine* 18: 271–282.
25. Chen Y, Kelton CML, Jing Y, Guo JJ, Li X, Patel NC (2008). Utilization, price, and spending trends for antidepressants in the U.S. Medicaid Program. *Research in Social and Administrative Pharmacy* 4: 244–257.
26. Jing Y, Kelton CML, Guo JJ, Fan H, Chen Y, Li X, Patel NC (2007). Price, utilization, and spending for antipsychotic medications in the Medicaid Program. *Drug Benefit Trends* 19: 27–41.
27. Jing Y, Klein P, Kelton CML, Li X, Guo JJ (2007). Utilization and spending trends for antiretroviral medications in the U.S. Medicaid Program from 1991 to 2005. *AIDS Research and Therapy* 4: 22.
28. Desai VCA, Cavanaugh TM, Kelton CML, Guo JJ, Heaton PC (2012). Trends in the utilization of, spending on, and prices for outpatient antifungal agents in U.S. Medicaid Programs. *Clinical Therapeutics* 34(10): 2118–2131.e1. http://www.ncbi.nlm.nih.gov/pubmed/23031625.
29. Jing Y, Kelton CML, Guo JJ, Chen Y, Li X, Wigle PR (2006). Price and utilization of statins in the Medicaid Program. *Drug Benefit Trends* 18: 580–592.
30. Gorevski E, Bian B, Kelton CML, Guo JJ, Martin-Boone JE (2012). Utilization, spending, and price trends for benzodiazepines in the U.S. Medicaid Program: 1991–2009. *Annals of Pharmacotherapy* 46: 503–512.
31. Vidt DG (2000). Is there an advantage to combination therapy with ACE inhibitors and angiotensin II receptor blockers? *Cleveland Clinical Journal of Medicine* 67: 89–91.
32. Matchar DB, McCrory DC, Orlando LA, Patel MR, Patel UD, Patwardhan MB, Powers B, Samsa GP, Gray RN (2007). *Comparative Effectiveness of Angiotensin-Converting Enzyme Inhibitors (ACEIs) and Angiotensin II Receptor Antagonists (ARBs) for Treating Essential Hypertension*. Comparative Effectiveness Review No. 10. Prepared by Duke Evidence-Based Practice Center under Contract No. 290-02-0025. Rockville, MD: Agency for Healthcare Research and Quality.

33. Ferrand Y, Kelton CML, Guo JJ, Levy MS, Yu Y (2011). Using time-series intervention analysis to understand U.S. Medicaid expenditures on antidepressant agents. *Research in Social and Administrative Pharmacy* 7: 64–80.
34. Kelton CML, Chang LV, Kreling DH (2013). State Medicaid Programs missed $220 million in uncaptured savings as generic fluoxetine came to market, 2001–05. *Health Affairs* 32: 1204–1211.
35. Kelton CML, Chang LV, Guo JJ, Yu Yan, Berry EA, Bian B, Heaton PC (2014). Firm- and drug-specific patterns of generic drug payments by US Medicaid Programs: 1991–2008. *Applied Health Economics and Health Policy* 12: 165–177.
36. Bian B, Gorevski E, Kelton CML, Guo JJ, Martin-Boone JE (2012). Long-term Medicaid excess payments from alleged price manipulation of generic lorazepam. *Journal of Managed Care Pharmacy* 18: 506–515.
37. Ohio Department of Job and Family Services (2000–2002). *Ohio Medicaid Expenditure Annual Report 2000, 2001, 2002.* Medicaid Department. Columbus, OH: ODJFS.
38. Dusing ML, Guo JJ, Kelton CML, Pasquale MK (2005). Competition and price discounts in anti-infective pharmaceutical markets in the United States. *Journal or Pharmaceutical Finance, Economics & Policy* 14: 59–85.
39. National Institute for Health Care Management Research and Education Foundation (June 2002). *A Primer: Generic Drugs, Patents and the Pharmaceutical Marketplace.* Washington, DC: NIHCM Foundation.
40. Federal Trade Commission (May 2000). *Antitrust Actions in Pharmaceutical Services and Products.* Washington, DC: FTC.
41. Office of the Attorney General (January 2003). *Attorney General Announces Cardizem CD® Settlement.* Richmond, VA: Office of the Attorney General.
42. Krishna RJ, Whalen J (April 1, 2013). Novartis loses glivec patent battle in India. *Wall Street Journal.* http://www.wsj.com/articles/SB10001424127887323296504578395672582230106.
43. Guo J, Kelton CML, Guo JJ (2012). Recent developments, utilization and spending trends for Pompe disease therapies. *American Health & Drug Benefits* 5: 182–188.
44. Villiger R, Bogdan B (2009). Licensing: Pros and cons for biotech. *Drug Discovery Today* 14: 227–230.
45. David JKM (2009). No Longer "If", but "When": The coming abbreviated approval pathway for follow-on biologics. *Food & Drug Law Journal* 64: 118–148.
46. Engelberg AB, Kesselheim AS, Avorn J (2009). Balancing innovation, access, and profits—Market exclusivity for biologics. *New England Journal of Medicine* 361: 1917–1919.
47. Kresse GB (2009). Biosimilars—Science, status, and strategic perspective. *European Journal of Pharmaceutics and Biopharmaceutics* 72: 479–486.
48. Malott SA, Chen Y, Pruemer J, Guo JJ (April 15, 2005). *Price Trends and Utilization Patterns of Breast Cancer Drug Therapy in the US Medicaid Systems.* Unpublished Poster Presentation. *Ohio Pharmacists Association Annual Conference.* Columbus, OH.
49. Coster JM (2010). Trends in generic drug reimbursement in Medicaid and Medicare. *U.S. Pharmacist* 35: 14–19.

Chapter 13

Structure and Dynamics of the Pharmaceutical Industry

Earlene Lipowski

Contents

Policy Relevance

Public policy initiatives affecting the industry provide some of the best examples of how government incentives foster innovations that have significant human and social value. These actions are also among the most thoroughly and systematically studied policies across their life cycle, from needs assessment to development, implementation, and impact analysis. Close examination by scholars and decision makers reveals the complex interplay between social welfare and the vicissitudes of economic, scientific, social, and political forces.

An examination of the structure and dynamics of the pharmaceutical manufacturing community illustrates how the industry continues to adapt to economic, political, and technological changes to preserve its functionality. Prior to WWII, pharmaceutical manufacturers in the United States operated as a segment of the chemicals industry. Unlike most industries in which innovation sprang from advancements in production, a distinct pharmaceutical industry evolved from discoveries in basic chemistry and innovations in chemical engineering.

The introduction of cimetidine (Tagamet) is an excellent example of a pharmaceutical innovation made possible by advances in science and technology in the early 1970s. Cimetidine was among the first drugs designed to target a specific biological receptor. Further application of the targeted drug design strategy resulted in novel treatments for herpes, AIDS, ovarian cancer, migraine, schizophrenia, depression, hypertension, and high cholesterol [1]. The pharmaceutical industry entered an era of unprecedented innovation and financial success based on this advancement.

By the start of the twenty-first century, pharmaceutical research was experiencing another paradigm shift driven by discoveries in biochemistry, cell biology, immunology, genetics, and molecular biology supported by advances in information and imaging technology. A biotechnology sector emerged within the pharmaceutical industry during the 1990s, and by 2005, all members of the Pharmaceutical Research and Manufacturers of America (PhRMA) were describing themselves as *bio*pharmaceutical firms.

Developments in science and technology do not occur in isolation but in conjunction with significant social and economic developments. Decades of rising health-care expenditures and maturing of the baby boom generation forced an examination of health policy and fostered attempts to restructure health-care delivery. Expanding government regulation, the evolution of managed care and investor-driven health care posed challenges to the pharmaceutical industry.

Legislation like the Hatch–Waxman Act of 1984 and regulations pursuant to the Food and Drug Administration (FDA) affect the U.S. pharmaceutical industry and provide some of the best examples of how government incentives foster innovations that have significant human and social value. However, government actions are not without controversy and criticism from a myriad of constituencies, including researchers, politicians, patients, payers, clinicians, and investors. Most notably, the aims of stockholders for a substantial return on investment (ROI) and the desire of consumers for readily accessible and affordable pharmaceuticals often conflict.

Ongoing adaptation of the pharmaceutical industry to scientific advances and societal pressures may be inevitable but nonetheless must take into account three traits that have been constants in the U.S. pharmaceutical industry: demand for continuous innovation, defense of intellectual property rights, and high profitability to fuel the enterprise [2].

Innovation through R&D

Although innovation has been a hallmark of success in the pharmaceutical industry, the necessity for continuous innovation was never more obvious than during the first decade of the twenty-first century. Industry expenditures for research and development (R&D) roughly doubled in real terms from 1982 to 1992 as measured in capitalized and uncapitalized dollars; the 1992 level of expenditures tripled by 2001. By 2013 R&D investment by the pharmaceutical industry totaled an estimated $(USD)51 billion [3]. However, despite the ever-increasing R&D expenditures and favorable public policy, introduction of innovative pharmaceutical products slowed [4–6]. Whereas the FDA approved an average of 37.2 new drugs and biologics annually from 1995 to 1999, approvals dropped to 22.6 per year from 2005 to 2009 [7].

The sales of the average new drug rise in a logarithmic pattern in the introductory period following FDA approval as depicted by the typical life cycle of a drug product in Figure 13.1. Drugs in the top decile of sales and profitability include products that eventually achieve blockbuster status by generating $(USD)1 billion or more in sales revenue per year. The top drugs tend

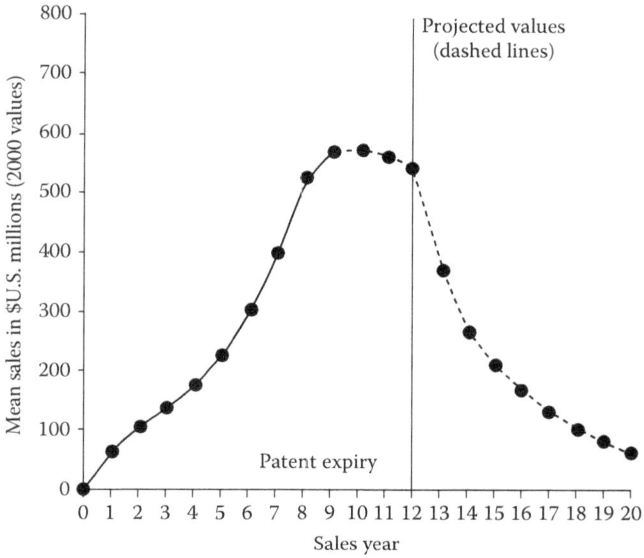

Figure 13.1 Actual and projected worldwide sales values for a representative sample product. (Reprinted from Grabowski, H., Vernon, J., and DiMasi, J.A., *Pharmacoeconomics*, 20(Suppl 3), 11, 2002. With permission from Wolters Kluwer Health.)

to represent therapeutic breakthroughs, i.e., they are the first agents in a therapeutic class and/or represent the best therapeutic option in the class. However, they are prime targets for cost containment measures, and sales revenues drop dramatically after the patents expire.

Managed care organizations, advised by pharmaceutical benefits managers (PBMs), increasingly promote the use of less-expensive alternatives and generic products in place of the brand-name innovators. Generics introduced in 1999–2000 could be expected to capture 50% of the market within 6 months, but by 2007–2008 the average generics accomplished a market shift of the same magnitude within the first month following FDA approval [8]. In addition PBMs apply strategies to encourage the use of generics as therapeutic alternatives for entire classes of drugs. When a generic drug is the first in its therapeutic class, the sales of all brands in an entire class drop [9].

Over the last decade the life cycle of a typical pharmaceutical product has shrunk in peak height and lifetime. Innovative products experience longer introductory phases due to safety concerns and constraints on promotions. Sales peak at lower levels due to pricing pressure and competition, and revenues fall off earlier as a result of more patent challenges occurring earlier in the life cycle [10,11]. Although there has been concern about innovator companies paying generic companies to postpone patent challenges and delay competition [12], recent research finds that the practice has not changed the effective market life of 12 years for drugs open to challenge between 2001 and 2010 [13].

Consequently, life cycle management strategy for manufacturers with top-selling drugs rests upon a vigorous defense of patents and market exclusivities that lengthen the effective patent life of the most successful innovations. Despite the efforts to defend intellectual property granted by law and regulation, the only true solution for sustaining gross revenues is to continuously replace older products with completely new ones that address previously unmet medical needs.

The results of published research examining the relationship between R&D spending and advances in therapeutics shows mixed results [6]. Some speculation even exists that modern industry practices have contributed to the apparent decline in R&D productivity. That is, firms operating under continuous pressure for novel and distinctive products but unsure that they can satisfy stockholders' demands rely more on aggressive marketing than pioneering research for their ROI.

The industry has in fact been accused of spending more on marketing than on R&D although definitive data and objective research are difficult to find [14]. PhRMA members reported sales and general administrative expense (including marketing) as 34.4% of revenue in 2013 and R&D at 17.8% of total sales [3]. On the other hand, PhRMA members lead in R&D expenditures not only in absolute dollars but also in terms of percentage of revenue. Of the top 20 spenders on R&D in 2013, 7 were PhRMA companies [15]. The pharmaceutical firms on the list of most innovative companies invested in a range of 11.4%–21.0% of revenue in R&D compared to 4%–5% reported by automakers and 6%–13% by computer firms [15].

U.S. public policy historically backs programs that provide economic incentives for pharmaceutical R&D, although the wisdom of some of these policies came under attack. For example, when the Orphan Drug Act was passed in 1983, it was generally viewed as a model piece of legislation for stimulating R&D by rewarding new treatments for rare diseases with provisions that protect the innovators' intellectual property rights. Incentives including waiver of filing fees, grants for clinical development, protocol assistance, and exclusive marketing rights for 7 years resulted in the approval of over 450 drugs designated as orphans by 2012 [17,18].

The majority of orphan drug products provide efficacious treatment, but the products presumably have limited sales potential to patient populations under 200,000 that defines an orphan condition. Manufacturers have also profited when products for conditions with few treatment options command high prices or if the innovation proves effective for treating other, more prevalent diseases [17]. Critics have questioned whether the Orphan Drug Act that represents a net benefit to society results in significant sales and profits [7].

The U.S. government provides further support of pharmaceutical R&D through cooperative agreements between federal agencies and the industry. The specific provisions were introduced in the Bayh–Dole Act of 1980, Stevenson–Wydler Act of 1980, and Federal Technology Transfer Act of 1986 [19]. Taken together, these acts supply the following directives and mechanisms for public–private collaboration:

1. Active promotion of technology transfer. Government-sponsored researchers are required to promote their discoveries to commercial firms. Each agency has a Technology Transfer Office whose role is to facilitate industry use and commercialization of publicly funded research.
2. Cooperative Research and Development Agreements. The National Institutes of Health (NIH) and government-funded university researchers are permitted to enter formal agreements with private entities for sharing personnel, services, equipment, resources, and knowledge on a specific project. The private sector partner is allowed to secure exclusive rights to the products produced under the arrangement.
3. Patent rights to government research. Government agencies assist industry partners in obtaining patent protection on publicly funded research results if the firms agree to invest in additional R&D to commercialize their discoveries.

4. Technology licensing. NIH and other government agencies can grant licenses to private companies that use government-funded research findings in proprietary research or to develop the ideas into commercial products. Under technology licensing the government recovers some of its research investment through licensing fees.

When the products of public–private collaboration are successful, critics argue that it is inappropriate for the private sector to profit without returning a share to the government [20]. Then again, if there is no commercial incentive for researchers who are employed or supported by the government, failure to bring an innovative product to market may represent an even greater loss to society [7]. Others maintain that government commercialization of discoveries is an unacceptable alternative in a free-market system.

The development of drugs to treat endemic diseases in developing countries is another circumstance when the economic incentive is not strong enough to drive R&D. Although large in number, the populations with the greatest need for drugs to treat malaria or dengue fever cannot afford to pay the prices that prevail in the developed world. This situation leads to demands to ignore patents and other intellectual property rights and provide early or selective approval of generic formulations in which the drugs are useful but high-price drugs [21]. Optimal public policy would seek to preserve a monopoly market as a reward for firms willing to accept the inherent risk in finding innovative products while reducing the likelihood of what is perceived as excessive profit.

The United States and Canada make up 65% of sales revenue for PhRMA members. Sales to Europe and Japan account for nearly 25% of PhRMA sales, while India and China together total merely 2% [3]. PhRMA has sought growth opportunities in the global marketplace, but disputes over intellectual property rights challenge the traditional business model. Large multinational corporations operating in developing countries face other challenges, including small markets, weak health-care systems, lax government regulation and enforcement, different disease environments as a result of geography and poverty, and widespread misuse of drugs [21]. Domestic manufacturers sell their generic products at prices that accentuate the price disparity with brand-name drugs generating strong competition often in the face of stiff price controls.

Global harmonization confronts the industry with yet another conundrum. Although the harmonization of requirements could open new markets for the industry, common standards would allow for parallel imports. The result, expressed in economic terms, would be the removal of regulatory barriers that allow innovator firms to engage in discriminatory pricing and collect monopoly rents. Harmonization also raises the prospect of all-or-none decision for marketing approval and price, posing one more threat to the traditional PhRMA business model and the conventional business strategy of global expansion.

In summary the pharmaceutical industry is strongly influenced by competitive and economic factors. Research over the past 4 decades is consistent and clear; financial success is directly linked to the success of R&D efforts and the profits generated by innovative products [2,7,22,23].

Intellectual Property Protection

The pharmaceutical industry depends on patent protection to achieve a return on the substantial investment of time and money required for new drug development. Current estimates are that an innovator firm can expect to spend 10–15 years and $(USD)1.8 billion or more in research, testing, and regulatory approval before receiving the first dollar of revenue for a new drug product [3,4].

Patent laws were designed to give firms the ability to collect monopoly rents on innovations, and the pharmaceutical industry is a prime example of the benefits the law intended. The innovator firm either commercializes the product directly or licenses the rights to another firm while blocking rivals from introducing a competing duplicate product.

However, initial patents are not the only form of intellectual property protection (IPP) critical to the success of the pharmaceutical industry. A succession of statutes supplements the patent system by (1) extending the term of the original patent, (2) shortening the period of time consumed by clinical testing and regulatory review, and (3) granting market exclusivity. At times laws and regulations produced by Congress and government agencies have resulted in multiple and additive protections for prescription drugs [7].

Arguably the "single most important piece of legislation to affect the modern pharmaceutical industry" is the Hatch–Waxman Act of 1984. The act restored nearly all of the patent life that had been lost by drugs to FDA requirements for clinical trials and evidence review [8,19,24]. Other measures passed in the 1990s considerably reduced the time required for FDA approval. The Prescription Drug User Fee Act of 1992 authorized the collection of user fees from pharmaceutical manufacturers providing additional resources to the FDA that expedites the market-approval process. The Food and Drug Administration Modernization Act (FDAMA) of 1997 renewed the user fees and added fast-track authority that allowed the FDA to move more quickly on priority drugs. FDAMA also conferred 6 months of market exclusivity to the end of an existing patent term for manufacturers that submit clinical studies specific to pediatric patients. Each of these acts proved to be a powerful motivator to the industry.

Through its regulations the FDA protects innovator firms by creating de facto barriers to prospective competitors [25]. It is difficult for other firms, especially small new companies, to enter particular therapeutic markets when compliance with regulations represents substantial capital and time investment, demands a high level of technical expertise, and gives competing firms time to develop defensive marketing strategies. Although government policies on IPP and regulatory approval of new drug products surely have direct social benefits, they also have strategic implications for the industry [7].

Profitability

The profitability of the pharmaceutical industry has been persistent and impressive, attractive to investors, and a target of criticism and scrutiny. The industry experienced a sharp rise in profitability during the 1970s and 1980s. From 1993 to 2002, it held first place in the Fortune 500 industry rankings in terms of net profit as a percent of revenues, peaking in 1999 at 18.9% and remaining above 18% through 2001. Rankings, however, reflect the median performance for the largest firms in the industry. Although profits are high in the aggregate, performance varies greatly across firms and across products within firms [26,27]. Less than one-third of products have present value in excess of the average R&D cost [3,23], so corporate profitability is highly skewed toward large returns for a small minority of products. Profits are the industry's primary source of funding for its ongoing R&D [28].

The profitability of the leading brand-oriented firms is driven by innovative products and best-in-class drugs. The mean ROI for the industry is 11.5%, which is slightly above the industry cost of capital of 11% as calculated by capital asset pricing model. Returns are described as modestly above cost of capital in the industry [29], in what Scherer describes in economic terms as a "virtuous rent seeking model" [16]. That is, when profits are high, the industry will increase R&D investments until profit margins fall in a self-regulating cycle.

What economists might describe as virtuous behavior vexes consumers and taxpayers. Increasing expenditures for insurers and consumers coupled with industry profitability has generated public controversy about the pricing policies of pharmaceutical firms. However, prescription expenses are not only the result of drug prices but also a combination of price, utilization, and adoption of innovation [30]. Expenditures for prescription drugs are driven not only by pricing practices but also by greater reliance on long-term use of prescription drugs to treat chronic diseases and the use of newer, higher-price drugs in place of older, less-expensive alternatives. Indeed, the annual number of prescriptions increased from 7.8 per person in 1993 to 12.2 in 2013 [31].

Prescription drugs are the most visible component of the health-care market because prescription drugs represent the greatest out-of-pocket health expenditure for most consumers. Managed care plans increase prescription price awareness through patient cost sharing in the form of deductions and co-payments, and government programs account for an increasingly larger proportion of the industry's products at prices that incense taxpayers. Not only are high prices a concern but price differentials are also potentially more infuriating. Consumers are abruptly confronted with the price differential between the brand and generic when high-price drugs are replaced by generics at nominal, or no, cost. Price differences between the United States and neighboring countries are not only inexplicably large and offensive to the public but also viewed by consumers as sustained only by FDA's prohibition on parallel trade [21,32]. In the end, the concern about the value received in return for the mounting expense persists.

More than one study of drug pricing suggests that products have higher introductory prices for compounds when they represent a gain over existing treatment modalities or are intended for short-term use [34]. Conversely, introductory prices are lower than the prices of existing drugs when the products are close substitutes. This pattern is consistent with the position that prices for new drugs bear some relation to their clinical value and are responsive to price sensitivity. Apart from new drug introductions, average drug prices generally have been at or below price inflation trends in the overall economy.

Individual corporate pricing decisions are determined by considerations that are difficult to quantify. Industry experts suggest that the factors determine drug prices take account of the company's market position and revenue targets, interest in the product, their current and future product portfolio, reimbursement trends among public and private insurers, switching costs in addition to production cost, clinical value, and patients' access to competing products. The impact of international price comparisons and price controls is an increasingly important consideration for setting prices [35].

Defense of pharmaceutical pricing is complicated by the inherent nature of the product. The manufacturers incur high costs for development, but generally the cost of production is quite low. When most drugs can be produced for just "pennies per pill," it is difficult to explain why a price greatly exceeds the cost of production to customers who do not view these as discretionary purchases [2].

Although prescription costs have declined, a new round of controversy over price appears to be underway. Biopharmaceuticals, some of which are orphan drug products, are being introduced at prices that manufacturers claim represent their value to society. However, the introduction of a treatment for hepatitis C that costs $(USD)1000 per dose in a population that is primarily politically and economically marginalized started a new round of criticism and congressional hearings [36].

Industry Evolution and Current Structure

The pharmaceutical industry has been characterized so far as being under constant pressure for innovation, highly dependent on intellectual property protection, and subject to scrutiny for its pricing practices. The firms that make up the PhRMA fit this profile. Not all firms classified as pharmaceutical manufacturers fit the prototype of PhRMA members. The most recent U.S. Census Bureau figures (2011) recorded 1825 entities as pharmaceutical manufacturers, but only 482 firms employed more than 100 persons. PhRMA lists 29 firms as members, large companies whose core activities involve basic and applied research that is followed by product development, clinical trials, FDA approval, and postmarketing surveillance [3]. Among PhRMA members, only 12 pharmaceutical manufacturers were among the Fortune 500 in 2013.

Nearly all the PhRMA members emerge from significant consolidation in the industry that occurred since 1980 [37]. From 1960 to 1980, companies in the industry differentiated themselves by divesting products for the consumer market, including over-the-counter medicines, toiletries, and cosmetics, in order to concentrate fully on the growth and profits available in the prescription drug market. After 1980, the PhRMA companies went through a process of consolidation that created greater uniformity among the remaining firms in terms of size and product portfolios [22]. More recently, the rising cost of R&D was often cited as the reason for major mergers. However, whether mergers produced efficiencies that increased R&D is not clear. Industry observers speculate that company cultures were not always compatible and that increased bureaucracy and morale problems stifled creativity within the research enterprise [38,39].

A recent analysis suggests that mergers prior to 2000 occurred between companies that were able to consolidate operations and cut operating cost. Mergers since that time have tended to provide a growth platform for the acquiring firm. All the mergers appear to have generated positive returns for shareholders although whether the emerged companies will meet expectations for improved productivity in R&D, and long-term success remains to be seen [37].

Thousands of biotechnology ventures were launched in the 1990s whereas the big PhRMA firms approached biotechnology more cautiously. Biotechnology was based on a different set of scientific disciples and required unique manufacturing facilities and competencies not possessed by the traditional firms. The biotechnology firms had neither the resources nor experience to bring new products through the regulatory process nor the marketing expertise to generate rapid and widespread use of innovative biological products [39]. The traditional PhRMA firms invested in the biotechnology sector and then pursued acquisitions and mergers with biotech firms when they delivered a promising drug prospect.

As the pharmaceutical industry adjusted and innovations shifted to biologicals, a new sector of specialty pharmaceuticals emerged with a distribution system designed to handle drugs with a different set of characteristics. Products produced through biotechnology are distinct from the drugs produced by chemical processes that defined the traditional pharmaceutical manufacturers. Biological products are often administered by injection, require special handling and storage, entail patient support and education of prescribers (primarily medical specialists), and have reimbursement schemes that differ from traditional oral chemical pharmaceuticals [31]. Specialty products are also known for bearing high prices with the top 10 products ranging from $(USD)150,000 to $(USD)410,000 per year of treatment [31].

Generic drug companies constitute the largest sector of the pharmaceutical industry in terms of number of firms. These companies make most generic drugs although some generics are made by divisions of major companies that also produce brand-name drugs. The Hatch–Waxman Act stimulated the development of the generic drug industry by introducing the Abbreviated

New Drug Application (ANDA), which streamlined the approval process for products with established clinical efficacy. Hatch–Waxman provisions also gave generic manufacturers the authorization to begin product development and to file an ANDA prior to the expiration of the patent of a brand-name drug. A firm that challenges a brand-name patent in order to be the first to market also is granted 180 days of market exclusivity as a reward for its initiative. In recent years generic firms have become more aggressive, filing patent challenges more frequently and earlier in the product life cycle [11]. On the strength of these incentives, the proportion of prescriptions dispensed as generics rose from 18% in 1980 to more than 50% in 2003 and reached 86% of all prescriptions in 2013 [16,31]. Then again, sales revenue going to generic firms is disproportionately low (29%) relative to their market share.

Early on generic firms focused on labeling and distributing their products, relying on supply-chain management and low-cost manufacturing for growth and success through 2012. However, their success leaves limited resources and opportunity for future growth. Competition is mounting domestically and from middle income countries that are expanding manufacturing capabilities and gaining experience with the predominant government-run health systems. It is estimated that 80% of all active ingredients and 40% of finished products sold in the United States are manufactured and imported from developing countries [33].

Manufacturing facilities in the United States are aging; purchasers are concerned about quality control and drug shortages, and new infrastructure that will be required to handle the complexity of the biological products making up the next wave of prescription drugs coming off patent. The Patient Protection and Affordable Care Act of 2010 enacted a system for approving bioequivalent alternatives to costly biologics but guaranteed 12 years of market exclusivity to the innovator product even if the drug's patent expires [19]. It is expected that both the biopharmaceutical and generic firms will be in competition to produce therapeutic alternatives for 38 biological products that will lose patent protection by 2017 and grow to 68 by 2020 [40].

Although biosimilars are attractive, growth target prognosticators are wary. Both the biopharmaceutical and generic sectors of the industry face uncertainty about the approval process for biosimilars, the evidence needed to establish bioequivalence and the acceptance of substitute products by prescribers and patients. The very first biosimilar application was submitted to the FDA late in July 2014 while regulations governing approval were not yet finalized.

Cost structures vary across industry sectors. Generic manufacturers have survived on high-volume sales with narrow profit margins and minimal outlays on both R&D and marketing. PhRMA members spend less on research than the biopharmaceutical firms, produce the bulk of the profitable products, and typically devote more resources to sales and marketing than other sectors. The primary activities of the biopharmaceutical firms include basic and applied research and product development, and they engage in clinical trials and new drug approvals to a lesser extent than traditional PhRMA members. Biotech firms have invested the most in research. Anticipated changes in the nature of medicines will lead to changes in each sector and potentially a more homogeneity across the industry.

Turning Point

Like the scientific and technical dilemmas, societal pressures are not new to the pharmaceutical industry. Since the 1960s, important constituencies have been making paradoxical demands. Medical professionals and consumers want safe products and the rapid introduction of new discoveries to the market; stockholders and prescription buyers (often the same individuals) want low prices and lucrative investment opportunities. The industry's initial response to rising social and political pressure at the turn of the century was to deploy tactics that maximized IPP, maintain opposition to parallel trade, and engage in aggressive marketing.

Eventually the pressure from external forces converged calling for fundamental changes to the traditional industry model. At least three themes emerged from the critics of the industry: (1) reduce the cost and increase the productivity of R&D, (2) rationalize prices and price differentials, and (3) increase accountability. In the short term, the industry responded through corporate restructuring, increasing investment in R&D, and trimming costs. For example, from 1995 to 2002 the industry had tripled number of sales representatives, peaking at a sales force of 95,000 in 2008. As the loss of patent protections and the influence of managed care reduced sales, PhRMA firms slashed their sales force by one-third and allocated additional funds to R&D [41].

Eventually the accumulation of pressures produced by the shift to biotechnology, the abrupt loss of sales from blockbuster products, and health reform initiatives coupled with an economic recession culminated in what is considered a turning point in the pharmaceutical industry. At least three strategies are emerging in the pharmaceutical industry with long-term implications: (1) efficiencies in R&D, (2) new business models, and (3) increased transparency.

Expertise in clinical trials and experience with the drug approval process serve as barriers to new firms entering the industry. However, substantially new technology emerging from biotechnology and other advances such as nanotechnology could create a new experience curve that would nullify the historical advantage held by the current industry leaders. The leaders need to find a way to make the same technological leaps to avoid being confronted with the new entrants [42].

Efficiencies in R&D

The cost of R&D has continued to climb in part due to the expense of clinical trials [3]. Drugs that are used for chronic conditions over long periods require longer trial periods to demonstrate the safety and compare effectiveness necessary to gain formulary access and assure product reimbursement. More complex studies are inherently more expensive, tend to require more subjects and increase the cost of patient recruitment. Firms restructure to achieve a more lean and flexible R&D operation, some outsourcing all but core activities.

Some firms attempted to mimic the small and more nimble biotechnology companies by reorganizing the R&D enterprise as a way to spark innovation and spur productivity. Others have opted to promote their unique competencies such as knowledge management, teamwork, and relationships with key leaders in science or practice. A number have confined their pursuits to clinical areas with unmet needs; although patient populations are less than 200,000 by definition, the values of orphan products to treat them are reflected in higher prices.

Theories of industrial organization suggest that two ways exist to manage risk in an industry heavily dependent on R&D. The first is to get larger. Increased size allows the firm to initiate and sustain more research projects, thereby increasing the chances that one project will pay off. An alternative strategy is to develop networks for the discovery and development of drugs. Networks reduce the risk posed to each firm and provide greater flexibility and adaptability. Evidence that suggests the industry is moving toward a more networked structure includes forming of strategic alliances between large firms and biotechnology companies, coordinating between firms with products that complement drug products such as medical devices, geographically locating new R&D facilities near major universities or research centers, and outsourcing of more R&D activities [43–45]. Big data presents opportunities to ignite innovation, but it comes with technical and regulatory risks [46].

New Business Models

Consolidation among the largest pharmaceutical manufacturers in conjunction with the mergers and acquisitions of biotechnology firms reduced the number of independent R&D centers in the industry. Questions are raised frequently about whether the newer, higher cost prescription drugs they produce represent a good value [47]. The mounting concern over the apparent slowdown in the industry spurred calls for new business models in addition to calls for greater efficiency [39,47]. Consequently there has been no shortage of recommendations for rethinking and potentially restructuring the enterprise [4,15,27,48–52].

Elements featured in the various new business models include integration and reliance on data from diverse sources and the analysis of that data to aid drug discovery, manage a drug development portfolio, and efficiently produce and distribute pharmaceuticals whose safety in use is monitored and managed. Partnerships and collaborations are a necessary part of these new business models and seen as a means to increase public trust in the industry.

Irrespective of the industry configuration that emerges, observers and commentators have begun to refer to pharmaceutical R&D not as an industry but as a research ecosystem involving the scientific, regulatory, investment and policy communities. New policy initiatives incorporate public–private partnerships, including industry, academia, government agencies, nonprofit foundations, venture capitalists, and patient advocates. Some of the earliest and most prominent collaborations include Accelerating Medicines Partnership to identify biological targets, the National Center for Advancing Translational Sciences for developing tools to promote common standards and best practices in science and medicine, the Cures Acceleration Network to fund priority initiatives and uncover impediments to innovation, and the Patient-Centered Outcomes Research Institute to identify societal priorities. In sum these policy interventions aim to foster more collaboration, faster R&D, and bold innovation focused on priorities identified by patients and society [3,47].

Munos summarizes the hope "… that one day soon industry will be able to link data in electronic medical records with patient-reported outcomes and genotypes to an era of truly personalized medicine" [47].

Transparency

Other long-time industry observers and scholars, Henry Grabowski and colleagues at Duke University, astutely anticipated that the introduction of personalized medicine could be accompanied by legal and ethical dilemmas as challenging as the scientific and technical hurdles [1,8]. Not only might there be differences in public opinion and controversial politics, but also the advancements could come at prices that create reimbursement dilemmas. Health reform initiatives come amid calls for improved health outcomes, a higher benefit-to-risk ratio, and concern for personal privacy and patient safety. Health-care providers are reacting to pay-for-performance programs that incorporate public reporting to drive quality improvement.

In September 2014 the Centers for Medicare and Medicaid Services (CMS) will begin posting industry-reported payments to teaching hospitals and physicians in compliance with the Physician Payment Sunshine Act [53]. The pharmaceutical industry is responding also to calls for increased reporting and access to clinical trial data. The pharmaceutical industry no doubt remains a powerful force but one that is willing to engage in cooperative ventures to maintain and enhance its position.

Prospects for the Pharmaceutical Market

The outlook for the pharmaceutical market is quite positive from a macro perspective. The aging of the baby boomers and long-term treatment needed for chronic diseases present a promising future for the industry. The expansion of insurance coverage under health reforms could increase the number of prescriptions and the ability to pay for them.

A more nuanced appraisal suggests that the pharmaceutical industry is undergoing significant structural changes. The implementation of a health reform measures poses some uncertainty for future profitability. Although the short-term impact will bring increased sales, price discounts and cost containment initiatives are sure to follow. Power shifts from sellers to buyers when revenues are concentrated in large-volume sales to a small pool of purchasers; expenditures become more significant, buyers acquire more information and expertise, and the public sector maintains pressure to keep costs low. The market could shift to a smaller number of better-coordinated purchasing systems and away from the diverse set of users, payers, and decision makers. Overall prospects for the pharmaceutical industry remain cautiously optimistic. Parts of the balancing act require being attentive to the demand for increased accountability and transparency while pursuing innovations with utmost efficiency.

Historically, public policy supported success in the pharmaceutical industry by nurturing strong intellectual property protection and maintaining a relatively free-market environment to accompany important discoveries in technology and science. The old system may give way to a revised business model with greater homogeneity across the industry sectors. The U.S. pharmaceutical industry is repositioning to take advantage of efficiencies in R&D to produce the next generation of drugs that represent first-line therapy. The ultimate balance between the industry and societal needs will be shaped by the strategy, skills, and resources that spring from collaborations in response to future changes.

References

1. Grabowski H. Are the economics of pharmaceutical research and development changing? *Pharmacoeconomics* 2004; 22(Suppl 2): 15–24.
2. Scherer FM. The pharmaceutical industry—Prices and progress. *New England Journal of Medicine* 2004; 3522: 927–932.
3. Pharmaceutical Research and Manufacturers of America. 2014 Profile Biopharmaceutical Research Industry. PhRMA, Washington, DC, 2014.
4. Paul SM, Mytelka DS, Dunwiddie CT, Persinger CC, Munos BH, Lindborg SR, Schacht AL. How to improve R&D productivity: The pharmaceutical industry's grand challenge. *Nature Reviews Drug Discovery* 2010; 9: 203–214.
5. Kaitin KI, DiMasi JA. Pharmaceutical innovation in the 21st century: New drug approvals in the first decade, 2000–2009. *Clinical Pharmacology & Therapeutics* 2011; 89: 183–188.
6. Kesselheim AS, Wang B, Avorn J. Defining "innovativeness" in drug development: A systematic review. *Nature* 2013; 94: 336–348.
7. Kesselheim AS. Using market-exclusivity incentives to promote pharmaceutical innovation. *New England Journal of Medicine* 2010; 363: 1855–1862.

8. Grabowski HG, Kyle M, Mortimer R, Long G, Kirson N. Evolving brand-name and generic drug competition may warrant a revision of the Hatch–Waxman Act. *Health Affairs* 2011; 30: 2157–2166.
9. Aitken M, Berndt ER, Cutler DM. Prescription drug spending trends in the United States: Looking beyond the turning point. *Health Affairs* 2009; 28: w151–w160.
10. Friedman D, Goldwasser R, Hooker D, Lewis DR, Risinger D, Simpson D, Urist M, McGinnis M. *The US Healthcare Formula Cost Control and True Innovation*. New York: Morgan Stanley, 2011.
11. Grabowski H, Long G, Mortimer R. Recent trends in brand-name and generic drug competition. *Journal of Medical Economics* 2014; 17: 207–214.
12. Wyatt E. Justices rule for the F.T.C. in generic drug case. *New York Times*, June 18, 2013, p. B1.
13. Hemphill CS, Sampat BN. Evergreening, patent challenges, and effective market life in pharmaceuticals. *Journal of Health Economics* 2012; 31: 327–339.
14. Lowe D. But don't drug companies spend more on marketing? In the Pipeline. May 20, 2013. http://pipeline.corante.com/archives/2013/05/20/but_dont_drug_companies_spend_more_on_marketing.php. Accessed August 1, 2014.
15. Jaruzelski B, Loehr J, Holman R. (2013). *The Global Innovation 1000: Navigating the Digital Future*. New York: Booz & Co.
16. Scherer FM. The link between gross profitability and pharmaceutical R&D spending. *Health Affairs* 2001; 20(5): 216–220.
17. Haffner ME, Torrent-Fanell J, Maher PD. Does orphan drug legislation really answer the needs of patients? *Lancet* 2008; 371: 2041–2044.
18. Kakkar AK, Dahita N. The evolving drug development landscape: From blockbusters to niche busters in the orphan drug space. *Drug Development Research* 2014; 75: 231–234.
19. Kesselheim AS. An empirical review of major legislation affecting drug development: Past experiences, effects, and unintended consequences. *Milbank Quarterly* 2011; 89: 450–502.
20. Treasure C, Avorn J, Kesselheim AS. What is the public's right to access medical discoveries based on federally funded research? *New England Journal of Medicine* 2014; 311: 907–908.
21. Kremer M. Pharmaceuticals and the developing world. *Journal of Economic Perspectives* 2002; 16(4): 67–90.
22. Achilladelis B, Antonakis N. The dynamics of technological innovation: The case of the pharmaceutical industry. *Research Policy* 2001; 30: 535–588.
23. Grabowski H, Vernon J, DiMasi JA. Returns on research and development for 1990s new drug introductions. *Pharmacoeconomics* 2002; 20(Suppl 3): 11–29.
24. Center for Medicare & Medicaid Services. Health care industry market update: Pharmaceuticals. Center for Medicare & Medicaid Services, Office of Research Development and Information, Baltimore, Maryland. January 10, 2003.
25. Eisenberg RS. The shifting functional balance of patents and drug regulation. *Health Affairs* 2001; 20: 119–135.
26. Miles T. What ails the pharmaceutical industry? July 8, 2013. http://blog.kinaxis.com/2013/07/what-ails-the-pharmaceutical-supply-chain/. Accessed August 3, 2014.
27. Kinch MS, Haynesworth A, Kinch SL, Hoyer D. An overview of FDA-approved new molecular entities: 1827–2013. *Drug Discovery Today* 2014; 19(8): 1033–1039.
28. Accenture. The future of pharmaceutical innovation. Tackling the R&D productivity gap. 2011. https://www.accenture.com/t20150527T203922_w_/us-en/_acnmedia/Accenture/Conversion-Assets/Microsites/Documents/Accenture-The-Future-of-Pharmaceutical-Innovation-Tackling-the-RD-Productivity-Gap-Online.pdf.
29. Baras AI, Baras AS, Schulman KA. Drug development risk and the cost of capital. *Nature Reviews Drug Discovery* 2012; 11: 347–348.
30. Kanavos P, Ferrario A, Vandoros S, Anderson GF. Higher US branded drug prices and spending compared to other countries may stem partly from quick uptake of new drugs. *Health Affairs* 2013; 32: 753–761.
31. IMS Institute for Healthcare Informatics. Medicine use and shifting costs of healthcare. A review of medicines us in the United States in 2013. April 2014. http://www.plannedparenthoodadvocate.org/2014/IIHI_US_Use_of_Meds_for_2013.pdf.

32. Danzon PM, Johnson SJ, Long G, Furukawa MF. Commercial importation of prescription drugs in the United States: Short-run implications. *Journal of Health Politics, Policy and Law* 2011; 36: 295–316.
33. Kramer DB, Kesselheim AS. User fees and beyond—The FDA Safety and Innovation Act of 2012. *New England Journal of Medicine* 2012; 367: 1277–1279.
34. Keyhani S, Diener-West M, Powe N. Do drug prices reflect development time and government investment? *Medical Care* 2005; 43: 753–762.
35. Gregson N, Sparrowhawk K, Mauskopf J, Paul J. Pricing medicines: Theory and practice, challenges and opportunities. *Nature Reviews Drug Discovery* 2005; 4: 121–130.
36. Koller C. The view from here: New hepatitis C drug, old problems. *Milbank Memorial Fund Newsletter*. June 2014. http://www.milbank.org/newsletter/current-newsletter. Accessed August 7, 2014.
37. Cha M, Lorriman T. Why pharma megamergers work, in *Regulatory Excellence. Achieving Public Health Impact through Distinctive Regulatory Management Systems*, Riefberg V, Singh N, Smith J, eds. Washington, DC: McKinsey Center for Government, 2014.
38. LaMatina JL. The impact of mergers on pharmaceutical R&D. *Nature Reviews Drug Discovery* 2011; 10: 559–560.
39. Comanor WS, Scherer FM. Mergers and innovation in the pharmaceutical industry. *Journal of Health Economics* 2013; 32: 106–113.
40. McKinsey & Company. Generating value in generics: Finding the next five years of growth. May 2013. http://www.mckinsey.com/. Accessed August 3, 2014.
41. Iskowitz M. A walk on the sales side. *Medical Marketing and Media (MM&M)* November 2013; 31–34.
42. Porter ME. *Competitive Strategy: Techniques for Analyzing Industries and Competitors*. New York: Free Press, 1980.
43. Tufts Center for the Study of Drug Development. Outlook 2013. *Boston, MA: Tufts University*, 2012.
44. Tufts Center for the Study of Drug Development. Outlook 2014. Boston, MA: Tufts University, 2013.
45. Kaitin KI, Honig PK. Reinventing bioinnovation. *Clinical Pharmacology & Therapeutics* 2013; 94: 279–283.
46. Cattell J, Chilukuri, Levy M. How big data can revolutionize pharmaceutical R&D, in *Regulatory Excellence. Achieving Public Health Impact through Distinctive Regulatory Management Systems*, Riefberg V, Singh N, Smith J, eds. Washington, DC: McKinsey Center for Government, 2014.
47. Munos BH. Pharmaceutical innovation gets a little help from new friends. *Science Translational Medicine* 2013; 5(168): 1–2.
48. Bonabeau E, Bodick N, Armstrong RW. A more rational approach to new product development. *Harvard Business Review* March 2008; 86: 96–102.
49. Timmerman L. 12 things the Pharma industry can do to rebuild real public trust. December 9, 2013. http://www.xconomy.com/national/2013/12/09/12-things-pharma-industry-can-rebuild-public-trust/. Accessed June 26, 2014.
50. Forda SR, Bergstron R, Chiebus M, Barker R, Andersen PH. Priorities for improving drug research, development and regulation. *Nature Reviews Drug Discovery* 2013; 12: 247–248.
51. Juliano RL. Pharmaceutical innovation and public policy: The case for a new strategy for drug discovery and development. *Science and Public Policy* 2013; 40: 292–405.
52. Alberts B, Kirschner MW, Tilghman S. Varmus H. Recuing US biomedical research from its systematic flaws. *Proceedings of the National Academy of Sciences* 2014; 111: 5773–5777.
53. Kirschner NM, Sulmasy LS, Kesselheim AS. Health policy basics: The physician payment sunshine act and the open payments program. Annals of Internal Medicine 2014; 161(7): 519–521.

Chapter 14

Health Policy and Economic Issues in Biotechnology and Personalized Medicine

Louis P. Garrison, Jr.

Contents

Introduction

Henry Aaron, a leading American health policy analyst at the Brookings Institution, has characterized America's ongoing tension between cost containment and technical advance in graphic terms:

> The drama of rising health care costs should be seen as a saga of rapid and even reckless advance in technology, fueled increasingly by an entrepreneurial sense of adventure.

There is no doubt that over the last nearly 50 years—since the initiation of the Medicare program in 1965—the U.S. health-care system has been the most supportive of innovation and technology in the world. And many would argue that this is what lies behind the fact that the share of GDP (now 17%) devoted to health care is significantly larger than in any other country.

But as Aaron suggests, Americans welcome innovation despite growing discomfort with total health-care costs and the overall functioning of the system. For example, in a recent Research!America poll, only 39% said America has the best health-care system in the world, but citizen support for medical science is considerable in their recent national telephone polls [2,3]:

- 54% would be willing to pay $(USD)1 per week more in taxes if they were certain that the money would be spent on additional medical research.
- 39% say we aren't making enough medical progress.
- 61% say that the cost of health care is the single most important health issue facing the nation.
- 51% think that research to improve health is part of the solution to rising health-care costs.
- 74% agree or strongly agree that basic scientific research is necessary and should be supported by the federal government.
- Only 30% think the FDA should move more quickly to approve new drugs.
- 48% say that we aren't making enough medical progress.

Americans generally view medical innovation favorably and see biotechnology and personalized medicine fields in this light. Yet increasing cost containment pressures are placing advances in these fields under the same scrutiny as traditional pharmaceuticals.

Since the cloning of the sheep Dolly in 1997, the completion of the sequencing of human genome in 2001, through to the ongoing hot debate about stem cell research, genetics and biotechnology have captured the imagination of Americans. These fields are seen as the cutting edge of medical innovation. The purpose of this chapter is to (1) define and describe biotechnology and personalized medicine, (2) discuss what makes them unique from economic and policy perspectives, and (3) identify and discuss the key policy issues in a U.S. context.

What Are Biotechnology and Personalized Medicine?

Ho and Gibaldi [4] define biotechnology as "An integrated application of scientific and technical understanding of a biologic process or molecule to develop a useful product. One can distinguish between traditional small molecule pharmaceuticals (Rx) and large (or 'macromolecule') biopharmaceuticals (BioRx)." Biopharmaceuticals, also called biologics, have some advantages and disadvantages versus small molecule products: by being similar to naturally occurring substances in the body, they may have better bioavailability and have less toxicity. Yet they are generally more complex to develop and especially to manufacture.

In the last 10 years, we have broadened our concept of *personalized medicine* beyond strictly pharmacogenetic measures to include any "biomarkers" that are predictive to respond to treatment. Still, genetics and pharmacogenetics remains the key in several of the important applications in personalized medicine, so it is useful to have some understanding of the terminology and concepts in this area. Furthermore, personalized medicine is also referred to by many names, including "stratified medicine" and even more recently "precision medicine."

Genomics and genetics are important to biotechnology as part of the production process, but we are using "pharmacogenetics" here in a narrower sense to mean how drug response in humans is influenced by genetic variation.

Simply put, individuals (except identical twins) vary in the DNA sequence of their genome. The genome is the complete set of genetic material found in the nucleus of cells inherited from their parents with half coming from the mother and half from the father. DNA is a long linear molecule made of bases of adenine, guanine, cytosine, and thymine. Particular stretches of base pairs can be identified as *genes*, and the actual nucleotide sequences in these stretches can vary among individuals sometimes providing *information* that is predictive of observable differences among humans, i.e., genotype can be a predictor of phenotype—the physical appearance or a specific manifestation of a trait. For our purposes here, it is very important to understand that, for most common, complex diseases, the predictive power of genotype alone is often limited and that environment (both at the cellular level and the level of individual lifestyle) is a significant contributor to phenotype—observable disease. The occurrence of single genes predicting disease with a very high likelihood is rare, e.g., Huntington's disease, cystic fibrosis, and Tay–Sachs disease. Nonetheless, these "monogenic" examples seem to dominate the public's perceptions and unduly influence their thinking about the potential impact of pharmacogenetics.

Although pharmacogenetics is currently the key to many of the important personalized medicine applications, several other types of "-omics" biomarkers are increasingly being considered and measured. In addition to genomics, these include proteomics, metabolomics, microbiomics, transcriptomics, and lipidomics, among others.

Biotechnology Industry and Its Products

As reported in Ho and Gibaldi [5], Amgen, the largest U.S. biotechnology company, had sales of $(USD)14.0 billion in 2010, spent $(USD)2.9 billion (20.0%) on R&D, and 17,400 employees. Pfizer, the largest pharmaceutical manufacturer, had sales of $(USD)67.8 billion, spent $(USD)9.4 billion on R&D (14%), and 110,600 employees. For Amgen, the revenue per employee is about $(USD)843,000, and for Pfizer it is about $(USD)613,000. Given the apparently smaller relative R&D workforce, Pfizer is likely devoting more staff to sales and marketing. To some degree, this reflects the need to market small molecules for common conditions to a broad audience of physicians and patients.

Although Amgen has remained the largest U.S. biotechnology company over the past 10 years, the marketplace is shifting substantially, as traditional pharma is investing in and acquiring biotechnology capability (see Table 14.1).

Between 2004 and 2013, there has a shift in the importance of biotechnology products. This is illustrated in Table 14.2, which lists U.S. sales for the top-selling small molecules and biopharmaceuticals in 2004 and 2013.

The top-selling small molecules are for the common chronic diseases of depression, high cholesterol, and gastrointestinal reflux, none of which are life threatening in an acute sense. Interestingly, the top-selling biologics are rheumatoid arthritis, with total sales of nearly

Table 14.1 Strategic Acquisition of Biotechnology Companies by Integrated Biopharmaceutical Companies

Originating Company	*Targeted Company*	*Technology or Products*	*Total Sales ($[USD] billions)*	*Year*
Roche	Genentech	MoAbs, Avastin, Herceptin, Rituxan, oncology	47	2009
Sanofi-Aventis	Genzyme	Cerezyme, Synvisc, Ceredase, orphan biologics	20	2011
AstraZeneca	MedImmune	MoAbs	15.6	2002
Merck	Serono	Biologics, Rebif, Erbitux	13.5	2006
Lilly and Co.	ImClone	Erbitux, MoAb, oncology	6	2008
Novartis	Chiron	Vaccines	5.8	2006
Johnson & Johnson	Centocor	MoAbs and derivatives: Remicade, Simponi	4.9	1999
Bristol–Myers Squibb	Medarex	MoAbs	2.4	2009
Johnson & Johnson	Crucell	Vaccines	2.3	2011
Amgen	Abgenix	MoAbs and humanized mouse platform	2.2	2006
Boehringer Ingelheim	MacroGenics	MoAbs	2.1	2010
GlaxoSmithKline	ID Biomed	Biologics	1.3	2005
AstraZeneca	Cambridge Antibody Technology	MoAbs and Ab phage display platform [Q]	1.3	2006

Source: Ho, R.J.Y. and Gibaldi, M.: *Biotechnology and Biopharmaceuticals: Transforming Proteins and Genes into Drugs*. 2013. Copyright Wiley-VCH Verlag GmbH & Co. KGaA. Reproduced with permission.

Abbreviation: MoAb, monoclonal antibody.

$(USD)15 billion for the top three alone. Clearly, blockbusters play a major role in both the pharma and biotech industries.

Economic Perspective on Biotechnology and Personalized Medicine

In seeking to understand the economic impact and policy implications of biotech and personalized medicine, it is useful to identify any distinguishing characteristics of them from an economic perspective.

Table 14.2 Selected Top-Selling Pharmaceutical and Biologic Products in 2004 and 2013

Rank	*Rx or BioRX*	*Product® (Company)*	*Indication*	*Sales ($[USD] billions)*
(a) 2004				
1	Rx	Lipitor (Pfizer)	Hypercholesterolemia	7.1
2	Rx	Zocor (Merck)	Hypercholesterolemia	5.5
3	Rx	Prevacid (Tap)	Gastrointestinal reflux	4.0
4	Rx	Nexium (AstraZeneca)	Gastrointestinal reflux	3.6
5	BioRx	Procrit (J&J)	Cancer anemia	3.3
6	Rx	Zoloft (Pfizer)	Antidepressant	3.0
12	BioRx	Epogen (Amgen)	Dialysis anemia	2.5
17	BioRx	Aranesp (Amgen)	Anemia	2.1
22	BioRx	Remicade (J&J)	Rheumatoid arthritis	1.8
24	BioRx	Neulasta (Amgen)	Low white blood cell count	1.8
106	BioRx	Herceptin (Genentech)	Breast cancer	0.47
(b) 2013				
1	Rx	Abilify (BMS/Otsuka)	Antipsychotic	6.5
2	Rx	Nexium (AstraZeneca)	GERD	6.2
3	BioRx	Humira (AbbVie)	Rheumatoid arthritis	5.5
4	Rx	Crestor (AstraZeneca)	Hypercholesterolemia	5.3
5	Rx	Cymbalta (Lilly)	Antidepressant	5.2
6	Rx	Advair Diskus (GSK)	Asthma/COPD	5.1
7	BioRx	Enbrel (Amgen/Pfizer)	Rheumatoid arthritis	4.7
8	BioRx	Remicade (Janssen)	Rheumatoid arthritis	4.1
9	BioRx	Copaxone (Teva)	Multiple sclerosis	3.7
10	BioRx	Neulasta (Amgen)	Low WBC count	3.6
11	BioRx	Rituxan (GenentechAV)	Lymphoma	3.3
16	BioRx	Avastin (Roche)	Cancers	2.7
20	BioRx	Epogen (Amgen)	Anemia	2.1
24	BioRx	Herceptin (Genentech)	Breast cancer	1.9

Sources: a, Adapted from NDC Health, The top 200 selling drugs in 2004 by US sales, NDC Health, Atlanta, GA, 2005, http://www.drugs.com/top200_2004.html; b, Brooks, M., Top 100 selling drugs of 2013, *Medscape*, January 30, 2014, http://www.medscape.com/viewarticle/820011, accessed on August 19, 2014. Accessed January 12, 2016.

Unique Economic Characteristics of Biotech Products

How do biologic products differ from traditional small molecule pharmaceuticals? The following characteristics stand out:

- Higher marginal costs of production
- Different safety profile
- Smaller markets
- Different regulatory pathway
- Less market competition

Of course, none of these characteristics—with the exception of the regulatory pathway—in and of themselves hold for all biotech products or fail to apply to some small molecules. Still, they can account for some of the unique structural features of the industry and related policy challenges.

Typically, biotech products are large molecules, such as monoclonal antibodies or specific receptor proteins, which are complex and costly to manufacture. This implies that at the margin (per each dose), the cost is much more significant than for small molecules. Of course, marginal cost to the health-care system also includes the costs of distribution. These can be high for both normal and biotech products, though the latter may be lower due to the generally smaller targeted audience. According to standard economic theory, a manufacturer with a patented product will behave as a profit-maximizing monopolist, setting price at the point where marginal revenue equals marginal cost. Thus, marginal cost has some influence on the price level. However, the demand curve for these products may be relatively more inelastic (i.e., less sensitive to price), so the margin between price and cost is often much higher than for small molecules. There is, however, little direct evidence on this, as marginal costs of production and distribution are not readily found.

Second, because biotech products often aim to copy or imitate naturally occurring proteins, they may be more likely to show efficacy and less likely to evoke certain types of adverse drug reactions (ADRs) in patients—though they can also carry risks of unwanted immune responses. An early but prominent example in Europe has affected thinking to this day. A change in the manufacturing process of one of the top-selling erythropoietins (EPOs) resulted in a severe ADR in some patients (which also is a major factor in explaining why policies about "generic" entry differ for biologics).

At least for conditions like anemia or neutropenia (white blood cell deficiency), it is reasonable to speculate that the proportion and degree of response are more pervasive in the target population and measurable than for many common small molecule products. The populations for the best-selling biologics tend to be smaller than for top-selling drugs that focus on highly prevalent conditions such as high cholesterol or gastrointestinal reflux. By implication, the prices of the biologics per year tend to be higher per year or course of treatment.

In the United States, review and approval of new drugs and therapeutic biologics is conducted by the Center for Drug Evaluation and Research (CDER), and the Center for Biologics Evaluation and Research (CBER) regulates other biologics, such as vaccines, blood products, certain devices, and cell- and tissue-based therapies. Review of therapeutic biologics was transferred from CBER to CDER in 2003 to ensure that the regulatory pathways for the product approval are the same. For most of the past decade, there has been one major difference with important economic implications: there was no regulatory path for "follow-on" biologics, analogous to the generic follow-ons that enter pharmaceutical markets after patents expire. The Hatch–Waxman Act (1984) facilitated generic entry (based on bioequivalence of the small molecule) by better defining and refining the processes around generic approvals. Generic compounds are not required to conduct a full-scale replication of the complete clinical trial program—Phase I to III. Generic companies can use the trial data from the patent-expired product to substantiate efficacy and safety. Up to now, there was no such process for follow-ons to biologics in the United States. In contrast, the EU has a more defined process, calling these "biosimilars."

Another FDA special program—for so-called "orphan drugs" for rare diseases—is also important to biopharmaceuticals. In the 31 years since the passage of the Orphan Drug Act in 1983, over 400 drugs and biologic products have received approval. Major biopharmaceuticals have obtained approval for specific conditions under the Orphan Drug Act, which provides R&D tax credits and awards "data exclusivity" for the first product in class for a period of 7 years if the target population is under 200,000 persons. The aim is to promote innovations for rare conditions, by limiting subsequent competition, by not allowing some in-class competitors during the exclusivity period. Both branded, in-class and generic follow-ons are excluded for this period. Approval under the Orphan Drug Act has limited competition for several major biological products.

Unique Economic Characteristics of Personalized Medicine Products

How do personalized medicine products differ from traditional small molecule pharmaceuticals? The following characteristics stand out:

- A greater role for the diagnostic industry
- Potential impact throughout the product development lifecycle—discovery, development, and marketing
- The paucity of current examples of products
- That pharmacogenetic-based diagnostics are not different (from an economic perspective) from diagnostics based on other biomarkers

Currently, there are many fewer personalized medicine applications than biologics. Indeed, the Royal Society in the United Kingdom recently concluded: "Personalized medicine is unlikely to revolutionize or personalize medical practice in the immediate future" [8]. We believe this is true for several reasons, though the impact of various factors is really an empirical question that remains open at the moment. Before turning and identifying those factors, let's first consider the state of the art.

Personalized Medicine Products

In the year 2000, Francis Collins, the current head of the U.S. National Institutes of Health, said, "In the next five to seven years, we should identify the genetic susceptibility factors for virtually all common diseases—cancer, diabetes, heart disease, the major mental illnesses—on down that list" [9]. This has not happened.

In 2005, a multidisciplinary exercise [10] at the University of Washington—including geneticists, physicians, pharmacists, and economists—reached a less optimistic view about the rate at which this promising future will reach us. In the *most likely* scenario for the year 2015, they predicted:

> By 2015, approximately 10 years from now, a variety of test kits using various biological markers testing will be feasible when rapid test results are needed. Yet, the discovery and validation of pharmacogenomic associations will likely continue at a similar measured pace. A notable development will be the identification of clinically useful pharmacogenomics associations in drug development trials outside of oncology. We expect that 10–5 pharmacogenomic tests will be in routine use in clinical practice. Although the majority will continue to be in oncology, evaluating both tumor and patient genetics, several tests outside of oncology will be used by primary care clinicians to guide treatment decisions.

This prediction is arguably still on target. It is clear that several genetic tests are widely used, mainly in oncology; however, the total number in routine clinical use remains fairly limited.

Current Personalized Medicine Applications

To this point, there are only a limited number of personalized medicine applications. Some of the more prominent ones are shown in Table 14.3. Many of the most important biopharmaceutical applications have been in oncology. Trastuzumab (*Herceptin*) for HER2-positive breast cancer is probably the most well-known and widely recognized example, which was established in the late 1990s metastatic breast cancer.

The basic approach of personalized medicine has been described many times as "finding the right drug for the right patient at the right dose" [11]. In order to prescribe the right drug for the right patient at the right dose, "responders" to the drug are identified using a diagnostic test. It was hoped and believed that an increased knowledge of genetic variations among individuals would allow us to predict a patient's response to specific medications, and although there has been

Table 14.3 Biopharmaceuticals and Other Examples in Personalized Medicine

Disease Association	*Drug(s)*
HER2 in breast cancer	*Herceptin* (trastuzumab)
BCR-ABL in chronic myelogenous leukemia	*Gleevec* (imatinib), *Sprycel* (dasatinib), and *Tasigna* (nilotinib)
Gene expression profiling in breast cancer	Oncotype DX/Mammaprint
EGFR in lung cancer	*Tarceva* (erlotinib) and *Iressa* (gefitinib)
KRAS mutations in colorectal cancer	*Erbitux* (cetuximab) and *Vectibix* (panitumumab)
ALK inhibitor in lung cancer	*Xalkori* (crizotinib)
BRAF mutation in melanoma	*Zelboraf* (vemurafenib)

Source: Garrison, Jr LP. 2013. Pharmacoeconomics and Drug Pricing, in Biotechnology and Biopharmaceuticals: Transforming Proteins and Genes into Drugs, Second Edition. Rodney J. Y. Ho, Milo Gibaldi (eds.), John Wiley & Sons, Inc.

considerable progress in recent years, progress has been slower than expected since 2003 when the human genome was sequenced.

It may well be that the number of cost-effectiveness analyses of pharmacogenetic applications has grown faster than the number of applications. A systematic review of the literature by Wong et al. [12] published in 2010 identified 34 articles. Most of which were published after 2004. Some 26% of the articles covered applications for thromboembolic-related diseases. They also found that there were many more studies to establish the clinical validity of personalized medicine biomarkers as opposed to establishing their clinical utility and also therefore cost-effectiveness.

The most commonly cited and recognized personalized medicine application is trastuzumab (Herceptin) for the 20%–25% of women with breast cancer whose tumors have a specific genetic change that leads to overexpression of the cell receptor HER2; this also happens to lead to a more aggressive form of the cancer. Their tumors can be tested for overexpression of this gene, qualifying them to receive a chemotherapy regimen that includes this targeted product. Recent findings indicate a survival advantage for use of trastuzumab in early-stage breast cancer for women whose tumors overexpress HER2 in addition to the initial benefit demonstrated in metastatic breast cancer. It is also noteworthy in this case that the mutation is in the tumor cells and is not due to a mutation in the individual's inherited genome: it is a "somatic" rather than a "germ line" mutation.

One of the most prominent examples in pharmacogenetics from several years ago was the recognition that individuals metabolize drugs differently: for example, some are "fast" metabolizers and others are "slow" metabolizers for certain kinds of medications. Seven or eight years ago, there was an expectation that these differences would lead to a wide range of testing applications. However, this has not panned out. The case of warfarin to prevent clots and for deep vein thrombosis is important and interesting one. Even the FDA was quite optimistic about the prospects for the application of pharmacogenetic testing for warfarin. But thus far the trials have not established its practical advantage over dose titration.

Economic Impact on Drug Development

An earlier broad overview [13] by Webster et al. in 2004 provides a thorough, balanced perspective on the state of the field at that time—that portends the slow progress that we have made over time. Economics was not their primary focus, but most of the issues they raise have an economic dimension. They introduce their piece by saying

> Pharmacogenomic (PGx) is on the threshold of making of major impact in commercial labs and in the clinic. But, despite its promise and the heavy investment made in the technology, many companies still question whether there is a coherent business, health policy, or regulatory model emerging to shape the future development of PGx.

Their search for a coherent model is aided by their useful taxonomy of areas of potential application of pharmacogenetics shown in Table 14.4.

They conclude that most large pharmaceutical companies focus their investments on improving the efficiency of drug development (options 1–3): "These companies have little commercial interest in the applications of PGx that are aimed at already licensed medicines, except where value can be added by extending product licenses...". Although they see greater interest in pre-prescription genotyping among providers of health care and specialist diagnostic firms, they suggest that this is likely to take place mostly after linked drug–test combinations have been tested in clinical trials, and that this linkage will be made primarily in situations where the linkage is required to make the drug viable for regulatory and commercial reasons.

Table 14.4 Taxonomy of Personalized Impacts

Option 1: using PGx to discover better drugs
1a. Discovering drugs for specific genomic subgroups (allelic variants of drug target)
1b. Discovering drugs that work in all subgroups (ensuring leads work in all allelic variants)
Option 2: PGx to improve the safety of new drugs in development
2a. Early-stage trial design and/or monitoring (for example, ensuring balanced trial population of cytochrome P450 variants)
2b. "Rescue" of drugs that fail clinical trials owing to safety problems
Option 3: PGx to improve the efficacy of new drugs in development
3a. Targeting late-stage trials as "good responders" (prospective)
3b. "Rescue" of drugs that fail clinical trials owing to lack of efficacy (retrospective)
Option 4: improving the safety of licensed drugs
4a. Pre-prescription patient testing for risk of ADRs (for example, thiopurine methyltransferase)
4b. Label and market extensions of drugs that have been restricted by ADRs (for example, abacavir)
4c. Improved postmarketing surveillance
Option 5: improving the efficacy of licensed drugs
5a. Pre-prescription patient testing to identify good responders
5b. The use of efficacy data in drug marketing

They see it as unlikely that PGx testing will be a regulatory requirement for all drugs:

> A drug that is highly efficacious across most of the population, has a wide therapeutic index and shows little inter-individual variability in kinetics and dynamics should not necessarily require PGx testing. It would not be cost-effective to do so.

Nonetheless, they expect that most applications will at least address the question of pharmacogenetic variability in the CYP450 enzymes.

Cost-Effectiveness of Personalized Medicine Products

One way to consider the potential impact of personalized medicine is to ask: what are the characteristics of technologies and diseases that are most likely to be cost-effective? This literature comes to one major conclusion: the cost-effectiveness of any given PGx-based or biomarker-based technology (such as a drug–test combination) will depend on the specific characteristics of that situation, and there are several factors that will play a major role.

A brief review of the relevant articles will illustrate the progression and refinement of the argument.

Veenstra et al. [14] applied a standard cost-effectiveness, decision analysis framework to the case of a linked PGx test and therapeutic intervention. They conclude that "... pharmacogenetics likely will be cost-effective only for certain combinations of disease, drug, gene, and test characteristics, and that the cost-effectiveness of pharmacogenetic-based therapies needs to be evaluated on a case-by-case basis." They also identify several examples of drug–disease areas where PGx may be cost-effective, such as trastuzumab for breast cancer, interferon/ribavirin for hepatitis C, and tacrine for Alzheimer's disease.

Phillips et al. [15] conducted parallel literature reviews of drugs associated with ADRs and of drug-metabolizing enzymes associated with poor metabolism. They identified 27 drugs with ADR problems and were able to link 16 of these to at least one enzyme with a variant allele that causes abnormal metabolism. They recognize that this association is not necessarily causal and that it does not necessarily follow that a commercially viable PGx test can be developed.

In 2004, Flowers and Veenstra [16] have refined the earlier Veenstra, Higashi, and Phillips analysis. They summarize the factors affecting cost-effectiveness in the Table 14.5.

Variant allele refers to a specific version or variant of the gene that affects the response to the drug: the more common it is, the more aggregate health impact exists from identifying

Table 14.5 Factors Affecting Cost-Effectiveness of Pharmacogenetic-Based Therapy Test Combinations

Factors and Their Features That Favor Cost-Effectiveness of Pharmacogenomic Strategies		
	Factor to Assess	*Features that Favor Cost-Effectiveness*
Gene	Prevalence	Variant allele is relatively common.
	Penetrance	Gene penetrance is high.
Test	Sensitivity, specificity, and cost	High specificity and sensitivity.
		A rapid and relatively inexpensive assay is available.
Disease	Prevalence	High disease prevalence in the population.
	Outcomes and economic impact	High untreated mortality.
		Significant impact on quality of life (QoL).
		High costs of disease management using conventional methods.
Treatment	Outcomes and economic impacts	Reduction in adverse events that significantly impact QoL or survival.
		Significant improvements in QoL or survival due to differential treatment effects.
		Monitoring of drug response is currently not practiced or difficult.
		No, or limited, incremental cost of treatment with pharmacogenomic strategy.

Source: Flowers, C.R. and Veenstra, D., *Pharmacoeconomics*, 22(8), 481, 2004.

responders and also avoiding the effects of adverse events and nonresponders. *Gene penetrance* refers to how often genotyped leads to a particular phenotypic response. In the end, although identifying the useful questions to evaluate any given PGx-based intervention, this analysis is still left with the conclusion that "it depends." Furthermore, the model takes the price of the therapeutics and the diagnostics as given. To understand better the incentives of pharmaceutical and diagnostic manufacturers to identify and pursue these opportunities, it is important to recognize that the prices charged for the drug and test are "endogenous"—chosen in the health-care system by a combination of market forces, regulatory procedures, and price controls.

Rather than focusing on specific PGx tests, one major study from Canada [17] examined their likely impact in the aggregate. They distinguished among three types of tests:

1. Tests for fully penetrant genes—high predictive power; mutation causes disease in all
2. Predisposition tests—highly, but not fully predictive; strong genetic component
3. Risk factor tests—lower predictive power; cost of testing the whole population amortized over responders

They pointed out that "predictive genetic tests cannot be meaningfully analyzed as one monolithic health technology." And they concluded that full penetrance tests (given the limited number of monogenic diseases) are likely to have the lowest aggregate cost impact, while the aggregate costs of risk factor tests are much less predictable. They argue that coverage decisions will have to be made on a case-by-case basis.

Two later articles highlight another variant on the notion of personalized medicine based on economic differences rather than biological ones. Economists and other outcomes researchers have long argued that therapy choices should vary among individuals depending on their preferences regarding risk and benefit. For example, Califf [18] says

> The anticipated effect of personalized medicine also fits with the increasing belief that people should be responsible for their own decision making to the greatest extent possible; if they are given information about the benefits and risks tailored to their biology and preferences... they would make more rational health care choices.

Bala and Zarkin [19] (2004) make a similar point, arguing that cost-effectiveness should be done at the individual level. Califf also argues that our current clinical trial system is ill suited to support a move to personalized medicine. He calls for more large pragmatic trials, coordination of regulatory and payment systems to support the needed studies, and provider education in probabilistic thinking. He recommends a two-track system whereby provisional approvals would be followed by required larger, longer-term economic and outcomes studies.

Economics of Personalized Medicine

Danzon and Towse [20] published an article in 2002 that explicitly addressed the issue of incentives to develop linked pharmacogenetic-based diagnostics and therapeutics. It is worthwhile to explain the framework they use.

The economic incentives for a drug manufacturer related to introducing a PGx test are intuitive and fairly obvious. If a drug is already on the market, the manufacturer has limited incentive to introduce a test that would restrict the market size. The main reasons for doing so would be (1) if a higher price could be obtained for this smaller subset and/or (2) if it is clear that some diagnostic test will be introduced during the life of the product.

Danzon and Towse formally analyze the economics of pharmacogenetics using a standard microeconomic framework. Using a simple framework, they are able to delineate the basic economic impacts of a new PGx test. In a theoretical model where a test can identify the responders, the "social value" of testing depends on (1) the expected health benefit per responder, (2) the averted costs of treating nonresponders, and (3) the cost of testing the entire population. They emphasize that the viability of the testing will depend crucially on the ability of the firm to capture the extra health benefit provided through the targeted therapy. Also, they highlight the importance of price flexibility, saying "if the final drug price is unchanged, the innovative firm has no incentive to invest in pharmacogenetic testing in development that will result in a narrower indication."

In 2007, Garrison and Austin [21] extended this model in two ways: (1) to recognize the value to the patient of reducing the uncertainty and (2) to allow the value to be captured by either the drug or diagnostic firm. Their results are discussed in the following sections under pricing and reimbursement challenges.

Health Policy and Economic Issues in Biotechnology

The major health policy issues facing biotechnology today are the following:

- Regulation and generic competition
- Orphan drug status and investment incentives
- Pricing and reimbursement challenges

We discuss each in turn.

Regulation and Generic Competition

The EPO products for treating anemia have been the biggest commercial success in biotechnology over the last decade. As indicated earlier, current sales for the three top-selling products in the United States totaled over $(USD)9.2 billion in 2004, but the Amgen patent expired in 2012. As indicated, the FDA has no defined path for follow-on products to enter as "biogenerics" or "biosimilars." Prices for generic pharmaceuticals are, as would be expected, typically far below the comparable branded products, as competitive pressures push price toward short-run marginal cost (including a competitive rate of return).

The lack of a defined pathway does not in itself totally rule out competition within a drug class: for example, several branded "anti-TNF" biologics for rheumatoid arthritis are on the market and in competition. On the other hand, the pressures to push price down substantially will only come through generic competition.

From a health policy perspective, it is important to keep in mind the role of the patents, as part of our intellectual property (IP) system. The need to encourage innovation through awarding IP rights has its origins in the U.S. Constitution. Article I, Section 8 says Congress shall have the power "To promote the progress of science and useful arts, by securing for limited times to authors and inventors the exclusive right to their respective writings and discoveries." Economists attribute this provision to the recognition by the founding fathers that information is a public good—one person's use of it does not make it unavailable to others, and it's difficult to control and prohibit use of it. In the absence of property rights, a free market will tend to undersupply a public good. Patents, in effect, grant temporary monopoly rights to inventors. Economic theory predicts that monopolists will set price higher than is socially optimal in the short run so that the quantity transacted will be smaller than is optimal as well. This results in a "welfare loss" in the short run that must be weighed against the social gain from having a higher rate of innovation in the long run.

On the pharmaceutical side, the Hatch–Waxman Act aimed to strike balance between protecting patents to encourage innovation and allowing generic entry to lower prices and improve access. Since the development of drugs typically takes 8–12 years of the 20-year patent life and follow-on branded drugs in the same class are common, effective patent life and monopoly power can be very limited. For biopharmaceuticals, these competitive pressures have been somewhat else, especially for those compounds approved as orphan drugs.

Beginning, however, with the Biologics Price Competition and Innovation Act of 2009, which was part of the Affordable Care Act of 2010 (ACA), the federal government has made substantial progress toward defining a biosimilar pathway for the United States [22]. The ACA specified a longer protection period for "data exclusivity" for biologics based on projections of what would be required to sustain biopharmaceutical enterprise [23]. As a result, the data exclusivity period for a biopharmaceutical will be 12 years rather than 5 years for small molecules. There was some controversy about the 12-year data protection period as the U.S. government tried, but failed, to shorten it as part of ACA reconciliation. Thus, the door is now open for biosimilar entry, but given the required comparative clinical trials against the originator biologic molecules, it remains to be seen what the result will be. In terms of impact on price, one instructive example in the United States is recombinant human growth hormone. Biosimilars are available, but the price differences between the innovator and biosimilar products are commercially significant—but only measured in percentage terms, not by several multiples. They are not as dramatic as the price declines for traditional generics versus small molecule brands.

Orphan Drug Status and Investment Incentives

The "success" of the Orphan Drug Act, aimed at rare and neglected disease, in stimulating drug development has probably far exceeded in the initial hopes of its supporters. Since enactment in 1983, over 400 products have been approved. Yet, there are critics who believe it has been abused [24]. Indeed, a recent article in the Wall Street Journal reports that nearly half of the pipeline drugs and biotech companies are for orphan indications. Prices can run into the hundreds of thousands of dollars for some patients for the rest of their lives. The article said that Genzyme Corporation had sales of $(USD)840 million on its drug for Gaucher's disease, which affects fewer than 10,000 people globally. Rep. Henry Waxman was reported to have commented: "we did not expect to see the high cost of orphan drugs," and he went on to say that the price of drugs "is unfair across the board, and Americans everywhere are getting fed up."

Pricing and Reimbursement Challenges

With recent increases in drug and medical care prices, cost containment pressures are increasing and drug prices are under the microscope. The high or "premium" prices for biologics are increasingly in the spotlight. Given the widespread support among the general public for medical innovation, biologics—perceived as among the most innovative products—have been somewhat immune from scrutiny and arguably have been able to attain some of the highest prices paid (reflected in a high cost-effectiveness ratio, meaning fewer health gains for the money spent). This is not necessarily inequitable or inefficient: it depends on many other factors, but it does mean that these companies are receiving greater rewards for their innovations.

Health Policy and Economic Issues in Personalized Medicine

The major health policy/economic issues related to personalized medicine today are the following:

- Uniqueness of pharmacogenetics
- Pricing and reimbursement challenges
- Patents
- FDA regulation

We discuss each in turn in the following texts.

The focus here will be on pricing and reimbursement. A brief comment is provided on each of the other three. First, however, it is necessary to review two concepts that color much of the debate around health policy issues related to genetics.

Background: Genetic Determinism and Exceptionalism

In thinking about health policy and economic issues in PGx, it is important to keep two prevalent views in mind—genetic determinism and genetic exceptionalism. Held in varying degrees by members of the public, they tend to influence their policy interests and prescriptions. We define these two views as follows:

1. *Genetic determinism*—the scientifically unfounded and inaccurate belief that genes determine every aspect of an individual: physical, psychological, emotional, and behavioral.
2. *Genetic exceptionalism*—the claim that genetic information is fundamentally different from other kinds of medical information, and, therefore, it deserves special protection, regulation, or other exceptional measures.

As discussed in Garrison et al. [25], "genetic determinism" is an erroneous position rooted in a monogenic (mis)perception of the impact of genetics. For most diseases and aspects of human behavior, genes alone have a very limited predictive power. Environment is at least—if not more—influential. Genetic exceptionalism is probably tied to genetic determinism in many people's minds: if genes are more highly predictive of disease or behavior, then they deserve special treatment.

Specifically, four characteristics of genetic tests are frequently cited to support policies that treat genetics exceptionally. None, however, of these characteristics are unique to genetic tests:

- *Predictive of future health*: Nongenetic factors can be just as predictive, e.g., plasma cholesterol levels, blood pressure, or exposure to radiation.
- *Permanent and immutable (i.e., out of personal control)*: Exposure to secondhand smoke as a child, or pollution, or a bad sunburn can irreversibly affect risk for certain diseases, such as skin cancer or asthma.

- *Uniquely identifying*: Fingerprints or other personal data yield similarly powerful information, and all require a reference point.
- *Informative about family and community members*: There are many examples for nongenetic predictors, e.g., infection with a communicable disease such as tuberculosis.

These misperceptions are not surprising if one considers that the vast majority of currently available genetic tests pertain either to rare cases of single-gene disorders where the relationship between the gene and health outcome is very strong or to paternity and forensic DNA testing. The public's current experience with genetic data and testing has therefore been highly biased toward genetic tests delivering information that is often more highly predictive than that encountered in many common medical tests. Conversely, the public has had no or very limited exposure so far to other applications of tests such as to help adjust drug dose. In approaching policy issues, these perceptions need to be recognized and acknowledged. At the very least, in thinking about policy, we should ask whether genes are needed and whether a special policy is needed.

Pricing and Reimbursement Challenges

Like Danzon and Towse, Garrison and Austin [26] argue that for products already on the market, given the limited ability to adjust market prices, drug companies have a very limited incentive to identify subgroups in which the benefit–risk ratio is better. Furthermore, diagnostic companies face an even more inflexible pricing and reimbursement system: reimbursement for diagnostics is more or less what economists would call an "administered pricing system" where amounts are reimbursed based on some approximate projection of perceived costs and bear little relation to added value.

Considering a number of scenarios, Garrison and Austin argue that incentives to develop a linked PGx-based diagnostics and therapeutics will depend on several factors: (1) whether the drug is already on the market (and priced) before the test is developed, (2) the extent to which drug and diagnostic prices are flexible and are value based versus cost based, (3) the competitiveness of the insurance market, and (4) the strength of the patent protection on the diagnostics versus the therapeutics.

There are substantial barriers in moving personalized medicine discoveries into real-world interventions. These include scientific, clinical development, and regulatory issues. The extent to which the current reimbursement system is a significant barrier remains an open question. However, the current reimbursement systems in most developed countries are not set up to reward the value created by an innovative personalized medicine test. In particular, the reimbursement systems in the United States and Europe for companion diagnostic tests are not fundamentally "value based." Instead, reimbursement levels are set based on expectations about the cost of providing the test, as reflected in the sequence of steps involved in the laboratory process, but the real value of a personalized medicine test is in the additional mortality improvements, morbidity reductions, and cost savings. Demonstrating these impacts requires an evidence base, and the development of that evidence base involves substantial fixed costs due to clinical trials. If the reimbursement system is based on expected marginal cost, then there will not be sufficient funds to support the needed trials.

In 2013 the Academy of Medical Sciences (AMS) in the United Kingdom held a symposium [27] to review the barriers to what they call "stratified medicine"—their equivalent to personalized medicine. The AMS prepared a report that included their recommendations to address these reimbursement shortcomings and the related barrier of IP. They not only recommended that companion diagnostics be reimbursed based on value, but they also addressed the practical problem of attributing value to the companion test versus the companion medicine—which are the two components of the stratified medicine product. From an economic perspective, the test and the medicine are complementary economic goods, and the division of their combined value is arbitrary—at least, from the perspective of the buyer [28,29], but from the perspective of the developers/manufacturers, the division greatly affects the incentives to invest in product development and evidence generation. The AMS report included following recommendation as a practical way forward for dividing the value, with an eye toward providing greater value for the diagnostics:

> Recommendation 15. To incentivize stratification, at least in the short term, we recommend that health technology assessment bodies develop a model to separate the value between the drug and the companion diagnostic. The medicine should be considered as the primary source of the health gain in responders. The diagnostic should be valued in terms of the cost savings and improvements in quality and length of life from reduced adverse drug reactions in non-responders, and in terms of increased certainty of response. Better patient adherence and greater overall appropriate use may also result, and this value could be divided similarly.

The "short term" identified in the recommendation is the recognition that this new approach would need some development and pilot testing. Indeed, the concept of a companion diagnostic test is evolving with the growth of whole gene sequencing technologies and their falling cost. The reimbursement model will most likely have to evolve as well. In any case, the key long-term issue remains providing sufficient incentives for efficient evidence generation for the right products over their life cycle, i.e., what economists refer to as dynamic efficiency.

While the preceding recommendation may offer a way forward regarding reimbursement of companion diagnostics, the advent of what is called "next-generation sequencing" (NGS) presents a new set of challenges [30]. NGS is a set of technologies that can identify—rapidly and at a relatively low cost—the DNA sequence of an individual. This information on an individual's genes, including mutations, may have both prognostic and predictive significance. Prognosis is the use of genetic information to forecast events in the individual's life course. Whereas the term "prediction" is used when the genetic information can forecast a response to an intervention, e.g., taking chemotherapy for cancer, but there is a statistical issue here that gives rise to an economic challenge. Given that there are so many genes, it is relatively easy to find correlations between genes and phenotypes (e.g., diseases) in small samples through what are called "genome-wide association studies," but many of these correlations will be spurious and have no biological or causal significance. Thus, very large studies or large numbers of replication studies are needed, but these are not inexpensive since collecting information on phenotype is costly. Furthermore, the validation of prediction of a response to treatment will require costly clinical trials.

NGS will produce a plethora of information on genetic makeup, but without appropriate validation studies, the information is of little value. Some type of IP protection will be needed to reward those who generate the evidence that validates a test. Once many of these are known, then a single NGS scan will produce multiple useful and actionable test results. The cost-effectiveness of each test will be unique but will vary among different tests. Each can be assessed independently, and will need to be, if value creation will be adequately rewarded, and evidence is needed to validate the test and to support its value.

Assessment of the value contribution of companion diagnostics or a drug will continue to require the use of the tools, such as decision modeling, benefit–risk analysis, budget impact analysis, cost-effectiveness analysis, and cost–utility analysis. It is important to remember that information has public good characteristics that require interventions, such as IP or research subsidies, to achieve an appropriate level of investment from a societal perspective [31]. Finally, the evidence base regarding the effectiveness of a personalized medicine product changes over time as more real-world experience is gained. As further information about the actual value delivered is gathered, reimbursement systems need to be flexible as well as being value based. Prices, which serve as rewards for innovation, need to be able to move either up or down as more is learned about the real-world cost-effectiveness of the drug–test combination.

In summary, it is clear that the role of economics in providing incentives or barriers to the development of personalized medicine is complex. It is doubtful that personalized medicine will bring about the widespread end of blockbuster drugs, dramatically speed the drug development process, or improve the cost-effectiveness of pharmaceutical drugs overall. However, a key role of the pharmaceutical industry is innovation, and as such, personalized medicine will offer opportunities for incremental improvements in all of these areas. The challenge will be in providing appropriate economic incentives, or reimbursements, for drug treatments that improve over time with the introduction of more biomarker testing, and in supporting an appropriate allocation of rewards to competing biotech and diagnostic manufacturers. For reimbursement for a personalized medicine technology to be related to the value it provides to patients and society, these reimbursement levels will have to be dynamic.

Patent Issues

A landmark legal case illustrates not only the need for IP protection but also the ultimate complexity of the legal issues involved. On June 13, 2013, the U.S. Supreme Court ruled that patent claims that covered naturally occurring DNA were invalid. The case involved Myriad Genetics BRCA1 and BRCA2 tests, for which the charge was about $(USD)4000, for the likelihood of developing breast cancer. The Myriad stock price fell from $(USD)32.92 on June 7, 2013, by 16.2% to $(USD)27.59 on June 14. As of August 8, 2014, the price had rebounded $(USD)37.74. Myriad has hundreds of related patent claims that apparently investors perceive to provide substantial IP protection and trade secrets, based in part of the testing database they have constructed over the years. However, it is clear that NGS will someday provide information on these genes at a low cost. The right to use or report that information may be under litigation for years to come. Furthermore, Myriad has moved on to develop a 25-gene test called "myRisk Hereditary Cancer test" that involves 25 genes, including the BRCA genes. They were able to use proprietary information to develop the weighting algorithm. This will presumably provide substantial competitive advantages over the longer term.

Another well-known case of a high-priced diagnostic personalized medicine diagnostics is Oncotype DX for use in predicting breast cancer recurrence. Indeed, this test has been called the "poster child" for a value-capturing personalized medicine test. It costs about $(USD)3500. It is a biomarker-based test based on a "23-gene signature" and a proprietary prediction formula. Competitors have entered by developing their own predictive index based on the different sets of genes. The challenge for payers becomes trying to decide which test for recurrence to use. However there are no head-to-head comparisons. It remains to be seen how this type of competitive marketplace will play out.

A related issue is the use of what are sometimes called "home brew" tests—or, more technically, called laboratory-developed tests (LDTs) in the United States and in-house tests in the United Kingdom. Once a set of genetic predictors or prognostic factors have been identified either in the literature or in another test, hospital pathology laboratories with the requisite sequencing technology can identify genes and mutations and then use them for prediction. Until recently, these have not been regulated by the FDA in the United States or regulatory authorities in Europe. In other words, these hospital laboratories can effectively enter the personalized medicine testing market without any IP by using general knowledge of existing genes to make predictions. However, this has two effects. First, for-profit test developers will have limited incentive to identify and develop an evidence base for biomarkers that are good predictors. Second, to the extent that the predictive biomarker knowledge is in the public domain, then these independent hospital laboratories can offer the test. This is equivalent to generic entry in the traditional small molecule pharmaceutical market. The situation is slightly different, however, in that LDTs do not have to be exact copies of previous or approved tests. The LDT supplier need only adds a few additional or different biomarkers to the panel to differentiate their test, and without some reporting or testing requirements, it is hard to contest whether the addition provides any additional value. In any case, all of this clearly undermines incentive for for-profit test developers to develop tests.

FDA Regulation

What should the FDA do to regulate and encourage the development of personalized medicine tests and their companion medicines? Until recently, the FDA has not taken a proactive role in this. They had guidance on voluntary genomic data submissions: companies were encouraged to collect genetic samples and to submit databases on these. Generally, the results from analyzing such samples will only be suggestive at best: clinical trials are powered to measure the primary endpoint and not in a subgroup of patients. In the case of Tarceva for non-small cell lung cancer, the FDA required the company to analyze subgroups *ex post* based on a biomarker test of the presence of epidermal growth factor receptors. The results were included in the label of the test but not required for prescription as its predictive power is still under debate.

The FDA has regulated in vitro diagnostic tests (IVDs), which are predictive tests that can be used on a large scale. IVD kits require more marketing authorization and are subject to some evidence requirements. Until recently, the FDA has abstained from regulating tests such as Oncotype DX or LDTs, but reserving the right to do so. On July 31, 2014 [32,33], the FDA rook steps to clarify its policies on both LDTs and IVDs. The FDA stated its intention to regulate LDTs, which is a change from the previous policy of selective enforcement. The policy would be phased in over 9 years with the level of oversight depending on the risk of the test. They define an LDT as "an IVD that is intended for clinical use and designed, manufactured and use it within a single laboratory." However, the proposed guidance does not apply to direct-to-consumer diagnostic tests such as "23andMe," which was ordered late last year to cease offering the test. This area remains uncertain and is under litigation. The FDA also finalized the draft guidance on IVDs that it had issued in 2011. The regulatory pathway for IVDs will use the risk-based criteria that apply to all medical devices: most IVD companion diagnostic devices will be class III devices, which can require premarket approval. The final guidance also calls for IVD companion diagnostic devices and their corresponding therapeutic products to generally be developed contemporaneously.

Conclusion

The health and economic policy challenges facing these two innovative related fields of biotechnology and personalized medicine have some commonalities, but there are also major differences. First, the incentives to innovate in both could be greatly affected by regulatory and reimbursement policies. For example, how the regulatory issues regarding biosimilars are being handled will have profound implications in the coming decades. Potential personalized medicine applications will be affected by recent regulatory changes at the FDA. Both biologics and personalized medicine products will also be affected by major changes in the reimbursement environment, for example, required cost-effectiveness evaluation to obtain coverage and reimbursement (as occurs in the United Kingdom). Indeed, a good argument could be made that to promote the optimal level of innovation, some policy changes are needed to provide a supportive regulatory, legal, and payment environment.

In his seminal 1978 book *Who Shall Live?* [34], Victor Fuchs identified the "technological imperative" as one of the major factors influencing how medical care is provided in the United States: physicians desire to use whatever technologies are at their disposal regardless of the benefit–cost ratio. This imperative continues to this day but is increasingly coming up against the pressure to contain costs. How this trade-off is handled in the policy realm will have much to say about whether these fields remain on the cutting edge of science and medical practice.

References

1. Aaron HJ. (January 2003). Should public policy seek to control the growth of healthcare spending? *Health Affairs* W3: 28–36.
2. Research!America. (2012). America speaks: Poll data summary, Vol. 13, Research!America, Alexandria, VA.
3. Research!America. (2013). America speaks: Polling data reflecting the views of Americans on medical, health and scientific research, Vol. 14, Research!America, Alexandria, VA.
4. Ho RYJ, Gibaldi M. (2003). *Biotechnology and Biopharmaceuticals: Transforming Proteins and Genes into Drugs*. Wilmington, DE: Wiley-Li.
5. Ho RJY, Gibaldi M. (2013). *Biotechnology and Biopharmaceuticals: Transforming Proteins and Genes into Drugs*, 2nd edn. Hoboken, New Jersey: John Wiley & Sons, Inc.
6. NDC Health. (2005). The top 200 selling drugs in 2004 by US Sales. NDC Health, Atlanta, GA. Available at: http://www.drugs.com/top200_2004.html. Accessed December 5, 2015.
7. Brooks, M. (January 30, 2014). Top 100 selling drugs of 2013. *Medscape*. http://www.medscape.com/viewarticle/820011. Accessed August 19, 2014.
8. The Royal Society. (September 2005). *Personalised Medicine: Hopes and Realities*. London, U.K.: The Royal Society.
9. Thirteen WNET New York. (2000). Human genome project. *Religion and Ethics Newsweekly*, Educational Broadcasting Corporation, New York.
10. Garrison LP, Veenstra DL et al. (February 2007). Backgrounder on pharmacogenomics for the pharmaceutical and biotechnology industries: Basic science, future scenarios, policy directions. Report, Pharmaceutical Outcomes Research Policy and Program, Department of Pharmacy, University of Washington, Washington, DC.
11. Garrison LP, Jr., Austin MJ. (2006). Linking pharmacogenetics-based diagnostics and drugs for personalized medicine. *Health Affairs* (*Millwood*) 25(5): 1281–1290.
12. Wong WB, Carlson JJ, Thariani R, Veenstra DL. (2010). Cost effectiveness of pharmacogenomics: A critical and systematic review. *Pharmacoeconomics* 28(11): 1001–1013.
13. Webster A, Martin P, Lewis G, Smart A. (2004). Integrating pharmacogenetics into society: In search of a model. *Nature Reviews Genetics* 5: 663–668.

14. Veenstra DL, Higashi MR, Phillips KA. (2000). Assessing the cost-effectiveness of pharmacogenomics. *AAPS PharmScience* 2(30): E29.
15. Phillips KA, Veenstra DL et al. (2001). Potential role of pharmacogenomics in reducing adverse drug reactions: A systematic review. *JAMA* 286(18): 2270–2279.
16. Flowers CR, Veenstra D. (2004). The role of cost-effectiveness analysis in the era of pharmacogenomics. *Pharmacoeconomics* 22(8): 481–493.
17. Miller F, Hurley J et al. (January 10, 2002). Predictive genetic tests and health care costs. Final report prepared for the Ontario Ministry of Health and Long-Term Care, Ontario, Canada. http://www.health.gov.on.ca/fr/common/ministry/publications/reports/geneticsrep02/chepa_rep.pdf.
18. Califf RM. (2004). Defining the balance of risk and benefit in the era of genomics and proteomics. *Health Affairs* 23(1): 77–87.
19. Bala MV, Zarkin GA. (2004). Pharmacogenomics and the evolution of healthcare: Is it time for cost-effectiveness analysis at the individual level? *Pharmacoeconomics* 22(8): 495–498.
20. Danzon P, Towse A. (2002). The economics of gene therapy and of pharmacogenetics. *Value in Health* 5(1): 5–13.
21. Garrison LP, Austin MJF. (2007). The economics of personalized medicine: A model of incentives for value creation and capture. *Drug Information Journal* 41: 501–509.
22. Blackstone EA, Fuhr JP. (2013). The economics of biosimilars. *American Health Benefits* 6(8): 469–478.
23. Grabowski H. (2008). Follow-on biologics: Data exclusivity and the balance between innovation and competition. *Natural Review Drug Discovery* 7(6): 479–488.
24. Anand G. (November 15, 2005). How drugs for rare diseases became lifeline for companies. *Wall Street Journal*, p. A1.
25. Garrison LP, Jr., Carlson RJ et al. (2008). A review of public policy issues in promoting the development and commercialization of pharmacogenomic applications: Challenges and implications. *Drug Metabolism Review* 40(2): 377–401.
26. Garrison LP, Jr., Austin MJF. (2007). The economics of personalized medicine: A model of incentives for value creation and capture. *Drug Information Journal* 41: 501–509.
27. Academy of Medical Sciences. (2013). *Realizing the Potential of Stratified Medicine*. London, U.K.: Academy of Medical Sciences.
28. Garrison LP, Towse A. (2014). Personalized medicine: Pricing and reimbursement as a potential barrier to development and adoption. In AJ Culyer, ed. *Encyclopedia of Health Economics*, Vol. 2. Amsterdam, the Netherlands: Elsevier, Location for Elsevier: Elsevier Radarweg 29, PO Box 211, 1000 AE Amsterdam, Netherlands The Boulevard, Langford Lane, Kidlington, Oxford OX5 1GB, UK 225 Wyman Street, Waltham, MA 02451, USA pp. 484–490.
29. Towse A, Garrison LP Jr. (September–October 2013). Economic incentives for evidence generation: Promoting an efficient path to personalized medicine. *Value in Health* 16(6 Suppl): S39–S43.
30. Phillips KA, Trosman JR et al. (2014). Genomic sequencing: Assessing the health care system, policy, and big-data implications. *Health Affairs* 33(7): 1246–1253.
31. Garrison LP, Jr., Mansley EC et al. (2010). Good research practices for measuring drug costs in cost-effectiveness analyses: A societal perspective: The ISPOR Drug Cost Task Force report—Part II. *Value in Health* 13(1): 8i–13i.
32. U.S. Food and Drug Administration. (August 6, 2014). In vitro companion diagnostic devices. Guidance for Industry, and Food and Drug Administration Staff, Silver Spring, Maryland. http://www.fda.gov/downloads/medicaldevices/deviceregulationandguidance/guidancedocuments/ucm262327.pdf.
33. U.S. Food and Drug Administration. (July 31, 2014). Framework for regulatory oversight of laboratory developed tests (LDTs). Anticipated details of the draft guidance for Industry, Food and Drug Administration Staff, and Clinical Laboratories. http://www.fda.gov/downloads/MedicalDevices/ProductsandMedicalProcedures/InVitroDiagnostics/UCM407409.pdf. Accessed December 5, 2015.
34. Fuchs VF. (1978). *Who Shall Live*? New York: Basic Books. U.S. Food and Drug Administration. Silver Spring, Maryland.

Chapter 15

Pharmaceutical Promotion in the United States

Alan Lyles

Contents

Introduction

Promoting pharmaceutical products has a long history. However, the types and amount of promotional activities vary by therapeutic indication, small or large molecule product, audience, market context, and regulatory guidance(s). Historically, they have focused on medical professionals, but more recently it includes the general public. Promotions range from the conventional activities of having a pharmaceutical company's pharmaceutical sales representative (PSR, previously called a *detail person*) meet with physicians, scheduling presentations for physicians' continuing education, arranging lunches and lectures for medical students and residents, and advertising in scientific journals, to social media, blogs, and broadcast advertisements that directly target potential consumers. Consumer-focused promotions have gained greater importance as patients have become responsible for more of the costs for pharmaceuticals. By 2011 branded products represented 46% of patients' out-of-pocket payments, disproportionate to their 18% of prescriptions.[1]

Promotional spending by the pharmaceutical industry has grown substantially, from $(USD)4.26 billion in 1996 to $(USD)10.74 billion in 2011—a 252% increase in unadjusted dollars (Tables 15.1 and 15.2). However, Kornfield et al. (2014) clarify that since 2004 promotion has declined as a percentage of revenue and was less for biological than for small molecule products.[2]

Professional journal advertising, PSR functions, and direct-to-consumer advertising (DTCA) are distinct activities, but the goal is a consistent, reinforced message across all communications. Brozak (2013), however, argues that large pharmaceutical companies lag as marketers and continue to search "for billion dollar blockbuster drugs that can support large bureaucratic organizations."[3] Moreover, changes in the marketplace and incentives under the Affordable Care Act mean that marketing communications alone will be less successful even if they might influence a physician to prescribe a product since the "fourth hurdle" of insurance plan coverage will require comparative effectiveness and value evidence.[4] For biosimilar products, there is a critical fifth hurdle of patient acceptability of the biosimilar versus the reference biological product.[5] More recently, social media are entering the mix but how it will influence segmented marketing to diverse demographic groups is uncertain. FDA issued draft guidance for the pharmaceutical industry in 2011 on interactive

Table 15.1 Total U.S. Promotional Spend by Type, 1996–2011 (in Millions $US)

	2011	*2010*	*2009*	*2008*	*2007*	*2003*[a]	*1996*[a]
Professional promotion	6,803	6,111	6,609	6,838	6,905	5,722	3,469
Direct-to-consumer advertising	3,934	4,074	4,364	4,429	4,907	3,235	791
Promotion total	10,737	10,185	10,973	11,267	11,812	8,957	4,260
Professional journal advertising	322	326	315	387	470	448	459
Sales rep details	6,481	5,785	6,294	6,451	6,435	5,274	3,010
Professional promotion	6,803	6,111	6,609	6,838	6,905	5,722	3,469
Direct-to-consumer advertising	3,934	4,074	4,364	4,429	4,907	3,235	791

Sources: Courtesy of IMS Health, Integrated Promotional Services, Danbury, CT; From IMS Health, Total US promotional spend by type, 2003, http://www.imshealth.com/deployedfiles/ims/Global/Content/Corporate/Press%20Room/Top-Line%20Market%20Data%20&%20Trends/2011%20Top-line%20Market%20Data/Promo_Spend_By_Type.pdf. Accessed January 13, 2014.

[a] For 2003 and 1996, sales rep details have been calculated from a prior report by summing office and hospital based promotional spending.

Table 15.2 Growth in Total U.S. Promotional Spend by Type, 1996–2011 (Percentages Compared to 1996)

	2011	*2010*	*2009*	*2008*	*2007*	*2003*[a]	*1996*[a]
Professional promotion (%)	196	176	191	197	199	165	100
Direct-to-consumer advertising (%)	497	515	552	560	620	409	100
Promotion total (%)	252	239	258	264	277	210	100
Professional journal advertising (%)	70	71	69	84	102	98	100
Sales rep details (%)	215	192	209	214	214	175	100
Professional promotion (%)	196	176	191	197	199	165	100
Direct to consumer advertising (%)	497	515	552	560	620	409	100

Sources: Courtesy of IMS Integrated Promotional Services, Danbury, CT; Data calculated from IMS Health, Total US promotional spend by type, 2003, http://www.imshealth.com/deployedfiles/ims/Global/Content/Corporate/Press%20Room/Top-Line%20Market%20Data%20&%20Trends/2011%20Top-line%20Market%20Data/Promo_Spend_By_Type.pdf. Accessed January 13, 2014.

[a] For 2003 and 1996, sales rep details have been calculated from a prior report by summing office and hospital based promotional spending.

postmarketing promotional media[6]; however, it is too soon to assess evidence about the influence of the delayed final guidance that was released in January 2014.[7]

Innovation as the pathway to revenue growth is challenging. This is captured in a 12-year analysis of new drug applications (NDAs) to the FDA. The National Institute of Healthcare Management examined NDAs covering 1989–2000: priority-review new molecular entities represented 15% of approvals for new drugs during this period (153 of 1035), while 65% contained already marketed active ingredients.[8] Consequently, expanding the use of existing products and engaging patients may be even more crucial over the next 10 years. The importance of marketing and advertising as an integrated strategy with research and development is apparent.

The scale of promotional activities has grown rapidly, precisely because research and development alone are less reliable for revenue growth.[9] Consolidations in the pharmaceutical industry through mergers and acquisitions have generally impeded rather than facilitated introducing new pharmaceutical products. For an industry whose members' shares are publicly traded, the consequence of slowing revenue generation can be swift and brutal—particularly when a past record of earnings has been stellar. The current flurry of mergers and acquisitions is more strategic than in the past, capturing focused strategic business and therapeutic and/or technological synergies rather than disintermediation alone.

Legislation, Regulation, and Oversight

The American Medical Association's (AMA) Council on Pharmacy and Chemistry, established in 1905, had a large impact on medical journal advertising policies and physician prescribing decisions. Recall that this precedes the Flexner Report on medical education in the U.S.' deficient, commercial foundations.[10] Although the council was established to fight patent medicines and their advertising, it also affected consumer access to drug information. "The council ... would not approve any drug that was directly advertised to the public, or whose 'label, package or circular' listed the diseases for which the drug was to be used."[11]

To place an advertisement in a medical journal, a manufacturer had first to comply with the AMA's requirement for disclosure of the product's content and its testing through the Bureau of Chemistry, which had been established by the Federal Food and Drugs Act of 1906.[12] As Paul Starr observed, the consequence of this requirement changed the direction of the Federal Food and Drugs Act of 1906. Instead of consumers having more accurate label information, they now had to rely on physicians as the source for drug information.[9]

The 1938 Food, Drug, and Cosmetic Act replaced the 1906 law: it mainly concerned requirements for proof of safety prior to marketing new drugs, but the Wheeler-Lea Act (1938) placed all drug advertising under the Federal Trade Commission (FTC), not the FDA.[13] FTC jurisdiction meant that the requirements and constraints were those of commercial rather than medical communications. It was not until the Kefauver–Harris Amendment (1962) that oversight of prescription drug advertising became an FDA authority,[14] and regulation then began to reflect the difference between drugs and consumer goods. Regulatory oversight of prescription drug promotions resided in FDA's Division of Drug Marketing and Advertising Communications, which was reorganized in 2011 into the Office of Prescription Drug Promotion (OPDP) to increase its visibility.[15]

Even something as basic as determining whether a drug was prescription only or over the counter (OTC) was inconsistent until the Durham–Humphrey Amendment of 1951.[16] Prior to this law, each pharmaceutical company could decide whether a drug was a prescription-only product or not, and manufacturers might come to a different decision regarding the same drug. The FDA could, of course, contest these decisions through the courts—a slow and costly regulatory option. Following the Durham–Humphrey Amendment, prescription-only products, known as legend drugs, were clearly and efficiently identified with the legend "CAUTION: Federal law prohibits dispensing without a prescription."

Advertising and promoting pharmaceutical products are restricted to approved uses, although physicians may legally prescribe marketed drugs for other, or off-label, uses. However, when off-label uses are promoted by manufacturers, or suspected of being promoted, possible actions include investigations ranging from communication reviews by OPDP to inquiries and possible justice department litigation. For example, court documents demonstrate integrated promotional strategies for gabapentin that included unapproved uses, resulting in a 2004 fraud settlement of $(USD)430 million with the Department of Justice.[17–19] Such settlements may also include *corporate integrity agreements (CIAs), certification of compliance agreements (CCAs),* and *settlement agreements with integrity provisions, a less complete category than a CIA*—a current and comprehensive set of these documents is maintained by the Office of Inspector General (OIG) on its website.[20] (See Appendix 15A for more details on CIAs and CCAs.)

Rapidly unfolding basic science discoveries and subsequent medical applications rest, in part, on the incentives of a patent system that protects the intellectual property of a patent award for the product or process. When patents are awarded to individuals who are employees, they are usually required by employment agreements to transfer the patent to their employer firm. U.S. legislation encourages researchers and universities to work with drug companies to file patents and bring the benefits of their discoveries to the public. As more of the products dispensed in pharmacies were manufactured by large drug companies rather than compounded by pharmacists, drug manufacturers became a more prominent stakeholder in setting prices for prescription products. Patent protection providing a period of potential monopoly on drugs, coupled with the costs of expanding manufacturing, research, and development infrastructure, led manufacturers

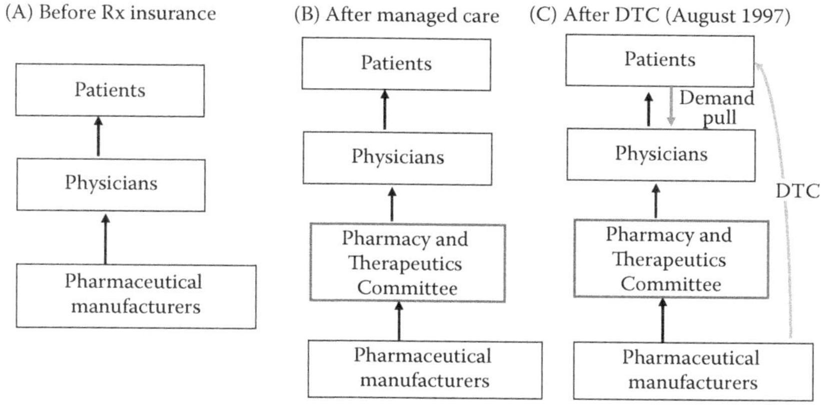

Figure 15.1 Evolution of pharmaceutical product communications.

to seek ways to increase revenues through more active product promotion. Initially these activities targeted physicians.

From the 1950s through the 1980s, drug product promotions consisted mainly of advertising in medical journals, sponsoring continuing medical education, and detailing physicians. Detail persons, or PSRs, are salespeople responsible for meeting with physicians, presenting information regarding their employer's products, answering doctors' questions, and, in the end, persuading physicians to write more prescriptions for the product(s) they are "detailing." Drug manufacturers' direct access to prescribing physicians has been the foundation of pharmaceutical product promotion for decades (Path A in Figure 15.1).

Prescription Drug Costs

Beginning in the early 1980s, cost containment efforts were relatively successful for hospital and physician expenditures. However, annual drug cost increases throughout the 1990s outpaced the rates of increase in hospital and in physician costs. As employers looked for more opportunities to reduce their operating costs, pressure to lower or at least restrain growth in their employees' health insurance costs grew.

Drug cost trends defied these pressures and required cross-subsidization through savings achieved in other sectors, such as hospital and physician payments. All national health expenditures rose between 1990 and 2012 (Table 15.4) and, except for 2011 and 2012, outpaced gross domestic product year-on-year growth. Recently cost increases have moderated, though this was missed by most Americans. Only 5% of respondents in a 2013 New York Times/CBS News Poll correctly said that health-care costs increased at a slower rate, while 50% reported that costs are increasing at a faster rate.[21]

Promoting Pharmaceutical Products

Virtually everyone in the United States has been exposed to prescription drug advertisements intended for consumers—these advertisements are on television, in newspapers and magazines, on the radio, and on the Internet. In addition, the same communication about the product should contain a balance of the most important evidence about both its therapeutic benefit and risks. However, the target of these promotions, consumers, cannot directly purchase the marketed products nor can most assess the information the advertisements contain. Drugs differ from other consumer products in that although *caveat emptor* may guide commerce, it is not applicable in medicine. Instead, behavioral models such as the physician being the agent for the patient, the *learned intermediary*, and ethical codes emphasizing *beneficence* provide guidance and expected standards in health care. Consequently, pharmaceutical advertisements and promotional activities should reflect the intended patient audience's general lack of medical sophistication. Currently, only the United States, New Zealand and Brazil allow DTCA, with varying regulations, restrictions and enforcement.[22]

DTC communications were just 19% of pharmaceutical marketing and advertising expenditures in 1996. However, this share rose to 36% in 2003 and peaked at 40% in 2008 and 2009 (Table 15.3). In unadjusted 2011 dollars, DTCA had increased to 497% of its 1996 amount.[23] Marketing pharmaceutical products directly to consumers (DTC or DTCA), although pervasive, is just the most visible aspect of pharmaceutical product promotion. In 2011, expenditures for pharmaceutical representatives and their activities represented 60% of promotional spending, DTCA 37% and professional journal advertising 3% (Table 15.3). The shift in the absolute amounts and blend of communication channels reflect strategic assessments of marketing constraints, opportunities, and trade-offs of short-term versus long-term prospects.

It is notable that professional journal advertising has declined in absolute dollars to the point that 2011 spending was only 70% of the 1996 baseline (Table 15.2).

The relative types of promotional spending have changed since FDA first issued a "Draft Guidance on Direct-to-Consumer Broadcast Advertisements" in 1997.[24] Although overall promotional spending grew 252% (in absolute dollars) from 1996 to 2011, the share for DTC increased from 19% to 37%. The promotional strategy shift is starkly reflected in the declining share for medical journal advertising—from 11% in 1996 to 3% in 2011 (Table 15.3).

Table 15.3 Total U.S. Promotional Spend by Type, 1996–2011 (Percentages of Total in Each Year)

	2011	*2010*	*2009*	*2008*	*2007*	*2003*[a]	*1996*[a]
Professional promotion (%)	63	60	60	61	58	64	81
Direct-to-consumer advertising (%)	37	40	40	39	42	36	19
Promotion total (%)	100	100	100	100	100	100	100
Professional journal advertising (%)	3	3	3	3	4	5	11
Sales rep details (%)	60	57	57	57	54	59	71
Professional promotion (%)	63	60	60	61	58	64	81

Sources: Courtesy of IMS Integrated Promotional Services, Danbury, CT; Data calculated from IMS Health, Total US promotional spend by type, 2003, http://www.imshealth.com/deployedfiles/ims/Global/Content/Corporate/Press%20Room/Top-Line%20Market%20Data%20&%20Trends/2011%20Top-line%20Market%20Data/Promo_Spend_By_Type.pdf. Accessed January 13, 2014.

[a] For 2003 and 1996, sales rep details have been calculated from a prior report by summing office and hospital based promotional spending.

Pressure to Reduce Pharmaceutical Expenditures: The Context

Private health insurance paid just 1% of prescription drug expenditures in 1960, public programs 3%, and the majority (96%) was paid directly by individuals.[25] During this period of predominantly out-of-pocket payments by patients for their prescription drugs, patients' independent access to prescription drug information was further limited by the American Pharmaceutical Association's Code of Ethics then in force: "the pharmacist does not discuss the therapeutic effects or composition of a prescription with a patient. When such questions are asked, he suggests that *the qualified practitioner* is the proper person with whom such matters should be discussed" [emphasis added].[26]

In recent years, third parties have had the risk and financial responsibility for larger portions of pharmaceutical costs. Insurance products that offered a prescription drug benefit, including managed care health insurance, have grown in popularity. By 1996 individual payments for prescription drug expenditures in the United States declined to just one-third of total expenditures. Managed care enrollment increased substantially during the last two decades of the twentieth century: from 1980, with enrollments of 9 million, to 81 million members of managed care plans by 1999.[27] This was a strategic shift in the pharmaceutical market: instead of having millions of individuals paying for prescription drugs that had been selected by individual physicians, large organizations became financially responsible for much of the cost of products covered under the insured person's policy (Path B in Figure 15.1).

Distinct trends began to converge. Purchasers became more powerful, control of pharmaceutical expenditures became a priority, and new product approvals slowed. The rise of DTC spending came in the context of rapid expansion of managed care plan enrollments in the 1980s and 1990s. Managed care insurance products provided the financial means for more people to obtain prescription drugs, yet for pharmaceutical manufacturers, managed care plans' benefit designs presented a barrier to their direct communications with physicians (Figure 15.1).

Managed care plans began with open access to FDA-approved pharmaceutical products, subject to nominal cost sharing by the insured—typically a fixed co-payment amount per prescription dispensed. During periods of expanding health plan enrollments, the rate of increase in prescription drug costs generally outpaced costs for other member benefits (Table 15.4). Drug cost trends prodded insurers and health plans to become more active in the oversight and management of pharmaceutical product use by those they insured and the physicians who treated them.

To maintain a clinical and safety rather than primarily a financial focus, a centralized decision-making body of drug therapy experts, the Pharmacy and Therapeutics Committee (P&T Committee), was interposed between the pharmaceutical company, its PSR(s), and the prescribing physician. As a form of oversight, the P&T Committee is a vital organizational resource (1) for assessing the adequacy or strength of evidence to support the use of alternative drugs and (2) for making recommendations to health plans, providers, employers, and insurance companies regarding their use. It is this committee that assesses the strength of the evidence for candidate products and whether or how each product's use fits the clinical needs of the covered population. P&T Committees increasingly requested evidence to support benefit coverage decisions and the extent of coverage of specific drug products, producing a rapid increase in the number of economic studies of pharmaceuticals[28] and the birth of pharmacoeconomics as a discipline. The absence of pharmacoeconomic practice guideline standards led Drummond to question whether pharmacoeconomics, as then practiced, was an applied science or just another form of marketing.[29,30]

Table 15.4 Average Annual Percent Change in National Health Expenditures and Gross Domestic Product from Previous Year, 1990–2012 (Selected Years)

Year	*All NHE*	*Hospital*	*Physician and Clinical Services*	*Rx Drugs*	*GDP*
2012	3.7	4.9	4.6	**0.4**	4.6
2011	3.6	3.5	4.1	**2.5**	3.8
2009	3.8	6.6	3.4	**4.9**	−2.1
2007	6.3	6.2	5.2	**5.1**	4.5
2005	6.8	7.7	6.1	**6.4**	6.7
2003	8.6	8.2	8.0	**11.3**	4.8
2001	8.4	8.1	8.5	**14.7**	3.3
2000	6.6	5.2	6.2	**11.6**	5.5
1990	11.0	9.6	12.8	**12.8**	7.6

Source: Centers for Medicare and Medicaid Services, National Health Expenditure Data, Tables 1 and 2, http://www.cms.gov/Research-Statistics-Data-and-Systems/Statistics-Trends-and-Reports/NationalHealthExpendData/Downloads/tables.pdf. Accessed June 23, 2015.

Health plans, insurance companies, and managed care plans turned to the use of drug lists, known as formularies, to influence prescription drug utilization and costs.[31] These formularies were, at first, *open*—meaning that the list was for information and posed no restriction or financial barrier to access for marketed drugs. Subsequent insurance benefit designs used *partially closed* and *closed* formularies, under which only selected products were covered by the individual's insurance policy. Formularies have been used to implement prescription drug benefits by linking the insured's increasing cost sharing to tiers or levels of product support within the formulary: two tiers consisting of generic and brand products; three tiers consisting of generic, brand, and nonpreferred brands; and four tiers consisting of generic, brand, nonpreferred brand, and lifestyle or other designated products.

Fourth tier products may require 100% payment by the insured, but including those products on a formulary may permit their costs to be applied toward a patient's deductible. These approaches to drug product selection influence the extent and specific use of pharmaceutical products. They were, over time, augmented by utilization management techniques such as physician prescription profiling, requiring prior authorization for certain drugs and limiting the prescribing of some classes or drugs to specific physicians or specialties.[32] The extent of the insured's cost sharing increases at each tier, clearly intending to influence the prescriber to use and the patient to request a product from a lower tier if possible.

These benefit changes created competition among pharmaceutical manufacturers for favorable formulary placement of its products. The insertion of the P&T Committee as a decision-making body and its influence on medication use within an insurance or health plan substantially also altered the relative effectiveness and mix of marketing activities. For example, physician detailing by PSRs as a marketing strategy based solely, or primarily, on physician communications, and their autonomous prescriptive decision authority has had to change.

Although physicians still have the professional prerogative to prescribe any marketed product they determine to be appropriate, as a practical matter, insurance coverage or the extent of coverage of specific products for their patients pressures them to prescribe products endorsed by P&T Committees.

Direct to Consumer

FDA mandated the inclusion of information on benefits and risks of oral contraceptives in a patient package insert (PPI) in 1970, but this was an isolated accomplishment for more accessible consumer information on approved drugs. A subsequent pilot PPI program was cancelled in 1982. Instead, the FDA elected to rely on voluntary, private sector actions to provide patients with product-specific information on risks and benefits.

During the period between definitively classifying drugs as prescription only or OTC and evolution of regulatory authority over their advertising, advertisements and promotional activity by pharmaceutical companies generally excluded the public. From the Durham–Humphrey Amendment (1951) to the early 1980s, marketing emphasized physicians and, to a lesser extent, physicians in training. Starting with a public advertisement of the price for a branded version of ibuprofen,[33] a pneumococcal vaccine advertisement, and then an advertisement for acyclovir, the move to promote prescription products directly to consumers had begun.[34] The shift from general or help-seeking promotions to those based on a specific product was influenced by the campaign for Oraflex® (benoxaprofen). Side effects and deaths attributed to this product led to its removal from the market—voluntarily, by the manufacturer—and then to the commissioner of the FDA's request in 1983 for a moratorium on DTCA. During the moratorium, the regulatory implications of communications that balanced safety with risk were assessed.

In ending the moratorium, the commissioner determined that consumers would receive sufficient protection if the guidelines for physicians remained in place but were applied to communications for all audiences.[35] These standards required *product-claim* advertisements to include a *brief summary* and to provide *fair balance* between the health benefits and risks posed by use of the product. In addition, a drug advertisement could not be false, misleading, or lacking in material facts.[36] These requirements, however, presented a dilemma for advertising claims for a specific product to a lay audience since the brief summary was an extensive compilation of a prescription drug's *adverse event profile, contraindications, warnings, and precautions*. The prospect of including all of this information in a broadcast communication, such as a television or radio advertisement, was impractical since the available time was too short to include it all. It was also unappealing to manufacturers since comprehensive discussion of all, or even rare side effects might defeat their purpose.

Besides a *product-claim* advertisement, the FDA also recognizes two other types: *help-seeking* (advertisements that only include information on medical conditions) and *reminder* advertisements (ones that mention the pharmaceutical product but make no claim regarding its uses).[37] These alternatives are not, in a strict sense, advertisements since they do not actively promote a particular product (unless it is the only treatment for the condition mentioned in the *help-seeking* advertisement or the general public already knows the use(s) of the product in the *reminder* advertisement). Other than benefiting from a possible class effect, pharmaceutical companies would gain little return from these types of promotional expenditures; therefore, they were a small component of the overall industry's promotional strategy.

The requirements and restrictions on broadcast drug advertisements intended for consumers were revised, and the FDA issued a draft guidance in 1997, with a provision for review after 2 years (the resulting final guidance was not materially different from the draft).[21] The Draft Guidance for Industry on DTC Broadcast Advertisements permitted such advertisements subject to several requirements: broadcast advertisements must contain a *major statement* of the most important risks and *adequate provision* by which consumers could obtain the full package label information. The *adequate-provision* requirement could be met by having four alternative sources for complete information identified in each advertisement, varied to accommodate different information-seeking preferences and abilities: (1) a telephone number (toll free) from which the complete information can be read to the caller, (2) a print advertisement in a widely available publication, (3) a suggestion to ask a physician or pharmacist, and (4) an Internet page.[21]

Marketing pharmaceutical products presents some of the most sophisticated examples of lessons learned from applied social science, yet pharmaceutical promotions to consumers, begun in earnest in 1997, pose unique challenges to a marketing industry built on hyperbole. The Food and Drug Administration Amendments Act of 2007 established the standard for a major statement as being *presented in a clear, conspicuous, and neutral manner* and directed FDA to promulgate regulations for determining whether an advertisement meets that standard. These were published in the March 29, 2010, issue of the *Federal Register*,[38] with an extended comment period so that a supplemental study on whether distractions such as added text, sounds, and/or dissonance between visual and auditory content influenced the consumer's comprehension of the product's risks, benefits, and trade-offs.[39] FDA assessed whether requiring risk information to be presented in text and audio and/or whether encouraging the reporting of adverse effects would interfere with the consumer's understanding, concluding that they do not.[40] A study of the results when they are used concurrently is next.

Current Practice

Direct-to-Consumer Advertising

Arguments by the proponents and opponents of DTCA have remained essentially the same since the draft guidance in 1999. Those who favor DTCA argue that it raises consumers' awareness of new therapies, motivates being seen by a physician, and reinforces medication adherence for those already taking prescription drugs. Some of the arguments raised by opponents to DTCA are as follows: it does not give sufficient attention to nonpharmacologic options, does not promote the use of generic medications when feasible, requires physician time to dissuade patients who make inappropriate medication requests, understates the risk(s) of pharmacotherapy, and leads some consumers to believe that they have all of the information needed to decide about their own pharmacotherapy (Path C in Figure 15.1).[41]

From DTCA's start under the FDA's 1997 guidance on broadcast communications, *Prevention* magazine surveyed consumer awareness, understanding, and reactions to DTCA. By 2011, 72% of persons who had seen or heard a DTC TV advertisement reported that its risk information was "very/somewhat useful," but only 67% felt that way about the benefit information. For magazine advertisements these percentages drop to 65% and 64%, respectively.[1]

Promotional activities are strategically designed to counteract forces that would otherwise reduce the use of sole-source branded pharmaceutical products. Poor economic conditions and consistently high unemployment are leading patients to reduce their prescription medicine costs, using tactics such as changing from a brand to a generic or from either to a nonprescription product (36%) and, to a lesser extent, deviations from their pharmacotherapeutic regimen.[1]

The effectiveness of product-specific DTCA appears to be declining—a lower percentage of people are discussing a specific advertised product with a doctor and those who have discussed it mostly talked about it (77%) rather than requested the product (23%).[1] One example of the adverse consequences of a patient's belief concerning risks and benefits comes from a September 2005 consumer survey. It reported that 31% of adults polled reported that they had not filled "a prescription that your doctor gave you because you felt it was unnecessary."[42] Fischer et al.[43] reported that 24% of e-prescriptions were not filled, suggesting that unfilled prescriptions continue to represent an unmet medical need, potentially requiring greater patient activation to fill and to follow their pharmacotherapeutic regimen.

DTCA coincides with waning confidence in the FDA's regulation of drug safety since some of the most actively litigated products were also some of the most heavily promoted. For example, rofecoxib (Vioxx®) promotional expenditures were $(USD)159.5 million in 2000, the year following marketing approval.[44] The subsequent discovery of potential exposure to cardiac risks by the millions of persons who had used rofecoxib has reinforced concerns about the safety of marketed drugs and how much is or is not known when they are approved by the FDA. In a July 21, 2005, survey by Harris Interactive, 52% of respondents agreed that *it is a good idea to forbid DTCA for some period of time after the FDA has approved a new drug so that doctors have time to become familiar with the drug;* 36% favored a mandatory ban, while 16% preferred a voluntary ban. For respondents aged 65 and older, the percent agreeing with some type of restriction increased to 55%.[45] Although 51% of respondents in that 2005 Harris Interactive poll thought that pharmaceutical and drug companies "should be more regulated by government," only 43% did by 2012. Nonetheless, that same 2012 survey reported that just 12% of respondents think pharmaceutical and drug companies are "generally honest and trustworthy" (compared to 20% for banks, 36% for hospitals, and 3% for tobacco companies).[46]

To provide more time to gain understanding and data about possible actions and side effects in a broader population, several drug manufacturing companies had announced that they would voluntarily forego DTCA in the initial period following a new product's marketing approval. For example, Bristol-Myers Squibb Co. decided to withhold DTCA for the first year following a new drug's marketing approval, and Pfizer pledged a 6-month moratorium.[47] The current voluntary Pharmaceutical Research and Manufacturers of America guiding principles,[48] which derive from the marketing guidelines developed by the International Federation of Pharmaceutical Manufacturers & Associations in Geneva, Switzerland,[1] state that "Companies are encouraged to consider individually setting specific periods of time, with or without exceptions, to educate health-care professionals before launching a branded DTC television or print advertising campaign." Legislation that would restrict DTC marketing of pharmaceuticals has been considered, but none was passed. According to the Congressional Budget Office, "a moratorium could affect public health. That impact is uncertain, depending on whether the benefits of fewer unexpected adverse health events were larger than the health costs of possibly reduced use of new and effective drugs."[49]

DTCA is effective. It does provide information, but its role in marketing communications is to influence: the main function of DTCA is to enhance sales of advertised products. Over the first 14 years of the *Prevention* survey, an annual average of 33% of respondents reported asking their doctor for an advertised drug, though that percentage was lower in two of the last three surveys.[1]

The bottom line … is the bottom line. In 2011, 27% of survey respondents reported discussing an advertised product with a physician.[1] Most of those who spoke with their doctor discussed lifestyle changes (78%) or nonprescription drugs (49%), but the larger question is as follows: how do physicians respond to patient conversations about an advertised prescription drug? The trend, based on annual consumer reports of their physician's prescribing the advertised product, tracks a decline from 50% in 2001 to 33% in 2011.[1]

Advertising legend drugs to consumers may deemphasize nonpharmacologic treatments or actions to take prior to using pharmaceutical products. However, some consumers who saw a DTC advertisement did speak with their doctor about a medical condition that they had not previously mentioned to their doctor (15%), and more sought additional information on their current medications (29%).[1]

To summarize, in 2011 a lower percentage of patients were following through after seeing a DTC advertisement for a pharmaceutical product and discussing it with a doctor, and a declining percentage of those who do discuss it actually receives a prescription for the advertised product.

The apparently positive financial return on investment for DTCA may represent an appropriate expenditure by society in meeting its citizen's needs for previously untreated disease—if rational pharmacotherapy is being practiced. Addressing this question requires moving beyond the conventional research methodology used in DTCA: much of the data regarding DTCA relies on surveys, opinions, and recall. A randomized trial provides empiric evidence on the prescribing consequences of DTCA.

Kravitz et al.[50] performed a randomized trial of DTCA-related prescription drug requests to family physicians and internal medicine physicians. Standardized patients (SPs) were calibrated with scripts that supported a diagnosis either of major depression or of adjustment disorder (that is, without major depression). Each SP made one of three different prescription drug requests to a primary care physician who had been randomly selected from a prior screened, representative panel of such physicians: (1) for an advertised, brand-name product; (2) for a drug to treat depression, but not specifying a particular product; or (3) no drug request. As might be expected, SPs with major depression frequently received antidepressant medication: 53% of those making brand-specific requests received an antidepressant, 76% of those making general drug requests received an antidepressant, but just 31% of those who made no drug request received an antidepressant. When a brand-name drug was requested by an SP with major depression, 27% received the requested brand, and 26% received a different antidepressant, while 47% received no pharmacotherapy.

However, 34% of those *without* major depression also received antidepressant drugs: 55% of those who had made a brand-specific request, 39% of those who made a general drug request, and 10% of those who had not requested a drug. Unexpectedly, 67% of persons *without* major depression who had requested a brand-name drug for depression received a prescription for that product. These data question both differential diagnosis and treatment of major depression in primary care practice. The impact of DTCA in primary care appears both to encourage appropriate pharmacotherapy and to stimulate inappropriate drug demands and prescribing.

Using a factorial design, McKinlay et al. (2013) developed videos for two scenarios to determine how primary care physicians would care for patient requests for specific pain medication versus a request "for something to help with the pain."[51] Patients who had symptoms of sciatic pain and requested a specific drug more often received that drug than did those who did not make the specific drug request. This was consistent in both scenarios and was not influenced by differences in patients, physicians, or organizational settings. However, Arney et al.[52] reported that physicians' likelihood of prescribing a requested medication increased if the medication was appropriate for the patient's condition and the patient understood the medication's risks. Furthermore, primary care physicians were more likely to accede to a patient's request for a specific drug than were specialists.

Promoting prescription drugs to consumers has some elements in common with selling brands of detergent—including free trial offers, rebates, and utilization incentives such as offering a free refill after a certain number of filled prescriptions for that product. Manufacturers provided patient assistance through vouchers and/or cost-sharing coupons for 395 branded products in 2011, for an average subsidy of \$(USD)24.28.[53] These subsidies reduce the cost barriers to initiating and persisting with the branded medications, blur the distinctions between formulary tiers, and lower the consumer/insured person's out-of-pocket costs for some branded products.

Such promotions potentially lead to greater utilization of these products than of multisource or generic drugs in the same therapeutic class. While pharmaceutical companies assert that these actions can raise consumer awareness of legitimate alternatives, opponents to such practices note the temporary savings relative to the longer-term costs once patients begin to refill their prescriptions without coupons or vouchers. In 2005 Massachusetts prohibited the use of coupons for prescription drugs, but a subsequent state law (H. 4200, 2012) removed most of the restrictions. This change reflects an insightful policy approach that aims to permit options that would reduce patient's out-of-pocket costs, but discourage promotion of sole-source branded products through this means—Massachusetts continues to prohibit manufacturers "from offering any discount, rebate, product voucher or other reduction in an individual's out-of-pocket expenses, including co-payments and deductibles, for any prescription drug that has an AB rated generic equivalent as determined by the United States Food and Drug Administration."[54,55]

Promotion to Physicians: Detailing

Promoting pharmaceutical products to consumers may create demand, but ultimately it is the physician who writes the prescription. Consequently, promotions to physicians and a search for the most effective ways to promote products to physicians have been a high priority of pharmaceutical manufacturers.

Data from Lehman Brothers, reported in Merx,[56] estimate the average sales per PSR in 2005 at \$(USD)1.9 million—a substantial amount individually and an impressive total when multiplied over the then approximately 100,000 sales representatives (according to Verispan as cited by Merx). These 100,000 salespeople worked with the approximately 782,200 physicians in the United States in 2000,[57] or about one sales person per 7.8 physicians. Since then there have been two main countervailing trends: (1) manufacturers' eliminating PSR positions and (2) increased reliance on the Internet, mobile applications, and digital tools.[58] For example, following loss of a patent on a leading product, in 2012 Pfizer eliminated 20% of its primary care sales representatives,[59] and in 2013 Eli Lilly announced plans to eliminate ~30% of its sales representatives.[60] As pharmaceutical companies receive marketing authorization for products used more by specialist than generalist physicians, Pines notes that a slimmed down sales force may be insufficient to reach primary care physicians as quickly and as fully as previously, nor will they reliably have access to the specialists who would prescribe the products.[61] Both the business and the marketing model are in transition—the old model does not fit the new environment, but there is no one new approach that has dominated promotional effectiveness.

A series of historically large settlements over marketing practices are influencing how pharmaceutical companies are organizing their PSR sales force and interacting with physicians. The PSRs who remain will likely face new compensation models and options for interacting with physicians. GSK removed PSR prescription targets (2011) and is removing sales targets from its PSR compensation algorithm (2013); AstraZeneca ceased funding physicians' international conference travel (2011), and GSK announced its intent to do so by 2016.[62]

Some health plans and providers restrict the frequency and content of sales representatives' contacts with physicians, residents, and others. The Johns Hopkins Hospital's *Pharmaceutical Sales Representatives Policy* (October 2004,[63] updated 2011[64]) requires a PSR to register with the Department of Pharmacy and to have scheduled the mandatory appointment at least 3 days in advance. PSRs "may provide information on their product if (1) They are qualified healthcare professionals or scientists, and (2) They are invited by a faculty physician and only in faculty-supervised, structured group settings" (Johns Hopkins Hospital[64]). The six-page document provides guidance that limit PSRs' roles, access, types of interactions, and exchanges. Policy violations are adjudicated through a three-level process: the first offense receives a warning, a second offense may result in a 6-month suspension of privileges to be on the hospital's grounds, and a third offense can lead to indefinite suspension. The severity of the violation may lead the hospital to bypass the phased escalation and may include both the PSR and potentially all PSRs from their firm.

Among other professional functions, a PSR provides free drug samples to physicians. The use of free drug samples of brand-name products might be supported as making a medication available to poor patients who otherwise may not be able to obtain the drug. However, noting that there were no free samples of generic drugs, Dr. Jack Billi of the University of Michigan Medical School explained that the use of brand-name drug samples actually complicate initiation and continued medication use by indigent patients since they will confront the branded product's price when a refill is needed.[53] The key principles in the Johns Hopkins Hospital's PSR policy has been extended to all of Johns Hopkins Medicine (JHM), which includes multiple hospitals, physician groups, home care, and international and other programs. The JHM Policy on Interaction With Industry[65] applies with a few caveats to all faculty, staff, and volunteers, whether full or part-time. Reasoning that free samples of pharmaceutical products may influence prescribing, the JHM policy prohibits accepting samples or vouchers.

There is a risk that some promotions to physicians may violate federal fraud, abuse, and antikickback statutes. The OIG of the Department of Health and Human Services developed compliance program guidance for federal health-care program participants to "encourage the development and use of internal controls to monitor adherence to applicable statutes, regulations and program requirements."[66] The OIG guidance provides both a structure and process for internal controls that would mitigate the risk of violations. The OIG's compliance program guidance for pharmaceutical manufacturers cautions manufacturers regarding the practice of paying physicians to meet with PSRs, to visit Internet sites, or similar activities as "highly susceptible to fraud and abuse and should be strongly discouraged."[63]

The OIG guidance also expressed concerns about arrangements where something of value might be given to physicians, such as "Entertainment, recreation, travel, meals, or other benefits in association with information or marketing presentations; and, gifts, gratuities, and other business courtesies" since they "potentially implicate the anti-kickback statute." [63]

The Physician Payments Sunshine Act, a part of health-care reform under the Patient Protection and Affordable Care Act of 2010,[67] requires public reporting and transparency of "transfers of value" (TOV) to physicians and teaching hospitals, beginning at $(USD)10.[68] Manufacturers who have a presence in the United States, both domestic U.S. and foreign owned, are responsible for reporting all TOVs. Physicians then have a 45-day review period during which they can correct the data prior to public release on the Centers for Medicare and Medicaid Services' National Physician Payment Transparency Program.[69] Data for August–December 2013 will be made public September 30, 2014; subsequently, annual data will be reported.

Gifts to Physicians

The AMA's Council on Ethical and Judicial Affairs provides guidance on Gifts to Physicians from Industry in Opinion 8.061.[70] Under AMA's ethics guidelines, a gift is only acceptable if it benefits a patient or is "of modest value." One of the AMA's goals for these guidelines is to provide the basis for industry to train its sales representatives regarding physician expectations. A second goal is to avoid even the appearance of conflict of interest as well as to prevent actual conflicts from arising. The AMA's position on transparency laws and industry interactions is that they "(1) not impose a regulatory and paperwork burden on physicians, (2) protect physician rights to challenge false and misleading reports, and (3) provide a meaningful, accurate picture of industry-physician interactions."[71]

Promotion to Physicians: e-Detailing

The Internet is a growing adjunct to in-person physician detailing. A 2002 survey of senior pharmaceutical company executives reported an anticipated decline in the importance of conventional marketing (advertising promotion, sales force, print media, conference events, and seminars) but increase in the importance of general websites, company websites, call centers, and e-detailing. Of those activities expected to grow in importance, the largest gain is expected to be in e-detailing due to cost and efficiency considerations and younger physician preferences.[72,73]

The difficulty of regulating the accuracy of Internet communications led the FDA to develop consumer guidelines for "Health Information On-Line" as early as 1996.[74] The draft guidance for industry on social media[5,6] continue this consumer/patient focus. The Internet can be a means to promote products to physicians, but it also provides patients with condition- and product-specific information. Eighty-five percent of U.S. adults use the Internet[75] with somewhat fewer in higher age groups and lower educational attainment. Of those who do use the Internet, 72% used it in 2012 for health information.[76]

Conclusion

Pharmaceutical product promotions will continue to be a "full court press" with specific communications for consumers, physicians, health plans, and pharmacy benefit management firms. These promotions will increase in amount, sophistication, and novelty as the opposing forces for cost control meet publicly traded companies' revenue growth requirements.

DTCA of prescription drugs will not be prohibited for two main reasons: (1) First Amendment protections on commercial communications that will likely supersede the FDA's claim to regulatory oversight and (2) some evidence that the public desires the information that is, perhaps imperfectly, communicated in these advertisements. The public's demand for more information and more credible information about prescription drugs will increase as baby boomers age and consumer-directed health plans with high deductibles push more prescription drug costs to patients' out-of-pocket expenses.[77]

Consequently, advertising and promoting pharmaceutical products will increase, innovate, and cover a broader spectrum. Recent initiatives such as e-detailing and social media marketing are just two examples that creatively employ technology. The ascendancy of advocacy and interest group politics assures that FDA and OIG guidelines will be tested. The content of promotional activities will continue to be assessed for balance and the absence of bias in communicating gains and risks from pharmaceutical products.

Next stages for social media will evolve as quickly as the technologies have and develop closer and more meaningful, interactive relationships with individual patients ... beyond the web pages, blogs, and now mainstream cluster of Facebook, Twitter, and Pinterest. As with existing laws governing drug efficacy, safety, and communications, regulations governing promotional activities will likely lag behind the rapid developments in digital options for product promotion.

Appendix: Corporate Integrity Agreements and Certification of Compliance Agreements Are Defined

Corporate Integrity Agreements

OIG negotiates CIA with health-care providers and other entities as part of the settlement of federal health-care program investigations arising under a variety of civil false claims statutes. Providers or entities agree to the obligations, and in exchange, OIG agrees not to seek their exclusion from participation in Medicare, Medicaid, or other federal health-care programs.

A comprehensive CIA typically lasts 5 years and includes requirements to

- hire a compliance officer/appoint a compliance committee
- develop written standards and policies
- implement a comprehensive employee training program
- retain an independent review organization to conduct annual reviews
- establish a confidential disclosure program
- restrict employment of ineligible persons
- report overpayments, reportable events, and ongoing investigations/legal proceedings
- provide an implementation report and annual reports to OIG on the status of the entity's compliance activities

Source: U.S. Department of Health and Human Services, Office of Inspector General, Corporate Integrity Agreements, https://oig.hhs.gov/compliance/corporate-integrity-agreements/cia-documents.asp#cia_list.

Certification of Compliance Agreements

The OIG has sometimes negotiated a CCA with health-care providers and other entities, in lieu of a comprehensive CIA, under appropriate circumstances. The terms of a CCA always includes a requirement that the entity maintain its existing compliance program. The organization must agree to a declaration related to their compliance program that is attached to the CCA.

The entity is also required to agree to certain compliance obligations that mirror those found in a comprehensive CIA, including (1) reporting overpayments, reportable events, and ongoing investigations and legal proceedings to the OIG and (2) providing annual reports regarding the entity's compliance activities to OIG during the term of the CCA.

Source: U.S. Department of Health and Human Services, Office of Inspector General, Corporate Integrity Agreements. http://oig.hhs.gov/compliance/corporate-integrity-agreements/cia-documents.asp. Accessed January 12, 2016.

References

1. Silvers C. 2011 DTC study. Prevention. Presentation information generously provided by Lauren Paul, Director of Communications. January 9, 2014. http://blog.advancemarketworx.com/wp-content/uploads/2011/07/dtc-2011-final.pdf. Accessed December 6, 2015.
2. Kornfield R, Donohue J, Berndt ER, and Alexander CG. Promotion of prescription drugs to consumers and providers, 2001–2010. *PLoS ONE* 2013;8(3):e55504. doi:10.1371/journal.pone.0055504. http://www.plosone.org/article/info:doi/10.1371/journal.pone.0055504. Accessed December 6, 2015.
3. Brozak S. Big pharma learned the wrong marketing lesson. *Forbes*. May 25, 2013. Retrieved from http://www.forbes.com/sites/stephenbrozak/2013/05/25/big-pharma-learned-the-wrong-marketing-lesson/. Accessed December 6, 2015.
4. Dunn Z. When sales force met marketing. *MM&M Medical Media & Marketing*. January 10, 2014. http://www.mmm-online.com/when-sales-force-met-marketing/article/328824/?DCMP=EMC-MMM_WeeklyDigest&spMailingID=7735814&spUserID=ODE5NjY3NjEwNzgS1&spJobID=113202571&spReportId=MTEzMjAyNTcxS0. Accessed December 6, 2015.
5. Lyles A. Biosimilars: Patient and physician acceptability is the fifth hurdle to market competition. *Generics and Biosimilars Initiative Journal* 2015;4(1):6–7. http://gabi-journal.net/biosimilars-patient-and-physician-acceptability-is-the-fifth-hurdle-to-market-competition.html. Accessed December 6, 2015.
6. Reisman M. The FDA's social media guidelines are here ... were they worth the wait? *Pharmacy & Therapeutics* 2012;27(2):105–106. http://www.ncbi.nlm.nih.gov/pmc/articles/PMC3351868/pdf/ptj3702105.pdf; U.S. Food and Drug Administration. Guidance for industry: Responding to unsolicited requests for off-label information about prescription drugs and medical devices. December 2011. http://www.fda.gov/downloads/Drugs/GuidanceComp%20liance%20RegulatoryInformation/Guidances/UCM285145.pdf. Accessed December 6, 2015.
7. U.S. Food and Drug Administration. Social media guidance. 2015. http://www.accessdata.fda.gov/FDATrack/track-proj?program=oc-administrative&id=OC-Admin-OEA-Social-Media-Guidance. Accessed December 6, 2015.
8. National Institute for Health Care Management. Changing patterns of pharmaceutical innovation. May 2002. http://www.nihcm.org/pdf/innovations.pdf. Accessed December 6, 2015.
9. Langreth R and Herper M. [Cover story] Pill pushers. *Forbes*. May 8, 2006. http://www.forbes.com/free_forbes/2006/0508/094a.html. Accessed December 6, 2015.
10. Duffy TP. The Flexner report—100 years later. *The Yale Journal of Biology and Medicine* 2011;84(3):269–276. http://www.ncbi.nlm.nih.gov/pmc/articles/PMC3178858/. Accessed December 6, 2015.
11. Starr P. *The Social Transformation of American Medicine*. Basic Books, New York, 1982. ISBN: 0-465-07934-2.
12. Federal Food and Drugs Act of 1906 (The "Wiley Act"). Pub. L. No. 59-384, 34 Stat. 768, 1906.
13. Federal Food, Drug, and Cosmetics Act. Pub. L. No. 75-717, 52 Stat. 1040 (1938), codified as amended 21 U.S.C. §§ 301 et seq. Federal Food, Drug, and Cosmetics Act, June 25, 1938.
14. Food, Drug, and Cosmetic Act 1962. Kefauver-Harris Amendment, 21 U.S.C. Section 355.
15. U.S. Food and Drug Administration. The office of prescription drug promotion. 2012. http://www.fda.gov/downloads/AboutFDA/CentersOffices/OfficeofMedicalProductsandTobacco/CDER/UCM330855.pdf. Accessed December 6, 2015.
16. Durham-Humphrey Prescription Drug Amendment of 1951. 1997. 21 U.S.C.§§ 353,355.
17. Steinman MA et al. Narrative review: The promotion of gabapentin: An analysis of internal industry documents. *Annals of Internal Medicine* 2006;145(4):284–293. Retrieved from annals.org/article.aspx?articleid=727539. Accessed December 6, 2015.
18. U.S. Department of Justice. Warner-Lambert to pay $430 million to resolve criminal & civil health care liability relating to off-label promotion. 2004. http://www.usdoj.gov/opa/pr/2004/May/04_civ_322.htm.
19. Armstrong D and Zimmerman R. Pfizer to settle Medicaid-fraud case: Drug maker agrees to pay about $430 million in fines over Neurontin marketing. *Wall Street Journal*. May 13, 2004. http://online.wsj.com/news/articles/SB108440099145209983.

20. U.S. Department of Health and Human Services. Office of Inspector General. Corporate integrity agreement documents. January 11, 2015. https://oig.hhs.gov/compliance/corporate-integrity-agreements/cia-documents.asp#cia_list. Accessed December 6, 2015.
21. Lowery A. Growth in U.S. health care spending slows. *New York Times*. December 18, 2013, p. A24. http://www.nytimes.com/2013/12/19/us/growth-in-us-health-care-spending-slows-but-out-of-pocket-costs-rise.html. Accessed December 6, 2015.
22. World Health Organization. Direct-to-consumer advertising under fire. Bulletin of the World Health Organization. 2009;87(8). http://www.who.int/bulletin/volumes/87/8/09-040809/en/. Accessed December 6, 2015. Wzorek, L. de F., Correr, C. J., Badaró Trindade, A. C., & Pontarolo, R. (2007). Analysis of medicine advertisement produced in Brazil. Pharmacy Practice, 5(3), 105–108. http://www.ncbi.nlm.nih.gov/pmc/articles/PMC4154743/. Accessed December 6, 2015.
23. IMS Health. Total US promotional spend by type, 1996–2011. http://www.imshealth.com/deployedfiles/ims/Global/Content/Corporate/Press%20Room/Top-Line%20Market%20Data%20&%20Trends/2011%20Top-line%20Market%20Data/Promo_Spend_By_Type.pdf.
24. Food and Drug Administration. Guidance for industry: Consumer-directed broadcast advertisements. August 1999. http://www.fda.gov/downloads/RegulatoryInformation/Guidances/ucm125064.pdf. Accessed December 6, 2015.
25. Smith C. Retail prescription drug spending in the National Health Accounts. *Health Affairs* January 2004;23(1):160–167. http://content.healthaffairs.org/content/23/1/160/T1.expansion.html. Accessed December 6, 2015.
26. American Pharmaceutical Association. Code of ethics of the American Pharmaceutical Association. *Journal of the American Pharmaceutical Association* 1952;41(2:2):20–21.
27. Centers for Disease Control and Prevention. Health, United States, 2003. Table 132: Health maintenance organizations (HMOs) and their enrollment according to model type, geographic region, and federal program: United States, selected years 1976–2002. www.cdc.gov/nchs/data/hus/hus03.pdf. Accessed October 20, 2004. Accessed December 6, 2015.
28. Elixhauser A, Halpern M, Schmier J, and Luce BR. Health care CBA and CEA from 1991 to 1996: An updated bibliography. *Medical Care* 1998;36(5 Suppl):MS1-9, MS18-147.
29. Drummond MF. Economic analysis of pharmaceutical: Science or marketing? *Pharmacoeconomics* 1992;1(1):8–13.
30. Drummond MF. A reappraisal of economic valuation of pharmaceuticals: Science or marketing? *Pharmacoeconomics* 1998;14(1):1–9.
31. Lyles A and Palumbo FB. The effect of managed care on prescription drug costs and benefits. *Pharmacoeconomics* 1999;15(2):129–140.
32. Lyles A. Formulary decision-maker perspectives: Responding to changing environments (Chapter 7). In Pizzi JT and Lofland JT (Eds.) *Economic Evaluation in U.S. Health Care: Principles and Applications*. Jones and Bartlett Publishers, Sudbury, MA, 2006. ISBN: 0-7637-Z746-6.
33. Pines WL. A history and perspective on direct-to-consumer promotion. *Food and Drug Law Journal* 1999;54:489–518.
34. Basara LR. Direct-to-consumer advertising: Today's issues and tomorrow's outlook. *Journal of Drug Issues* 1992;22(2):317–330.
35. Federal Register. Direct-to-consumer advertising of prescription drugs; Withdrawal of moratorium. *Federal Register* September 9, 1985;50(174):36677–36678.
36. Food and Drug Administration. Prescription drug advertising. 21 Code of Federal Regulations Pt. 202.1(e), 1999.
37. Federal Register. Direct-to-consumer promotion: Public hearing. *Federal Register* August 16, 1995; 60(158):42581–42584.
38. 21 CFR Part 202. Direct-to-Consumer Prescription Drug Advertisements; Presentation of the Major Statement in Television and Radio Advertisements in a Clear, Conspicuous, and Neutral Manner. *Federal Register*; 75(59): 15376–15387. March 29, 2010. http://www.gpo.gov/fdsys/pkg/FR-2010-03-29/pdf/2010-6996.pdf. Accessed December 7, 2015.

39. U.S. Food and Drug Administration. Experimental evaluation of the impact of distraction on consumer understanding of risk and benefit information in direct-to-consumer prescription drug television advertisements. June 2011. http://www.fda.gov/downloads/AboutFDA/CentersOffices/OfficeofMedicalProductsandTobacco/CDER/UCM285377.pdf. Accessed December 6, 2015.
40. U.S. Food and Drug Administration. [Noptice] Federal Register Agency information collection activities; Proposed collection; Comment request; Eye tracking study of direct-to-consumer prescription drug advertisement viewing. November 29, 2013. https://www.federalregister.gov/articles/2013/11/29/2013-28599/agency-information-collection-activities-proposed-collection-comment-request-eye-tracking-study-of. Accessed December 6, 2015.
41. Lyles A. Direct marketing of pharmaceuticals to consumers. *Annual Review of Public Health* 2002;23:73–91.
42. Prescription drug compliance a significant challenge for many patients, According to New National Survey. 2005. http://www.harrisinteractive.com/news/allnewsbydate.asp?NewsID=904. Accessed April 16, 2006.
43. Fischer MA, Choudhry NK, Brill G, Avorn J, Schneeweiss S, Hutchins S, Liberman JN, Brennan T, and Shrank WH. Trouble getting started: Predictors of primary medication nonadherence. *American Journal of Medicine* 2011;124:1081.e9–1081.e22.
44. IMS Health. Leading 10 products by U.S. DTC spend, 2000. http://www.imshealth.com/ims/portal/front/articleC/0,2777,6599_40054629_1004776,00.html. Accessed April 24, 2006.
45. Majority of U.S. adults think it is a good idea to forbid direct-to-consumer advertising for new prescription drugs when they first come to market. *Wall Street Journal* 2005;4(14):1–5. http://www.harrisinteractive.com/news/newsletters/wsjhealthnews/WSJOnline_HI_Health-CarePoll2005vol4_iss14.pdf. April 9, 2006.
46. Harris Interactive. Oil, pharmaceutical, health insurance, tobacco, banking and utilities top the list of industries that people would like to see more regulated. December 18, 2012. Retrieved from http://www.harrisinteractive.com/vault/Harris%20Poll%2068%20-%20Industry%20Regulation_12.18.12.pdf.
47. Hensley S. Drug makers seek to transform advertising. *Wall Street Journal Online*. August 29, 2005. http://online.wsj.com/article-print/JB112526814442925007.html. Accessed October 14, 2005.
48. Pharmaceutical Research and Manufacturers of America. PhRMA guiding principles: Direct to consumers advertisements about prescription medicines. 2008. http://www.phrma.org/sites/default/files/pdf/phrmaguidingprinciplesdec08final.pdf. Accessed December 6, 2015.
49. Congressional Budget Office. Potential effects of a ban on direct-to-consumer advertising of new prescription drugs. Economic and Budget Issue Brief. May 2011. Retrieved from http://www.cbo.gov/sites/default/files/cbofiles/ftpdocs/121xx/doc12164/5-25-prescriptiondrugadvertising.pdf.
50. Kravitz RL, Epstein RM, Feldman MD, Franz CF, Azari R, Wilkes MS, Hinton L, and Franks P. Influence of patients' requests for direct-to-consumer advertised antidepressants: A randomized controlled trial. *Journal of the American Medical Association* 2005; 293(16):1995–2002.
51. McKinlay JB, Trachtenberg FL, Marceau LD, Katz JN, and Fischer MA. Do patient medication requests affect primary care physician prescribing? Results from a factorial experiment. Abstract 284467. *American Public Health Association 141st Annual Meeting*, Boston, MA, November 4, 2013. https://apha.confex.com/apha/141am/webprogramadapt/Paper284467.html.
52. Arney J, Street RL Jr, and Naik JD. Factors shaping physicians' willingness to accommodate medication requests. Evaluation & the Health Professions. 2014; 37(3):349–365. http://ehp.sagepub.com/content/37/3/349.abstract. Accessed December 6, 2015.
53. IMS Institute for Healthcare Informatics. The use of medicines in the United States: Review of 2011. April 2012. Retrieved from http://www.imshealth.com/ims/Global/Content/Insights/IMS%20Institute%20for%20Healthcare%20Informatics/IHII_Medicines_in_U.S_Report_2011.pdf.
54. Krasner J. Drug coupons may be no bargain: Legislators fear they could push health costs up. *The Boston Globe*, April 6, 2006. https://www.highbeam.com/doc/1P2-7961366.html.

55. Massachusetts Bill H. 4200. An act making appropriations for the fiscal year 2013 for the maintenance of the departments, boards, commissions, institutions and certain activities of the commonwealth, for interest, sinking fund and serial bond requirements and for certain permanent improvements. Section 130(b)(2). Retrieved from https://malegislature.gov/Bills/187/House/H4200. Accessed December 6, 2015.
56. Merx K. Drug marketing: Freebies for doctors curbed. *Detroit Free Press*. July 12, 2005.
57. Bureau of Health Professions, Health Resources and Services Administration, U. S. Department of Health and Human Services. National Center for Health Workforce Analysis: U.S. Health Workforce Personnel Factbook. Table 101. Estimated supply of selected health personnel and practitioner-to-population ratios, selected years: 1970–2000. http://bhpr.hrsa.gov/healthworkforce/reports/factbook.htm. Accessed April 15, 2006.
58. Whalen J. Drug makers replace reps with digital tools. *Wall Street Journal*. May 10, 2011. http://online.wsj.com/news/articles/SB10001424052748703702004576268772294316518. Accessed December 6, 2015.
59. Armstrong D. Pfizer said to fire 20% of U.S. Primary-Care Sales Force. *Bloomberg News*. December 18, 2012. Retrieved from http://www.bloomberg.com/news/articles/2012-12-18/pfizer-to-fire-about-20-percent-of-u-s-primary-care-sales-force. Accessed December 6, 2015.
60. Rockoff JD. Lilly plans to lay off 30% of its sales reps. *Wall Street Journal*. April 11, 2013. Retrieved from http://online.wsj.com/news/articles/SB10001424127887324240804578417111074635032. Accessed December 6, 2015.
61. Pines N. Therapeutic focus 2014: Cardiovascular. *MM&M Medical Marketing & Media*. January 1, 2014. http://www.mmm-online.com/therapeutic-focus-2014-cardiovascular/article/326164/. Accessed December 6, 2015.
62. Hirschler B. GSK to stop paying doctors in major marketing overhaul. *Reuters*. December 17, 2013. Retrieved from http://www.reuters.com/article/2013/12/17/us-glaxosmithkline-payment-idUSBRE9BG03620131217. Accessed December 6, 2015.
63. Johns Hopkins Hospital. Johns Hopkins Hospital Pharmaceutical Sales Representatives Policy. Johns Hopkins Hospital, Baltimore, MD, October 1, 2004.
64. Johns Hopkins Hospital. The Johns Hopkins Hospital Interdisciplinary Clinical Practice Manual. Pharmaceutical Sales Representatives (PSRs) Policy. Johns Hopkins Hospital, Baltimore, MD, Effective September 1, 2011.
65. Johns Hopkins Hospital. The Johns Hopkins Medicine Policy on Interactions with Industry. Johns Hopkins Hospital, Baltimore, MD, Effective September 1, 2011.
66. U.S. Department of Health and Human Services, Office of Inspector General. Compliance Guidance. http://oig.hhs.gov/compliance/compliance-guidance/index.asp and, Federal Register. OIG compliance program guidance for pharmaceutical manufacturers. *Federal Register* May 5, 2003;68(86):23731–23743.
67. Federal Register. Medicare, medicaid, children's health insurance programs; Transparency reports and reporting of physician ownership or investment interests. *Federal Register* February 8, 2013;78(27): Part II. https://www.federalregister.gov/articles/2013/02/08/2013-02572/medicare-medicaid-childrens-health-insurance-programs-transparency-reports-and-reporting-of. Accessed December 6, 2015.
68. Agarwal S, Brennan N, and Budetti P. The Sunshine Act—Effects on physicians. *The New England Journal of Medicine* 2013;368(22):2054–2057.
69. Centers for Medicare and Medicaid Services. National Physician Payment Transparency Program. http://www.cms.gov/Regulations-and-Guidance/Legislation/National-Physician-payment-Transparency-Program/index.html. Accessed December 6, 2015.
70. American Medical Association Council on Ethical and Judicial Affairs. Opinion 8.061—Gifts to physicians from industry. http://www.ama-assn.org//ama/pub/physician-resources/medical-ethics/code-medical-ethics/opinion8061.page. Accessed December 6, 2015.
71. American Medical Association. Sunshine Act: Physician financial transparency reports. http://www.ama-assn.org/ama/pub/advocacy/topics/sunshine-act-and-physician-financial-transparency-reports.page? Accessed December 6, 2015.

72. IMS Health. How relevant is e-detailing? August 9, 2004. http://www.imshealth.com/ims/portal/front/articleC/0,2777,6599_54702271_54703501,00.html. Accessed April 5, 2006.
73. Capgemini and Quantia. The paradigm shift in pharma-physician interactions: Key findings from Capgemini Consulting and Quantia study. File dated November 22, 2013. http://www.quantia-inc.com/markets/life-sciences/the-paradigm-shift-in-pharma-physician-interaction.pdf.
74. Food and Drug Administration. Health information on-line. *FDA Consumer Magazine* 1996;30(5). Revised January 1998 and April 1999. https://www.highbeam.com/doc/1G1-18375225.html.
75. PEW Internet and American Life Project. Trend data (Adults). http://www.pewinternet.org/data-trend/internet-use/internet-use-over-time/. Accessed December 6, 2015.
76. PEW Internet and American Life Project. Health Online 2013. http://www.pewinternet.org/~/media//Files/Reports/PIP_HealthOnline.pdf. Accessed December 6, 2015.
77. Berndt ER. To inform or persuade? Direct-to-consumer advertising of prescription drugs. *New England Journal of Medicine* 2005;352:325–328.
78. IMS Health. Total US promotional spend by type. 2003. http://www.imshealth.com/deployedfiles/ims/Global/Content/Corporate/Press%20Room/Top-Line%20Market%20Data%20&%20Trends/2011%20Top-line%20Market%20Data/Promo_Spend_By_Type.pdf.

Chapter 16

Health Technology Assessment

Laura T. Pizzi and Tony Amos

Contents

Learning Objectives

1. Define health technology assessment as a tool for informing decisions regarding pharmaceutical and biotechnology products.
2. Discuss the main components of health technology assessment.
3. Explain the history and rationale for health technology assessment in the United States.
4. Review key applications of health technology assessment in the United States by the Office of Technology Assessment, Patient-Centered Outcomes Research Institute, and the Academy of Managed Care Pharmacy.
5. Discuss applications of health technology assessment outside of the United States, including Australia's Pharmaceutical Benefits Advisory Committee, the Canadian Agency for Drugs and Technologies in Health, the Haute Autorité de Santé (French National Authority for Health), Germany's Institute for Quality and Efficiency in Health Care, and the UK National Institute for Health and Care Excellence.

Introduction

Health technology assessment (HTA) is a form of policy research, which has been defined by the Institute of Medicine (IOM) of the National Academies, a congressionally chartered nongovernmental entity "that works outside of government to provide unbiased and authoritative advice to decision makers and the public," (Institute of Medicine 2015) as "any process of examining and reporting properties of a medical technology used in health care, such as safety, effectiveness, feasibility, and indications for use, cost and cost-effectiveness, as well as social economic, and ethical consequences, whether intended or unintended" (Institute of Medicine 1985). Attributes assessed can also include patient-reported outcomes as well as legal and political impacts (O'Donnell et al. 2009; Sullivan et al. 2009). The main purpose of this multifaceted approach to policy analysis is to inform public and private sector technology-related policymaking in health care. This approach is conducted within "interdisciplinary groups using explicit analytical frameworks drawing from a variety of methods" (Goodman 2014). Unfortunately, achieving consensus regarding standards on how this work should be performed continues to evolve. The United States does not have an official standards-setting government agency or legislation; instead, this work consists mostly of *de facto* practices in the private sector.

HTA is often used synonymously with *cost-effectiveness analysis* (CEA) and *evidence-based medicine* (EBM), but they are not the same. CEA focuses on quantifying the incremental cost per outcome achieved by a new drug or medical technology compared to the standard of care or some other alternatives, whereas EBM refers to the evaluation of the strength of clinical evidence to facilitate medical decisions, or the development of protocols and/or guidelines (Sullivan et al. 2009). While all three approaches entail analysis of clinical evidence, HTA is a broader and more formal process than CEA and EBM and typically considers not only clinical evidence but also economic and quality-of-life evidence.[4] The result of these decisions can be full acceptance,

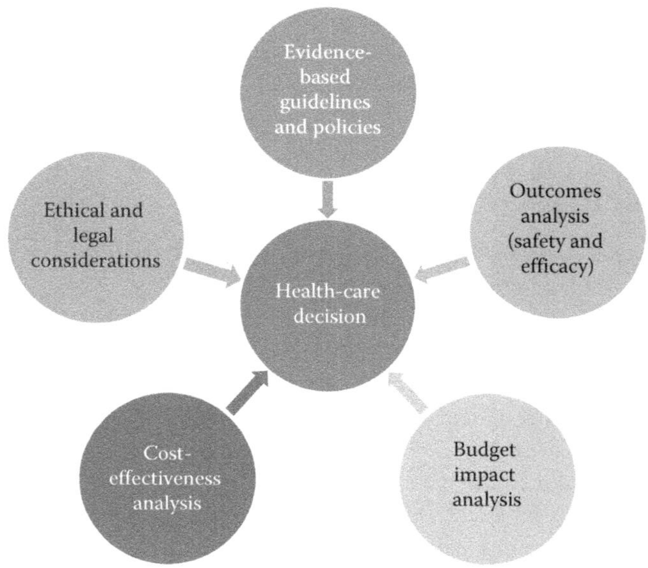

Figure 16.1 Stages of health technology assessment.

modification, or rejection of the medical technology (Oberlander 2012), marketing approval, benefit inclusion and/or the extent of coverage, and, in some cases, price. Essentially, HTAs serve as a vehicle for systematically and comprehensively assessing and communicating the comparative value of a drug, device, or other medical technology.

The HTA process can be utilized by authoritative bodies to facilitate informed decisions concerning the coverage of technologies. A full HTA appraisal has, by convention, five conceptual parts. These five components of technology assessment are shown in Figure 16.1. In practice, performing HTAs involves iteration between these components, as insight is gained when information regarding the treatment emerges (Eddy 2009).

The combined learnings from these components permit decision-makers to understand more completely the effects of health-care technologies on outcomes of interest (Eddy 2009). Ideally, the process will be transparent, credible, and consistently applied, which would eventually support credibility with stakeholders and manages potential conflicts of interest.

Economic costs and product prices vary substantially across nations, reflecting differences in market conditions, public pharmaceutical policies, public–private requirements and authorities, and treatment guidelines. Consequently, HTAs have limited direct utility across national boundaries.

Rationale for Health Technology Assessment

The historical rise in health-care costs over the recent decades is said to stem from America's unrestrained use of health-care services (Fineberg 2012); a reimbursement system whose evolution, pricing, and utilization follow market-based and political economic guidance rather than objective guidance. It has been said that it is "hardwired" to be expensive—it actually rewards inefficiency while incenting the development of new and more expensive pharmaceuticals and other medical technologies.

The evidence HTAs provide offers an opportunity to reduce health-care costs while optimizing patient health outcomes (Shi and Singh 2012). Recognizing this, the Congress created the Office of Technology Assessment (OTA) in the United States in 1972 (Eddy 2009). This endeavor produced over 50 assessments per year from 1972 to 1995; the technologies spanned medicine, telecommunications, agriculture, materials, transportation, and defense (Sullivan et al. 2009). However, in 1995, the U.S. Congress withdrew OTA's funding because of political controversy over the content of several reports and pushback from the emergent commercial health-care technology industry (Institute of Medicine 1985). Now, with the rollout of the provisions of the Patient Protection and Affordable Care Act of 2010 over the coming decade, coupled with rising drug and device costs, HTA is reemerging as a national priority (Fineberg 2012; Sorenson et al. 2013).

The U.S. Food and Drug Administration (FDA) and the more recent Patient-Centered Outcomes Research Institute (PCORI) are specifically prohibited from cost or economic assessments. Once a product receives marketing approval, however, such assessments are a commonplace, and pharmacy and therapeutics (P&T) committees may use these to determine insurance and program coverage decisions. Consistency is elusive as the analyses occur in numerous organizations that may use differing assumptions, models, and decision evaluation criteria.

Health Technology Assessment Applications in the United States

Unlike nations in which the central government has a prominent role in paying for health care and has commensurate authority to dictate prices or exclude from coverage based on cost, the United States' use of HTA for economic assessments is more prominent in the private sector.

Academy of Managed Care Pharmacy Format for Formulary Submissions

To meet the needs of pharmacy benefit management (PBM) organizations, insurers, and provider organizations, the *Academy of Managed Care Pharmacy* (AMCP) commissioned a technical report on the elements and information relevant to HTA and benefit coverage decisions.

The initial version of the *AMCP Format*, presented at the *AMCP Annual Meeting* in San Diego in October 2000 and reported in the July/August 2001 issue of the *Journal of Managed Care Pharmacy*, was to "[improve] the timeliness, scope, quality, and relevance of information provided to the P&T committees and streamline the process of acquiring data and reviewing products for health plan staff pharmacists" (Sullivan et al. 2001). The Format serves as a vehicle for pharmaceutical manufacturers to provide systematic and comprehensive evidence to inform the formulary decision-making process. In compliance with the Food and Drug Modernization Act of 1997 section 114, information not on the product label can be shared from manufacturers to health plans only if the plans "explicitly request" the information (i.e., make an unsolicited request to the manufacturer) (U.S. Food and Drug Administration 2009).

The Format is intended for use by manufacturers of pharmaceuticals, biologics, vaccines, and companion diagnostic tests when responding to unsolicited requests (Sullivan et al. 2001). The evidence contained in the Format enables P&T committees and other health decision-making bodies to make informed decisions regarding medical technology coverage and reimbursement strategies. AMCP has made it clear that they do not endorse any particular product that uses the Format. Furthermore, the Format should be viewed as a "living document" that provides guidance for individual health-care systems and may change as new data evolve (Academy of Managed Care Pharmacy 2013).

Initially, it was uncertain whether manufacturers would provide the information requested in the Format. Early adopters, however, saw it as a means of gaining competitive advantage where they had innovative products and, they determined, a material advantage over competitors if their clients understood the details.

Additional inducements for manufacturers to participate in this voluntary exercise include the following: (1) as the requests for the dossiers were unsolicited and from an expert body (the P&T committee), the response could include both unpublished studies and economic analyses; (2) if their product was not added to the formulary, they expected to receive an explanation for the adverse decision; and, in the early versions of the Format, (3) there is a section for a value statement by the manufacturer—how it saw the information demonstrating the value of its product.

The latest version of the AMCP dossier is 3.1, in which insurers, health plans, and PBMs were invited to begin using as of February 1, 2013. Components of the dossier include an executive summary, clinical and economic value of the product, product information and disease description, supporting clinical evidence, economic value and modeling reporting, other supporting evidence, and supporting information (Academy of Managed Care Pharmacy 2012). More details on these components are readily available on the ACMP website (http://amcp.org/practice-resources/amcp-format-formulary-submisions.pdf).

Qualified health-care decision-makers (HCDMs) are now given easy access to a web platform called the AMCP e-dossier system, which was launched in October 2009. This platform affords the opportunity for HCDMs to easily "access, review, and evaluate research to make informed, evidence-based decisions" (Academy of Managed Care Pharmacy 2010). The e-dossier system shares the same fundamental format as the paper-based dossier, yet with this system, the use of a dossier is more flexible and interactive. The electronic format makes it easier to navigate through the plethora of information within product dossiers. HCDMs gain access to the tool upon log-in and registration. The e-dossier system abides by the FDA provisions governing the release of product information from manufacturers only through unsolicited requests from HCDMs (Academy of Managed Care Pharmacy 2010).

U.S. Patient-Centered Outcomes Research Institute

The *PCORI*, a private sector entity, was developed as part of the Affordable Care Act, section 6301, to fund research whose results would help individuals and entities make better informed health-care decisions, presumably leading to improved health-care delivery and outcomes (Fleurence et al. 2013). It is governed by a 21-member board of governors that includes the directors of the National Institutes of Health and the Agency for Healthcare Research and Quality (AHRQ), as well as individuals from private stakeholders. What makes PCORI unique is that it approaches research with the stakeholders' input as the basis of the research (Shi and Singh 2012). By producing and promoting high integrity, evidence-based information that comes from research guided by patients, caregivers, and the broader health-care community, PCORI provides patients and the public with the information they need to make decisions that reflect their desired health outcomes (Patient-Centered Outcomes Research Institute 2014).

PCORI is funded through the Patient-Centered Outcomes Research Trust Fund (PCORTF), which was created in 2010, and is currently funded at a rate of $(USD)150 million per year through 2019. Part of PCORI's ongoing funding is derived from an assessment of each health insurance premium under the theory that these are investments that will provide future returns that will reduce insurance costs (Patient-Centered Outcomes Research 2012). PCORI is an independent, nonprofit corporation, and these funds will be mostly used to support research and pilot projects. The research from PCORI does not focus on the typical study end points, but instead supports research that reports clinical outcomes that matter the most to patients and caregivers/clinicians (Fleurence et al. 2013). For example, evidentiary needs for Alzheimer's disease should include patient-centered measures such activities of daily living in addition to traditional measures such as women, children, older adults, and patients with multiple chronic conditions. In addition, PCORI's comparative effectiveness research (CER) will expand the use of pragmatic clinical trials to better understand how effectiveness of various products and services differ in the heterogeneous populations encountered in usual community practice. This comes, of course, with diminished internal validity (a particular strength of randomized clinical trials [RCTs]). Consequently, PCORI is also funding projects examining more robust methodologies for this type of research.

Taking public input into account, PCORI's Board of Governors endorsed 11 new methodology standards aimed at providing valid, trustworthy, and useful determinations that will facilitate better clinical decisions and subsequently better patient outcomes. The 11 methodology standard topics, which are included in PCORI's November 2013 document, are detailed in Tables 16.1 and 16.2 and are as follows (PCORI 2013):

- Cross-cutting standards for Patient-Centered Outcomes Research (PCOR)
  - Standards for formulating research questions
  - Standards associated with patient centeredness
  - Standards for data integrity and rigorous analyses
  - Standards for preventing and handling missing data
  - Standards for heterogeneity of treatment effects
- Standards for specific study designs and methods in PCOR
  - Standards for data registries
  - Standards for data networks as research-facilitating structures
  - Standards for causal inference methods
  - Standards for adaptive and Bayesian trial designs
  - Standards for studies of diagnostic tests
  - Standards for systematic reviews

To inform its initial research agenda, PCORI's Board of Governors conducted a national survey aimed at identifying specific medical conditions and treatments, which required additional patient-focused evidence. From this initial survey, PCORI developed a research agenda that included five broad research priorities for which the organization planned to give 25 awards from a $(USD)40.7 million fund over 3 years (Fleurence et al. 2013). The five priorities include (1) assessing options for prevention, diagnosis, and treatment, (2) improving health-care systems, (3) addressing disparities, (4) communicating and disseminating research, and (5) improving patient-centered outcomes, research methods, and infrastructure. PCORI then set criteria describing which aspects of these priorities represented critical gaps in current medical evidence. Together, the priorities and the criteria were evaluated in order to identify PCORI's research agenda and, consequently, the research PCORI funds (Figure 16.2) (Shared Health Data 2012).

PCORI is also actively reaching out to key stakeholders such as patients, clinicians, caregivers, and policymakers via web portals, workshops, and/or social media to solicit questions for future research that matter most to them (Fleurence et al. 2013). PCORI has the potential to affect decision-making, but the success of the program depends on the continued enthusiasm and engagement of key stakeholders (D'Arcy 2012). That will depend of the quality, utility, and timeliness of the results of the research that it funds.

CER that is precluded from using outcome metrics such as quality-adjusted life years (QALYs) or performing economic analyses would seem to have limited potential impact. However, having unbiased and strong results for the effectiveness part of an HTA provides an excellent starting point for a more complete HTA that could include economic consequences.

U.S. Agency for Health-Care Research and Quality

The AHRQ has three research networks that support HTA: (1) the Evidence-based Practice Centers (EPCs), (2) the Centers for Education and Research on Therapeutics (CERTs), and (3) the Developing Evidence to Inform Decisions about Effectiveness (DEcIDE) Networks. These networks support a three-part structure that connects AHRQ's Effective Health Care Program initiative. The EPCs review literature to produce technology assessments and reports to inform

Table 16.1 Cross-Cutting Standards for Patient-Centered Outcomes Research

Standards for Formulating Research Questions	*Standards Associated with Patient Centeredness*	*Standards for Data Integrity and Rigorous Analyses*	*Standards for Preventing and Handling Missing Data*	*Standards for Heterogeneity of Treatment Effects*
Identify gaps in evidence.	Engage people representing the population of interest and other relevant stakeholders in research-appropriate ways.	Assess data source adequately.	Describe methods to prevent and monitor missing data.	State the goals of HTE analyses.
Develop formal study proposal.	Identify, select, recruit, and retain study participants representative of the population of interest and ensure that data are collected thoroughly and systematically from all study participants.	Describe data linkage plans, if applicable.	Describe statistical methods to handle missing data.	Prespecify the analysis plan or prespecify hypotheses and supporting evidence base.
Identify specific populations and health decision(s) affected by the research.	Use patient-reported outcomes when patients or people at risk of a condition are the best source of information.	A priori, specify plans for data analysis that correspond to major aims.	Use validated methods to deal with missing data that properly account for statistical uncertainty.	All HTE claims must be based on appropriate statistical contrasts among groups being compared.
Identify and assess participant subgroups.	Support dissemination and implementation of study results.	Document validated scales and tests.	Record and report all reasons for dropout and missing data, and account for all patients in reports.	For any HTE analysis, report all prespecified analyses and the number of post hoc analyses.

(*Continued*)

Table 16.1 (*Continued*) Cross-Cutting Standards for Patient-Centered Outcomes Research

Standards for Formulating Research Questions	*Standards Associated with Patient Centeredness*	*Standards for Data Integrity and Rigorous Analyses*	*Standards for Preventing and Handling Missing Data*	*Standards for Heterogeneity of Treatment Effects*
Select appropriate interventions and comparators.		Use sensitivity analyses to determine the impact of key assumptions.	Examine sensitivity of inferences to missing data methods and assumptions, and incorporate into interpretation.	
Measure outcomes that people representing the population of interest notice and care about.		Provide sufficient information in reports to allow for assessments of the study's internal and external validity.		

Source: PCORI, The PCORI methodology report: Appendix A Methodology Standards, 2013, http://www.pcori.org/assets/PCORI-Methodology-Standards1.pdf, accessed June 2014.

decision-making. The gaps in evidence identified by EPCs then become part of the research agenda for DEcIDE Networks to perform studies to address the specific needs. The CERTs generate evidence on the safe and effective use of therapeutics (Agency for Healthcare Research and Quality 2006). The individual research groups funded by AHRQ conduct HTAs that typically take 15–18 months to complete. Reports are then posted on the agency's website for ease of access and rapid dissemination. Nevertheless, the information is oftentimes too late to be used by private sector payers that need the information sooner. Having more comprehensive, reliable information but receiving it too late for immediate decisions has, in the past, been a limitation of using government reports (Lyles et al. 1997; Sullivan et al. 2009).

While the Centers for Medicare and Medicaid Services (CMS) requests external HTA reports at times, the Medicare Evidence Development and Coverage Advisory Committee is an internal CMS body that provides recommendations for national coverage polices on new technology (Centers for Medicare and Medicaid Services 2015). CMS also has an interagency agreement with AHRQ to review HTA reports. CMS will typically request this type of assessment if the body of evidence to review is extensive or if it requires expertise not available in the CMS staff (Centers for Medicare and Medicaid Services 2006).

Other Applications of HTA in the United States

Outside of the large-scale efforts of AMCP, PCORI, and AHRQ, there are other examples of publicly funded HTA applications in the United States. The Oregon Health and Sciences

Table 16.2 Standards for Specific Study Designs and Methods in Patient-Centered Outcomes Research

Standards for Data Registries	*Standards for Data Networks as Research-Facilitating Structures*	*Standards for Causal Inference Methods*	*Standards for Adaptive and Bayesian Trial Designs*	*Standards for Studies of Diagnostic Tests*	*Standards for Systematic Reviews*
Requirements for the design and features of registries	Requirements for the design and features of data networks	Define analysis population using covariate histories.	Specify planned adaptations and primary analysis.	Specify clinical context and key elements of diagnostic test study design.	Adopt the IOM standards for systematic reviews of CER, with some qualifications.
Selection and use of registries	Selection and use of data networks	Describe population that gives rise to the effect estimate(s).	Evaluate statistical properties of adaptive design.	Study design should be informed by investigations of the clinical context of testing.	
Robust analysis of confounding factors		Precisely define the timing of the outcome assessment relative to the initiation and duration of exposure.	Specify structure and analysis plan for Bayesian adaptive RCT designs.	Assess the effect of factors known to affect diagnostic performance and outcomes.	

(Continued)

Table 16.2 (*Continued*) Standards for Specific Study Designs and Methods in Patient-Centered Outcomes Research

Standards for Data Registries	*Standards for Data Networks as Research-Facilitating Structures*	*Standards for Causal Inference Methods*	*Standards for Adaptive and Bayesian Trial Designs*	*Standards for Studies of Diagnostic Tests*	*Standards for Systematic Reviews*
		Measure confounders before start of exposure and report data on confounders with study results.	Ensure clinical trial infrastructure is adequate to support planned adaptation(s).	Structured reporting of diagnostic comparative effectiveness study results.	
		Report assumptions underlying the construction of propensity scores and the comparability of the resulting groups.	Use the CONSORT statement, with modifications, to report adaptive RCTs.	Focus studies of diagnostic tests on patient-centered outcomes, using rigorous designs and RCTs.	
		Assess the validity of the instrumental variable and report the balance of covariates in the groups by the instrumental variable.			

Source: PCORI, The PCORI methodology report: Appendix A Methodology Standards, 2013, http://www.pcori.org/assets/PCORI-Methodology-Standards1.pdf, accessed June 2014.

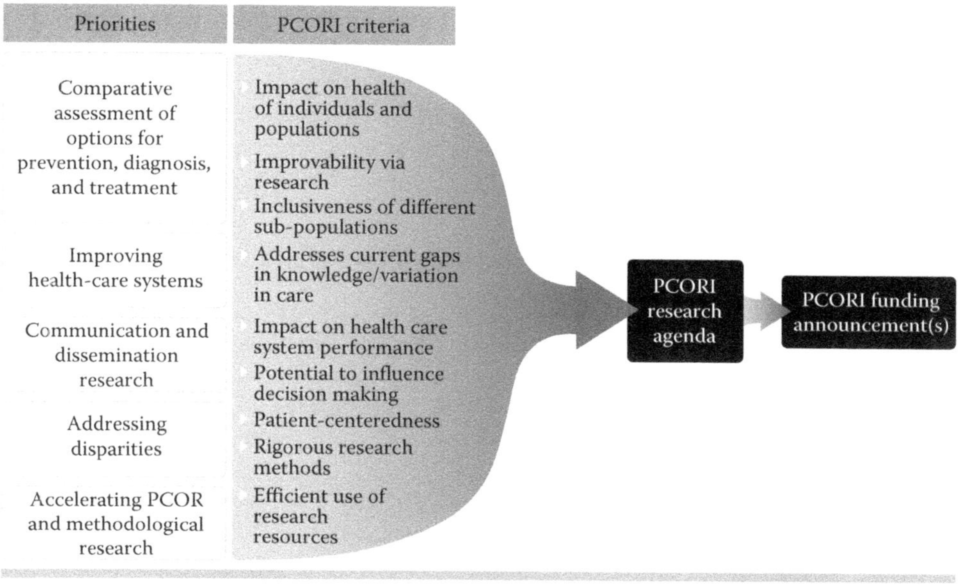

Figure 16.2 Patient-Centered Outcomes Research Institute research implementation process. (From Shared Health Data, Calling all patient advocates: Patient Centered Outcomes Research Institute needs your feedback, 2012, http://www.sharedhealthdata.com/2012/01/31/calling-patient-advocates-patient-centered-outcomes-research-institute-needs-your-feedback/, accessed June 2014.)

University—Drug Effectiveness Review Project (DERP) is one such example. The DERP program contracts with 14 state Medicaid programs to support decisions regarding pharmaceuticals. The evidence regarding a specific technology is presented to each state, and each state then makes its own coverage decisions based on the clinical and economic evidence provided. The DERP program has strict guidelines and requirements for having a sufficient published evidence base to meet the standard to support a decision. As a result, their HTAs take significant time and effort to complete, but may be more reliable (Sullivan et al. 2009).

The Department of Veterans Affairs' (VA) Pharmacy Benefits Management Strategic Healthcare Group supports pharmaceutical technology assessment decisions that ultimately determine national drug formulary coverage for the VA, in addition to treatment guidelines and contracting decisions. Another example of a federal program is the Military Health System, which uses the Department of Defense (DoD) Pharmacoeconomic Center in conjunction with the DoD P&T committee to complete evaluations of pharmaceuticals to aid in the decision-making process (Sullivan et al. 2009).

In terms of private applications of HTA, it is a common practice for the larger health plans to complete their own internal HTA research. This typically includes a review of the new product's clinical attributes compared to other alternatives, as well as a budget impact model to project the financial impact of adopting the new product to the plan's formulary.

The Blue Cross Blue Shield Technology Evaluation Center (TEC) was founded in 1985 to conduct formal evaluations on medical technologies with the strategic goal of informing decision-makers across all Blue Cross Blue Shield plans, as well as other stakeholders. The TEC is another resource for both private and public sectors in need of scientifically rigorous technology evaluations for various agendas. The TEC pioneered criteria based on clinical and scientific measures to determine if the technology improves health outcomes. However, the TEC does not use evidence based on costs such as cost containment, comparative cost, or price in the evaluation of medical technologies (Ziegler et al. 2005; BlueCross BlueShield 2015). While organizations like Wellpoint have published their HTA guidelines, the process at other health plans is generally not transparent, and the evidence reports are generally not available to the public (Sullivan et al. 2009).

Health Technology Assessment Initiatives Outside of the United States

HTA in the developed countries outside the United States are typically developed using formal processes and bridge the evidence on the value of medical technologies to health-care decision-makers (Battista and Hodge 1999; Fattore et al. 2011). Globally, there is significant country-to-country variation in the application of HTA due to differing political and social priorities, public and private sector authorities and constraints, and differences in the technical workforce available to perform these assessments (O'Donnell et al. 2009). However, the overarching purpose of HTA is shared, which is to inform real-world decisions from the evidence about the value (i.e., health outcomes and costs) of medical technologies. To this point, the universal acknowledgement of HTA necessity is growing rapidly as stakeholders strive to contain costs. The projected annual spending of medications by 2016 is $(USD)1.2 trillion (IMS Institute for Health Informatics 2012), which places a great responsibility on HTA systems from a global perspective on developing robust and transparent methodologies to facilitate evaluation and rational decision-making. In addition, this pressure is coupled with the ongoing demands from patients, a growing elderly population, and the ongoing challenge of managing chronic diseases. Thus, policymakers are faced with the challenge of working through the constraints in the health-care system by reining in spending through HTA programs, while also ensuring patients have access to treatments that deliver the greatest value (O'Donnel et al. 2009; Fattore et al. 2011; IMS Institute for Healthcare Informatics 2012).

The introduction of HTA emerged in Europe in the late 1970s, with the first HTA bodies in France and Spain initiated in the early 1980s. This initial formation spearheaded several other countries like England and Germany to form their own HTA bodies or institutions. Today, many countries, especially in Europe, have established HTA bodies that undertake a range of activities that provide national guidance to improve health and social care (Garrido-Velasco and Busse 2005). Moreover, other countries such as Australia and Canada have developed formal HTA processes to assess whether and how new pharmaceuticals and biotechnologies will be reimbursed with government health-care dollars. The International Society for Pharmacoeconomics and Outcomes Research maintains a directory of HTA efforts across the world. A summary of countries with formal processes is provided in Table 16.3, with a discussion of key countries here.

The National Health Services commissioned the National Institute for Health and Care Excellence (NICE) to provide insight on health technologies. HTA is just one of the NICE's main responsibilities; other activities include developing clinical guidelines, public health guidance regarding disease prevention, quality standards, and information services. NICE's existence represents an acknowledgment by the United Kingdom that its universal health-care systems must set priorities in order to maximize the quality and efficiency of care for the population (Rawlins 2013). NICE's processes involve both technical and scientific evaluations of pharmaceutical and biotechnology products, as well as incorporation of social values by involvement of a citizen's counsel. HTA includes both rigorous clinical evaluation as well as a formal cost-effectiveness

Table 16.3 Summary of Countries That Have Formal Health Technology Assessment

Country	*Organization*	*Purpose*
Australia	PBAC	Required by the National Health Act to consider the effectiveness and cost of a proposed benefit compared to alternative therapies.
Canada	CADTH	To facilitate the appropriate and effective utilization of health technologies within health-care systems across Canada. To provide timely, relevant, rigorously derived, evidence-based information to decision-makers and support for the decision-making processes.
France	The Haute Autorité de Santé (French National Authority for Health)	To improve the quality of care delivered to patients through measures such as the production of good practice guidelines, the development of disease management programs for chronic conditions, continuing professional development, and accreditation of health-care organizations.
Germany	IQWiG	The IQWiG is an independent scientific institute that evaluates the quality and efficiency of health care. The institute investigates what therapeutic and diagnostic services are feasible and meaningful and communicates its findings to the health-care professions, patients, and the general public.
United Kingdom	NICE	NICE is the independent organization responsible for providing national guidance on the promotion of good health and the prevention and treatment of ill health.

Source: International Society for Pharmacoeconomics and Outcomes Research, Directory of health technology assessment organizations worldwide, 2015, http://www.ispor.org/htadirectory/index.aspx, accessed June 2014.

evaluation, where the latter is reported as cost per QALY. Its methods are reviewed and revised every 3 years. Guidance developed by NICE is completed by employees of the UK National Health Service, as well as universities within the country. In 2013, the scope of NICE's responsibilities was expanded to include guidelines and performance standards for social services. A goal of this initiative is to foster better coordination of health and social services.

Germany's Institute for Quality and Efficiency in Health Care (IQWiG) is commissioned by the Federal Joint Committee or the Ministry of Health to assess the quality and efficiency of medical treatments (Conrad 2006). In the past, IQWiG primarily evaluated the published results of randomized controlled trials and focused on morbidity, mortality, and health-related quality of life to inform their decisions (Conrad 2006; IQWiG 2014). However, the guidelines were changed in 2007 and 2010 to include economic evaluations (IQWiG 2015). HTA is commissioned by a committee of physicians and insurance funders or the country's health ministry (Conrad 2006). The scope of evidence reviewed for each HTA varies; in some cases, a subset of evidence is considered, which is focused on the priorities of these health-care decision-makers. While developing the HTA, external peer reviews may be conducted to promote the highest quality of technical and scientific review. IQWiG then publishes a draft HTA that is made available for public comment and may or may not be discussed at a hearing at which revisions will be recommended. In contrast to NICE, IQWiG has not focused on cost per QALY as a measure of cost-effectiveness. Though the level of transparency and stakeholder involvement has been perceived as a weakness of IQWiG, the organization continues to improve its policies and procedures and has made important strides since its inception.

The guidelines for health technology evaluations provided by the Canadian Agency for Drugs and Technologies in Health (CADTH) allow the use of the five most common types of economic evaluations to inform their decision: cost-utility analysis, cost–consequence analysis, cost minimization analysis, cost–benefit analysis, and CEA. While not all five of these evaluations have to be reported by manufacturers, the guidelines recommend that the reported analytic choice be justified. Along with economic evaluations, CADTH guidelines also recommend that manufacturers chose and justify their outcomes. "Final outcomes" such as QALYs and "important clinical outcomes" are the preferred "important patient outcomes" that should be reported. However, CADTH will also accept "surrogate outcomes" such as cholesterol levels, depending on available evidence and insights from clinically relevant research (Canadian Agency for Drugs and Technologies in Health 2006; Australian Government Department of Health and Ageing 2008).

In Australia, the relevant factors of the Pharmaceutical Benefits Advisory Committee's (PBAC) guidelines include CEA and cost-effectiveness assessment of comparative health gains. These assessments are a precondition to price determination and marketing. PBAC then uses this information to make recommendations to the Minster of Health for drugs that should be subsidized (Australian Government Department of Health and Ageing 2008).

Future Directions

HTA is critical to informing public and private stakeholders who must make decisions based on both evidence and values regarding the clinical and economic support for pharmaceutical products. The importance of HTA is increasing in the United States and worldwide, with governments increasingly involved in formal HTA implementation. Though wealthier nations have invested in HTA thus far, it can be argued that middle- and low-income countries have as great a need, if not greater. While one reason for this is constrained health-care funds in emerging nations, another is the idea that health is a societal goal that countries can only achieve through global efforts to promote access to safe and effective treatments at the lowest cost. Consistent with this societal goal is the evolution of universal health coverage in emerging nations. A key to the global success of HTA will be communication and translation of evidence from country to country in an accurate and timely manner. Further, HTA's future impact can be maximized by using its components to set clinical and economic benchmarks, which, in turn, can be measured to determine the outcomes of treatments evaluated.

Statement of the Policy Issue

Rising health-care costs coupled with pharmaceutical and biotechnology advances have challenged health-care budgets in the United States and abroad. HTA refers to policy research aimed at informing health-care decision-makers about the costs and effects of new treatments. While

HTA approaches vary between decision-makers, there is a shared goal of promoting the safe and effective use of pharmaceuticals at the lowest cost.

References

A format for submission of Clinical and Economic Evidence of Pharmaceuticals in Support of Formulary Consideration, Alexandria, VA. http://amcp.org/practice-resources/amcp-format-formulary-submisions.pdf (accessed January 12, 2016).

Academy of Managed Care Pharmacy. 2010. AMCP eDossier system pilot program launches. http://www.amcp.org/Tertiary.aspx?id=8546 (accessed June 2014).

Academy of Managed Care Pharmacy. 2012. The AMCP format for formulary submissions Version 3.1: A format for submission of clinical and economic evidence of pharmaceuticals in support of Formulary consideration. Alexandria, VA: Academy of Managed Care Pharmacy.

Academy of Managed Care Pharmacy. 2013. AMCP releases revised AMCP format for formulary submissions. http://amcp.org/Tertiary.aspx?id=16065 (accessed June 2014).

Agency for Healthcare Research and Quality (AHRQ). 2006. The new effective health care program at AHRQ. http://www.ispor.org/news/articles/june06/ahrq.asp (accessed June 2014).

Australian Government Department of Health and Ageing. 2008. Guidelines for preparing submissions to the pharmaceutical benefits advisory committee (version 4.3). Canberra, Australian Capital Territory, Australia: Commonwealth of Australia.

Battista R. N. and M. J. Hodge. 1999. The evolving paradigm of health technology assessment: Reflections for the millennium. *Canadian Medical Association Journal* 160(10):1464–1467.

BlueCross BlueShield. 2015. Technology evaluation center (TEC). http://www.bcbs.com/blueresources/tec/ (accessed June 2014).

Canadian Agency for Drugs and Technologies in Health. 2006. HTA guidelines for the economic evaluations of health technologies: Canada. Ottawa, Ontario, Canada: Canadian Agency for Drugs and Technologies in Health.

Centers for Medicare and Medicaid Services. 2006. Factors CMS considers for commissioning external technology assessments. http://www.cms.gov/medicare-coverage-database/details/medicare-coverage-document-details.aspx?MCDId=7&McdName=Factors+CMS+Considers+in+Commissioning+External+Technology+Assessments&mcdtypename=Guidance+Documents&MCDIndexType=1&bc=BAAIAAAAAAAA& (accessed June 2014).

Centers for Medicare and Medicaid Services. 2015. Medicare evidence development & coverage advisory committee. http://www.cms.gov/Regulations-and-Guidance/Guidance/FACA/MEDCAC.html (accessed June 2014).

Conrad, C. 2006. German IQWiG—It's not NICE Benefit Assessment in Germany. ISPOR Connections. http://www.ispor.org/news/articles/oct06/germanpolicy.asp (accessed June 2014).

D'Arcy, L. P. and E. C. Rich. 2012. From comparative effectiveness research to patient-centered outcomes research: Policy history and future directions. *Neurosurgical Focus* 33(1):E7. doi:10.3171/2012.4.FOCUS12106; 10.3171/2012.4.FOCUS12106.

Eddy, D. 2009. Health technology assessment and evidence-based medicine: What are we talking about? *Value in Health* 12:S6–S7. doi:10.1111/j.1524-4733.2009.00551.x.

Fattore, G., Maniadakis, N., Mantovani, L. G., and G. Boriani. 2011. Health technology assessment: What is it? Current status and perspectives in the field of electrophysiology. *Europace* 13(Suppl. 2):ii49–ii53. doi:10.1093/europace/eur083.

Fineberg, H. V. 2012. Shattuck lecture. A successful and sustainable health system—How to get there from here. *New England Journal of Medicine* 366(11):1020–1027. doi:10.1056/NEJMsa1114777.

Fleurence, R., Selby, J. V., Odom-Walker, K. et al. 2013. How the patient-centered outcomes research institute is engaging patients and others in shaping its research agenda. *Health Affairs (Millwood)* 32(2):393–400. doi:10.1377/hlthaff.2012.1176; 10.1377/hlthaff.2012.1176.

Garrido-Velasco, M. and R. Busse. 2005. Policy brief: Health technology assessment, an introduction to objectives, role of evidence, and structure in Europe. Geneva, Switzerland: World Health Organization.

Goodman, C. S. 2014. HTA 101: Introduction to health technology assessment. Bethesda, MD: National Library of Medicine (US).

IMS Institute for Healthcare Informatics. 2012. The global use of medicines: Outlook through 2016. Parsippany, NJ: IMS Institute for Healthcare Informatics.

Institute of Medicine. 1985. Assessing medical technologies. Washington, DC: National Academy Press.

Institute of Medicine. 2015. About IOM. http://www.iom.edu/About-IOM.aspx (accessed June 2014).

International Society for Pharmacoeconomics and Outcomes Research. 2015. Directory of health technology assessment organizations worldwide. http://www.ispor.org/htadirectory/index.aspx (accessed June 2014).

IQWiG. 2014. Institute for quality and efficiency in health care: General methods. https://www.iqwig.de/download/IQWiG_General_Methods_Version_%204-1.pdf (accessed June 2014).

IQWiG. 2015. International network of agencies for health technology assessment (INAHTA). http://www.inahta.org/Members/IQWiG/ (accessed June 2014).

Lyles, A., Luce, B. R., and A. M. Rentz. 1997. Managed care pharmacy, socioeconomic assessments and drug adoption decisions. *Social Science & Medicine* 45(4):511–521. doi:S0277953696003929 [pii].

O'Donnell, J. C., Pham, S. V., Pashos, C. L., Miller, D. W., and M. D. Smith. 2009. Health technology assessment: Lessons learned from around the world—An overview. *Value Health* 12(Suppl. 2):S1–S5. doi:10.1111/j.1524-4733.2009.00550.x; 10.1111/j.1524-4733.2009.00550.x.

Oberlander, J. 2012. The future of Obamacare. *New England Journal Medicine* 367(23):2165–2167. doi:10.1056/NEJMp1213674; 10.1056/NEJMp1213674.

Patient-Centered Outcomes Research Institute. 2012. How we're funded. Last modified June 16, 2015. http://www.pcori.org/about-U.S./how-were-funded/ (accessed June 2014).

Patient-Centered Outcomes Research Institute. 2014. Governance. http://www.pcori.org/about-U.S./governance-and-leadership/ (accessed June 2014).

PCORI. 2013. The PCORI methodology report: Appendix A Methodology Standards. http://www.pcori.org/assets/PCORI-Methodology-Standards1.pdf (accessed June 2014).

Rawlins, M. D. 2013. NICE: Moving onward. *New England Journal of Medicine* 369(1):3–5.

Shared Health Data. 2012. Calling all patient advocates: Patient Centered Outcomes Research Institute needs your feedback. http://www.sharedhealthdata.com/2012/01/31/calling-patient-advocates-patient-centered-outcomes-research-institute-needs-your-feedback/ (accessed June 2014).

Shi, L. and D. Singh. 2012. *Delivering Health Care in America: A Systems Approach*. Sudbury, MA: Jones & Bartlett.

Sorenson, C., Drummond, M., and B. Bhuiyan Khan. 2013. Medical technology as a key driver of rising health expenditure: Disentangling the relationship. *Journal of ClinicoEconomics and Outcomes Research* 5:223–234. doi:10.2147/CEOR.S39634.

Sullivan, S. D., Lyles, A., Luce, B., and J. Grigar. 2001. AMCP guidance for submission of clinical and economic evaluation data to support formulary listing in U.S. health plans and pharmacy benefits management organizations. *Journal of Managed Care Pharmacy* 7(1):272.

Sullivan, S. D., Watkins, J., Sweet, B., and S. D. Ramsey. 2009. Health technology assessment in health-care decisions in the United States. *Value Health* 12(Suppl. 2):S39–S44. doi:10.1111/j.1524-4733.2009.00557.x; 10.1111/j.1524-4733.2009.00557.x.

U.S. Food and Drug Administration. 2009. Full text of FDAMA law. http://www.fda.gov/RegulatoryInformation/Legislation/FederalFoodDrugandCosmeticActFDCAct/SignificantAmendmentstotheFDCAct/FDAMA/FullTextofFDAMAlaw/default.htm#SEC (accessed June 2014).

Ziegler, K. M., Flamm, C. R., and N. Aronson. 2005. The blue cross blue shield association technology evaluation center: How we evaluate radiology technologies. *Journal of the American College of Radiology* 2(1):33–38. doi:1546-1440(04)00293-5 [pii].

Chapter 17

Pharmacoeconomics as a Response to Market Failure: An International Perspective

Ruth Lopert

Contents

Introduction

Irrespective of the structure of the health system—whether a "single-payer" system like the UK National Health Service, a social health insurance (Bismarck) model such as in the Netherlands, or a market-based, heavily privatized model as in the United States—all countries face challenges in ensuring affordable care for their populations. In health care, it is axiomatic that resources will always be finite, and thus, payers and decision makers must make informed choices when allocating funds. *Health economics* is a discipline that supports the optimization of health-care resource allocation decisions, and an important component of health economics is the microeconomic evaluation of the value of individual interventions or treatments. Just as governments must make budgetary decisions to allocate funds among different portfolios, health-care decision makers may assign different health policy priorities and apply these when choosing to allocate resources among prevention and treatment options, therapeutic domains, and treatment modalities. Within individual programs, this may mean prioritizing some interventions and outcomes ahead of others.

When this form of economic valuation is applied to medicines, it is referred to as *pharmacoeconomics*. Pharmacoeconomics is a discipline that combines the principles of evidence-based medicine, clinical economics, and decision analysis to support rational decision making around the coverage and reimbursement of new medicines. The diffusion of new medicines is usually among the key drivers of health-care expenditure growth, and pharmacoeconomics is increasingly important in countries of varying stages of economic development and across different health system models. In addition to helping payers assess value for money, pharmacoeconomics offers a powerful mechanism for responding to "market failure" in medicines.

Market Failure in Medicines

In 2012, the global pharmaceutical industry was estimated to be worth $(USD)858 billion.* Although highly profitable, the industry has long maintained that the processes of discovery and research and development (R&D) of new medicines are both expensive and highly risk prone. Today, the *billion dollar pill* is a familiar term, though attempts to analyze actual R&D costs systematically have been hampered by commercial confidentiality, sparse and unverifiable data, extensive assumptions, and substantial methodological controversy.[2–4] Some analyses have made countervailing claims based on deconstructing previous published estimates—though these too have relied on broad assumptions in concluding that costs are both exaggerated and investment risks largely offset.[5–7]

Nevertheless, the costs of R&D are often cited to justify high prices, particularly for new medicines—so high that today few, if any, new medicines brought to market are likely to be affordable to an individual—and must therefore be subsidized by an insurer or *third-party payer.* Irrespective of the costs of R&D, the value of any good or service is determined by purchasers' willingness to pay. How then is it possible for the price of that good or service to significantly exceed the ability of an individual to afford it?

In theory, prices result from the interactions between supply and demand, with consumers seeking to maximize their utility (well-being) and producers to maximize their profits. The efforts of the latter will be mitigated by the presence of competition in the market. Using prices as signals in a perfectly competitive market, demand and supply will fluctuate until equilibrium is reached in which the supply of a product matches the demand at the current price. This equilibrium is referred to as *Pareto optimal*,† meaning that neither consumers nor producers can be made better off without someone being made worse off.

In order to achieve this equilibrium, certain minimum conditions must be met:

- There must be multiple consumers and producers in the market.
- Producers must be able to freely enter and exit the market.
- Consumers must have complete information about products and prices and be able to compare them and make informed choices.

In the real world, the situation is more complex of course, and markets are far from "perfect." Many factors influence both the prices charged by producers and the willingness to pay of consumers. Price elasticity of demand—a measure of the sensitivity of consumer demand to changes in price—is an important concept here, first described by economist Alfred Marshall.[8] Demand for a product is said to be *inelastic* when changes in price have no or only modest impact on the

* Figure refers to ex-factory prices. See Reference 1.
† Named after Italian sociologist and economist Vilfredo Pareto (1848–1923).

quantity demanded and *elastic* when changes in price have a relatively large effect. Where demand is elastic, consumer preferences will vary with only modest differences between the prices of competing products.

The medicine market is a particularly compelling case of what is referred to as *market failure.* First, the need for effective regulation to ensure the efficacy, safety, and quality of medicines acts as a barrier to producers entering the market. As noted earlier, both development costs and risks are high, and a significant proportion of products do not make it into the market at all.[3,9] Furthermore, regulatory processes intended to ensure the quality, efficacy, and safety of marketed medicines are a significant hurdle.

Second, there is significant asymmetry in the information available about medicines. *Information asymmetry* occurs when one party to a transaction has more or better information than the other party. Not all information generated in the drug development process is available to prescribers and consumers.[10] Moreover, there is usually only limited, if any, information about the *comparative* performance of new medicines available at the time of market launch. Generally speaking, consumers do not have sufficient information to enable them to make fully informed choices about which medicines to take, and they are usually dependent on third parties (prescribers) to facilitate their access (referred to as an *agency relationship*). Prescribers may also have incomplete information about the benefits and may be indifferent to the costs of different treatment options. This lack of information with which to compare treatments limits both rational choice and effective competition.

Significant barriers to market also exist in the form of monopolies conferred by intellectual property protections (Chapter 17). In a market with only one (a monopoly) or few (an oligopoly) producers, consumers will have limited choices and prices can become significantly distorted. Moreover, competition between patented medicines is rare, particularly in the absence of evidence from clinical trials directly comparing them, and this also allows prices to become, or remain, elevated.[11] Increasing interest in comparative effectiveness research in the United States and the establishment of the Patient-Centered Outcomes Research Institute may ameliorate this evidence gap to some extent.* Conversely, a market with only one, or one dominant buyer (a monopsony), can create significant downward pressure on prices.[13]

Market failure has also been blamed for the paucity of effective treatment for many diseases that principally afflict developing countries. These "neglected" diseases, such as leishmaniasis, malaria, trypanosomiasis, and multidrug-resistant tuberculosis, have been largely ignored in the R&D programs of major research-based pharmaceutical companies. As these conditions mainly affect countries of limited wealth, even market exclusivity cannot assure high prices and sufficiently competitive profits.

Perhaps the most important of all, health-care purchasing is rarely discretionary, and therefore, willingness to pay is often heightened and demand highly inelastic. Postponing the purchase of a new television until the "Black Friday"† sales may be merely inconvenient, but delaying the acquisition of a life-saving drug may be catastrophic. That said, where a third-party payer (insurer) is involved, consumers may be largely or, at times, completely shielded from the actual cost of

* The Patient-Centered Outcomes Research Institute (PCORI) was established by a provision of the 2010 Patient Protection and Affordable Care Act (ACA). PCORI is an independent, not-for-profit, private entity authorized by the Congress to fund and disseminate research that will provide information about the best available evidence to help patients and their health-care providers make more informed decisions. See Reference 12.

† "Black Friday" is the name given to the Friday following Thanksgiving Day in the United States (the fourth Thursday of November), a day on which major retail stores offer promotional sales to kick off the holiday shopping season. See Reference 14.

treatment, further distorting the elasticity of demand.[15] Together, these factors mean that the normal market mechanisms are significantly disturbed and thus fail to allocate resources efficiently. This is market failure.

Government Responses to Market Failure in Medicines

In most industrialized countries, governments have recognized that the high prices of medicines are a significant and enduring burden to individuals and families and that government intervention in response to market failure is both desirable and necessary to promote affordability and access. With demand for medicines largely inelastic, the capacity for a producer to exploit a monopoly position has led almost all high-income and many middle-income countries to subsidize medicines for some or all of their populations, although the extent of subsidization varies considerably.[16] Where governments purchase, subsidize, or reimburse part or all of the costs of large quantities of medicines, they have considerable market power; in some countries, this approaches an effective monopsony. This market power can be used to regulate prices directly, or as a means of moderating them indirectly.

Across the OECD, there is substantial variation in cost sharing; however, consumers typically assume less than half the cost of their medicines. This gives rise to far greater utilization than would be likely to occur if the costs were borne entirely out of pocket.[16] Drug coverage programs in most OECD countries require manufacturers to accept direct or indirect moderation of prices in exchange for the inclusion of the products in reimbursement program *formularies*.* This is true even in the United States, where manufacturers must accept a degree of price regulation in order to have products reimbursed in Medicaid (Chapter 26) and Veterans Administration programs, although market-based competition occurs in nonpublic programs.[16]

Within Europe, countries apply some form of direct price regulation at a national level or employ measures at moderate prices indirectly. Mechanisms for moderating prices include competitive tendering, profit controls, and reference pricing. Until recently, free pricing was the norm in the United Kingdom, with the pharmaceutical industry subject instead to profit controls via the Pharmaceutical Price Regulation Scheme (PPRS). Under the PPRS, firms negotiated an overall rate of return, but profit margins could be varied across a portfolio of drugs.[17] The disadvantage of this type of approach is that there may be little or no relationship between the price of a drug and its therapeutic value.

A more common approach is to use *external reference pricing* to set wholesale or retail price ceilings by benchmarking prices against those in one or more countries selected for geographic proximity, similar economic background, or simply transparent availability of pricing information.[18] Prices may be set as the average or lowest in a basket of countries, and in some cases, the referenced price may be adjusted to reflect differences in national wealth as a proxy for affordability.

Many countries also utilize *therapeutic* (also known as internal) *reference pricing*. Among a group of drugs considered clinically equivalent, subsidy is limited to the lowest priced product in the group, with consumers paying out of pocket for any difference between the price of the "benchmark" product and that of the product preferred by or prescribed for them. Where consumers resist

* A formulary is a list of drugs explicitly covered by a third-party payer; it is sometimes referred to as a positive list. Occasionally, a payer may instead define a negative list, which sets out those drugs explicitly excluded from coverage.

these "gap" payments, this creates pressure on producers to lower prices toward the benchmark—or risk losing market share.[18] The significance of this approach is that it establishes an important nexus between the clinical performance of a drug and its price. Not surprisingly, therapeutic reference pricing is unpopular with the pharmaceutical industry, particularly as patented and off-patent medicines within a therapeutic class may be grouped together.[19] This, it is argued, undermines the value of the market exclusivity enjoyed by the patented product but can also be viewed as a rational approach by payers to the valuation of products offering equivalent health outcomes. In 2011, 20 EU member states were applying some form of therapeutic reference pricing for determining prices for reimbursement of groups of therapeutically interchangeable products.[18]

What Is Pharmacoeconomics?

Rather than focusing simply on the price of a medicine, an increasingly widespread approach is to consider a medicine's price in relation to the benefits it offers and use this to determine whether, at a given price, it represents reasonable value for money. This is particularly relevant where new, patented products are first-in-class compounds without obvious therapeutic equivalents (though a first-in-class drug may not necessarily offer a clinical advantage over drugs in an existing class). Too often in these circumstances, drug selection decisions are driven by estimates of acquisition costs or budget impact, rather than by a systematic assessment of the relationship between anticipated costs and benefits. The acquisition costs of a medicine used to prevent or delay the long-term sequelae of a disease may well be offset by downstream medical and hospital costs. That said, distributional impacts can cloud decisions if near-term costs are disproportionately borne by one payer but the long-term cost offsets are enjoyed by another—a common occurrence when private insurance is a large part of the market, and switching between insurers is common. This is particularly true where pharmaceutical coverage is stand-alone, as is the case in most Medicare Part D plans.

Economic evaluation in health care has been described as the comparative analysis of alternative courses of action, in that it seeks to identify, measure, value, and compare the costs and consequences of the alternatives being considered.[20] Pharmacoeconomics also deals with costs and consequences, is implicitly about informing choices, and, by identifying opportunity costs and maximizing efficiency, supports decision making on the disposition of finite resources. Pharmacoeconomic analyses are thus inherently comparative—usually, a new medicine is compared with the existing standard of care, which may be another medicine or a nondrug therapy—and comprise a set of methods for assessing the overall value proposition, taking into account both immediate and future costs and benefits. The perspective taken in the analysis is critical to the result and is determined by the question that the analysis is attempting to address. This will determine which benefits and costs will be taken into account; a pharmacoeconomic analysis performed from a payer's point of view will only consider benefits and costs accruing to or borne by that payer, whereas an analysis performed from a societal perspective will attempt to consider costs and benefits to society as a whole.

Whatever the question being addressed, ultimately the decision must also take into account political, fiscal, and commercial realities, and maximizing efficiency in every case may not be achievable.[13] It's also important to understand that pharmacoeconomics is not principally concerned with *saving* money but rather with how to obtain the best value in *spending* it.

There are four main techniques of pharmacoeconomic analysis. In *cost-minimization analysis* (CMA), the outcomes of treatment with the medicines being compared are expressed in the same or equivalent units, and all options under consideration must produce equivalent outcomes. It addresses the question: *of two or more medicines with equal effectiveness, which is the least expensive?* While this may seem straightforward, in reality it can be quite complex. First, defining an acceptable standard for therapeutic equivalence can be particularly challenging, particularly if there are no head-to-head clinical trials directly comparing the alternatives under consideration or existing trials are designed to demonstrate differences rather than equivalence between treatments. Usually, the test is one of noninferiority, that is, evidence that shows that the new treatment is no worse than existing therapeutic options after determining a noninferiority boundary that represents the maximum degree of acceptable difference beyond which the two products could not be considered to be equivalent. Once the doses at which the respective drugs have been shown to be equivalent (the "equi-effective doses") are identified, these can be used to establish the comparative costs of the products, taking into account not just the costs of the medicines but also any differences in costs of administration or in managing adverse effects.

Like CMA, *cost-effective analysis* (CEA) is a technique for comparing two or more competing therapies for which the benefits are expressed using a common outcome measure (usually natural units such as fractures avoided or life years gained) but where the extent of the expected benefits differs. The purpose of the analysis is to determine the treatment option with the least cost per unit of additional benefit. It is a particularly useful technique in formulary decision making when confronted with a new medicine thought to be superior to existing options but with a price substantially higher, where the question arises as to whether the additional costs represent reasonable value in light of the anticipated additional benefits. The ratio of the difference in costs to the difference in benefits is called the *incremental cost-effectiveness ratio* (ICER). The ICER represents the additional cost needed to achieve each additional unit of benefit.

CEA is less informative when the benefits of the treatments being compared are measured using different outcome metrics. It is difficult to determine how well $(USD)1500 per nonvertebral fracture avoided stacks up against $(USD)2500 per myocardial infarction averted. Which has better value? When comparing different diseases, *cost-utility analysis* (CUA) is a more useful technique. It is a form of CEA in which outcomes are expressed using a common metric that encompasses patient utility, usually the *quality-adjusted life year* (QALY) or the *disability-adjusted life year* (DALY). The QALY allows the effects of an intervention on mortality and morbidity to be combined into a single metric, with the survival weighted by the "quality of life" of those years. The DALY also combines the impact of an intervention on mortality and morbidity into a single metric, by weighting the survival gain by a measure of the amount of disability associated with the condition. It is a metric more commonly used in analyses of interventions in lower- and middle-income countries as, unlike the QALY, the DALY does not require context-relevant health state valuation estimates.

In *cost-benefit analysis* (CBA), both costs and outcomes are monetized. While this has the advantage of enabling the comparison of treatment alternatives with different outcome measures, it is less commonly used in pharmacoeconomics because of the difficulties in ascribing a monetary value to, for example, life years saved.[20] Both CEA and CMA are techniques most suited to addressing questions of *technical efficiency*, or how best to use given resources to deliver a program or to achieve a given objective, whereas CUA and CBA may be applied to questions of *allocative efficiency*. Allocative efficiency is concerned with achieving the right mix and type of health-care programs to maximize the health of a society.

A key question is how should a decision-maker interpret an incremental cost-effectiveness (or cost-utility) ratio? Recall that the ICER is a measure of the additional expenditure needed to acquire one unit of additional health gain produced by one treatment compared with another (usually the next most effective option). Broadly speaking, a cost-effectiveness threshold is a value judgment that will depend on who the decision-maker is, the purpose and perspective of the analysis, and the resources available.[21]

There is a substantial body of literature on different approaches to the derivation of thresholds for cost-effectiveness,* beginning with the articulation of the concept of a threshold, attributed to Weinstein and Zeckhauser in 1973.[23] One approach is to consider the threshold as a measure of the opportunity cost, in terms of health forgone, arising from directing expenditure to a new treatment from within a fixed budget. That is, the adoption of the new treatment requires disinvestment elsewhere within the system, and the threshold represents the amount of additional expenditure imposed on the system that will lead to the displacement of one QALY's worth of health.[24] Other approaches involve attempting to elicit societal willingness to pay to achieve a QALY's worth of health *improvement*.[25] Critics of this approach have argued that while it can provide useful information on the value of health gains, it cannot inform resource allocation decisions within a program that is subject to a fixed budgetary constraint.[24] Of course, adopting a new drug or other technology in this circumstance would not necessarily displace an existing intervention; funds may be redirected from some other program or sector of the economy or may be supported, for example, via a new tax or a tax increase—which would then supplant a degree of private consumption. In the latter case, the value of the threshold willingness to pay for a QALY will be the degree of utility of private consumption forgone equivalent to the utility gained from an increase of one additional QALY.[25]

Drawing on recommendations of the Commission on Macroeconomics and Health in 2002,[26] the World Health Organization proposed the use of per capita gross domestic product (GDP) as an indicator of cost-effectiveness, with the following threshold values for different interventions: highly cost-effective (less than GDP per capita/DALY), cost-effective (up to three times GDP per capita/DALY), not cost-effective (more than three times GDP per capita/DALY).[27]This approach has the advantage of utilizing an objective metric that ostensibly reflects affordability, thus facilitating comparisons of interventions across countries of different degrees of national wealth. Arguably, the use of purchasing power parity (PPP)-adjusted GDP per capita provides a measure more reflective of the capacity to pay. However, critics of this general approach point to the fact that as GDP per capita (whether PPP adjusted or not) is an average value; it cannot accurately reflect value or capacity to pay across the entire population in any given country.

In practice, most European jurisdictions utilizing fourth hurdle systems for drug selection and formulary listing have not declared fixed thresholds[16,28]; in several, attempts have been made to discern implicit thresholds from retrospective analyses[29,30] but in no case has the implicit or explicit threshold had an empirical basis. The UK National Institute for Health and Care Excellence currently utilizes a threshold within the range of £20,000–£30,000[31]; however, a recent analysis suggested that the true value of a QALY in the UK context may be as low as £18,000 or even less,[24] substantially below the UK GDP per capita.[32]

Wherever the threshold is set, it is important to recognize that no matter how cost-effective a drug is, it may yet be unaffordable if the scale of treatment is large. This can occur where the upfront costs of a treatment are high, but the benefits mainly accrue over a longer period. This is often the case with vaccines, for example.

---

* For a comprehensive discussion, see Reference 22.

Conclusion

Where the results of pharmacoeconomic analysis of a new drug are unfavorable, the decision maker may decline to approve the listing of the medicine or may seek to negotiate conditions that improve the cost-effectiveness of the drug. Better evidence of benefit in the proposed indication may be pursued through additional clinical trials, or the target population may be narrowed to those patients with the greatest capacity to benefit. The third option to improve the ICER is to reduce the price of the drug. Since in many countries the public formulary represents not only the largest market for a drug but also a market with guaranteed buyers, a producer whose drug is denied formulary listing may be strongly motivated to discount, particularly if the alternative is a limited private market.

By assessing the comparative effectiveness and comparative cost-effectiveness of medicines in the decision-making process around coverage or subsidization of a drug, decision makers can mitigate, to a degree, the power imbalance that arises from the imperfections that characterize the pharmaceutical market, as described earlier.

Beginning with Australia in the early 1990s (see Case Study 17.1), pharmacoeconomic analyses have been adopted increasingly by public payers around the world to support decision making on the inclusion of new drugs in public programs and, in some cases, by private payers to inform formulary and benefit design for private drug plans. Australia was followed quickly by the Canadian province of Ontario and several European countries. In the United Kingdom, the National Institute for Health and Care Excellence was established in 1999, and today, fourth hurdle processes are widely used in Europe, Asia, and Latin America. In most countries, pharmacoeconomic analyses are used to determine whether new medicines represent reasonable value for money and whether the expenditure associated with their adoption is both efficient and affordable, as well as to inform listing and pricing negotiations. Today, despite some of the highest drug prices in the world,[33] the United States remains the only major industrialized country where this does not occur to any significant extent, with the use of CUAs to support coverage decisions by public payers expressly prohibited by the Affordable Care Act.[34]

CASE STUDY 17.1 Australia—Over 20 Years of Pharmacoeconomics in Formulary Decision Making

In Australia, pharmacoeconomics has been used in the assessment of new medicines proposed for formulary listing in the country's national drug subsidy program, the Pharmaceutical Benefits Scheme (PBS), since 1993. The PBS was first established more than 60 years ago and today forms a key component of Australia's single-payer health insurance system called Medicare.[35] The PBS formulary consists of more than 4000 different items, covering most medical conditions for which drug therapy is appropriate. In the late 1980s, amid concern over high prices and rising costs, the PBS became the first national pharmaceutical coverage program to introduce a mandatory pharmacoeconomic assessment, and the demonstration of comparative cost-effectiveness, a prerequisite for formulary listing.[36] The PBS evaluation process is often referred to as a "fourth hurdle" system—so-called because the requirement to demonstrate comparative cost-effectiveness is assessed separately and generally subsequent to regulatory processes intended to ascertain quality, safety, and efficacy for entry to market.

Submissions proposing listing of new medicines on the PBS (or for making changes to existing listings) are considered by the Pharmaceutical Benefits Advisory Committee (PBAC). The PBAC is a statutory, independent, expert panel established under the National Health Act (1953) to make recommendations to the Minister for Health about medicines to be included in the PBS formulary and any conditions that should apply. A 1987 legislative amendment introduced a provision that when considering a proposal for listing a medicine on the PBS formulary, the PBAC must consider its effectiveness and cost compared with other drug (or nondrug) therapies and specifies that a medicine that is substantially more costly than available alternatives may not be recommended for subsidy unless for some patients, at least, it provides a significant increase in efficacy, reduction in toxicity, or both.[37] Importantly, the legislation also stipulates that the Minister of Health may not add a drug to the PBS formulary in the absence of a positive recommendation from the PBAC.

The development of formal pharmacoeconomic guidelines for applicants seeking the listing of medicines on the PBS formulary began in the late 1980s, with the first version released in 1992 and with an ongoing and continuous process of revision and update.[38] They provide applicants (usually pharmaceutical companies) with a detailed guidance as to the nature, content, and presentation of the evidence of comparative effectiveness and comparative cost-effectiveness. The required information consists of clinical evidence (data on comparative effectiveness against the appropriate comparator), economic evidence (comparative cost-effectiveness), and budget impact (anticipated utilization and costs both to PBS and government heath budgets). As part of the application, the pharmaceutical company proposes both a price and the conditions—treatment population, indication(s), and treatment algorithm—under which it is seeking addition to the formulary for its drug.

The PBAC's role is to determine whether and under what conditions the drug in question may represent reasonable value for money at the price proposed. A key metric is the incremental cost-effectiveness ratio, or the additional cost associated with each additional unit of benefit, usually expressed as an incremental cost per additional QALY. However, comparative cost-effectiveness is a necessary but not a sufficient condition for listing; the PBAC weighs several other quantitative and qualitative factors, including the degree of clinical need, the availability of other treatments for the indication, and affordability of the new drug in the absence of a subsidy as well as the uncertainty in the estimate of comparative cost-effectiveness. Importantly, the PBAC does not use a fixed threshold for cost-effectiveness and thus is able to apply flexibility by weighing these additional factors in reaching its decision to recommend or reject a submission. In Australia, the prices of new medicines are not regulated directly, but the "fourth hurdle" process has had a significant indirect effect in moderating them. Importantly, the requirement to demonstrate comparative cost-effectiveness was not intended as a mechanism of cost containment, but rather, as a means of ensuring that any additional expenditure associated with the uptake and diffusion of new medicines represented reasonable value for money—that is, that expenditure growth would give rise to commensurate improvements in health outcomes.[39] The result is that some first-in-class drugs that represent substantial innovations in treatment prices may approximate those in the United States; for others that are later entrants in existing classes or for which patents have expired, prices may be considerably lower.[40]

References

1. European Federation of Pharmaceutical Industries and Associations (2013). The Pharmaceutical Industry in figures: Key data 2013. Available at: http://www.efpia.eu/uploads/Figures_Key_Data_2013.pdf. Accessed June 15, 2014.
2. Mestre-Ferrandiz J, Sussex J, Towse A (2012). *The R&D Cost of a New Medicine* (London, U.K.: Office of Health Economics).
3. DiMasi JA, Hansen RW, Grabowski HG (2003). The price of innovation: New estimates of drug development costs. *J Health Econ* 22:151–185.
4. DiMasi JA, Grabowski HG, Vernon J (2004). R&D costs and returns by therapeutic category. *Drug Inform J* 38(3):211–223.
5. Love J (2003). Evidence regarding research and development investments in innovative and non-innovative medicines (Washington, DC: Consumer Project on Technology). Available at: http://www.cptech.org/ip/health/rnd/evidence regardingrnd.pdf. Accessed December 6, 2015.
6. Light DW, Warburton R (2011). Demythologizing the high costs of pharmaceutical research. *BioSocieties* 6:34–50.
7. Light DW, Lexchin JR (2012). Pharmaceutical research and development: What do we get for all that money? *BMJ* 34(1):e4348.
8. Marshall A (1920). *Principles of Economics* (London, U.K.: Macmillan). Available at: http://www.econlib.org/library/Marshall/marP.html. Accessed July 30, 2014.
9. Adams C, Brantner VV (2003). New drug development: Estimating entry from human clinical trials. FTC Bureau of Economics Working Paper No. 262. Social Science Research Network (SSRN). Available at: http://ssrn.com/abstract=428040. Accessed December 6, 2015.
10. Goldacre B (2013). Are clinical trial data shared sufficiently today? *BMJ* 347:f1880.
11. United States Government Accountability Office (2009). Brand-name prescription drug pricing. Lack of therapeutically equivalent drugs and limited competition may contribute to extraordinary price increases. GAO-10-201 (Washington DC: Government Accountability Office).
12. Washington EA, Lipstein SH (2011). The Patient-Centered Outcomes Research Institute—Promoting better information, decisions, and health. *N Engl J Med* 365:e31.
13. Henry D (2012). Chapter 10: Economics for pharmaceutical management. In *MDS3-Managing Access to Medicines and Health Technologies* (Arlington, VA: Management Sciences for Health). A Kumarian Press Book, Lynne Rienner Publishers. Boulder, Colorado.
14. Simpson L, Taylor L, O'Rourke K, Shaw K. An Analysis of Consumer Behavior on Black Friday. *American International Journal of Contemporary Research* 2011;1(1) http://www.aijcrnet.com/journals/Vol._1_No.1_July_2011/1.pdf http://www.aijcrnet.com/journals/Vol._1_No.1_July_2011/1.pdf. Accessed December 6, 2015.
15. Henry DA, Lexchin J (2002). The pharmaceutical industry as a medicines provider. *Lancet* 360:1590–1595.
16. Docteur E, Paris V, Möise P (2008). Pharmaceutical pricing policies in a global market (Paris, France: Organisation for Economic Co-operation and Development).
17. Claxton K, Sculpher M, Carroll S (2011). Value-based pricing for pharmaceuticals: Its role, specification and prospects in a newly devolved NHS. CHE Research Paper 60 (York, U.K.: Centre for Health Economics, University of York). Available at: http://ideas.repec.org/p/chy/respap/60cherp.html. Accessed July 30, 2014.
18. Ruggiero K, Nolte E (2013). Pharmaceutical pricing: The use of external reference pricing (Cambridge, U.K.: RAND Europe). Available at: http://www.rand.org/content/dam/rand/pubs/research_reports/RR200/RR240/RAND_RR240.pdf. Accessed June 28, 2014.

19. Pharmaceutical Research and Manufacturers of America (PhRMA) (2014). PhRMA special 301 submission, 2014. Available at: http://www.phrma.org/sites/default/files/pdf/2014-special-301-submission.pdf. Accessed July 30, 2014.
20. Drummond MF, Sculpher MJ, Torrance GW, O'Brien BJ, Stoddart GI (2005). *Methods for the Economic Evaluation of Health Care Programmes*, 3rd edn. (Oxford, U.K.: Oxford University Press).
21. Owens DK (1998). Interpretation of cost-effectiveness analyses. *J Gen Intern Med* 13(10):716–717.
22. Eichler H-G, Kong SX, Gerth WC, Mavros P, Jönsson B (2004). Use of cost-effectiveness analysis in health-care resource allocation decision-making: How are cost-effectiveness thresholds expected to emerge? *Value Health* 7:518–552.
23. Weinstein M, Zeckhauser R (1973). Critical ratios and efficient allocation. *J Public Econ* 2:147–157.
24. Claxton K, Martin S, Soares M, Rice N, Spackman E, Hinde S et al. (2013). Methods for the estimation of the NICE cost effectiveness threshold. Revised report following referees comments (York, U.K.: University of York). Available at: http://www.york.ac.uk/media/che/documents/reports/resubmitted_report.pdf. Accessed July 29, 2014.
25. Ryen L, Svensson M (2014). The willingness to pay for a quality adjusted life year: A review of the empirical literature. *Health Econ* 24(10):1289–1301. doi:10.1002/hec.3085.
26. World Health Organization, Commission on Macroeconomics and Health (2001). Macroeconomics and health investing in health for economic development. Report of the Commission on Macroeconomics and Health (Geneva, Switzerland: World Health Organization).
27. World Health Organization. Cost effectiveness and strategic planning (WHO-CHOICE): Tables of Costs and Prices used in WHO-CHOICE Analysis. (n.d.) http://www.who.int/choice/costs/en/. Accessed December 6, 2015.
28. Boersma C, Broere A, Postma MJ (2010). Quantification of the potential impact of cost-effectiveness thresholds on Dutch drug expenditures using retrospective analysis. *Value Health* 13(6):853–856.
29. Harris AH, Hill SR, Chin G, Li JJ, Walkom E (2008). The role of value for money in public insurance coverage decisions for drugs in Australia: A retrospective analysis 1994–2004. *Med Decis Making* 28(5):713–722.
30. Rocchi A, Miller E, Hopkins R, Goeree R (2012). Common drug review recommendations: An evidence base for expectations? *Pharmacoeconomics* 30(3):229–246.
31. McCabe C, Claxton K, Culyer AJ (2008). The NICE cost-effectiveness threshold. *Pharmacoeconomics* 26(9):733–744.
32. http://data.worldbank.org/indicator/NY.GDP.PCAP.CD.
33. The Economist. Pharmaceutical pricing: The new drugs war. *The Economist*, January 4, 2014. Available at: http://www.economist.com/news/leaders/21592619-patents-drugs-are-interests-sick-well-industry-protection-should-not. Accessed December 6, 2015.
34. The Patient Protection and Affordable Care Act. PL 111-148, March 23, 2010.
35. Sloan C (2005). A history of the pharmaceutical benefits scheme, 1947–1992 (Canberra, Australian Capital Territory, Australia: Department of Human Services and Health).
36. Lopert R (2009). *Evidence-Based Decision-Making within Australia's Pharmaceutical Benefits Scheme* (New York: The Commonwealth Fund).
37. National Health Act 1953, S101. Available at: http://www.austlii.edu.au/au/legis/cth/consol_act/nha1953147/s101.html. Accessed December 6, 2015.
38. Australian Government Department of Health. Guidelines for preparing submissions to the Pharmaceutical Benefits Advisory Committee. (Version 4.4). June 2013. http://www.pbac.pbs.gov.au/content/information/printable-files/pbacg-book.pdf. Accessed December 6, 2015.
39. Lopert R, Elshaug AG (2013). Australia's 'Fourth Hurdle' drug review comparing costs and benefits holds lessons for the United States. *Health Affairs* 32(4):778–787.
40. Roughead EE, Lopert R, Sansom LN (2007). Prices for innovative pharmaceutical products that provide health gain: A comparison between Australia and USA. *Value Health* 10(6):514–520.

Chapter 18

Market for Pharmaceuticals

David H. Kreling

Contents

Introduction

The market for pharmaceuticals can be characterized as being complex and unique. The aspects that contribute to the complexity of the market include the number and kinds of firms or entities that operate and interact in the market and how those firms or entities interact. This complexity, plus peculiarities in the demand for pharmaceuticals, contributes to the uniqueness of the market. An understanding of some relevant characteristics of the market for pharmaceuticals can provide context for policy and policy making related to pharmaceuticals.

The goal of this chapter is to provide a brief description and introduction to some relevant characteristics of the market for pharmaceuticals, covering some of the *who*, *what*, *where*, and *how* questions about pharmaceuticals and hopefully providing basis for a sense of *why* related to pharmaceuticals and pharmaceutical policy.

This chapter includes a description of the position and characteristics of expenditures for pharmaceuticals in health care, an overview of different kinds of firms and entities as structural components of the market, and some aspects and characteristics that make pharmaceuticals and the market for pharmaceuticals unique.

Expenditures and Payments for Drugs

Prescription drugs play a key role in health care. They represent the most common therapeutic intervention in both community-based and hospital-based medical care. However, prescription drugs consistently have been a relatively small part of health-care expenditures. As shown in Figure 18.1, expenditures for prescription drugs have been a much smaller proportion of personal health-care spending than hospital care or physician and clinical services. From the late 1960s through 1999, prescription drugs comprised less than 10% of personal health-care expenditures in the United States.* Annual growth rates in expenditures for drugs that exceeded the percent changes in expenditures for hospital care and physician and clinical services in the 1990s heightened

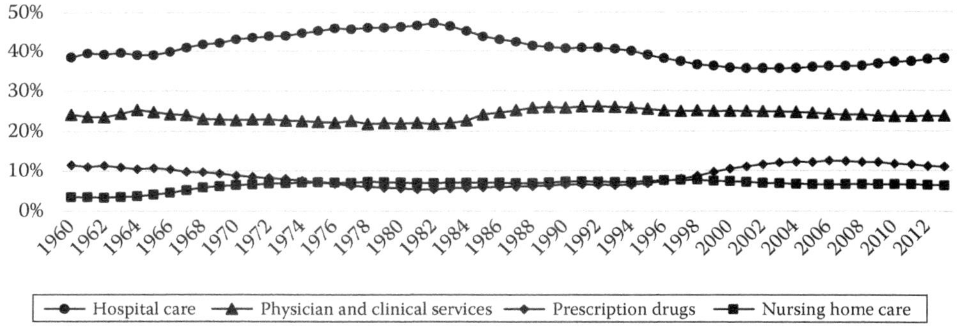

Decade averages	1960s	1970s	1980s	1990s	2000s	2010s
Hospital care (%)	39.9	44.8	44.3	38.9	35.9	37.7
Physician and clinical services (%)	24.0	22.5	23.6	25.5	24.5	23.7
Prescription drugs (%)	10.5	7.3	5.8	7.3	11.8	11.2
Nursing home care (%)	4.3	6.9	6.9	7.4	6.8	6.4

Figure 18.1 Percent of spending for personal health-care expenditures: hospital care, physician and clinical services, prescription drugs, and nursing home care, 1960–2013. (From Centers for Medicare and Medicaid Services, National Health Statistics Group.)

* In these national estimates, expenditures for prescription drugs are ambulatory expenditures; the total proportion is higher if drugs dispensed to hospitalized patients are included. Expenditures for drugs are not itemized as part of hospital expenditures, and thus the total amount of combined prescription expenditures cannot be derived from these expenditure data. Data from market research firms, such as IMS health, would suggest that approximately 10%–15% of total manufacturer sales are made to hospitals and other institutional purchasers.

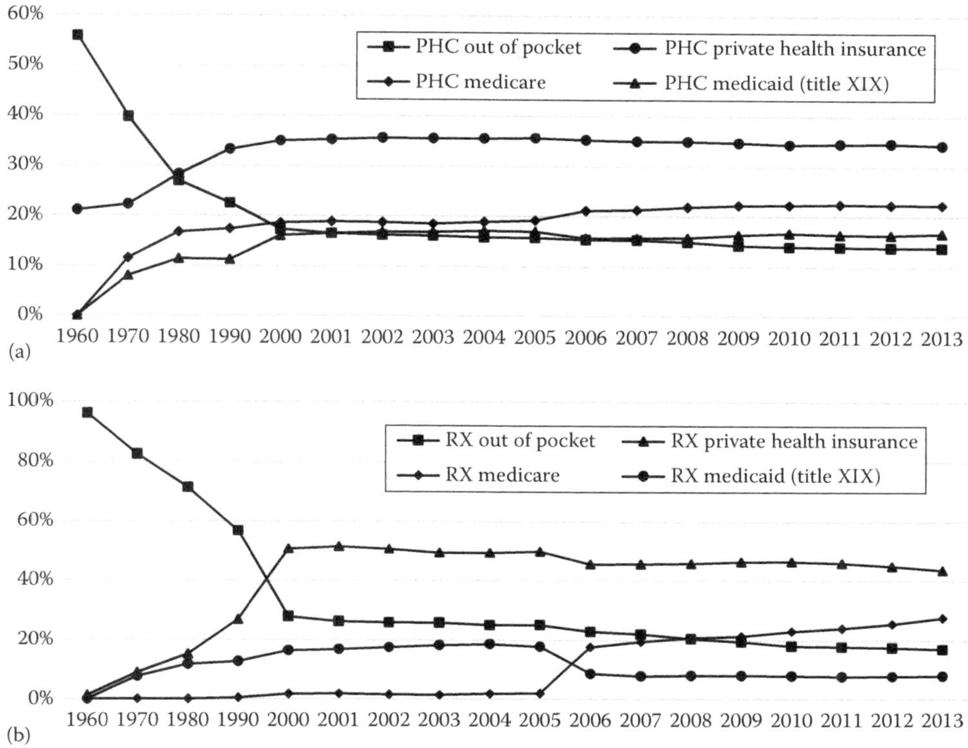

Figure 18.2 Source of payment for (a) personal health care and (b) prescription expenditures, on selected years, 1960–2013. (From Centers for Medicare and Medicaid Services, National Health Statistics Group.)

awareness and concern about spending for prescription drugs. That sensitivity has continued as the percent of total health-care expenditures for drugs exceeded 12% in the mid-2000s, levels not experienced in the previous 50 years (Figure 18.1). The increases in prescription spending have been a primary reason why policy makers have focused on drugs and policies aimed at curbing growth in expenditures.

The responsibility for drug spending also has been changing, as reflected in the proportion of payments for drug expenditures by source of payment. (See Figure 18.2.) In the past 50 years, the proportion of expenditures for prescription drugs that has been out of pocket for consumers has declined from 96% (in 1960) to 17% (in 2013). Private health insurance as a source of payment grew to just over 50% of expenditures in the early 2000s, with a slight decrease since then. Medicaid as a source of payment grew to nearly one-fifth of the expenditures in 2005, the year before Part D drug coverage under Medicare began. In 2006, Medicare became the source of payment for nearly 18% of prescription drug expenditures with the advent of Part D coverage for prescriptions and has grown steadily since then.* The combined role of government (Centers for Medicare and Medicaid Services [CMS]—Medicaid, Medicare, and Children's Health Insurance

* Medicare represented a nonzero, but very small (less than 2%), proportion of prescription drug expenditures before 2006 due to coverage of nonelderly disabled individuals, so the nearly 18% Medicare spending for 2006 was substantially, but not totally, due to Part D.

Program [CHIP]) as a source of payment for prescription drugs was almost 36% in 2013 (some retraction in Medicaid spending resulted from dual eligible elderly citizens gaining drug coverage under Medicare).*

The recent pronounced shifting to government (e.g., Medicaid and Medicare) as a source of payment for prescription drug expenditures has contributed to recent changes in the source of payment for health expenditures overall. The proportion of total personal health-care expenditures represented by Medicare spending grew to represent 3.5% more of total expenditures since 2005, and combined CMS spending (with Medicaid and CHIP added in) totaled nearly 40% of the total personal health-care expenditures for 2010 through 2013 (also shown in Figure 18.2a). As with prescription drug expenditures, the proportions of private health insurance and out-of-pocket spending for personal health care declined slightly from around 2002 through 2013. The increased role of government (e.g., CMS) as a source of funding for health-care expenditures and the contribution of prescription drugs to these changes elevate the potential policy attention given to drugs.

From an economic perspective, expenditures or spending for prescription drugs can be considered simply the product of price (P) and quantity (Q) of drugs consumed. Growth or change in expenditures results from changes in three factors: (1) inflationary changes in product prices for pharmaceuticals; (2) changes in the quantity of drugs used, that is, intensity of use; and (3) changes in which products are used, that is, the mix of products (which has a separate price effect). Intensity of use can be thought of as a quantitative aspect of utilization, and the mix of products used can be considered a qualitative aspect of utilization.

Change in utilization from a quantitative perspective captures increased intensity of use, from either more prescriptions dispensed and used or more doses per day, or both. The commonality of prescription drugs as a part of primary care is fundamental to the quantitative utilization aspect as a contributor to expenditures and changes in expenditures. In the majority of instances, a patient visit or contact with a physician results in an order for a prescription drug. According to the 2010 National Ambulatory Medical Care Survey, 75.1% of physician visits by ambulatory patients in the United States resulted in a drug being prescribed.† For patients with chronic conditions requiring drug therapy, one physician visit generates multiple pharmacy visits for an original dispensing and refills of any prescription drug(s) being taken by the patient. Increased intensity of prescription drug use has been evident. Between 1994 and 2014, the number of prescriptions dispensed doubled. On a per capita basis, utilization grew from 7.9 prescriptions per capita in 1994 to 13.3 in 2014; prescriptions grew at an annual rate of 3.5%, while the population grew at 0.9% annually.‡

The qualitative aspect of utilization changes as the composition or mix of products used varies. As the mix of drug products used or market basket of goods changes, it drives change in the average price of a prescription in an aggregate sense. The effect of a change in product mix on the average price of a prescription is independent of and in addition to the effect of inflationary changes in the prices of pharmaceuticals on a year-to-year basis; both product mix and inflation contribute to the price component of the price (P) times quantity (Q) determination of expenditures and changes

* Other payors, including some that could be considered government sources of payment—Indian Health Service, Department of Defense, and Department of Veterans Affairs—are not included in the CMS government spending. All these other payors were less than 2% in any year individually and always less than 5% cumulatively.

† Table 21. Medication therapy and number of medications mentioned at office visits, by patient sex (United States, 2010, National Ambulatory Medical Care Survey: 2010 Summary Tables, www.cdc.gov/nchs/ahcd.htm).

‡ Based on the numbers of prescriptions dispensed reported by IMS Health and the U.S. population from the Census Bureau.

in expenditures for prescription drugs. The relative consequences of inflationary price changes for the individual products and the mix of products used vary depending on the prescription price and expenditures; however, typically for a mix of products, the qualitative aspect of utilization has tended to have a larger impact on the average change in price for an average prescription from year to year, and thus expenditures also change.* Such changes in the mix of drugs dispensed likely contributed to more than 20% increase in the average prescription price, from $(USD)61.02 in 2011 to $(USD)75.92 in 2013 (as reported in the *Healthcare Distribution Management Association* [*HDMA*] *Factbook* based on National Association of Chain Drug Stores (NACDS) analysis of IMS Health data).

A variety of phenomena could be considered underlying factors that contribute to expenditures and changes in expenditures for prescription drugs. Some of the factors affect price or utilization aspects of prescription expenditures or both, and some of these underlying factors may be having synergistic effects in driving expenditure growth. The aging of the U.S. populace is one overall contributor to prescription expenditures and expansion in prescription spending as well as other health-care spending. With increased population age, more age-related morbidity is present, and correspondingly, more drugs are consumed. Increased prevalence of insurance coverage for prescription drugs has reduced price barriers to the use of prescription drugs, creating a moral hazard or insurance effect that affects the quantity and, potentially, quality of drugs used. Promotion of drug products has been a hallmark of pharmaceutical manufacturers, and changed interpretations of marketing regulations in the mid-1990s led to the increased consumer-directed advertising, in addition to the continued emphasis on physicians as traditional promotional message targets. Advances in technology and emphasis on those advances that have been core aspects of health care and pharmaceuticals are no exception. The imperative to ever increase technology has contributed to higher costs for developing new pharmaceutical products that are reflected in product prices. Advances in technology also have led to different mechanisms for treating conditions (e.g., biotechnology), new diagnostic procedures, and therapeutic agents for previously untreatable conditions or additional complementary treatments to enhance outcomes. Substantial shifts have occurred recently in the emphasis on innovation for therapies and treatments in new technology areas and more focused markets, such as orphan drugs, which have resulted in dramatically increased costs for new treatments and potentially high new spending areas for pharmaceuticals.

Although the factors noted earlier have contributed to increasing expenditures for pharmaceuticals, there also have been some recent phenomena with contrary implications. The proportion of prescriptions dispensed as generic drugs has increased substantially as prior blockbuster drugs have lost patent protection, opening the door for lower-cost generic versions of those drugs to substitute in the market (with an increase from 50% to 82% of prescriptions dispensed as generic drugs between 2005 and 2014).† Some cost-sharing requirements and benefit structures in some insurance drug coverage programs have changed to increase consumers' contributions to their drug spending and to sensitize them to the cost of their drug use.‡ Cost-effectiveness reviews and findings have sensitized coverage programs and consumers about relative values and benefits of drugs and whether they or other approaches are preferred or necessary. Economies in dispensing

---

* For a depiction of inflation and product mix impact on prescription price changes, see *Prescription Drug Trends—A Chartbook*, Kaiser Family Foundation, July 2000, or Fulda and Wertheimer.[1]

† Declining medicine use and costs: For better or worse? A review of the use of medicines in the United States in 2012, May 2013; and medicines use and spending shifts: A review of the use of medicines in the U.S. in 2014, April 2015, IMS Institute for Healthcare Informatics, Parsippany, NJ, www.theimsinstitute.org.

‡ See, for example, copays and trends that have been reported in the annual Drug Trend Reports produced by Express Scripts, St. Louis, MO (www.lab.Express-Scripts.com), and by Pharmacy Benefit Management Institute (PBMI) in the 2013–2014, Prescription drug benefit cost and plan design report, www.pbmi.com.

prescriptions have resulted from automated systems and substitution of supportive personnel and strategic deployment of pharmacists in pharmacies. Whether and to what extent these factors that can dampen expenditure growth will or can continue remains to be seen.

Market for Pharmaceuticals: Structural Overview

In general, the market for pharmaceuticals has structural components and a channel of distribution similar to other consumer goods. Channel member include manufacturers, distributors, and retailers; these entities engage in functions that generate the flow of consumer goods from production to consumption. Pharmaceuticals are considered highly regulated products because specific and special regulations and regulatory processes and procedures apply throughout the channel. In addition, more than just the buyer and seller can be involved in transactions for pharmaceuticals at the consumer level, adding an aspect of complexity not present in other markets. Public and private insurance-type coverage programs and sponsors or funders of these programs often also have a financial stake, in addition to the consumer, when individuals purchase pharmaceutical products.

Manufacturers

The market can be characterized as having two main groups of companies that manufacture pharmaceuticals: innovator or brand name manufacturers and generic manufacturers. Further distinction especially among brand name manufacturers of pharmaceuticals often is made based on the firm's emphasis on the types of drugs produced, such as traditional, biotechnology, or specialty pharmaceuticals. Traditional or *small molecule* pharmaceuticals are the classic or historic type of pharmaceutical products in the market and represent the most common drug products. Biotechnology pharmaceuticals are distinct by virtue of the products themselves being biologics or having molecular biology or biotechnology processes involved in their production. Specialty pharmaceuticals often are biotechnology drugs but can include traditional, small molecule compounds, and they typically are administered by injection or infusion and thus are not used in traditional self-dosing ways. As their name implies, specialty products are intended for special therapeutic situations and conditions and fall into therapeutic categories such as oncologics, antivirals, immunosuppressants, immunostimulants, and autoimmune modulators.

Brand name manufacturers emphasize innovation and generation of new drug products. They concentrate on research and development of new products for the market and promotion of those products to engender market success for their innovations. Brand name manufacturers obtain patents for their innovations that result from their research and development. When a drug is covered by a patent, only the firm with the patent can produce and market the drug, effectively establishing a monopoly for the company that holds the patent for the period of time (up to 20 years, maximum) that the patent is in effect.* Since only the company holding the patent can produce and sell a *patent-protected* drug, these drugs often are referred to as single-source products. When the patent for a drug expires, additional firms can begin manufacturing the drug; thus, such drugs are referred to as off-patent or multisource drugs. After the patent for a drug expires, the brand name manufacturer that discovered the drug typically continues to market the drug, and their version

* The standard patent time for an original patent is 20 years, but manufacturers can apply for patent extensions, for example, if additional testing is done for use of drugs in children. See the United States Patent and Trademark Office, www.uspto.gov/.

of the drug is referred to as the multisource innovator product. Versions of the drug manufactured by other firms that enter the market after the patent expires are referred to as multisource generic versions of the drug, and those manufacturers are referred to as generic manufacturers.*

Brand name manufacturers are noted for their marketing and promotional efforts, and it can be useful to think of their *products* as being not only pharmaceutical agents and the physical drug products but information about those agents and their use. Generic manufacturers focus on making off-patent drug products and seek market success by efficiently producing and competitively pricing their versions of brand name manufacturers' products. These two groups of manufacturers are counterparts to manufacturers in many other consumer good product categories: major label or original equipment manufacturers and secondary or *off-label* manufacturers.†

Brand name and generic manufacturers generally are considered distinct and separate from each other, but they are closely interrelated. In theory, the corresponding manufacturers compete for market share since they sell the same, *identical* products. However, often there are efforts to maintain a distinction between brand name and generic versions of drug products. Typically, a large difference in price between brand name and generic versions of a drug product develops, and consequently, brand name manufacturers lose a considerable market share to generic competitors' products.‡ The often dramatic and rapid reduction in the brand name manufacturer's revenue after patent expiry due to generic competitors' products drives brand name manufacturers to divert their attention and marketing efforts to other products they sell, sometimes even to the extent of demarketing their older, off-patent products. Another interrelationship between brand name and generic manufacturers is that brand name companies may have subsidiaries producing generic versions of their own or other products or they may apply excess manufacturing capacity and contract out for production of generic versions of their product for generic firms. An important issue for manufacturers is how innovation and research and development can be encouraged while at the same time advantage can be taken of opportunities from demand for generic versions of their drugs in the marketplace.

The genesis of many contemporary firms in the pharmaceutical manufacturing market was with entrepreneurial efforts of individual pharmacists, physicians, or drug distributors as they moved into standardized manufacturing of drug products and discovery of novel therapies. Companies such as Merck, Lilly, and Pfizer all have this common theme in their history. The market also can be considered a global market because both domestic and internationally headquartered firms are present in both brand name and generic manufacturer ranks, with drugs being produced for export and sourced from import to be marketed. The Pharmaceutical Research and Manufacturers' Association is the trade organization that represents innovative biopharmaceutical research and discovery companies—the brand name manufacturer segment of the U.S.

---

* Some manufacturers of generic products promote and sell their products with their own brand name for the generic version of the product. These products are considered "branded generics" as a subset of the generic drug market and they represent a small and declining proportion (from 11% of all prescriptions dispensed in 2003 to 6% in 2014) of generic prescriptions dispensed. IMS Institute for Healthcare Informatics. Declining medicine use and costs: for Better or worse?—A review of the use of medicines in the United States in 2012, May 2013; and medicines use and spending shifts: A review of the use of medicines in the U.S. in 2014, April 2015.

† A major contributor to generic manufacturers' production efficiencies is that they are not required to conduct their own clinical trials for their versions of innovators' products, and thus they avoid those costs. In addition, the innovator has promoted the drug and established it in the marketplace; thus generic firms tend to have lower marketing expenses.

‡ Branded generic drug products typically will have considerably lower prices than the brand name innovator's version of the drug, but higher than prices of *unbranded* generic products. Thus, branded generic manufacturers compete with both innovators' products and unbranded generic manufacturers' products.

pharmaceutical market.* The Generic Pharmaceutical Association is a counterpart trade organization for manufacturers and distributors of generic drugs.†

According to IMS Health, a market research firm concentrating on the pharmaceutical market and health care, the total U.S. market for prescription drugs in 2014 was $(USD)373.9 billion, valued at the wholesale level.‡ The majority of these sales were for brand name products and their companies; in 2014, brand name drug products comprised 72% of sales and generic products represented 28% of the market.[§,3] Another way to consider the composition of the market is by dosage or administration form; traditional forms of pharmaceuticals were most common but specialty pharmaceuticals have been increasing and in 2014 represented 33% of total sales. A ranking of the top 20 companies in 2013 by sales volume is shown in Table 18.1. Brand name companies dominate the top 20 list; only 3 firms, Actavis, Mylan, and Teva, are generic firms among the top 20 list. A nearly opposite result occurs when the market is considered from the perspective of prescriptions dispensed. In 2014, 88% of prescriptions dispensed through retail pharmacies were for generic drugs (82% for unbranded and 6% for branded generics),[3] and the top 20 ranking of firms in 2013 by prescriptions dispensed has generic firms holding the top 3 spots and 12 generic manufacturers in total (shown in Table 18.1).

Some recent changes in the market have contributed to the different representations of brand name and generic drug manufacturers when considering the market. Patent expirations for popular drugs have contributed to increased proportions of generic drugs dispensed; generic versions are rapidly adopted and effectively replaced the prior brand name counterparts. Higher prices, and often higher margins on specialty and biotechnology drugs, have made them desirable for sellers at several levels in the channel of distribution, and use of these agents has grown as administration of specialty drugs has moved beyond physician offices and clinics to patient homes and home care administration with more pharmacy retailer distribution of these supplies. Consequently, an increased number of less commonly dispensed, but high-cost biotechnology and specialty, drugs have moved up in rankings of products by sales, often bringing manufacturers with smaller, focused product lines into the high sales spotlight. In the top drug products by sales in 2014, 14 of the top 20 products were biotechnology or specialty drugs.¶

What has resulted is divergence of the market and impact of brand name and generic firms when viewed from sales versus prescription volume perspectives. Brand name drugs represent a large proportion of sales, yet a small fraction of prescriptions dispensed.[**,4] The disproportionate

* See the Pharmaceutical Research and Manufacturers of America website, www.PhRMA.org.

† See the Generic Pharmaceutical Association website, www.gphaonline.org/.

‡ IMS conducts audits of wholesaler sales, thus capturing the amounts of sales of manufacturers at the wholesaler level in the channel of distribution. The IMS National Sales Perspectives (NSP)™ measures spending within the U.S. pharmaceutical market by pharmacies, clinics, hospitals, and other health-care providers. NSP reports 100% coverage of the retail and nonretail channels for national pharmaceutical sales at actual transaction prices. Sales are reported at wholesaler invoice prices and do not reflect off-invoice discounts and rebates, www.imshealth.com.

§ The 28.3% of market sales for generic drugs was composed of 11.1% for branded generics and 17.2% for unbranded generics. IMS Institute for Healthcare Informatics. Medicines use and spending shifts: A review of the use of medicines in the U.S. in 2014, April 2015, www.imshealth.com.

¶ In contrast, only 2 of the Top 20 Drugs ranked by sales in 2004 were specialty drugs.

** For example, only 14 of the Top 200 Drugs in 2012 ranked by sales were generic drugs, with the highest ranking generic drug at number 37. Conversely, when ranked by the number of dispensed prescriptions, 157 of the Top 200 Drugs in 2012 were generic drugs and 43 were brand name drugs. Brand name drugs in the Top 200 by prescription volume have decreased; in 2004 more than twice as many drugs, 103, were brand name drug products.

Table 18.1 Top 20 Pharmaceutical Manufacturers, Ranked by U.S. Sales and by Prescription Volume, 2013

	By Sales	*Total Sales[a] ($[USD] Billions)*	*Market Share (%)*	*By Dispensed RXs*	*Total Prescriptions[b] (Millions)*	*Market Share (%)*
1	Novartis	18.8	5.7	Teva	559	13.3
2	Pfizer	17.0	5.2	Mylan	370	8.8
3	Merck & Co.	16.5	5.0	Actavis	302	7.2
4	AstraZeneca	15.9	4.8	Novartis	258	6.1
5	Genentech (Roche)	15.8	4.8	Endo Pharm.	198	4.7
6	Teva	15.4	4.7	Lupin Laboratories	176	4.2
7	Eli Lilly & Co.	15.3	4.6	Pfizer	144	3.4
8	Amgen	14.8	4.5	Amneal Pharm.	138	3.3
9	Johnson & Johnson	13.9	4.2	Zydus Pharm.	103	2.4
10	GlaxoSmithKline	12.8	3.9	Aurobindo Pharma	96	2.3
11	Sanofi U.S.	12.2	3.7	Dr. Reddy's Lab	93	2.2
12	AbbVie U.S.	12.1	3.7	Boehringer Ingelheim	87	2.1
13	Actavis	10.3	3.1	Mallinckrodt Pharm.	83	2.0
14	Novo Nordisk	7.9	2.4	Apotex Corp.	80	1.9
15	Mylan Inc.	7.8	2.4	Daiichi Sankyo	75	1.8
16	Boehringer Ingelheim	7.7	2.3	Camber Pharm	69	1.6
17	Gilead Sciences	7.6	2.3	AstraZeneca	58	1.4
18	Otsuka America	6.8	2.1	GlaxoSmithKline	56	1.3

(Continued)

Table 18.1 (*Continued*) Top 20 Pharmaceutical Manufacturers, Ranked by U.S. Sales and by Prescription Volume, 2013

	By Sales	*Total Sales[a] ($[USD] Billions)*	*Market Share (%)*	*By Dispensed RXs*	*Total Prescriptions[b] (Millions)*	*Market Share (%)*
19	Bristol-Myers Squibb	5.6	1.7	Sun Pharma USA	53	1.3
20	Shire Pharmaceuticals	4.2	1.3	Wockhardt America	53	1.3

Source: Healthcare Distribution Management Association (HDMA). *85th Edition HDMA Factbook—The Facts, Figures, and Trends in Health Care (2014–2015),* Center for Healthcare Supply Chain Research, Alexandria, VA.

Sales: Top companies by nondiscounted spending (United States), IMS national sales perspective.

Prescriptions: Top companies by dispensed prescriptions (United States), IMS National Prescription Audit plus.

[a] Represents prescription pharmaceutical purchases, including insulin at wholesale prices by retail, food stores and chains, mass merchandisers, independent pharmacies, mail services, nonfederal and federal hospitals, clinics, closed-wall Health Maintenance Organizations (HMOs), LTC pharmacies, home health care, and prisons/universities. Excludes comarketing agreements. Joint ventures assigned to product owner. Data run by custom redesign to include completed mergers and acquisitions.

[b] Prescriptions dispensed reflects prescription-bound products, including insulin and excluding other products such as OTC. Include all prescriptions dispensed through retail pharmacies, including independent and chain drug stores, food store pharmacies, and mail orders, as well as LTC facilities.

sales and dispensed prescription volumes for brand name and generic drugs are related to the differences in prices of brand name and generic drugs. Applying the proportions of sales (71% and 29%) and prescription volumes (13% and 87%) noted earlier for brand name and generic drugs, the relative prices of brand name and generic drug prescriptions can be derived; that determination reveals about a 17-fold difference in price between a brand name and generic drug.*

Distributors: Drug Wholesalers

Drug wholesalers serve as the middleman link between drug manufacturers and pharmacies. They perform what marketers refer to as the logistics function in the channel of distribution for pharmaceuticals; they assemble, sort, and disperse drug products. According to the HDMA (the trade association for drug wholesalers), 90.4% of all U.S. prescription sales were completed through pharmaceutical distributors in 2013.† The drug wholesaling industry is very specialized, with prescription

* This calculation is based on sales valued at the wholesaler level—the pharmacy retailer's cost to purchase the drug. With prescription margins included, the price multiple between a brand prescription and generic prescription will be less, but still a substantial difference to generate the disparity in sales and prescription volume that occurs for brand and generic drugs.

† The remaining sales primarily were directed to pharmacies and other purchasers from manufacturers.

drugs comprising all but a few percent of their sales. The drug wholesaler industry also is quite concentrated, with three firms (AmerisourceBergen, Cardinal Health, and McKesson) dominating the market. There has been a continued consolidation in the drug wholesaling industry; for 2014, HDMA reported 32 distribution companies as members, and these companies operate 153 distribution centers in the United States (down from 39 members and 200 distribution centers in 2007).*

Although the role of distributor that wholesalers play is essential, as an intermediary in the channel of distribution with a somewhat limited scope of function and value added, they less often are a policy focus. Generally, policy related to drug wholesalers tends to be relevant regulations and requirements to ensure the integrity of the drug distribution system and supply chain. For example, there are strict requirements about distribution of prescription drugs only to pharmacies and practitioners licensed to prescribe or dispense drugs and special handling procedures and controls for narcotics and controlled substances. In addition, drugs distributed in the United States have to be approved for use and sale, raising issues about drug imports and possible counterfeit drug products.

Historically, the drug wholesaling industry has been very competitive and that characteristic continues. Since competing wholesalers generally sell the same products and function predominantly as a distributional middleman, price has been a primary competition variable and they have focused on efficiency in their operations to ensure they can price competitively. The HDMA reports that wholesaler operating expenses have averaged just over 1% of revenues in recent years, with gross profit margins approximately 3%.† The low overhead costs and margins also have tended to limit the policy attention that the drug wholesaling industry has been given.

Retailers: Pharmacies

Pharmacies comprise the *retail sector* or terminal seller in the channel of distribution for pharmaceuticals. Pharmacies engage in the final transfer of title to consumers for pharmaceutical products. This sector of the market for pharmaceuticals is quite diverse; it encompasses different types of pharmacies (including independent and chain community pharmacies, institutional hospital and long-term-care [LTC] pharmacies, and mail-service pharmacies) and a variety of ownership structures (independent entrepreneurs, publicly traded corporate businesses, not-for-profit and for-profit private organizations, and government and military). The sales of pharmaceutical manufacturers to different types of pharmacies that is summarized in Table 18.2 provides a sense of diversity of pharmacies and their relative sizes in the market.

The table is broken down to represent a classic distinction for types of pharmacies that has been based on the kind of patient served, with institutional pharmacies (hospital and LTC pharmacies) serving patients confined to beds with professional or technical staff administering doses contrasted with community pharmacies serving ambulatory, self-dosing patients. This kind of distinction by type of patient is useful because it conceptually reflects the relevant competitors and business units in the market. However, this simple distinction is violated when market measures are taken and information is reported. For example, although patients in nursing homes (LTC facilities) are considered institutionalized patients, their prescription drug supplies often are provided by community pharmacies and quantified as dispensed prescriptions from retail pharmacies in market measures of prescription activity in pharmacies. Also, although clinics

* In addition, drug wholesalers specialize in distributing prescription pharmaceuticals; nearly all (98%) of drug wholesalers' sales are for prescription drugs (with the remainder primarily OTC and health and beauty products).[2]

† Figures are weighted averages taking into account the proportional relevance of company size; unweighted averages are slightly higher. See the HDMA Factbook for additional financial and operational information about drug wholesalers.

Table 18.2 Sales of Manufacturers to Different Classes of Customers, 2010–2014

	2010	2011	2012	2013	2014 ($[USD])	2014 (%)
Total U.S. Market	$(USD) 315.7	$ (USD) 328.7	$ (USD) 319.6	$ (USD) 330.5	$ (USD) 373.9	100.0
Retail channels	226.8	236.3	229.2	236.8	268.6	71.8
Chain stores	108.1	112.6	110.6	115.2	124.0	33.2
Mail service	59.4	63.9	60.9	63.1	79.9	21.4
Independent	38.1	38.3	36.5	36.7	41.9	11.2
Food stores	21.3	21.5	21.2	21.8	22.8	6.1
Institutional channels	88.9	92.4	90.4	93.7	105.2	28.1
Clinics	36.7	38.6	39.5	42.2	48.1	12.9
Nonfederal hospitals	28.0	28.2	28.1	28.4	30.2	8.1
LTC	14.7	15.2	13.9	14.0	16.2	4.3
Federal facilities	2.1	2.6	2.8	3.1	3.9	1.0
Home health care	2.5	2.7	2.7	2.7	3.2	0.9
HMO	3.9	4.2	2.5	2.4	2.7	0.7
Miscellaneous	1.0	1.0	0.9	0.9	1.0	0.3

Source: IMS Institute for Healthcare Informatics, Medicines use and spending shifts: A review of the use of medicines in the U.S. in 2014, April 2015, National Sales Perspective, reported in the IMS Health Institute Report. http://www.theimsinstitute.org/en/thought-leadership/ims-institute/reports/medicines-use-in-the-us-2014. Accessed December 6, 2015.

Channel distribution by nondiscounted spending (United States). Data represent sales from manufacturers at the wholesale level (exfactory) in billion dollars for prescription-bound products, including insulins and excluding other products such as OTC.

represent a substantial proportion of the institutional sales sector of the market in Table 18.2, they serve ambulatory patients and can include clinic-based pharmacy operations that are not included as retail pharmacies in market measures.* Further, as health systems have developed, they have included inpatient and outpatient services with clinic-affiliated or free-standing outpatient pharmacies, and although they can be considered competitors for other community pharmacies, they are not part of the traditional market sectors included in community retail market measures.

Within the community pharmacy sector of the market, a traditional chain versus independent ownership distinction has been used to characterize community retail pharmacies. That distinction remains relevant for some aspects of these pharmacies, such as how dependent the

* As described by IMS, their National Prescription Audit Plus (NPA Plus) captures elements of the prescription details recorded in retail pharmacies of all types, including independent and chain drug stores, food store pharmacies, and mail order, as well as long-term care facilities (www.IMSHealth.com).

overall operation is on the prescription department or professional services aspect of their business. However, independent pharmacies commonly belong to buying groups that give them substantial purchasing power akin to chain pharmacies and others are part of franchise organizations, giving them merchandising and operational capacities and additional similarity to chain pharmacies.* In addition, corporate (chain) pharmacies themselves can be quite diverse, including pharmacies in mass merchandiser stores and food stores. It has been suggested that operational characteristics, such as daily prescription volume may be better classifying variables for community pharmacies instead of independent and chain ownership. The distinction between mail-service and community pharmacies also becomes blurred when independent and chain community pharmacies offer extended-day supplies or mail delivery service for prescription patrons. The diversity and "blurring of the lines" between types of pharmacy operations can make it difficult to predict or measure the implications of policies on the market.

Important market trends have occurred within the community pharmacy market sector. Although the total number of community retail pharmacies has been stable or slightly growing in recent years, there has been ongoing redistribution of outlets between corporate (including chain, mass merchandiser, and supermarket) pharmacies and independent pharmacies. This *corporatization* of pharmacies has been occurring for many years and is reflected in the numbers of prescriptions dispensed by the type of community retail pharmacy as shown in Figure 18.3. Also, there has been growth in prescriptions dispensed from mail-service pharmacies, with some of this growth a reflection of policies by insurers and drug coverage plans requiring or encouraging patients to obtain prescriptions from mail-service pharmacies. There also has been movement of the community retail prescription market to an *insured* market. With the addition of Part D coverage for prescriptions under Medicare, the market has become a nearly totally covered market. In 2014, only 8% of all prescriptions dispensed in community pharmacies were self-pay prescriptions.

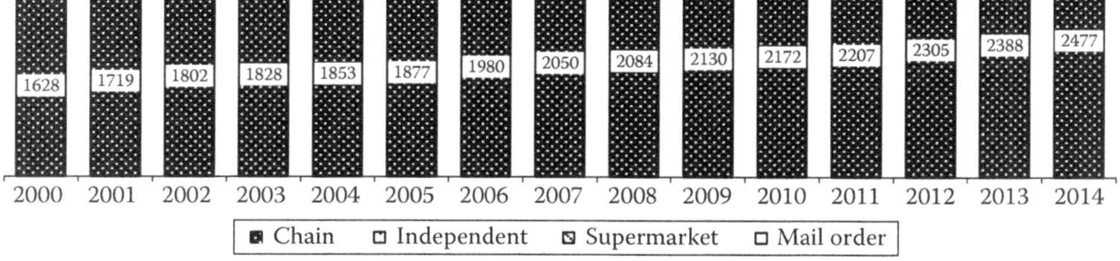

Figure 18.3 Trends in prescriptions dispensed in retail pharmacies, 2000–2014. (From 2000–2008 data from NACDS Industry Profile 2009, 2009–2014 data from IMS Health, Top Line Data, or IMS Health Institute Reports via their website, www.imshealth.com.)

* See, for example, the Independent Pharmacy Cooperative (IPC), a buying group with more than 4,000 independent pharmacy members (*IPC Newsletter*, "Advantage Advisor" June 2013, www.ipcrx.com).

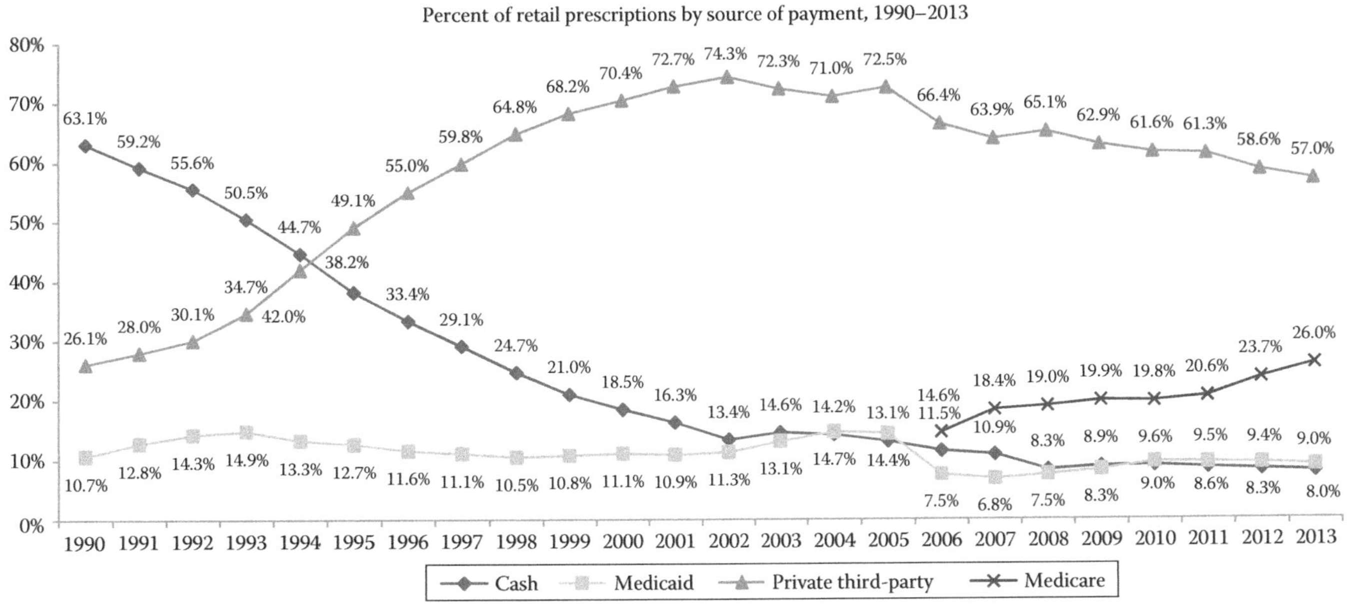

Figure 18.4 Prescriptions dispensed in community pharmacies by payor type, 1990–2013. ***Note*****: Data reflect prescription-bound products including insulins and excluding other products such as OTC. Medicare Part D reflects only retail pharmacy prescriptions. Mail order deliveries of Medicare Part D prescriptions are not distinguished from other commercial third parties. Medicaid includes both fee for service and managed Medicaid. (From dispensed prescriptions by payment type from various sources based on IMS Health National Prescription Audit; Sources include** ***NWDA Factbook*****, NACDS Chain Pharmacy Industry Profile, and IMS Health Institute Year in Review reports, accessed at the source websites over several years.)**

(See Figure 18.4.) In contrast, in 1993, half of all prescriptions were paid for out of pocket by consumers. Consequently, the market has been commoditized with pharmacies becoming *price takers* as drug coverage plans with an eye toward program cost control have established reimbursement rates and policies with a bulk purchasing, volume discount mentality, and set prices to reflect their purchasing power. This has generated interest and movement within pharmacies to diversify into patient care services beyond dispensing, such as immunizations and medication therapy management services, fitting nicely into initiatives and increased emphasis on interdisciplinary care models.

Other Peripheral Market Parties

An additional aspect of the market for pharmaceuticals that adds to its complexity is a variety of other organizations or entities that play a role or are interconnected with firms and transactions in the channel of distribution for pharmaceuticals. These other parties typically are not involved with the physical distribution of pharmaceuticals and thus never hold title to the drug products as they move through the channel of distribution, but they can affect the flow of goods or the actions of channel members who do take and transfer title to the goods.

Physicians are central to the sale and use of pharmaceuticals, especially prescription drugs. They write orders for prescriptions that provide consumers with access to prescription drugs. They also make recommendations for use of nonprescription drugs. However, physicians (or, generically, prescribers) neither use nor pay for the drugs that consumers use. The government, via the Food and Drug Administration (FDA), determines which drugs will be available and whether a prescription is required for obtaining the drug.*

The financial aspects of pharmaceuticals and consumer purchase of drugs bring a range of entities into the picture related to private insurance or public coverage programs. Private insurance coverage connects employers, insurers, and insurance-related organizations such as claims processors or pharmacy benefit managers (PBMs) to the market for pharmaceuticals. Consumers can purchase insurance coverage for prescription drugs or acquire coverage through their employment as a fringe benefit and part of their overall compensation (as an alternate form of income). Employers offer coverage to employees through selected insurers (which may take the form of traditional insurers, managed care organizations, etc.). Insurers or managed care organizations may utilize PBMs to process claims and administer the specialized drug coverage aspects of the benefit. PBMs often are connected to pharmaceutical manufacturers through rebate arrangements related to formularies and drug use policies.

Publicly funded coverage for drugs includes Medicare Part D and state Medicaid programs. Drug coverage under Medicare began in 2006 as plans offered by private insurers that met the general framework and coverage requirement parameters established for Medicare coverage. The specifics and how the benefit is operationalized are up to private firms that offer prescription drug plans for Medicare coverage. The Medicare plans have premiums and coverages that vary based on how the individual plans choose to meet or exceed the basic coverage requirements. In state Medicaid programs, there are broad programmatic aspects and parameters set by the federal government, and states individualize and detail specific policies and procedures for unilateral statewide implementation in pharmacies. State Medicaid programs may involve insurers and insurance-related organizations similar or parallel to the private insurance scenario, or they may

* Other countries have agencies similar to the FDA in the United States. which determine whether a drug requires a prescription or not for sales.

undertake some or all of the roles or functions themselves. Ultimately, citizens are connected to the publicly funded programs because their tax payments fund the coverage.

As noted earlier, an important trend related to these other parties involved in the market for pharmaceuticals has been an increase in the proportion of prescriptions that are covered by public or private insurance. This trend is shown in Figure 18.4. Increased coverage for prescriptions has had a large impact on community retail pharmacies, because the insurance programs establish reimbursement systems that set the prices they will pay for prescriptions. The reimbursement levels set by insurers have reflected a *large purchaser* philosophy, extracting volume discounts from pharmacies as sellers. Insurers make payment to pharmacies for dispensed prescriptions; thus, reimbursement cuts to pharmacies initially seemed the only way they could respond to increased costs. More recently, insurers have devised other methods in attempt to contain costs, some with intent to affect the "upstream" cost in the channel of distribution such as formularies and rebates, and thus, manufacturers also have been affected by policies related to coverage.

Private insurance coverage is dominant in the market for prescriptions, at least in aggregate, and although a single private third-party program might not represent as large a proportion of an individual pharmacy's business as Medicaid, the private third-party business combined greatly surpasses the public programs. The dominance of private insurance coverage plans for prescriptions carries over to the prominence in the policy arena. Early in the evolution of drug coverage programs (i.e., through the 1970s and early 1980s), the trend was for private plans to adopt public policies (e.g., the Federal Maximum Allowable Cost Program). More recently, private plans have led the way with changes, including seeking deeper discounted payment rates to pharmacies and implementing more aggressive drug use policies or restrictions. Since Part D is administered by private insurers offering prescription drug programs, the more recent and current trend of private plans leading the way with policies and programs likely will continue.

Unique Aspects and Characteristics of Pharmaceuticals

Compared to other consumer goods, there are a number of characteristics of pharmaceuticals and the market for pharmaceuticals that are unique and that can make policy interesting and/or challenging. Some of these characteristics have been mentioned or alluded to earlier in this chapter. Many of the aspects that make pharmaceuticals and the market for pharmaceuticals unique relate to the demand for pharmaceuticals, in terms of both the quantity of drugs demanded and the type of drugs demanded.

Derived/Directed Demand

The demand for pharmaceuticals is considered a derived demand, derived from the demand for health because pharmaceuticals can contribute to producing health. Health can be considered a consumption commodity and health inputs are demanded for health's intrinsic utility. Another view considers health as an investment commodity such that investing in health yields time for other activities, including simply more time or life years. The investment view toward health includes the notion that individuals begin their life with an initial stock of health and they allocate resources to health care in an attempt to maintain their health capital or return to or retain their initial health stock. Consequently, it is not pharmaceuticals they necessarily demand, but they consume pharmaceuticals for the role they can play in affecting their health.

The demand for prescription drugs also is directed by physicians and others authorized to prescribe. Consumers may have varying degrees of input to prescribing decisions, but they do not have the ability to access prescription drugs without a prescription order. Physicians are granted the authority to choose drugs and prescribe them for patients in their role as *learned intermediaries*, helping consumers with decisions too involved or complex for them to make on their own. Individual patients are considered to be lacking in knowledge or information about diagnoses, drugs, and drug effects to be able to make decisions about their use. An alternate to this traditional, quite paternalistic view of the role of physicians and prescribers is a perspective with more emphasis on self-care and based more on concordance as a way of thinking about medical decisions that includes the patient and their input as being important, useful, and even equal in the decision-making process. Concordance does not remove the prescriber from the process or alter the directed demand aspect of prescription drugs, but instead expands or accentuates the role that consumers, as patients, play in having input about choices. Broader access to information, such as via the Internet, also can contribute to an increased role of consumers in medical decisions.

With the demand for prescription drugs directed by physicians, physicians act as agents for patients in making decisions. A physician acting as a perfect agent for the patient will act in the patient's best interest when making decisions, presumably with full and accurate information about the patient's or principal's resources and preferences. However, the physician may not have full information and this asymmetry between the principal and agent can yield erroneous decisions or imperfect agency. Imperfect agency also can result if the prescriber has different motivations and violates their agency role, such as attempting to influence their revenues or preserve consumer resources for themselves by selecting lower-cost treatments. There could also be dual agency situations, where the physician may be required or requested to engage in cost control measures by an employer or managed care program to save resources either for themselves or for others; this can put the prescriber in a dilemma about which agent is sovereign. These agency phenomena are common in medical care and typically absent in other transactions where consumers select and purchase goods and services on their own.

Information Issues

There are several aspects or issues related to information that are a characteristic of pharmaceuticals and prescription drugs. Some of these information issues relate particularly to the directed demand and agency situations described earlier and to the idea of information asymmetry.

In their role as agents and directing demand for prescription drugs, prescribers have to rely on available information to base their decisions. Manufacturers or producers serve as primary information sources about products in practically all markets for goods and services, including pharmaceuticals, and promotion is the means by which information is communicated. This places manufacturers of pharmaceuticals in a position to control the amount and type of information available, and, as mentioned previously, this information role, promotion, is an important aspect of the business of pharmaceutical companies.

Studies have shown that industry-provided materials are one of the primary sources that physicians rely on for information about drugs, and that physicians often have not been knowledgeable about costs or relative costs of drugs. Sometimes it seems too much information is available; it can be difficult for prescribers to keep up with the volume of journal articles and other information available. In other cases, there may be not enough medical evidence about what is appropriate. Reliance on industry sources is understandable, because promotion is active dissemination of information; information about drugs typically is the most available and accessible via manufacturer's promotional efforts. Alternate sources of information about drug actions and effects, such as the FDA, do not take as much of an active, visible role as an information source. Journal articles or information from colleagues about drugs that prescribers access may be based on clinical studies about drugs in development. Often these authors or individuals sharing information are researchers involved in studies sponsored by the manufacturer ultimately interested in marketing the drugs; the information provided will be related to the objectives of the research, proving the worthiness of the drug for use. It could be argued that testing of new drugs and the benefits or outcomes from a drug focus on differentiating aspects of the drug that ultimately will stimulate market success. The information about benefits of new drugs from clinical studies is used, in part, to justify approval and indications for use; it also can provide the foundation for promotional campaigns.

Criticisms have been raised about a paucity of cost-effectiveness information or evidence of the comparative value of drugs. Such information is not required as part of the FDA approval process to market drugs, nor is it typically necessary or used to ensure coverage in public or private insurance plans. In clinical trials for safety and effectiveness, the tested drug may be compared with placebo only or typically with comparative agents in a narrow therapeutic subclass, restricted to agents within a basic molecular structure group. There has been increased interest and emphasis on the idea of comparative effectiveness of health-care treatments and interventions. Comparisons of drugs across a broader range of therapeutic class agents are becoming more available as such examinations or clinical studies are being performed and evidence-based evaluations of existing available data are occurring. However, there is no accepted compilation or "gold standard" evaluation mechanism for drugs. In addition, placebo effects and idiosyncratic reactions or effects of drugs in individual patients make it difficult to make broad sweeping generalizations about the "one best" drug in a therapeutic class or for a given condition.

There is tacit development of information asymmetry about drugs by what is emphasized in clinical trials and approvals (benefits), by which drugs are promoted and what is emphasized in promotions (new drugs and differentiating aspects/advantages), and by limited objective and comparative evaluations of drugs and their relative values. This puts pharmaceutical manufacturers (especially) and prescribers in critical positions relative to the role and use of information in decision making about drugs. Prescribers use industry sources for information, directly and indirectly; they also may have limited cost information and/or awareness. Promotion by pharmaceutical manufacturers generally occurs only for newer, patented drugs, generics are not promoted, and promotional efforts are reduced on brand name drugs as patent expiration nears. When prescribers choose the drugs to prescribe for consumers, the information asymmetry, skewed toward the manufacturer as the source of information, is actualized.

Demand Elasticity

Generally, the demand for pharmaceuticals (prescription drugs) is considered to be inelastic with respect to price; quantities demanded for drugs do not change to the same degree as any price changes. Several factors contribute to this price inelasticity. First, morbidity, or nonhealth, is the reason individuals seek to purchase drugs, consistent with the notion of derived demand described previously. Individuals generally have a high preference for health; thus, price becomes a secondary issue, and they will seek medical care in spite of the price of that care. Second, since demand is directed and physicians as prescribers seek first to do no harm (as part of their Hippocratic oath) and they neither consume nor pay for the drugs they select for patients, price is relegated to a more secondary role in selecting therapeutic agents. A lack of available comparative value information and a low awareness of drug cost levels by physicians also contribute to reduce the role that price plays in physician prescribing decisions. Patients cannot access prescription drugs without a physician's order; thus, consistent with their high preference for health (and risk aversion to avoid nonhealth), they follow through with purchasing prescribed medicines and minimize thoughts of substitute drugs or alternate courses of action. It even is possible to think that when elderly patients purchase prescribed drugs, they are purchasing "hope" for extending their life or improving the quality of their life. Rational thinking about purchases may be replaced with emotion, reducing the role of price in decision making. Priorities, perspectives, and preferences can change with age.

Insurance coverage also can contribute to price inelasticity of demand. Coverage shields individuals from the true cost of care, particularly if there is no cost sharing or the cost sharing is a copayment where the cost of resources used is not reflected in the out-of-pocket cost that consumers experience. The shielding of costs by insurance can lead to increased use or the use of more expensive drugs (moral hazard or insurance effects). The trends of increased insurance coverage for prescriptions over time and the prevalence of copayment cost sharing in drug coverage programs likely have exacerbated the price inelasticity of demand for pharmaceuticals.

Finally, a kind of *incrementalism* can be thought of as contributing to the demand and the inelasticity of demand for pharmaceuticals. New drugs are introduced to the market with potential benefits and advantages that represent incremental advances. The new drugs are tried and adopted to gain from the incremental advances; it is a part of the innovation–adoption process. However, unless there is a failure or major problems with trial of a new therapeutic agent, rarely, if ever, is a recursive thinking or analysis applied to question whether there really was a gain or whether returning to an older agent would yield outcomes similar (equivalent or even better, clinically) to the adopted innovation. Information asymmetry issues such as the type of information available about drugs and especially a lack of comparative value information contribute to this *incrementalism* adoption imperative, with limited or no consideration of price. Since newer drugs typically cost more than the older drugs they replace within a therapeutic category, this adoption process of newer, more costly drugs reflects a kind of demand inelasticity for new drugs.

"Patent Cliff"

When the patent expires for a drug, the brand name firm that discovered and originally marketed the drug faces what has been referred to as the "patent cliff." Sales fall precipitously for the brand name product as the generic manufacturers' products enter the market and are adopted.* Although the producers of any and all patented products face a time when their patent expires and other firms can produce and market the same item, there are unique aspects to this phenomenon for drug products. First, the effective patent life for a brand name drug product is shortened considerably by the long development time for clinical trials and approval that are required before a product can be marketed. Half or more of the 20-year patent life for a drug can be consumed by these developmental activities. In other industries, the time for product development leading to the market is shorter. Second, the cost of development is a high operational expense for the

* For an analysis of some recent patent expirations and this phenomenon, see Aitken et al.[5]

brand name manufacturer.* Generic firms have a much lower level of these developmental costs because they can rely on the innovator's clinical trials for approval; they need to only show that their generic version of the drug is bioequivalent and reaches blood levels within a tolerance window of the innovator's product. With lower-cost structure, a generic firm can be profitable with substantially lower prices and resulting revenues, and this is borne out in the relative prices of brand name and generic versions of a drug.† Finally, aside from the trademarked characteristics of the brand name product, such as the color, size, and shape of the tablet or capsule, the generic version of a drug product essentially is the same—the active ingredient, dosage strength, and dosage form are consistent—making the brand name and generic versions of a drug substitutable, homogenous products. This homogeneity coupled with substantial price difference has combined to create nearly complete market shifts from brand name to generic after a drug patent expires.

Of note, during the patent life of a product, that drug's manufacturer faces the same kind of competition faced by manufacturers in all markets, that of similar, but distinct products that serve as alternate offerings in the market. Like manufacturers of other products, brand name manufacturers promote the features and benefits of their products versus competing products. And like manufacturers of other products, their promotion can be substantial and intensive to attract buyers to one product over another.

Prescription Price Uniqueness

As retailers, community pharmacies are an anomaly when it comes to pricing. Although community pharmacies appropriately are considered merchandising entities, a dispensed prescription is thought of as a combination of a physical good and a service. Prescription pricing techniques used by pharmacists typically are different than customary retailing approaches where selling prices are established via markups with percentage relationships between the price and the retailer cost of acquiring the product. Instead, pharmacists incorporate service enterprise pricing methods, where fees are assessed for services rendered. Typically, the price of a prescription will somehow include a professional services dispensing fee amount added to the cost of the dispensed drug. As a result, the prices of prescriptions for different quantities of a given drug do not vary in straight-line extrapolation based on quantity; doubling (or halving) the quantity dispensed would not result in an exact doubling (or halving) the original quantity price, and costs per unit vary based on the number of units dispensed. The *mixed pricing* approach makes analyses of prescription price and expenditure trends more challenging in projecting or determining the implications of policy changes, especially if the policy impact would change the quantities of drugs dispensed in prescriptions. Also, pricing with a dispensing fee component contributes to decreased margins for community pharmacies when the average cost of the drug dispensed increases, driven by changes in the mix of drugs prescribed to include higher-cost products. In Figure 18.5, the breakdown of a prescription dollar revenue that goes to the manufacturer, wholesaler, and retail pharmacy is shown, and it reveals why community retail pharmacies have tended to be considered as low-margin enterprises.

* Although it is enticing to accept the notion that brand name manufacturers' prices are set to recoup discovery and development costs, the reality is that they rely on revenues from their current products for their current, ongoing research and development and operating costs. The current operational costs for development are important. Thus, a product discovered years before, with high costs invested to ready the product for market, generates sales revenues for similar or higher costs for the next wave of products to join the market and currently under development.

† Producers of products in other industries do not have such a differential in costs related to bring a product to market; thus a *knock-off* version of a competitor's product often will not have such a steep price discount.

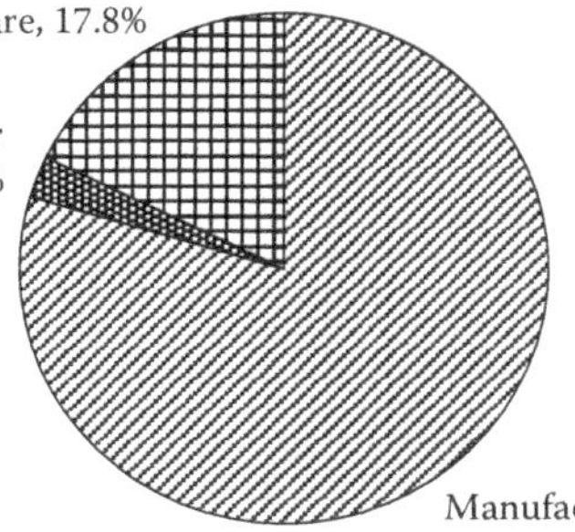

Figure 18.5 Breakdown of an average retail prescription price, 2013. (From *HDMA Factbook*, 2014–2015, analysis by NACDS Economics Department based on data from IMS Health.)

Most of an average prescription price is represented by the manufacturer's revenue for the drug and less than 20% of a prescription price is the pharmacy's margin. Over the last few decades, profit margins in pharmacies (particularly gross profit) have declined.[6]

Pricing and reimbursement for prescriptions in insurance coverage programs also have been handled differently for pharmacies and pharmacists than for other health-care providers. Perhaps because of the mixed good and service aspect of a dispensed prescription, pharmacy payment for prescriptions typically has had cost-based, formulaic approach to determining the reimbursement amount for prescriptions. Reimbursement for prescriptions has been specified as an amount for the ingredient cost of the drug dispensed plus a professional dispensing fee, with both components based on market cost referents (e.g., published pricing lists or market levels for drugs and cost of dispensing study results for fees) and the amounts thus determined set as an established price. For other health-care providers such as physicians, dentists, and hospitals, a discounted, charge-based reimbursement approach has been applied for determining payments. The starting point for reimbursement has been the charge that the provider has determined, although these charges may be bounded by market levels and/or discounted (often substantially) for determining reimbursement. As pharmacists begin to develop specific patient-based services separate from dispensing, a charge-based approach may be more relevant if those services will be covered events, and efforts to establish and implement such an approach will be needed.

One additional comment with regard to pricing and insurance is worth making. In light of recent changes in the prescription drug market where a high proportion of prescriptions dispensed are for low-cost generic drugs, some might question the role of insurance coverage for prescriptions. Insurable hazards typically are thought of as low-probability, high-risk events. Many prescriptions, as with much of primary care, do not have these characteristics. If recent market changes and conditions persist, fundamental thinking about some aspects of the market for pharmaceuticals may be prime for reconsideration.

Conclusion

Pharmaceuticals and the market for pharmaceuticals have characteristics that make them unique. The manufacturing sector of the market for pharmaceuticals includes brand name and generic manufacturers that are interrelated in important ways but also distinct and separate. Brand name and generic manufacturers may produce the same product, but with substantial difference in costs and consequent prices that are much larger than seen for other types of consumer products. This contributes to a very different distribution of products that are important in the market when considering the market on the basis of product sales revenue versus unit sales volume, as prescriptions dispensed. The demand for pharmaceuticals is not determined by the consumer, but directed by prescribers, and the demand is inelastic with respect to price. Consumer purchase of pharmaceuticals nearly always has a third-party, insurer-type entity that has a financial stake and influence in the transaction that is atypical in markets for other consumer goods. These unique aspects and characteristics contribute to make policy and policy making related to pharmaceuticals interesting and challenging.

References

1. Fulda TR and Wertheimer AI. *Handbook of Pharmaceutical Public Policy*, Pharmaceutical Products Press, New York, 2007.
2. Center for Healthcare Supply Chain Research. *85th Edition HDMA Factbook—The Facts, Figures, and Trends in Health Care (2014–2015)*, Center for Healthcare Supply Chain Research, Alexandria, VA. 2014. http://www.hcsupplychainresearch.org/projects/factbook.asp. Accessed December 6, 2015.
3. IMS Institute for Healthcare Informatics. Medicines use and spending shifts: A review of the use of medicines in the U.S. in 2014, April 2015, www.imshealth.com.
4. Bartholomew M. Top 200 drugs of 2012, *Pharmacy Times*, published online July 17, 2013, http://www.pharmacytimes.com/publications/issue/2013/july2013/top-200-drugs-of-2012. Accessed December 6, 2015; Vaczek D. Top 200 prescription drugs of 2004, *Pharmacy Times*, May 2005. http://www.pharmacytimes.com/publications/issue/2005/2005-05/2005-05-9582. Accessed December 6, 2015.
5. Aitken ML, Berndt ER, Bosworth B, Cockburn IM, Frank R, Kleinrock M, and Shapiro BT. The regulation of prescription drug competition and market responses: Patterns in prices and sales following loss of exclusivity, National Bureau of Economic Research Working Paper 19487, October 2013, http://www.nber.org/papers/w19487. Accessed December 6, 2015.
6. *Prescription Drug Trends: A Chartbook*, The Henry J. Kaiser Family Foundation, Menlo Park, CA, July 2000. http://kff.org/health-costs/report/prescription-drug-trends-a-chartbook/. Accessed December 6, 2015; Talsma J. Greater PBM leverage: Despite acute margin pressure, retail pharmacies fight to stay in the game, *Drug Topics*, 157(4) (April 2013), 24–32. http://drugtopics.modernmedicine.com/drug-topics/news/tags/mac/pbm-squeeze. Accessed December 6, 2015.

Chapter 19

Managed Care Pharmacy and Pharmacy Benefit Management

Perry Cohen and Mary Claire Wohletz

Contents

Introduction

Pharmacy benefit management (PBM) companies are a lynchpin in the managed care pharmacy industry. They are responsible for processing and paying prescription medication claims on behalf of their clients (managed care organizations, employers, and government agencies), while providing services including developing and maintaining drug formularies, contracting with community and mail service pharmacies, and negotiating discounts and rebates with pharmaceutical manufacturers. PBMs aggregate the purchasing power of millions of enrollees on behalf of their clients, obtaining lower prices for their prescription medications through maximizing efficiencies in the medication distribution system. PBMs also implement and manage clinical pharmacy programs, which are used to reduce inappropriate prescribing by physicians, reduce medication errors, and improve member compliance.

PBMs serve as intermediaries between their clients, pharmacies, and pharmaceutical manufactures. In this position, they decrease medication costs to their clients and their clients' members. Three of the key means used by PBMs to lower medication costs are (1) maintaining discounts with a network of pharmacies where members can obtain their prescription medications, (2) contracting with pharmaceutical manufacturers for rebates to reduce the net costs of brand name medications, and (3) managing the use and reimbursement for generic medications.

Before electronic claims processing, as developed and advanced by PBMs, patients and pharmacies submitted considerable paperwork to health plans and other third-party administrators for payment. The evolution of electronic claims processing for pharmacy claims introduced efficiencies in payment, where a pharmacy now knows within seconds whether a medication is covered for a patient, what they will be paid, and what the patient has to pay (out-of-pocket expenditures). They also know what the dispensing fee is, and if the medication is not covered, many times a point-of-service (POS) message alerts the pharmacy whether there is a preferred alternative or why the medication is not covered as submitted. Electronic claims processing has provided efficiencies for pharmacies and payers (e.g., employers and government agencies) that helped to develop the current PBM industry.

Electronic drug claims processing also allows for easily obtained data from prescription medication claims, with data fields including the patient name, doctor name, drug name, strength, quantity, days supply, data filled, and every other data field sent by the pharmacy to the PBM for processing. The data have become a powerful tool for drug use reviews (DURs) to encourage appropriate medication use and other analyses.

PBM Clients

A PBM's client base is typically managed care health plans, such as Blue Cross Blue Shield plans, employer groups, Medicare plans, and frequently managed Medicaid plans. In addition, PBMs, via their health plan clients, are creating drug formularies for the individual market. However, PBMs also consider that retail pharmacies are a customer, as is the member served.

PBM's clients will continue to look to their PBM for help in managing the cost trend of prescription medications, which is continually increasing. PBMs use a variety of tools to achieve low-cost trends for their clients. In addition, PBMs will forge new territory by helping their clients understand and manage medically administered medications (medications administered in a clinic setting and billed via medical coding). The challenge faced by PBM clients is how to deal with rising medication costs while ensuring access to those medications that improve therapeutic outcomes and health-related quality of life.

Overview of PBM Activities

While claims adjudication (prescription claims processing) is still a primary function of a PBM, there are many other clinical and operational areas that have been developed, refined, and enhanced by PBMs as a service to their clients, to improve medication use and patient care. PBMs have evolved into highly sophisticated, multifaceted, full-service organizations that offer their clients effective pricing strategies and economies of scale in order to improve operations performance and reduce administrative costs. A list of PBM core functions is included in Table 19.1.

PBM Clinical Activities

PBM's clinical activities are a vital part of a PBM's functions. By employing clinical experts, PBMs are in a position to help their clients understand the efficacy and safety of the new medications and the value a new medication has in comparison to other medications used for the same condition. Clinical expertise is also used in the discussions with pharmaceutical manufacturers, to ensure that each covered medication is fully appraised for safety and efficacy.

PBMs employ clinical writers, most often pharmacists, who are responsible for the review and analysis of all clinical written material produced by the PBM. PBM clinical writers use comparative effectiveness review methods. The written products created include new drug reviews, drug class (or therapeutic) reviews, and criteria-for-use guidelines. The clinical teams ensure policies, utilization protocols, and formularies reflect current best practices and offer valuable insight, expertise, and resources to encourage appropriate medication use.

P&T Committee

The pharmacy and therapeutics (P&T) committee is a committee made up of pharmacists and physicians, who serve both an advisory and educational role within the PBM, but they are not employees of the PBM. The P&T committee meets on a regular basis and provides governance for creating and managing the drug formulary and clinical policies. P&T committees, through the direction of the PBM clinical leadership, review all new medications for clinical and safety issues.

Table 19.1 Pharmacy Benefit Management Core Functions

Clinical services
• P&T committee activities
• New drug reviews
• Drug class reviews
• Drug formulary development
• Drug formulary maintenance
• Preferred drug lists
• Drug utilization management programs
• Clinical review call center
• Medication use management, including physician and patient interventions
• Disease management programs
Operational
• Prescription claims processing
• Benefits operations
• Member eligibility maintenance
• POS online edits
• Retail, mail order, and specialty pharmacy network management
• Pharmacy network audits, including identification of fraudulent pharmacies and fraudulent billing
• Drug analysis and reporting
• Drug rebate programs
• Contracting—pharmaceutical manufacturers
• Contracting—clients
• Client engagement/account management
• Pharmacy and member help desk operations
• Compliance

Often, large P&Ts will have specialist members (e.g., geriatrics, oncology, rheumatology) or subcommittees to help the larger group understand nuances of a drug or disease state.

Specific responsibilities of the P&T committee may include, but are not limited to, the following:[1]

1. To select new items for inclusion in the medication formulary based on an objective evaluation of therapeutic efficacy, safety
2. To advise PBM clinical teams about programs that ensure optimum standards for rational and cost-effective medication therapy
3. To assist in the development of educational programs
4. To assist in the development and periodic review of drug use evaluation (DUE) programs

Drug Formulary: Creation and Management

A drug formulary is a continually updated list of medications and related information, representing the clinical judgment of physicians, pharmacists, and other experts.[1] Drug formularies ensure that members have access to medications in all therapeutic areas, while helping to control costs. A drug formulary publication not just often includes the list of covered medications but also indicates the utilization management (UM) programs that are applied to each covered medication.

For example, a drug formulary would show the quantity limits (QL) allowed per prescription and identify which medications are subject to prior authorization (PA). A formulary may also include the applicable tier or preferred status of medications within a class.

Some drug formularies (i.e., formularies for Medicare or Medicaid beneficiaries) include coverage of certain over-the-counter (OTC) medications, typically those that have a therapeutic benefit such as pain relievers, fever reducers, and topical corticosteroids. One of the reasons that government plans cover OTC products is that they are less costly than a prescription alternative. However, other drug formularies, such as those for commercial clients, have no OTC coverage, and some exclude prescription medications that are also available OTC.

Medicare Part D plans limit a PBM's ability to manage some medication classes via formulary methods by deeming some medication classes a "protected class".[2] Drugs that are categorized to be in a protected class must be added to the Medicare plan sponsor's drug formulary. The protected medication classes defined by the Centers for Medicare & Medicaid Services (CMS) at the initiation of the Medicare Part D program are as follows:

- Antidepressants
- Antipsychotics
- Anticonvulsants
- Antiretrovirals used for the treatment of HIV and AIDS
- Antineoplastics used for the treatment of cancers
- Immunosuppressants used to prevent the rejection of organ transplants

Pharmacy Benefit Design: Drug Formulary Tiers

Pharmacy benefit design, including deductibles and co-payment tiers, is overlaid on a drug formulary to encourage the use of clinically appropriate but lower cost medication choices. Medications are assigned to a tier based on use, cost, and clinical effectiveness. The tiers direct co-pay structure and member responsibility where the lowest tier is associated with the lowest co-payment and the highest tier with the highest co-payment. Common categories of tiers (lowest to highest) are generics, preferred brands, nonpreferred brands, and specialty (Table 19.2).

Another aspect of pharmacy benefit design includes decisions about whether certain medication classes are excluded from coverage. For example, most Medicaid plans have state laws that dictate certain excluded therapeutic categories, such as medications that promote hair growth, medications for weight loss, and medications to enhance fertility.

Member Cost Sharing

Member cost sharing via co-payments and coinsurance is a tool that has been enhanced in recent years as the cost of medications continues to rise. One of the purposes of member cost sharing is

Table 19.2 Typical Formulary Tiers

Tier 1 usually includes generic medications.
Tier 2 usually includes preferred brand name medications.
Tier 3 usually includes nonpreferred brand name medications.
Tier 4 usually includes specialty medications (3-tier programs do not have a unique tier for specialty medications).

to encourage the use of a lower cost medication within a therapeutic category. Some plans employ a pharmacy benefit design that allows members to request a PA or formulary exception to the high co-payment for the approved (nonpreferred) medication so that the lower member cost share would apply.

Utilization Management Tools

UM helps improve safety and lowers costs of pharmaceutical medications and diabetic supplies. UM encompasses three main areas: PA, QL, and step therapy.

Prior Authorization

Prior authorization (referred to as "coverage determination," under Medicare Part D) is a process used by PBMs on behalf of their clients to ensure that a medication paid for by the client is being used for a clinically appropriate reason, at a clinically appropriate dose, without exposing the patient to avoidable risk. Often, the medications that are subject to PA are those with a potential for misuse or inappropriate use. PA procedures and requirements for coverage are based on clinical need and therapeutic rationale, and the PA approval for use criteria follow FDA-approved indications and also take published evidence and clinical guidelines into consideration. The PA process gives the prescriber the opportunity to justify the therapeutic basis for the prescribed medication.[3]

Guidelines and administrative policies for PA are developed by pharmacists and other qualified health professionals. Each PBM develops guidelines and coverage criteria that are clinically appropriate. Well-designed PA programs consider the workflow impact on health-care system users and minimize inconvenience for patients and providers.[3] Requiring PA in a medication benefit can avoid inappropriate medication use and promote the use of evidence-based medication therapy encouraging efficient and effective use of health-care resources.[3]

Quantity Limits

Quantity limits is a term used to describe the amount of medication (e.g., number of tablets) allowed for payment over a period of time (e.g., 30 days).QLs are in place to encourage appropriate medication use and contain medication costs. QLs are based on the product's approved dose and use, as well as to limit overpayment due to errors when submitting claims (e.g., submitting a claim for 300 tablets instead of 30). For example, Medication Z, with a half-life of 72 h, is approved for use as one tablet per day and is indicated for a chronic condition. The QL would be 30 tablets for 30-day supply. If the prescriber believes that his or her patient's condition requires an amount that exceeds the set QL, he or she may submit an exception request to the PBM.

Step Therapy

A step therapy program mandates the use of a clinically recognized first-line medication before the approval of a more complex and often more expensive medication. Step therapy requirements ensure that an established and cost-effective therapy is used prior to progressing to other therapies. If the required therapeutic benefit is not achieved by the use of the first-line medication, the prescriber may request the use of a second-line medication.

Electronic Claims "Look Back": Automatic Prior Authorization/Step Therapy

Claims processing has reached a level of sophistication that allows pharmacy-submitted claims to be electronically reviewed at the point-of-sale for the patient's previous prescription medication use. PBM claims systems can assess a patient's medication use history against the submitted claim to verify whether the patient meets the criteria for use. For example, if Medication A has similar efficacy to Medication B for the same condition, but costs significantly more, a PBM may place step therapy on Medication A so that the patient has to have tried Medication B or have a contra-indication to use it. If a patient has tried Medication B within the past 12 months, the electronic claims look back will allow payment for Medication A, with no need for the pharmacy to call for a PA or other override. This would also hold true if the patient had been taking Medication A and continued to have prescriptions filled for Medication A. While this sophisticated "look-back logic" is often used for step therapy rules, it can be used for other types of PA rules as well.

Disease Management Programs

Disease management programs that are administered by PBMs have evolved over the past 20 years. Disease management programs are based on a retrospective analysis of a member's medication claims and typically make assumptions about a member's medical status based on the list of medications that have been filled. A key example of a PBM disease management program is an asthma program where members who use rescue inhalers at a high frequency are targeted for educational interventions, as are their doctors, about using asthma controller medications. The main goals of PBM-based disease management programs are to provide physicians with drug claims history of their patients, to provide patient education about the value of medication therapy for disease management, and to encourage patients to be adherent to their medication regimen. The main methods of communication are mailed campaigns and telephone-based communication, or a combination of these.

Cost Management Tools

Prior to implementation of the aggressive cost management tools by PBMs, the costs for traditional drugs were increasing at double-digit rates year after year. To help clients find the lowest net cost within a therapeutic area, while minimizing member disruption, PBMs must understand the market dynamics of how prescription medications are priced and purchased, as well as understand each medication's competitive market to manage the cost of medications and pass savings on to their clients.

MAC Program for Generic Medications

PBMs use several programs to promote the use of generic medications when the generic offers a cost savings for the plan. One of the most successful programs is the MAC—or maximum allowable cost—program. A MAC is a maximum amount that will be paid to a pharmacy for a generically available, multiple source, medication name, strength, and dose form (e.g., one tablet of zolpidem 10 mg). When an ingredient is formulated in both tablets and capsules, a MAC should be specific to the dose formulation.

When a pharmacy submits claims to a PBM, the claim is submitted with a base price, usually an average wholesale price (AWP), which is a list price of the medication. The PBM's adjudication system is most often programmed to read the claim and adjust the paid amount to the lesser of the contracted retail rate (e.g., a percentage of AWP), the submitted amount, or the MAC. Because there is no relationship between the AWP of a generic and the purchase price to the pharmacy, it is important for the PBM to implement MACs on generic drugs to balance reimbursement to a level that is closer to the wholesale purchase price, while still allowing profit on the claim. For example, a tablet of fluoxetine 20 mg may cost the pharmacy $(USD)0.10, but the AWP on the same tablet is $(USD)3.50. Setting a MAC at $(USD)0.30 allows profitability on the claim, but without a MAC, every fluoxetine 20 mg tablet pays with a profit of $(USD)3.40 per tablet multiplied by a 30-day supply.

MAC price lists are established by PBMs for private sector clients and by many states for their Medicaid and other state-funded programs. Private sector MACs are usually considered confidential, whereas state-based MAC lists can often be found online. No standardized definition for MAC exists, but a variety of formulae, including wholesale acquisition cost–based and federal upper limit–based approaches, as well as market surveys targeting distributors and pharmacies are used to set MACs.[4]

Pharmaceutical Manufacturer Contracting and Rebating

Even though only about 10%–15% of prescriptions are filled with brand name drugs, and 80%–85% with generics, brand name drugs make up the largest percentage of prescription drug costs.[5] Therefore, it is important for PBMs to get discounts from pharmaceutical manufacturers. PBMs have been instrumental in finding the lowest net cost medication in a therapeutic class, and for brand name medications, this involves negotiating with pharmaceutical manufacturers for rebates.

A rebate is an amount paid by the pharmaceutical manufacturer after a claim has been paid for the contracted medication. PBMs offer data collection and invoicing services to their clients. It is of utmost importance that PBMs are transparent to their clients about the net cost of medications after rebates, and that clinical decisions are the overriding policies for medication use and formulary placement. PBMs and plans have been fined for driving utilization to medications that have an overall higher cost to their clients but offer the PBM rebate income.

Rebates to PBMs are negotiated in a variety of ways. Some pharmaceutical manufacturers offer rebates on a per unit (e.g., tablet) basis, and some contracts are structured to pay a higher level of rebate depending on market share. Rebates may be impacted by the UM criteria placed on the medication or how many medications share preferred status (i.e., one of one preferred medication, one of two preferred medications, or one of three preferred medications in a therapeutic class).

In a transparent PBM model, the PBM develops a process that allows pharmaceutical manufacturers to compete with other manufacturers of similar medications on best net price for their product. In this model, manufacturers submit bids for their product for the preferred placement. By understanding the best net cost scenario for each product, the health plan can make cost-informed decisions and understand the financial impact of these decisions. Understanding the net cost of the medication is critical in maintaining a manageable medication trend.

Medicaid Rebates

Most states offer a pharmacy benefit through their Medicaid program, which is a government program jointly funded by federal and state governments and managed by the individual states.

A state may contract with a managed care plan (i.e., managed Medicaid) for health-care services for the Medicaid member or pay for health-care services directly with state funds, (i.e., fee for service). Many states use a combination of managed Medicaid and fee-for-service methods.

For a drug to be considered covered on a state's Medicaid drug plan, the pharmaceutical manufacturer must, as mandated by federal law, enter into, and have in effect, a national rebate agreement with the secretary of the Department of Health and Human Services. The Medicaid Drug Rebate Program is a partnership between CMS, state Medicaid agencies, and participating pharmaceutical manufacturers.

A simplified explanation of the fee-for-service Medicaid prescription medication plan is that if a medication is made by a manufacturer that rebates with the federal government, the medication is covered by Medicaid (i.e., "on formulary"). Conversely, if a manufacturer does not participate in the federal rebate program, then their medication cannot be covered by a Medicaid plan. It is important to remember that even if a medication has "covered" status, UM criteria, such as PA and QL, can still be applied.

On a quarterly basis, manufacturers are responsible for paying rebates on medications purchased on behalf of Medicaid patients. The collected rebates are then shared between the states and the federal government to offset the overall cost of prescription medications under the Medicaid program. With the passage of the Affordable Care Act 2010, the Medicaid rebate is also applied to medications purchased on behalf of the managed Medicaid population (i.e., those lives in managed care plans). In addition to expanding the population whose prescription medication use is eligible for Medicaid rebates, the 2010 federal legislation also increased the base level percentage, for which a larger share is paid to the federal government.

Pharmaceutical manufacturers are also required to enter into agreements with two other Federal programs in order to have their medications covered under Medicaid pharmacy programs: the 340B medication pricing program administered by the Health Resources and Services Administration and a master agreement with the secretary of Veterans Affairs (VA) for the federal supply schedule, which allows the VA to purchase medications at even lower prices than Medicaid.[6]

Medicaid Unit Rebate Amount Calculation

The CMS Medicaid drug rebate system calculates the unit rebate amount for each product using the pharmaceutical manufacturer's sold costs.[6] The specific methodology used is determined by law and depends upon whether a medication is classified as an innovator single source, a line extension, a noninnovator multiple source, a clotting factor medication, or an exclusively pediatric medication. CMS provides this URA information to states as a courtesy; however, pharmaceutical manufacturers remain responsible for correctly calculating the URA for their covered outpatient medications.[6] The amount of rebate due for each unit of medication is based on statutory formulas as shown in Table 19.3. Because of consumer price index (CPI) penalties, the federal rebate increases over time as price increases are applied to the branded medication. Frequently the net cost of a branded medication in the Medicaid environment is lower than its generic equivalent when the first generic enters the market.

Specialty Pharmacy

Specialty pharmacy is a distinct business arm of pharmacy. While there is no industry definition of a specialty medication, it is generally accepted that specialty medications are indicated for a limited population, require special handling, and are high cost. Many specialty medications are

Table 19.3 Unit Rebate Amount for Medicaid Prescription Medication Claims

Innovator (branded) medications	The greater of 23.1% of the average manufacturer price (AMP) per unit or the difference between the AMP and the best price per unit and adjusted by the consumer price index-urban (CPI-U) based on launch date and current quarter AMP.
	The limit on the total rebate amount for each innovator medication is 100% of AMP.
Blood-clotting factors	The greater of 17.1% of the AMP per unit or the difference between the AMP and the best price per unit and adjusted by the CPI-U based on launch date and current quarter AMP.
Medications approved by FDA exclusively for pediatric indications	The greater of 17.1% of the AMP per unit or the difference between the AMP and the best price per unit and adjusted by the CPI-U based on launch date and current quarter AMP.
Line extensions	For a medication that is a new formulation (line extension) of a brand name medication that is an oral solid dosage form, the rebate is the amount computed under Section 1927 of the Act or, if greater, the product of the following: • The AMP for the line extension medication. • The highest additional rebate for any strength of the original brand name medication. • The total number of units of each dosage form and strength of the line extension medication (Section 1206 of HCERA, which replaced Section 1927[c][2][C] as added by Section 2501[d] of PPACA).
Noninnovator (generic) medications	13% of the AMP per unit.

Source: Adopted from Medicaid.gov. Medicaid Drug Rebate Program. Accessed at http://www.medicaid.gov/medicaid-chip-program-information/by-topics/benefits/prescription-drugs/medicaid-drug-rebate-program.html. Last updated October 13, 2015. Last accessed December 6, 2015.

biologics that are delivered via an injection or an infusion and are used to treat chronic, complex diseases.[7] Some of the common diseases treated by specialty medications are multiple sclerosis, rheumatoid arthritis, growth deficiency, and many types of cancer. Specialty medications require extensive patient education to teach self-administration, to limit administration adverse events (e.g., injection site reactions), and to minimize toxic adverse events (e.g., body rash, hand and foot syndrome, high blood pressure).

Whereas traditional medication spending increases are projected to be 2%–6% per year, specialty medication trend is projected to be 17%–19% per year.[8] Health plans are verifiably concerned about the cost impact of specialty medications being introduced to the market. Specialty medications are now routinely launched at monthly costs of $(USD)7,000 or $(USD)10,000, or higher. Medications for orphan disease are even more expensive. Furthermore, manufacturers continued to attain expanded FDA-approved indications, increasing overall use, which increases a payer's financial risk.

Specialty medications are used by about 1% of any population but account for approximately 30% of total medication expenditures.[7] While some of the new specialty medications offer advancements in therapy, it is important to note that the clinical efficacy of many of the specialty medications is far from 100%. Yet, payers are continually being asked to pay for these new medications. This is why a thorough clinical evaluation and UM tools are employed to ensure appropriate use.

Because of the increased cost pressures, in addition to the clinical complexity of specialty medications, most health plans are requiring more sophisticated approaches to managing specialty pharmacy use and spend. Specialty pharmacy is an area that PBMs have become more adept at managing, but it will continue to require dedicated resources to achieve continued success. PBMs apply traditional UM criteria (PA for FDA-approved indication and QL) to specialty medications but have found that even more robust tools are needed to ensure appropriate use, encourage patient adherence while limiting stockpiling, and reduce waste. In some drug classes, where there is a growing number of therapeutically equivalent products, and thus increased market competition, PBMs are engaging the pharmaceutical manufacturers to rebate for the preferred placement. Usually, the preferred placement is defined within step therapy protocols.

Some PBMs own their own specialty pharmacy, which often becomes the primary specialty pharmacy in a health plan's pharmacy network. A limited specialty pharmacy network offers the PBM's clients a larger discount than retail pharmacy channels of dispensing. In addition, specialty pharmacies are patient- and service-centric with resources for patient education and refill reminder for patient outreach. Patients with specialty diseases often require a higher level of clinical service than can be offered by high-volume retail pharmacies. Thus, specialty pharmacies often have 24 h on-call services and have ongoing patient touch points for check-in about clinical issues and data collection about effectiveness or side effects. Specialty pharmacies also have shipping and tracking expertise, billing expertise, and knowledgeable staff to provide the appropriate supplies.

Pharmacy Networks

PBMs develop and manage pharmacy networks for their clients. The networks offer clients cost savings by governing costs that are charged by pharmacies. While retail pharmacies generally protest the PBM-contracted reimbursement rates and dispensing fees, without the contracted oversight of the PBM, PBM clients and their members are subject to paying for their prescription medications at retail rates or list prices of medications as charged by the pharmacy. Most patients are not aware of the tremendous markup built into the list prices of medications. Thus, the PBM's knowledge about how medications are priced and sold brings value to their clients and their client's members.

Because of the increased cost pressures from areas, such as medication price increases, and the increased use of high-cost specialty medications, clients have been asking about other ways to reduce overall costs. One method is to offer a limited pharmacy network. The pharmacies that are contracted trade patient volume for higher dispensing fees because patients tend to purchase OTC or sundry items while in the store.

Mail Order/Home Delivery

Most PBMs own a mail order pharmacy or contract to provide mail order service for their client's membership. Mail order pharmacy, also called home delivery, offers PBM clients' cost savings and their members the convenience of home delivery (Table 19.4). Their purpose is to provide refills

Table 19.4 Advantages of Mail Order/Home Delivery

• Lowest-cost channel
• High-volume purchasing power
• High level of accuracy
• Home delivery convenience
• Alignment to get all medications in one shipment
• Adherence programs

for maintenance prescriptions, and many plans design the benefit with a 90-day supply. In order to encourage the use of mail order services, some plans charge only two 30-day co-payments instead of three co-payments for the 90-day (3 months) supply. Some medications are not available through the mail order benefit, such as those used for acute purposes (e.g., antibiotics), and these are dispensed through retail channels.

Mail order/home delivery pharmacies offer their members similar clinical services as offered by retail sites and also have adherence/compliance programs. While auto filling is not allowed by Medicare rules, members receive refill reminder mailings and phone calls. Medicare Part D members, and many who are covered by state Medicaid plans, are not required to use mail order services. Some commercial insurers mandate the use of mail order pharmacy for their members for all medications that are used chronically.

Owners of retail pharmacies, including America's largest chain stores, have raised concerns about the impact on business due to health plans' mandates that their members use mail order pharmacies.[9,10] Yet, they have found ways to compete with mail order, and with each other, such as by implementing $(USD)4.00 generic drug lists and loyalty programs.

Specialty Pharmacy Networks

An area where PBMs have had more success in limiting the number of pharmacies that can fill specialty medications is in the specialty pharmacy arena. Using a specialty pharmacy network, which is typically limited to one or two specialty pharmacies, offers plans a larger discount than retail rates. In addition, a specialty pharmacy should have sophisticated patient education programs that help the patient self-administer their medication as well as manage side effects to prevent patient self-discontinuation and monitor the effectiveness of the therapy.

Limited distribution drugs (LDD) is a term used to describe medications made by the manufacturers that have chosen to limit the number of pharmacies that are allowed to dispense their drug. This is often because the medication is used in a small population, and the manufacturer uses a limited dispensing network to manage inventory and production. Thus, a PBM must have contracts with all of the pharmacies that have LDD-dispensing arrangements with manufacturers.

Currently, Medicare Part D plans do not allow a PBM to offer a closed specialty pharmacy network, but, there are some indications that CMS may be considering allowing Medicare D plans to use a preferred specialty pharmacy network, which may be preferred but not closed, in order to reduce costs.

Data and Data Analysis

Because of the core function of claims adjudication, PBMs must have the capabilities to read and price almost all claims that are sent for payment. In order to accommodate this function, PBMs purchase drug data from drug data warehouse firms. These companies house and manage all of the fields of old and new drug data, which are too numerous to name but include such pertinent fields as each drug's individual national drug code, brand and generic name, strength, formulation, unit of use, manufacturer's name, date introduced to the market, pricing, price increases, and date of price increase. New drug data are introduced daily, but a PBM may collate the data for weekly review.

PBMs have an incredibly powerful tool in the ownership of pharmacy claims data. PBMs use the data for clinical and cost analyses, which are important to identify areas for new clinical programs as well as identify cost savings opportunities. PBMs have a responsibility to their clients to provide reporting about medication use and cost regularly (e.g., monthly or quarterly basis) as well as patterns and trends over time. PBMs also provide aggregate data to help their clients understand the clinical and financial impacts of their formulary and UM benefits.

Drug Use Evaluation

Drug use evaluation, also referred to as drug use review, is a quality improvement activity that uses an ongoing cyclical process to improve quality use of medicines or decrease overall prescription medication costs. It involves monitoring and reviewing medication use, evaluating and comparing it with the best practice guidelines, and using multifaceted interventions to improve medication use and overall patient care.

DUE programs play a key role in helping managed health-care systems understand, interpret, and improve the prescribing, administration, and use of medications. DUE programs are valuable because the results are used to foster more efficient use of scarce health-care resources. Pharmacists play a key role in this process because of their expertise in the appropriate and inappropriate use and costs of medications. DUE also allows a PBM the opportunity to identify trends in prescribing within groups of patients such as those with asthma, diabetes, or high blood pressure. Pharmacists, in collaboration with physicians and other members of the health-care team, initiate action to improve medication therapy for both individual patients and covered populations.[11]

DUE may be categorized as prospective and retrospective. Prospective DUE is based on clinical edits that are prospectively programmed to flag claims as the medication is being dispensed. Typical criteria reviewed in prospective studies include the following:

- Dose
- Duration of therapy
- Therapeutic duplication
- Quantity dispensed
- Contraindications
- Drug–drug interactions

Retrospective DUE programs analyze claims data over a defined time set (e.g., previous 3 months) to find clinical opportunities. Some of the issues commonly addressed by retrospective DUE include

- Overutilization and underutilization
- Cost management opportunities
- Therapeutic duplication
- Drug–disease contraindications

- Drug–drug interactions
- Incorrect dosage
- Inappropriate extended treatment
- Identification of nonadherence
- Clinical abuse/misuse

Some PBMs are also able to obtain medical data via their health plan clients and are developing sophisticated methods to integrate medical and pharmacy claims that are proving to be beneficial for member health while offering cost savings to the plan. The activities of PBMs to continue development of such programs will enhance care for patients, particularly fractured care when patients are being treated by multiple physicians or are using multiple pharmacies.

PMPM Calculation

To normalize* the amount of drug spent over different populations, with different medication needs and usage patterns, PBMs use a per member per month (PMPM) comparison, which is a cost averaged over the health plan's total population. The PMPM is used for both cost outlays and cost savings calculations, for example, cost savings of implementing a UM program. The PMPM calculation can be adjusted to measure the cost PMPM or the number of medications used PMPM. It can further be broken into brand and generic medication use.

Medicare Part D

Medicare Part D is a federally funded outpatient prescription medication benefit under the Medicare program, which is closely overseen and managed by CMS. Private health insurers enter into contracts with Medicare to administer this prescription medication benefit and are referred to as Part D sponsors. To provide pharmaceutical coverage, the Part D sponsors often enter into contractual relationships with PBMs to help administer the medication benefit.

Medicare Part D sponsor plans and their PMBs are subject to strict oversight by CMS to ensure that they are meeting all the statutory and regulatory requirements of Medicare Part D programs.[11] CMS has close oversight of all Medicare Part D formularies and formulary rules, such as rules about the number of drugs that need to be covered per therapeutic class, defining a protected class, and covering all drugs in protected classes.[2]

Medicare Part D and Star Ratings

The U.S. health-care system is moving from fee-for-service-based purchasing toward value-based purchasing. The value is the balance of quality and cost; thus to optimize value, a plan must improve quality while reducing costs. Yet defining and measuring quality uniformly is one of the major challenges facing all parties. For now, CMS has defined it for plan sponsors and has put it in terms of star ratings.

---

* *Normalize*: To develop a comparable measure.

The five-star rating system is a quality and performance scoring method used for certain pharmacy benefit plans offered to Medicare beneficiaries. It is used to provide a scored assessment of individual quality components as well as aggregate overall performance.

Quality-based payments and quality bonus payments are offered by CMS as an incentive to encourage plan sponsors and are awarded to plans achieving or exceeding a star rating of four or five.[12,13] A higher star rating also improves plans' competitive advantage in the marketplace.

PBMs are engaged to help their clients meet a higher star rating. Since the pharmacy benefit is the primary objective of Medicare Part D plans, attention has shifted to the pharmacy department to deliver strategies to improve sponsor plans' star ratings. The primary data that PBMs can provide revolve around medication utilization and adherence. A PBM can also marry medication and medical claims data if a health plan has capabilities to share that data. PBMs provide prescription-level claims information that offers both a qualitative and quantitative view of patient and physician activity.

An integrated approach to quality requires that PBMs have a team knowledgeable about the star rating system, its quality measures, and processes. PBMs are helping their Part D clients meet star ratings by developing star-based formularies and also instituting policies that help plans stay compliant with stars measures.

The Future of PBMs

The current health-insurance system has evolved over time, since the 1970s. At that time, Americans received only the medical benefit, which covered office visits and hospitalizations. Drugs administered in the hospital or physician's office were covered; however, outpatient prescription drugs usually were not covered by insurance.

By 1990, it became clear that having a medical benefit alone was in adequate. The growth and success of health-insurance products that managed the cost and improved the quality of care prompted employers to want similar programs to manage the cost of providing a prescription drug benefit. During the 1990s, prescription drugs were developed for chronic diseases affecting large populations of patients (for example, asthma, diabetes, and hypertension). In addition, there was a surge of drug discovery and new chemical entities to treat chronic diseases, as well as an increase in competition among pharmaceutical manufacturers for these new markets.

The pharmacy benefit thus emerged. Its purpose was to manage outpatient prescription drugs for populations of people. Forward-thinking systems that took advantage of data standards for prescription drugs were more sophisticated than the old systems used in the medical benefit. Technology became the backbone of the newly emerging PBM operations. Ultimately, PBM operations developed into data-mining systems that used advanced processing providing evidence of what was really happening in healthcare.

Today, the country's needs are no longer being fully met with a combination of the medical and pharmacy benefits. Technology and the need to increase patients' involvement in their own healthcare will necessitate new models and unique approaches. Medical benefits and pharmacy benefits are addressing chronic diseases for large patient populations, but now, a third area is appearing: specialty health benefits.

Experts indicate that the 1% of patients who will use specialty drugs will account for up to 30% of medically administered drugs and specialty drug costs.[8] Because spending on specialty drugs is growing rapidly—much faster than drug spending in general—a coverage category specifically for specialty health benefits is needed. This piece of the benefit set would include specialty drugs, certain diagnostic tests, and genetic profile testing but would be managed with PA criteria and co-payments.[14]

Providers will need advanced electronic tools, including decision support at the point of care to provide emerging specialty health-care services. The most reasonable approach will be to build on systems developed in the medical and pharmacy benefit models. The implications for healthcare will be the following: new cost-sharing mechanisms; technology infrastructures that integrate, transfer, and share data; distribution systems that are seamless to patients; expanded disease management programs; and data collection and analysis will be even more important because the results of specialty service activities will demonstrate outcomes and help clinicians make reasonable decisions. As new health-care technology enters the marketplace, specialty health benefits will grow to provide access to these new services.

Several other factors will impact PBMs over the next 5–10 years, such as drug-mix changes driven by increased generic competition and increased specialty drugs. PBM's evolution as successful pharmacy benefit managers will involve creative clinical and cost solutions for their clients. PBMs will have to consider incorporating ways to involve and educate the consumer in pharmacy decision making. In addition, PBMs that have methods to integrate medical and claims data, and that are successful in helping their plans manage the medically administered drugs, will have a competitive advantage over PBMs that do not have this capability. PBMs will have continued opportunities to encourage use of the least costly pharmacy channel.

Conclusion

PBMs are a vital part of the American health-care system. By understanding the dynamics of pharmaceutical drug delivery, PBMs bring value to their clients and to the American health-care system. PBMs develop, implement, and continually improve clinical, operational, and financial tools that help to ensure the right patient receives the right drug while improving efficiencies and reducing waste in the delivery of prescription medications to patients. Yet, PBMs will be pushed to continue to enhance clinical service offerings to help their clients manage specialty drug cost trends as well as manage medically infused drugs. The future of PBM will likely include management of a third benefit set, outside of pharmacy and medical benefits. A specialty pharmacy benefit will be modeled on the claims adjudication platforms of traditional drug adjudication but will also include capability to manage and pay for genetic testing. The PBM business model must continue to evolve, and PBMs will have to seek new ways to achieve competitive differentiation and improving delivery of pharmacy benefits.

References

1. American Society of Health-System Pharmacists. ASHP guidelines on the pharmacy and therapeutics committee and the formulary system. *Am J Health-Syst Pharm.* 2008; 65:1272–1283. Accessed at http://www.ashp.org/DocLibrary/BestPractices/FormGdlPTCommFormSyst.pdf. Accessed December 6, 2015.
2. Medicare prescription drug benefit manual chapter 6—Part D drugs and formulary requirements. Accessed at http://www.cms.gov/Medicare/Prescription-Drug-Coverage/PrescriptionDrugCovContra/Downloads/Chapter6.pdf. Last updated November 6, 2015. Last accessed December 6, 2015.

3. Academy of Managed Care Pharmacy (AMCP). 2012. Concepts in managed care pharmacy prior authorization. What is prior authorization and why is it an essential managed care tool? Accessed at http://www.amcp.org/prior_authorization/. Accessed December 6, 2015.
4. Academy of Managed Care Pharmacy. AMCP guide to pharmaceutical payment methods, update (Version 2.0). *J Manage Care Pharm.* August 2009; 15(6) (Suppl):S1–S57. Accessed at http://www.amcp.org/WorkArea/DownloadAsset.aspx?id=9854. Accessed December 6, 2015.
5. IMS Institute for Healthcare Informatics. 2012. The use of medicines in the united states: Review of 2011. Revised 053012. Accessed at: http://www.environmentalhealthnews.org/ehs/news/2013/pdf-links/IHII_Medicines_in_U.S_Report_2011-1.pdf. Accessed December 6, 2015.
6. Medicaid.gov. 2015. Medicaid Drug Rebate Program. https://www.medicaid.gov/Medicaid-CHIP-Program-Information/By-Topics/Benefits/Prescription-Drugs/Medicaid-Drug-Rebate-Program.html. Accessed January 12, 2016.
7. Stettin G. (May 21, 2013). Specialty medication spending to jump 67% by 2015. Accessed at http://lab.express-scripts.com/insights/specialty-medications/specialty-drug-spending-to-jump-67-percent-by-2015. Accessed December 6, 2015.
8. Prime Therapeutics. (2013). Specialty drug trend insights. Accessed at https://www.primetherapeutics.com/PDF/specialtydtr2013/index.html.
9. Dearment A. (September 8, 2011). Pennsylvania legislation would ban mandatory mail order. Accessed at http://www.drugstorenews.com/article/pennsylvania-legislation-would-restrict-mail-order-pharmacy. Accessed December 6, 2015.
10. New York Senate Bill S3510B-2011. 2012. Prohibits health insurers from requiring that the insured purchase prescribed drugs from mail order pharmacy. Accessed at http://www.nysenate.gov/legislation/bills/2011/s3510b. Accessed December 6, 2015.
11. Academy of Managed Care Pharmacy (AMCP). 2009. Concepts in managed care pharmacy. Drug use review. Accessed at http://www.amcp.org/WorkArea/DownloadAsset.aspx?id=9296. Accessed December 6, 2015.
12. Lee H. CMS oversight. *J Manage Care Pharm.* 2008; 14(6)(Suppl S-c):S22–S24. Accessed at http://www.amcp.org/data/jmcp/Aug%20suppl%20C_S22-S24.pdf. Accessed December 6, 2015.
13. Green J., for the Pharmacy Quality Alliance (PQA), Inc. (2013). Executive update on medication quality measures in medicare Part D plan ratings 2013. Accessed at http://pqaalliance.org/measures/cms.asp. Accessed December 6, 2015.
14. Cohen P. (November 1, 2012). The path to specialty benefits. *Managed Healthcare Executive.* Accessed at http://managedhealthcareexecutive.modernmedicine.com/managed-healthcare-executive/content/path-specialty-benefits. Accessed December 6, 2015.

Chapter 20

Drug Insurance Design and Management

Earle "Buddy" Lingle and William N. Yates

Contents

Introduction

The sources of payment for pharmaceuticals have greatly evolved over the past 40 years. When Congress passed Medicare and Medicaid in 1965, only about 7% of retail expenditures for pharmaceuticals were paid by insurers and public programs, i.e., third-party payers [1]. However, by 2012 the percentage of retail prescription drug payments by third parties had climbed to 81% [2]. This substantial increase has provided third parties with influence over the prescribing, dispensing, and use of prescription drugs. This change has contributed to an ongoing struggle over controlling costs involving employers, government agencies, pharmacy providers, and the pharmaceutical industry.

Controlling the cost of a drug benefit is important to increasing the profits of employers (by limiting their employee benefit costs) and third parties (who act on behalf of employers) as well as restraining the expenditures of publicly funded programs. In this chapter, references to *third parties* will be directed to organizations that are responsible for benefit management and/or the payment of services in lieu of the patient. These may include private insurance companies, managed care organizations, pharmacy benefit managers (PBMs), and government programs such as Medicaid and Medicare.

The purpose of this chapter is to provide the reader with information regarding the different policies and programs third parties utilize to help control costs. These may be mechanisms that directly control reimbursements or others that are intended to assure the appropriate use of therapies. For our purposes, these policies and programs are divided into the following categories:

- Prescribing restrictions
- Patient cost-sharing
- Utilization controls
- Product cost controls
- Pharmacist reimbursement

Prescribing Restrictions

Prescribing restrictions are controls put in place by payers that limit the choice of pharmaceutical products available to be prescribed. They may vary from rigid lists of drug products that may not be prescribed to lists of suggested products. Most allow some appeals process by which a patient may receive a restricted product. The following are the typical programs used to restrict prescribing in drug benefit programs.

A *formulary* may be defined as a preferred list of drug products that are deemed essential for the rational treatment of patients. Formularies were first developed for use in the hospital setting and were formed to decrease inventory costs and promote prescribing of appropriate therapy. As third-party drug benefit programs increased in number and size, formularies became more accepted for use in outpatient care settings.

Generally, formularies vary by the amount of information they provide and their restrictiveness. Formularies may be lists that provide guidance as to which drug products will be reimbursed by a third party, and/or they may be designed to provide a prescriber with therapeutic information about a drug product. With the advent of personal digital assistants and other electronic systems, formularies may also provide cost comparisons of various products within a therapeutic category.

One method used to characterize the restrictiveness of formularies is through the use of the terms *open formulary* and *closed formulary*. An *open formulary* is one that is perceived to be fairly unrestrictive and/or its use is voluntary. It is usually little more than a list of most prescribed products and serves as a guide to prescribing and payment. A *closed formulary* is more restrictive regarding the number of medications included and it is usually mandatory. The drug products that are allowed are usually organized by therapeutic category.

Decisions regarding the inclusion and exclusion of drugs from a formulary are usually made by a Pharmacy and Therapeutics Committee (P&T Committee). This committee typically consists of members who are knowledgeable about pharmacotherapeutics and includes practicing physicians and clinical pharmacists. Managed care groups and PBMs many times also include medically trained professionals with an expertise in pharmacoeconomics. A P&T Committee will usually make formulary decisions based on the primary criteria of safety, efficacy, and effectiveness. If various drug products have similar safety and efficacy profiles, then product cost will also be a factor in decision-making.

Most formulary policies also include an appeals process by which a physician or patient can appeal the exclusion of a drug product from a formulary. Approval of this appeal is usually based on the medical necessity of the patient receiving the excluded drug.

Formularies have been criticized for various reasons. Physicians have maintained that they hinder their ability to prescribe the most appropriate medicine for a patient, and therefore, they negatively impact patient care. Prescribers and the pharmaceutical industry also express a concern that some therapeutically effective pharmaceuticals are omitted because of their cost. Some opponents, including the pharmaceutical industry, maintain that restriction of access to pharmaceuticals may not have the desired impact on expenditures since other medications or services are substituted if the preferred drug cannot be prescribed [3]. Such criticism has led many insurers to evolve from using formularies to employing prior approval and preferred drug lists (PDLs).

Prior approval programs (also known as prior authorization [PA]) have been used by some third parties as a stand-alone program or in conjunction with a formulary. Most PA programs consist of access restrictions for drug products within certain therapeutic categories. As with formularies, if a specific drug is not included as a covered drug, then the physician or pharmacist must justify its need. Some third parties also have PA programs related to restrictions on prescribing of products or certain dosage forms, length of therapy, diagnoses, and/or patient's age.

State Medicaid programs have used PA programs because they are not allowed by law to employ a formulary. With the passage of the Omnibus Budget Reconciliation Act of 1990 (OBRA-90), state Medicaid programs were limited in restricting Medicaid recipients' access to most prescription drugs. The act provided that state Medicaid programs must cover drug products if they are marketed by companies with federal drug rebate agreements. However, several drug classes were allowed to be restricted, including agents for weight gain or anorexia, agents to promote fertility, agents for cosmetic purposes or hair growth, agents for symptomatic relief of cough and colds, agents for smoking cessation, prescription vitamins and mineral products (except prenatal vitamins and fluoride products), nonprescription drugs, outpatient drugs requiring purchase of tests or monitoring services from the same manufacturer, DESI drugs, barbiturates, and benzodiazepines. States were required to cover all new drug products approved by the FDA for at least 6 months after approval. After the 6-month period expired, PA programs were popular methods by which states attempted to control utilization. The subsequent passage of OBRA'93 repealed the requirement that new drugs be covered without restriction. It allowed states to exclude, restrict, or place on PA recently approved drugs. OBRA'93 did establish various criteria a state must meet when establishing a formulary, including the requirement that drugs excluded from a formulary (except from the categories listed earlier) must be made available by way of a prior approval program.

In many ways, prior approval programs have become *de facto* formularies. The requirements of OBRA'93 made formularies and PA programs essentially the same in functionality. In some instances, the process of making a PA request may be more restrictive than overriding a formulary exclusion.

A *PDL* is another method used to restrict prescribing. A PDL is essentially a group of prior approval programs. Each therapeutic category will have *preferred* drugs that will not require prior approval before being dispensed.

A *step therapy* program (also known as step protocol) is often used in conjunction with a formulary or prior approval program. Its purpose is to initiate a patient's therapy with a drug product that is deemed to be the most cost-effective. Patients would begin their therapy with a *first-line* drug product. If therapeutic failure occurred, the prior approval process would allow the dispensing of a *second-line* drug product. Step therapy has become a particularly popular program as new generic products enter the market and as prescription-only products become available over the counter (OTC). For example, as proton pump inhibitors became available OTC and at a lower cost, many third parties made them a first-line therapy.

Aside from the prescribing restrictions mentioned earlier, most third-party programs make decisions that will not allow prescribing of certain drug products or drug categories. Most of these decisions are based on concerns about the safety of a drug product or because its use is not considered medically necessary. For example, many plans do not cover barbiturates or benzodiazepines because there are alternative therapies that are considered more effective and safer. Certain therapeutic categories of drug products that are thought of as *lifestyle* drugs may also be excluded from coverage. These include drug products used for cosmetic purposes as well as those used to treat erectile dysfunction.

The *coverage of OTC products* is another decision that third parties must make. Traditionally, third parties have been hesitant to cover OTCs because of difficulty controlling the reimbursement process, the potential for fraud by patients, the large number of products and difficulty in knowing their ingredients, and the inability to provide the information to health-care professionals for inclusion in their patient profiles.

Because of the potential cost differential between OTC products and prescription-only drug products, some third parties have covered selected medications if prescribed by physicians. The switch from prescription-only status to OTC status for an allergy medication was actually initiated by WellPoint Health Networks, a managed care organization, which petitioned the FDA for switching the drug product to an OTC medication. Some third parties believe that the coverage of OTCs is such a cost-effective strategy that they require a prescription be written for the OTC and a dispensing fee is paid to the pharmacy. However, many insurers discontinued coverage of prescription formulations of products when an OTC formulation became available. In other situations, physicians will prescribe an OTC medication even if it is not covered by insurance so that a patient may claim the expense of the medication under a medical flexible spending account.

Patient Cost-Sharing

Almost all drug insurance plans require the patient to share in the cost of their prescriptions. By doing so, third parties believe that excessive and/or unnecessary utilization will decrease. The basis for this is that when a good or service is fully covered (i.e., price equals zero), the patient will demand the quantity of goods or services corresponding to a price of zero. Co-payments are used to make a patient evaluate the financial cost for using a drug compared to the need or potential benefit to the patient. Hopefully, this will deter excess utilization. However, if the cost-sharing amount is too high, the concern that arises is that both necessary and unnecessary utilization will be decreased. If this occurs, then a patient's health may worsen and more expensive medical care services may be ordered.

There are several different forms of patient cost-sharing that a third party may implement. A common type is a *deductible*. This is the amount of eligible expense that a patient must pay from his or her own pocket before benefits begin. For example, if a patient has a $(USD)250 deductible, then he or she must pay the first $(USD)250 of *eligible* expenses before insurance claims are paid.

Although not a method of cost-sharing, the concept of *eligible expenses* is important to the understanding of cost-sharing and various other aspects of third-party drug benefit programs. Examples of noneligible expenses include payments for a drug that is not on the third party's formulary. Therefore, if a prescribed drug is not on the formulary, then the amount the patient pays for that prescription would not be included toward the deductible the patient must meet.

A second type of patient cost-sharing is *coinsurance*. This represents a portion of prescription costs that a patient must pay and is usually implemented as a fixed percentage of the costs. When combined with a deductible, coinsurance will be paid by the patient once the deductible has been met. For example, a 20% coinsurance policy will result in a $(USD)20 payment for a $(USD)100 prescription once the deductible is met.

Another example of cost-sharing is the *co-payment* (or co-pay). A co-payment is a specific, fixed amount a patient must pay per prescription. It is usually paid by the patient to the pharmacy when services are rendered. For example, if a patient has a drug benefit plan that includes a $(USD)10 co-payment per prescription, then the patient would be expected to pay $(USD)30 if she has three prescriptions dispensed. A complication with co-payments is that the actual cost of generic prescriptions may be less than the co-payment. Many third parties have established policy that the co-payment is lower than the prescription actual cost (product cost plus pharmacist's fee for dispensing) or the co-payment.

Most private third-party drug benefit plans and Medicare Part D plans have implemented the use of *tiered co-payments*. The purpose of a tiered co-payment system is to steer patients away from using more expensive medications to using lower-cost drugs. Only a small minority of drug benefit plans do not currently use tiered co-payments.

Tiered systems may include two-tier, three-tier, or four-tier plans. A two-tier plan will have two categories of drugs, usually preferred drugs (generics) and nonpreferred (brand-name drugs). The nonpreferred tier will have a higher co-payment than the preferred tier. A three-tier plan may have a preferred drug (generics), preferred brands (brand-name drug without a generic substitute), and nonpreferred brands (brand-name drug with a generic substitute) tiers, and there will be three different co-payments. The intent is to drive utilization away from the more expensive nonpreferred brand drugs. In 2013, the average co-payments for a three-tier plan were $(USD)10 for generics, $(USD)29 for preferred brands, and $(USD)52 for nonpreferred brands [4]. A four-tier plan may include the three tiers described earlier as well as a fourth tier that includes lifestyle drugs, cosmetic drugs, and/or injectable drugs. In 2013, the average co-payment for a fourth-tier drug was $(USD)80, but frequently, a patient will be responsible for the full prescription cost for these medications [4].

In many drug benefit plans, a deductible will be used in combination with either a co-payment or coinsurance. However, it is infrequent that a drug benefit will require co-payments and coinsurance be collected from patients for the same prescription.

Insurance plans and their PBMs are concerned about the effects that *co-pay coupons* and *cards* have on the utilization of nonpreferred drug products. These coupons reduce patient cost-sharing for at least the first prescription of the higher-tier product. Manufacturers provide co-pay coupons in an attempt to increase the number of prescriptions and sales for their products. Insurance plan administrators maintain that such discount vehicles may decrease patient costs in the short term, but they will eventually increase a plan's net cost by decreasing drug rebate revenue and increasing the use of nonpreferred products [5].

Utilization Controls

Although many cost-containment tools used by third parties attempt to indirectly control drug utilization, there are some that directly limit use. Some of these methods include limits on the number of prescriptions a patient may receive, the quantity of doses that may be dispensed, or a patient's annual prescription drug expenditures. These utilization controls limit access or make the patient share in the costs. Other methods limit utilization after a review and evaluation of a patient's therapy regimen. These mechanisms control utilization by requiring the use of a therapeutically equivalent but lower-cost option.

Limiting the number of prescriptions a patient may receive over some time period (most frequently per month) is found in public programs such as Medicaid more often than in private programs. Limits on days' supply or quantity of doses per prescription can be either minimum or maximum limits. A maximum quantity limit (e.g., 30-day supply or 100 doses) is used to help prevent wastage in the event a medication order is stopped because of ineffectiveness or adverse drug events. A common reason why a minimum limit might be implemented is to supply greater quantities of chronic medications. For example, a third party may require a 90-day supply of medication to treat hypertension in lieu of a 30-day supply. This would be implemented to decrease the number of dispensing fees paid to pharmacies and/or decrease the handling and shipping charges for mail-order prescriptions.

Some drug benefit programs have placed dollar reimbursement limits that may be implemented on a monthly, quarterly, semiannual, or annual basis. The standard drug insurance plan for the Medicare Part D drug benefit in 2014 has a $(USD)310 deductible and then coverage with coinsurance; however, when a recipient reaches a monetary limit of $(USD)2850, he or she has no coverage until an additional $(USD)3841 in prescription drug expenditures occurs. Therefore, the standard Medicare drug benefit uses a unique structure with an expenditure limit that serves as a coverage gap until an additional *catastrophic* benefit begins when total expenditures reach $(USD)6691.

Although these direct controls on utilization should decrease a third party's prescription drug costs, the principal concern with their use is what happens once patients meet their limits. For example, Soumerai et al. found an increase in admissions to nursing homes when a prescription limit was put in place in the New Hampshire Medicaid program [6]. However, the higher admission rates returned to normal when the limits were removed a year later. When a limit is met, the concern is that a patient will not get the medication needed and that the utilization of other medical care services will be substituted resulting in greater costs. This is the main reason these controls are not frequently used.

Drug utilization review (*DUR*) is another method by which utilization may be controlled. With the passage of the OBRA-90, all state Medicaid programs were mandated to institute prospective and retrospective DUR programs in their outpatient drug programs. The use of DUR programs by private third parties also has greatly expanded.

DUR may take various forms, but in general, it includes any system that is used for monitoring and managing drug utilization. DUR serves two general purposes: (1) facilitate appropriate drug use and (2) manage costs by reducing inappropriate drug use. Although DUR has frequently focused on assuring appropriate physician prescription, it also focuses on pharmacist dispensing as well as patient's adherence to drug therapy regimens.

Product Cost Controls

There are two components to prescription drug costs: (1) the cost of the drug product and (2) reimbursement to the pharmacy for services rendered. Because a significant cost of the pharmacy benefit is the drug product cost, payers give significant attention to determining the proper method by which they should reimburse for drug products. However, the landscape of product reimbursement is littered with attempts to find a method that contains product costs while providing a fair reimbursement to pharmacy providers (Table 20.1).

Third parties attempt to reimburse pharmacies at their actual cost to purchase. This is also known as the *actual acquisition cost* (AAC). Reimbursing product costs at the pharmacy's AAC is difficult to achieve because of the complexity of determining various discounts, rebates, and deals that pharmacies receive. In addition, these factors vary if the drug product is purchased from a wholesaler or directly from the manufacturer in addition to the volume of product ordered. The most accurate method for determining AAC is to perform audits of pharmacies' invoices; however,

Table 20.1 Comparison of Drug Product Reimbursement Methods

Benchmark	*Pros*	*Cons*
Average wholesale price (AWP)	Nationally standardized price, widely accepted, frequently updated, comprehensive	Not transparent, not reflective of actual prices, subject to manipulation, not durable at this time
Average acquisition cost (AAC)	Represents average true acquisition cost from targeted purchasers on a transactional basis, includes discount and rebates, comprehensive	Varies by purchasing entity (chain vs. independent), not standardized as prices will vary from state to state, not frequently updated, high administrative burden, may require legislation to implement
Average sales price (ASP)	Transactional basis calculated by CMS, weighted average prices	Not comprehensive as use was intended for Medicare Part B drugs, not frequently updated, considerable lag time in reporting, not stratified for class of trade, not transparent
Average manufacturer cost (AMP)	Transactional basis calculated by CMS, specific per NDC, comprehensive	Only weighted average AMP, not NDC-specific AMR, is publicly available, considerable lag time in reporting, no transparency
Wholesale acquisition cost (WAC)	Nationally standardized price (codified in legislation), broadly accepted, brands frequently updated, tied in supplemental rebates (increases to WAC will result in increases in supplemental rebates)	Semitransparent, no oversight, not reflective of actual prices for brand or generic (but closer than AWP for brand), not comprehensive, generics not frequently updated, NCPDP endorsed replacement benchmark.

Source: AMCP Task Force on Drug Payment Methodologies, AMCP guide to pharmaceutical payment methods, 2013 Update (version 3.0), Academy of Managed Care Pharmacy, Alexandria, VA, April 2013.

this is cost prohibitive because of the large number of pharmacies that would need to be audited and because prices are dynamic. Therefore, third parties have developed different product cost estimates in an attempt to reimburse pharmacies at their approximate purchase price. The following are various methods that have been used and are proposed.

Third parties have used the average wholesale price (AWP) of a drug product to assist in calculating a product reimbursement. AWP is a suggested wholesale price of a drug. In other words, it is the manufacturer's published price recommended for wholesalers to sell a drug product to a pharmacy. However, because of discounts that wholesalers provide to pharmacies, the AWP is a higher price than what the pharmacy usually pays. Because of this reason, it is rarely used alone as the method for determining drug product reimbursement.

Because AWP is not an accurate estimate of product cost and AAC is too expensive and too difficult to determine, third parties have employed a calculation using AWP to determine the *estimated acquisition cost* (EAC). EAC uses an estimate of the discounts a pharmacy receives expressed as a percentage and deducts that from the AWP. For example, a third party may reimburse pharmacies for drug products at AWP-15%. Even though this estimate only approximates pharmacies' actual costs, it is simple and inexpensive to implement.

In state Medicaid programs, the EAC formulae vary from AWP-16% in New Hampshire to AWP-5% in Alaska [7]. Some states have established different EAC calculations for brand-name versus generic drugs. For example, Connecticut's Medicaid program calculates product reimbursement at AWP-16% for brand-name drug products and AWP-72% for generics. Some states also vary their EAC formulae by the type of pharmacy submitting prescription drug claims. Michigan reimburses independent pharmacies and small chain pharmacies (1–4 stores under the same ownership) at AWP-13.5% while it reimburses chain pharmacies (5 or more pharmacies under the same ownership) at AWP-15.1%.

EAC has also been calculated using the *wholesale acquisition cost* (WAC). It also is a published price but it is defined by law as a manufacturer's price to a wholesaler or direct purchasers [8]. It does not include discounts, rebates, or other reductions in price. Third parties reimburse pharmacies based on the WAC plus a specified percentage that represents the markup that a wholesaler would add to their cost before selling the drug product to a pharmacy. For example, the Ohio Medicaid program reimburses pharmacies at a lower cost of WAC+9% or AWP-12.8% [7].

The *average manufacturer price* (AMP) is another attempt to move away from the use of AWP in determining product reimbursement for generic drug products paid by Medicaid. Although the definition of AMP has evolved, the current definition was established in the Patient Protection and Affordable Care Act (PPACA; PL 111–148), and it represents the price paid by wholesalers to manufacturers for drug products sold to retail pharmacies as well as the price paid by retail pharmacies when they purchase directly from manufacturers. The PPACA excluded various discounts, rebates, and payments to more accurately reflect the cost of drugs to retail pharmacies. The final regulations for setting AMP were expected in May 2014 [9].

The *average sales price* (ASP) has replaced AWP in establishing the payment for most drugs covered under Medicare Part B such as those used in physicians' offices. ASP is based on the prices of products sold by manufacturers and includes most discount and rebates. The use of ASP has been controversial as the prices can be outdated by the time they go into effect and because many smaller physician offices and other providers are unable to purchase at or below a product's ASP [5].

In an attempt to resurrect the use of AAC, the Center for Medicare and Medicaid Services (CMS) contracted with a public accounting firm to provide a monthly national survey of retail pharmacies and their prescription drug prices. Its purpose was to provide state Medicaid agencies with pricing files to assist them in comparing their drug cost reimbursement methods and payments to the findings of the survey. In July 2013, CMS suspended one part of the survey (national average retail prices) that collected information on consumer purchase prices regarding approximately 4000 of the most commonly dispensed brand and generic drug products, customer cost-sharing amounts, and dispensing fees [10]. The second part of the survey (national average drug acquisition cost [NADAC]) concentrates on retail community pharmacy purchase prices for all Medicaid-covered outpatient drugs, and they are based on invoices from wholesalers and manufacturers. Discounts and other price concessions not included on the invoice are not calculated into the prices. The NADAC survey's purpose is to establish a national benchmark for which state Medicaid programs may base their reimbursements to pharmacy providers [11]. In addition, several states (including Alabama, Colorado, Idaho, Iowa, Louisiana, and Oregon) have developed their own average acquisition cost surveys [7].

The *federal upper limit* (FUL) program was established so that the federal government would achieve savings by acting as prudent buyers of generic drug products. It provides the maximum amount of reimbursement for certain multiple-source drugs that the federal government will recognize when calculating federal Medicaid matching funds being provided by the states. For example, assume that a state receives a 70% federal match under Medicaid. Also assume that the state reimburses $(USD)10 for a prescription for a generic drug although the FUL for the same drug is only $(USD)5. In this example, instead of the state receiving a match of $(USD)7 ($[USD]10 × 70%) for this prescription, the federal match will only amount to $(USD)3.50 ($[USD]5 × 70%). The FUL program has been controversial as it has evolved and as the FUL calculations have decreased reimbursement to pharmacies. Most recently, the PPACA revised the calculation of FULs for multisource drug products purchased by retail pharmacies to no less than 175% of the weighted average (weighted by utilization) of the most recent month's AMP data. After comments from pharmacy organizations, CMS developed a rolling three-month average FUL to help alleviate problems pharmacies might have in monthly price variations [12]. The final CMS regulations regarding FUL were expected in mid-2014.

The use of maximum allowable cost (MAC) payments was first introduced in the Medicaid program in the 1970s. It was an attempt to take advantage of variation in prices of multiple-source products. MAC limits are payment limits for multisource drug products that have different market prices. MAC limits will vary based on the drug entity as well as strength and dosage form. MACs take advantage of the difference in prices of brand-name drugs and generic drugs and limit the product cost reimbursement to the lowest price at which the product is available. MAC limits undergo periodic review and may either be increased, decreased, or discontinued depending upon the availability and prices of generic drug products. Pharmacies may dispense a more expensive brand-name drug, but they will only be reimbursed at the MAC limit. In the private sector, MACs are utilized by health insurance and PBMs, but the method of determining the MAC limits may vary among various plans. Lists of MAC limits will differ across state Medicaid programs and the MAC limits are often lower than the FUL prices.

Most third parties use a *lowest of* provision in their contracts with pharmacies to assure that they are paying the pharmacy's best price. The third party will reimburse the pharmacy the lowest prescription price based on (1) the EAC plus a dispensing fee, (2) the MAC limit (if available) plus a dispensing fee, or (3) the pharmacy's *usual and customary* charge. The usual and customary charge is the pharmacy's price to a cash-paying customer.

The use of a third party's selected method of product reimbursement is not readily apparent to a patient. However, it may be an important issue regarding the patient's access to pharmacy services. If a third party reimburses a pharmacy at a lower price than the pharmacy's actual cost for a drug product or provides an inadequate dispensing fee, the pharmacy may decide to not participate in that drug benefit plan. This may be particularly disruptive to access in rural areas.

Related to drug product costs but not a pharmacy reimbursement method, manufacturer *rebates* have become an important tool by which third parties recoup product costs they have paid. Rebates are payments from a manufacturer to a third party based on the utilization of the manufacturer's drug products over a period of time. This results in a discount back to the third party.

Third parties will often require rebates in order for a manufacturer to have its drug products available to the benefit plan's insured patients. Usually, access to a drug product is related to including the product on a restrictive formulary or granting the product *preferred* status on a PDL. Rebates are negotiated between the third party and the manufacturer and may be based on a specific drug or on a bundle of drugs. Manufacturers prefer to negotiate based on a bundle and will use their newer, innovative drugs as leverage to get their other drugs covered by the plan [13]. Third parties prefer to negotiate by the specific drug.

Rebates were mandated for the Medicaid program through the OBRA-90 legislation in an attempt to ensure that Medicaid would receive the *best price* that manufacturers offer public or private third parties. Some states recognized the potential to produce additional savings for drug product costs and implemented *supplemental* rebates. States persuaded manufacturers to provide these additional rebates by excluding them from their PA programs if supplemental rebates were provided to the state.

Rebates are also utilized in the private sector to assist insurance plan sponsors (employers) in reducing drug benefit costs. Employers may receive rebates via a flat amount per prescription or a percentage share of the rebates with the PBM receiving the remaining share. A 2013 survey found that more than one-third of employers received 100% of the rebates collected by PBMs while 22% of employers received no rebate [14].

The use of *mail order* may be included in several different sections of this chapter. It could be discussed under "Prescribing Restrictions" since formularies and PA programs are used extensively in mail-order programs. It may be discussed in the "Utilization Controls" section as mail order often uses quantity limits. It might even be discussed under "Patient Cost-Sharing" as mail order offers lower co-payments to entice patients to receive their prescription drugs in such a manner. However, it is included under this section, "Product Cost Controls," because a major reason for mail order's professed cost savings is due to lower product costs. Because of the large volume of prescriptions that mail-order facilities dispense, they are able to purchase medications in bulk resulting in larger product discounts. In addition, the economies of scale for such facilities provide lower operating costs and enable them to accept lower reimbursement for their dispensing functions than other pharmacies.

Pharmacy Services Reimbursement

In addition to reimbursing pharmacies for the drug product, third parties also pay pharmacies for their services. Although most of the payments are to reimburse for dispensing of the medication, pharmacies are also being compensated for other services they provide.

The most common form of pharmacy reimbursement is the *dispensing fee*. The advantages for third parties paying for pharmacy services through a dispensing fee include the simplicity to administer, good predictability of dispensing costs, and no incentives for the pharmacy to dispense a more expensive drug product, and it is viewed by pharmacy as being *professional*. The dispensing fee offered to a pharmacy should cover the pharmacy's cost to process and dispense a prescription (including personnel and building expenses) and provide a profit. Some pharmacies may not be concerned about a low dispensing fee if they are able to profit by purchasing the drug product at a price below what the third party reimburses.

Dispensing fees in state Medicaid programs range from $(USD)1.75 in New Hampshire to $(USD)5.77 in Louisiana [7]. To encourage the dispensing of generic drug products, some states provide higher dispensing fees for generics than for brand-name products. States may also differentiate their dispensing fees based on whether the dispensing pharmacy is a retail pharmacy, institutional pharmacy, or long-term care pharmacy. Utah also provides higher dispensing fees for rural pharmacies compared to pharmacies in urban areas.

Some third parties may also pay pharmacies for nondispensing services such as medication therapy management and patient education. The challenge for a third party is to differentiate between services provided by pharmacists when dispensing a prescription medication and those services that are not related to this function. When third parties have reimbursed for nondispensing services, they have usually based payments on the resources used and the time spent in providing the services. A later chapter covers this topic in more depth.

A rarely used form of pharmacy reimbursement is *capitation*. Capitation is a payment for services to be rendered over a specific period of time and is based on the number of patients who will receive services at that pharmacy. Capitation reimbursement holds several advantages for pharmacies. With capitation, a pharmacy is paid for services before services are provided thereby alleviating potential cash flow problems resulting from the filing of prescription claims. Also, the pharmacy is paid whether or not a patient receives any services during the specified time period. There are also advantages for third parties in that administrative costs are decreased since claims are not processed and the third party will have a more predictable expenditure for pharmacy services. In addition, the third party expects that the pharmacy would have an economic incentive to eliminate unnecessary utilization and decrease costs since it is only being paid one capitation fee per patient.

Even though there are advantages for pharmacies and third parties, capitation has failed to become a popular reimbursement mechanism. The main reason for its lack of use is because the proper amount of reimbursement is difficult to estimate. With the high price of prescription drug products, a change or addition of one prescription for a patient could produce a significant loss for a pharmacy. Because pharmacists do not have final authority to change a physician's prescription, their ability to influence utilization and expenditures is limited. Therefore, an unnecessary burden of risk would be placed on pharmacies unless third parties would allow capitation payments to vary with utilization. However, this would negate the advantages of the capitation reimbursement method.

Pharmacy reimbursement is still evolving as third parties attempt to implement product reimbursement that most closely approximates actual product acquisition cost. However, pharmacies have long relied on product reimbursements to be greater than acquisition costs in order to offset inadequate dispensing fee reimbursements. This difference is being lessened as third parties refine their product reimbursement methods. Pharmacists also continue to promote reimbursement for their nondispensing services. The Medicare Part D drug benefit and its Medication Therapy Management program may facilitate the recognition of pharmacy services and their reimbursement.

As with mail order, *pharmacy benefit networks* could be categorized in several ways; however, since participating in a network has direct implications for pharmacies' reimbursement, it has been included in this section. An *open pharmacy network* is one in which almost all retail pharmacies can participate in a drug benefit plan. In this type of network, an enrollee will pay the same cost-sharing at any pharmacy that is chosen. A *closed pharmacy network* only contracts with pharmacies that agree to provide pharmacy services at a lower dispensing reimbursement. These pharmacies are often referred to as in-network pharmacies. In-network pharmacies may also be categorized as being preferred and nonpreferred pharmacies. Enrollees in preferred plans generally have lower cost-sharing than those in nonpreferred plans. The use of pharmacy networks in the private sector as well as in Medicare Part D plans has rapidly increased. For example, Part D saw the proportion of prescription drug plan enrollees using a preferred pharmacy network increase from 14% in 2012 to 53% of enrollees in 2013 [15].

Fein lists several reasons why drug benefit plans are shifting toward preferred drug networks: (1) there are decreased drug benefit costs, (2) availability of pharmacies do not normally affect enrollees' accessibility, (3) enrollees are willing to switch pharmacies to reduce their cost-sharing, (4) pharmacies will accept lower reimbursement in order to attract patients, and (5) insurance plans are familiar with provider networks as they have been used by them for other medical services [16]. However, not all pharmacy providers and patients are supportive of networks. Some providers maintain that they are not allowed to join all networks even if they are willing to agree to a health plan's terms and that prices are sometimes higher in preferred networks [17]. They also insist that accessibility to pharmacy services is negatively impacted, especially in rural areas.

Summary

The evolution of drug benefit programs continues as the share of prescriptions paid by third parties continues to grow. As prescription drug spending is expected to increase at a greater rate than inflation, third parties will continue to work to decrease expenditures. The influence of third parties and their use of methods to control prescribing, utilization, product costs, and reimbursement will shape the future of drug benefits. However, it is imperative that third parties and health-care providers remember that a drug benefit will directly affect the utilization and expenditures for other medical care. In some instances, a more expensive drug benefit will result in a complete benefit package that will provide higher-quality care at a reduced total cost.

References

1. Centers for Medicare and Medicaid Services (2013). National health expenditure data. Available at: http://www.cms.hhs.gov/NationalHealthExpendData/. Accessed December 5, 2015.
2. Martin A et al. (2014). National health spending in 2012: Rate of health spending growth remained low for the fourth consecutive year. *Health Affairs* 33:67–77.
3. Murawski MM, Abdelgawad T (2005). Exploration of the impact of preferred drug lists on Hospital and Physician Visits and the Costs to Medicaid. *American Journal of Managed Care* 11:SP35–SP42.
4. Kaiser Family Foundation/Health Research and Educational Trust (August 2013). Employer health benefits, 2013 Annual survey. Available at: http://kaiserfamilyfoundation.files.wordpress.com/2013/08/8465-employer-health-benefits-20132.pdf.
5. AMCP Task Force on Drug Payment Methodologies (April 2013). AMCP guide to pharmaceutical payment methods, 2013 update (version 3.0). Academy of Managed Care Pharmacy, Alexandria, VA.
6. Soumerai SB et al. (1991). Effects of Medicaid drug-payment limits on admission to hospitals and nursing homes. *New England Journal of Medicine* 325:1072–1077.
7. Centers for Medicare and Medicaid Services (2014). Medicaid covered outpatient prescription reimbursement information by state—Qtr ending December 2013. Available at: http://www.medicaid.gov/Medicaid-CHIP-Program-Information/By-Topics/Benefits/Prescription-Drugs/Downloads/revised-SampleMedicaidDrugRebateAgreement.pdf. Accessed December 5, 2015.
8. Office of Inspector General, Department of Health and Human Services (June 2005). *Medicaid Drug Price Comparisons: Average Manufacturer Price to Published Prices* (U.S. Department of Health and Human Services, OEI-05-05-00240). Washington, DC: Government Printing Office.
9. Centers for Medicare and Medicaid Services. Covered outpatient drugs. Available at: http://www.reginfo.gov/public/do/eAgendaViewRule?pubId=201310&RIN=0938-AQ41&operation=OPERATION_PRINT_RULE Fall 2013. Accessed December 5, 2015.
10. Centers for Medicare and Medicaid Services (December 5, 2012). Survey of retail prices: Payment and utilization rates and performance rankings. Available at: http://www.medicaid.gov/Medicaid-CHIP-Program-Information/By-Topics/Benefits/Prescription-Drugs/Survey-of-Retail-Prices.html. Accessed December 5, 2015.
11. Centers for Medicare and Medicaid Services, Myers and Stauffer LC. (2012). Draft three-month rolling average federal upper limits. *Webinar* presented December 5, 2012. Available at: http://www.medicaid.gov/medicaid-chip-program-information/by-topics/benefits/prescription-drugs/downloads/december-5-2012webinarpresentation.pdf. Accessed December 5, 2015.

12. Centers for Medicare and Medicaid Services (November 20, 2014). Federal upper limits. Available at: http://www.medicaid.gov/Medicaid-CHIP-Program-Information/By-Topics/Benefits/Prescription-Drugs/Federal-Upper-Limits.html. Accessed December 5, 2015.
13. Hoadley J (2005, March). *Cost Containment Strategies for Prescription Drugs: Assessing the Evidence in the Literature*. Washington, DC: Kaiser Family Foundation.
14. Pharmacy Benefit Management Institute (2013). 2013–2014 prescription drug benefit cost and plan design report. Pharmacy Benefit Management Institute, Plano, TX.
15. Medicare Payment Advisory Commission (March 2014). Report to the congress: Medicare payment policy. Available at: http://medpac.gov/documents/reports/mar14_entirereport.pdf. Accessed December 5, 2015.
16. Fein A (May 2013). The big squeeze, Pharmaceutical Executive. Available at: www.PharmExec.com. Accessed May 1, 2014.
17. National Community Pharmacists Association (December 4, 2013). Let community pharmacies compete as preferred providers in Medicare drug plans. Available at: http://archive.ncpa.co/index.php/ncpa-commentary/1857-let-community-pharmacies-compete-as-preferred-providers-in-medicare-drug-plans. Accessed December 5, 2015.

Chapter 21

Electronic Information Technology

Role in Supporting Drug Use and Policy

Gordon Schiff, Tewodros Eguale, and Bill G. Felkey

Contents

Introduction

Electronic information technology (IT) is such an integral factor and force in medication prescribing and utilization in that it is a difficult topic to isolate and package into a separate chapter. The need for high-quality timely information is vast, and information management is a common denominator that permeates all aspects of medication use and policy. A further challenge is presenting an accurate, balanced, and up-to-date snapshot of the state of the art, given its dynamic nature, uneven implementation, and all of the hype and failed promises. A final challenge for this chapter, but one of our aims in writing it, is bringing together the varied but overlapping perspectives and vantage points of the three authors—medicine, pharmacy, health IT, pharmacoepidemiology, patient safety, and health policy disciplines—whose professional activities, workflows, and, in the case of physicians and pharmacists, information databases have often been more siloed and disconnected rather than synergistically shared (Schiff and Rucker 1998; Schiff et al. 2003).

Technologies are continually evolving making it difficult to make accurate predictions about how a technologically transformed health-care landscape will look, even a few years into the future. Yet at the same time, progress in the actual implementation of available technologies has been slow and uneven with false starts, dead ends, and numerous barriers and safety issues that will be touched on in this chapter (Martich et al. 2004). However, understanding general principles, as well as specific directions and issues, can assist policy makers, no matter how quickly the specific features and benefits of new technologies emerge (Detmer and Safran 2005).

Given these challenges, only a high-level overview that attempts to give big picture lessons and perspectives, yet is grounded in clinical realities, can best serve the readers of this volume. Thus, we will focus less on particular technologies and more on broad trends, issues, and insights.

Coming at the end of this book's journey through the various aspects of our pharmaceutical care system, this chapter will both draw upon issues raised by these pharmacy policy topics generally, as well as point to the specific impact of electronic IT on pharmacy policy formation. Our comments reflect our view that IT will continue to play a major role in both shaping ways how policy is going to be developed, implemented, and integrated into a myriad of clinical care settings and itself being shaped by broader policy directions. But it also is based on our experiences and views that unless health IT is approached wisely, critically, and with a relentless commitment to learning about how it is actually working, it will fail to reach its potential and can actually harm patients. Because choices and direction must be first and foremost guided by the needs of the patients and their practitioners, we will be focusing on clinical applications of computer technology and how it can make healthcare safer and more efficient and effective.

It is important to understand the far-reaching impact of information and technology. At the most fundamental level, information plays a role in reducing uncertainty during decision making and communicating across time, distance, and people. However, technology is also often a battleground where issues over control of work are manifest, as it is a tool that can transform the way people work together as well as exercise control over their work. As such, it can either be used to enhance the work of a human being or replace work done by humans (Felkey and Barker 1996). Depending on the context and implementation methods, these two purposes may either conflict or converge (Schiff and Goldfield 1994). While much of the historical introduction of new labor-saving technologies have been experienced as a threat to workers and their jobs, and thus met with resistance, we believe that empowering health-care practitioners, particularly physicians and pharmacists, to creatively use these tools and innovations to enhance the quality of the care they deliver and the ways they work together, should be the most important goal of their introduction. Even those who consider cost savings to be their primary aim will be missing the real opportunities for savings that can be achieved by a broader quality-directed, rather than a narrow labor saving, cost-cutting focus.

The American Recovery and Reinvestment Act of 2009 (ARRA) and a component of the legislation included over $(USD)20 billion in funding to advance for the Health Information Technology for Economic and Clinical Health Act (HITECH) (Blumenthal and Tavenner 2010). The following year, the Patient Protection and Affordable Care Act of 2010 was legislated. These two historical pieces of U.S. federal legislation are significantly accelerating the adoption of health-care technology in the United States by creating technology adoption incentives and penalties while concurrently attempting to expand health insurance to millions more Americans. Millions of citizens who previously did not have health-care insurance and thousands of providers who had not adopted electronic health records will be both helped, and others will face penalties. A stimulus program for eligible providers (although excluding pharmacists) provides incentives for the adoption of electronic health records. But simply purchasing technology, however, will not be rewarded with stimulus dollars.

Thus, there is increasing attention being paid to *how* these technologies are actually being used (in the language of the legislation, defining and measuring whether there is "meaningful use"), which is discussed in detail in this chapter and is the stimulus to accelerating adoption of various technologies discussed in the following text.

Five Generic Functions of Health-Care/Medication Information Technology

Experience in patient safety and quality improvement have identified a number of complementary potentials for IT for preventing errors and adverse events as well as facilitating earlier recognition and reporting of problems (Bates and Gawande 2003). While most are self-evident, none are trivial and each worth pausing to consider how health information technology (HIT) can best be designed and leveraged to accomplish better, more reliable, and efficient carrying out of these functions (Table 21.1).

Table 21.1 Linking Lab and Pharmacy Data

Core Function	*Ways Lab–Pharmacy Data Linkages Can Improve Medication Uses*
Drug selection	1. Lab contraindicates drug—Automatic alerts to prevent inappropriate prescription or administration 2. Lab suggests indication for drug—Alerts clinicians of patients whose regimen is missing and indicated medication
Dosing	3. Lab affecting drug dose—Automates adjustment of dosing for patients with preexisting risks such as renal insufficiency 4. Drug requiring lab for titration—Feedback of international normalization ratio (INR) or anticonvulsant drug levels to automate intelligent dose adjustments
Monitoring	5. Abnormal lab signaling toxicity—Screen for changes in lab parameters that are relevant for that drug, such as liver abnormalities for patients on TB Rx 6. Drug justifying lab monitoring for toxicity—Oversee regular monitoring of electrolytes, or CBC for patients on drugs that
Lab interpretation	7. Drug influencing or interfering with lab 8. Drug impacting on response to lab
Improvement	9. Drug toxicity/effects surveillance 10. Quality oversight

Source: From Schiff, G.D. et al., *Arch. Intern. Med.*, 163(8), 893, 2003.

Access to Information

Access to information such as searchable patient-specific list of medications, demographics, allergies, insurance plans, and instantaneous access to reference materials such as dosing regimens, side effects, or generic/brand names is such a powerful and ubiquitous function that we take the idea of having such access for granted. Yet just a few years ago, most of this either was unavailable or required a lookup in often outdated drug reference manuals on the pharmacist's shelf (Ambizas et al. 2009). But, as most of the rest of this chapter will make clear, particularly in case of searching for a complete up-to-date patient information, nirvana has hardly been reached.

Enhanced Reliability/Efficiency of Processes

To forget, overlook, get distracted, or err is human (Mcdonald 1976; Kohn et al. 2000). Instead of exclusively depending on these frail human qualities to ensure fail-safe recall and quality, technology can help ensure standardization and reliability. (Although unlike the computer, a human cannot forget everything!) Thus, the need to decrease reliance on human memory is a paramount rationale and function for health IT. Leaders in the field of evidence-based medicine understand that the complexity of practice is such that it has exceeded the capacity of the unaided human mind (Sackett 1998). Clearly the computer and IT are key to overcoming this limitation.

Improved Communication among Caregivers

One major requirement for more effective and safe care is efficient and reliable communication between physicians, pharmacists, and patients—something that can be radically transformed by IT. At the most basic level, communication about a patient's medicines requires everyone to be "working off the same page," regarding which medications to take and how they are to be taken. This requires creation of a shared, continuously updated, and reconciled medication profile list. Currently, patients can have a dozen different "medication profiles". HIT can dramatically enhance communication between pharmacies and physicians' offices, for example, related to medication refills or asynchronously answering questions.

Monitoring Both Individual Patients and Aggregated Outcomes

Monitoring both individual patients and aggregated outcomes to connect patient's experiences to overall learning. Every prescription should be viewed as drug trial, an experiment to be appropriately monitored, from which we need to be learning. Thus, individual patients need to be carefully and systematically monitored, and we need to be aggregating this experience and analyzing such large-scale epidemiologic data. Linking large medication-prescribing databases with outcomes databases (e.g., of subsequent hospitalizations or laboratory records) is the basis of the expanding discipline and function of pharmacoepidemiology (Strom 2006; Eguale et al. 2008; Avorn 2013; Forster et al. 2013). It could be used to answer simple questions such as how many patients fail to fill a prescription (conservatively at least one in four) or more nuanced policy questions such as whether drug cost and socioeconomic status and government support for poor patients have roles in the ability to fill a prescription (Fischer et al. 2010; Tamblyn et al. 2014) or whether patients persist in taking a chronic medication after 6 or 12 months (often more than half) (Avorn 2004) or longer-term drug therapy health outcomes (often requiring complex drug exposure measurement and risk adjustments for analysis of these observational databases). Because most clinical trials seldom look beyond a few weeks or months, longer-term data are sorely needed. Learning from linkages to other electronic outcomes data and using this to feedback to change practice are essential for improving the use and safety of drugs, yet have received relatively scant support from policy makers. Additionally, the consumer electronics industry has developed and marketed various monitoring technologies that can capture and transmit data, such as blood pressure readings, blood glucose measurements, and electrocardiograms, in online, real-time feedback and monitoring to health-care system. If all of these data are properly integrated, every patient should be able to benefit from each patient who has gone before and contribute to better care for those that follow.

Oversight and Accountability

Many aspects of medication use are highly individualized, which is a good thing if this is based on individual patient characteristics. However, if variations stem instead from a lack of clear standards, personal preferences based on no, or contradictory, evidence or, worse yet, irrational factors or impulses (promotional ads or drug rep pitches), then drug therapy can be irrational, wasteful, and potentially dangerous. Identifying the lack of conformity with best evidence in drug prescription decision making is the first step in better aligning practices with evidence-based practice, and electronic data are the key to unlocking this door. This logically can also help experts working with prescribers prospectively grapple with specifying more standardized approaches that align treatment practices with recommended evidence-based and most cost-effective approaches. HIT again is key for helping bringing together the three important inputs—patient information, best practice, physician judgment at the moment prescribing decisions are being made.

This is not about mandating overly rigid inflexible treatment. Instead, HIT should mean "help individualized therapy" in a way that broader patterns are evident at the prescribing (sharp) end as well as the oversight (blunt) end (Cook and Woods 1994) (with real-time delivery and capture of data along with tools to facilitate collaboration to overcome gaps (often chasms), between these two ends), and frankly current "unknown" at both ends. Under this scenario, healthcare can become a closed-loop system with online, real-time connectivity driving appraisal, intervention, and evaluation of outcomes in the long term (Garg et al. 2005; Harpaz et al. 2013).

Key Medication Use HIT Technologies/Function

In this section we review six key technologies and tools that policy makers need to understand to how drugs are ordered and used. Each builds on the others but if fully integrated provides the powerful pillars for new infrastructure for safer, more effective, and more efficient medication use.

Computerized physician order entry (CPOE)—Ordering medication via the computers rather than handwritten prescriptions. This technology has spread from the earliest more limited stand-alone programs in the 1990s that would simply compose, record, store, and print out a legible prescription (Schiff and Rucker 1998) to what is now the widespread adoption of CPOE in both inpatient and outpatient settings. This spread has been catalyzed by funding from the affordable care act (ACA), and the implementation of electronic prescribing has increased from 240 million e-prescribing messages in 2008 to 788 million in 2012 (Surescripts 2012). There have been various attempts to classify and differentiate more primitive from more advanced systems for electronic prescribing, but they, such hierarchies, generally center around the following elements and functions:

1. Extent to which the CPOE system is stand-alone vs. integrated into other elements of the electronic medical record

2. Whether and how the prescriptions are transmitted from the ordering clinician to the pharmacy (via printed paper script or via fax or fully electronically into the pharmacist's computer)
3. How robust are the clinical decision support (CDS) capabilities and how effective they are if being used
4. Extent to which CDS is customized/individualized to incorporate patient-specific information (demographics, labs, diagnoses, other drugs, patient's drug plan formulary) into the CDS functions
5. Design and role for other non-MD staff in interacting with the CPOE system in key workflows (such as for medication renewals, reconciliation, nursing medication administration)
6. Vendor roles in designing, maintaining (the CPOE system, updating the drug databases), and even storing the data (on-site vs. remotely)

The U.S. Congress sought to ensure that minimum standards for what constituted "meaningful use" of CPOE were being met in order for offices and hospitals to qualify for subsidies for installing CPOE systems. They commissioned the Office of the National Coordinator for Health Information Technology (ONC) to designate graded timetable levels for progressively more comprehensive use. Their published stages of meaningful use levels (Blumenthal and Tavenner 2010) represent a good framework for understanding varying levels of use, as well as represent as a barometer for the policy tug-of-war battles and compromises between various stakeholders (e.g., clinicians who may be resisting too high a bar and enthusiasts who feel patients would benefit more from more comprehensive implementation and use).

CDS—Tools to assist clinicians in safe and appropriate prescribing. CDS can be broadly defined as "a process for enhancing health-related decisions and actions with pertinent, organized clinical knowledge and patient information to improve health and healthcare delivery" (Osheroff et al. 2012). This functionality is designed to fill the gap between practice guidelines and actual prescribing and limitations prescribers face and put guidelines in gear to change prescribing practices. Medication-related CDS includes electronic and automated tools to check for drug allergies, interaction, duplicates, incorrect dosing, as well as automated monitoring of patients on medications. While often narrowly depicted solely as the "firing of alerts"—many of which clinicians complain are annoying, inaccurate or inapplicable to that specific patient, and therefore disruptive to their workflow—CDS represents a much broader collection of tools and functions. The additional functions include the following:

1. *Support for accurately and completely composing orders* such as default or adjusted (e.g., if renal, pediatric, or geriatric) dosing and unit (milligrams or micrograms), calculated pill quantities (e.g., 180 pills for a 3-month twice daily prescription), and standard instructions for patients (e.g., do not take with alcohol, or drive when taking this medication). Evidence has shown that help in constructing the orders "before the fact" is more effective than alerting the prescriber "after the fact" in terms of acceptance and acceptability of the advice (Seidling et al. 2011).
2. *"Prepackaged" order sets* to quickly and easily enter a predefined order or group of commonly used ("favorites" either personal favorites or ideally institutionally standardized, evidence based) orders (Payne et al. 2003; Bobb et al. 2007; McGreevey 2013).
3. *Intelligent data displays* that can arrange, customize, filter, highlight, and simplify key information to make it easier for users to find or not overlook key pieces of information (most recent INR for warfarin prescription; display in red if outside the therapeutic range) (Samal et al. 2011; Mathew et al. 2012).

4. *Info buttons* that offer a one-click instant access to the context-specific reference information, typically in the case of medications, can access online monographs for the drug being prescribed, so the user can review indications and side effects or even access online guidelines or original articles or studies. As opposed to alerts and reminders, which might be considered "uninvited" by a clinician (although they can be welcomed or even lifesaving), info buttons represent a type of CDS vehicle driven by the clinician who decides when and whether to access these additional sources of information (Maviglia et al. 2006; Del Fiol et al. 2014).

Ideally, much of the CDS functionality is working in the background, hardly noticeable by physicians, pharmacists, and patients (Van Der Sijs et al. 2006; Jung et al. 2013). CDS should be intelligently filtered and presented at the appropriate times to the appropriate people (the so-called five rights of CDS: right, patient-specific information, to the right person, in the right intervention format, through the right channel, at the right time in the workflow; Osheroff et al. 2007).

Electronic transmission of prescriptions—Standards and channels for electronically transmitting CPOE-generated prescriptions to (and from) pharmacies. Early electronically generated prescriptions resulted in a printed paper script that the patient carried to the pharmacy or that would be faxed (electronically from the CPOE or manually by the office staff). In the early 1990s, pioneering dedicated systems were piloted the transmitted prescriptions directly via dedicated links to a contracted pharmacy (Walgreens 1999). Obvious shortcomings of paper or "glorified fax" CPOE transmissions included potential transcribing errors during manual pharmacy entry and the inflexibility of a prescriber being "locked in" to a particular pharmacy or chain (Walgreens 1999). This led in 2001 to a consortium of pharmacies including the National Association of Chain Drug Stores and the National Community Pharmacists Association coming together to create Surescripts, a set standard and a network that allowed pharmacies and CPOE systems to exchange information and enable true e-prescribing. This in turn enabled and fueled the growing adoption of electronic transmission of prescriptions over the past decade. In 2008, Surescripts merged with another key component of the health IT system, a consortium of drug insurance benefit benefits managers (PBM's) who had created RxHub to capture "back-end" prescription claims data. As of 2012, nearly 800 million prescriptions for 240 million patients representing 40%–74% (depending on which state) of prescriptions are now electronically transmitted to pharmacies (Surescripts 2012).

In theory, this bidirectional information exchange (prescription flow into pharmacies and information back to prescribers on fill history) can permit true closed-loop information flow, whereby a clinician can, at the push of a button, transmit prescriptions to the pharmacy of the patient's choice as well as instantly access and view all of the patient's pharmacy transactions. This also permits the assessment of patient adherence based on when they were last filled, as well as inappropriately early refills/overuse/abuse of medications (Tamblyn et al. 2014). However, multiple issues still remain, including (high on the list of many frustrated clinicians) requirements in most states to use paper prescriptions for controlled drugs (Fishman et al. 2004); barriers in usability and use in accessing claims data prescription profiles; persistence of fax, phone calls, and pharmacy and office variations related to refills; complexities in mail order vs. community pharmacy routing; incomplete capture of prescription drug fills when patient is out of pocket (rather than billing to drug insurer, thus no "claim" is generated); and ambiguities related to medication discontinuation (discontinuation information from physicians' CPOE fails to flow to pharmacy systems). In addition, there currently are barriers preventing the use of such refill data for safety and research purposes (Surescripts 2014).

Medication reconciliation—Tools/modules to reconcile patient medication profiles across various care venues (Table 21.2). Straightening out the mass (and mess) of data regarding which drugs a patient has been prescribed and actually taking is quite complex—more so than the joint commission ever imagined when they attempted to require (and later had to back off) this from being an accreditation standard for all patients at admission, discharge, and all transitions within the hospital. IT plays an essential role in supporting each for the steps in this "med rec" process (Schnipper et al. 2009; Fernandes and Shojania 2012). These include (1) collecting all of the sources that need to be queried to assemble a complete medication history; (2) organizing this list in a coherent way that distinguishes active from inactive medications and physically brings together similar (or identical in the case of the same medication ordered by both brand and generic name) drugs and ideally grouping those for the same condition; (3) decision making, recording, and carrying out desired actions (i.e., deciding which drugs to continue, discontinue, change); and (4) conveying those decisions/actions to the pharmacy, other staff, and most importantly, the patient. At each step in this process, interoperability and tools are needed (Allen et al. 2014) but are generally poor, incomplete, difficult to use, and therefore time-consuming

Table 21.2 What Medication Is the Patient Taking: Multiple Unreconciled Sources of Truth for Meds List

Outpatient	MDs (PCP, specialists) medication office chart med lists, text notes—either electronic and/or handwritten
	Transaction med list in retail pharmacy computer
	Pill bottles ("brown bag") of meds patients may (or may not) be taking
	Handwritten or electronic medication pocket cards or information/instruction leaflets
	Aggregated pharmacy benefit insurance claims (pooled transactions from multiple sources); mail order purchaser data
	OTC/alternative/herbal remedies patient may (or may not) be taking
	Barcode-scanned OTC drug data (from drug or grocery store checkout)
	Web-based (provider or patient maintained) profiles, including personal health records and smartphone apps
	"Free samples" from a variety of sources
	Medications "borrowed" from relatives, illegal street meds
Inpatient	Inpatient profiles (ER, wards, ICU)
	Nurse medication administration record; Cardex
	Electronic dispensing cabinet (e.g., Pyxis) profiles
	Discharge prescriptions, medication lists
	Anesthesia records

and underused. Pharmacies and pharmacists are generally treated as a "back end" rather than seen as playing a primary role in the medication reconciliation process (Practice et al. 2013), while many physicians (e.g., surgeons and medical subspecialists) are understandably resistant to any requirements that they reconcile all the patient's medications every visit (Haig 2006). Transitions into and out of the hospital are particularly vulnerable times for regimen changes, leading to patient confusion, which thus has been the focus of considerable effort, though still sharing evidence of widespread challenges. The need for improved interoperability and usability has been widely noted, but it is unclear who will take the lead to provide the standard and software to make the major transformations needed for addressing each of these elements for more efficient and reliable medication reconciliation. What is needed (assuming privacy, confidentiality, security concerns can be adequately addressed) is a "single source of truth" with one continuously updated medication list (e.g., in the "cloud") from which all prescriptions are written from which the regimen is modified (Gleason et al. 2012).

Patient portals/other tools—Ways for patients to view and interact with their medication regimens and improve their quality and safety. Patients (and their families) are using "online portals" to view their test results or request/schedule appointments, as well as view and give feedback on their electronic medical record (EMR) medication list. Patients are the closest and often the most accurate source of truth about what medications they are actually taking, side effects they may be experiencing, renewals (timing, which drugs) that are needed, and questions they may be having regarding their medications (Heyworth et al. 2014). Each of these functions requires careful system design, intuitive interfaces, capable patients (Internet access, training), and efficient and effective use of the data. For example, if a patient reports an adverse effect, whose job will it be to follow up with the patient without overwhelming providers on one hand or creating important liability risks (if ignored) on the other hand. Only a minority (in 2011 only 20% of physician offices have "live" patient portals) (Wynia et al. 2011) of practices and patients have fully functional portals, and even fewer are using these capabilities effectively to support safer prescribing and more efficient practice. Practice portals need to, but often fail to communicate with pharmacies for med renewals (which are often poorly synchronized with different medications expiring at differing times (Linsky and Simon 2013) adverse effects, questions that pharmacist are best suited to answer). Trends toward empowering patients to play an enhanced role in their own care as well as giving them greater access to their EMR information/records are unmistakable (Delbanco et al. 2012). Health IT can support and empower patients in a variety of ways outlined in Table 21.3.

Outcomes data/linkages—Learning from each drug prescription. Premarketing data on drugs leave much to be desired for fully informing drug prescribing and policy decisions. There are a myriad of shortcoming that can *only* be overcome by systematically capturing and analyzing postmarketing experience using large, longitudinal electronic databases. While the labeled information developed, preapproval may be a reasonable initial best guess of the drug's benefits, indications, adverse effects, and clinical effectiveness, only longer-term, real-world use data can provide information about (1) rarer, but potentially serious, adverse effects; (2) risks and benefits in populations typically excluded from premarketing studies (e.g., patients with multiple comorbid conditions being treated with other potentially interacting drugs, younger/older patients); (3) how appropriately clinicians use the drug particularly appropriateness of patient selection (to assess the risk of overuse and/or treatment of conditions lacking evidence for benefit); (4) how carefully clinicians follow monitoring recommendations and whether this adversely impacts outcomes; (5) patient adherence—its reasons and impact; (6) longer-term

Table 21.3 Tools to Assist/Aid Patient Engagement

• Medication lists, organized by indication plus instructions for safe use
• Medication information/leaflets
• Pictures to identify (actual product patient is receiving) medications
• Tools for synchronizing medication regimens
• Ways to record, transmit concerns about potential adverse effects
• *Adherence aids*: Regimen displays, electronic alerts
• Tools to identify whether patients taking medications as prescribed
• Ways for patients (or families) to ask questions about medications
• Technologies to monitor, record, and transmit physiologic parameters
• *Outcomes metrics*: Ways to capture drug- and disease-specific outcomes to determine if effective

outcomes; (7) and overall effectiveness and safety considering all of these variables in comparison to alternative treatment strategies.

Mining of big databases to efficiently answer these questions is a widely shared aim (or perhaps a better word would be "dream") for all medication use stakeholders. Pharmacoepidemiology is a discipline well described in the pages in this book (Chapters 5, 9 and 24) with its first generation of contributions focused mainly on adverse effects and relying on insurance claims rather than clinical databases. A threshold has now been crossed with wider use of electronic medical records making possible much more powerful and clinically rich postmarketing, monitoring, and learning. Prominent examples of initiatives taking advantage of such large databases include European adverse drug reaction alliance (EU-ADR) with surveillance with coverage of 30 million people; the U.S. FDA's Mini-Sentinel with records for 100 million individuals, 3 billion prescriptions from 2.4 billion medical encounters (Platt and Carnahan 2012); the Observational Medical Outcomes Partnership, a private–public partnership launched by the Foundation for the National Institutes of Health partnership with Pharmaceutical Research and manufacturers of America (PhRMA) and the FDA; and the Centers for Disease Control and Preventions (CDC's) PROTECT initiative to monitor unintentional medication overdoses in children (collecting emergency department electronic visit data) representing more than 70,000 emergency visits annually. Each of the "big data" pharmacoepidemiology initiatives is both blessed and cursed with huge databases that can play a role in hypothesis generation and testing but are also susceptible to limitations that may lead to falsely incriminating or exonerating a particular drug, indication, or treatment in a subset of patients. These include confounding by indication (sicker people may be prescribed the drug, leading to erroneous causality conclusions), protopathic bias (an early symptom of the disease leads to starting a drug that is then mistakenly implicated in causation of the disease and is later fully manifest and diagnosed), and database limitations (patient discontinuities, missing, or inaccurate data).

To understand the direction medication-related HIT is taking, we conclude this chapter by reviewing selected issues and trends to illuminate from readers' areas of activity and controversy that are likely to shape both HIT policy direction and outcomes in the future.

HIT Trends Shaping Drug Use, Policy, and Outcomes

Patient Involvement

Patients are increasingly IT tech savvy and involved in their own care using computer searches, patient portals, mobile apps, chat rooms, and other social medias (Frost and Massagli 2008; Sarasohn-Kahn 2008). Because the most important "ingredient" in an effective medication regimen is an involved patient, these are welcome developments. While "adherence" is clearly a basic component of effective patient medication use—and various tools noted earlier can support patients taking prescribed medicine—proactive and educated patients are taking advantage of IT to "take medicines" to higher, previously unimaginable levels. This involvement means, for example, that patients may have more knowledge about their medication than their physicians as a result of extensive online searching and interacting with other patients. This enhanced access comes with a cost of information overload, including a plethora of nonevidence-based, inaccurate, or even surreptitiously misrepresented information. It also potentially widens disparities between access, knowledge, and behaviors of better vs. less resourced and educated patients with variability and gaps in being able to navigate the most affordable, effective, and safest medication options (DesRoches et al. 2012).

Government Stimulus and Oversight

The U.S. HITECH, enacted as part of the ARRA, gave subsidies of up to $(USD)44,000 per physician backed up by so-called meaningful use requirements for EMRs. This has had two catalytic impacts on evolution of electronic prescribing. The first is to increase the numbers and percentage of physicians' writing prescriptions on paper vs. electronically; the second is its mandating and accelerating functionality that might otherwise not have been as rapidly adopted (Blumenthal and Tavenner 2010; Terry 2013; Wright et al. 2013; Kaushal and Blumenthal 2014). Previously, a number of other countries had a substantial lead over the United States. For example, in the United Kingdom and the Netherlands, the majority of outpatient prescriptions have been written electronically for nearly a decade, often driven more via a grass roots bottom-up adoption of electronic prescribing (Van Dijk et al. 2011). The steep rise in U.S. adoption, from the top-down stimulus of incentives and penalties, has resulted in a tipping point being crossed. Thus, the focus of attention now needs to be more not on *whether* EMRs/HIT is adopted, but *how* the quality, safety, and efficiency of electronic prescribing tools can be optimized. Currently, there is considerable clinician dissatisfaction with various aspects of the EMR, although perhaps less so with the electronic prescription-writing component than other data entry burdens (such as clinical documentation) (Friedberg et al. 2013; Sinsky et al. 2014). Just as with patient adoption of new technologies, there are disparities in physician uptake with continuing barriers of resources and affordability, infrastructure support, along with a (shrinking) minority of MDs that are still reluctant to move to electronic prescribing (DesRoches et al. 2012; Fosso Wamba et al. 2013). Because current systems fall short in usability and efficiency (Armijo et al. 2009), many fear that the current push makes risk bolstering harder-to-use systems that will ultimately have to be replaced in the future at considerable cost (Kellermann and Jones 2013).

Interoperability Issues and Data Fragmentation

Unfortunately the current health IT systems that dominate the market are not designed to talk to each other (Kellermann and Jones 2013). Hospitals across the street from each other often cannot share medication lists or other electronic data. There have been various federal initiatives in the United States led by the ONC, but progress has been slow due to a host of barriers, including resistance from vendors, costs, and governance issues in setting up regional health exchanges (RHIOs) (Adler-Milstein et al. 2013). A recent survey found that although there are a growing number of regional health information exchanges, only a small number of hospital and practices participate in one of these information exchange initiatives, and these exchanges are struggling to develop a "sustainable business model" (Adler-Milstein et al. 2013). Particularly, successful examples such as the network in Indianapolis, built incrementally over the past decade, illustrate the value of such exchanges for real-time clinical care (access of citywide data for a patient going to any emergency room), public health (tracking infection and antibiotic resistance patterns), and pharmacoepidemiology research (McDonald et al. 2005; Kho et al. 2013). Other efforts have led to the creation of standards for a Continuity of Care Record, which has now been implemented as an HL-7 standard called the Continuity of Care Document. This alternative approach (to building centralized data repository exchanges) can enable sharing a standardized "packet" of basic clinical health information (medications, problem lists) in an exchangeable format (D'Amore et al. 2012).

HIT Limitations and Side Effects

These include increased recognition of IT-related errors, vulnerability, CDS limitations, and alert fatigue. Many of the promises of health IT have yet to be realized and remain to be demonstrated in carefully designed studies. There is also growing appreciation that implementing electronic solutions is much more complex and difficult than previously understood. It can also introduce new, both predictable and unanticipated problems and safety risks (IOM 2011; Kushniruk et al. 2013). Thus, what appeared to be simpler and more straightforward technical fixes have turned out to belie more challenging sociotechnical systems' issues that involve complex organizational, human, technology, political, and societal interactions (Ash et al. 2004, 2007; Koppel et al. 2005; Carayon 2006; Waterson 2014). While the list is much longer, we highlight just a few of the challenges that have arisen that will require multidisciplinary continuous improvement efforts in addition to perhaps new paradigms to achieve breakthrough and sustainable improvements in reliability and safety (Table 21.4). At the very least, these problems call for a shared awareness of their frequency and serious consequences, transparency, and collaboration in efforts to address and a respect for clinicians, patient, clinical uncertainties and workflow and teamwork complexities.

Internet Marketing of Drugs

Targeting MDs and (especially) patients is increasingly ubiquitous, sophisticated, and often covert. The so-called "free" websites, search engines, and email providers support themselves by selling data on site visitors. A leading purchaser of these data is the pharmaceutical industry. The industry collects data on not only users' general and health-related searches but also personal data such as social networks, geographic data (cell phones can collect data tracking everywhere the user has been), email (e.g., Gmail) content, purchases, and even information from online chat rooms and discussions (Greene and Kesselheim 2010; Lenzer 2011). In addition, the industry has, for years, collected electronic data from pharmacies on every prescription written by each physician (except the <2% of those who are aware of this surveillance and have opted out) (Fugh-Berman 2008; Mello and Messing 2011).

Table 21.4 Examples of Medication HIT Shortcomings and Challenges

Failure to communicate outpatient medication discontinuation orders	Current systems fail to transmit orders to the pharmacy when a drug is discontinued (for example, due to an adverse reaction) by the physician in the EMR CPOE system.
Alert fatigue	Most clinical decision support warnings are ignored or overridden, at times appropriately but at other times inappropriately, placing patient (and prescriber) at risk.
Lack of indication on prescription	A potential for errors (since no cross-check if right drug was chosen), and patient confusion (not knowing what drug is for), and medication lists not grouped indication making such lists confusing to patients and staff.
Wrong patient errors	Because providers can inadvertently select the wrong patient from a menu, or because interrupted/distracted while working with more than one patient's chart open at a time, resulting in thousands of wrong patient electronic orders in one hospital system in a single year (Adelman et al. 2013).
Medication reconciliation challenges	Not only is this a problem to integrate multiple currently noninteroperable data sources (pharmacy, specialists, PCPs, OTCs), but IT systems lack robust tools for clinicians to organize, clean up, and make decisions on which drugs to continue, change, or discontinue.
Medication refill coordination and synchronization	Many patients on chronic medications are having medications running out at different dates making it difficult to coordinate with pharmacies and physicians' offices.
Failures in surveillance to detect adverse reactions	While not technically a health IT failure, it represents a major problem, that is, well-designed HIT should, but is failing to, realize its potential role, both on an individual patient level—up to ¼ of patients have some sort of reaction, but these mostly go undetected by MDs—and the fact that large-scale pharmacoepidemiological surveillance and the HIT infrastructure are currently lacking.

Considering that the majority of Americans now use the Internet as their primary source of health information, even surpassing physicians as the leading source consulted (Sarasohn-Kahn 2008), this ability to collect, collate, and analyze very personal data with powerful analytics has the potential to radically transform pharmaceutical marketing. In turn, these result in the ability to influence patients by targeting them with individualized messages aimed at their health and personal vulnerabilities. These practices raise various regulatory, ethical, privacy, and practical issues (Greene and Kesselheim 2010). Particularly, When sponsorship and authorship of online information are unclear, it is particularly difficult to regulate and enforce a balanced presentation of risks and benefits (Liang and Mackey 2011). The FDA is struggling to create guidelines related to ensuring such balance on third-party sites that a drug company may or may now sponsor or be providing content for, but are difficult to determine who is responsible for the content and messages (Chernaik and Ford 2014).

Conclusion

Medication IT is deeply woven into the fabric of the present and future prescribing and policy environment. Rather than a "fix" for the myriad of problems it was designed to address, it should best be viewed as a tool with many applications and contradictions. The next generation of clinicians, pharmacists, and policy makers will both shape and be shaped by the potentials, challenges, and limitation we outlined here.

References

Adelman, J. S., G. E. Kalkut et al. (2013). Understanding and preventing wrong-patient electronic orders: A randomized controlled trial. *Journal of the American Medical Informatics Association* 20(2): 305–310.

Adler-Milstein, J., D. W. Bates et al. (2013). Operational health information exchanges show substantial growth, but long-term funding remains a concern. *Health Affairs* 32(8): 1486–1492.

Allen, A., T. R. Des Jardins et al. (2014). Making it local: Beacon communities use health information technology to optimize care management. *Population Health Management* 17(3): 149–158.

Ambizas, E., D. Ezzo et al. (2009). Drug information resources for the community pharmacist. US Pharmacist. http://www.uspharmacist.com/continuing_education/ceviewtest/lessonid/106043/. Accessed December 6, 2015.

Armijo, D., C. McDonnell et al. (2009). Electronic health record usability: Interface design considerations. AHRQ Publication (09)10. Rockville, MD: Agency for Healthcare Research and Quality.

Ash, J. S., M. Berg et al. (2004). Some unintended consequences of information technology in health care: The nature of patient care information system-related errors. *Journal of the American Medical Informatics Association* 11(2): 104–112.

Ash, J. S., D. F. Sittig et al. (2007). Categorizing the unintended sociotechnical consequences of computerized provider order entry. *International Journal of Medical Informatics* 76: S21–S27.

Avorn, J. (2004). The role of pharmacoepidemiology and pharmacoeconomics in promoting access and stimulating innovation. *Pharmacoeconomics* 22(2): 81–86.

Avorn, J. (2013). The promise of pharmacoepidemiology in helping clinicians assess drug risk. *Circulation* 128(7): 745–748.

Bates, D. W. and A. A. Gawande (2003). Improving safety with information technology. *New England Journal of Medicine* 348(25): 2526–2534.

Blumenthal, D. and M. Tavenner (2010). The "meaningful use" regulation for electronic health records. *New England Journal of Medicine* 363(6): 501–504.

Bobb, A. M., T. H. Payne et al. (2007). Viewpoint: Controversies surrounding use of order sets for clinical decision support in computerized provider order entry. *Journal of the American Medical Informatics Association* 14(1): 41–47.

Carayon, P. (2006). Human factors of complex sociotechnical systems. *Applied Ergonomics* 37(4): 525–535.

Chernaik, T. and S. Ford (2014). # ThinkAgain: How regulator guidance can impact social media marketing. *Journal of Digital & Social Media Marketing* 2(1): 40–47.

Cook, R. I. and D. D. Woods (1994). Operating at the sharp end: The complexity of human error. *Human Error in Medicine* 13: 225–310.

D'Amore, J. D., D. F. Sittig et al. (2012). How the continuity of care document can advance medical research and public health. *American Journal of Public Health* 102(5): e1–e4.

Del Fiol, G., T. E. Workman et al. (2014). Clinical questions raised by clinicians at the point of care: A systematic review. *JAMA Internal Medicine* 174: 710–718.

Delbanco, T., J. Walker et al. (2012). Inviting patients to read their doctors' notes: A quasi-experimental study and a look ahead. *Annals of Internal Medicine* 157(7): 461–470.

DesRoches, C. M., C. Worzala et al. (2012). Small, nonteaching, and rural hospitals continue to be slow in adopting electronic health record systems. *Health Affairs* 31(5): 1092–1099.

Detmer, D. E. and C. Safran (2005). AMIA's White paper policy series on timely issues in informatics. *Journal of the American Medical Informatics Association* 12(4): 495.

Eguale, T., R. Tamblyn et al. (2008). Detection of adverse drug events and other treatment outcomes using an electronic prescribing system. *Drug Safety* 31(11): 1005–1016.

Felkey, B. G. and K. N. Barker (1996). Technology and automation in pharmaceutical care. *Journal of the American Pharmaceutical Association* NS36(May): 309–314.

Fernandes, O. and K. G. Shojania (2012). Medication reconciliation in the hospital: What, why, where, when, who and how? *Healthcare Quarterly* 15: 42–49.

Fischer, M. A., M. R. Stedman et al. (2010). Primary medication non-adherence: Analysis of 195,930 electronic prescriptions. *Journal of General Internal Medicine* 25(4): 284–290.

Fishman, S. M., J. S. Papazian et al. (2004). Regulating opioid prescribing through prescription monitoring programs: Balancing drug diversion and treatment of pain. *Pain Medicine* 5(3): 309–324.

Forster, A. J., C. Auger et al. (2013). Using information technology to improve the monitoring of outpatient prescribing. *JAMA Internal Medicine* 173(5): 382–384.

Fosso Wamba, S., A. Anand et al. (2013). A literature review of RFID-enabled healthcare applications and issues. *International Journal of Information Management* 33(5): 875–891.

Friedberg, M. W., P. G. Chen et al. (2013). *Factors Affecting Physician Professional Satisfaction and Their Implications for Patient Care, Health Systems, and Health Policy*. Santa Monica, CA: Rand Corporation.

Frost, J. H. and M. P. Massagli (2008). Social uses of personal health information within PatientsLikeMe, an online patient community: What can happen when patients have access to one another's data. *Journal of Medical Internet Research* 10(3): e15.

Fugh-Berman, A. (2008). Prescription tracking and public health. *Journal of General Internal Medicine* 23(8): 1277–1280.

Garg, A. X., N. K. J. Adhikari et al. (2005). Effects of computerized clinical decision support systems on practitioner performance and patient outcomes—A systematic review. *Journal of the American Medical Association* 293(10): 1223–1238.

Gleason, K. M., H. Brake, V. Agramonte, and C. Perfetti (2012). Medications at transitions and clinical handoffs (MATCH) toolkit for medication reconciliation. Rockville, MD: Agency for Healthcare Research and Quality.

Greene, J. A. and A. S. Kesselheim (2010). Pharmaceutical marketing and the new social media. *New England Journal of Medicine* 363(22): 2087–2089.

Haig, K. (2006). Medication reconciliation. *American Journal of Medical Quality* 21(5): 299–303.

Harpaz, R., W. DuMouchel et al. (2013). Performance of pharmacovigilance signal-detection algorithms for the FDA adverse event reporting system. *Clinical Pharmacology & Therapeutics* 93(6): 539–546.

Heyworth, L., A. M. Paquin et al. (2014). Engaging patients in medication reconciliation via a patient portal following hospital discharge. *Journal of the American Medical Informatics Association* 21(e1): e157–e162.

IOM (2011). *Health IT and Patient Safety: Building Safer Systems for Better Care*. Washington, DC: National Academies Press.

Jung, M., A. Hoerbst et al. (2013). Attitude of physicians towards automatic alerting in computerized physician order entry systems. *Methods of Information in Medicine* 52: 99–108.

Kaushal, R. and D. Blumenthal (2014). Introduction and commentary for special issue on health information technology. *Health Services Research* 49(1pt2): 319–324.

Kellermann, A. L. and S. S. Jones (2013). What it will take to achieve the as-yet-unfulfilled promises of health information technology. *Health Affairs* 32(1): 63–68.

Kho, A. N., B. N. Doebbeling et al. (2013). A regional informatics platform for coordinated antibiotic-resistant infection tracking, alerting, and prevention. *Clinical Infectious Diseases* 57(2): 254–262.

Kohn, L. T., J. M. Corrigan et al. (2000). *To Err is Human: Building a Safer Health System*. Washington, DC: National Academies Press.

Koppel, R., J. P. Metlay et al. (2005). Role of computerized physician order entry systems in facilitating medication errors. *Journal of the American Medical Association* 293(10): 1197–1203.

Kushniruk, A. W., D. W. Bates et al. (2013). National efforts to improve health information system safety in Canada, the United States of America and England. *International Journal of Medical Informatics* 82(5): e149–e160.

Lenzer, J. (2011). Big Pharma would like to befriend you. *British Medical Journal* 342: d4075.

Liang, B. A. and T. Mackey (2011). Direct-to-consumer advertising with interactive internet media: Global regulation and public health issues. *Journal of the American Medical Association* 305(8): 824–825.

Linsky, A. and S. R. Simon (2013). Medication discrepancies in integrated electronic health records. *BMJ Quality & Safety* 22(2): 103–109.

Martich, G. D., C. S. Waldmann et al. (2004). Clinical informatics in critical care. *Journal of Intensive Care Medicine* 19(3): 154–163.

Mathew, G., A. Kho et al. (2012). Concept and development of a discharge alert filter for abnormal laboratory values coupled with computerized provider order entry: A tool for quality improvement and hospital risk management. *Journal of Patient Safety* 8(2): 69–75.

Maviglia, S. M., C. S. Yoon et al. (2006). KnowledgeLink: Impact of context-sensitive information retrieval on clinicians' information needs. *Journal of the American Medical Informatics Association* 13(1): 67–73.

Mcdonald, C. (1976). Protocol-based computer reminders, the quality of care and the nonperfectability of man. *New England Journal of Medicine* 295(24): 1351–1355.

McDonald, C. J., J. M. Overhage et al. (2005). The Indiana network for patient care: A working local health information infrastructure. *Health Affairs* 24(5): 1214–1220.

McGreevey, J. D., 3rd (2013). Order sets in electronic health records: Principles of good practice. *Chest* 143(1): 228–235.

Mello, M. M. and N. A. Messing (2011). Restrictions on the use of prescribing data for drug promotion. *New England Journal of Medicine* 365(13): 1248–1254.

Osheroff, J. A., J. M. Teich et al. (2007). A roadmap for national action on clinical decision support. *Journal of the American Medical Informatics Association* 14(2): 141–145.

Osheroff, J. A. T., J. M. Teich, D. Levick, L. Saldana, F. T. Velasc, K. M. Rogers, and R. A. Jenders (2012). *Improving Outcomes with Clinical Decision Support: An Implementer's Guide*. Chicago, IL: HIMSS.

Payne, T. H., P. J. Hoey et al. (2003). Preparation and use of preconstructed orders, order sets, and order menus in a computerized provider order entry system. *Journal of the American Medical Informatics Association* 10(4): 322–329.

Platt, R. and R. Carnahan (2012). The US food and drug administration's mini-sentinel program. *Pharmacoepidemiology and Drug Safety* 21(S1): 1–303.

Practice, D. t. t. A. C. o. P., approved by the ASHP Board of Directors on April 13 et al. (2013). ASHP statement on the pharmacist's role in medication reconciliation. *American Journal of Health-System Pharmacy* 70(5): 453–456.

Sackett, D. L. (1998). Evidence-based medicine. *Spine* 23(10): 1085–1086.

Samal, L., A. Wright et al. (2011). Leveraging electronic health records to support chronic disease management: The need for temporal data views. *Inform Prim Care* 19(2): 65–74.

Sarasohn-Kahn, J. (April 22, 2008). The wisdom of patients: Health care meets online social media. Retrieved May 28, 2014, from http://www.chcf.org/publications/2008/04/the-wisdom-of-patients-health-care-meets-online-social-media.

Schiff, G. D. and N. I. Goldfield (1994). Deming meets Braverman: Toward a progressive analysis of the continuous quality improvement paradigm. *International Journal of Health Services* 24(4): 655–674.

Schiff, G. D., D. Klass et al. (2003). Linking laboratory and pharmacy: Opportunities for reducing errors and improving care. *Archives of Internal Medicine* 163(8): 893–900.

Schiff, G. D. and T. D. Rucker (1998). Computerized prescribing: Building the electronic infrastructure for better medication usage. *Journal of the American Medical Association* 279(13): 1024–1029.

Schnipper, J. L., C. Hamann et al. (2009). Effect of an electronic medication reconciliation application and process redesign on potential adverse drug events: A cluster-randomized trial. *Archives of Internal Medicine* 169(8): 771–780.

Seidling, H. M., S. Phansalkar et al. (2011). Factors influencing alert acceptance: A novel approach for predicting the success of clinical decision support. *Journal of the American Medical Informatics Association* 18(4): 479–484.

Sinsky, C. A., J. W. Beasley et al. (2014). Electronic health records: design, implementation, and policy for higher-value primary CareEHRs for higher-value primary care. *Annals of Internal Medicine* 160(10): 727–728.

Strom, B. L. (2006). *Pharmacoepidemiology*. Hoboken, NJ: John Wiley & Sons.

Surescripts (2012). The National Progress Report on E-prescribing and Safe-Rx Ranking. http://surescripts.com/docs/default-source/national-progress-reports/national-progress-report-on-e-prescribing-year-2012.pdf.

Surescripts (2014). Privacy Policy, from http://surescripts.com/privacy-policy. Accessed December 6, 2015.

Tamblyn, R., T. Eguale et al. (2014). The incidence and determinants of primary nonadherence with prescribed medication in primary care: A cohort study. *Annals of Internal Medicine* 160(7): 441–450.

Terry, N. P. (2013). Meaningful adoption: What we know or think we know about the financing, effectiveness, quality, and safety of electronic medical records. *Journal of Legal Medicine* 34(1): 7–42.

Van Der Sijs, H., J. Aarts et al. (2006). Overriding of drug safety alerts in computerized physician order entry. *Journal of the American Medical Informatics Association* 13(2): 138–147.

Villalba Van Dijk L, De Vries H, Bell DS. Electronic prescribing in the United Kingdom and in the Netherlands. (Prepared by RAND Europe under Contract No. RD-141-AHRQ.) AHRQ Publication No. 11-0044-EF. Rockville, MD: Agency for Healthcare Research and Quality. February 2011. https://healthit.ahrq.gov/sites/default/files/docs/citation/europe-e-prescribing-report.pdf.

Walgreens (1999). Media backgrounder on electronic prescriptions, from http://lobby.la.psu.edu/044_Internet_Prescriptions/Organizational_Statements/WG/WG_Media.htm. Accessed December 6, 2015.

Waterson, P. (2014). Health information technology and sociotechnical systems: A progress report on recent developments within the UK National Health Service (NHS). *Applied Ergonomics* 45(2): 150–161.

Wright, A., S. Henkin et al. (2013). Early results of the meaningful use program for electronic health records. *New England Journal of Medicine* 368(8): 779–780.

Wynia, M. K., G. W. Torres et al. (2011). Many physicians are willing to use patients' electronic personal health records, but doctors differ by location, gender, and practice. *Health Affairs* 30(2): 266–273.

Chapter 22

Assessing Medicare Part D after 10 Years*

Jack Hoadley

Contents

* This chapter is based in part on testimony given to the Senate Special Committee on Aging, May 2013. It also draws on material prepared for and funded by the Kaiser Family Foundation.

Introduction

In 2015, the Medicare Part D prescription drug benefit marked its 10th year of operation and thus represents one of the newer components of a Medicare program that has delivered benefits for 50 years. Medicare beneficiaries include Americans who are age 65 or older and are eligible for Social Security, who have received Social Security disability for at least 2 years, or who are diagnosed with end-stage renal disease.

History of Medicare Part D

Part D was signed into law by President George W. Bush on December 8, 2003, as part of the Medicare Prescription Drug, Improvement, and Modernization Act of 2003 (MMA). The program's birth was a challenging one, as passage took place in a contentious, partisan environment with close votes in both the House and the Senate. Final passage in the House of Representatives occurred on November 22, 2003, by a vote of 220 in favor and 215 against, but this margin was accomplished only after the House vote was held open for about 3 h in the middle of the night. The Senate passed the legislation on November 25, 2003, by a 54–44 vote, after clearing an earlier procedural by one vote over the required 60 votes.

The dispute over passage was not about the idea of adding a drug benefit to Medicare, a concept that enjoyed relatively broad support. But some questioned the scope of adding a new and potentially costly program to an entitlement program. Beyond that, members of the Congress disagreed over the design of the benefit, especially over the idea of delivering the drug benefit only through private health plans.

The history of outpatient drug coverage in Medicare is far longer. By one account, such coverage was omitted from the original Medicare program in 1965 "on the grounds of unpredictable and potentially high costs."*[1] Other opportunities to address outpatient drug coverage came and went until the Congress added an outpatient drug benefit to Medicare as part of the Medicare Catastrophic Coverage Act of 1988. This benefit, which would have provided coverage after an initial $(USD)600 deductible, never went into effect because the underlying legislation was repealed in 1989 as a result of public pressure. Because the benefit provided only catastrophic coverage, many seniors objected to paying for coverage that they believed was of no benefit to them.

* For more information on the history of Medicare drug coverage.

President Bill Clinton included Medicare drug coverage in his unsuccessful effort in 1993 to enact the broader health reform legislation known as the Health Security Act. Then in 1999, President Clinton proposed a Part D drug benefit. This proposal did not become law, but included many but not all of the elements that were part of the program that passed in 2003, including the idea that it would be a voluntary benefit.*

Adding drug coverage to Medicare became one of the key issues in the 2000 presidential election campaign. With high public support for the idea of adding drug coverage to Medicare, both candidates felt the need to have a credible proposal. Al Gore's proposal followed roughly the lines of the Clinton proposal, while George Bush envisioned a more limited program to assist low-income Medicare beneficiaries purchase coverage through private insurers.

As finally enacted in 2003, Medicare Part D marked several firsts. Not only was it is the first program to offer outpatient prescription drug benefits to Medicare beneficiaries, but it was the first part of Medicare to be made available solely through competing private health plans, rather than being part of traditional, fee-for-service Medicare. Those beneficiaries who get their other Medicare benefits through traditional, fee-for-service Medicare are able to enroll in a stand-alone prescription drug plan (PDP). Those who have selected to get their Medicare benefits through a Medicare Advantage managed-care plans may enroll for prescription drug coverage through that same Medicare Advantage plan.

Part D also marked the first time that assistance for low-income beneficiaries was offered directly through Medicare, not through supplemental coverage provided through Medicaid. Although everyone is eligible for the Part D benefit without any type of means test, those at lower income levels are eligible for a low-income subsidy (LIS) that provides more highly subsidized coverage, typically without a monthly premium and with low cost sharing on their drug purchases. As a result of later changes in law, those at higher income levels pay a premium surcharge.

The standard Part D benefit includes a deductible and beneficiary cost sharing. But it also includes the unusual feature of a coverage gap or "doughnut hole," in which beneficiaries are required to pay the entire cost of their drugs. Those who make it through the gap become eligible for catastrophic coverage with more modest cost sharing. As a result of the Affordable Care Act, the coverage gap is currently being phased out and will no longer exist as of 2020. Plans offering Part D have the flexibility to modify the benefit design, within specified limits. Many plans eliminate the standard deductible, most plans substitute tiered cost sharing with flat co-payments for the 25% coinsurance in the standard benefit, and most also include a specialty tier for selected high-cost drugs. In addition, some plans offer enhanced benefits, for example, to provide coverage for some drugs in the coverage gap or to reduce overall cost-sharing levels.[3]

Part D Program Today†

In 2015, about 39 million Medicare beneficiaries (over two-thirds of all Medicare beneficiaries) enrolled in Medicare Part D. About 61% of them (24.0 million) are in PDPs; the others are enrolled in Medicare Advantage drug plans. In addition, about 6% of Medicare beneficiaries maintain comparable retiree drug coverage through a former employer. The government provides a subsidy to these companies to support that coverage. Medicare beneficiaries have a choice of about 30 stand-alone PDPs. The exact number varies by region, but since most companies offering

* For more information on the history of Medicare drug coverage, see Oliver et al.[2]

† Most of the descriptive data in this section are taken from analysis conducted for the Kaiser Family Foundation.[3]

Part D plans do so nationally, the array of PDP choices is generally similar in all regions. There is more variation in the availability of Medicare Advantage drug plans, but on average, beneficiaries have access to about 20 Medicare Advantage drug plans. In addition, about one-sixth of Part D enrollees (6.6 million in 2015) are in drug plans organized by a former employer and open only to the retirees of one or more particular employers.

The Part D marketplace has been somewhat concentrated. In 2015, about half of all Part D enrollees are in plans sponsored by just three firms: UnitedHealth, Humana, and CVS Health. UnitedHealth and Humana have had the most enrollees from the first year onward, while CVS Health has built up its enrollment through a series of acquisitions. The 10 firms with the most enrollees collectively account for about 80% of all enrollees. The program has been dominated by national firms, but in a few parts of the country, regional companies have maintained a substantial market share (Exhibit 22.1).

The average monthly premium for the stand-alone drug plans, weighted by enrollment, in 2015 is $(USD)37.02. Premiums have been generally flat since 2010. Between 2006 and 2010, however, premiums rose about 9% per year, from $(USD)25.93 to $(USD)37.25. Premiums for Medicare Advantage drug plans are lower, in part because they can apply savings from other health services to reduce their drug costs (Exhibit 22.2).

The basic design of the drug benefit was established in statute, but plans have some flexibility to modify the design. The basic design combines an initial deductible ($[USD]320 in 2015), followed by an initial coverage period in which beneficiaries pay 25% coinsurance on each drug purchase. After accumulating a certain amount ($[USD]2960 in 2015) in total drug purchases, beneficiaries enter a coverage gap (often referred to as the "doughnut hole"). Prior to 2011, beneficiaries were required to pay the full cost of drugs while in the gap. As a result of the Affordable Care Act, the gap is being phased out and will be gone in 2020. Once beneficiaries have reached a threshold for out-of-pocket costs ($[USD]4700 in 2015, equivalent to about $(USD)7062 in total drug costs), the coinsurance is set at the greater of 5% of drug costs or a fixed co-payment ($[USD]2.65 for a generic or multisource drug or $(USD)6.60 for all other drugs) (Exhibit 22.3).

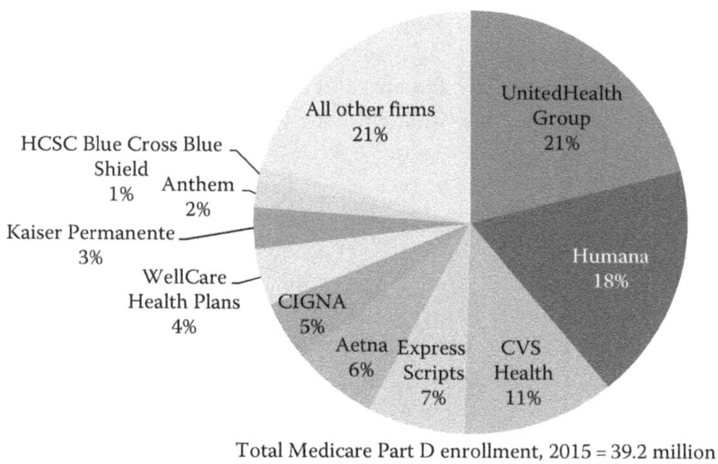

Exhibit 22.1 Distribution of Medicare Part D enrollment, by firm, 2015. ***Note*****: Includes plans in the territories and employer group plans. (From Georgetown analysis of CMS Enrollment Files, 2015, for the Kaiser Family Foundation.)**

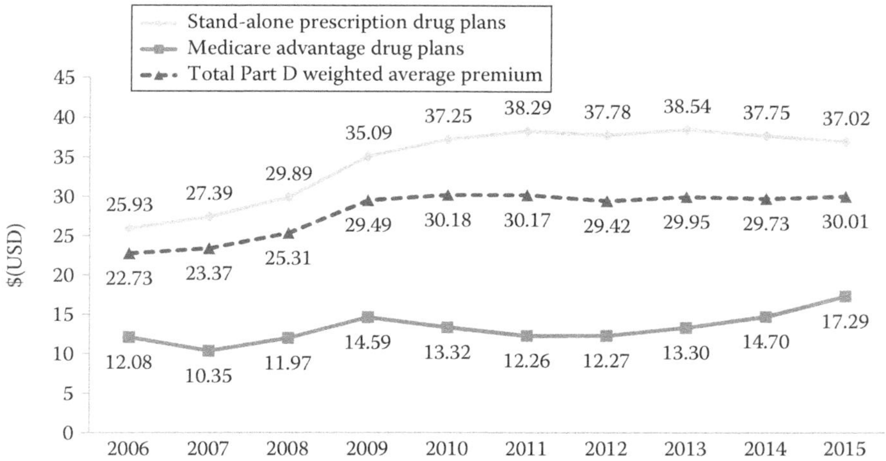

Exhibit 22.2 Medicare Part D weighted average monthly premiums, by plan type, 2006–2015. ***Note*****: Average premiums are weighted by enrollment in each year. Excludes Part D plans in the territories. (From Georgetown analysis of data from CMS for the Kaiser Family Foundation.)**

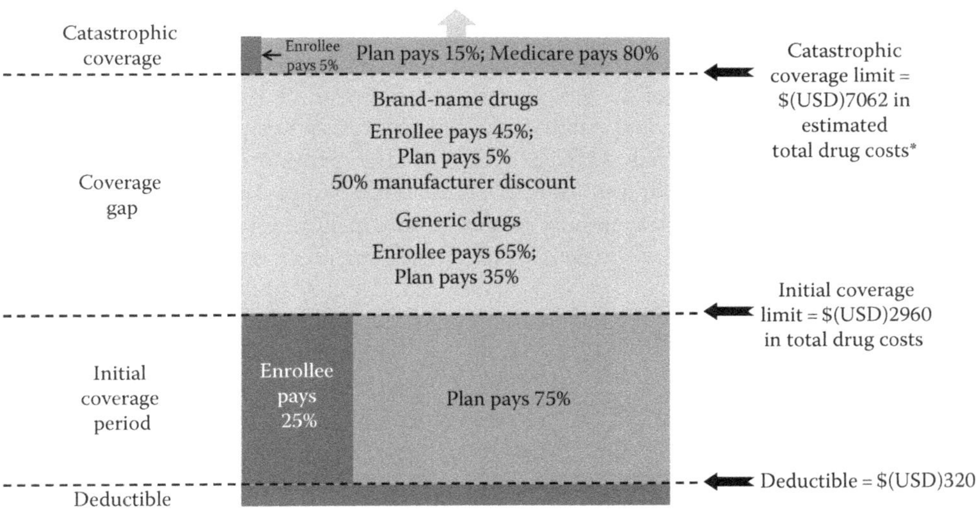

Exhibit 22.3 Standard Medicare prescription drug benefit, 2015. ***Note*****: *Amount corresponds to the estimated catastrophic coverage limit for non-low-income subsidy (SIL) enrollees ($[USD]6680 for LIS enrollees), which corresponds to true out-of-pocket spending of $(USD)4700 (the amount used to determine when an enrollee reaches the catastrophic coverage threshold, amounts rounded to nearest dollar). (From Kaiser Family Foundation illustration of standard Medicare drug benefit for 2015.)**

Plans are permitted to modify this standard design in one of two ways. Some plans offer a more generous or enhanced benefit. The greater value typically involves some combination of a reduced or eliminated deductible, lower cost sharing, and increased coverage during the coverage gap. Other plans offer a design that is actuarially equivalent to the basic benefit design, meaning that it includes the same overall amount of out-of-pocket costs for plan enrollees. For most plans, this means substituting for the fixed coinsurance a system of tiers with different cost-sharing amounts for preferred and nonpreferred generic drugs and for preferred and nonpreferred brand-name drugs. Some plans also lower or eliminate the deductible in exchange for higher cost-sharing levels.

In 2015, no prescription drug plans (PDPs) and 2% of medicare advantage prescription drug access (MA-PDs) use the standard benefit design. In earlier years, this design was somewhat more common, but even in the program's first year, a majority of plans have used some alternate design. Plan enrollees tend to prefer flat and thus predictable co-payments as opposed to the 25% coinsurance in the standard benefit. Thus, competitive pressures pushed plans in this direction. About 55% of PDPs and about 80% of MA-PDs offer enhanced benefits.

In 2015, nearly half of all PDPs use the standard deductible, while most other PDPs eliminate the deductible completely. By contrast, only 16% of MA-PDs use the standard deductible. Use of a deductible has grown modestly over the history of the program, but even in the program's first year, one-third of PDPs used the standard deductible.

Over time, plans' use of cost sharing has evolved considerably. In the program's first year, the most common approach was four cost-sharing tiers: generic drugs, preferred brand-name drugs, nonpreferred brand-name drugs, and specialty drugs. But some plans used just one tier for brand-name drugs, and some plans did not have a separate tier for specialty drugs. Within a year, most plans adopted specialty tiers, and the use of the four-tier system had become nearly universal by 2009. After that date, some plans started dividing generic drugs into preferred and nonpreferred tiers. By 2013, this five-tier approach had become the most common approach.

Among plans offering an enhanced benefit design, some plans have offered some coverage for drugs in the coverage gap. Mostly, plans with additional coverage in the gap have included only a subset of drugs in that coverage. In the program's first year, several plans offered generous gap coverage for both generics and brand-name drugs, but these plans attracted mostly enrollees with high use of drugs. As a result, these plans experienced large premium increases, followed either by departure from the program or a substantial reduction in gap coverage. In 2015, about three-fourths of plans have no gap coverage; those that do mostly include only generics in that coverage. Because premiums for these plans are much higher than for plans without such coverage, they have attracted few enrollees.

Part D plan formularies typically include more than the minimum drugs required by Centers for Medicare and Medicaid Services (CMS) standards. Some plans list all or nearly all drugs on their formularies, while other plans are more selective with as few as two-thirds of all drugs on formulary. Plans with more restrictive formularies often limit coverage of brand-name drugs in those drug classes where several generic drugs are available. Plans with less restrictive formularies may include those brand-name drugs, but place them in a formulary tier with substantially higher cost sharing. Beneficiaries retain the option of requesting an exception to have the plan cover an off-formulary drug or can purchase the drug by paying out of pocket.

Formularies also vary in their use of utilization management. Even if a drug is listed on a plan's formulary, utilization management rules, including step therapy, prior authorization, and quality limits, may restrict a beneficiary's access to the drug. Since 2007, PDPs have applied utilization management restrictions to an increasing share of on-formulary brand-name drugs. The presence of such rules has increased since 2007, with 39% of drugs subject to some utilization management in 2015, up from 18% in 2007. Quantity limits (e.g., limiting a prescription to 30 pills for 30 days) are applied to 18% of drugs in 2015, prior authorization is applied to 23% of drugs, and step therapy to 1% of drugs, on average across all PDPs.

Overall access to pharmacies is high; most PDPs contract with at least 95% of all available pharmacies. In contrast to the first years of Medicare Part D, however, a growing number of PDPs are using preferred pharmacy networks, whereby enrollees pay lower cost sharing for their prescriptions if they use preferred pharmacies. The idea behind these arrangements is that Part D plans are able to negotiate discounted prices at certain pharmacies in exchange for higher volume of sales at those pharmacies. The lower cost sharing creates an incentive for enrollees to use the preferred pharmacies.

This trend has gained prominence with the market entry in 2011 and 2012 of co-branded PDPs featuring relationships with specific pharmacy chains, such as the Humana Walmart-Preferred Rx PDP and the Aetna CVS/Pharmacy PDP. In 2015, 87% of all PDPs—representing 81% of all enrollees—have a preferred pharmacy network. By contrast, only 7% of PDPs (6% of enrollees) had a preferred pharmacy network in 2011. Medicare Advantage drug plans are much less likely to use preferred pharmacy networks.

In addition to creating the Part D program, the Medicare Modernization Act established a subsidy for companies offering their former employees drug coverage as least as generous as the basic Part D benefit. Initially, these subsidies encouraged many such companies not to drop their drug coverage. In the program's first year (2006), about seven million beneficiaries had subsidized retiree drug coverage from a former employer. In the Affordable Care Act, a change to the tax treatment of this subsidy made it less attractive for companies to accept the subsidy. As a result, the number of Medicare beneficiaries with subsidized retiree coverage decreased rapidly to an estimated two million in 2015.[4] The Medicare Trustees estimate that the use of subsidized retiree coverage will drop further to one million by 2018. Instead, many employers are working with insurers to create Part D plans tailored to the needs of their retirees and partially paid by the company.

In 2012, the average drug expenditure per month for Part D enrollees was $(USD)235, based on 4.3 prescriptions filled per month.[5] Average spending for beneficiaries qualifying for the LIS was about double that for non-LIS beneficiaries, in part because of differences in health status and in part because LIS beneficiaries select brand-name drugs over generics more frequently. About one-fourth of all prescriptions filled by Part D enrollees, representing about 16% of all drug spending, are for cardiovascular drugs, including those used to treat hypertension, hypercholesterolemia, and other cardiovascular conditions.[6] Psychotherapeutic drugs, including antidepressants and antipsychotic drugs, are the next most used class of drugs—representing about 8% of prescriptions and 13% of spending.

Successes of Medicare Part D

In key respects, Part D can be considered a success, although several ongoing problems limit our ability to call the program an unqualified success. The remainder of this chapter outlines both the program's successes and its ongoing challenges.

Success: The Cost of Part D Has Been Lower Than Expectations

A key element of the debate over the creation of Part D was the potential cost of the program. At the time of passage, the Congressional Budget Office (CBO) estimated the 10-year budget impact of the drug benefit as $(USD)407 billion for fiscal years 2004–2013, while the Bush Administration's estimates were 25% higher. It also projected an initial average premium of $(USD)35 per month, rising to $(USD)58 by 2013. Estimating these costs was challenging, since there was no precedent for the program's stand-alone private drug plans. Trends in drug spending were also a concern, with annual growth at the time standing at around 12%—a combination of both price increases and higher utilization.*[7]

The reality is that Part D spending has been considerably lower.[7a] Based on spending numbers from the 2012 Medicare Trustees Report, total spending on Part D benefits and administration was about 74% of projected levels in the program's first year (2006) and averaged 68% of projections over the program's first 6 years (Exhibit 22.4). In 2011, actual program spending was $(USD)60 billion, compared to the projected level of $(USD)95 billion. The average Part D premium, as measured by the base beneficiary premium used by the program to set the federal subsidy level, was about $(USD)30 in 2006 and has fluctuated between $(USD)26 and $(USD)33 through 2015. The $(USD)31 average premium in 2013 fell well below the CBO estimate of $(USD)58 for 2013.

Several factors have contributed to lower Part D costs. One of the most important was that the growth of drug spending across all payers (public and private) has been considerably slower than projected in the past 10–15 years.[7a] CBO projected 12% growth per capita between the law's passage in 2003 and the 2006 start of the benefit and 9% per capita from 2006 onward. In fact, the actual trend has been 10% and 4%, respectively. The Part D program has contributed to the trends, but also benefited from broader system-wide trends, especially the greater availability of

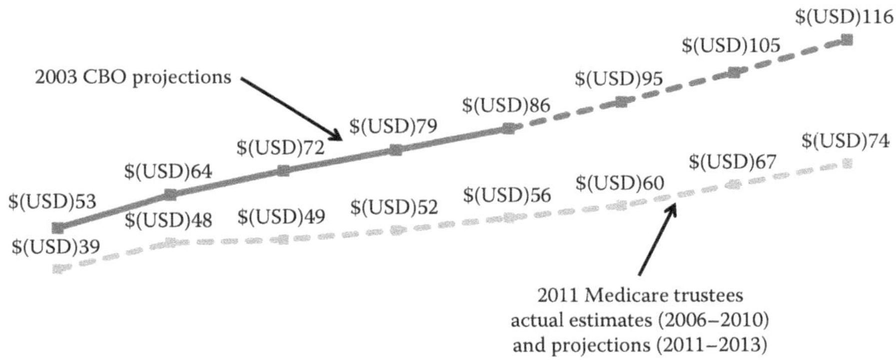

Difference, estimate less actual	2006	2007	2008	2009	2010	2011	2012	2013
$	13.9	16.0	22.9	26.6	30.4	34.7	37.9	41.8
%	74	75	68	66	65	63	64	64

Exhibit 22.4 Comparison of projected and actual Medicare Part D benefit spending, 2006–2013: Congressional Budget Office (CBO) (2003) and Medicare trustees (2011) (billions of dollars). ***Note*****: CBO projections are adjusted from fiscal years to calendar years. Medicare Trustees actual spending amounts are adjusted for reconciliation payments. All totals exclude offsetting receipts from beneficiary premium amounts and state "clawback" payments for dual eligibles. (From Congressional Budget Office, July 2004; 2011 Medicare Trustees Report.)**

* Similar conclusions have been noted elsewhere.

generic drugs. Lower drug use was also affected by factors such as the recession that started in 2008 and concerns about the safety of some popular drugs.

Underlying the lower overall growth rate in drug spending has been the wider availability of generic drugs. The start of Part D coincided with patent expirations for many of the most commonly prescribed brand-name drugs—sometimes referred to as the "patent cliff"—and the relatively slow pipeline for new drugs. The share of generic drugs for Part D enrollees rose from 60% in 2006 to 77% in 2011 and is higher today.[6*] Because the cost of the average generic drug is about 25% of the chemically equivalent brand-name drug, higher generic use translates into lower drug spending both for beneficiaries and for the program as a whole. Some of the trend to more generics, resulting from the direct substitution of a generic drug for the chemically equivalent brand-name drug (referred to as generic substitution), is automatic as a result of state laws. Part D plans have further encouraged substitution of generic drugs for brand-name drugs in the same drug class (but not chemical equivalents) through tiered cost sharing and other management techniques. This type of therapeutic substitution is higher when plans lower the cost sharing for generic drugs, and there is some evidence that eliminating generic co-payments altogether increases that effect.[8] It appears that Part D plans are not taking all steps that have the potential for maximizing generic use.

Based on available evidence, claims that spending is lower because of the program's use of competing private plans seem overstated. There is some tendency for plan enrollees to switch to lower-premium plans, though not as clearly to plans that have low overall costs. For example, when plan enrollees faced a premium increase of $(USD)20 per month or more over the period from 2006 to 2010, they were two to four times more likely to switch plans than the average PDP enrollee. Still over two-thirds of enrollees facing these higher premiums stayed with their current plan.[9]

In general, the relatively few PDP enrollees who switched to a different plan between 2006 and 2010 were more likely than those who did not switch to end up in a plan that lowered their costs.[9] But they were more likely to find a plan that lowered premiums than a plan that lowered their overall out-of-pocket costs. This fits with a broader observation that beneficiaries do not end up in plans that optimize their lowest possible spending.[10] Although some decisions by beneficiaries help to encourage cost efficiency in the Part D market, the general tendency to avoid changing plans—strengthened what the perceived complexity of the benefit choices—weakens one potential source of market discipline.

One additional contributing factor to lower costs—but not a sign of program success—is that initial program enrollment was significantly below projected levels in 2006. Whereas CBO projected close to universal drug coverage for Medicare beneficiaries, a share of beneficiaries did not take advantage of the new opportunity to enroll in Part D. Enrollment growth from year to year, however, has been at projected levels. Later in the chapter, we discuss the ongoing gap in uptake. Lower enrollment translated to lower program costs, although it also may have translated into some people going without protection from out-of-pocket drug costs.

Success: Part D Has Improved Access to Prescription Drugs for Part D Enrollees in General and for Low-Income Enrollees in Particular

A significant motivation for creating a prescription drug program for Medicare beneficiaries was evidence that some beneficiaries had no access to coverage and that they were going without some needed

---

* A new measure introduced by CMS for what drugs are counted as generics lowers the generic rate for 2011 to 70%.

drugs as a result. Before the program was created, 25% of Medicare beneficiaries had no drug coverage.[11] Coverage was available to some retirees through their former employers, and others obtained coverage through privately purchased Medicare supplemental insurance (Medigap), which tended to be costly and provided only limited coverage. Those who qualified based on their low incomes received drug coverage through Medicaid. But for others, there was simply no good coverage available.

When coverage was lacking, two things happened. First, when beneficiaries without coverage purchase drugs, not only did they pay the entire cost out of pocket, but they faced higher prices at the pharmacy than those with insurance coverage.[12] Health plans that provide a drug benefit typically negotiate lower prices with pharmacies in exchange for directing customers to those pharmacies. Those with no coverage lack access to those lower prices. Second, without drug coverage, people are more likely to skip some necessary drugs and to take others less frequently than prescribed.[13]

The introduction of the Part D program has increased access, both in terms of having coverage for their drugs and in terms of taking more of their prescribed drugs. Under Part D, use of drugs grew considerably for those without a prior source of coverage.[14] Nearly every Part D enrollee (92%) fills at least one prescription during the year.[6] One study found that after the introduction of Part D, plan enrollees with no previous drug coverage experienced large drug spending increases.[15] Another study showed that there were significant increases (11%–37%, depending on the drug class) in use for nearly all drugs in four classes of medications for those without prior coverage.[16]

Before Part D, many Medicare beneficiaries with low incomes were dually eligible for Medicare and Medicaid; as a result, they received drug coverage through Medicaid. Under the MMA, this coverage was transferred to Part D, and all dually eligible beneficiaries were automatically deemed to be enrolled for the program's LIS. For these LIS beneficiaries, the shift to a new program was a disruption of existing coverage. For some who faced no cost sharing at all under their state Medicaid program, it meant having to pay small co-payments to obtain drugs. The LIS subsidy, however, opened up subsidized drug coverage to another 1.5 million low-income Medicare beneficiaries without coverage under Medicaid. For both groups, the LIS program offers access to plans with no premium and reduced cost sharing to much more modest levels, eliminates the coverage gap, and offers a true out-of-pocket cap.

Success: Part D Has Lowered the Out-of-Pocket Costs of Prescription Drugs for Many Part D Enrollees

For Medicare beneficiaries previously lacking any drug coverage and for some whose previous drug coverage was not generous, Part D has reduced the amounts they pay out of pocket to obtain needed drugs.[14] For example, one study found declines in the amounts spent out of pocket of 37%–58%, depending on the drug class.[16] Although more research is needed, there is some evidence that increased use and adherence to medications by Part D enrollees are saving money elsewhere in Medicare as a result of fewer hospitalizations and less use of other services.[17] This literature was reviewed by CBO in 2012, leading to the conclusion that it is reasonable to attribute overall Medicare savings to increase use of prescription drugs.[18]

Success: Overall, Medicare Beneficiaries Participating in Part D Have Been Satisfied with the Program

At first, many Medicare beneficiaries were skeptical about the new program.[19] According to a poll in April 2005, 34% of seniors had an unfavorable impression of the program, compared to only

21% with a favorable impression.[20] Ratings had improved modestly just before implementation, but there were still more unfavorable ratings than favorable.[21] Understanding of the new drug benefit and how it worked was also lacking. As open enrollment for the new program began, a majority of those polled said they did not have enough information to understand how the new benefit would affect them personally.

After a year's experience with the program, however, Medicare beneficiaries had grown to understand the program better, leading them to view it more favorably. In November 2006, half of the seniors polled said the program was working well or that just minor changes were needed, although more chose the latter.[22]

In 2012, over three-fourths of Part D enrollees reported that there were satisfied with the drug benefit.[23] Over 90% said they would recommend their plans to other people. Other surveys conducted by stakeholders have consistently shown high rates of satisfaction.[24]

Success: A Big Design Flaw in Part D—The Coverage Gap—Is Being Fixed

In the Affordable Care Act, the Congress addressed one of the least-liked features of Part D. The benefit's coverage gap, also called the doughnut hole, constituted a segment of the benefit when enrollees were responsible for paying the full cost of their drugs out of pocket. This gap fell between the benefit's initial coverage period and the start of catastrophic coverage. The coverage gap was included when policymakers wanted to limit the projected cost of Part D while also seeking to maintain both front-end coverage that was politically popular and back-end (catastrophic) coverage that was an important element of insurance coverage. Some have suggested that the coverage gap has helped to contain costs by creating more cost exposure for program enrollees, while others have pointed to its creation of an impediment to access.

The coverage gap has not been well understood by enrollees,[25] but one in five Part D enrollees typically reaches the gap in any 1 year and experiences higher out-of-pocket costs. Many enrollees in this situation respond by stopping some of their prescribed drugs or by taking them less often.[26] Some beneficiaries in these situations may be eliminating unnecessary drugs at the advice of a physician, and others may be substituting free samples or drugs bought for cash from cheaper sources. It is harder to know whether this reduction in use has health consequences.[27]

The Affordable Care Act's reduction of the gap started in 2011 with lower beneficiary costs for brand-name drugs, accomplished by requiring manufacturers to reduce the price of these drugs by 50% for purchases made during the gap. In addition, Part D plans gradually cover an increasing share of the cost of drugs purchased in the gap. By 2020, enrollees will face the same cost sharing at the spending levels now associated with the gap as they do at lower spending levels—so that the Part D benefit will have no coverage gap after that date (Exhibit 22.5a and b from/http://kff.org/health-reform/issue-brief/explaining-health-care-reform-key-changes-to/. Accessed December 7, 2015).

Success: Coverage of Drugs in Part D is Reasonably Robust

Formularies used by Part D plans are reviewed by CMS based on several criteria. These include the statutory rule that plans must cover at least two drugs in each drug class, another provision in statute requiring that a plan's design and benefits, including the formulary, not substantially discourage enrollment of certain beneficiaries (the nondiscrimination rule), and additional rules set forth in program guidance by CMS.[28] The most significant of the these rules (later included in statute through an amendment to the original Part D legislation) is that plans must include in their formularies all or substantially all drugs in certain protected classes (currently including

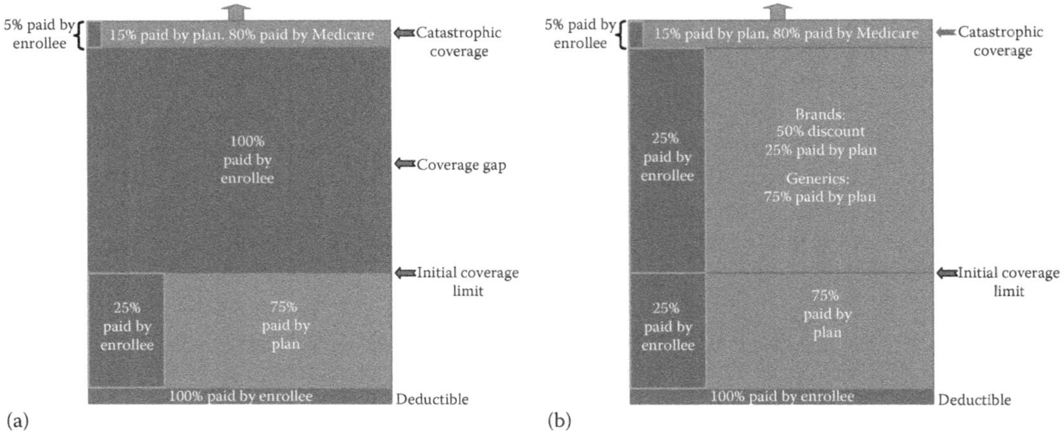

Exhibit 22.5 (a) Standard Medicare prescription drug benefit, 2020 without health reform. (From Kaiser Family Foundation illustration of standard Medicare drug benefit in 2020 without health reform legislation.) (b) Standard Medicare prescription drug benefit, 2020 with health reform. (From Kaiser Family Foundation illustration of standard Medicare drug benefit for 2020 under the Patient Protection and Affordable Care Act, as amended by the Health Care and Education Reconciliation Act of 2010.)

drugs used to treat mental health conditions, HIV/AIDS, and cancer). Furthermore, beneficiaries retain the option of requesting an exception to have the plan cover an off-formulary drug or can purchase the drug by paying out of pocket.

The reality is that plan formularies tend to be well above the required minimum levels.[3] In 2014, the average PDP enrollee was enrolled in a plan where the formulary lists 83% of eligible drugs, slightly below the average in recent years. The average enrollee in MA-PD plans is in a plan with slightly more drugs (87%) on formulary than PDPs. The scope of formulary coverage does vary considerably across plans. Some plans list all or nearly all eligible drugs on their formularies, while other plans list as few as two-thirds of these drugs.

For the most part, Medicare beneficiaries seem satisfied that drug coverage is reasonably robust. In 2012, 80% of Part D enrollees reported that they were satisfied with their plan's list of drugs covered. Only 7% reported that there was a medication they had not obtained, most often due to cost or because a drug was not on the plan's formulary.[29]

Outstanding Issues for Medicare Part D

Notwithstanding a record of significant success for Part D, various policy issues remain for the program. Congress and CMS have made adjustments to lessen some of the outstanding concerns, but there is still room for improvement.

Issue: Not Every Beneficiary Has Drug Coverage

According to the most recent estimate, 88% of Medicare beneficiaries had drug coverage in 2011, either through a Part D plan or some other source of equivalent or better coverage.[21,30] One reason for this high level is a penalty for late enrollment, created in law as an incentive for Medicare beneficiaries to enroll when they are first eligible. Those who do not enroll and have no other source of comparable coverage face a 1% premium surcharge for each month that they have not enrolled. Thus, a beneficiary who defers enrollment for 2 years and maintains no comparable coverage will pay a 24% premium surcharge for the entire time he or she is enrolled in Part D.

Nevertheless, 12% of beneficiaries lacked drug coverage in 2011; about 1 beneficiary in 10 has been without drug coverage starting in the program's first year. Although we lack extensive information on why some people decline to sign up for coverage, research indicates that beneficiaries who do not enroll in Part D tend to be healthier and have lower drug spending.[31] Appropriately, those with greater needs were the most likely to enroll. And some of those with low drug spending may be making rational decisions to forgo purchasing coverage, even taking into account the late enrollment penalty. But others go without coverage because they found that premiums were too costly, the enrollment process was too difficult, and information was too hard to obtain.[32] There is also some evidence of different rates of enrollment for certain population groups. For example, one survey shows that Hispanics were 35% less likely to have drug coverage in 2011 from either Part D or some other source than non-Hispanic whites, whereas there was no difference between non-Hispanic blacks and non-Hispanic whites.[30]

It seems important that the program reach out to all beneficiaries and determine whether some are unaware of the help they could receive from Part D. One option would be to increase outreach and counseling efforts, with a particular focus on hard-to-reach populations. Another option would be some form of default enrollment with an opt-out option, at least for new Medicare beneficiaries.[33]

Issue: Some Beneficiaries Who Are Eligible for the Low-Income Subsidy Are Not Signed Up for This Extra Help

The LIS in Part D provides assistance with the cost of drug coverage for about 11 million Medicare beneficiaries. Many get this extra help automatically as a result of receiving benefits from Medicaid (dual eligible), Medicare Savings Programs, or Supplemental Security Income. But not everyone who is eligible receives the subsidy. The most recent estimate from CMS showed that only 40% of eligible low-income beneficiaries who are not deemed eligible were enrolled for the LIS in 2009—meaning that 2.3 million beneficiaries may be missing out on the benefits for which they are eligible.[34]

There is some evidence that some of those lacking the subsidy are still enrolled in a drug plan, meaning that they are paying much more than necessary for their drug coverage.[35] Poor cognitive abilities and numeracy skills are apparently factors associated with failure to sign up.[36] Although improved outreach can play a critical role, it seems that some type of automatic sign-up may be the only means to increase take-up substantially. The lessons learned from establishing eligibility for insurance subsidies under the Affordable Care Act may offer guidance for Part D.

Issue: Part D Remains Complex and Confusing to Many Beneficiaries

Many beneficiaries think there are too many plans to choose from in Part D—each of which has a different premium, a different mix of deductibles and cost-sharing amounts, and different drugs on its formulary. When there are many choices, evidence from psychology and behavioral economics suggests that people often have more difficulty making decisions, make poorer choices, and may in fact fail to make a decision.[37] This line of thinking says that there are circumstances where adding more choices reduces the likelihood that people will actually make any choice. Seniors report that they appreciate the opportunity to have a choice a plan and do not want the government or others to limit the number of available choices.[38] But they also find it frustrating to compare plans due to the volume of information they receive and because the process for reviewing and choosing plans is confusing. Only 6 in 10 seniors say they (or someone on their behalf) review their plan options every year; one-fourth say they rarely or never do so.[39] Some plan enrollees could be better off financially by reacting to these changes and selecting a different plan, and not doing so can increase the cost difference between the chosen plan and other available alternatives.

As a result, only a small fraction of enrollees are enrolled in the lowest-cost Part D plan available to them, based on the specific drugs they take.[40] Many Part D enrollees incur higher out-of-pocket costs than would be the case with a different plan selection. This is true especially in situations where the plan premium is not a good indicator of overall value, such as plans that include coverage for generic drugs in the coverage gap or plans with no deductible.[41] Furthermore, plan selection does not improve in later years after the initial plan selection.*[11,42] Part D enrollees often have difficulty with the plan selection process and find the decision-making complicated, especially because of the large number of available plans.[43]

CMS has taken some important steps to limit the array of plan offerings by encouraging sponsors to eliminate plans with low enrollment and requiring that multiple plans offered by the same plan sponsor are meaningfully different from each other. Although these steps have helped keep the choice environment more constrained and easier to understand, Medicare beneficiaries still have many choices. On average in 2015, beneficiaries have a choice of 30 stand-alone drug plans and about 20 Medicare Advantage drug plans.[44] But the amount of choice is higher, for example, in Miami-Dade County, Florida, where beneficiaries have a choice of 60 plans.

In selecting a plan, beneficiaries should consider benefit and formulary differences, cost levels, the availability of pharmacies, and plan reputations both when making an initial selection and should reconsider that selection in later years. Yet few Part D enrollees (13% each year, on average) chose a new plan during the annual enrollment period from 2006 through 2010.[10] Furthermore, 7 out of 10 Medicare beneficiaries enrolled in PDPs from 2006 to 2010 never made a voluntary change of plans in any of the four enrollment periods. Those who did switch were more likely to end up in a plan with a lower premium, but only slightly more likely to have lower costs overall (Exhibit 22.6).

One solution is to reduce the total number of options, but this might be difficult to accomplish or be viewed as overly paternalistic. Less intrusive options include simplifying the choice environment, such that CMS has been attempting in requiring that multiple options from the same sponsor be meaningfully different, or improving the existing online tools with clearer language and a better means of making apples-to-apples comparisons.[38,45] Increased access to in-person counseling is another option, beyond those available today from insurance brokers and plan representatives and federally funded state health insurance assistance programs. Other decision tools could be made available to help beneficiaries better understand the consequences of their actions or inactions, as well as to provide easy ways to research and make a choice.

---

* Another study suggested that Part D enrollees dramatically improved their plan choices in the program's second year. But because this study uses data from only a single plan manager with a limited range of plan offerings, it is not generalizable to the broader Part D population.

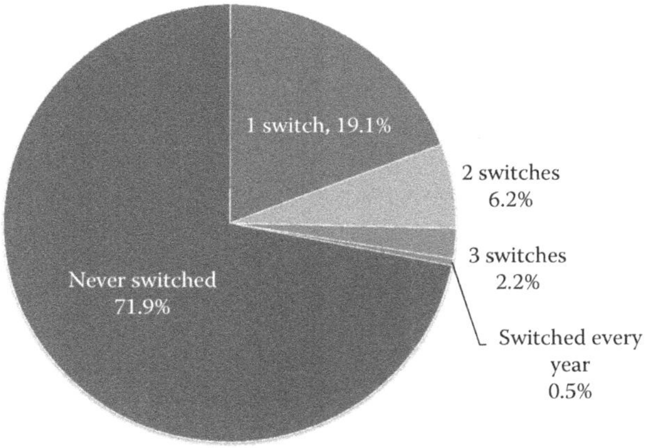

Exhibit 22.6 Share of non-LIS Medicare Part D enrollees, continuously enrolled in PDPs, by total number of plan switches, 2006–2010. *Notes:* LIS is low-income subsidy. PDP is prescription drug plan. Analysis includes non-LIS Medicare Part D enrollees in a PDP continuously from 2006 to 2010 (n = 313,418). (From Georgetown/NORC/Kaiser Family Foundation analysis of Medicare Beneficiary Summary Files and Plan Characteristics Files, 2006–2010.)

Issue: Some Low-Income Beneficiaries Experience Significant Volatility in Coverage to Maintain Their Low-Cost Plans, While Others Are Paying More Than Necessary

Low-income Medicare beneficiaries who qualify for the LIS are eligible to enroll in a Part D plan with no monthly premium as well as paying significantly reduced cost sharing for their drug purchases.[34] In order to avoid a premium, they must enroll in a benchmark plan, one that offers only the basic Part D benefit and has a premium below a benchmark calculated for each region based on average premiums in the region. In 2015, however, about 1.2 million beneficiaries with the LIS are paying a premium unnecessarily for their Part D coverage because they have not selected one of the qualifying benchmark plans.* Nearly three-fourths pay a premium of at least $(USD)10 per month, and some pay much more. Some of these beneficiaries may have chosen to pay a premium because they benefit from other features of the particular plan, but others may have selected the plan when it qualified as a benchmark plan but have stayed with it even though it no longer has benchmark plan status.

LIS beneficiaries who do not select a plan when initially joining Part D are randomly assigned to a benchmark plan. If these plans lose benchmark status for a given year, CMS randomly assigns these beneficiaries to new plans (for example, 425,000 of these reassignments were effective in 2015) in order to preserve their ability to pay no premium. But this occurs only for beneficiaries who have never made a voluntary plan selection.

The advantage of either a reassignment or voluntary plan switch is that it avoids the situation of paying a monthly premium for drug coverage, thus avoiding unnecessary costs for the beneficiary.

---

* Benchmark plans are drug plans that are available for no monthly premium to LIS enrollees, defined as below a regional average premium.[3]

The drawback is that it means a disruption of one's current coverage. A new plan usually means new formularies and new coverage rules, new procedures, and a different pharmacy network. While such disruptions can be minor inconveniences, they sometimes lead to situations where one or more of the beneficiary's drugs are not covered by the new plan.

Although the LIS has been an enormous help to many low-income Medicare beneficiaries, critical design improvements could make this program even more effective. The Congress and CMS have taken steps to increase the number of benchmark plans that are available, but other changes are needed to help reduce the degree of disruption. For example, CMS could base plan reassignments on a beneficiary's current drug use and choice of pharmacy instead of a random assignment, thus reducing the degree of disruption and potentially saving dollars for both the beneficiary and government.[46] The program could also take more aggressive steps to notify those who pay a premium unnecessarily that other options with potentially lower costs are available to them.

Issue: Higher Spending Trends for Specialty Drugs and Biologics Are Likely to Increase Pressures on Program Spending in the Coming Years

Although Part D costs to date have been considerably lower than the original projections, lower costs have resulted in great part from the patent cliff and the substitution of low-cost generic drugs for brand-name alternatives. In 2015, a substantial share of commonly used drugs, other than biologics, are available as generics or at least have a generic alternative in the same drug class. As forecast by the Medicare Trustees, drug cost growth is likely to be higher in the coming years, although not as high as in the 1990s. Whereas the Trustees reported average per enrollee growth of just 0.5% over the past 7 years, they have forecast 6.0% annual growth per enrollee over the next decade.[4]

Biologics and other specialty drugs—typically with prices far higher than conventional drugs—will contribute significantly to this higher growth. According to one pharmacy benefit manager, the growth trend for specialty drugs in Medicare in 2014 was 46%, compared to a much lower 6% for nonspecialty drugs.[47] The growth for specialty drugs was mostly driven by increases in unit cost, rather than utilization, and was strongly influenced by the newly available treatment for hepatitis C. Although specialty drugs are expensive, they remain a relatively small segment of all Part D spending. These new drugs may offer important treatments, especially for some health conditions lacking effective medications today. The pipeline of new drug approvals will be an ongoing challenge for Medicare Part D.

Managing cost growth will be critical to keeping the program affordable for both plan enrollees and taxpayers. But it is equally vital that high cost sharing for specialty drugs does not create an impediment for the appropriate and timely use of these drugs and prevent the health benefits of their use. The use of percentage-based coinsurance in Part D plans for most specialty drugs makes it costly for beneficiaries to start treatment with these drugs, even though cost sharing is reduced (but not eliminated) once they reach an out-of-pocket spending threshold.

One proposal to reduce Part D spending increases would require manufacturers to reduce prices through payment of a new federal Part D rebate for drugs purchased by LIS beneficiaries. The regulatory approval of follow-on biologics (a process starting with the new approach that became law in the Affordable Care Act) offers another route to controlling the cost of biologics. But ensuring that newly approved follow-on biologics will be accepted and used by patients and their physicians will require further steps.

Issue: Managing the Cost of High-Cost Beneficiaries is a Challenge for Health Plans and Has Implications for Managing Overall Program Costs

About 1 in 12 Medicare Part D enrollees have total drug costs high enough to reach the catastrophic spending threshold (about $[USD]7000 in 2015). On average, these beneficiaries fill about nine prescriptions per month and incur nearly $(USD)1300 in monthly drug costs.[29] Compared to enrollees with lower drug costs, these beneficiaries take more different drugs. So they seem driven less by using a few high-cost drugs and more by use of multiple drugs treating different health conditions.

By law, Part D plans are required to operate medication therapy management (MTM) programs to help ensure appropriate use of high-cost medications (see Chapter 24 on MTM). To date, these programs have not been able to demonstrate much in the way of results. Development of more robust MTM programs might not only help manage high drug utilization and high costs but also improve health outcomes by increasing adherence to needed medications and eliminating use of unnecessary drugs.

One complicating factor is the separation of drug coverage under stand-alone Part D plans from coverage for other health services under Medicare Parts A and B. The separation reduces the incentives for plans to manage drug utilization with an eye toward the impact on other health services. It also means that Part D plans lack a direct relationship with physicians that is critical for manage utilization of drugs.

Issue: Although Access to Pharmacies Has Been Good under Part D, the Emergence of Preferred Pharmacy Networks Raises New Questions for Both Access and Costs

In 2012, 92% of Part D enrollees said they were satisfied with the ease of finding a pharmacy that accepts their drug plan.[29] Because Medicare policy requires plans to accept for their network any pharmacy willing to accept the terms and conditions used by the plan, plan pharmacy networks tend to include most pharmacies in the region. Although overall access to pharmacies is good, the trend toward use of preferred pharmacy networks raises new access questions. On average, PDPs with preferred pharmacy networks designated only about one-fourth of their network pharmacies as preferred in 2014.[48] For example, one plan in 2015 designates only Walmart pharmacies as preferred pharmacies, which means that plan enrollees who live in some cities must travel to the outer suburbs to find a preferred pharmacy. Using a pharmacy that is not part of the preferred pharmacy network increases the amount paid out of pocket. In this particular example, coinsurance for a brand-name drug goes up from 20% to 25% and cost sharing for a generic drug rise from $(USD)1 to $(USD)10.

Plans have introduced preferred pharmacy networks with the goal of obtaining lower prices and lower overall program costs, but it remains important that beneficiaries understand both the benefits and potential consequences of selecting this type of plan. Furthermore, the program may need to consider revising pharmacy access standards to ensure that all plan enrollees have reasonable access to the plan's preferred pharmacies.

Issue: More Information Is Needed to Understand Whether the Process for Exceptions and Appeals Works Adequately

A key part of providing access to needed prescription drugs is an effective and efficient process for exceptions and appeals. Part D rules allow enrollees to request an exception in order to obtain a drug that not on the plan's formulary or to pay for that drug at a lower level of cost sharing as long as the request is supported by medical necessity. Enrollees who are not satisfied with their plan's decision have rights to appeal that decision (with some limits) first to the plan, then to an independent external review entity, and eventually to an administrative law judge or the court. An analysis of these processes by the Medicare Payment Advisory Commission found insufficient data available to make an assessment of these procedures.[23] Beneficiary advocates report that denials of coverage and appeals constitute a frequent source of calls by beneficiaries to their telephone helplines.[49] Beneficiaries do not always understand their rights to request exceptions or make appeals, even when they do, they find the process challenging. Successful requests and appeals typically require input from the prescribing physician to support the case for medical necessity, but this can become a burden on physicians.

Improving the process for exceptions and appeals starts with making more data availability so that researchers can study the process and identify what works and what does not. Awareness of beneficiary rights might be increased if denials received at the pharmacy used clear and standardized language to explain the reason behind the coverage denial with specific information on how to file an appeal. A further option would treat this denial as the starting point for initiating an appeal, rather than requiring a further coverage determination by the plan.[50] In 2015, CMS initiated a process to explore improvements in the process for exceptions and appeals.

Conclusion: The Bottom Line for Part D

In the 10 years after the Medicare Part D program was created by the Congress, there have been clear successes. More Medicare beneficiaries are able to take prescription drugs that may be improving their health and extending their lives. They are spending less out of pocket, meaning they are not forced to make difficult choices between medications and other needs. Many low-income beneficiaries receive extra help beyond the basic help available to all beneficiaries. Thanks to a lower growth rate for drug spending, we have accomplished these results at a cost lower than originally projected.

But it is critical that we not rest on this record of success. Steps should be taken to ensure that new cost pressures, such as those posed by expensive specialty drugs, do not challenge the program's affordability in the future. Steps should also be taken to ensure that every Medicare beneficiary who is eligible for both Part D and its LIS has a real opportunity to participate. Recent actions by the Congress and the Administration have helped to improve the benefit by phasing out the coverage gap and simplifying the program, but further changes can help make sure that Part D enrollees get access to needed drugs without paying unnecessary costs out of pocket.

References

1. T.R. Marmor, *The Politics of Medicare*, 2nd ed., New York: Aldine de Gruyter, 2000.
2. T.R. Oliver, P.R. Lee, and H.L. Lipton, A political history of medicare and prescription drug coverage, *Milbank Quarterly* 82(2): 283–354, June 2004.
3. J. Hoadley, L. Summer, E. Hargrave, J. Cubanski, and T. Neuman. 2014. Medicare part D in its ninth year: The 2014 marketplace and key trends, 2006–2014, Report, Kaiser Family Foundation, Washington, D.C. http://kff.org/medicare/report/medicare-part-d-in-its-ninth-year-the-2014-marketplace-and-key-trends-2006-2014/.
4. Boards Of Trustees of the Federal Hospital Insurance and Federal Supplementary Medical Insurance Trust Funds. 2014 annual report of the boards of trustees of the federal hospital insurance and federal supplementary medical insurance trust funds, July 2014. https://www.cms.gov/research-statistics-data-and-systems/statistics-trends-and-reports/reportstrustfunds/downloads/tr2014.pdf. Accessed on December 6, 2015.

5. Medicare Payment Advisory Commission, *A Data Book: Health Care Spending and the Medicare Program*, Washington, DC: Medicare Payment Advisory Commission, June 2014.
6. Centers for Medicare and Medicaid Services (CMS). 2011 Medicare Part D Drug Utilization Trends. Last updated April 8, 2015. https://www.cms.gov/Medicare/Prescription-Drug-Coverage/PrescriptionDrugCovGenIn/ProgramReports.html. Accessed on December 6, 2015.
7. (a) J. Hoadley, *Medicare Part D Spending Trends: Understanding Key Drivers and the Role of Competition*, Menlo Park, CA: Kaiser Family Foundation, Issue Brief, May 2012; (b) E. Park, Misleading claim about Medicare Part D relies on faulty arithmetic, Blog posting, Center on Budget and Policy Priorities, June 12, 2012; (c) D. Elmendorf, The accuracy of CBO's budget projections, CBO Blog, March 23, 2013; (d) A contrary position is advocated by J.C. Capretta, The case for competition in Medicare, Heritage Foundation, September 2011.
8. J. Hoadley, K. Merrell, E. Hargrave, and L. Summer, In Medicare part D plans, low or zero copays and other features to encourage the use of generic statins work, could save billions, *Health Affairs* 31(10): 2266–2275, October 2012; J.S. Haas et al., Potential savings from substituting generic drugs for brand-name drugs: Medical expenditures panel survey 1997–2000, *Annals of Internal Medicine* 142(11): 891–897, 2005.
9. J. Hoadley et al., *To Switch or Not to Switch: Are Medicare Beneficiaries Switching Drug Plans To Save Money?* Menlo Park, CA: Kaiser Family Foundation, October 2013.
10. J. Abaluck and J. Gruber, Evolving choice inconsistencies in choice of prescription drug insurance, National Bureau of Economic Research Working Paper 19163, June 2013.
11. B. Stuart et al., Riding the rollercoaster: The ups and downs in out-of-pocket spending under the standard Medicare drug benefit, *Health Affairs* 24(4):1022–1031, July 2005.
12. Department of Health and Human Services, Prescription drug coverage, spending, utilization and prices, Report to the President, April 2000.
13. (a) P. Neuman et al., Medicare prescription drug benefit progress report: Findings from a 2006 national survey of seniors, *Health Affairs* 26(5): w630–w643, August 21, 2007; (b) S.B. Soumerai et al., Cost-related medication nonadherence among elderly and disabled Medicare beneficiaries: A national survey one year before the Medicare drug benefit, *Archives of Internal Medicine* 166(17): 1829–1835, September 25, 2006; (c) C.L. Schur, M.M. Doty, and M.L. Berk, Lack of prescription coverage among the under 65: A symptom of underinsurance, Issue Brief, Task Force on the Future of Health Insurance, The Commonwealth Fund, February 2004; (d) R. Tamblyn et al., Adverse events associated with prescription drug cost-sharing among poor and elderly persons, *Journal of the American Medical Association* 285(4): 421–429, January 24–31, 2001.
14. (a) J.M. Polinski et al., Changes in drug use and out-of-pocket costs associated with Medicare Part D: A systematic review, *Journal of the American Geriatrics Society* 58(9): 1764–1779, September 2010; (b) J.M. Polinski et al., Medicare Part D's effect on the under- and overuse of medications: A systematic review, *Journal of the American Geriatrics Society* 59(10): 1922–1933, October 2011; (c) W. Yin et al., The effect of the Medicare Part D prescription benefit on drug utilization and expenditures, *Annals of Internal Medicine* 148(3): 169–177, February 5, 2008; (d) J.M. Madden et al., Cost-related medication nonadherence and spending on basic needs following implementation of Medicare Part D, *JAMA* 299(16): 1922–1928, April 23/30, 2008; (e) J.M. Madden et al., Cost-related medication nonadherence after implementation of Medicare Part D, 2006–2007, *JAMA* 302(16): 1755–1756, October 28, 2009; (d) D.G. Safran et al., Prescription coverage, use and spending before and after Part D implementation: A national longitudinal panel study, *Journal of General Internal Medicine* 25(1): 10–17, January 2010.
15. Y. Zhang et al., The effect of Medicare Part D on drug and medical spending, *New England Journal of Medicine* 361(1): 52–61, July 2, 2009.
16. S. Schneeweiss et al., The effect of Medicare Part D coverage on drug use and cost sharing among seniors without prior drug benefits, *Health Affairs* 28(2): w305–w316, February 3, 2009.
17. J. Michael McWilliams et al., Implementation of Medicare Part D and nondrug medical spending for elderly adults with limited prior drug coverage, *JAMA* 306(4): 402–409, July 27, 2011; C.C. Afendulis et al., The impact of Medicare Part D on hospitalization rates, *Health Services Research* 46(4): 1022–1038, August 2011.

18. Congressional Budget Office, *Offsetting Effects of Prescription Drug Use on Medicare's Spending for Medical Services*, November 2012.
19. J. Hoadley, S. Corlette, L. Summer, and L. Monahan. *Launching the Medicare Part D Program: Lessons for the New Health Insurance Marketplaces*. The Center on Health Insurance Reforms, Georgetown University Health Policy Institute. Washington, D.C. June 2013. http://chir.georgetown.edu/rapid_response.html.
20. Kaiser Family Foundation, March/April 2005 Kaiser health poll report—Toplines, April 1, 2005, http://kff.org/medicare/poll-finding/marchapril-2005-kaiser-health-poll-report-toplines/. Accessed December 6, 2015.
21. Kaiser Family Foundation and the Harvard School of Public Heath, *The Medicare Drug Benefit: Beneficiary Perspectives Just before Implementation*, Menlo Park, CA: Kaiser Family Foundation, October 31, 2005, http://kff.org/medicare/poll-finding/the-medicare-drug-benefitbeneficiary-perspectives-just-3/.
22. Kaiser Family Foundation and the Harvard School of Public Health, *The Public's Health Care Agenda for the New Congress and Presidential Campaign*, Menlo Park, CA: Kaiser Family Foundation, November 29, 2006, http://kff.org/health-costs/poll-finding/the-publicshealth-care-agenda-for-the/.
23. Medicare Payment Advisory Commission, *Report to the Congress: Medicare Payment Policy*, Washington, DC: Medicare Payment Advisory Commission, Chapter 14, March 2014.
24. KRC Research for the Healthcare Leadership Council, Seniors' opinions about Medicare prescription drug coverage: 9th year update, July 2014.
25. J. Hsu et al., Medicare beneficiaries' knowledge of Part D prescription drug program benefits and responses to drug costs, *JAMA* 299(16): 1929–1936, April 23/30, 2008.
26. J. Hoadley et al., *Understanding the Effects of the Medicare Part D Coverage Gap in 2008 and 2009*, Kaiser Family Foundation, August 2011; J.M. Polinski et al., Changes in drug use and out-of-pocket costs associated with Medicare Part D: A systematic review, *Journal of the American Geriatrics Society* 58(9): 1764–1779, September 2010; V. Fung et al., Falling into the coverage gap: Part D drug costs and adherence for medicare advantage prescription drug plan beneficiaries with diabetes, *Health Services Research* 45(2): 355–375, April 2010; S. Schneeweiss et al., The effect of Medicare Part D coverage on drug use and cost sharing among seniors without prior drug benefits, *Health Affairs* 28(2): w305–w316, March/April 2009; Y. Zhang et al., The effects of the coverage gap on drug spending: A closer look at Medicare Part D, *Health Affairs* 28(2): w317–w325, March/April 2009.
27. G.F. Joyce et al., Digesting the doughnut hole, *Journal of Health Economics* 32(6): 1345–1355, December 2013.
28. J. Hoadley, The effects of formularies and other cost management tools on access to medications: An analysis of the MMA and the final rule, Kaiser Family Foundation, March 2005.
29. Medicare Payment Advisory Commission, *Report to the Congress: Medicare Payment Policy*, Washington, DC: Medicare Payment Advisory Commission, Chapter 14, March 2015.
30. B.E. McGarry, R.L. Strawderman and Y. Li, Lower hispanic participation in Medicare Part D may reflect program barriers, *Health Affairs* 33(5): 856–862, May 2014.
31. Medicare Payment Advisory Commission, *Report to the Congress: Medicare Payment Policy*, Washington, DC: Medicare Payment Advisory Commission, March 2013.
32. A.J. Davidoff et al., Lessons learned: Who didn't enroll in Medicare drug coverage in 2006, and why? *Health Affairs* 29(6): 1255–1263, June 2010.
33. L. Summer, P. Nemore, and J. Finberg, *Improving the Medicare Part D Program for the Most Vulnerable Beneficiaries*, New York: Commonwealth Fund, 2007.
34. L. Summer, J. Hoadley, and E. Hargrave, *The Medicare Part D Low-Income Subsidy Program: Experience to Date and Policy Issues for Consideration*, Menlo Park, CA: Kaiser Family Foundation, September 2010.
35. J. Samantha Shoemaker et al., Eligibility and take-up of the Medicare Part D low-income subsidy, *Inquiry* 49: 214–230, Fall 2012.
36. I.O. Kuye, R.G. Frank, and J. Michael McWilliams, Cognition and take-up of subsidized drug benefits by Medicare beneficiaries, *JAMA Internal Medicine* 173(12): 1100–1107, June 24, 2013.

37. S. Iyengar and M. Lepper, When choice is demotivating: Can one desire too much of a good thing? *Journal of Personality and Social Psychology* 79(6): 995–1006, December 2000; B. Schwartz, *The Paradox of Choice—Why More Is Less*, New York: Ecco, 2004.
38. G. Jacobson et al., How are choosing and changing health insurance plans? Kaiser Family Foundation, May 2014.
39. Kaiser Family Foundation, Key findings from the Kaiser Family Foundation 2012 National Survey of Seniors: Seniors' knowledge and experience with Medicare's open enrollment period and choosing a plan, October 2012, Available at http://www.kff.org/medicare/issue-brief/seniors-knowledge-and-experience-with-medicares-open/. Accessed December 6, 2015.
40. Y. Hanoch, T. Rice, J. Cummings, and S. Wood, How much choice is too much? The case of the medicare prescription drug benefit, *HSR* 44(4): 1157–1168, August 2009; Y. Hanoch et al., Choosing the right Medicare prescription drug plan: The effect of age, strategy selection, and choice set size, *Health Psychology* 30(6): 719–727, November 2011; J.R. Kling et al., Comparison friction: Experimental evidence from Medicare drug plans, *Quarterly Journal of Economics* 127(1): 199–235, January 2012; J.T. Abaluck and J. Gruber, Choice inconsistencies among the elderly: Evidence from plan choice in the Medicare Part D program, *American Economic Review* 101(4): 1180–1210, June 2011; F. Heiss, A. Leive, D. McFadden, and J. Winter, Plan selection in Medicare Part D: Evidence from administrative data (No. w18166), National Bureau of Economic Research, 2012.
41. C. Zhou and Y. Zhang, The vast majority of Medicare Part D beneficiaries still don't choose the cheapest plans that meet their medication needs, *Heath Affairs* 31(10): 2259–2265, October 2012.
42. J.D. Ketcham et al., Sinking, swimming, or learning to swim in Medicare Part D, *American Economic Review* 102(6): 2639–2673, 2012.
43. Y. Hanoch, T. Rice, J. Cummings, and S. Wood (2009). How Much Choice Is Too Much? The Case of the Medicare Prescription Drug Benefit. *Health Services Research*, 44(4), 1157–1168. http://doi.org/10.1111/j.1475-6773.2009.00981.x http://www.ncbi.nlm.nih.gov/pmc/articles/PMC2739022/. Accessed December 6, 2015.
44. J. Hoadley et al., *Medicare Part D: A First Look at Part D Plan Offerings in 2013*, Data Spotlight, Menlo Park, CA: Kaiser Family Foundation, November 2012.
45. J. Hoadley, *Medicare Part D: Simplifying the Program and Improving the Value of Information for Beneficiaries*, The Commonwealth Fund, May 2008.
46. Y. Zhang, C. Zhou, and S.H. Baik, A simple change to the Medicare Part D program low-income subsidy could save $5 Billion, *Health Affairs* 33(6): 940–945, June 2014; J. Hoadley et al., Beneficiary-centered assignment and Medicare Part D, Presentation to MedPAC, September 4, 2008; J. Hoadley et al., The role of beneficiary-centered assignment for Medicare Part D, Contractor report for MedPAC, June 2007.
47. Express Scripts, The 2014 drug trend report, March 2015.
48. Centers for Medicare & Medicaid Services, Analysis of Part D beneficiary access to preferred cost sharing pharmacies, April 2015.
49. C. Sutton et al., Medicare trends and recommendations: An analysis of 2012 call data from the Medicare Rights Center's National Helpline, Medicare Rights Center, January 2014.
50. Medicare Rights Center, Refused at the pharmacy counter: How to improve Medicare Part D appeals, Winter 2013.

Chapter 23

Medicaid

Brian K. Bruen and Linda Elam

Contents

Introduction

Established in 1965 as Title XIX of the Social Security Act, Medicaid is the nation's public health insurance program for low-income people. It is a means-tested entitlement; any applicant who meets the financial and/or categorical eligibility requirements must be allowed to enroll. Referring to Medicaid as one program is somewhat inaccurate; each state administers its own program with federal oversight through the Centers for Medicare and Medicaid Services (CMS) in the U.S. Department of Health and Human Services (HHS). The federal government helps states pay for covered services and program administration. State programs have to meet certain standards to receive federal funds, but each state sets its own Medicaid eligibility rules, selects which services it covers for eligible groups, and determines payment rates for those services, resulting in considerable variation between state programs. State participation is voluntary, but all 50 states, the District of Columbia, and the 5 U.S. territories participate.*

Medicaid originally targeted recipients of cash assistance in "welfare" programs, but the Congress and the states have expanded eligibility to more low-income groups and vulnerable populations over the years. The federal health-care reform legislation passed in 2010, the Patient Protection and Affordable Care Act, more commonly referred to as the Affordable Care Act, or ACA, and sometimes colloquially as "Obamacare," made a number of noteworthy changes to Medicaid eligibility and benefits.† The ACA expands the population eligible to enroll in Medicaid, and it allows states to provide a more limited set of benefits to newly eligible groups. With regard to drug benefits, it affects the amounts Medicaid programs will pay to community retail pharmacies for drugs dispensed to beneficiaries and increases the scope and size of the mandatory rebates that Medicaid receives from drug manufacturers.

Today, Medicaid is the largest source of health and long-term care financing in the United States. In 2013, states covered approximately 59 million low-income children, parents, pregnant women, people with disabilities, and persons age 65 and older—roughly one in six Americans—at an annual cost of about $(USD)450 billion.[1] Enrollment and expenditures increased significantly in 2014 because of the eligibility expansions authorized by the ACA. The CMS Office of the Actuary projects that Medicaid will cover more than 77 million people in 2020.‡

Medicaid is a major component of state budgets. On average, states spend about 19% of their general funds on Medicaid, making it second only to elementary and secondary education in

* Unless noted otherwise, the term "state" in this chapter refers any of the 50 states, the District of Columbia, and the U.S. territories (American Samoa, Guam, the Northern Mariana Islands, Puerto Rico, and the Virgin Islands).

† Two separate pieces of legislation comprise the Affordable Care Act: The Patient Protection and Affordable Care Act (P.L. 111–148) and the Health Care and Education Reconciliation Act of 2010 (P.L. 111–152).

‡ Unless noted otherwise, the term "state" in this chapter refers any of the 50 states, the District of Columbia, and the U.S. territories (American Samoa, Guam, the Northern Mariana Islands, Puerto Rico, and the Virgin Islands).

terms of its share of state budgets.[3] The addition of federal funding for eligible expenditures makes Medicaid's impact on states' total budgets and economies even greater. Medicaid's size and growth have prompted ongoing federal and state efforts to manage costs. For example, rapid growth in Medicaid expenditures for prescribed drugs in the 1990s and early 2000s spurred the adoption of tactics designed to encourage use of less expensive drugs and efforts to elicit larger discounts from drug manufacturers. The economic recession of 2007–2009 and the slow recovery afterward brought more challenges, as Medicaid enrollments grew while government revenues fell and then struggled to recover.

This chapter begins with an overview of the Medicaid program, including its role in the health-care system, eligibility, covered services, administration, and financing. The remainder of the chapter focuses on Medicaid drug benefits, including trends in expenditures and utilization, covered drugs, methods used to influence prescribing and utilization, beneficiary cost sharing, payments and rebates, and notable issues for states as of 2015. Within the applicable sections, we discuss changes made by or expected to occur due to the ACA.

Medicaid's Role in the Health-Care System

Medicaid is a major contributor to the health-care economy. In 2013, Medicaid accounted for 17% of all personal health-care expenditures, 17% of spending on hospital care, 9% of spending for physician and clinical services, 8% of spending for prescribed drugs, 30% of spending on nursing homes and continuing care retirement communities, and 36% of spending on home health care.[1] Medicaid is a vital source of funding for safety net providers—hospitals and health centers serving large numbers of low-income and uninsured people—by way of payments for services provided to beneficiaries and supplemental payments intended to mitigate costs of uncompensated care. Eligibility expansions authorized by the ACA added millions of new enrollees, broadening Medicaid's role in the health-care system.

By insuring people and paying for services that are not adequately covered through other financing options, Medicaid moderates the number of people without health insurance and helps other health insurance programs function. Compared to low-income people covered by private insurance and the uninsured, Medicaid beneficiaries are more likely to live below the poverty line, much more likely to be in fair or poor physical or mental health and much more likely to have health conditions that limit their ability to work.[4] Medicaid provides coverage to millions of children and parents in low-income families and childless adults who do not have access to private insurance due to either lack of employer offerings or unaffordable premiums and out-of-pocket costs. Additionally, Medicaid picks up many children and families who lose insurance coverage due to economic downturns, job losses, and the erosion of employer-based insurance.[5]

Medicaid also covers millions of low-income aged (65+) and younger persons with chronic conditions, mental illnesses, and/or physical disabilities that limit or prevent work opportunities. About one-quarter of Medicaid beneficiaries are either aged or persons with disabilities, but nearly two-thirds of Medicaid spending on benefits is for these groups (Figure 23.1). Long-term care is a major component of this spending: Medicaid pays for approximately 40% of all long-term care services and supports in the United States, including home health, community-based, and personal care services and institutional services such as nursing homes.[6]

Prior to the ACA insurance reforms, many people in these vulnerable populations were unable to get affordable private health insurance because of their high health-care utilization and expenses, often a consequence of their preexisting conditions. Even with the new protections

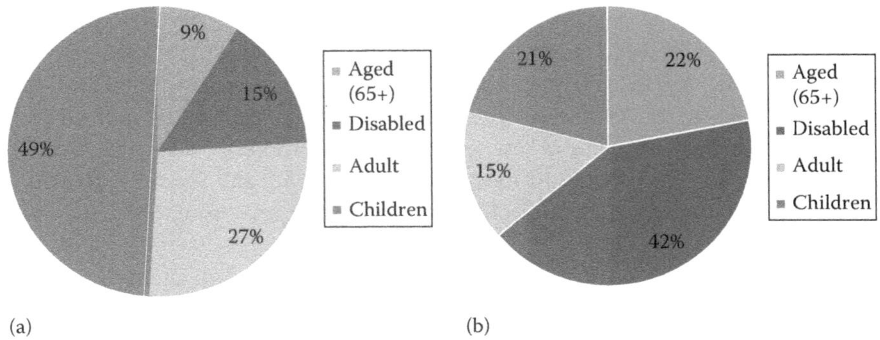

Figure 23.1 Distributions of Medicaid (a) enrollees and (b) payments by enrollment group, FY 2011. (Data from The Henry J. Kaiser Family Foundation, State health facts: Medicaid and CHIP, Retrieved June 26, 2015, http://kff.org/state-category/medicaid-chip/, no date.)

under the ACA, many would likely not be able to afford the premiums and out-of-pocket costs for private insurance. Others require long-term care services and supports, such as personal care or nursing facility services, which traditional private health plans usually do not cover. Because of these gaps in affordability and coverage, Medicaid is the foundation upon which the ACA marketplace is built, providing essential benefits to people the market is most unlikely to serve.

Eligibility

Medicaid is an important source of health-care financing for people with low incomes, but not all low-income people qualify for coverage. States determine eligibility for Medicaid based on financial criteria such as income and assets and nonfinancial criteria such as disability status or age, within the parameters established by the federal law. There are several categories of people that states must cover to receive federal matching payments for their Medicaid programs (mandatory groups) and many other groups that they may choose to cover and receive federal matching payments for (optional groups).* Mandatory groups include

- Families (children and their parents/caretaker adults) who meet standards states had in effect in 1996 for the Aid to Families with Dependent Children cash assistance ("welfare") program†
- Pregnant women and children under age 6 with family incomes at or below 133% of the federal poverty level (FPL)
- Children 6–19 years of age with family income up to 100% of the FPL
- Most people receiving cash assistance through the federal Social Security Income (SSI) program serving the low-income aged, blind, and disabled populations

* 42 U.S.C. 1396a(10).

† Temporary Assistance to Needy Families (TANF) replaced Aid to Families with Dependent Children (AFDC) in 1996, but the Congress retained the mandatory Medicaid eligibility for families with children at the former AFDC standards rather than the new, typically more restrictive, TANF eligibility standards.

Optional groups include children, parents, and pregnant women with incomes that exceed the federal cutoffs for mandatory eligibility, persons age 65 or older and younger persons with disabilities with incomes under the FPL, and nursing home residents and individuals at risk for needing institutional long-term care at incomes up to 300% of the limit for Social Security Income (SSI). Most states have expanded eligibility for children and pregnant women to income levels well above the minimum federal standards, through either Medicaid or the Children's Health Insurance Program.* Another important optional group is the "medically needy," individuals who meet nonfinancial standards but who have incomes or assets that exceed the thresholds for categorical eligibility. The medically needy qualify for Medicaid by incurring medical expenses until their health-care spending surpasses another threshold, a process known as "spending down."

The ACA expanded eligibility to all individuals under age 65 with family incomes up to 133% of the FPL, except Medicare beneficiaries and certain immigrants (see the following texts). It added a standard 5% income disregard for these applicants, making the effective income limit 138% of the FPL. As passed by the Congress, the ACA made these expansions mandatory and authorized the secretary of HHS to take away *all* Medicaid funding for any state that did not comply. However, in the case of *National Federation of Independent Business v. Sebelius*, the U.S. Supreme Court ruled that the threat of losing existing Medicaid funding was an unconstitutional coercion of the states, and the Court precluded the secretary from enforcing the penalty, thus making the expansion optional for states. As of June 2015, 29 states and the District of Columbia had expanded or planned to expand, two states were considering expansions, and 19 states were not expanding coverage.[7]

Many aged and disabled Medicaid beneficiaries also qualify for Medicare and are known as "dually eligible." Full "dual eligibles" rely on Medicaid to pay for Medicare premiums and cost sharing and services not covered by Medicare, especially long-term care services and supports. Additional low-income Medicare beneficiaries whose incomes are higher than the limit for full dual eligibility are served by Medicare Savings Programs, which use Medicaid funds to provide assistance to with premiums and cost sharing for Medicare benefits. Known as Qualified Medicare Beneficiaries, Specified Low-Income Medicare Beneficiaries, Qualifying Individuals, and Qualified Disabled and Working Individuals, these groups receive varying levels of assistance, and most get an extra help paying for Medicare prescription drug coverage, but they do not receive full Medicaid benefits.

Federal law bars states from using federal Medicaid funds to pay for services for lawfully present immigrants who have been in the United States for less than 5 years. Undocumented immigrants are not eligible for Medicaid except to pay for limited emergency services.

Benefits

Federal law requires Medicaid programs to cover some services (mandatory services) and permits federal matching payments for additional services that states are not required to provide (optional services). Examples of mandatory services include inpatient and outpatient hospital services, physicians' services, federally qualified health center and rural health clinic services, nursing facility services for persons age 21 and older, early and periodic screening diagnosis and treatment (EPSDT) services for children, and pregnancy-related services. Examples of optional services

* The Children's Health Insurance Program, Title XXI of the Social Security Act, provides federal matching funds for states to provide health coverage for children in families with incomes too high for Medicaid.

include prescribed drugs, dental services, home- and community-based services, personal care, intermediate care facility services for individuals with intellectual disabilities, and hospice services.[8] "Optional" means that states are not required to cover these services, not that they are elective or discretionary based on current standards of care. Certain "optional" services, such as prescription drugs, reflect the 1960s-era establishment of the program—it is hard to imagine a contemporary mainstream health-care practitioner deeming prescription drugs an optional modality. Moreover, federal law requires states to cover any optional service for a child when it is medically necessary to correct or ameliorate a defect, illness, or condition that is identified by screening of that child under EPSDT, even if the state does not cover that service otherwise.

States must observe four basic federal guidelines in the provision of Medicaid benefits:

- *Amount, duration, and scope*: Services must be sufficient in amount, duration, and scope to achieve their intended purpose. The state may not arbitrarily deny or limit services to a beneficiary based on diagnosis or condition; however, the state may limit service delivery based on medical necessity or with appropriate utilization controls.
- *Comparability*: Services available to those within the categorically needy group must be comparable, and services available to those within the medically needy group must be comparable; in addition, services available to the categorically needy must not be less in amount, duration, or scope than services available to the medically needy.
- *Statewideness*: The amount, duration, and scope of coverage must be uniform statewide.
- *Freedom of choice*: A state must allow beneficiaries to exercise freedom of choice among providers or plans, with certain exceptions.

States may provide different benefit packages to beneficiaries qualifying as medically needy or to members of special groups (such as women eligible for Medicaid through a diagnosis of breast cancer) than they provide to categorically eligible beneficiaries under the traditional Medicaid program. States also have discretion to vary the package of services offered to different groups of medically needy beneficiaries; however, all members of a group, as defined by the state, must have access to the same set of services.

Section 1937 of the Social Security Act gives states considerable flexibility to implement different benefit packages for certain groups of Medicaid beneficiaries. Initially called Medicaid Benchmark or Benchmark Equivalent Plans, these options are now known as Alternative Benefit Plans (ABPs). ABPs must be at least equal to one of the four benchmark plans named in statute or include certain specified services and be actuarially equivalent to one of the named benchmark packages. Effective January 1, 2014, ABPs must include the 10 essential health benefits established by the ACA and subsequent regulations and meet the requirements of the Mental Health Parity and Addiction Equity Act. States cannot require certain groups to enroll in ABPs—primarily aged, blind, and disabled individuals—but they may offer voluntary enrollment for these groups. ABPs will be the standard for coverage of low-income adults eligible under the ACA-mandated expansions.

Administration and Financing

Each state is responsible for the day-to-day operations of its Medicaid program. Within the parameters set by the federal government, states determine their own eligibility requirements, covered services, and provider payment rates, process applications and enroll eligible persons, and oversee operations and compliance with laws. Each state has a contractual agreement with CMS called a state plan, which describes how its program operates and assures that the state follows federal rules and can claim federal matching funds for eligible expenditures. States file a state plan amendment when they wish to implement changes to their programs or to provide updates, corrections, or other allowable changes. CMS engages in numerous regulatory, financing, and administrative functions, including collecting program data from states, ensuring that states get federal matching funds, reviewing and approving state plan amendments, and overseeing program compliance by states, providers, and plans.

Under Medicaid's joint financing structure, the federal government reimburses each state for at least half of the state's expenditures on covered services and administrative functions. The federal share is called the federal medical assistance percentage (FMAP). Each state's FMAP is adjusted annually using a statutory formula that reflects the per capita income of the state relative to per capita income of the United States; however, FMAPs for the U.S. territories (55%) and District of Columbia (70%) are fixed.* The FMAPs for 2015 range from 50%, the statutory minimum that applies to the wealthiest states, up to 73.6% (the statutory maximum is 83%). The Congress has authorized exceptions to the regular FMAP rates for certain states (e.g., Alaska from 1998 to 2007), situations (e.g., state fiscal relief), populations (e.g., certain women with breast cancer, Medicaid expansion population under ACA), providers (e.g., Indian Health Service), services (e.g., family planning), and administrative activities (e.g., fraud control units).[9]

Historically, the federal government covered about 57% of Medicaid expenditures nationwide on average; the Congressional Budget Office expects this percentage to be around 60–62% in 2015 and in the later years, because the ACA established higher FMAPs for populations newly eligible for Medicaid under that law, as well as temporary FMAP increases for primary care payment rates and certain other services.[10] There is no limit to federal matching payments for covered services, other than the amount of eligible state spending incurred, except in the U.S. territories. Federal matching payments from Medicaid are the largest source of grant funds received by states, accounting for 46.6% of state spending from federal funds in 2013.[3]

States pay for covered services either on a fee-for-service basis (e.g., by paying claims submitted by providers) or through contracts with managed care plans to administer and pay for a package of covered services on the state's behalf. Some plan operators are commercial groups that also serve non-Medicaid clients, while others are Medicaid-only plans. The most common types of managed care in Medicaid are comprehensive managed care organizations (MCOs), limited benefit plans, and primary care case management (PCCM). MCOs receive fixed payments per beneficiary from the state Medicaid agency for a set of covered services, usually on a per-member-per-month basis, and then pay providers for those services. Limited benefit plans operate in a similar fashion to the comprehensive MCOs, but may only cover one or two benefits such as mental health or dental services. PCCMs are entities that monitor beneficiaries' use of covered primary care services and are less risk based than MCOs.

Medicaid programs have considerable flexibility to exclude ("carve out") populations and benefits from managed care, meaning that these groups or services remain in fee-for-service Medicaid. While managed care enrollment varies considerably by state, in July 2011, more than 74% of Medicaid beneficiaries were in some form of managed care and 49% were in MCOs.[11] Many states require parents and children to enroll in some form of managed care. Fewer states require managed care participation by beneficiaries age 65 or older or younger persons with disabilities, but enrollment of these groups is growing, and many states are now turning toward managed care

* Section 1101(a)(8)(B) and Section 1905(b) of the Social Security Act describe the federal medical assistance percentage computations and limitations.

- Section 1115 research and demonstration waivers are vehicles states can use to test new or existing ways to deliver and pay for health care services in Medicaid.
- Section 1915(b) waivers enable states to provide services through managed care delivery systems or otherwise limit choice of providers.
- Section 1915(c) waivers allow states to provide LTSS in home and community settings rather than institutional settings.
- States may offer a continuum of services to elderly and disabled beneficiaries using concurrent section 1915(b) and 1915(c) waivers.

Exhibit 23.1 Common types of Medicaid waivers.

programs to provide long-term services and supports (LTSS), services that traditionally were not in managed care benefit packages.

Most states use either state plan amendment authority under Section 1932(a) of the Social Security Act or waiver authority to implement managed care. States may ask the federal government to waive the general rules for populations and services concerning statewideness, comparability of services, and freedom of choice. The secretary may grant exceptions to rules on a state-by-state basis, making federal matching funds available for services or populations not mandated by Medicaid statute. States also have received various types of waivers to limit the services provided to certain groups of beneficiaries (Exhibit 23.1). In applying for a waiver, states must demonstrate that the actions they are proposing will be budget neutral and not cost the federal government any more than it would have paid without the waiver. For example, a state must be able to demonstrate that provision of LTSS in the community will not cost more in the aggregate than institutional care provided to the same population.

Medicaid Outpatient Drug Benefits

Prescription drugs are an optional benefit, but all states currently cover them. Consistent with Medicaid policies more broadly, states have wide latitude to design their own drug benefits, but there are some federal guidelines to which they must adhere. Medicaid programs paid for more than 550 million prescriptions in 2013.[12] The CMS Office of the Actuary estimates that Medicaid spent $(USD)21.2 billion for prescribed drugs in that same year, 7.8% of the $(USD)271.1 billion in total expenditures for prescribed drugs nationwide.[2] As is the case across almost all Medicaid services, a relatively small share of beneficiaries incurs a majority of prescription drug expenditures. These individuals tend to have multiple medical and/or mental health conditions.

Trends in Drug Benefit Use and Expenditures

Historically, the prescription drug benefit has been one of the fastest growing components of Medicaid (Figure 23.2). Rapid growth in the 1990s and early 2000s reflected broader market trends, such as the proliferation of widely used "blockbuster" drugs, and the integral role of drug therapies in contemporary treatment protocols for physical and mental health conditions. Enrollment also grew significantly during this period because of eligibility expansions, health-care cost increases, and declining private insurance coverage. States and the federal government focused intently on cost containment and utilization management of the Medicaid drug benefit during this period.

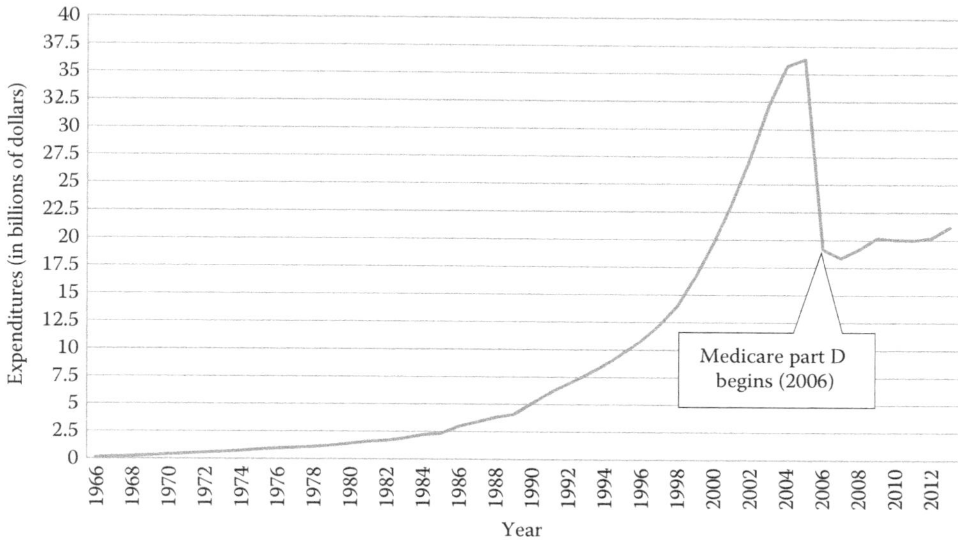

Figure 23.2 Medicaid expenditures for prescription drugs, 1966–2013. (Data from Centers for Medicare and Medicaid Services, National health expenditure accounts: Historical, Retrieved June 28, 2015, http://www.cms.gov/Research-Statistics-Data-and-Systems/Statistics-Trends-and-Reports/NationalHealthExpendData/NationalHealthAccountsHistorical.html, 2015.)

Prior to 2006, roughly half of Medicaid's prescription drug expenditures were on behalf of dually eligible beneficiaries enrolled in Medicaid and Medicare. Because Medicare did not cover prescription drugs, Medicaid provided "wraparound" coverage through its comprehensive drug benefit for this population. The launch of Medicare Part D, the Medicare drug benefit, on January 1, 2006, relieved some of the burden on states as Medicare supplanted Medicaid as the primary source of drug coverage for dual eligibles, but states must still contribute funds to help cover costs for these individuals.*

Medicaid drug expenditures grew slowly from 2006 to 2013 and even declined from year to year at times during this period. The slowdown reflected general trends in the marketplace—notably the arrival of generic versions of many highly utilized drugs and some very expensive ones, which reduced costs per prescription/unit dispensed. Additionally, the economic recession of 2007–2009 and the subsequent slow recovery witnessed a prolonged period of reduced healthcare utilization. States also implemented or expanded numerous cost containment efforts aimed at prescribed drugs, motivated by revenue shortfalls and rapid Medicaid enrollment growth.

States and the federal government continue to monitor Medicaid drug benefits and to look for opportunities for better management and cost control. One area of focus, especially at the federal level, is reimbursement to retail pharmacies and discounts from drug manufacturers. Other targets include beneficiary cost sharing and continued efforts to influence utilization and prescribing practices. Better management of specialty drugs is a growing concern in many states.[13] In its *2014 Drug Trend Report*, pharmacy benefit management firm Express Scripts observed that

* States must make "phased-down state contribution" or "clawback" payments to the federal government to offset part of the cost of drug coverage for dual eligibles under Medicare Part D. Each state pays a percentage of the projected Medicare drug payments for dual eligibles in the state. That percentage, which started at 90% in 2006, will be lowered each year until 2015, when it will be fixed at 75%.

per-member-per-year (PMPY) prescription drug expenditures increased by 10.2% from 2013 to 2014 among Medicaid beneficiaries covered by its plan sponsors. Although utilization was slightly lower per person, expenditures were driven by a 37% increase in per unit costs PMPY for "specialty" drugs.[14] We discuss these issues in more detail later in this chapter.

Covered Populations

States can choose to cover different benefit packages for different populations, but they generally offer full or supplemental prescription drug coverage to all Medicaid beneficiaries, so the covered populations are diverse. Most are children, pregnant women, parents, and caretaker adults; these groups are generally low volume in terms of their prescription drug needs, although the relatively high psychotropic medication use in children on Medicaid is a common concern. Persons with physical and mental disabilities account for a majority of Medicaid prescription drug expenditures. These individuals tend to be older (ages 45 and up), and an increasing age is associated with higher use of prescription drugs, even among nondisabled populations. Other high-use, high-cost groups include children with special needs, patients with HIV/AIDS, and other individuals with complex health needs, including physical, behavioral, and/or cognitive ailments that lead to long-term use of drug therapies.[15]

Covered Drugs

Federal Medicaid regulations define prescribed drugs as follows:

> [S]imple or compound substances or mixtures of substances prescribed for the cure, mitigation, or prevention of disease, or for health maintenance that are (1) prescribed by a physician or other licensed practitioner of the healing arts within the scope of this professional practice as defined and limited by Federal and State law; (2) dispensed by licensed pharmacists and licensed authorized practitioners in accordance with the State Medical Practice Act; and (3) dispensed by the licensed pharmacist or practitioner on a written prescription that is recorded and maintained in the pharmacist's or practitioner's records.*

This definition includes over-the-counter products ordered with a prescription, and most states provide at least limited coverage of these products such as antihistamines, cough and cold preparations, or gastrointestinal products.

States are required to cover all drugs manufactured by companies that have entered into a rebate agreement with the secretary of HHS, with the exception of certain categorical exclusions (Exhibit 23.2). ABPs must offer the greater of (1) one drug in every category or class established by the U.S. Pharmacopeia or (2) the same number of drugs in each category and class as offered by the essential health benefit benchmark plan. States must allow beneficiaries to request and gain access to clinically appropriate drugs not covered by the ABP.† Whether in traditional Medicaid, MCOs, or ABPs, beneficiary access to covered drugs may be subject to prior authorization, other forms of utilization management, or cost sharing within the limitations described later in this chapter.

Analgesics and antipyretics for the management of pain, fever, and inflammation are the most commonly used drugs worldwide—and in Medicaid. Additionally, many leading drugs

* 42 CFR 440.120.

† 45 CFR 156.122.

Medicaid law allows states to exclude the following categories of drugs from their Medicaid formularies (subject to updates from the Secretary of HHS):

- Drugs where the prescribed use is not for a medically accepted indication.
- Agents when used for anorexia, weight loss, or weight gain.
- Agents when used to promote fertility.
- Agents when used for cosmetic purposes or hair growth.
- Agents when used for the symptomatic relief of cough and cold.
- Prescription vitamins and mineral products, except prenatal vitamins and fluoride preparations.
- Nonprescription (OTC) drugs, except certain agents when used by pregnant women to promote tobacco cessation.
- Drugs where the manufacturer seeks to require as a condition of sale that associated tests or monitoring services be purchased exclusively from the manufacturer or its designee.
- Agents when used for the treatment of sexual or erectile dysfunction, unless such agents are used to treat another condition for which the agents have been approved by the FDA.

The ACA eliminated long-standing provisions that allowed states to exclude barbiturates, benzodiazepines, and drugs used to promote smoking cessation; states must cover these drugs after January 1, 2014.

Exhibit 23.2 Drugs subject to restriction in Medicaid. (From 42 U.S.C. 1396r-8(d).)

used by Medicaid beneficiaries—measured by either numbers of prescriptions or expenditures—target mental health and behavioral concerns; these include antidepressants and antipsychotics, benzodiazepines and other drugs often used to treat anxiety and insomnia, anticonvulsants, and popular treatments for attention deficit hyperactivity disorder and narcolepsy. Additional high-use and high-expenditure drugs in Medicaid target many different acute illnesses and chronic conditions, including anti-infective agents, cardiovascular drugs, hormones and synthetic substitutes, autonomic drugs, and gastrointestinal drugs. A few high-expenditure drugs in Medicaid have low-to-moderate levels of use, such as antihemorrhagic agents and antineoplastic drugs, but many of these are biologic and specialty products with very high average costs per prescription.[16]

Drug Utilization Review

Federal rules require states to have drug utilization review (DUR) programs for outpatient drugs that ensure that prescriptions are appropriate, medically necessary, and unlikely to result in adverse medical outcomes. Prospective DUR programs target inappropriate drug access at the point of sale; retrospective DUR programs generally track prescribing practices and both use of and expenditures for drugs using data from completed transactions. All DUR programs are designed to identify problems such as drug interactions, duplicate prescriptions, and improper prescribing practices. In addition to addressing patient safety, these efforts can help contain costs. Providers with unusual or inappropriate prescribing practices may receive targeted information or educational materials intended to change their behavior. States must file an annual report with CMS reflecting their DUR activities, including trends in prescribing habits, cost savings generated by the program, and general program operations.

Combating Fraud and Abuse

DUR programs are integral to federal and state efforts to identify potential cases of fraud and abuse. Drug diversion, the redirection of prescription medicines obtained legally and for medically necessary reasons to illegal and typically not medically necessary uses, is a significant concern for Medicaid agencies. Opioid pain relievers are the most commonly diverted drugs but diversion of mental health drugs is also a significant problem. Federal law prohibits Medicaid programs from paying for any covered drug based on a written prescription that does not come from a tamper-resistant pad or electronic system.* States are allowed to use "lock-in" programs that restrict prescribers or pharmacy choices for beneficiaries identified as potential abusers. The ACA gave states additional authority to combat fraud and abuse by requiring suspension of payment in cases where there is a credible allegation of fraud and by giving additional options for oversight of providers and limits on those identified as being high risk for fraud and abuse.

Utilization Management

Medicaid law gives states flexibility to apply an array of other mechanisms to manage drug utilization and costs within their programs (Exhibit 23.3). States implement many of these tools to steer use toward preferred drugs. Although states grant preferred status to certain drugs for a variety of reasons, including improving or maintaining quality of care, these products frequently offer cost savings relative to nonpreferred products. Other utilization management tools are blunter instruments, such as caps on the numbers of prescriptions that the state will pay for on behalf of a beneficiary at a point in time. Although states may rationalize these caps as fraud control measures, they are widely perceived as attempts to limit costs. Medicaid law does not allow unfettered use of any of these controls, primarily to protect vulnerable populations.

Requiring or Encouraging Generic Substitution

Many brand-name drugs have generic counterparts that provide therapeutic equivalence at lower cost. States can mandate generic substitution at the pharmacy level, although they may allow prescribers to override substitution through prior authorization or "dispense as written" orders. They may provide incentives for pharmacists to encourage use of generics—for example, through additional fees or favorable reimbursement rates—either by substitution (if appropriate but not mandated) or by talking about generic options with patients or prescribers. Additionally, some states conduct provider or patient education programs to promote the value of generics and encourage their use when medically appropriate. States also may set beneficiary cost sharing for generic drugs lower than for brand-name products.

- Provide feedback to providers based on drug utilization review (DUR) programs
- Encourage or require the use of generics
- Institute prior authorization
- Establish formularies or preferred drug lists (PDLs)
- Apply fail first or step therapy requirements
- Set limits on numbers of prescriptions or quantities per prescription

Exhibit 23.3 Selected strategies states use to influence utilization and prescribing patterns.

* 42 U.S.C. 1396b(i)(23).

Prior Authorization and Preferred Drug Lists

States may require that prescribers obtain prior authorization (approval) from the agency or its designated agent before a pharmacist can dispense certain drugs. States may mandate prior authorization for any covered drug, although they must respond to requests within 24 h and make a 72 h supply of the drug available in emergencies.*

A preferred drug list (PDL) or Medicaid formulary is typically a list of drugs that can be prescribed without prior authorization. In order to institute a PDL, states must (1) establish a committee of physicians, pharmacists, and others to create and modify the list, (2) exclude only those drugs that do not have a clinically meaningful therapeutic advantage over other drugs on the list, and (3) have a prior authorization program for excluded drugs.† The amount of variation between states' PDLs implies that the factors for selection are not all related to evidence-based drug reviews.[17] States may use several criteria to compile PDLs, including safety and therapeutic outcomes, manufacturer price concessions or rebates above the federal rebate, value-added programs such as disease or case management, and burden on certain patient populations (e.g., people with HIV/AIDS or mental illness).

Prior authorization can reduce utilization of targeted medications, improve patient safety and quality of care by reducing access to unnecessary or dangerous drugs, and generate savings. However, it can also give rise to unanticipated problems.[18–22] If a physician or other provider prescribes a drug that is not on the PDL or that otherwise requires prior authorization, the pharmacist or patient must get the prescriber to change the prescription or obtain prior authorization for the medication of choice. Either action requires intervention by the prescriber and creates a potential roadblock to access, depending on providers' workloads and their willingness and ability to navigate Medicaid's prior authorization procedures.

Several studies have shown that use of PDLs typically (but not invariably) has the intended effect of shifting use away from nonpreferred drugs to those on the list.[23–25] Unintended consequences can arise, such as increased use of other services, or higher program costs.[26,27] For example, net reductions in the use of clinically important medications can result if patient access is delayed or prevented, or the available "preferred" medication is less effective for their condition—although the latter may be an indicator that the PDL is not well designed. Consequently, savings in drug expenditures may be modest or even outweighed by other program costs.[28] On the other hand, rational and efficient prior authorization and PDL policies can deliver a more cost-effective benefit, which is why they are popular.

Implementing "Fail First" Policies

Fail first or step therapy policies require a prescriber to demonstrate that a drug favored by the agency is inappropriate for a patient before the patient is able to try another, nonpreferred option. Fail first policies may be used for classes of drugs that have several less expensive alternatives, such as antiulcer drugs or antihistamines; states may also use these policies to require failure on lower cost, traditional drug therapies before granting access to expensive biologics. Under some circumstances, requiring patients to fail first-line medications may cause unnecessary delays in access and subsequent compromises to care, but this strategy is defended by states citing patient and provider demand for newer, not always better, but generally more expensive treatments.

---

* 42 U.S.C. 1396r-8(d)(5).

† 42 U.S.C. 1396r-8(d)(4).

Prescription Limits

States may limit the quantity of medication paid for by Medicaid, either by capping days' supply per prescription, the number of refills allowed on a prescription, or the number of prescriptions allowed per month or per year. As of 2012, 16 states limited the number of active prescriptions for at least some beneficiaries.[29] Some states applied caps to brand-name drugs only. Some states had "soft caps" that allowed beneficiaries to get additional drugs with prior authorization, in contrast to "hard caps," which are absolute limits. Most states also made exceptions for individuals with HIV/AIDS and other serious conditions. Even with exceptions, prescription limits are often viewed as an imprecise way to identify and target overuse, whether through waste or abuse. Prescription limits can deny people with multiple illnesses access to necessary medications and have been linked to both increased institutionalization[30] and abrupt changes in drug regimens.[31]

Quantity limits on certain medications may be appropriate for safety reasons. However, for the patient, limits on the quantity of medication dispensed or the number of refills permitted can mean more trips to the pharmacy or the doctor, a particular problem for some beneficiaries, particularly those with disabilities or transportation difficulties. Moreover, a quantity limit translates into a greater number of refills, which, if copayments are imposed, compounds the logistical burden with a financial one.

Beneficiary Cost Sharing

States have the option to impose beneficiary cost sharing for many Medicaid covered services, subject to several limitations. Federal law limits cost sharing for individuals with incomes up to 150% of the FPL to "nominal" amounts and prohibits cost sharing for children under 18; individuals in foster care or for whom adoption or foster care assistance is made; terminally ill patients receiving hospice care; inpatients in hospitals, nursing homes, and other institutions; and women eligible for breast or cervical cancer treatment. Cost sharing is also prohibited for pregnancy-related services for pregnant women, emergency services (although cost sharing is allowed for nonemergency services provided in emergency departments), and family planning services and supplies.

The Deficit Reduction Act of 2005 (DRA) gave states the option to increase cost sharing for individuals with incomes above 150% of the FPL and indexed federal cost-sharing limits to keep pace with inflation. The DRA also allowed states to give providers the ability to withhold services from certain beneficiaries who did not pay cost sharing, a practice previously prohibited by law. Part of the rationale for these changes was to increase beneficiaries' sensitivity to health-care spending and to discourage wasteful consumption. CMS issued regulations in July 2013 to simplify the resulting cost-sharing provisions. The new rules set nominal limits at up to $(USD)4 for preferred drugs regardless of family income; for nonpreferred drugs, the new limits are $(USD)8 for individuals with incomes at or below 150% of the FPL and up to 20% of the cost of the drug for individuals with incomes above 150% of the FPL. The new caps are still indexed to inflation and all of the excluded groups are still exempt from most cost sharing.

Today, almost all state Medicaid programs and MCOs charge nominal copayments for prescription drugs for adults. It is unclear how many states will take up the new, higher cost-sharing options. However, existing evidence suggests that increased cost sharing for prescription drugs typically reduces utilization, including appropriate use, and may lead to higher costs for other services.[32–37] Price sensitivity to cost sharing is likely to be a function of the type of medication, pattern of adverse effects, and various patient characteristics, including income. There may be less sensitivity to price when medications have clear and relatively immediate effects on symptoms than when medications treat conditions that are largely asymptomatic.

Pharmacy Reimbursements and Manufacturer Rebates

The policies described to this point primarily affect utilization of prescribed drugs. States and the federal government have two main ways to influence the amounts paid for those drugs: reimbursement to pharmacies and rebates from manufacturers.

Payments to Retail Pharmacies

Medicaid reimburses retail pharmacies based on a complex set of federal and state policies. With the exception of multiple-source drugs* for which there are specific federal or state limits, federal regulations require Medicaid programs to reimburse pharmacies based on the lesser of (1) the estimated acquisition cost (EAC) plus a reasonable dispensing fee or (2) the pharmacy's "usual and customary charge" to the public.† The EAC is intended to reflect the price generally and currently paid by providers (retail pharmacies) to procure a particular drug from suppliers. The dispensing fee is intended to cover reasonable costs associated with providing the drug to a Medicaid beneficiary, including the pharmacist's services and overhead associated with maintaining the facility and equipment necessary for operation.

Most states determine EAC using formulas that apply prices from commercially available drug pricing compendia, such as a percentage reduction from the average wholesale price (AWP) for the drug or a percentage increase to the wholesale acquisition cost (WAC).[38] For many years, critics and experts alike have noted that AWP is akin to the sticker price on a car; it represents a starting point for negotiations, but a common joke is that AWP stands for "ain't what's paid." In the early 1990s, the Health Care Financing Administration (now known as CMS) pressured states to improve their estimates of acquisition costs based on evidence that AWP was higher than pharmacies' actual costs of acquiring drugs.[39] Investigations over the next two decades continued to show that AWP-based payments exceeded pharmacies' acquisition costs, despite states' efforts to bring reimbursement in line with costs.[40–43]

In 2009, First DataBank and Medi-Span, publishers of the most widely used drug price compendia, settled lawsuits that alleged that they had inflated AWPs to benefit pharmacies and wholesalers with higher payments, at the expense of purchasers (including Medicaid). Those lawsuits support claims that AWP does not reflect actual costs and confirms suspicions that it may be subject to manipulation. WAC seems to suffer criticism because of its close relationship to AWP, but there is evidence that WAC is a relatively accurate pricing measure for many sole-source drugs (brand-name medications with market exclusivity). WAC is less accurate, if even reported, for many multiple-source drugs (generic versions of brand-name drugs).[44]

In February 2012, CMS issued proposed rules that would require states to pay pharmacies based on actual acquisition cost (AAC) plus a "professional" dispensing fee, instead of EAC plus a "reasonable" dispensing fee.[45] CMS defined AAC as the state agency's determination of the actual prices paid by pharmacy providers to acquire drug products sold or marketed by a

* Multiple-source drugs are products available from two or more manufacturers; most are generic versions of older brand-name drugs and the originator brand-name drugs themselves.

† 42 CFR 447.512(b); note that the EAC is applied as an aggregate limit on payments and need not apply to each prescription. Separate EAC certifications are required for single-source and multiple-source drugs.

specific manufacturer. To determine AAC, CMS suggested that states might use invoices collected from a sample of pharmacies, or use average manufacturer price (AMP), which is defined by statute as the average price paid to the manufacturer for the drug in the United States by (1) wholesalers for drugs distributed to retail community pharmacies and (2) retail community pharmacies that purchase drugs directly from the manufacturer.* Final rules had not been released at the time of this writing (June 2015).

Federal Upper Limits

The federal upper limit (FUL) program limits reimbursement for certain multiple-source drugs and seeks to ensure that government acts as a prudent buyer by taking advantage of market prices for these drugs. CMS calculates maximum payment amounts for specific forms and strengths for each multiple-source drug that meets the established criteria; currently, about 700 drugs, including both generic drugs and originator brands for which generic substitutes, are available. These FUL drugs accounted for $(USD)2.4 billion in Medicaid expenditures in 2010.[46]

Traditionally, the FUL for a multiple-source drug was set at 150% of the lowest price for the drug published in national drug pricing compendia (usually an AWP or a WAC). The Congress legislated changes to the FULs in 2005, based in part on research indicating that FULs based on published prices were significantly higher than pharmacies' acquisition costs.[47] CMS did not implement these rules because of an injunction and subsequent changes to federal law. The ACA and subsequent rules limit FULs to no less than 175% of the weighted average of the most recently reported AMPs for that drug; these changes also include new definitions for the terms "average manufacturer price," "multiple-source drug," "retail community pharmacy," and "wholesaler," reflecting efforts to make the new rules more palatable to pharmacies and other stakeholders in the pharmaceutical supply chain.[48,49]

State Maximum Allowable Costs

Nearly all Medicaid programs apply state maximum allowable cost (SMAC) limits to multiple-source drugs; like FULs, these are ceilings on reimbursement for the drug products. They are generally part of a complex "lesser of" formula, where the state agency sets reimbursement at the lowest amount for each drug based on (1) the state's EAC formula, (2) the FUL (if applicable), (3) the SMAC, or (4) the pharmacy's usual and customary charge to the public. A 2013 analysis found that SMAC programs included 50%–60% more drugs than FULs, and most states used pharmacy acquisition costs as part of the benchmark to set SMAC prices.[48]

Dispensing Fees

In addition to paying for the drug product or ingredient costs, states pay dispensing fees to pharmacies that fill prescriptions for Medicaid beneficiaries. In 2015, these fees ranged from $(USD)2 or less in five states to more than $(USD)10 in eight states; the average fee in most other states was around $(USD)5 per prescription.[38] In setting their fees, states look to the fees paid by other state Medicaid programs, private insurance programs, and Medicare Part D plans. Variation in fees also reflects differences in states' approaches to EAC: except for Alaska, the states with the highest fees also use AAC-based reimbursement.

* Section 1927(k)(1) of the Social Security Act, as amended by §2503 of the Affordable Care Act, P.L. 111–148.

A pharmacy's "cost of dispensing" includes its operating costs of staffing and maintaining the pharmacy location and any costs for equipment, licensing, and other materials required to dispense prescriptions. A nationwide study supported by retail pharmacies estimated that retail pharmacies' average cost of dispensing in 2006 was $(USD)10.50 per prescription (each pharmacy's average cost weighted by prescription volume) and $(USD)12.10 per pharmacy (each pharmacy's average cost counted once). State-specific averages per pharmacy ranged from $(USD)10.36 to $(USD)15.91.[49] A state-funded study in Alabama estimated an average cost of dispensing in 2009 of $(USD)12.97 per pharmacy.[50] A state-funded study in Oregon estimated an unweighted average cost of dispensing in 2009 of $(USD)11.15 per pharmacy.[51]

Manufacturer Rebates

Since 1991, states and the federal government have received mandatory rebates from pharmaceutical manufacturers based on the volume of their drugs purchased by Medicaid, as established by the Omnibus Reconciliation Act of 1990. The federal rebate program is an important source of Medicaid cost savings, returning a total of $(USD)104 billion to states and the federal government from 2002 to 2012.[52] In exchange for the rebates, manufacturers receive a guarantee that state Medicaid programs will cover all of their products, except those explicitly excluded from coverage as noted earlier in this chapter.

The ACA increased the minimum required rebates, established additional rebates for new formulations of existing drugs, and extended the mandatory discounts to include drugs purchased for Medicaid beneficiaries by MCOs. The federal rebate amount is based on the AMP for each drug, reported by manufacturers to the federal government. Rebates for "innovator" (brand name) drugs are the larger of (1) 23.1% of the AMP or (2) the difference between the AMP and the lowest price the manufacturer offers to most other purchasers (known as the "best price"). Manufacturers must pay additional rebates when price increases for these drugs exceed inflation. Rebates for multiple-source (generic) drugs are calculated by multiplying the AMP by 13%; as of mid-2015, there is no additional rebate for generic drugs when price increases exceed inflation, although this adjustment has been proposed on several occasions. There are also special federal rebate amounts for blood clotting factors, drugs approved by the Food and Drug Administration exclusively for pediatric indications, and new formulations ("line extensions") of brand-name drugs that are in oral solid dosage forms.

Many states have negotiated rebates in addition to those received through the federal rebate program. These "supplemental" rebates are frequently mediated through use of PDLs, where manufacturers may have their products added to the preferred list through payment of rebates to the states. The effectiveness of individual states' efforts to negotiate varies. Small states do not have the leverage of larger states. States have increased their bargaining power by pooling drug purchases, either between states (e.g., "multistate purchasing" by Medicaid programs in several states) or within a state (e.g., Medicaid, state employees, corrections).

Coordination of Rebates with the Federal 340B Drug Discount Program

The federal 340B Drug Discount Program requires manufacturers of drugs, biologics, and insulin to give significant discounts to "covered entities," including safety net hospitals and community health centers, as a condition of having their products covered by Medicaid. For patients covered by Medicaid, federal regulations mandate oversight to prevent covered entities from receiving drug discounts and Medicaid rebates for the same drug.* The Health Resources and Services Administration (HRSA), which oversees the 340B program, requires covered entities to "carve in" or "carve out" the use of 340B drugs for Medicaid patients. Those that carve in must file their provider number(s) in HRSA's Medicaid Exclusion File so Medicaid does not reimburse all 340B drugs billed to this number. Entities that carve out must purchase drugs for Medicaid patients outside of the 340B program and receive only Medicaid rebates. Entities are prohibited from carving in or carving out certain drugs on a case-by-case basis. Coordination between Medicaid and the 340B program is increasingly important for states. The number of covered entities nearly doubled from 2001 to 2011 (8,605–16,572 entities),[53] and program data indicate there were more than 25,000 covered entities as of April 2014.[54]

Challenges to Manufacturers' Prices

States, consumers, and the federal government have all taken legal action against pharmaceutical companies, alleging unfair or illegal marketing and pricing strategies for both generic and brand-name drugs. Several states have sued manufacturers, alleging the companies misrepresented their AWPs by inflating both inpatient and outpatient drug costs. Class action antitrust lawsuits have also been filed on behalf of consumers against pharmaceutical companies, charging that companies overpriced their drugs by stifling generic competition, price fixing, and other illegal and unfair practices. Typically, action at the federal level regarding fraudulent pricing practices is based upon the Federal False Claims Act, which levies significant fines against contractors that submit false or fraudulent claims to the federal government.

Bringing More Transparency to Drug Pricing in Medicaid

As with other provider payments, prescription drug reimbursement and dispensing fees are frequent cost-cutting targets. Many contend that the big winners from inflated AWPs, FULs, and other reimbursement metrics are retail pharmacies because they retain the "spread"—the difference between what they actually pay to acquire drugs from manufacturers or wholesalers and the amounts they are reimbursed by Medicaid. Inflated AWPs and FULs provide more revenues for pharmacies, but manufacturers also benefit when larger spreads encourage pharmacies to sell their products. In efforts to bring more transparency to drug acquisition costs, several states and the federal government collect invoices from retail pharmacies to evaluate the amounts that pharmacies pay to acquire drugs from manufacturers or wholesalers. These surveys are not perfect as they do not account for rebates or discounts that are not included on invoices and, by the time they are collected and the results are tabulated, may reflect outdated prices.

Pharmacies assert that total reimbursement must factor in all of the costs to pharmacies of acquiring and dispensing drugs. They tend to resist decreases in ingredient reimbursement unless such reductions are offset with higher dispensing fees, arguing that current fees are inadequate compensation for the services they provide to Medicaid beneficiaries. Pharmacies also argue that they already face the burdens of other cost containment initiatives (e.g., prior authorization, prescription caps, and cost-sharing enforcement), and they maintain that reimbursement reductions threaten access to and/or quality of pharmacists' services.

---

* 42 USC 256b(a)(5)(A)(i).

Managed Care Plans and Prescription Drug Coverage

Nearly all states enroll at least some of their Medicaid beneficiaries in comprehensive MCOs; nearly two-thirds of Medicaid beneficiaries nationwide were in such plans in 2010.[55] States continue to expand managed care, citing reasons such as anticipated savings, better predictability of expenditures, and improved access, care coordination, and quality of care. Most adults eligible under the Medicaid expansions supported by the ACA are expected to enroll in MCOs. Although the majority of managed care enrollees traditionally have been children and nondisabled adults, states are also increasingly enrolling more medically complex patients, such as persons with disabilities.

A fundamental decision for states enrolling beneficiaries into managed care is whether to include outpatient prescription drugs as part of the benefit package of services for which plans receive capitated payments from the state Medicaid agency or to carve out drug benefits and keep them in the fee-for-service system. Arguments in favor of incorporating drug benefits into the package of managed care services tend to highlight advantages from integration of medical and prescription drug benefits and improved coordination and management of medication utilization. States may still choose to carve out drug benefits because management by health plans can lead to differences in formularies, pharmacy audits, DUR, and prior authorization processes. Other concerns related to drug coverage through managed care plans center around the fact that plans are at risk for drug payments and therefore may have a financial incentive to reduce access to care. Another area of concern is plan coordination, as in the case of coordinating drug regimens between primary care providers and types of care that may be carved out—for example, mental health.

When managed care plans cover drugs, the terms of that coverage are governed by plans' contracts with the states. Plans set their own retail pharmacy reimbursement levels. Contractual requirements and oversight of managed care plans' formularies and utilization management strategies vary considerably by state. However, federal regulations charge states with ensuring that plan enrollees have access to all prescription drugs covered by the state Medicaid plan, even if the MCO formularies do not normally include them.

Prior to passage of the ACA, several states with comprehensive Medicaid managed care plans carved out prescription drug benefits in order to collect federal drug rebates from manufacturers for those purchases, because these discounts were not required when MCOs covered drugs. The ACA extended federal rebates to Medicaid-covered drugs purchased by MCOs for their Medicaid enrollees in 2010. In 2011, four states that previously carved out drug benefits—Kentucky, New Jersey, New York, and Ohio—turned over pharmacy management to Medicaid MCOs. IMS Health reported that the number and percentage of Medicaid prescriptions paid for by MCOs surged from 4.9 million (19%) per month in September 2011 to 12.5 million (46%) per month in June 2012. The switch affected the types of medications received by patients, although effects varied by state and disease category. The study did not assess impacts of these changes on health outcomes and overall program costs.[56]

Specialty Drugs

The rapid growth of expenditures for so-called "specialty" drugs is a major area of focus for federal and state policymakers. One challenge in assessing trends for these drugs is there is no universally accepted definition of specialty drugs. Although Medicaid programs use varying definitions, products designated as specialty drugs tend to have at least one of the following characteristics:

high cost, difficult medication delivery, or complex treatment maintenance.[57] The Academy for Managed Care Pharmacy (AMCP) *Format for Formulary Submissions* defines specialty drugs as those that require either of the following:

- A difficult or unusual process of delivery to the patient (preparation, handling, storage, inventory, distribution, risk evaluation and mitigation strategy programs for known or potential dangers, data collection, or administration)
- Patient management prior to or following administration (monitoring, disease, or therapeutic support systems)

The AMCP acknowledges that price is frequently a consideration in definitions used by individual organizations, but the Academy does not include price in its definition and argues that price alone should not be used to define specialty drugs.[58]

Express Scripts' *2014 Drug Trend Report* noted that specialty drugs accounted for 28% of overall PMPY expenditures for Medicaid beneficiaries in plans managed by Express Scripts plan sponsors, but this percentage ranged from 17% for children ages 0–19 to 31% for adults ages 35–64. The company also reported that 1-year increases in costs for specialty drugs (+36.7%) far outpaced those for traditional drugs (+3.2%) used by Medicaid beneficiaries, leading to much higher overall growth in total expenditures for specialty drugs (+35.8%) compared to traditional drugs (+2.8%).[14]

Physician-Administered Drugs

The Deficit Reduction Act of 2005 required states to collect rebates under the federal drug rebate program on claims for physician-administered drugs, including all single-source drugs and the top 20 multiple-source (generic) drugs ranked by expenditures—although CMS encourages states to collect rebates on all multiple-source drugs administered by physicians. A federal survey found that about one-quarter of state Medicaid programs (13 of the 49 who responded) did not meet the requirements as of early 2009.[59] States continue to face challenges carrying out these mandates: providers may not report all of the information needed to support rebate claims, state systems may not accurately capture relevant information or may accept claims without complete documentation, and manufacturers may challenge claims because of concerns over the accuracy of claims information.[60]

Coordination of outpatient drug benefits and physician-administered drugs covered under the medical benefit raises another set of issues for states, including choices about coverage of specific drugs under either the outpatient drug benefit or medical benefit. Many drugs classified by states as specialty drugs require a physician to administer or supervise dosing. The number of specialty drugs is expected to increase significantly in future years, which will likely bring issues of management, coordination of benefits, and payment for physician-administered drugs to the forefront of state Medicaid drug policy decisions.

Institutional Drug Benefit

Most residents in long-term care facilities are dually eligible for Medicaid and Medicare and receive their drugs from Medicare Part D. However, beneficiaries residing in nursing homes who are only eligible for Medicaid are still covered by Medicaid prescription drug benefits. To serve this population, nursing homes typically contract with institutional pharmacies, which are tailored to fill special needs, such as 24 h drug delivery or unit dose packaging. Medicaid reimburses drugs dispensed in nursing homes using a formula similar to that used in fee-for-service—an ingredient cost plus a dispensing fee. However, institutional pharmacies may get an additional payment in recognition of the extra services they typically provide, whether an increased ingredient cost payment or higher dispensing fees.

Conclusion

As a major component of state budgets, Medicaid faces ongoing pressure to limit cost growth, even as medical inflation maintains an upward trend and the program continues to serve the poorest and sickest Americans. Medicaid faces the same pressures experienced by all payers for health-care services: increased prices, the introduction of new technologies, and changing U.S. demographics—in particular, the aging of the population. However, Medicaid's countercyclical nature—enrollment and expenditures grow during periods of economic downturn as workers lose jobs and health coverage—also leaves it vulnerable to increased scrutiny by cash-strapped states because the program costs tend to increase more rapidly when states have fewer resources to expend. At the same time, Medicaid is vitally important to the provision of drugs for the low-income and vulnerable populations that qualify for coverage, particularly given the greater burden of illness borne by these populations.

Medicaid's comprehensive coverage provides access to medical care and mental health services that would likely otherwise be beyond the reach of the vulnerable populations it serves, but this inclusiveness makes controlling utilization difficult. States are increasingly seeking ways to better manage high-use, high-cost beneficiaries. There are likely to be opportunities for significant cost savings among these patients by addressing issues such as polypharmacy and inappropriate (even dangerous) prescribing, but a challenge is focusing efforts in ways to avoid both *over*use and *under*use of prescription drugs, and that also take into account potential effects beyond the drug benefit. Targeting these beneficiaries with the intent to cut drug spending may be counterproductive if the approaches used result in higher costs to other parts of the Medicaid budget. In some cases, it may be appropriate to spend more money on prescription drugs to try to avoid more costly care (e.g., it is less expensive and better for a beneficiary with severe mental illness to be stabilized in the community using mental health drugs than to be hospitalized).

State Medicaid programs use a variety of benchmarks to determine their reimbursements to pharmacies for prescribed drugs. Many states have changed the methods they use to determine reimbursement in recent years, both in response to concerns about the accuracy and long-term availability of commercially available prices and as a way of controlling cost growth. States and the federal government continue to explore new reimbursement options. Regardless of which benchmark best approximates the final transaction prices at which retail pharmacies purchase drugs, the right benchmark for acquisition costs does not alone resolve the issue of what constitutes "appropriate" Medicaid reimbursement. Retail pharmacies incur costs to safely and accurately dispense medications to patients from convenient locations. The total compensation they receive, including reimbursement for the cost of the drug and the dispensing fee, should be sufficient to support ongoing operations.

With the traditional, fee-for-service delivery model shrinking as a share of Medicaid program enrollments and drug benefits being folded back into comprehensive managed care programs where they were previously carved out, managed care plans are increasingly assuming the role of being the principal managers of pharmacy benefits and negotiators of reimbursement rates for prescriptions dispensed to Medicaid patients through retail pharmacies. This conversion, and the influx of new adult enrollees resulting from the ACA, will require states to make adjustments to the oversight and management of drug benefits.

Many new drugs and biologics are "specialty" medications, dispensed through specialty pharmacies and administered by physicians or other health-care providers, and thus covered via medical benefits. Involvement of providers in the administration or monitoring of specialty drug products adds a layer of complexity because of the necessary coordination of benefits, payments, and rebate collections. These products tend to be much more expensive than traditional drugs, so accurate reimbursement is important, regardless of whether the state pays for them directly through pharmacies or indirectly as part of a larger reimbursement to a medical provider or health-care facility. With the increasing numbers of specialty products, growing utilization, and generally high costs of these products, managing specialty drugs will be crucial to limiting state and federal Medicaid expenditures for prescribed drugs in the near future.

The Medicaid program is always evolving to meet federal mandates, state preferences, technological changes, and beneficiary needs. What remains the same is that Medicaid fills gaps in other forms of coverage, covers populations that cannot otherwise receive coverage, and pays for services, such as long-term care, which are inadequately provided through other sources. Unless these other critical coverage needs can be addressed through other avenues, Medicaid will remain the workhorse of the U.S. health-care system.

References

1. Centers for Medicare and Medicaid Services. (2015). National health expenditure accounts: Historical. Retrieved June 26, 2015, from https://www.cms.gov/research-statistics-data-and-systems/statistics-trends-and-reports/nationalhealthexpenddata/nationalhealthaccountshistorical.html. Accessed on December 5, 2015.
2. Centers for Medicare and Medicaid Services. (2015). National health expenditure accounts: Projected. Retrieved June 26, 2015, from http://www.cms.gov/Research-Statistics-Data-and-Systems/Statistics-Trends-and-Reports/NationalHealthExpendData/NationalHealthAccountsProjected.html.
3. National Association of State Budget Officers. (2014). State expenditure report. Washington, DC: National Association of State Budget Officers.
4. Coughlin, T., Long, S.K., Clemans-Cope, L., and Resnick, D. (2013). What difference does Medicaid make? (No. 8440). Washington, DC: Kaiser Commission on Medicaid and the Uninsured.
5. Holahan, J. and Garrett, B. (2009). Rising unemployment, Medicaid, and the uninsured. (No. 7850). Washington, DC: Kaiser Commission on Medicaid and the Uninsured.
6. Medicaid and long-term care services and supports (2012) (No. 2186-09). Washington, DC: Kaiser Commission on Medicaid and the Uninsured.
7. KFF State Health Facts. (June 22, 2015). Status of state action on the Medicaid expansion decision. Retrieved June 26, 2015, from http://kff.org/health-reform/state-indicator/state-activity-around-expanding-medicaid-under-the-affordable-care-act/.
8. Centers for Medicare and Medicaid Services. (2014). Medicaid benefits. Retrieved February 14, 2014, from http://www.medicaid.gov/Medicaid-CHIP-Program-Information/By-Topics/Benefits/Medicaid-Benefits.html.
9. Mitchell, A. and Baumrucker, E.P. (2013). Medicaid's federal medical assistance percentage (FMAP), FY2014 (CRS Report for Congress No. R42941). Washington, DC: Congressional Research Service.
10. Congressional Budget Office. (2015). The budget and economic outlook: 2015 to 2025 (Publication 49892). Washington, DC: Congressional Budget Office.

11. Centers for Medicare and Medicaid Services. (2013). 2011 Medicaid managed care enrollment report. Retrieved June 26, 2015, from http://www.medicaid.gov/medicaid-chip-program-information/by--topics/data-and-systems/medicaid-managed-care/medicaid-managed-care-enrollment-report.html.
12. Centers for Medicare and Medicaid Services. (2015). Medicaid drug programs data and resources. Retrieved June 28, 2015, from http://www.medicaid.gov/Medicaid-CHIP-Program-Information/By-Topics/Benefits/Prescription-Drugs/Medicaid-Drug-Programs-Data-and-Resources.html.
13. Smith, V., Kramer, S., and Rudowitz, R. (2011). Managing Medicaid pharmacy benefits: Current issues and options. Washington, DC: Kaiser Commission on Medicaid and the Uninsured.
14. Express Scripts, Inc. (2015). 2014 drug trend report. Retrieved June 28, 2015, from http://lab.express-scripts.com/drug-trend-report/.
15. Bruen, B. and Miller, L. (2008). Changes in medicaid prescription volume and use in the wake of Medicare part D implementation. *Health Affairs*, 27(1):196–202.
16. Bruen, B. and Young, K. (2014). What drives spending and utilization of Medicaid drug benefits in states? Washington, DC: The Henry J. Kaiser Family Foundation.
17. Ketchan, J. and Ngai, J. (2008). How similar are states' Medicaid preferred drug lists? *American Journal of Managed Care*, 14(11 Suppl):SP46–SP52.
18. Farley, J., Cline, R., Schommer, J., Hadsall, R., and Nyman, J. (2008). Retrospective assessment of Medicaid step-therapy prior authorization policy for atypical antipsychotic medications. *Clinical Therapeutics*, 30(8):1524–1539.
19. Law, M., Ross-Degnan, D., and Soumerai, S. (2008). Effect of prior authorization of second-generation antipsychotic agents on pharmacy utilization and reimbursements. *Psychiatric Services*, 59(5):540–546.
20. Lu, C., Soumerai, S., Ross-Degnan, D., Zhang, F., and Adams, A. (2010). Unintended impacts of a Medicaid prior authorization policy on access to medications for bipolar illness. *Medical Care*, 48(1):4–9.
21. Hartung, D., Touchette, D., Ketchum, K., Haxby, D., and Goldberg, B. (2004). Effects of a prior-authorization policy for celecoxib on medical service and prescription drug use in a managed care Medicaid population. *Clinical Therapeutics*, 26(9):1518–1532.
22. Lu, C., Law, M., Soumerai, S., Graves, A., LeCates, R., Zhang, F., Ross-Degnan, D., and Adams, A. (2011). Impact of prior authorization on the use and costs of lipid-lowering medications among Michigan and Indiana dual enrollees in Medicaid and Medicare: Results of a longitudinal, population-based study. *Clinical Therapeutics*, 33(1):135–144.
23. Virabhak, S. and Shinogle, J. (2005). Physicians' prescribing responses to a restricted formulary: The impact of Medicaid preferred drug lists in Illinois and Louisiana. *American Journal of Managed Care*, 11(1):SP14–SP20.
24. Law, M., Lu, C., Soumerai, S., Graves, A., LeCates, R., Zhang, F., Ross-Degnan, D., and Adams, A. (2010). Impact of two Medicaid prior-authorization policies on antihypertensive use and costs among Michigan and Indiana residents dually enrolled in Medicaid and Medicare: Results of a longitudinal, population-based study. *Clinical Therapeutics*, 32(4):729–741.
25. Ridley, D. and Axelson, K. (2006). Impact of Medicaid preferred drug lists on therapeutic adherence. *Pharmacoeconomics*, 24(Suppl 3):65–78.
26. Murawski, M. and Abdelgawad, T. (2005). Exploration of the impact of preferred drug lists on hospital and physician visits and the costs to Medicaid. *American Journal of Managed Care*, 11(1):SP35–SP42.
27. Johnson, T. and Stahl-Moncada, S. (2008). Medicaid prescription formulary restrictions and arthritis treatment costs. *American Journal of Public Health*, 98(7):1300–1305.
28. Abouzaid, S., Jutkowitz, E., Foley, K., Pizzi, L. Kim, E., and Bates, J. (2010). Economic Impact of prior authorization policies for atypical antipsychotics in the treatment of Schizophrenia. *Population Health Management*, 13(5):247–254.
29. The Henry J. Kaiser Family Foundation. (2012). Medicaid benefits: Prescription drugs. Retrieved March 14, 2014, from http://kff.org/medicaid/state-indicator/prescription-drugs/.
30. Soumerai, S., Ross-Degnan, D., Avorn, J., McLaughlin, T., and Choodnovskiy, I. (1991). Effects of Medicaid drug-payment limits on admission to hospitals and nursing homes. *The New England Journal of Medicine*, 325(15):1072–1077.

31. Martin, B.C. and McMillan, J.A. (1996). The impact of implementing a more restrictive prescription limit on Medicaid recipients: Effects on cost, therapy and out of pocket expenditures. *Medical Care*, 34:686–701.
32. Newhouse, J. (1996). *Free For All? Lessons from the Rand Health Insurance Experiment*. Cambridge, MA: Harvard University Press.
33. Ku, L. and Wachino, V. (2005). The effect of increased cost-sharing in Medicaid: A summary of research findings. Washington, DC: Center on Budget and Policy Priorities.
34. Swartz, K. (2010). Cost-sharing: Effects on spending and outcomes. Robert Wood Johnson Foundation Synthesis Report Number 20, Princeton, NJ.
35. Hartung, D.M., Carlson, M.J., Kraemer, D.F., Haxby, D.G., Ketchum, K.L., and Greenlick, M.R. (2008). Impact of a Medicaid copayment policy on prescription drug and health services utilization in a fee-for-service Medicaid population. *Medical Care*, 46(6):565–572.
36. Wallace, N.T., McConnell, K.J., Gallia, C.A., and Smith, J.A. (2008). How effective are copayments in reducing expenditures for low-income adult Medicaid beneficiaries? Experience from the Oregon Health Plan. *Health Services Research*, 43(2):515–530.
37. Subramanian, S. (2011). Impact of Medicaid copayments on patients with cancer: Lessons for Medicaid expansion under health reform. *Medical Care*, 49(9):842–847.
38. Centers for Medicare and Medicaid Services. (2015). Medicaid prescription reimbursement information by state—Quarter ending March 2015. Retrieved June 28, 2015, from http://www.medicaid.gov/medicaid-chip-program-information/by-topics/benefits/prescription-drugs/state-prescription-drug-resources.html.
39. Pracht, E.E. and Moore W.J. (2003.) Interest groups and state Medicaid drug programs. *Journal of Health Politics, Policy and Law*, 28(1):9–39.
40. U.S. Department of Health and Human Services—Office of Inspector General. (1997). Medicaid pharmacy: Actual acquisition cost of prescription drug products for brand name drugs (A-06-96-00030), Washington, D.C.
41. U.S. Department of Health and Human Services—Office of Inspector General. (2001). Medicaid pharmacy: Actual acquisition cost of brand name prescription drug products (A-06-00-00023), Washington, D.C.
42. U.S. Department of Health and Human Services—Office of Inspector General. (2002). Medicaid pharmacy: Additional analyses of the actual acquisition cost of prescription drug products (A-06-02-00041), Washington, D.C.
43. U.S. Department of Health and Human Services—Office of Inspector General. (2002). Medicaid pharmacy: Actual acquisition cost of generic prescription drug products (A-06-01-00053), Washington, D.C.
44. U.S. Department of Health and Human Services—Office of Inspector General. (2005.) Medicaid drug price comparisons: Average manufacturer price to published prices (OEI-05-05-00240), Washington, D.C.
45. Medicaid Program. (February 2, 2012). Covered outpatient drugs; proposed rule. *Federal Register*, 72(22):5317–5367.
46. U.S. Department of Health and Human Services—Office of Inspector General. (2012). Analyzing changes to Medicaid federal upper limit amounts (OEI-03-11-00650), Washington, D.C.
47. U.S. Department of Health and Human Services—Office of Inspector General. (2005). Comparison of Medicaid federal upper limit amounts to average manufacturer prices (OEI-03-05-00110), Washington, D.C.
48. U.S. Department of Health and Human Services—Office of Inspector General. (2013). Medicaid drug pricing in state maximum allowable cost programs (OEI-03-11-00640), Washington, D.C.
49. Grant Thornton LLP. (2007). An independent comparative analysis of U.S. prescription dispensing costs. http://mpi-group.com/wp-content/uploads/2015/01/Research-GT-CostofDispensingStudy.pdf.
50. Health Information Designs. (2010). Cost of dispensing prescription drugs in Alabama, Auburn, Alabama.
51. Myers and Stauffer LC. (2010). Survey of dispensing costs of pharmaceuticals in the state of Oregon. http://www.oregon.gov/OHA/pharmacy/reimburse-method/docs/rpt-2010.pdf.

52. Centers for Medicare and Medicaid Services. CMS-64 quarterly expense report. Retrieved April 2, 2014, from http://medicaid.gov/medicaid-chip-program-information/by-topics/financing-and-reimbursement/expenditure-reports-mbes-cbes.html.
53. U.S. Government Accountability Office. (2011). Manufacturer discounts in the 340B program offer benefits, but federal oversight needs improvement (No. GAO-11-836). U.S. Government Printing Office. Washington, D.C.
54. Health Resources and Services Administration. (2014). Covered entities database. Retrieved April 2, 2014, from http://opanet.hrsa.gov/opa/CESearch.aspx. Accessed January 12, 2016.
55. Gifford, K., Smith, V., Snipes, D., and Paradise, J. (2011). A profile of Medicaid managed care programs in 2010: Findings from a 50-state survey. Washington, DC: Kaiser Commission on Medicaid and the Uninsured.
56. IMS Institute for Healthcare Informatics. (2013). Shift from fee-for-service to managed Medicaid: What is the impact on patient care? Parsippany, NJ: IMS Institute for Healthcare Informatics.
57. Blaser, D., Lewtas, A., Ousterhout, M., Lee, K., Hartman, S., and Gagnon, J. (2010). How to define specialty pharmaceuticals—A systematic review. *American Journal of Pharmacy Benefits*, 2(6):371–380.
58. Academy of Managed Care Pharmacy. (2012). AMCP format for formulary submission guidelines (version 3.1), Alexandria, Virginia. Retrieved October 16, 2013, from http://www.oregon.gov/OHA/pharmacy/reimburse-method/docs/rpt-2010.pdf.
59. U.S. Department of Health and Human Services Office of Inspector General. (2011). States collection of rebates for physician-administered drugs (No. OEI-03-09-00410), Washington, D.C.
60. Nebraska Department of Health and Human Services. (2013). Medicaid Drug Rebate Program—National Drug Code (NDC) reporting requirement for physician administered drugs new quantity limits (Provider Bulletin No. 13–63) http://dhhs.ne.gov/medicaid/Documents/PB1363.pdf.
61. The Henry J. Kaiser Family Foundation. (no date). State health facts: Medicaid and CHIP, Retrieved June 26, 2015, from http://kff.org/state-category/medicaid-chip/.

Chapter 24

Medication Therapy Management Services

Brian J. Isetts

Contents

Introduction

The ineffective and unfortunate consequences of medication use, referred to as drug-related morbidity and mortality (DRM&M), are an insidious public health nemesis that has persisted for many years. It's almost as if consumers perceive the unfortunate consequences of medication use as inevitable and a typical cost of doing business. The magnitude of this problem came to light with a study published in 1995 [1]. Additional research and analyses followed indicating that DRM&M is a nearly $(USD)300 billion annual burden in the United States [2–4]. In other words, we spend almost as much to fix the bad things that happen when patients take medications as we do to purchase pharmaceutical products.

This alarming reality begs the question, "how did this happen?" One answer is that "every system is perfectly designed to get the results it gets"[5]. A few years from now, we may look back and reflect on the days when we merely threw drugs at patients and hoped that good things would happen. Prior to 1974, airline crashes occurred fairly regularly until a "systems safety" approach was applied so that passengers now safely reach their destination on time with very few accidents [6]. It can be argued that medication use is at similar crossroads as that of airline travel prior to 1974.

The personal and financial toll of DRM&M is now being recognized as an urgent national crisis. An analysis of emergency hospitalizations for adverse drug events (ADEs) in older Americans published in the *New England Journal of Medicine*, coupled with the comprehensive report from the office of inspector general, resulted in a congressional call to do more to coordinate and ensure that ADEs experienced by Medicare beneficiaries become the exception rather than the norm [4,7–9]. Subsequently, a Federal Interagency Workgroup on Adverse Drug Events was convened in the fall of 2012 to develop a national action plan for ADE prevention [10].

If we were able to go back and start over to consciously design a true medication use system, we would look to apply key systems engineering concepts and methods to improve health-care delivery generally, and medication management specifically. This approach was the subject of a joint report from the National Academy of Engineering (NAE) and Institute of Medicine (IOM) advocating for the widespread application of systems engineering tools to improve health-care delivery [11]. Systems engineering focuses on the design, control, and coordination of system activities to meet performance objectives. When the medication management is viewed from this systems engineering focus, performance objectives can be articulated specific to the manner in which patients take medications.

This chapter presents and discusses medication therapy management services in the context of systems engineering. Performance objectives for a medication use system are similar to those of the airline industry, in which passengers expect to safely reach their destination on time with high reliability. The same can be said for the use of medications, in which patients should expect to reliably achieve their drug therapy treatment goals with zero tolerance for medication harms.

Historical Perspective

DRM&M is defined as the incidence and prevalence of disease, illness and harm, and death associated with drug therapy [12]. The history of DRM&M dates back many years. A number of approaches have been implemented to address harms caused by medications. The emergence of clinical pharmacists functioning on health teams in hospitals is one example. Another response to DRM&M includes requirements that a consultant pharmacist review the records of skilled nursing facility residents at least monthly to assess the appropriate use of medications.

DRM&M encompasses both the ineffective use of medicines and unfortunate consequences of medication use. These consequences span from ADEs and drug interactions to the ineffective use of medications and lack of access to effective therapies. It has become apparent that we do not have a medication management system in place to reliably ensure patients' achievement of desirable drug therapy outcomes. An important article published in 1990 on opportunities and responsibilities in pharmaceutical care highlighted the need for a consistent and systematic patient care process specific to drug therapy, as well as the need for individuals and organizations to be held accountable and responsible for patient outcomes of medication use [13].

One of the first attempts to study medication management in a systems context includes the Minnesota Pharmaceutical Care Demonstration Project [14]. Similar to services provided by all other health professionals, medication management must also be supported by a practice management system. Important lessons have been learned from various attempts to address isolated aspects of dysfunctional medication use that were uncoordinated with a patient's medical care system. For instance, medication adherence interventions disconnected from medical care have the potential to increase DRM&M and cause harm to the patient by increasing adherence to medications that may not have an intended medical use or are ineffective or unsafe for the patient.

One of the most important take-home messages of this chapter is that medication therapy management services cannot be effectively or efficiently provided outside of a systems context. The following sections of this chapter discuss the impact and results of medication therapy management services within redesigned systems of health care, and it is the practice of pharmaceutical care that supports the effective and efficient delivery of medication therapy management services in a rational medication use system.

Origins of Medication Therapy Management Services

The origins of the term medication therapy management services are not entirely certain and are somewhat of an urban myth. In the 1990s, legislation was introduced in the Congress intended to reimburse pharmacists for pharmaceutical care services utilizing terms such as medication management, drug management, and collaborative drug therapy management.

In 2002, the Medicare Payment Advisory Commission (MedPAC) prepared a report for the Congress on Medicare payment of nonphysician providers. This report recognized DRM&M and the inappropriate use of medications among the elderly. Drug management was described as "an evolving approach to care in which drug therapy decisions are coordinated collaboratively by physicians, pharmacists, and other health professionals together with the patient" [15]. The report addressed the need to optimize the drug therapy of Medicare beneficiaries with complex drug regimens and also set the stage for initiating a Medicare drug benefit with medication therapy management services.

An important development in defining and describing the medication therapy management service has been addressed in the same manner as that of all other health-care services. Official health-reporting nomenclature exists in the United States as a means for systematically classifying and reporting health procedures and services. *Current Procedural Terminology* (CPT®) was established in 1966 in response to the need for standardizing health procedures and services [16]. The primary purpose of CPT is to codify official health-reporting nomenclature. Other secondary administrative functions of CPT include use in health-care billing and reimbursement and in the development of performance benchmark measurements.

The journey toward recognition of medication therapy management as a health service and acknowledgment of pharmacists as providers of medication therapy management services, in official health-reporting nomenclature, can be traced to the Health Insurance Portability and Accountability Act of 1996 (HIPAA) regulations. In August 2000, the U.S. Department of Health and Human Services released the final rule for the implementation of HIPAA with electronic data interchange transaction standards for professional services claims from all health professionals, including pharmacists. These professional services transaction regulations created an opportunity for the profession of pharmacy to petition for inclusion in CPT coding.

The American Medical Association (AMA) oversees the proceedings of the CPT Editorial Panel as the publisher of CPT. In 2002, a coalition of eight national pharmacy organizations was created to work with the AMA and the CPT Editorial Panel to begin the process for submitting a formal medication therapy management services code proposal. The original CPT code proposal petition submitted in 2004 requested a permanent Category I medication therapy management services (MTMS) coding system based on patient complexity using tiered intensity, or more accurately stated a resource-based relative value scale. Evidence of the effectiveness and safety of MTMS in the original CPT code proposal was derived directly from literature on the practice of pharmaceutical care [17].

The consistent and systematic patient care process, serving as a centerpiece for the practice of pharmaceutical care, was adopted and codified by the CPT Editorial Panel. Fundamental components of MTMS codified in CPT include (i) pharmacists performing a face-to-face comprehensive medication review (CMR) and assessment, (ii) to identify, resolve, and prevent drug therapy problems, (iii) formulating a medication treatment plan to achieve patients' goals of therapy, (iv) monitoring, and (v) follow-up evaluation of patient outcomes of therapy. "MTMS is provided to optimize the response to medications or to manage treatment-related medication interactions or complications" [17–19].

In its deliberations on the initial CPT Code Proposal Petition, the CPT Editorial Panel recognized the safety and effectiveness of MTMS but was not convinced that the service was widely available. Due to the lack of evidence of widespread availability, CPT codes for MTMS provided by pharmacists were assigned Category III (temporary) CPT code status. This unfamiliarity with MTMS provided by pharmacists also resulted in assigning time-based, rather than tiered intensity or resource-based relative value scale, CPT codes.

In response to this decision, a provider and a payer survey were developed and disseminated to gather information on the number of pharmacists providing MTMS as defined in *CPT 2006*. Practices offering MTMS, as specified in the complete and comprehensive service definition, were identified in all 50 states, the District of Columbia, and Puerto Rico. And the vast majority of responses (86%) originated from ambulatory care practice sites. Results of this survey revealed that there were a total of nearly 2.8 million MTMS encounters over the prior 2-year study period (2005 and 2006) [17]. Based on the results of this survey, a code change proposal was submitted to the CPT Editorial Panel, and the MTMS CPT codes were assigned permanent Category I status in 2007. However, dissonance between time-based MTMS CPT codes and actual resources required to provide MTMS for patients with complex medical and drug-related needs remains unresolved.

Policy Solutions to Drug-Related Morbidity and Mortality

Medicare Part D Medication Therapy Management Program

To fully appreciate current and future approaches for addressing DRM&M, it is instructive to analyze the evolving policy focus on appropriate medication use. When Medicare was enacted in 1965, it included coverage for hospitalizations and physician office visits in elderly citizens. However, coverage of prescription medications was not included in the Medicare legislation. Factors influencing this decision included the small average cost of a typical prescription in 1965, competing priorities related to devastating hospitalization costs of individual retirees, and an aggressive attack on Medicare legislation as "socialized medicine" [20].

As time elapsed, it was recognized that Medicare beneficiaries desperately needed a drug benefit. The MedPAC report of 2002 on payment of nonphysician providers highlighted the importance of including medication management in a future Medicare drug benefit noting that "as part of multi-faceted program reforms, the Congress could consider drug management services together with comprehensive care coordination for Medicare beneficiaries," and the report went on to specifically state that "as the Congress contemplates creating a Medicare drug benefit, including a drug management benefit may provide a mechanism to optimize drug therapy for a subset of Medicare beneficiaries who have complex drug regimens" [15].

The Medicare Modernization Act of 2003 under title 42 Code of Federal Regulations (CFR) Part 423, Subpart D, established a Medicare Part D prescription drug benefit along with requirements that Part D plans and sponsors must meet to control costs and improve quality through medication therapy management programs (MTMPs).* The MTMPs of Medicare Part D plans and sponsors include a person-to-person CMR and targeted medication therapy management interventions such as communications with prescribers. A unique policy decision was made to fund the Medicare Part D MTMP as a component of the administrative fees paid to Part D plans and sponsors, as compared to payments for other health services, which are paid to health providers or health-care organizations, and the initial Code of Federal Regulations (CFR) regulations for MTMPs established a general framework that allowed sponsors' considerable flexibility for incorporating a MTMP into their plan's benefit structure.

Permitting Part D plans flexibility in defining MTM services coupled with program funding through administrative fees has resulted in predictably restrictive beneficiary access to the Part D MTMP, as well as wide variations in service delivery standards. Evidence that the Part D MTMP improves quality and generates medical savings supports the CMS aim that more than 25% of enrollees will benefit from MTM services [21]. However, even as enrollee eligibility criteria mandated by CMS have increasingly expanded, access to MTM services remains low with MTMP eligibility rates of less than 8% in 2011 [21]. Despite the MTMP's improvements and an emphasis on outcome measures in rating plan quality and performance, MedPAC Commissioners "continue to be concerned about the quality of pharmaceutical care received by beneficiaries with multiple medications" [22]. In 2014, MedPAC Annual Report to Congress, wide variations in Part D MTMP eligibility criteria and kinds of interventions provided to enrollees are noted, while also recognizing that "the current risk-sharing arrangement may limit how aggressively or successfully plan sponsors manage drug utilization for beneficiaries who take many medications" [22].

As CMS strives to hold plans and providers accountable for service level expectations consistent with official MTMS health-reporting nomenclature of CPT, there is a focus on measuring the comprehensive nature of CMRs. Findings from a mixed methods MTM study conducted through the CMS Center for Medicare and Medicaid Innovation (CMMI) are influencing evolving approaches for holding plans and providers accountable [23]. The CMMI MTM study found that MTMPs, which effectively targeted high-risk individuals with CMRs, "experienced significant improvements in drug therapy outcomes when compared to beneficiaries who did not receive MTM services" [21,23]. These findings are supporting the hypothesis that the CMR may be one of the more crucial elements of MTM and that significant cost savings associated with all-cause hospitalizations may be due to MTM's comprehensive, rather than disease-specific approach [21].

The proposed rules of January 10, 2014, signal a more intense focus on measuring comprehensive MTM service level expectations of plans and providers. Other best practices identified in the CMMI MTM study expected to influence CMS MTMP measures include [21]

- Establishing persistent and proactive CMR recruitment efforts
- Aggressively targeting and recruiting beneficiaries for CMRs based on information from medical events such as hospital stays, emergency room visits, and readmissions
- Utilizing existing working relationships within a beneficiary's medical care system and coordinating care through trusted community relationships among pharmacists and prescribers

* The Medicare Prescription Drug Benefit program was established by Section 101 of the Medicare Prescription Drug, Improvement, and Modernization Act of 2003 and is codified in Sections 1860D-1 through 1860D-42 of the Social Security Act. The Medication Therapy Management Program is authorized in under Part D (§ 423.153(d)), Section 1860D-4(c)(2) of the Act.

Innovations Influencing National MTMS Policy Decisions

Federal policy is substantially influenced by State innovations, demonstration projects, large-scale tests of change, and multistakeholder initiatives. One important multistakeholder initiative is focusing on standards for delivering complete and comprehensive medication therapy management services. The Patient-Centered Primary Care Collaborative (PCPCC) is promoting MTMS service level standards and expectations through a broad coalition of providers, payers, and consumers. Standards for comprehensive medication management are an integral component of the PCPCC mission for advancing a health system built on a strong foundation of primary care and the patient-centered medical home [24,25].

Demonstration projects and State Medicaid Program waivers continue to have an important influence on national MTMS policy. The Asheville Project, Project ImPACT, and the Minnesota Pharmaceutical Care Demonstration Project are three examples of projects with enduring lessons learned [14,26,27]. And early State Medicaid Program waivers designed to pay pharmacists in Mississippi, Wisconsin, Iowa, North Carolina, and elsewhere were important to build the body of evidence and experience shaping today's efforts [28–31].

An analysis by the National Alliance of State Pharmacy Associations provides a high-level state-by-state snapshot of pharmacist recognition in managing medications. Of the 34 states included in this analysis that recognize pharmacists as providers or practitioners, the majority do so through state statute, but a handful also recognize pharmacists within their state Medicaid provider manuals [32]. In addition, a detailed case study description of the 2005 Minnesota State Law specifying MTMS service level expectations, standards of practice, and a resource-based relative value scale reimbursement system for Medicaid recipients is readily available [33,34].

Characteristics of a Highly Reliable Medication Use System

Progress toward implementing a true medication use system focuses on engineering principles of highly reliable organizations currently reshaping health-care delivery and financing [11]. Principles of high reliability organizations have been critical to the success of clinical quality and safety initiatives among leading edge health-care systems [35,36]. A highly reliable medication use system combines evidence-based medicine with the science of continuous quality improvement to consistently do the right things so patients routinely achieve their drug therapy treatment goals with zero tolerance for preventable medication harms.

A summary of desirable medication use system characteristics in value-based, or outcomes-based, health-care delivery and financing has been described from a health-care organization perspective. In redesigned health-care systems, patient-specific drug therapy treatment goals are embedded in care model redesign across the care continuum [37]. Effectively working with patients and families to engage them in comprehensive medication therapy management services becomes the responsibility of all health-care team members. Establishing drug therapy treatment goals with objective and subjective measures that are important to patients and families is essential for improving clinical outcomes at reduced total cost of care expenditures [38,39].

And the careful integration of MTMS at critical transitions of care has been shown to improve medication reconciliation processes and procedures. A study was conducted to assess the impact of MTMS in medication reconciliation for patients postdischarge in terms of hospital readmission rates, financial savings, and medication discrepancies. At Group Health Cooperative in Seattle,

WA, the integration of MTMS with medication reconciliation was associated with a statistically significant reduction in hospital readmission rates at 7 and 14 days postdischarge, net financial savings of $(USD)354 per patient projected to save Group Health $(USD)1.5 million annually, and more than 80% of patients had at least one medication discrepancy resolved by a pharmacist [40]. The take-home message is that analyzing a patient's medication list across transitions of care to detect medication discrepancies is important, but it's what you do with a well-reconciled medication list that makes all the difference.

Future Policy Implications

In order to build a medication use system, this country deserves a number of challenging policy decisions loom on the horizon. Movement from volume-based to value-based reimbursement, concerted national action to address DRM&M, and inter- and intragovernment collaboration are great news for individuals who need medications to improve their quality of life. And it is now recognized that one of the biggest barriers to high-value health care rests in a pathway to reduce destructive self-interest. It has been documented that workers pay almost all of the costs of their health care, doing so through employee contributions to premiums, out-of-pocket payments, a shift of compensation dollars from wages to benefits, and state and federal payroll taxes that support Medicare [41], and rather than serving workers' best interest in providing the best care at the lowest cost, industry stakeholders have acted more like adversaries.

The pathway to lower total costs with better outcomes, recognizing that all stakeholders are in a common system with a common pool of limited resources, can be applied to the Medicare Part D Program generally, and the Part D MTMP specifically. As mentioned previously, funding MTMPs through administrative fees, restricting beneficiary eligibility, and permitting insurance plans to define MTM services will need a fundamental policy reanalysis. In addition, recognizing that best practices in the Part D MTMP improve quality and generate total cost of care savings, it stands to reason that the Medicare drug benefit should not reside in a separate silo as a stand-alone service, but rather integrated with the Medicare Part A and Part B (e.g., hospital and medical care) benefits.

Conclusions

DRM&M has been a persistent and growing public health nemesis that is now being addressed as an urgent national crisis. The NAE and the IOM have advocated for the widespread application of a systems approach to improve our health-care delivery system. These systems approach methods call for a continuous process analysis for improvement. The use of medications can also be viewed from this process improvement perspective.

Policies for redesigning health-care delivery and financing through value-based reimbursement are generating intense interest in accountability for what happens to patients when they take medications. Medication therapy management services have emerged as a rational approach for ensuring that patients routinely achieve their drug therapy treatment goals with zero tolerance for preventable medication harms. Studies on the outcomes of MTMS integrated in care model redesign are consistent with national aims of better care and better health at reduced per capita expenditures.

The Medicare Part D MTMP represents one of the first large-scale public policy solutions for improving medication safety and effectiveness in elderly Americans. However, programmatic decisions permitting Part D plans flexibility in defining MTM services combined with funding through administrative fees have resulted in predictably restrictive beneficiary access to the Part D MTMP, as well as evidence of substandard service delivery. A pathway to lower total costs with better outcomes recognizes that stakeholders are in a common system with a common pool of limited resources. Integrating the Medicare Part D drug benefit and MTMP with Medicare Parts A and B in value-based health-care delivery and financing may be one pathway for overcoming the challenges of destructive self-interests by embedding patient-specific drug therapy treatment goals as standard operating procedure across the care continuum.

Therefore, if we are serious about building a medication use system this country deserves, then it is time to invest in our medication management infrastructure. One potential policy solution for investing in a national medication management infrastructure is currently available in the Medication Therapy Management Services Grant Provisions of the Affordable Care Act (Section 3503). The Patient Protection and Affordable Care Act, also known as the Affordable Care Act (ACA) was not appropriated for funding by the Congress, it may be time to reexamine this solution in light of concerted national action to aggressively combat DRM&M.

References

1. Johnson JA, Bootman JL. Drug-related morbidity and mortality: A cost-of-illness model. *Arch Intern Med.* 1995; 155:1949–1956.
2. Ernst FR, Grizzle AJ. Drug-related morbidity and mortality: Updating the cost-of-illness model. *J Am Pharm Assoc.* 2001; 41:192–199.
3. NEHI. Improving patient medication adherence: A $290 billion opportunity. 2011; Accessed March 1, 2014, Available at: http://www.nehi.net/bendthecurve/sup/documents/Medication_Adherence_Brief.pdf.
4. Levinson DR. Adverse events in hospitals: National incidence among Medicare beneficiaries. U.S. Department of Health and Human Services, Office of Inspector General, OEI-06-09-00090, Washington, DC, November, 2010. Accessed June 1, 2015, Available at: https://oig.hhs.gov/oei/reports/oei-06-09-00090.pdf.
5. Paul Batalden MD. Quotation etched on the walls of the Institute for Healthcare Improvement, Boston, MA. Accessed June 1, 2015, Available at: http://www.dartmouth.edu/~cecs/hcild/hcild.html.
6. Airline Transport Association (ATA). Chapter 6: Safety. In *Airline Handbook.* Washington, DC: Air Transport Association. http://libraryonline.erau.edu/online-full-text/books-online/1064.pdf Last modified June 7, 2008; last accessed December 5, 2015.
7. Budnitz DS et al. Emergency hospitalizations for adverse drug events in older Americans. *N Engl J Med.* 2011; 365:2002–2012.
8. United States Senate. Letter from Senators Michael F. Bennet and Olympia J. Snowe to Secretary Kathleen Sebelius, December 28, 2011. Accessed March 15, 2014, Available at: http://thehill.com/images/stories/blogs/healthwatch/hhsdrugsletter.pdf.
9. Pecquet J. Senators call for joint government task force on adverse drug events. Healthwatch, The Hill, December 29, 2011. Accessed March 15, 2014, Available at: http://thehill.com/blogs/healthwatch/medical-devices-and-prescription-drug-policy-/201715-senators-call-for-joint-government-task-force-on-adverse-drug-reactions.
10. U.S. Department of Health and Human Services. National action plan for adverse drug event prevention. 2014; Accessed June 1, 2015, Available at: http://www.health.gov/hai/pdfs/ade-action-plan.pdf.
11. Proctor P, Compton WD, Grossman J, Fanjiang G. *Building a Better Delivery System: A New Engineering/Health Care Partnership.* Washington DC: National Academy of Engineering and Institute of Medicine, National Academy Press, Committee on Engineering and the Health Care System, 2005. Accessed June 1, 2015, Available at: http://www.iom.edu/Reports/2005/Building-a-Better-Delivery-System-A-New-EngineeringHealth-Care-Partnership.aspx.

12. Cipolle RJ, Strand LM, Morley PC. *Pharmaceutical Care Practice: The Patient Centered Approach to Medication Management*, 3rd ed. New York: McGraw-Hill, 2012.
13. Hepler CD, Strand LM. Opportunities and responsibilities in pharmaceutical care. *Am J Hosp Pharm.* 1990; 47:533–543.
14. Cipolle RJ, Strand LM, Morley PC. *Pharmaceutical Care Practice: The Clinician's Guide.* New York: McGraw-Hill, 2004.
15. Medicare Payment Advisory Commission, Hackbarth GM (Chair). Report to the congress: Medicare coverage of nonphysician practitioners. Washington, DC: Medicare Payment Advisory Commission, June 2002, pp. 21–26.
16. American Medical Association. About CPT®. Accessed June 1, 2015, Available at: http://www.ama-assn.org/ama/pub/physician-resources/solutions-managing-your-practice/coding-billing-insurance/cpt/about-cpt.page? Accessed January 12, 2016.
17. Isetts BJ, Buffington DE. CPT code-change proposal: National data on pharmacists' medication therapy management services. *J Am Pharm Assoc.* 2007; 47:491–495.
18. American Medical Association. *CPT Changes 2006: An Insider's View.* Chicago, IL: American Medical Association, 2005, pp. 309–312.
19. Pharmacist Services Technical Advisory Coalition. Medication therapy management service codes. Accessed January 12, 2016, Available at: http://www.pstac.org/services/mtms-codes.html.
20. Oliver TR, Lee PR, Lipton HL. A political history of Medicare and prescription drug coverage. *Milbank Quart.* 2004; 82(2):283–354. Accessed June 1, 2015, Available at: http://www.amcp.org/WorkArea/DownloadAsset.aspx?id=11196.
21. CMS-4159-P, Medicare Program. Contract Year 2015 Policy and Technical Changes to the Medicare Advantage and the Medicare Prescription Drug Benefit Programs. *Fed Reg.* January 10, 2014; 79(7):1947–1953.
22. Medicare Payment Advisory Commission, Hackbarth GM (Chair). Report to the congress: Medicare payment policy. Washington, DC: Medicare Payment Advisory Commission, March 2014; Chapter 14, Status Report on Part D, pp. 355–384.
23. U.S. Department of Health and Human Services, Centers for Medicare and Medicaid Services, and Center for Medicare and Medicaid Innovation. Medication therapy management in chronically ill populations: Final report, August 2013. Accessed June 1, 2015, Available at: http://innovation.cms.gov/Files/reports/MTM_Final_Report.pdf.
24. McInnis T, Webb E, Strand L. The patient-centered medical home: Integrating comprehensive medication management to optimize patient outcomes. Patient-centered primary care collaborative, June 2012. Accessed June 1, 2015, Available at: http://www.pcpcc.org/sites/default/files/media/medmanagement.pdf.
25. McInnis T, Webb E, Strand L. The patient-centered medical home: Integrating comprehensive medication management to optimize patient outcomes. Appendix A: Guidelines for the practice and documentation of comprehensive medication management in the patient-centered medical home. Patient-centered primary care collaborative, June 2012. Accessed June 1, 2015, Available at: http://www.pcpcc.org/sites/default/files/resources/Appendix_A_Guidelines_for_the_Practice_and_Documentation.pdf.
26. Cranor CW, Bunting BA, Christensen DB. The Asheville project: Long-term clinical and economic outcomes of a community pharmacy diabetes care program. *J Am Pharm Assoc.* 2003; 43:173–190.
27. Bluml BM, McKenney JM, Cziraky MJ. Pharmaceutical care services and results in Project ImPACT: Hyperlipidemia. *J Am Pharm Assoc.* 2000; 40:157–165.
28. Medicaid to pay Mississippi pharmacists for disease management. *Am J Health Syst Pharm.* 1998; 55:1238–1239.
29. HMOs adopt Wisconsin Medicaid pilot project for commercial enrollees. *Paym Strat Pharm Care.* 1998; 3:1,2,5–8.
30. Chrischilles EA et al. Evaluation of the Iowa Medicaid pharmaceutical case management program. *J Am Pharm Assoc.* 2004; 44:337–349.
31. Michaels NM, Jenkins GF, Pruss DL, Heidrick JE, Ferreri SP. Retrospective analysis of community pharmacists' recommendations in the North Carolina Medicaid medication therapy management program. *J Am Pharm Assoc.* 2010; 50:347–353.

32. Weaver K. NASPA finds state-level provider status is widespread, but not necessarily linked to payment, February 1, 2014. Accessed June 1, 2015, Available at: http://www.pharmacist.com/naspa-finds-state-level-provider-status-widespread-not-necessarily-linked-payment.
33. State of Minnesota Medicaid Medication Therapy Care Program documents and information. 2015; Accessed June 1, 2015, Available at: http://www.dhs.state.mn.us/main/idcplg?IdcService=GET_DYNAMIC_CONVERSION&RevisionSelectionMethod=LatestReleased&dDocName=dhs16_13688.
34. Isetts BJ. Chapter 12: The global perspective, United States. In Cipolle RJ, Strand LM, Morley PC (Eds.), *Pharmaceutical Care Practice: The Patient Centered Approach to Medication Management*, 3rd ed. New York: McGraw-Hill, 2012, pp. 627–644.
35. Weick KE et al. Organizing for high reliability: Processes of collective mindfulness. In BM Staw, LL Cummings (Eds.), *Research in Organizational Behavior*, Vol. 21. Greenwich, CT: JAI Press Inc., 1999, pp. 81–123.
36. Weick K et al. *Managing the Unexpected: Resilient Performance in an Age of Uncertainty*. San Francisco, CA: Jossey Bass, 2007.
37. Isetts BJ, Brummel AR, Ramalho de Oliveira D, Moen DW. Managing drug-related morbidity and mortality in a patient-centered medical home. *Med Care*. 2012; 50:997–1001.
38. Isetts BJ, Schondelmeyer SW, Artz MB, Lenarz LA, Heaton AH, Wadd WB, Brown LB, Cipolle RJ. Clinical and economic outcomes of medication therapy management services: The Minnesota experience. *J Am Pharm Assoc*. 2008; 48:203–211.
39. Isetts BJ, Brown LM, Schondelmeyer SW, Lenarz LA. Quality assessment of a collaborative approach for decreasing drug-related morbidity and achieving therapeutic goals. *Arch Intern Med*. 2003; 163:1813–1820.
40. Kilcup M, Schultz D, Carlson C, Wilson B. Postdischarge pharmacist medication reconciliation: Impact on readmission rates and financial saving. *J Am Pharm Assoc*. 2013; 53:78–84.
41. Martin LA, Berwick D, Nolan T. The big barrier to high-value health care: Destructive self-interest. *Harvard Business Review*. HBR Blog Network, November 15, 2013. Accessed June 1, 2015, Available at: http://blogs.hbr.org/2013/11/the-big-barrier-to-high-value-health-care-destructive-self-interest/.

Chapter 25

The Affordable Care Act: Potential Impacts on Pharmaceutical Markets

Steven H. Sheingold and Pierre L. Yong

Contents

Introduction

On March 23, 2010, President Obama signed the landmark Affordable Care Act (ACA). The implementation of ACA is having and will continue to have a substantial impact on the financing and delivery of health-care services in the United States. Its coverage expansion provisions will significantly reduce the number of uninsured Americans over the next few years and will expand access to health-care services. For those already insured, the ACA's insurance market reform provisions will assure continued access to high-quality and affordable health insurance coverage. In addition to the insurance changes, the ACA contained a number of provisions intended to drive change in the way health care is reimbursed and delivered in the United States. Together, these changes have the potential to impact pharmaceutical markets in several ways in the coming years.

The initial view in the policy and financial communities was that the pharmaceutical industry had emerged from the ACA legislative process as clear winners Milne and Kaitlin. The industry agreed to a variety of fees, discounts for Medicare, increased Medicaid rebates and an abbreviated licensure pathway for biological products that are demonstrated to be ***biosimilar*** to or *interchangeable* with an FDA-licensed biological product. They avoided major provisions that they had opposed in the past such as increased government role in negotiating drug prices, relaxed restrictions on drug reimportation, and prohibition of certain methods used to delay the market entrance of generic competitors, however (Cacciotti and Mozeson, 2011). In addition, the significant expansion of insurance coverage was expected to increase the demand for prescription drugs and, thus, be very good for overall sales volume. As the many provisions of ACA unfold, however, a more complex analysis of their long-run effect on pharmaceutical markets may be useful. Indeed, while markets for drugs are likely to expand, the changing incentives for delivering health care may have a variety of other impacts on sales and innovation whose overall magnitude and direction are less certain. In this chapter, we discuss the many potential ways in which the provisions of ACA may affect pharmaceutical markets in the future. In particular, we focus on their direct and indirect impacts that may be related to insurance coverage expansion, reimbursement and delivery system changes, and the greater availability of comparative effectiveness research (CER) to inform decision making. These changes are likely to affect utilization through formulary and practice decisions, pricing, and eventually research and development decisions by pharmaceutical manufacturers.

As a backdrop to the discussion of these potential effects, it is noteworthy that we have witnessed a substantial slowdown in health-care cost growth over the past few years (Martin et al., 2014). Clearly, the deep recession that began in 2008 has had some effect on health spending, but numerous other factors more systemic to health-care delivery have likely played a substantial role (Iglehart, 2013). While it is too early to fully assess the role that ACA has played through its value-based purchasing policies and the innovations in health-care financing and delivery being tested under its new authorities, it is reasonable to assume some early impact of the law on cost growth (Altman, 2013). Another likely important factor, however, is the slowdown in medical technology diffusion that has occurred in recent years. Indeed, the limited number of new blockbuster drugs since 2006 as well as the availability of generic competitors to high use drugs for the elderly has been integral to the ability of Medicare's Part D program to control costs since its implementation in 2006. While the average price per drug increased by 8% between 2007 and 2009, the average price per prescription increased by half that amount due to generic substitution (Sheingold and Nguyen, 2013). It is also reasonable to assume that the pace and composition of medical technology innovation in the coming years, and how they interact with the financial incentives of the changing reimbursement and delivery environment, will be critical to whether the recent favorable cost trends can be sustained or whether health spending growth once again accelerates. These same trends and interactions will ultimately determine the full effect that ACA has on pharmaceutical markets.

Framing the Issues: Pharmaceutical Economics, Public Policy, and the Affordable Care Act

Pharmaceutical pricing presents difficult and controversial policy issues in the United States. As pharmaceuticals grew as a share of national health expenditures and Medicare added a prescription drug benefit in 2006, the issue of cost containment became more visible. The United States pays higher prices for brand-name drugs and adopts them faster than do other countries (Kavanos et al., 2013). Nonetheless, the United States remains one of the only developed nations without some form of drug price controls or government price negotiations. Clearly, this distinct direction in policy is related to political philosophy regarding government interference in private markets, but there are a number challenging economic factors to consider as well.

Whether relying on the interaction of private market participants or on price control policies, navigating the trade-off between static and dynamic efficiency in pharmaceutical markets is critical. While the marginal costs of producing a pill are usually very low, bringing a drug to market can involve substantial investments in R&D. Static efficiency refers to a single time period in which price equal to marginal cost provides optimal allocative efficiency in terms of value to consumers. Dynamic efficiency refers to value over multiple time periods and a price in each period that contains sufficient incentives for R&D that improves future capacity to prevent health conditions and cure diseases in the future. The trade-off is often put simply as "today's prices bring tomorrows miracles"—that is, a short-run cost containment policy directed at the price of existing drugs may reduce investment in new effective drugs for the future.

Patent protection provides monopoly pricing power to manufacturers for some time period, potentially providing means for setting prices high enough to earn a sufficient rate of return on investment. In textbook monopoly markets, the consumer demand curve provides a constraint on monopoly pricing power in a way that equates price with the marginal value placed on the product—albeit at a less optimal equilibrium than would exist in a competitive market. For a number of well-known reasons—e.g., third-party coverage and consumer uncertainty about the product benefits—many believe that the traditional consumer demand schedule for many drugs does not exist and monopoly power may lead to prices well above those required to provide a fair rate of return on investment. While other nations use a variety of national policy methods such as technology assessment–based evaluations of product benefits and pricing strategies to represent a countervailing demand side of the market, in the United States, such approaches are left to individual health plans and pharmaceutical benefit managers (PBMs). As discussed later in this chapter, the decentralized U.S. approach appears to be somewhat successful in classes of drugs for which there are a number of therapeutically substitutable alternatives (brand and generic). For unique and specialty drugs, however, PBMs and health plans have few tools to combat monopoly pricing.

Of course, cost control (or cost management) can be achieved through managing quantity and price. Health plans have some tools such as prior authorization, quantity limitations, and step therapy, but these approaches may be limited by FDA labeling, practice guidelines, and evidence. More importantly, prescribing and use of pharmaceutical are largely in the hands of health-care providers who often face a different set of financial incentives than do PBMs and health plans. It is here that the ACA may play a substantial role in pharmaceutical markets, despite the fact that it does not directly address drug pricing or cost containment in any major way.

Quite simply, the ACA is likely to accelerate payment reform and delivery system transformation in a manner that more closely aligns incentives between health plans and provider organizations. A goal of many ACA provisions is to move toward a delivery system in which significantly more of health-care dollars (and patients) go to provider organizations that are held financially accountable for both cost and quality. These organizations will likely look for ways to use pharmaceuticals in the most cost-effective manner possible. In the following sections, we discuss key aspects of ACA that may affect pharmaceutical markets.

Background: Key Provisions of ACA

The new legislation made significant changes to financing and delivery of health-care services in the United States. Its many provisions might be summarized into three groups that are not independent with regard to their objectives: insurance market reforms and coverage expansion, delivery system transformation, and CER.

Coverage Expansions

The insurance market reforms were intended to assure that individuals and families would have continued access to affordable, high-quality insurance plans. In part, these requirements were aimed at minimizing or eliminating what were considered less desirable features of insurance plans such as annual and lifetime limits, policy decisions, preexisting condition restrictions, underwriting, and exclusion of dependents under the age of 26. A key feature of the law was to make insurance markets function more competitively for individuals and small groups through insurance exchanges that are now known as marketplaces. The marketplaces, along with a variety of rules for eligible health plans to participate, were intended to provide individuals and small groups with the same advantages that were available to large group purchasers. Individual and employer responsibility requirements, premium discounts (subsidies) within the marketplaces, and Medicaid expansion are expected to expand coverage to millions in the next few years. As of March 2015, approximately 11.7 million individuals had signed up through the marketplaces (U.S. Department of Health and Human Services and Office of the Assistant Secretary for Planning and Evaluation [ASPE], 2015a). The number of individuals gaining coverage through Medicaid was approximately 11.2 million from October 1, 2013, to April 30, 2014 (U.S. Department of Health and Human Services and Office of the Assistant Secretary for Planning and Evaluation [ASPE], 2015b).

While the ultimate impact on coverage is still uncertain, the latest projections are that the number of uninsured will be significantly reduced in the near future. Recent estimates by the Congressional Budget Office suggest that 24 million will gain coverage through insurance marketplaces and 13 million through Medicaid programs (CBO, 2014). The net reduction in the number of uninsured is expected to be 25 million after accounting for reductions in current employer coverage. Despite the uncertainties in these projections, one can expect new coverage to result in significantly increased demand for health care, including prescription drugs.

Driving Payment and Delivery System Transformation

Beyond the health insurance coverage provisions, the ACA's prescription for delivery system innovation and transformation has the potential to fundamentally change the way health care is provided in this country. As an important part of many patient care regimens, pharmaceutical purchasing and utilization are bound to be affected as stakeholders will have new incentives to carefully determine their value. In this section, we summarize key value-based purchasing initiatives underway and the key role of the new Center for Medicare and Medicaid Innovation (the Innovation Center).

The Innovation Center was established by Section 1115A of the Social Security Act (as added by section 3021 of the ACA). Congress created the Innovation Center for the purpose of testing "innovative payment and service delivery models to reduce program expenditures...while preserving or enhancing the quality of care" provided to those individuals who receive Medicare, Medicaid, or Children's Health Insurance Program (CHIP) benefits—about one in three Americans. The Innovation Center's mandate gives it flexibility within these parameters to select and test the most promising innovative payment and service delivery models. The statute provides $(USD)10 billion in direct funding for these purposes in fiscal years 2011 through 2019. It is expected that successful innovations will diffuse to private insurers as well and thus impact the entire delivery system.

The Centers for Medicare and Medicaid Services (CMS) published a Statement of Organization, Functions, and Delegations of Authority for the Innovation Center in the November 17, 2010, Federal Register (75 FR 70274). Since that time, the Innovation Center has focused on four main priorities:

- Developing and testing new payment and service delivery models
- Effectively developing and managing congressionally mandated and authorized demonstrations and related initiatives
- Rapidly evaluating results and advancing best practices
- Engaging a broad range of stakeholders to develop additional models for testing

The broad underlying principles for addressing these priorities have been well publicized as the *triple aim*: (1) improve the individual experience of health care, (2) improve the health of populations, and (3) reduce per capita costs of health care for populations. Accordingly, the center strives to test models of care and payment approaches that reduce costs through care improvement—consistent with the statutes' call for preference being given to models that improve coordination, quality, and efficiency of services.

It is important to note that many programs being implemented by CMS, including the Innovation Center initiatives, represent a new paradigm for policies that would moderate cost growth and achieve health system value. Our current delivery system is often fragmented, leaving patients to seek care from multiple providers who often have little information or incentive to carefully coordinate the care. In this environment, fee-for-service payment may incentivize medical practice that emphasizes quantity of care rather than quality. Past cost control efforts that often focused on pricing mechanisms relied on changing incentives and behaviors within this system. In contrast, the Innovation Center's initiatives recognize the need and are geared toward incentives for restructuring the delivery system to provide high-quality, less costly care. Value-based health care relies on the concept that buyers should hold providers of health care accountable for both cost and quality of care.

The basis of the new value paradigm can be related to another triple, which might be called the three Is—information, infrastructure, and incentives:

1. *Information*—Includes a variety of technology, evidence, and tools to inform decision making. These include health information technology, CER, patient education tools, and the availability quality/performance data
2. *Infrastructure*–Includes support for a variety of delivery approaches, including accountable care organizations (ACOs), primary care medical homes, and public/private collaboration for diffusion of best practices
3. *Incentives*—Payment mechanisms that reward quality and value, including pay for performance (bonuses), penalties for bad performance, and bundled payment approaches

Both through their existing payment systems and through the initiatives of the Innovation Center, CMS has developed and fielded an impressive array of initiatives in just a few short years. This section briefly describes the value-based policies and some of the key Innovation Center initiatives.

Hospital Value-Based Payments

As required by the ACA, beginning in October 2012, Medicare began adjusting payments to acute care hospitals according to how well they meet Medicare's standard for quality. Medicare uses quality measures covering a range of domains, including clinical care process and outcome measures, patient experience of care, and efficiency measures. Examples of these measures include appropriate antibiotic use for community-acquired pneumonia, 30-day mortality rates for heart failure, and communication with doctors. These measures are consistent with evidence-based clinical practice for the provision of high-quality care. Hospitals are scored on improvement as well as achievement on a variety of quality measures. The higher a hospital's performance score during a performance period, the higher the hospital's value-based incentive payment will be for a subsequent fiscal year. The Hospital Value-Based Purchasing Program is a carefully crafted program that incorporated significant stakeholder feedback. The Hospital Value-Based Purchasing (VBP) Program will redistribute an estimated $(USD)963 million to hospitals based on their quality performance in the FY 2013 payment year (Blum, 2013).

Second, the ACA established the Hospital Readmissions Reduction Program (HRRP), which reduces Medicare payments to hospitals that have high rates of hospital readmissions beginning in October 2012. Currently, CMS measures the readmission rates for three very common and very expensive conditions for Medicare beneficiaries—heart attack, heart failure, and pneumonia. Beginning in fiscal year 2015, CMS has the authority to expand the program so that additional measures could be included. Though the payment adjustments took effect only recently, hospitals have been preparing for this program for some time and results suggest it is already having a positive impact. After 5 years of relative stability, the Medicare readmission rate began to drop across the country in the final quarter of 2012 (ODIPA paper).

Bundled Payments

Traditionally, Medicare makes separate payments to providers for each of the individual services they furnish to beneficiaries for a single illness or course of treatment. This approach can result in fragmented care, lack of coordination across health-care settings, and increased costs. The Innovation Center recently developed and launched the Bundled Payments for Care Improvement initiative, a new payment model for related hospital, physician, and postacute care services. The research is designed to test whether bundled payments can align incentives for providers—hospitals, postacute care providers, physicians, and other practitioners—encouraging them to work closely together across all specialties and settings. Over the course of the 3-year initiative, CMS will work with participating organizations to assess whether the models being tested result in improved patient care and lower costs to Medicare.

Accountable Care Organizations

ACOs are one of the ACA's key reforms to improve the delivery of care. ACOs are groups of doctors and other health-care providers that have agreed to work together to treat individual patients and better coordinate their care across care settings. In the ACO models being tested, the contacting entity is responsible for the health of the population, which is defined as patients who receive care from primary care physicians who are part of the ACO. All providers continue to be paid by Medicare through their normal payment methodology. The ACO will presumably implement care management processes aimed at coordinating care for each individual in ways that improve the health of the population while maintaining quality and reducing cost. The payments made by Medicare for services provided to this population are compared to a target established by CMS that takes into account the severity of illness of the population. If the cost of the ACO patients is more than 2% lower than the target, the ACO can receive a bonus payment of half of the cost savings, with Medicare retaining the remainder. Various laws and regulations concerning payments to providers and ability of providers to form organizations are expected to be reduced or waived to allow these organizations to be created. They share—with Medicare—any savings generated from lowering the growth in health-care costs while improving quality of care, including providing patient-centered care.

Over 360 organizations are participating in the Medicare ACOs, serving approximately 5.3 million Medicare beneficiaries. As existing ACOs choose to add providers and more organizations join the program, participation in ACOs is expected to grow. They are located in 47 states and territories—from the most remote community in Montana to as far away as Puerto Rico (Centers for Medicare and Medicaid Services [CMS], 2014).

The Shared Savings Program requires that participants—which can be providers, hospitals, suppliers, and others—coordinate care for all services provided under Medicare fee-for-service (FFS) and encourages investment in infrastructure and redesigned care processes. ACOs that lower their growth in health-care costs, while also meeting clearly defined performance standards on health-care quality, are eligible to keep a portion of the savings they generate for the program. As a result of these efforts, we are seeing providers developing strategies to work together to redesign care process, promote preventive care, and better coordinate services for patients with chronic disease and high-risk individuals. Medicare ACOs participating in the Shared Savings Program generated $(USD)128 million in net savings for the Medicare trust fund to date (CMS, 2014).

In addition to the ACOs participating in the Shared Savings Program, the CMS Innovation Center is testing a different payment model for ACOs, the Pioneer ACO model. The Pioneer ACO model is designed for health-care organizations that have experience coordinating care for patients across care settings. This model tests alternative payment models that include escalating levels of financial accountability. One purpose of the Pioneer ACO model is to inform future changes to the Shared Savings Program. Thirty-two organizations initially participated in the testing of the Pioneer ACO model—nine left the program after the first year likely due to concerns that they would be unable to meet targets and therefore face financial penalties. A preliminary evaluation of the Pioneer ACOs estimated that they generated gross savings of $(USD)147 million in their first year while continuing to deliver high-quality care. Results showed that of the 23 Pioneer ACOs, nine had significantly lower spending growth relative to Medicare fee for service while exceeding quality reporting requirements (HHS Press Release, 2014).

Primary Care Medical Homes: Comprehensive Primary Care Initiative

CMS is also testing various patient-centered medical home (PCMH) models to strengthen primary care by improving care coordination across providers. The PCMH is a care delivery model intended to better coordinate patient care through their primary care physician practices. Approximately 500 primary care practices in 7 markets are participating in the Comprehensive Primary Care initiative—a multipayer model testing the effectiveness of enhanced payments to primary care practices in improving care coordination for people enrolled in Medicare and Medicaid.

CMS consulted extensively with other payers to design a model that would be suitable for adoption by Medicare, commercial, and Medicaid payers.

Under this initiative, primary care practices are given the resources they need to transform their practices to better serve their patients, such as developing care plans and using a team-based approach to care. Participating practices receive an additional payment from CMS and are eligible for shared savings beginning in the second year of the initiative, in addition to enhanced payment the practice might receive from other payers.

Evaluation

The results from rigorously designed impact evaluations are critical to the Innovation Center's mission to test new models and drive change. The statute requires the Innovation Center to conduct an evaluation of each new payment and service delivery model tested. The statute also specifies that measures in each evaluation must include an analysis of the quality of care furnished under the model (including the measurement of patient-level outcomes and patient-centeredness criteria) and changes in spending. In order to expand the scope or scale of a model tested by the Innovation Center, the secretary of HHS must determine that such expansion is expected to reduce spending under Medicare, Medicaid, or CHIP without reducing the quality of care, or improve the quality of patient care without increasing spending. Before any expansion can take place, the CMS Office of the Actuary must certify that expansion of the model would reduce—or not result in an increase in—net program expenditures.

Potential Impact on Provider Incentives, Care Coordination, and Integrated Delivery

The Innovation Center's initiatives, along with other value-based policies implemented by CMS and private payers, certainly have the potential to drive the U.S. delivery system toward increasingly integrated and value-conscious care. To what extent these initiatives will be successful in driving change on a widespread basis and over the long term will likely depend on a number of factors, however. The evidence that will be forthcoming from various evaluation efforts will be critical. Evidence of improved value will allow CMS to rapidly expand the scale of bundled payment, ACOs, and primary care medical home initiatives to reach millions of Medicare beneficiaries. Another critical factor will be the extent to which private insurers adopt these models and expand them to the non-Medicare population. Here again the strength of the evaluation evidence and its widespread dissemination will be important to whether the private stakeholders see a strong business case for adopting these innovations. Finally, recent health system history teaches us that perhaps the most important factor for new financing/delivery arrangements is continued buy-in by stakeholders. Thus, it will be important to monitor quality of care, including the satisfaction of patient and providers that participate.

While it is not clear that the future environment for health care will contain the exact delivery organizations and payment mechanisms described earlier, it is less likely that fragmented, fee-for-service care will ever dominate the landscape again. Unlike promising past changes in financing and delivery that have failed to take hold, there seems to be closer alignment today among payers (public and private) and providers around cost consciousness (Cacciotti and Mozeson, 2013). This alignment is evidenced by the rapid growth in ACO arrangements both for Medicare and among private payers (Muhlstein et al., 2012). Moreover, many past changes took place in anticipation of major legislation that did not pass the Congress. The ACA was passed by the Congress and is being implemented, reinforcing the anticipatory impacts (Altman, 2013).

Thus, it is likely that whatever configuration evolves, providers will be held financially accountable for cost and quality. There will be strong incentives for delivery organizations to integrate and coordinate care and carefully consider the cost-effectiveness of the items and services they provide. As discussed later, health-care suppliers such as pharmaceutical manufacturers may be operating in a business environment more synergistic in terms of insurers and providers having common interest in being cost and value conscious than in the past. In this new environment, both the short-term marketing and pricing policies and long-run R&D strategies of pharmaceutical manufacturers may have to change in order to maintain financial viability.

Comparative Effectiveness Research

A necessary component for all of the payment and delivery strategies described earlier is high-quality information to enhance value-based decision making. This is particularly true for guiding coverage, formulary, and practice decisions. Acknowledging the importance and need for more comparative data about the effectiveness of clinical interventions to drive improved quality, the Patient Centered Outcomes Research Trust Fund (PCORTF) was authorized by ACA. PCORTF provides a significant pool of funds for a period of 10 years to invest in patient-centered CER. CER has been thought of containing several key elements:

1. There is a comparative element to the research, though the elements being compared may range from specific clinical interventions like medications or procedures to health system and population-level interventions.
2. The research is focused on effectiveness, where interventions are studied under real-world conditions as compared to the narrow-spectrum *ideal* conditions of most randomized clinical trials.
3. There is a focus on outcomes of meaning to patients and providers, including benefits and harms.

Section 6301(e) of the ACA established the PCORTF within the U.S. Department of the Treasury and identified three sources of funding: (1) transfers from general revenues, (2) transfers from the Medicare Federal Hospital Insurance and Federal Supplementary Medical Insurance Trust Funds, and (3) transfer from health insurance and self-insured plans.

Funding of the PCORTF began in Federal Fiscal Year (FFY) 2010 and extends through 2019. Funding gradually builds and plateaus in FFY 2015. Beginning in FFY 2010, the PCORTF is solely funded by transfers from general revenue—\$(USD)10 million in FFY 2010, \$(USD)50 million in FFY 2011, and \$(USD)150 million in FFY 2012. Beginning in FFY 2013, transfers from Medicare and private plans begin. The transfers amount to the average number of individuals enrolled in a plan annually (e.g., Medicare, health insurance, and self-insured plans) multiplied by \$(USD)1 for FFY 2013 and \$(USD)2 for FFY 2014 and beyond. The amount is adjusted for applicable annual medical inflation. But funding does not go into perpetuity. No funding will be available after September 30, 2019, and any amounts in the PCORTF at the end of FFY 2019 will be returned to the general fund of the U.S. Department of the Treasury. A rough estimation of the amount of funding for patient-centered outcomes research via the PCORTF is approximately \$(USD)4.8 billion.

The ACA identified broad activities to be funded by the PCORTF. First, it created a nongovernmental entity called the Patient-Centered Outcomes Research Institute (PCORI). PCORI was created to identify research priorities and to advance patient-centered outcomes research (PCOR).

The ACA also identified tasks complementary to those of PCOR for the U.S. Department of Health and Human Services (DHHS)—dissemination and incorporation of PCOR findings in practice, the training of researchers in PCOR methods, and investment in building data infrastructure to conduct PCOR. Responsibility for dissemination and training has been assigned to the Agency for Healthcare Research and Quality (AHRQ), and responsibility for data infrastructure has been assigned to the secretary of DHHS.

Each of these activities has important implications so we'll describe each in turn. PCORI's main purpose is to carry out research, ranging from primary clinical trials to observational studies and systematic reviews, which can help address national priorities for PCOR. Recognizing that a successful PCOR enterprise requires engagement and cooperation between multiple stakeholders, including private and public industry, the ACA requires diverse representation among the board. Members of the board are selected by the U.S. Government Accountability Office, and the ACA explicitly requires board representation from pharmaceutical, device, and diagnostic manufacturers or developers.

PCORI has identified five national priorities for research:

1. Assessment of prevention, diagnosis, and treatment options, focusing on comparative assessments of the effectiveness and safety of clinical interventions
2. Improving health-care systems, focusing on comparing system-level approaches, including use of health information technology, care coordination, and workforce deployment
3. Communication and dissemination research, focusing on supporting use of information and supporting shared decision making
4. Addressing disparities, focusing on identifying differences in effectiveness and outcomes between patient populations and potential solutions
5. Accelerating patient-centered outcomes research and methodological research, focusing on capacity building through creation of data infrastructure, improvement in analytic methods, and training of researchers, patients, and other stakeholders to enhance participation in PCOR

Thus far, PCORI has funded 279 awards totaling more than $(USD)460 million across its five priorities. And over the next year, PCORI will commit as much as $(USD)1.5 billion to research projects (Selby and Lipstein, 2014). Research projects involve and have implications for pharmaceuticals in a number of different ways. The most straightforward way is a head-on comparative study of drug A vs. drug B. But it is important to note that several other types of funded studies have implications for drugs even though they may not be studying the comparative effectiveness of specific individual drug or drug combinations. For example, one currently funded project addressing disparities is comparing the impact of decision support tools for human papillomavirus (HPV) vaccines to usual care, with the goal of increasing HPV vaccination rates among Latinas. If this research finds effective methods of increasing vaccination rates, the use of HPV vaccines may increase with broader implementation of the study findings (PCORI, 2014).

While the head-to-head comparison studies tend to be funded in the assessment of options priority, studies with direct impact on medications occur throughout the first four priorities. In addition to the example mentioned earlier about HPV vaccinations, another example is a study on the use of geriatric assessment surveys to capture patient-centered outcomes that can help improve communication that could impact chemotherapy outcomes. This study is being funded under a health systems project (PCORI, 2014). It is important to note that medications are an important aspect of multiple projects in the first four priorities and will likely play an important role in research conducted through the data networks being created and linked in PCORI's data infrastructure initiative (PCORnet). Indeed a representative from the pharmaceutical industry is a member of the PCORnet Steering Committee (PCORnet, 2014). The importance of these examples is that they highlight the opportunities and the importance of thinking about how PCORI-funded research will impact the generation of research about medications and potentially how medications will be used in clinical practice once findings are implemented.

How will all the research funded by PCORI be used? While PCORI funds research, the ACA has identified AHRQ as having a lead role on broadly disseminating the research findings that are produced by PCORI and other research organizations. AHRQ will develop information tools that organize and disseminate research findings for a variety of audiences, including physicians and health-care providers, payers, and policy makers. AHRQ will develop a publicly available resource database of PCOR, which will be an immensely helpful resource for stakeholders as a central inventory of PCOR (Affordable Care Act, 2010). Currently, to find PCOR findings, one has to go to a resource like PubMed, which was not developed specifically to identify PCOR findings. The benefit of the resource as described in the ACA is that it will provide a central resource whose explicit goal is to help with dissemination of PCOR findings and thus will be designed with particular attention to details of particular interest to PCOR, such as research methodology, subpopulations, and limitations of the research.

PCORI announced the creation of PCORnet, a large, over $(USD)90 million investment to create a highly representative, national network of networks to conduct PCOR. With an emphasis on engaging cross-institutional networks with representation from patients, health systems, clinicians, and payers, the initial phase of PCORnet will include 18 patient-powered research networks and 11 clinical data research networks. The goals of this initiative are to promote broader participation among multiple participants in the research progress; promote more comprehensive, complete, and longitudinal data collection; and enable a new model of conducting PCOR in the United States that will allow for large-scale research at lower costs.

It will be important to watch the development of the network as it matures. If it achieves the vision of becoming a large, representative, national network that provides a foundation for conducting observational and clinical research, the potential for studies that range from direct comparative drug studies to system-level interventions that have impacts on drug utilization will be tremendous.

Potential Impact on Pharmaceutical Markets

In this section, we discuss the potential impacts of the changes described earlier throughout pharmaceutical markets. The various ACA-related changes potentially affect the number of prescriptions used per capita, the mix of those prescriptions, prices, profits, and both the level and composition of R&D spending. The coverage expansion, changing payment/delivery environment, and the availability of CER will most likely interact with each other to have potentially significant effects on pharmaceutical markets. Clearly, the expansion of comprehensive insurance coverage to millions of individuals will expand markets for pharmaceuticals. Previously uninsured individuals will have better access to health-care services meaning better prevention and treatment regimens, including the access to and affordability of prescription drugs. Currently insured individuals will have the certainty of continued affordable coverage regardless of employment changes or other economic issues. Thus, demand for prescription drugs should increase and investment in R&D becomes potentially more favorable. Recent estimates of the impact of insurance expansions demonstrate the potential effect. These estimates suggest that past coverage expansions through the Medicare and Medicaid programs may have accounted for 25% of the growth in R&D spending over the time period (Clemens, 2013). The overall effect of the ACA coverage expansion may be more nuanced and difficult to predict this time, however, because of the numerous other changes in payment and delivery and the associated changes in purchase and practice decision making at all levels that may occur.

Indeed, the potential effects need to be discussed in terms of the public and private insurers directly affected by the coverage expansions (state Medicaid programs and marketplace insurers) and potential policies, economic factors, and decisions that may affect these sectors. Moreover, the separate financial incentives that provider organizations will face and how they complement the incentives that will drive insurer decision making need to be analyzed. Finally, the market factors and policies potentially affecting pharmacy drugs and those affecting provider administered drugs (e.g., Medicare Part B drugs) need to be considered separately.

The dynamic interaction between insurance coverage expansion and medical technology innovation was first analyzed by Weisbrod (1991). The innovation in new and effective technologies often provides medical possibilities for improved patient outcomes that did not previously exist and significantly raise the cost of care at the same time. Thus, innovation tends to increase the demand for health insurance. At the same time, expanding insurance coverage increases the demand for health care, including the consumption of new technologies, and encourages both greater R&D spending and more rapid diffusion of its products. Thus, medical technology diffusion has historically been recognized as a significant driver of health-care cost growth (CBO, 2008).

Another important aspect to these analyses, however, is the recognition that how providers are reimbursed by public and private payers may affect the relationship between insurance coverage and technology innovation. In the distant past, reimbursement of reasonable costs was the principal method of determining payment to providers. Providers had little incentive to look for cost-saving or cost-effective methods of practice and could purchase expensive new technologies with little financial risk. Innovators had every incentive to invest in quality-enhancing or outcome-oriented technologies regardless of their cost. The advent of prospective payment systems and growth in capitated reimbursement during the 1980s and 1990s, both which potentially increased provider risk, were expected to modify these relationships and perhaps create demand for more cost-saving technologies (Weisbrod, 1991).

Arguably, these expectations were not met entirely as new technologies continued to drive costs into the twenty-first century (CBO, 2008). Pricing and payment under Medicare's inpatient prospective payment system (PPS) adapts relatively quickly to the use of new technologies during inpatient stays, reducing long-run risks to hospitals from adopting them. Likewise, the managed care backlash of the late 1990s may have limited the amount of risk being shifted to the providers. But perhaps the most important factor concerning insurance and reimbursement was not fully considered in these predictions. That being the methods and criteria used by insurers to make coverage decisions for new services and the legal/public relations environment in which they are made. Indeed, Medicare and private insurers remained under great pressure to cover any new technology thought to be effective, regardless of the cost (Neumann, 2004; Sheingold and Sheingold, 2010). Despite the configuration of payments between insurers and providers, the nature of the coverage decisions continued to send signals that costly, outcome-oriented innovations could still be profitable.

One change in coverage decision-making processes almost certainly had some impact on the innovation/diffusion process. In recent years, Medicare and other large payers have implemented evidence-based decision-making frameworks for their coverage decisions—raising the bar for the quality of evidence needed to demonstrate effectiveness and obtain a positive decision (Foote and Town, 2007; Neumann et al., 2012). Medicare continues to make positive decisions despite weaker evidence, but often with conditions limiting use or requirements for further evidence development (Chalkidou et al., 2008). These processes, as discussed later, will potentially be better informed by the availability of CER.

As a lens for looking at possible futures for medical technology and formulary decisions in the emerging health-care market through these past changes, consider four definitions of *innovation* applicable to making positive coverage and payment decisions:

- New technologies (or new uses of existing technologies) thought (e.g., expert opinion) to be effective
- New technologies (or new uses of existing technologies) whose effectiveness in terms of patient outcomes is demonstrated by strong evidence
- New technologies that are more effective than existing technologies for the same uses as demonstrated by strong evidence, if they are more costly than the existing technologies
- New technologies that are more effective than existing technologies for the same uses as demonstrated by strong evidence and for which it is determined that the incremental effectiveness exceeds incremental costs

In terms of medical benefits, including facility-administered pharmaceuticals (e.g., Part B drugs under Medicare), decisions are now mostly based on the second level earlier. That is, evidence of effectiveness must meet accepted scientific standards for when it is reasonable to conclude that a technology will improve patient outcomes. Making coverage and pricing decisions based on comparing the effectiveness of these technologies to others used for the same purpose has been difficult, however. Indeed, recent legal decisions have greatly restricted Medicare's use of least costly alternative pricing based on paying the lowest price available for equally effective therapies (MedPAC, 2010). On the other hand, it is reasonable to conclude that formulary policy for private health plans (including Medicare's Part D plans) and pharmacy benefit managers has gone one level further, basing pricing, co-payments, and benefit management practices on comparative effectiveness information. That is, they actively use these tools to shift utilization toward lower-cost drugs—such as generic competitors of favored brands—that are considered equally effective. Due to a combination of legal and public relations issues, the fourth definition is seldom used explicitly to make either medical benefit or formulary decisions (Neumann, 2005). As discussed later, this issue may become important to pharmaceutical markets in the future.

The immediate impact of the coverage expansions on pharmaceutical markets is likely to depend to a large degree on how Medicaid and private insurers respond to cost and competitive pressures by extending the use of these formulary tools. It will also depend on how provider organizations such as ACOs implement strategies for controlling the costs of facility administered (e.g., Part B drugs) and to the extent that competing health insurers adopt new methods of reimbursing these drugs.

A significant share of the coverage expansion will occur through the Medicaid program. States have the choice of expanding Medicaid to cover all individuals within 133% of the federal poverty level with a significant federal subsidy. For the first 3 years, the federal government will provide 100% of the funding for the newly eligible population. After that, states that choose to undertake the expansion will be responsible for 10% of the total. Moreover, even states that do not choose to expand Medicaid may see a larger eligible population; the requirements of ACA will likely produce a *woodwork* effect in which those who were eligible under the states' pre-ACA criteria but did not apply for the program may now do so. In either case, the larger Medicaid population is likely to mean closer attention to cost control in the near future and examining new pricing and other formulary policies to assist these efforts.

Currently, states use a variety of pricing and formulary policies and have greatly increased generic dispensing rates (Smith et al., 2011). They are considering a variety of other strategies, including preferred drug lists, ingredient pricing policies, prior authorization, step therapy requirement, and cost sharing (NCSL, 2013). It is reasonable to assume that the cost concerns described earlier will intensify these efforts, meaning further shifts toward lower-price alternatives when they are available. Thus, Medicaid markets for drug manufacturers will clearly expand in terms of the number of insured individuals. The net effect on the level and composition of sales is more difficult to predict, however, as more aggressive state policies will likely result in some offsetting effects in terms of numbers and mix of drugs per insured person.

Similar factors may determine the net effect on pharmaceutical sales through expansion of private insurance. Qualified health plans offered through federally facilitated or state-based marketplaces will need to provide drug coverage that meets essential health benefit requirements while facing a potentially competitive market—meaning that offering a quality benefit at the lowest cost possible will be critical. Thus, it is reasonable to expect aggressive formulary management policies.

Like the Medicaid programs, private plans, including those providing the Part D benefit, have achieved very high generic dispensing rates in many therapeutic classes. They also seem to quickly move toward new generics when they become available (Sheingold and Nguyen, 2013). The majority of dollars still goes to the brand drugs, however, due to the large price differentials. Moreover, there is some evidence that PBMs may still favor some brand drugs to increase their rebate dollars despite the fact that health plan and consumer costs would be higher than if they used a generic drug substitute (Pharmacy Times, 2011). Health plans will have greater incentive to scrutinize these arrangements in a more competitive environment. Although 100% generic dispensing is not likely in many therapeutic classes due to patient-specific factors, there are estimates that billions of dollars in savings are still available through increasing the generic dispensing rates (CBO, 2010; Sheingold and Nguyen, 2013). Thus, more aggressive efforts to increase generic dispensing in these therapeutic classes might be expected. Moreover, as current brand-name drugs lose patents in the near future, it can be expected that private plans will shift utilization to generics very quickly, shrinking the market for the brand names at a rapid rate.

The aggressive efforts to reduce pharmaceutical costs by generic substitution and other formulary management tools will be enhanced by a potential alignment in incentives between the health plans and PBMs on the one hand and providers on the other hand (Caccioti and Mozeson, 2013). As described earlier, new payment and delivery models will focus on provider accountability for value, meaning coordinating care, focusing on prevention and carefully managing a range of chronic illnesses. To the extent that drug costs are a part of total spending used to determine financial risk under various ACO and bundled payment arrangements, providers will also have incentive to modify their prescribing habits in a more value and cost-conscious manner. While the current Medicare ACO models described earlier do not include Part D spending, including these costs in next-generation models would certainly be a logical option.

Within this evolving delivery system, brand manufacturers may have to reconsider their current pricing and marketing strategies to become more competitive and maintain market share. Traditionally, manufacturers of drugs whose patents have expired have resisted direct price competition with their generic counterparts. Instead, they have chosen to segment the market and keep prices high for brand loyal consumers (Frank and Salkever, 1997; Regan, 2008). The ability of health plans and PBMs to use co-payments and other tools to rapidly shift their enrollees to the generics, and the incentives for providers to assist in this effort, may mean that brand manufacturers will need to rethink this pricing strategy. A good recent example is Pfizer's aggressive policies to maintain market share for Lipitor when its patent expired. They aggressively increased their rebates for exclusive contracts with health plans and subsidized co-payments for patients (Jackevicious et al., 2012).

In addition to simply being concerned with price competitiveness, pharmaceutical companies may have to begin regularly demonstrating value across the care spectrum for different types of patients (Daemmrich 2011; Caccioti and Mozeson, 2013). As provider organizations are held accountable for the full range of care, they will also be concerned with the impact of pharmaceutical use on the utilization of other services, total patient care cost, and outcomes. Indeed, it has been argued that in contrast to the *stovepipe* approach other countries take to price negotiation, the emerging delivery system may offer pharmaceutical companies a real opportunity to demonstrate the health system value of their products in a very comprehensive manner (Daemmrich, 2011).

Another area that delivery system organizations may look to reduce spending is in facility-provided drugs, such as those under Medicare Part B. Currently, Medicare pays for these drugs at their average sales price (ASP) plus 6% in physicians' offices and hospital outpatient departments. Compared to unrestricted fee-for-service payment, organizations such as ACOs will now have greater incentive to aggressively negotiate for lower prices on these drugs as well as to look for therapeutically equivalent, lower-cost substitutes when they are available. Moreover, nothing in legislative history or research studies can be found to support the 6% add-on to ASP. If proposals to reduce this percentage were implemented, these incentives would be enhanced. For example, the President's Budget for 2014 proposed a reduction to a 3% add-on.

Potential Effects of Comparative Effectiveness Research

Information is a key component to the three Is (information, infrastructure, and incentives) described earlier (see the section on Driving Payment and Delivery System Transformation), and CER has the potential to strongly support value-based formulary, coverage, payment, and treatment decisions. The overall impact of the CER supported by PCORI will depend on a number of factors related to broad-based acceptance of the research support for using it in decision making. These factors include gaining consensus on the scientific methods for conducting CER, prioritizing funding in a way that targets the most important clinical areas and interventions, and the extent to which legal, regulatory, and public relations factors support or inhibit the ability of health plans and providers to use the information in decision making.

An example of the latter is the legislative clarity, or lack thereof, in using CER in coverage and payment decisions. The ACA explicitly prohibits PCORI from developing or using quality-adjusted life-years (QALYs) *as a threshold* to determine effectiveness of interventions. QALYs are a frequently used metric for comparing the impact of interventions across diseases and conditions. QALYs measure impact in terms of the number of life-years that would be added by the intervention and factors in not just quantity but quality of life gained or lost. The ACA also prohibits the secretary of HHS to using QALYs or similar metrics as a threshold to determine coverage, reimbursement, or incentive programs.

One reason for this prohibition may be that QALYs are used in cost-effectiveness analyses, which can guide decision making on resource allocation. Any apprehension that cost-effectiveness data could be used to limit benefits coverage for beneficiaries served by federal programs was compounded by political controversies that occurred during the passage of the law such as fear of so-called death panels. While the use of QALYs has limitations in terms of potentially favoring younger, healthier populations that might benefit more from an intervention, QALYs and cost-effectiveness analyses are frequently in coverage and determination decisions in many countries, including the United Kingdom's National Institute for Health and Clinical Excellence (NICE) (Drummond, 2013). However, in the context of rising health-care costs, the lack of clarity on whether measures of adjusted life-years like QALYs might be considered as part of any PCORI research or Medicare coverage and payment decisions even if they are not the determining *threshold* factor limits the ability of policy makers to understand the relationship between benefits and costs of specific interventions (Neumann and Weinstein, 2010).

In addition, a number of lessons can be learned from the experience to date of the Drug Effectiveness Review Project (DERP). In 2001, researchers at Oregon Health and Science University began conducting evidence reviews of drugs for the Oregon Medicaid Program. DERP emerged from this effort in 2003 with the vision of engaging states and other partners in conducting and using comparative research reports—focusing on efficacy, effectiveness, and safety—to assist policy makers in making drug coverage decisions. Limited evidence suggests that DERP has had some impact on state Medicaid program formulary decisions (VanLare et al., 2013). Nonetheless, the overall impact on decision making and health system outcomes is quite uncertain (Neumann, 2006). Moreover, there have been criticisms and controversies about DERP's methods from both the pharmaceutical industry and patient advocacy groups. These include methods of systematic review, assuming equivalency of all drugs within a therapeutic class, the appropriate use of surrogate endpoints, and whether costs should be explicitly recognized in CER. Because of these issues, as well as a decision not to explicitly include costs, critics charge that the DERP reviews are a thinly disguised cost containment vehicle for Medicaid programs (Neumann, 2006). Thus, for ACA's new CER structure to have a positive impact, resolving these issues will be critical.

Pharmaceutical Markets, Prices, and R&D in the Future: What Are the Uncertainties

The earlier discussion suggests that both direct and indirect effects of ACA could have substantial impacts on pharmaceutical markets. These markets will undoubtedly expand, but pharmaceutical companies may have to modify their business models in order to be competitive and profitable in the changing environment. For the most part, however, the discussion has assumed some degree of competitiveness in drug markets, largely through the availability of competing brand drugs and/or generic equivalents that provide health plans, PBMs, and delivery system tools for cost control and some leverage in price negotiations. The market environment could be quite different if a number of new and unique drugs become available in the near future, however. These would be drugs that are demonstrated to be effective in terms of FDA approval and for which there are no viable therapeutic alternatives, or drugs seen as significantly more effective than any alternatives.

Manufacturers would have considerable monopoly pricing power on these drugs, and purchasers have little leverage to negotiate rebates or apply formulary management tools for cost containment. In part, this situation is related to the political, legal, and optical issues associated with denying or restricting use of effective or even marginally effective medical therapies.

Neither public nor private purchasers are likely to have at their disposal real ability to refuse coverage of these new products because they are too costly. Moreover, it has not been possible to use the fourth-level definition of innovation described previously by applying cost-effectiveness analyses to coverage and payment decisions—meaning that real value considerations do not enter decision making whether at the purchaser or provider level (Neumann, 2005). Positive FDA approval and health plan coverage decisions can be based on statistically significant improvements in outcome measures that might be relatively small in magnitude or clinical importance—without regard to overall cost. A number of recent cancer drugs fit this profile (Siddiqi and Rajkhumar, 2012). Even drugs for more conventional uses, such as Flomax for the treatment of benign prostatic hyperplasia, can exhibit unique drug properties. Until a generic equivalent (tamsulosin) became available late in 2009, Flomax demonstrated rapid increases in both price and utilization (Sheingold and Nguyen, 2013). Thus for the foreseeable future, new and unique drugs are likely to remain profitable and look favorable for R&D investment.

Examining the current situation for specialty drugs may offer clues to these potential market effects. Specialty drugs are typically high-cost biologics used to treat serious conditions such as cancer and blood diseases. Due to the nature of the diseases treated and the lack of competing therapies, most of the formulary management tools that have been used to contain costs are not applied or are relatively ineffective. The number of specialty drugs and spending on them had grown rapidly in recent years and is projected to grow rapidly as drugs in development come to market (Payer Perspectives, 2013). They currently account for 12%–16% of commercial prescription drug spending despite being used for a relatively small number of patients (Tu and Divya, 2012).

The bottom line is that if a number of unique drugs enter the marketplace in the near future, whether specialty or conventional, pharmaceutical costs could begin to increase rapidly. Risk-sharing delivery organizations would likely put pressure on payers to increase payment targets and bundled payment rates, or carve high-cost drugs out of the financial arrangements entirely. Medicare, Medicaid, and private insurers would also experience pharmaceutical-related cost pressures from their remaining fee-for-service sectors. The new class of hepatitis C drugs provides an early example. These drugs are more effective than current alternatives but entered the market costing $(USD)1,000 per pill or $(USD)84,000 per course of treatment. Private insurers and Medicaid managed care plans have already expressed significant concerns with absorbing this. Members of Congress are demanding that the manufacturer provide justification for their pricing. More importantly, the introduction of this one drug is causing greater concern that it is the tip of the iceberg and that several very-high-cost drugs will enter the market in the near future (Kaiser Health News, 2014).

It should be stated clearly that ACA does not directly address these issues in any way, meaning that new legislation would be needed if a public policy response was to be considered. It would be purely speculative at this point to consider what, if any, legislative responses might result from these cost pressures. One possibility is that new political impetus would arise for legislation targeted at government drug price negotiations, reimportation, or more rapid availability of generics. Again, these are all issues that would affect profitability and have been aggressively opposed by the industry in the past. Another possibility is that we, as other countries already have, would consider developing new processes and institutions that might integrate public values and cost-effectiveness considerations for making decisions on high-cost drugs (Cohen et al., 2013). In any case, while the near-term market for these drugs should remain financially advantageous for manufacturers, accelerated pharmaceutical expenditure growth may lead to a more uncertain picture for sales and investment due to the political and policy reaction.

Conclusion

That the continuing implementation of the ACA will have far-reaching effects on the financing and delivery of health care in the United States is certain. A significantly greater share of Americans will have continuous and affordable insurance coverage. In addition, a growing number of patients will receive care from delivery organizations that are financially accountable for providing well-coordinated, high-value care. There is little doubt that effective pharmaceuticals will continue to play a critical role in developing an optimal mix of preventive, curative, and palliative care within this evolving system.

ACA's insurance coverage expansions, in conjunction with legislative provisions that favored pharmaceutical manufacturers by not being included in the law, mean continued opportunities for expanding markets and investment in R&D. Nonetheless, the emphasis that is being placed on accountability for high-value care means that manufacturers may have to adapt new business models with regard to pricing strategies and research in order to fully benefit from these opportunities. This is particularly true where specific drugs are in competitive situations, meaning there are viable alternative brand or generic competitors, and thus, formulary management tools are most effective. While there is still considerable uncertainty over what impact CER will have, it does have the potential to greatly enhance the use of these formulary practices by better informing decision-making processes. Moreover, research efforts by manufacturers to demonstrate effectiveness may need to be directed at demonstrating favorable cost and quality outcomes across the full spectrum of care for specific patients rather than more narrowly defined effectiveness measures.

Perhaps the greatest uncertainties for pharmaceutical markets lie in the potential impact new and unique drugs will have as they become available in the coming years. These drugs are likely to be profitable in the near future as they have been in the past. To the extent they put pressure on overall cost growth and the risk-sharing arrangements of delivery systems however, the potential for policy reaction certainly exists. New proposals for government price negotiation or new pathways to speed generics to markets might arise very quickly. In the past, concern over upsetting the innovative process and potentially derailing development of new and effective remedies has had a dampening effect on public and political reaction to cost increases. The emerging system spreads financial risk and accountability more broadly than in the past, meaning that public and private purchasers, insurers, providers, and even patients will share the impact of rising costs. The ability to introduce effective new drugs at very high prices may once again remind Americans of the impact monopoly power can have on markets. Whether the adage "today's prices result in tomorrow's miracles" can still dominate the policy reaction in this new environment is difficult to predict at the current time.

References

Altman, D., How Obamacare may be holding down costs, *Politico*, September 26, 2013. http://www.politico.com/story/2013/09/why-obamacare-could-be-holding-down-costs-097354.

Baker, S. Obamacare enrollment tops 6 million, *National Journal*, March 27, 2014. http://www.nationaljournal.com/health-care/2014/03/27/obamacare-enrollment-tops-6-million.

Blum, J., Delivery system reform: Progress report from CMS, Before the U.S. Senate Finance Committee, February 28, 2013.

Cacciotti, J., Mozeson, M. How ACA could transform the U.S. pharmaceutical marketplace. *Oliver Wyman Company*. 2011. http://www.oliverwyman.com/content/dam/oliver-wyman/global/en/files/archive/2011/ACA_and_the_Pharma_Marketplace.pdf.

Centers for Medicare and Medicaid Services (CMS), Lower costs, better care: Reforming our health care delivery system, CMS Fact Sheet, Released January 30, 2014a.

Centers for Medicare and Medicaid Services (CMS), Medicaid enrollment shows continued growth in April–June 4, 2014b, http://www.hhs.gov/healthcare/facts/blog/2014/06/medicaid-chip-enrollment-april.html. Accessed July 9, 2015.

Chalkidou, K., Lord, J., Fischer, A., and Littlejohns, P., Evidence- based decision making: When should we wait for more information? *Health Affairs* 2008; 27(6):1642–1653.

Clemens, J., The effect of U.S. health insurance expansions on medical innovation, NBER Working Paper No. 19761, Issued in December 2013.

CMS.gov. Medicare ACOs continue to succeed in improving care, lowering cost growth. November 10, 2014. https://www.cms.gov/Newsroom/MediaReleaseDatabase/Fact-sheets/2014-Fact-sheets-items/2014-11-10.html.

Cohen, J., Malins, A., and Shahpurwala, Z., Compared to US practice, evidence based reviews in Europe appear to lead to lower prices for some drugs, *Health Affairs* 2013; 32(4):762–770.

Congressional Budget Office, Technological change and the growth of health care spending, Congressional Budget Office, Washington, DC, January 2008.

Congressional Budget Office, Effects of using generic drugs on Medicare's prescription drug spending, Congressional Budget Office, Washington, DC, September 2010.

Congressional Budget Office, The budget and economic outlook: 2014 to 2024, Congressional Budget Office, Washington, DC, February 2014.

Daemmrich, A., U.S. healthcare reform and the pharmaceutical industry, Harvard Business School Working Paper 12-015, September 14, 2011.

Drummond, M., Twenty years of using economic evaluations for drug reimbursement decisions: What has been achieved?, *Journal of Health Politics, Policy and Law* 2013; 38(6):1081–1102.

Foote, S.B. and Town, R.J., Implementing evidence-based medicine through Medicare coverage decisions, *Health Affairs* 2007; 26(6):1634–1642.

Frank, R.G. and Salkever, D.S., Generic entry and pricing of pharmaceuticals, *Journal of Economics and Management Strategy* 1997; 6:75–90.

Iglehart, J.K., Are unsustainable trends finally coming to a stop? *Health Affairs* 2013; 32(5):830.

Jackevicius, C.A., Chou, M.M., Ross, J.S., Shah, N.D., and Krumholz, H.M., Generic atorvastatin and health care costs, *New England Journal of Medicine* 2012; 366:201–204.

Kaiser Health News, There's a life-saving hepatitis C drug. But you may not be able to afford it, March 3, 2014. http://khn.org/news/insurers-debate-who-should-get-costly-hepatitis-c-drug/. Accessed December 5, 2015.

Kanavos, P., Ferrario, A., Vandoros, S., and Anderson, G.F., Higher US branded drug prices and spending compared to other countries may stem partly from quick uptake of new drugs, *Health Affairs* April 2013; 32:753–761. doi:10.1377/hlthaff.2012.0920.

Martin, A.B., Hartman, M., Whittle, M., Catlin, A., and the National Health Expenditure Accounts Team, National health spending in 2012: Rate of health spending growth remained low for the fourth consecutive year, *Health Aff*airs 2014; 33:67–77.

Medicare Payment Advisory Commission (MedPAC), Report to congress: Aligning incentives in Medicare, June 2010. Washington DC. http://www.medpac.gov/-documents-/reports/page/2/.

Milne, C.P. and Kaitin, K.I., Impact of the new U.S. health care reform legislation on the pharmaceutical industry: Who are the real winners? *Clinical Pharmacology and Therapeutics* 2010; 88(5):589–592.

Muhlstein, D., Croshaw, A., Merrill, T., and Pena, C., Growth and dispersion of accountable care organizations: June 2012 update, Leavitt Partners, Salt Lake City, UT.

National Conference of State Legislatures (NCSL), Recent Medicaid prescription drug laws and strategies, Updated 2012; Selected material added August 2013.

Neumann, P.J., Why don't Americans use cost-effectiveness analysis?, *American Journal of Managed Care* 2004; 10(5):308–312.

Neumann, P.J., *Using Cost-Effectiveness Analysis to Improve Health Care: Opportunities and Barriers.* New York: Oxford University Press, 2005.

Neumann, P.J., Emerging lessons from the drug effectiveness review project, *Health Affairs* 2006; 25:W262–W271.
Neumann, P.J., Bliss, B.K., and Chambers, J.D., Therapies for advanced cancers pose a special challenge for health technology assessment organizations in many countries, *Health Affairs* 2012; 31(4):700–708.
Neumann, P.J., Kamae, M.S., and Palmer, J.A., Medicare's national coverage decisions for technologies, 1999–2007, *Health Affairs* 2008; 27(6):1620–1631.
Neumann, P.J. and Weinstein M.C., Legislating against the use of cost-effectiveness, *New England Journal of Medicine* 2010; 363:1495–1497.
Payer Perspectives, The growing cost of specialty pharmacy—Is it sustainable? *American Journal of Managed Care*, February 18, 2013. http://www.ajmc.com/payer-perspectives/0213/the-growing-cost-of-specialty-pharmacyis-it-sustainable.
PCORI, PCORI funding awards. Accessed February 23, 2014. http://pfaawards.pcori.org/.
PCORnet, About PCORnet. Accessed February 23, 2014. http://pcornet.org/about-pcornet/.
Regan, T.L., Generic entry, price competition, and market segmentation in the prescription drug market, *International Journal of Industrial Organization* 2008; 26:930–948.
Selby, J.V. and Lipstein, S.H., PCORI at 3 year—Progress, lessons, and plans, *New England Journal of Medicine* 2014; 370:592–595.
Sheingold, S.H. and Nguyen, N.X., Impacts of generic competition and benefit management practices on spending for prescription drugs: Evidence from Medicare's part D benefit, *Medicare and Medicaid Research Review* 2013; 4(1):E1–E14.
Sheingold, S.H. and Sheingold, B.H., Medical technology and the U.S. healthcare system: Is this the road to Abilene? *World Medical and Health Policy* 2010; 2(2):Article 5.
Siddiqui, M. and Rajkumar, S.V., The high cost of cancer therapies and what we can do about it, *Mayo Clinic Proceedings* 2012; 87(10):935–943.
Smith, V.K., Kramer, S., and Rudowitz, R., Managing Medicaid pharmacy benefits: Current issues and options, Kaiser Commission on Medicaid and the Uninsured, Washington, DC, September 2011.
The Growing Cost of Specialty Pharmacy—Is it Sustainable? February 18, 2013. http://www.ajmc.com/payer-perspectives/0213/the-growing-cost-of-specialty-pharmacyis-it-sustainable#sthash.5x8l8X7I.dpuf.
Tu, H.T. and Divya, S.R., Limited options to manage specialty drug spending, Center for Studying Health System Change Research Brief No. 22, April 2012.
U.S. Department of Health and Human Services and Office of the Assistant Secretary for Planning and Evaluation (ASPE), Health insurance marketplace: Summary enrollment report for the 2015 open enrollment period, ASPE issue brief, May 1, 2015a, http://aspe.hhs.gov/health/reports/2015/MarketPlaceEnrollment/Mar2015/ib_2015mar_enrollment.pdf.
U.S. Department of Health and Human Services and Office of the Assistant Secretary for Planning and Evaluation (ASPE), Medicaid Enrollment and the Affordable Care Act, March 2015b, http://aspe.hhs.gov/health/reports/2015/MedicaidEnrollment/ib_MedicaidEnrollment.pdf.
VanLare, JM., Wong, HH., Gibbs, J., et al. Comparative effectiveness research in practice: the Drug Effectiveness Review Project experience. *J Comp Eff Res.* 2013 Nov; 2(6):541–50.
Weisbrod, B.A., The health care quadrilemma: An essay on technological change, insurance, quality of care and cost containment, *Journal of Economic Literature* 1991; 29(2):523–552.
What the PBMs Aren't Telling the Press and Employers about Rebates. Pharmacy Times December 2, 2011. http://www.pharmacytimes.com/blogs/pharmacists-united-for-truth-and-transparency/1211/what-the-pbms-arent-telling-the-press-and-employers-about-rebates.

Chapter 26

Role of Government as Regulator, Payer, and Provider of Care

W. Mike Heath and John Spain

Contents

DoD

In order to better understand pharmaceutical policy within the Department of Defense (DoD), it is first important to understand the basics about the delivery of health care and organizational structure of the DoD Military Health System (MHS).

This chapter will begin with a description of recent transformational changes to DoD health care. Additional discussions will provide a general overview of DoD health care with specific emphasis on pharmaceutical policy and its application in the DoD as it pertains to pharmacy benefit management and the provision of pharmaceutical care for all patients served.

Governance and Reform of the Military Health System

Numerous transformations have occurred in the MHS over the past several years, including Base Realignment and Closure, consolidation of medical functions and facilities in the National Capital Region (NCR), and fiscal imperatives. Such transformation has resulted in necessary changes in the governance, organization, and processes of the MHS. On September 15, 2011, a task force was implemented that focused on reforming MHS governance. The output from the task force was recommendations for dramatic changes to the MHS, which are described later in this section. On March 2, 2012, a memorandum signed by the deputy secretary of Defense directed the under secretary of Defense for Personnel and Readiness, and the chairman of the Joint Chiefs of Staff to stand up a planning team to develop an implementation plan for changes in governance. These changes included a new centralized Defense Health Agency (DHA), commanded by a three-star general (currently U.S. Air Force Lieutenant General Robb, a physician) [1]: the transition of TRICARE Management Activity to the DHA, which remains under the leadership of the assistant secretary of Defense for Health Affairs (ASD-HA) (currently Dr. Jonathan Woodson), and the designation of DHA as a Combat Support Agency with oversight by the Chairman of the Joint Chiefs of Staff (CJCS). Under the new DHA structure, 10 "shared services" were established. Included in this initial effort was the establishment of Pharmacy Shared Services. The DHA assumed the responsibility for the performance of these shared services [2,3].

The DHA implementation of the DHS also included provisions for multimarket services and a formalized NCR organizational command and control structure. The multimarket services have a market manager who is appointed with the mission to create and sustain a cost-effective, coordinated, high-quality health-care system, with enhanced authority to manage and allocate the budget for the market, and direct workload and personnel between the various markets. For the NCR, the DHA assumes all authority, direction and control over all military medical treatment facilities within the NCR. The previous joint task force CapMed becomes known as the NCR Medical Directorate. The position of director of the NCR Medical Directorate will be a two-star (general officer) level.

DHA Restructure Major Milestones

August 21, 2013: Rehearsal of concept drills presented to ASD-HA and Surgeons General.

August 31, 2013: Coordinated Concept of Operations approved, including organizational alignment, manpower, and personnel requirements.

October 1, 2013: Initial operating capability (IOC)—five shared services begin operations within the DHA.

October 1, 2015: Full operating capability (FOC).

Medical Mission of the DoD Remains [4]

Create a healthy and fit force: When the DoD puts a pair of muddy boots somewhere or deploy any war fighter, they are physically, mentally, and socially able to accomplish any mission our nation calls upon them to perform.

Deploy with them to protect: The battlefield is the *office place* of the warrior, who deserves the best possible protection from risks that could prevent mission success.

Restore health for service members deployed and at home: The DoD is with them to deliver world-class care: treatment, stabilization, and medical evacuation. At exactly the same time and level of importance, the DoD delivers care to the families at home.

DoD Health Plan

America is a grateful nation that thanks its retired warriors by giving them and their families' health care for life. Health care within the DoD is an entitlement based on Title Ten of Federal Law specifically as contained in the Code of Federal Regulations Section 32. As previously mentioned, the MHS has been restructured organizationally under the DHA. The ASD-HA, a presidential appointee, remains responsible to the secretary of Defense for the oversight and management of the MHS. Each of the armed services (army, navy, and air force) is led by a senior medical three-star flag officer (general or admiral), each of whom is the respective surgeon general (SG) of those services. Of significance, for the first time in the history of any of the armed services, the current army SG is a nurse. The SGs are also appointed by the president and are directly responsible and report to their respective senior line officer (chief of staff of the army, chief of staff of the air force, and chief of naval operations). Although there are no direct command and control lines of authority from the DHA or the ASD-HA to each of the service SG, all five of these senior MHS leaders work closely together in providing the highest-quality and cost-effective health care to all patients eligible through the DoD.

TRICARE remains the health plan for all uniformed service members (active duty, family members of active duty, and retired service members and their families) [5]. Currently, there are approximately 9.6 million eligible beneficiaries (patient lives) covered under TRICARE. The benefit is provided through a combination of military treatment facilities and partnerships with three regional managed care support contractors in the United States and one managed care contractor covering Eurasia–Africa, Latin America–Canada, and the Pacific. TRICARE offers several health and dental plans as well as a pharmacy benefit to eligible beneficiaries. Patient enrollment and coverage options under TRICARE include the following [6]:

Prime

- Similar to HMO plan.
- Active duty service members must enroll in this option.
- Patient care is directed by a primary care manager (PCM).
- Enrollment fee only for age 65 retirees and family members.
- Lowest out-of-pocket cost; portable coverage.
- Priority access to military hospitals and clinics.

- Civilian network option for those service and family members living in remote locations in the United States.
- In select areas within the United States, the U.S. Family Health Plan is an available alternative to prime coverage and provides comprehensive services. Enrollees not eligible to use military care or military pharmacies.

Extra

- Similar to PPO plan.
- Greater choice of network providers; however, access not guaranteed.
- No enrollment fee.
- Deductibles, co-pays/cost shares.

Standard

- Similar to indemnity plan, fee for service.
- Greatest choice to include nonnetwork providers.
- No enrollment fee.
- Deductibles, higher co-pays/cost shares.

Young adult

- Premium-based health plan for qualified young adult dependents who have aged out of TRICARE.
- Includes medical and pharmacy benefits, does not include dental benefits.
- Not available for those eligible for employer-sponsored coverage or above the age of 26.

TRICARE for life

- Must have Medicare Part A and B; TRICARE acts as last payer.
- No enrollment fee.
- Choice of Medicare and non-Medicare providers, military care on space-available basis.
- Responsible for Medicare and TRICARE deductibles.

Reserve Select/Retired Reserve

- Premium-based plan; enrollment is required.
- Available to qualifying members of the reserves, retired reserves, and family members.
- Access to any TRICARE provider.

DoD Pharmacy Benefit, Organization, Structure, and Leadership

The strategic objective of the DoD pharmacy benefit is to "uniformly, consistently, and equitably provide appropriate and safe drug therapy to meet patients' clinical needs in an effective, efficient, and fiscally responsible manner" [7]. This objective remains relevant as the DOD Pharmacy Working Group (PWG) continues to advance patient outcomes while optimizing pharmacy expenditures [8].

The pharmacy benefit within the department is provided to patients through multiple points of service that include military treatment facility (MTF) pharmacies located on the various post and bases, one centralized TRICARE Home Delivery (formerly TRICARE Mail Order Pharmacy), and over 55,000 retail network pharmacies and nonnetwork retail pharmacies. Pharmacy leadership, who provide senior level advice and recommendations to the ASD-HA and the service SG in the department is provided through the DoD Pharmacy Board of Advisors [9], which consists of the chief pharmacist/pharmacy consultant to each of the service SG, the chief of the DHA Pharmacy Operations Directorate, the director of the DoD Pharmacoeconomic Center, and the pharmacy consultant for the coast guard. This group in collaboration with the DoD Pharmacy and Therapeutics (P&T) committee, the DoD Pharmacoeconomic Center, and others is responsible for monitoring and making recommendations to senior DHA health-care leadership on opportunities to include potential policies to ensure a readily accessible, cost-effective pharmacy benefit. Similar to other civilian health plans, the expenditures on pharmaceuticals in the DoD have increased at a significant rate during the past several years.

DHA Shared Pharmacy Services Priorities

The DHA Pharmacy Shared Services Work Group (PWG) was established as a result of the transition to the DHA structure and replaces the previously established DOD pharmacy board of directors. Similar to this board, the PWG provide a forum for pharmacy leaders to coordinate and collaborate in order to direct the pharmacy benefit in support of the MHS mission. This PWG aims at improving the delivery of pharmacy services in terms of advancing patient outcomes while optimizing pharmacist costs to the enterprise. The PMG priorities include (1) redirecting beneficiary prescriptions for maintenance medications from retail to mail order and MTF points of service, (2) increasing MTF outpatient pharmacy compliance with centralized drug purchasing rules, (3) decreasing spending on decentralized pharmacy automation contracts, and (4) integrating clinical pharmacy into patient-centered care. At final operational capability (FOC), the DHA will (1) develop guidance for MTF pharmacy beneficiaries as well as a standard staffing model for MTF outpatient pharmacy use; (2) define structures and processes needed to centrally program, budget, execute, and manage pharmacy program funds; (3) receive, review, and consolidate pharmacy staff support contracts as well as *develop a centralized contract vehicle for* acquiring pharmacy automation equipment and *services*; and (4) receive detailed drug purchasing reports through Defense Logistics Agency (DLA) and identify and provide corrective feedback on any compliance deviation. At FOC, the Services will (1) continue to execute MTF outpatient pharmacy services, (2) support the DHA in identifying funding requirements, (3) provide automation contract needs and requirements and execute those contracts, and (4) continue to define and establish their formularies, purchase necessary drug inventories through the DLA, and dispense those drugs to beneficiaries.

Pharmacy Opportunities under Shared Services

- Seven different savings initiatives have been identified to achieve $(USD)1384 M in cumulative net savings between FY14 and FY19.
- Approximately 50% of the estimated savings are related to directing beneficiaries to lower-cost (for both the beneficiary and the government) points of service (MTF and mail order). Other major opportunities include centralizing the checkbook for MTF outpatient pharmacy, consolidating pharmacy automation contracts, and centralizing drug purchasing rules.

Future Vision for DHA (DoD) Pharmacy

The longer-term vision for MHS Pharmacy is to integrate pharmacists into the patient-centered medical home (PCMH) team in order to improve patient outcomes and reduce overall health-care costs. With this comes reduced variability, reduced cost of medications, products and services, and optimization of drug therapy. Pharmacist's roles in the PCMH model include comprehensive disease management, collaborative drug therapy management, medication management (MM), health promotion/disease prevention and care coordination, and follow-up patient care. The potential clinical pharmacy return on investment is estimated at 481% [10].

The DHA pharmacy includes four major initiatives: (1) pharmacy benefit channel management, (2) a centralized checkbook for MTF outpatient pharmacy, (3) consolidation of pharmacy automation contracts, and (4) centralization of drug purchasing rules. Pharmacy savings initiatives have the potential to achieve $(USD)1384 M in cumulative net savings between FY14 and FY19. The largest opportunity is directing beneficiaries to lower-cost points of service. The initiatives also provide savings from greater headquarters oversight and control of pharmacy resources. The main changes from the current state to IOC are as follows: (a) DHA pharmacy will have the ability to direct beneficiaries to lower-cost points of service and (b) the DHA pharmacy will provide oversight and corrective feedback for drug purchasing rules at MTFs. The main changes from IOC to FOC are as follows: (a) the DHA pharmacy will centrally program, budget, execute, and manage pharmacy program funds and (b) the DHA pharmacy will have direct oversight and control of pharmacy resources across the enterprise [11].

DoD Pharmacy Standards of Practice

With the focus on appropriate and safe drug therapy for all patients served by the DoD, the standards of practice and expectations for pharmacy and the provision of pharmaceutical care mirror those of national practice standards, which include compliance with applicable federal and state laws, DoD and service-specific pharmacy regulations, and nationally accepted standards of practice as identified in the national policies and procedures of the American Pharmacists Association and the American Society of Health System Pharmacists in addition to other applicable federal or national organizations that are accepted as defining a national practice standard (e.g., the U.S. Pharmacopoeia [USP] as it relates enacted federal standards pertaining to any sterile product preparation as contained in USP, Chapter 797).

Compliance with Joint Commission Medication Management Standards

As with many civilian health-care organizations and civilian hospitals, the majority of DoD medical treatment facilities (hospitals, clinics, etc.) are accredited by the Joint Commission (JC). Therefore, all aspects for the provision of pharmaceutical care within DoD health-care facilities are expected to comply with the JC MM standards. Policies and procedures must meet the intent of these stringent standards, and it is expected that MM within military health-care facilities is patient centered, multidisciplinary, and collaborative. The JC coordinates the accreditation survey schedule, which now includes unannounced surveys [12].

Formulary Management

In 2004, the Uniform Formulary (UF) rule was finalized and implemented for the DoD. This final rule (a federal statute) directed the establishment of a UF to include three-tier co-pays (generic, formulary, nonformulary). The UF was mandated by the Congress as part of the National Defense Authorization Act (NDAA) of 2000, but because of significant public comment, it was some 4 years later (2004) when the UF became a final rule and was implemented. The UF was legislated 1 year prior to the TRICARE Senior Pharmacy Program, which was implemented on April 1, 2001, for all over age 65 DoD beneficiaries. The TRICARE Pharmacy benefit access standards have become a national benchmark and in fact were utilized as the standard that was incorporated into the Medicare Part D Prescription Drug Program, which began its implementation in January 2006. The TRICARE Senior Pharmacy Program also known as TSRx was legislated by the 2001 NDAA for DoD retirees and dependents over the age of 65 who meet eligibility requirements [13]. This program provided equal access for these DoD seniors to the TRICARE Home Delivery and retail (network and nonnetwork) and retained their access to military medical facility pharmacies. The prescription co-pays for this program are the same as of those DoD patients under age 65. This revolutionary program, which was the first of its size in America to provide a comprehensive robust pharmacy benefit to over 1.6 million eligible patients, was implemented on April 1, 2001.

The UF provides a standardized and centralized formulary management process for the department that enhanced patient access to clinically appropriate, cost-effective medications. The UF also established the DoD P&T committee and Beneficiary Advisory Panel (BAP). The DoD P&T committee is comprised of military and civilian health-care professionals from each of the services. The primary responsibility of this committee is to evaluate drugs by reviewing the therapeutic class for consideration of inclusion on the UF. The DoD P&T committee is charged based on explicit provisions contained in the UF to evaluate drugs first based on their clinical effectiveness and then based on their cost-effectiveness. The BAP is comprised of civilian medical and professional lay personnel. This group meets after each DoD P&T committee during a public meeting held in Washington, DC, and reviews and comments on the formulary recommendations of the DoD P&T committee. Both the DoD P&T and the BAP meet quarterly. Upon review and comment on the DoD P&T minutes and recommendations by the BAP, both the DoD P&T minutes (recommendations) and BAP comments are forwarded to the ASD-HA for their consideration and review. Upon approval and signature by the assistant secretary, the minutes become final with the formulary recommendations fully implemented.

The initial Institute of Medicine report *To Err is Human* and subsequent follow-on publications opened America's eyes to the staggering problem of medical errors: a significant subset of those medical errors has been documented to be medication errors [14].

Interestingly and perhaps of no surprise to health-care providers is the fact that medication errors are one of the leading causes of deaths in the United States. The tragedy of course is the fact that medication errors are most often preventable and the result of a series of breakdowns in the medication use process.

The DoD has embraced the need to first do no harm in preventing and reducing medical and medication errors. To this end, the DoD implemented a patient safety center and a multidisciplinary patient safety committee. The DoD has been a national leader in patient safety. Specifically, for decades the DoD has included electronic physician order entry for medications as a component of the department's standardized electronic health record (eHR), the composite health-care system. The next generation of this system is scheduled to be implemented by 2015 with full implementation by 2023. Pharmacy will be a major module with the new eHR and will also include a much needed inventory management component as well as enhancements to differentiate true allergic reactions from nonallergic adverse drug reactions. Additionally, the DOD seeks a mechanism to document pharmacogenetic information to facilitate drug screening and selection and dose determination.

From the MM perspective, DoD's focus is the appropriate and safe use of medications. The DoD has taken an integrated health-care system focus in reporting, evaluating, and developing medication use process improvements based on data trend analysis. In 2001, the DoD implemented the pharmacy data transaction service (PDTS). The primary purpose of this initiative was patient safety—it facilitated DoD's ability to monitor its patients' medication use regardless of where the patient received their medication. PDTS connected the three primary points of service of the DoD pharmacy benefit, which are either the medical treatment facility pharmacy, the TRICARE Home Delivery pharmacy, or one of the 55,000 retail network pharmacies nationwide. Because PDTS electronically integrates all three points of service, this process includes provider (physician and pharmacist) warnings on dangerous drug–drug interactions or duplicate drug therapies. Once the system identifies a clinically significant level one drug–drug interaction or duplicate drug therapy, a review and hard edit override by either the pharmacist or physician must occur in order for the prescription to be released from the system allowing a label to then be printed and the prescription filled. As of 2010, the PDTS system had documented the identification of over 100,000 level one drug–drug interactions.

Deployment of Medication Management Policies

As previously discussed in this chapter, pharmacy policies in the DoD are often based on federal and state law and other applicable and nationally accepted standards of practice. Operational policies and procedures are typically service (army, air force, navy) based and are deployed and implemented at the local level.

Additionally, there are DoD directives and regulations applicable to the pharmacy in the DOD. Finally, there are health affairs policies that are signed under the authority of the ASD-HA. These policies are primarily focused on the DoD pharmacy benefit to ensure standardization of procedures and the provision of a uniform and consistent benefit to all patients. These health affairs policies, once staffed through the services and approved by the DHA and ASD-HA, are routed to the service SG for deployment and implementation.

Emergency Preparedness and Homeland Defense

Readiness is always a number one priority of the DoD, which also includes pharmacy. There is much joint planning among the services and other federal and state agencies, particularly post–September 11, 2001. Pharmaceuticals are widely used in the wartime environment during natural disaster and humanitarian relief efforts and in emergency preparedness and homeland defense. For example, data from the Army Medical Department for soldiers deployed to Iraq and Afghanistan post 9/11 documents that approximately one out of every five mobilized and deployed soldiers is taking at least one medication for a chronic medical condition [15]. This led to development and implementation of policies and procedures by the army to ensure that a deployment medication policy and process was in place to screen all soldiers for their medications, electronically record their medications necessary to treat any chronic medical conditions, and dispense an initial 6-month supply of medications with a process in place to provide any refills during their deployment. This process is now referred to by army pharmacists as the wartime provision of pharmaceutical care, which means appropriate and safe drug therapy for all deployment service members. Within the DoD, which works closely with the Department of Homeland Defense and multiple other federal agencies, there is ongoing coordination and collaboration on the development of national policy applicable to the utilization of pharmaceuticals for various emergency preparedness scenarios. These include policies related to potential threats such as a chemical, biological, radiological, nuclear, or explosive attack as well as other potentially high-risk threats like the avian flu. These policies are developed and coordinated at the agency secretary or assistant secretary level.

Conclusion

The DoD pharmacy and its dedicated pharmacists and pharmacy technicians have a proud tradition of selfless service performed with duty and honor in providing excellence in pharmaceutical care and service, never forgetting all of those who serve from the "soldier walking point" to the retiree at home. DHA (DoD) pharmacy challenges in the future will include four major initiatives: (1) pharmacy benefit channel management, (2) a centralized checkbook for MTF outpatient pharmacy, (3) consolidation of pharmacy automation contracts, and (4) centralization of drug purchasing rules. Pharmacy savings initiatives have the potential to achieve $(USD)1384 M in cumulative net savings between FY14 and FY19. The largest opportunity is directing beneficiaries to lower-cost points of service. The initiatives also provide savings from greater headquarters' oversight and control of pharmacy resources.

Additional future challenges faced by the DoD pharmacy community include the need to develop a right-sized twenty-first century DoD pharmacy workforce, standardized documentation practices that validate the need for pharmacists in supporting the services readiness mission, and preventative care and wellness imperatives. Development of enhanced organizational productivity policies with local business plans, consideration for manpower realignment, ongoing regional monitoring of performance metrics, and oversight through the services in collaboration with the DHA summarize additional challenges to the DOD pharmacy community. To be successful in the future, DoD pharmacy and the DoD medical professionals must continue to gain a better understanding of effective formulary management strategies with the development and implementation of policies that improve patient access to needed specialty medications. The development and implementation of business planning policies and tools within the high-cost specialty market will continue to play a critical role in this future success. These include the development of a strategic business planning process that focuses on appropriately mitigating expenditures on pharmaceuticals, and the appropriate utilization of pharmacy personnel resources with a focus on deploying pharmacists in more direct patient care roles. Additionally, the strategic business planning process should include the development of sound internal clinical business practice policies in compliance with JC MM standards that ensure all patient medication orders are reviewed by a pharmacist and involvement of the pharmacist at the beginning of the prescription order to provide drug expertise that results in the appropriate utilization of drug therapy. Prudent financial management policy development and monitoring will ensure improved utilization of resources. There must be a renewed emphasis on the customer service component in the delivery of pharmaceutical care within the department, which includes medication error prevention strategies, appropriate resourcing of DoD pharmacies that results in improved pharmacy patient waiting times, and improvements to the DoD pharmacy benefit delivery processes.

Additionally, the paradigm must shift from taking drugs off the formulary to a focus on pharmaceutical cost drivers and ensuring patients are first properly evaluated and placed on clinically appropriate medications. The focus for the future of DoD pharmacy and the effective management of the pharmacy benefit should be on best practices in managing pharmaceutical costs [16]. The primary changes from the current state are that DHA (DoD) pharmacy will have the ability to direct beneficiaries to lower-cost points of service, and DHA (DoD) pharmacy will provide oversight and corrective feedback for drug purchasing rules at MTFs. The DHA pharmacy will centrally program, budget, execute, and manage pharmacy program funds and will have direct oversight and control of pharmacy resources across the MHS enterprise with an overriding focus on providing a readily accessible, quality, cost-effective pharmacy benefit to all patients eligible for care through the MHS [11].

References

1. Kime P. New Defense Health Agency takes on support functions formerly run by services. Army Times, January 20, 2014. http://archive.armytimes.com/article/20140120/BENEFITS06/301200027/New-Defense-Health-Agency-takes-support-functions-formerly-run-by-services.
2. Carter AB. Deputy Secretary of Defense. Planning for the Reform of the Governance of the Military Health System. Memorandum Office of the Deputy Secretary of Defense, March 2, 2012.
3. Health.mil. DoD submits military health system reform plan to congress, December 13, 2013. http://www.health.mil/Reference-Center/Articles/2013/12/13/DoD-Submits-Military-Health-System-Reform-Plan-to-Congress. Accessed May 5, 2014.
4. U.S. Department of Defense. Military Health System Mission Statement, Office of the Assistant Secretary of Defense for Health Affairs 2004. http://prhome.defense.gov/HA.
5. TRICARE, Your Military Health Plan. Introduction to TRICARE, Power Point presentation, Updated May, 2015. http://www.tricare.mil/.
6. TRICARE Policy Manual 2008. https://assets.documentcloud.org/documents/20381/tricare-policy-manual-february-1-2008.pdf.
7. DoD Pharmacy Board of Director's Mission/Vision Statement, 2004.
8. DoD Pharmacy Work Group (PWG) Charter, June 2015.
9. DoD Pharmacy Transformation Plan, Office of the Assistant Secretary of Defense for Health Affairs and Director, TRICARE Management Activity, March 22, 2005.
10. Giberson S, Yoder S, and Lee MP. Improving patient and health system outcomes through advanced pharmacy practice. A Report to the U.S. Surgeon General, Office of the Chief Pharmacist, U.S. Public Health Service, December 2011. http://www.accp.com/docs/positions/misc/improving_patient_and_health_system_outcomes.pdf.
11. Defense Health Agency shared Pharmacy Working Group: Defining the future of military pharmacy, COL John Spain, Presentation to the Association of Military Surgeons, Sustaining Members, August 29, 2013.
12. Joint Commission Accreditation Manual 2013. Kansas City, MO. http://www.jointcommission.org/accreditation_guide_for_hospitals_hidden.aspx.
13. Public Law 106-65. National Defense Authorization Act of 2000, Section on the Uniform Formulary. https://www.congress.gov/bill/106th-congress/senate-bill/1059.
14. Kohn L, Corrigan J, and Donaldson, M. *To Err is Human: Building a Safer Health System*. Institute of Medicine, National Academy Press, Washington, DC, 1999.
15. DoD Pharmacoeconomic Center, Predeployment medication analysis and reporting tool [PMART], 2004–2005.
16. DoD Pharmacy Consultants, Combined forces pharmacy seminar, October 2004.

Chapter 27

Department of Veterans Affairs Pharmacy Programs

Vaiyapuri Subramaniam and Michael A. Valentino

Contents

VA Pharmacy Programs

Mission

To provide the highest-quality care to veterans by ensuring safe, effective, and medically necessary use of medications.

Vision

To provide the highest-quality, value added pharmaceutical care services to veterans.

Department of Veterans Affairs (VA) pharmacy program is an essential component of the patient-focused health-care team. This is accomplished by creating a practice environment that fosters education, research, and professional development. The VA pharmacy programs utilize innovative technologies to ensure consistent, accurate, and reliable medication distribution, education, and information systems. Use of these innovations ensure that VA pharmacy programs will continue to provide pharmaceutical services during national emergencies, disasters, and other events that adversely affect our veterans. By continuing these achievements, VA pharmacy will be an employer of choice for pharmacists, pharmacy technicians, and supportive staff by providing a compassionate, progressive work environment.

Introduction

The Department of Veterans Affairs (VA) continues to be the benchmark of excellence and value in health care and benefits by providing exemplary services that are both patient centered and evidence based for veteran patients. The care delivered is accomplished by engaged and collaborative teams in an integrated environment that supports learning discovery and continuous improvement in the framework of public health that emphasizes prevention and population health that contributes to the nation's well-being through education, research, and services in national emergencies.

The VA pharmacy programs are led and supported nationally by the pharmacy benefits management (PBM) services. The PBM is part of the Veterans Health Administration (VHA) that is dedicated to ensuring the full continuum of health care comprising of health promotion, disease prevention, diagnostics, therapeutics and rehabilitative care, recovery and palliative care. These initiatives of care are provided through policy and program development that promotes dignity and respect and is achieved by utilizing innovative approaches and technologies through interdisciplinary collaboration both within and outside of VHA. The PBM joins the VHA in the provision of leadership and policy to enable the VA to provide the best possible health care for the nation's veterans and advice on pharmacy matters to a wide variety of stakeholders. Major pharmacy programs of PBM include pharmacy practice, consolidated mail outpatient pharmacies (CMOPs), drug benefits design, formulary management, drug safety and VA Center for Medication Safety (VA MedSAFE), pharmaceutical compounding and hazardous drug management, pharmacy recruitment and retention, advancing clinical pharmacy programs, and pharmacy informatics.

Background

The VA was established on March 15, 1989, succeeding the Veterans Administration.[1] The department is responsible for providing federal benefits to veterans and their families—meeting the challenge President Abraham Lincoln laid out for the nation in 1865 "to care for him who shall have borne the battle, and for his widow, and his orphan." The VA is the second largest of the fifteen U.S. Cabinet Departments and operates the largest integrated health-care delivery system in the country. The VA provides a broad range of primary care, specialized care, and related medical and social support services. The VA is also the nation's largest integrated provider of health-care education and training for physician residents, pharmacy residents, and other health-care trainees. The VA advances medical research and development in areas that most directly address the diseases and conditions that affect veterans and eligible beneficiaries.

As of 2008, about 36% total living veterans received VA benefits and/or services in fiscal year (FY) 2008 of which 81% were 45 years old or older.[2] Of the 22 million veterans alive in late 2013, nearly three-quarters served during a war or an official period of conflict.[2] Veterans are predominately male and white. This will change over the next 30 years; women will make up almost one-fifth of the veteran population and nearly 35% will be nonwhite. Gulf War veterans will overtake Vietnam veterans as the largest cohort. The age distribution of veterans will remain stable over time, with the largest segment being those over 65 years old. However, the age distribution of women veterans will shift from the largest segment being the 30–49 years old range to those 65 years and older. Increases in the diversity of the veteran population will result in the need for more diverse services, outreach, communications, and research and development. Utilization of services and benefits is unique to the individual, but, on average, increases with age. The sustained percentage of veterans over the age of 65, and the increasing percentage of women veterans over the age of 65, means geriatric care will continue to be a significant portion of VA's health care.

The most visible of all VA benefits and services is health care. From 54 hospitals in 1930, VA's health-care system, managed by the VHA, now includes 154 medical centers, with at least one in each state, Puerto Rico, and the District of Columbia. The VA operates over 1700 sites of care, including services and benefits provided from 820 ambulatory care and community-based outpatient clinics (CBOCs), 135 community living centers, 103 residential rehabilitation centers, and 300 veteran centers. Each year, over 200,000 VHA leaders and health-care employees provide exceptional care to over 6.3 million veterans and other beneficiaries. VA's health-care facilities provide a broad spectrum of medical, surgical, and rehabilitative care.[1]

Since 1979, VHA has operated Vet Centers, which provide psychological counseling for war-related trauma, community outreach, case management, and referral activities, plus supportive social services to veterans and family members. Veteran centers are open to any veteran who served in the military in a combat theater during wartime or anywhere during a period of armed hostilities.

While providing high-quality health care to America's veterans, VHA also conducts an array of research on some of the most difficult challenges facing medical science today. The VA is a world leader in such research areas as aging, women's health, AIDS, posttraumatic stress disorder (PTSD), and other mental health issue. VA researchers played key roles in developing the cardiac pacemaker, the CT scan, radioimmunoassay, and improvements in artificial limbs.

VHA receives most of its funding from the Congress, through annual authorizing legislation that serves as the basis for operating the administration, and provides guidance to the House and Senate Appropriations Committees as to an appropriate level of funding for its services.

Until the mid-1990s, the VA operated largely as a hospital system providing general medical and surgical services, specialized care in mental health and spinal cord injury, and long-term care through directly operated or indirectly supported facilities. Medical centers and other facilities operated relatively independently of each other, even competitively duplicating services. Anachronistic laws required that virtually all of VA's health-care services should be provided in hospitals—which ran counter to changes in the remainder of the health-care industry, which had already begun to move most care into the ambulatory environment.

In 1996, the Veterans Health Care Eligibility Reform Act was passed, enabling the VA system to be restructured from a hospital system to a health-care system. The changes that followed were predicated on the assumption that providing effective, efficient care required coordination among VA's facilities and that resources should be used synergistically—including the requirement that care to veterans be provided in the most appropriate environment.

To accomplish this task, the VA created 22 (now 21) geographically defined Veterans Integrated Service Networks (VISNs). These networks allowed the VA to redirect its resources in two ways: first, to follow the veteran population, which was shifting from the Northeast and Midwest to the Sunbelt and elsewhere, and second, to allow resources to be allocated to networks instead of facilities. This allowed VHA to create financial incentives to coordinate care and resources among facilities that previously competed with each other.

A central strategy in accomplishing VHA's goals is the use of information technology. This is a continuing evolutionary process that also involves PBM's pharmacy informatics program. The VA strives to use technology to implement best practice, support team-based care coordination, clinical decision making, medical device integration, and ancillary service integration. The Veterans Health Information Systems and Technology Architecture (VistA) electronic health record (EHR) is the core component of the VA's system of medication management. The Computerized Patient Record System (CPRS), Pharmacy VistA, and Bar Code Medication Administration (BCMA) are three integral and tightly integrated systems in the VA EHR, VistA that provide medication therapies. The CPRS has other capabilities to support improvements in performance and patient safety, including computerized provider order entry, clinical alerts, enhanced order checks, the ability to view data remotely from other facilities, and a clinical reminder system that provides real-time, point of care clinical decision support. VistA imaging provides a multimedia, online patient record that integrates traditional medical chart information with medical images of all kinds. This system is fully operational at all VA sites of care.

Today, a secure patient portal known as My Health*e*Vet provides patients access to their personal health record, online health assessment tools, mechanisms for prescription refills, requesting appointments, and access to high-quality consumer health information. The consumer information is evidence based and consistent with clinical practice guideline recommendations and, ideally, inspires patients to participate in their own health care. My Health*e*Vet is part of VHA's effort to make the patient the focus of control of his or her own health care and to make the experience of care seamless across the various environments in which it is provided—including not only the hospital and clinic but also the patient's home, workplace, and community. Patient-centered care coordination extends the focus of disease management to better and more efficiently integrate every patient's disease-specific and general health needs with the resources of the health system.[3] The VA Blue Button provides patients with more timely access to information, expands the types of self-reported information that all registered users can include, and enhances user-friendly functionalities. This includes more timely access to VA laboratory results, radiology reports, and VA notes and problem lists, and now, all registered users can include the "My Goals" option in their VA Blue Button and access and monitor their health information. For example, a patient with heart failure can enter his or her daily weight from home for review by a care coordinator. Should his or her weight exceed a clinical threshold, he or she would then be called to visit a clinic, or even be visited at home. This enables him or her to be seen just as he or she begins to retain fluid, instead of on an arbitrary appointment schedule that is likely to fail to identify an impending crisis.

Pharmacy Practice

The VA offers a broad scope of pharmacy services across all patient care settings. The PBM services leads and supports pharmacy program activities in VHA and provides advice on pharmacy issues to a wide variety of stakeholders. As part of its mission to improve the health status of veterans in the appropriate use of medications, VA's pharmacy programs offers a broad range of services and is committed to provide and deliver to veterans personalized, proactive, patient-driven care. This includes the provision to veterans of reliable, evidence-based medication information in an efficient manner to enable veterans with their health-care team to make informed decisions about their medications in the overall improvement of their health. Major pharmacy program areas are described and presented in the following sections.

PBM Consolidated Mail Outpatient Pharmacies

With the exception of some of its CBOCs, the VA operates pharmacies and provides pharmacy services in all of its medical care facilities. In addition, the VA operates seven large, highly automated CMOPs, where prescriptions originating at VA medical care facilities are filled and delivered to veterans' homes. CMOP fills 80% of all the outpatient prescriptions in VHA (117 million in FY 2013). Every workday, over 310,000 veterans receive a parcel at their home containing prescriptions from the CMOP. The extensive use of automation enables the CMOP to fill a prescription for $(USD)1.52 in personnel and operating cost. The CMOP delivers this service with greater than six sigma accuracy. The average cost of mailing a prescription to the veteran's home is $(USD)1.71. CMOP personnel pride themselves in providing exceptional customer service. The customer survey firm of J.D. Powers and Associates conducts an annual customer satisfaction survey of mail order pharmacy providers. Veterans gave the CMOP the highest customer satisfaction score of any mail order pharmacy in the country in 2010, 2011, 2012, and 2013.

In the outpatient setting, VA pharmacists deliver care through both primary care and specialty care clinics. In primary care, VA pharmacists are fully integrated in VA's primary care delivery model, conducting prospective and concurrent pharmacy therapy reviews, making recommendations, and/or implementing medication therapy changes under a scope of practice (SOP) agreement. Additionally, VA pharmacists have assumed very active and leadership roles in focused clinics, such as anticoagulation clinics, lipid clinics, and a variety of other clinics designed to deliver focused care for drug therapy–intensive disease states. It is estimated that greater than 90% of VA's dedicated anticoagulation clinics are pharmacist managed where the pharmacist assumes complete responsibility for achieving the primary care or specialty care physician's anticoagulation goals.

Drug Benefit Design

The VA offers over 1502 molecular entities and a large number of medical/surgical supply items and prosthetic supplies through its national formulary.[4] These molecular entities include legend drugs, over-the-counter drugs as well as biological products, and in some cases, drug-containing medical devices. The VA's National Formulary (VANF) is a "core" formulary in that the drugs listed *must* be made available through all VA medical treatment facilities.

To provide an affordable and comprehensive prescription drug benefit, the VA uses generic substitution, therapeutic substitution, mandatory national standardization for high-cost/high-volume branded drugs, and evidence-based utilization management. VA patients pay $(USD)8 for each 30-day supply of medication ($[USD]9 for veterans in priority groups 7–8), regardless of the cost of the drug, or its legend or over-the-counter status. Some veterans are exempt from co-payments by virtue of their military service, income, or other factors. In FY 2012, the VA dispensed over 266 million 30-day equivalent prescriptions (84% via VA's CMOP home delivery pharmacies) at a drug ingredient cost of $(USD)3.5 billion.

Formulary Management

Prescription drugs constitute a large percentage of the country's overall health-care spending. Many U.S. citizens receive pharmaceuticals through some form of PBM to help achieve cost-effective and high-quality pharmaceutical care. By necessity, the VA is a leader in the PBM movement, having the responsibility to provide all "needed" care to enrolled patients under Public Law 104-262, the *Veterans' Health Care Eligibility Reform Act of 1996*.[5]

The VA offers a broad array of pharmacy benefits to its patient population and, like many other health-care organizations, has seen its pharmaceutical expenditures rise in recent years. Drug expenditures in FY 2005 increased to $(USD)3.4 billion dollars from $(USD)1.6 billion in FY 1999, a 112% increase, largely driven by rising enrollment of new patients. To cope with the increased use of pharmaceuticals, the VA implemented a national PBM program in 1995 to (1) reduce geographic variability of access to pharmaceuticals across the system, (2) improve the distribution of pharmaceutical agents, (3) promote appropriate drug therapy, (4) reduce inventory carrying and drug acquisition costs, (5) promote improvements in drug-related patient safety issues, and (6) design and carry out drug outcomes assessment projects. As a result of the national PBM program, during a continued (though less pronounced) rise in enrollment of new patients, from FY 2005 to FY 2013, drug expenditures decreased from $(USD)3.4 billion dollars to $(USD)3.3 billion, a 4% decrease.

Evolution of the VA Formulary Drug Process

Prior to 1995, each of VA's more than 170 individual VA facilities managed its own pharmaceutical coverage via a local pharmacy and therapeutics (P&T) committees. The VA Headquarters Drug Product and Pharmaceuticals Management (DPPM) division, based in Hines, Illinois, managed and monitored drug usage and purchasing options for those facilities, but had no utilization oversight responsibilities. In September 1995, Dr. Kenneth Kizer, then VA's undersecretary for health, established the VA Pharmacy Benefits Management Strategic Healthcare Group (PBM), directing it to develop and implement a national formulary; manage pharmaceutical costs, utilization, and related outcomes; and oversee pharmacologic guideline development of common diseases within the VA system. To do so, clinical pharmacists employed at DPPM headquarters collaborated with a newly established consultative body of 11 field-based VA physicians and VA clinical pharmacist specialists called the VA medical advisory panel (MAP).

Formulary decisions fall under the purview of two groups: the MAP and the VISN pharmacist executives (VPEs). The VPEs are pharmacy leaders who manage the pharmacy benefit for VA's 21 regional care systems. Each VISN includes a variety of health-care centers such as tertiary facilities, ambulatory care centers, and associated community clinics. Under the oversight of the

VPEs, each VISN's formulary committee collaborates with the P&T committees of its health-care centers to allow for integrated multilevel decision making. Thus, VISNs and local facilities can communicate and provide guidance to the PBM, and vice versa, on policies determining drug use within the VA system.

Implementing the VANF evoked considerable scrutiny from stakeholders and a series of hearings at the congressional level ensued. In 1999 and 2000, the Senate and House Committees on Veteran Affairs each requested an outside review of the national formulary from the Institute of Medicine (IOM) and the U.S. Government Accountability Office (GAO), respectively, to assess the clinical and economic integrity of the VANF and the formulary management process.

The IOM report, released in 2001, concluded that the VANF was not "overly restrictive" with respect to "formulary size and quality, coverage of drugs in different classes, timeliness of new drug additions, fairness and responsiveness of the non-formulary exceptions process, and sensitivity of therapeutic interchange policies and procedures." According to this report, within its first 2 years, the VANF saved approximately $(USD)100 million via its closed and preferred drug classes.[8] Per the IOM report, during July 1997–July 1999, only 0.4% (2,385 out of 570,937) of all complaints to patient representatives about the VA involved a pharmacy issue.[6]

A second study, conducted by the GAO, noted that VANF drugs accounted for 90% of outpatient prescriptions dispensed between October 1999 and March 2000 and that the VANF met veterans' needs.[7,8] The VANF continues to be an important utilization management tool. In FY 2013, VANF drugs accounted for approximately 94% of the outpatient prescriptions dispensed.

Both reports had recommendations for improved processes in the areas of use of nonformulary drugs and therapeutic interchange policy. The VA acknowledged that changes were needed to its rapidly evolving formulary management processes and, in many cases, efforts to make those changes predated the IOM and GAO reviews. These changes included eliminating local facility formularies, eliminating a 1-year moratorium on adding new molecular entities (NMEs) to the VANF, taking steps to reduce variation across the system regarding the addition of new products, and conducting timely system-wide reviews of all newly approved NMEs. Finally, the PBM began to develop an expanded research/outcomes assessment agenda to measure the effects of the VANF on patient outcomes and safety.

Pharmaceutical Standardization and Contracting

By competitively sourcing branded products within a given drug class, the VA achieved nearly $(USD)5.4 billion in pharmaceutical national contract cost savings from FY 1999 through 2012. Standardization contracts have a compelling effect on adherence in the VA. After awarding a national standardization contract, VISNs encourage providers to switch to the contracted agent if clinically appropriate. This, in turn, leads to significant drug acquisition cost savings. As an example, after competitive bidding for proton-pump inhibitors (PPI) in 2001, 95% of patients switched to the contracted agent within 6 months. Patients tolerated this switch well, with only 5% needing another PPI due to suboptimal response or intolerance. This therapeutic interchange generated over $(USD)45 million in cost savings in FY 2001.

Through careful competitive bidding and other cost-effectiveness measures (such as promoting use of generic drugs and the most cost-effective branded drugs whenever clinically possible), according to internal VA data, the average acquisition cost per 30-day fill for drugs and the average outpatient drug ingredient cost per patient have remained relatively stable for approximately 13 years (Figures 27.1 and 27.2).

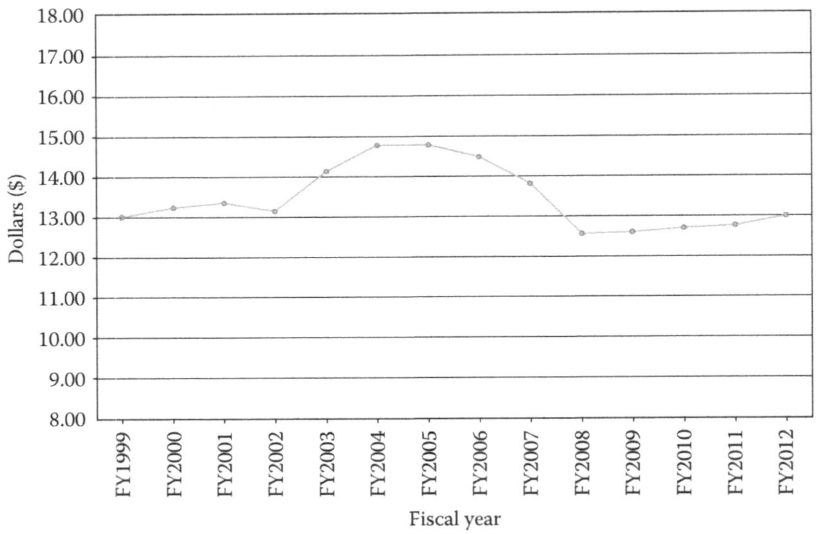

Figure 27.1 Average cost per 30-day equivalent prescription in the Department of Veterans Affairs—fiscal years 1999–2012.

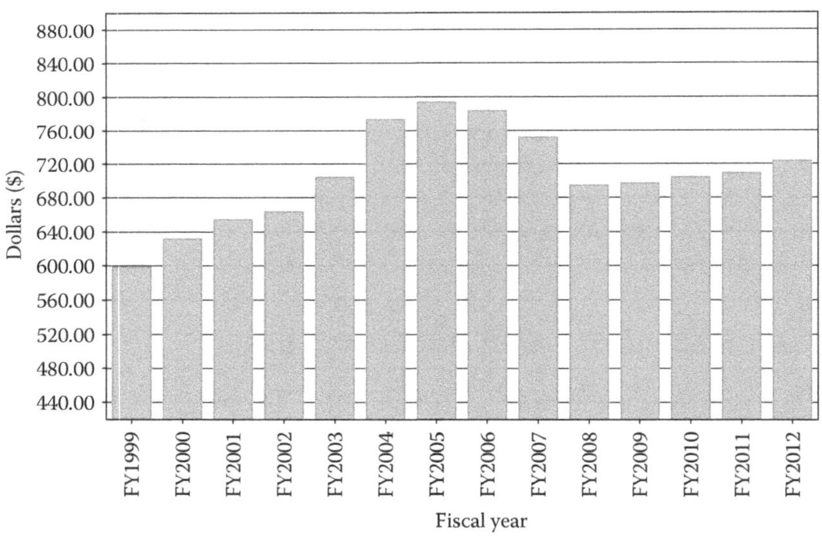

Figure 27.2 Average drug ingredient cost per pharmacy user per fiscal year—fiscal years 1999–2012.

Evidence-Based Reviews

One of the first issues addressed by PBM was to develop pharmacologic management guidelines for the most prevalent and most costly disease states observed in the VA population.[7,8] These clinical documents and algorithms of drug use initiated by the PBM rely on a process of peer review by the MAP, VPEs, and field-based experts (therapeutic advisory groups). The finalized drug and disease-state policies, together with utilization statistics from its national prescription utilization database, assist the VA in advancing its national purchasing power to contract for quality drug products at competitive prices and to help assure equal access to specific drugs, for specific conditions. The PBM posts are available for general use and can be found on the PBM website.[4] PBM clinical pharmacists regularly monitor these drug use documents, and updates occur according to PBM directors/advisors and VA health-care system needs on an as-needed basis as new information become available in published, peer-reviewed literature.

Outcomes Assessment

Early in VA's formulary evolution process, it became apparent that assessments of past formulary decisions were needed to (1) gain credibility among providers and oversight bodies for decision-making quality and (2) to make improvements in medication-related patient safety issues. It was further realized that using existing data to prospectively evaluate the likely impact of anticipated formulary decisions would be superior to retrospective analyses. By virtue of a relatively closed health-care delivery model and the ubiquitous use of an advanced electronic medical record (EMR) system, the VA was able to undertake formal assessments of its past and future formulary initiatives.

Over time, PBM developed and improved its ability to conduct outcomes assessment and research to support and reinforce formulary and policy decisions in a variety of ways. Most outcomes assessments address quality improvement (QI) and patient safety initiatives using a pharmacy database developed by the PBM. This patient/provider-specific database includes information on all outpatient drugs dispensed from any VA pharmacy and provides a detailed profile of medications, dosing, quantities, and drug costs. Prescription use can be tracked on a macro (national, VISN, or facility) or micro (individual patient and provider) level. Further, when required, merging these data with larger VA administrative and clinical databases can provide further information such as diagnosis, procedures, hospitalization, clinic visits, comorbidity, mortality, and laboratory data. In addition, the PBM utilizes data management software to create views of relational pharmacy databases, allowing quick queries of data on selected pharmaceuticals for questions requiring urgent responses.

Within the VA, the PBM has spearheaded the nationwide monitoring and management of clinical pharmacy and pharmacy-related patient outcomes. The PBM's Outcomes Research group and VA MedSAFE design formal research evaluations looking at safety, appropriateness of use, effectiveness, and cost-effectiveness of prescription drugs in the veteran population for retrospective, real-time, and prospective analyses. The VA MedSAFE has developed an infrastructure that allows the conduct of both passive and active medication safety surveillance, real-time intervention to prevent potential adverse events, and a national medication safety communication plan to disseminate pertinent medication safety information. Passive surveillance is conducted through the national web-based VA Adverse Drug Event Reporting System (VA ADERS) that was initiated in FY 2007.[4] This system allows patient-reported or provider-identified adverse events to be reported. Active medication safety surveillance is achieved through rapid cycle database evaluations, which allows for evaluation of suspected adverse event signals for identified drugs. The VA's risk reduction program allows for real-time intervention to prevent potential adverse drug events (ADEs) through various mechanisms, including the VA's medication utilization evaluation tracker (MUET). Finally, PBM educates the VA on pertinent medication safety issues through its National PBM Bulletins and Medication Safety in Seconds Newsletter. PBM has published several articles describing its outcomes, safety, and QI efforts.[4,9–24]

Patient Safety

The VA is a recognized leader in patient safety, having undergone a transformational cultural change from punishment to prevention. In addition to the medical error philosophical changes underway within VA and the careful data collection and analysis necessary for the reduction of medical errors, the VA is also a leader in the deployment of technology to reduce the risk of medical errors. Through the use of its innovative EMR, VA clinical and informatics staff have in many ways been the vanguard of EMR-based patient safety and clinical QI efforts. Pace setting improvements in drug-related safety is also occurring within VA pharmacy, where major system improvements have been achieved with the pioneering use of a system-wide BCMA system.[25]

When used as designed, VA's BCMA system has the potential to virtually eliminate medication administration errors in the inpatient setting.

VA pharmacists also developed a highly automated home delivery pharmacy CMOP system in the early 1990s. Almost immediately and for several years after implementation, VA's CMOPs served as *the* home delivery system prototype in both the public and private sectors in the United States and abroad. VA CMOP continues to evolve in regard to efficiency and safety and is operating very near the six sigma threshold for accuracy. Additional improvements are currently being deployed that could further increase VA CMOP accuracy.

Pharmaceutical Compounding and Hazardous Drug Management Programs

The Pharmaceutical Compounding and Management Standards Program Office in the VHA PBM services fulfills the VA pharmacy program's emerging needs to provide oversight and technical expertise to ensure compliance and best practices by VA medical centers (VAMCs) in pharmaceutical compounding and pharmaceutical waste and hazardous drug management. Following the establishment of pharmacy compounding standards in the United States Pharmacopeia (USP) on pharmaceutical compounding, the program office implements compliance monitoring and educational programs through the provision of subject matter expertise and the development of guidelines, training, and policy guidance to ensure compliance with practice standards on compounded sterile and nonsterile preparations in accordance with VA policy and standards delineated in USP Chapters 797 and 795, respectively.[26] The program office provides educational tools and training to VAMC pharmacy staff to ensure compounded sterile preparations are prepared with assurance of environmental control standards, personnel competency requirements, and quality assurance monitoring.[27–29] To meet needs of VAMC pharmacy services for compounded sterile preparations in pharmaceutical and parenteral drug compounding or when commercially available drug products are not available, the program office provides ongoing guidelines, consultations, presentations, and webinar-based educational programs to VA pharmacists and pharmacy technicians to ensure that best practice approaches and pharmaceutical quality standards are implemented in compounding sterile preparations by VAMC pharmacy services in compliance with USP Chapter 797 or, if necessary, to purchase compounded sterile preparations from outsourced compounding pharmacies. The program office developed guidelines to ensure best practices in the utilization of outsourced compounding establishments to procure compounded sterile preparations in accordance with pharmaceutical compounding quality provisions of the Drug Quality and Security Act of November 27, 2013. In the area of pharmaceutical waste and hazardous drug management, the program office ensures best practice approaches by VAMCs by communicating and providing technical expertise and guidance on proper disposal and management of pharmaceutical waste and hazardous drug products in compliance with regulations under the Resource Conservation and Recovery Act (RCRA).[30,31] Initiatives include working with VHA stakeholders on hazardous drug classification of pharmaceutical products in VA drug formulary system to ensure proper disposal and handling at the point of care. The program office took the lead to establish a Pharmaceutical Management Work Group (PMWG) composed of VA interdisciplinary subject matter experts to address topics related to pharmaceutical and environmental programs areas and on pharmaceutical and occupational safety and health. Through the PMWG, the program office initiated ongoing collaborations with VHA stakeholders representing pharmacy, environmental, and industrial hygienist disciplines to conduct and evaluate findings from assessment of selected VAMC sites to identify and improve waste management practices. This collaboration resulted in the development of VHA Green Environmental Management Systems guidance initiatives in 2010 on training curriculum and performance metrics on pharmaceutical waste management practices. Together with VHA stakeholders, the program office contributed in the development and educational structure of a nationwide online training program on pharmaceutical waste management principles and practices within VHA's web-based talent management system. In partnership with a local VHA environmental protection program office, a study evaluation was made in 2013 on management of empty containers of acutely hazardous waste pharmaceuticals related to warfarin drug products based on regulatory guidelines from the local regional Environmental Protection Agency (EPA) office. Integration of study evaluations from EPA regulatory guidelines resulted in proper management controls for managing empty warfarin containers that can be utilized in a pharmacy operation for proper classification of VHA facility "hazardous generator status." The term "hazardous generator status" given to a facility is based upon the size or volume of hazardous waste produced. Three categories describe the "hazardous generator size" assigned to a facility based on size or volume produced, viz., large quantity generators, small quantity generators, or conditionally exempt small quantity generators.[30,31]

Education and Training

VA's medical education program began in the postwar years of World War II. By forming affiliations with medical schools and universities, the VA has become the largest provider of health-care training in the United States. VA's graduate medical education (GME) is conducted through affiliations with university schools of medicine. Currently 152 VHA medical facilities are affiliated with 126 of the nation's 141 allopathic medical schools. Through these partnerships, almost 38,000 medical residents and 20,000 medical students receive some of their training in VA every year. Accounting for approximately 9% of U.S. GME, the VA supports 10,250 physician resident positions in almost 2,000 residency programs accredited in the name of our university partners. VA physician faculty have joint appointments at the university and at the VA and see patients at VA, supervising students and residents and conducting research. It would be difficult for the VA to deliver its high-quality patient care without the physician staff and residents that are available through these affiliations.

The VA has been a leader in the training of associated health professionals as well. Through affiliations with individual health professions schools and colleges, clinical traineeships and fellowships are provided to students in more than 90 professions, including nurses, pharmacists, dentists, audiologists, dietitians, social workers, psychologists, physical therapists, optometrists, podiatrists, physician assistants, respiratory therapists, and nurse practitioners. Over 32,000 associated health students receive training in VA facilities each year and provide a valuable recruitment source for new employees. The greatest majority (90%) of associated health trainees receive clinical experiences on a without-compensation (WOC) basis. For additional information regarding WOC or funded trainee positions, contact the education office or the clinical discipline office at the desired VA facility.

Pharmacy Residency Education

The Pharmacy Residency Program Office (PRPO) oversees the strategic planning of pharmacy residency programs nationwide. To support VHA strategic initiatives, the PRPO has expanded the Mental Health Pharmacy Residency programs and is now the largest trainer of mental health pharmacy residents with the highest percentage of board certified psychiatric pharmacists in the country. For 2012, the VA will have a total of 579 pharmacy residency positions that also include specialty training programs in geriatrics, mental health, oncology, pharmacy administration, infectious disease, internal medicine, and ambulatory care. The VA also expects to train an additional 5800 pharmacy students. VA offers a small number of pharmacy fellowships in the areas of pharmacoeconomics, palliative care, and patient safety. Additional pharmacy fellowships in pharmacy automation, pharmacy information technology, pharmacoepidemiology, pharmacy administration, and war-related illness and injury are being considered.

Pharmacy Recruitment and Retention Programs

The Pharmacy Recruitment and Retention Office was established to provide guidance and support to VA facilities facing pharmacy recruitment and retention challenges. At the end of FY 2012, the VHA had 6755 pharmacist employees on board. Onboard strength for pharmacists grew by 2.7% in FY 2011 and 2.6% in FY 2012. In total, onboard strength is projected to increase by 7.7% over the next 7 years. Of the current workforce (FY 2011), approximately 31% will be eligible for retirement or will retire by FY 2018. Because of the strength of VHA's pharmacist workforce, VHA was able to successfully achieve a wide array of strategic goals for maximizing quality of care, access to care, and patient-centered care for veterans. These initiatives have positively impacted numerous aspects of VA's health-care delivery, including, among others, clinical pharmacy services, CMOP and Meds by Mail, formulary management, medication safety, emergency pharmacy services, informatics, student and residency training programs, medication reconciliation, and recruitment and retention of a high-quality workforce.

Advancing Clinical Pharmacy Practice

In response to the changing roles of clinical pharmacists, the PBM developed a new program office in April 2010, the Clinical Pharmacy Program Office (CPPO), to align clinical pharmacy practice system-wide. The strong clinical practice and leadership that existed in VHA served as the springboard for the program office to further develop clinical pharmacy practice roles in areas where gaps in patient care exist.

The VA offers a broad scope of pharmacy services across all patient care settings. With the exception of some of its CBOCs, the VA operates pharmacies and provides pharmacy services in all of its medical care facilities. In addition, the VA operates CMOPs, where prescriptions originating at VA medical care facilities can be filled. In the outpatient setting, VA pharmacists deliver care through both primary care and specialty care clinics. In primary care, VA pharmacists are fully integrated into VA's Patient Aligned Care Team delivery model where they often practice at the top of their license conducting prospective and concurrent pharmacotherapy reviews, performing disease and population management, conducting shared medical appointments and group visits, and implementing medication therapy changes under a SOP agreement. Additionally, VA pharmacists have assumed very active and leadership roles in many specialty clinics, such as pain management, anticoagulation, mental health, hepatitis C, heart failure, nephrology, and a variety of other clinics designed to deliver patient-focused care for drug therapy–intensive disease states. The strong clinical practice and leadership that existed in VHA served as the springboard for the program office to further develop clinical pharmacy practice roles in areas where gaps in patient care exist.

The VA/VHA has long recognized the need for team-based care and the importance of the role of the clinical pharmacist. Since the early 1990s, VHA policy has existed system-wide to allow clinical pharmacy specialists (CPS) providing direct patient care to be granted a SOP with prescriptive authority. The direct patient care activities covered by a SOP include all functions that are carried out autonomously by a pharmacist in an advanced practice role and are above and beyond those functions considered a routine part of pharmacist professional practice. The SOP delineates medication prescriptive authority and the ability to order laboratory tests, screenings, referrals, appointments, and other items pertinent to monitoring and assessing the patient's drug therapy.

A SOP allows the pharmacist to function at the top of their licensure and scope as a direct care provider. The VHA has worked with facilities to develop standardized SOP documents for pharmacists with similar responsibilities. Activities that require a SOP include, but are not limited to, the following:

1. Developing, documenting, and executing therapeutic plans utilizing the most effective, safest, and most economical medication treatments
2. Ordering and subsequent review and interpretation of appropriate laboratory tests and other diagnostic studies necessary to monitor, support, and modify the patient's drug therapy
3. Prescribing medications, devices, and supplies to include initiation, continuation, discontinuation, monitoring, and altering therapy
4. Performing the physical measurements necessary to ensure the patient's appropriate clinical responses to drug therapy
5. Ordering and administering vaccines as necessary for the provision of pharmaceutical care
6. Taking independent corrective action for identified drug-induced problems
7. Ordering consults (i.e., dietician, social work, specialty provider), as appropriate, to maximize positive drug therapy outcomes
8. Providing clinical pharmacy expertise, comprehensive medication management, and monitoring for practice-based areas to include clinics and wards in conjunction with the attending physician or team (e.g., home-based primary care, internal medicine, critical care, community living centers)

Demographics of VA Pharmacists with a Scope of Practice

Pharmacists with a SOP are broadly distributed geographically within the VA, although the number of them in any one geographic location varies broadly. Some sites have only a few pharmacists with a SOP, while others have in excess of 70 pharmacists practicing in this manner. Figure 27.1

is a graphical representation of that distribution of more than 2700 practicing pharmacists at the VA with a SOP as of February 1, 2013.

In addition to the geographical distribution, the VHA has further delineated the types of scope categories based on the disease state and patient population most commonly managed by the CPS at each location. Figure 27.2 is a graphical representation of the most common ($n > 60$) disease states managed by the CPS in the VA as of February 1, 2013. As one may have predicted the most commonly managed individual, disease states are those encountered in the primary care setting: anticoagulation, lipids, diabetes, and hypertension. However, there is surprising diversity of other disease states and medications that pharmacists managed throughout the country.

More recently, the duties assigned to these individual pharmacist clinicians has grown, and increasingly the scopes for these pharmacists have migrated away from limited, disease-specific scopes of practice in primary care (e.g., hypertension) toward broader or "global" SOP. This allows the pharmacist to treat and manage multiple disease states, including many of the ones depicted in Figure 27.2. There has been an increased use of a "global" SOP for pharmacists working in primary care from 207 pharmacists in 2011 to 1021 pharmacists in February 2013 (an 80% increase). Figure 27.3 represents the change in the number of pharmacists working under a SOP from July 2011 until February 1, 2013. This spectacular 40% growth is yet another validation that the health-care team is changing within the VHA to recognize the value and role of the pharmacist in medication and disease management as a nonphysician provider is well received by the health-care system.

Knowing the number of pharmacists with a SOP in a given disease state does not (alone) provide an adequate picture of how pharmacists are utilized system-wide. To acquire a more comprehensive picture of these additional metrics, one must include the percentage of time pharmacists work in their practice using their SOP that they utilize. These data show that over half

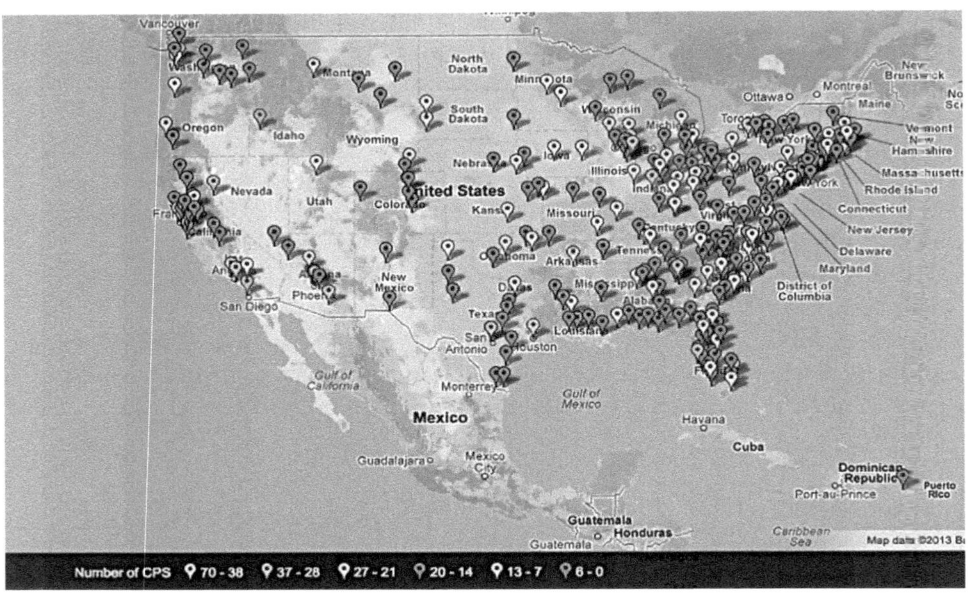

Figure 27.3 Geographic distribution of Veterans Health Administration pharmacists with a scope of practice.

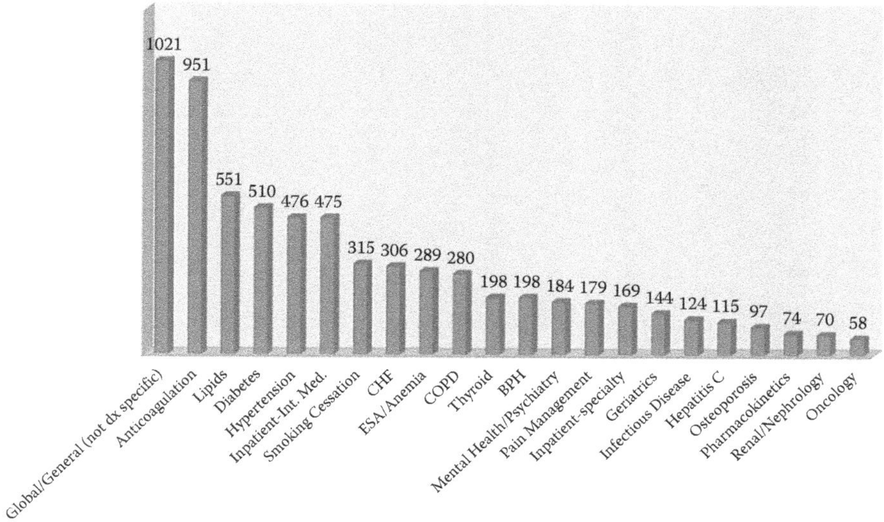

Figure 27.4 Veterans Health Administration pharmacist scope of practice by disease state.

of the pharmacists with a SOP spend 75%–100% of their time working under their scope as the medication use expert and performing comprehensive medication management for the health-care team and its patients, as represented in Figure 27.4.

In addition to metrics for disease state management and measurements of success, PBM sought to better understand and describe the credentials of pharmacists with a SOP in the VA to include qualifications such as PharmD degree, postgraduate residency training, and board certification. This information will be useful to assess differences in how the pharmacist is utilized within the teams (primary care vs. specialty care) and whether or not there are differences in outcomes achieved by these individuals. As depicted in Figure 27.5, the pharmacist workforce with a SOP is highly trained with over 88% having a PharmD degree, 61% resident trained, 33% board certified, and an impressive 72% with an aggregate of residency and/or certification.

Figure 27.6 outlines the demographic distribution of pharmacists with a SOP relative to their education, training, and certification.

Pharmacy Informatics

Pharmacy informatics is part of VHA's goals in the use of information technology to implement best practice, support team-based care coordination, clinical decision making, medical device integration, and ancillary service integration (Figure 27.7).

In 1989, VA PBM program office developed the largest open source electronic drug file. The VA National Drug File (NDF)/Pharmacy Product System (PPS) combines medication information and terminologies with clinical knowledge systems for medication prescribing and ordering within its VistA EHR. Key features of the system are nationally standardized and coded medication terms, formulary status, restricted use status, drug classifications, and links to drug interactions and dosage knowledge systems and improvement of interoperability for data sharing. The NDF/PPS contains 22,000 medication and supply names. PPS data support patient safety and formulary management in the VA and the Indian Health System. The contained enterprise

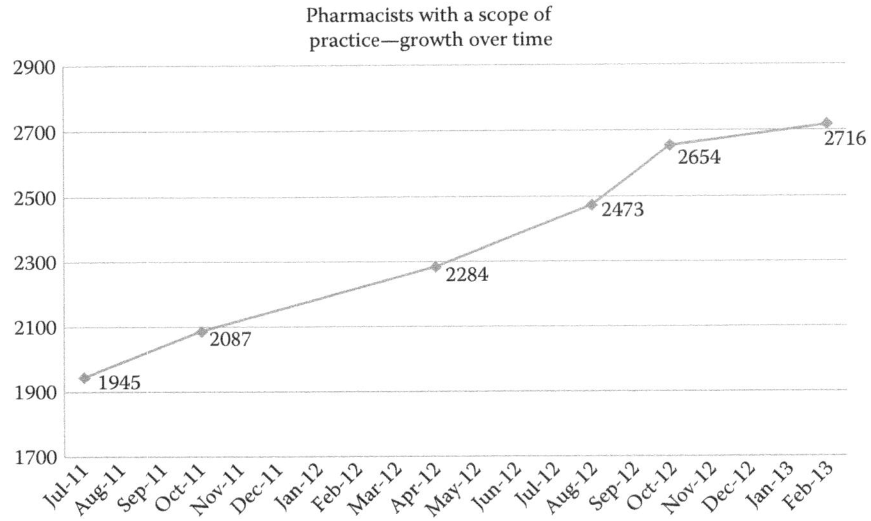

Figure 27.5 Growth of Veterans Health Administration pharmacist scope of practice.

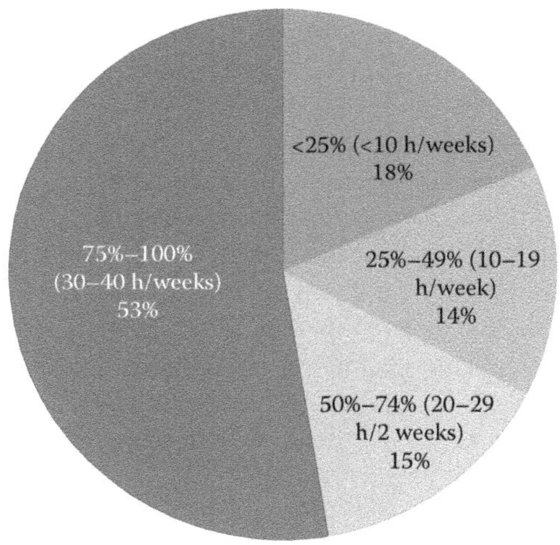

Figure 27.6 Percentage of time Veterans Health Administration pharmacists practice under their scope of practice.

product list is available to health-care systems such as the National Library of Medicine where terminologies are matched to RxNorm.

Pharmacy VistA contains multiple information systems for medication order fulfillment and dispensing, formulary management, inventory, analytics, and reporting. The pharmacy suite of applications provides functionality to allow pharmacy to manage medications from ward stock to dispensing directly to our veterans, from receiving medication orders from providers and dispensing to the nurse for medication administration. Our software allows us to manage the drug nomenclature and inventory as well as meet all Drug Enforcement Administration (DEA)

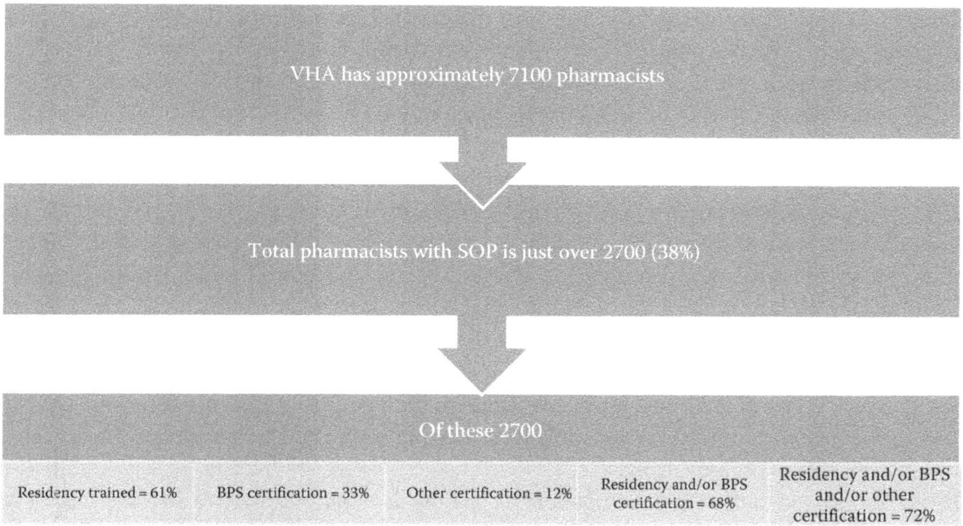

Figure 27.7 Credentials of Veterans Health Administration pharmacists with a scope of practice.

requirements for e-prescribing of controlled substances and fulfillment. The PBM has national reporting services to monitor all pharmacy dispensing activity as well as allowing local documentation of interventions to improve medication therapy. The CMOP application allows a centralized distribution with multiple fulfillment centers to dispense outpatient prescriptions, freeing up workload and resources at the local medical centers. VAMCs utilize numerous commercially available dispensing and medication storage systems internal to the VA pharmacy as well as in the clinic and direct patient care environments that interface with the VistA and nursing informatics systems.

The PBM continues to modernize its pharmacy system program and provides business owner oversight of pharmacy development activities to improve and transform health care through information technology. The primary initiative has been to modernize to its Pharmacy VistA system component of VA's EHR. One project in this effort is the VA Medication Order Check Healthcare Application (MOCHA). This application provides clinical decision support for drug interactions and excessive dosing, including access to drug interaction monographs, and initially became operational across all VAMCs for drug interaction decision support in 2012. VHA Product Effectiveness Program Office indicated that 48% of providers and 58% of pharmacists were satisfied with the MOCHA. The percentages of those who believed that MOCHA improves patient safety are 61% of the providers and 71% of the pharmacists. Continued development to enhance the order check system to improve efficiency and patient safety is underway. Prescribers will receive an alert when the maximum single dosage of a medication is exceeded. The MOCHA generates over 1000 order checks per site per day to help prevent ADEs due to incorrect drug dosage, unnecessary therapeutic duplication, and potential drug–drug interactions.

When fully deployed, it is expected that ADEs and overdoses will be reduced by approximately 10%. MOCHA enhancements were released to improve order check alerts and reduce alert fatigue.

One aspect of the VA medication safety system is its BCMA system. In 1994, the Colmery-O'Neil VA Medical Center in Topeka, Kansas, piloted the use of bar codes to match patients positively with their medications. All dispensed drugs carry bar codes, and nurses scan these at the bedside, along with the bar code on the patient's wristband, to ensure the correct patient receives the correct medication at the correct administration time. In 2000, senior VA leadership demonstrated its commitment to this patient safety technology by implementing BCMA throughout all inpatient VA hospitals. Studies demonstrate that the BCMA system reduces medication errors to one-third of preimplementation levels. The technology relies on computerized medication carts and VA-developed software. This system is available in inpatient care areas and in outpatient clinics. The system significantly reduces medication errors and has been adopted by the Department of Indian Health Services was described as "Patient Safety and Usability, Experiences in the U.S. Department of Veterans Affairs."[32]

The VA health data repository (HDR) creates a true longitudinal health-care record including data from VA and non-VA sources, supporting research and population analyses, improving data quality and security, and facilitating patient access to data and health administration. The VA system has the ability to provide interoperable data sharing with the Department of Defense (DoD) and other health-care organizations.

The consolidated health data repository (CHDR) is a joint initiative between the VA and DoD that enables the bidirectional exchange of computable allergy and pharmacy data between the DoD clinical data repository (CDR) and the VA HDR for over two million veterans and their families who use health-care services from both the VA and DoD. The CHDR acronym was derived by combining the VA and DoD repository acronyms (CDR/HDR) since CHDR provides the link for exchanging data when the DoD or VA sets a patient's active dual consumer (ADC) status to "active." ADC patients are the portion of the dual treatable population that has been treated by both DoD and VA medical facilities. The CHDR uses matching traits (social security number, date of birth, first name, and last name) to identify and mark patients as ADC. The automated process targets 1200 new ADC patient activations per day to the system.

The CHDR exchanges computable data that supports drug–drug and drug–allergy interagency warnings and alerts. In addition, CHDR reduces costs by eliminating duplicate tests ordered for the veteran. The CHDR is an important step forward toward "interoperability" and represents an alternative to "view-only" data.

VA obtained regulatory permission to query from and transmit data to state prescription drug monitoring programs in February 2013. Testing to perform daily automated transmissions has been successful in four states. It is anticipated that the system will be available at all VAMCs by August 2014.

The ePharmacy claims system allows the VA to dispense outpatient medications and bill non-VA payers for those prescriptions. Electronic Prescribing of Controlled Substances (EPCS) is another VA advancement. At this time, the VA is one of a few organizations approved by DEA for EPCS. This system reduces paper processing of prescriptions and improves the ability to monitor prescribing and dispensing of controlled substances.

For the future, the VA has been developing its VistA Evolution Program that is a joint program between the VHA and the VA Office of Information and Technology.

The VA recently released several health-care apps for its operating systems. The apps address various health issues that veterans may face, including difficulty sleeping, PTSD, psychological first aid and smoking cessation. In the future, the VistA Evolution Program will deliver a next-generation VistA product entitled VistA-4. VistA-4 will provide the tools necessary for the VA to maintain its track record as a highly acclaimed health-care technology. Upon implementation of VistA-4, the VA will be well positioned to interoperate with the DoD and other health-care partners using modern, flexible technologies and standards. This enhances VA efforts to improve the health status of veterans through the delivery of a longitudinal integrated health record that supports the continuum of care.

The VA is transforming its human capital to meet the goals of health-care reform through technology. The VHA PBM uses information technology to provide education and training for its workforce through numerous Internet and intranet sites. There is also a partnership with DoD, Indian Health Services, and affiliated universities to provide access to education through Moodle-based websites.[33] *Moodle*, viz., the modular object-oriented dynamic learning environment, is a learning management system or e-learning platform that serves educators and learners.

The VA maintains its internal web-based education system, My VeHu (VA eHealth University), which provides online education and training. Each year VHA PBM trains an average of 200 VA employees through its online interactive informatics training in four areas of informatics and analytics.

Conclusion

The VA is the second largest federal executive department with a workforce over 327,000 employees. VA operates the largest integrated health-care delivery system in America and manages its services and benefits through a nationwide network of its medical centers, veteran centers, CBOCs, and various regional health-care centers that provide care to veterans. The VA provides a broad range of primary care, specialized care, and related medical and social support services. The VA is also the nation's largest integrated provider of health-care education and training for physician residents, pharmacy residents, and other health-care trainees. The VA advances medical research and development in areas that most directly address the diseases and conditions that affect veterans and eligible beneficiaries. The VA administers compensation benefits, pension benefits, fiduciary services, education benefits, vocational rehabilitation and employment services, transition services, and home loan and life insurance programs. Programs are administered by its three major line organizations: Veterans Health Administration, Veterans Benefits Administration, and National Cemetery Administration. The VA is the second largest federal department. The PBM services provide leadership for pharmacy activities in the VHA and advice and support regarding pharmacy services to a wide variety of stakeholders, veterans, VA leadership, VAMCs, and clinical staff across the system. Through its major pharmacy program offices, the PBM works to enhance the clinical outcomes from medication use and improve the health of veteran patients through the appropriate use of pharmaceuticals.

List of Acronyms

ADC	Active dual consumer
ADE	Adverse drug event
BCMA	Bar Code Medication Administration
CDR	Clinical data repository
CHDR	Consolidated health data repository
CMOP	Consolidated mail outpatient pharmacy
CPRS	Computerized Patient Record System
DEA	Drug Enforcement Administration
DoD	Department of Defense
DPPM	Drug Product and Pharmaceutical Management

EHR	Electronic health record
EMR	Electronic medical record
EPCS	Electronic Prescribing of Controlled Substances
GAO	Government Accountability Office
HDR	Health data repository
IOM	Institute of Medicine
MOCHA	Medication Order Check Healthcare Application
MUET	Medication utilization evaluation tracker
My VeHu	VA eHealth University
NCA	National Cemetery Administration
NDF	National Drug File
NME	New molecular entities
OIT	Office of Information and Technology
P&T committee	Pharmacy and therapeutics committee
PBM	Pharmacy Benefits Management Services
PFA	Psychological first aid
PPS	Pharmacy Product System
PTSD	Posttraumatic stress disorder
RCRA	Resource Conservation and Recovery Act
SOP	Scope of practice
USP	United States Pharmacopeia
VA MAP	Department of Veterans Affairs Medical Advisory Panel
VA MedSafe	VA Center for Medication Safety
VA	Department of Veterans Affairs
VAADERS	VA Adverse Drug Event Reporting System
VANF	Department of Veterans Affairs National Formulary
VBA	Veterans Benefits Administration
VHA	Veterans Health Administration
VISN	Veterans Integrated Service Networks
VistA	Veterans Health Information Systems and Technology Architecture
VPE	VISN Pharmacist Executive
WOC	Without compensation

Acknowledgments

Vaiyapuri Subramaniam, PharmD, MS; Michael Valentino, RPh, MHSA; Anthony Morreale, PharmD, MBA; Vincent Calabrese, PharmD; Francesca Cunningham, PharmD; Lynn Sanders, PharmD; Lori Golterman, PharmD; Julie Groppi, PharmD; Heather Ourth, PharmD; Kenneth Siehr, RPh, MPA; Carolyn Stephens, PharmD, MBA; and Timothy Stroup, RPh, BS Pharm are gratefully acknowledged for contributing toward the development of this chapter.

References

1. Department of Veterans Affairs Home Page. Facts about the Department of Veterans Affairs. Washington, DC. Accessed January 12, 2016. http://www.va.gov/opa/publications/factsheets.asp.
2. Department of Veterans Affairs. Office of the Actuary. Vet Data. Washington, DC. Accessed January 12, 2016. http://www.va.gov/vetdata/Veteran_Population.asp.

3. Department of Veterans Affairs. MyHealth*e*Vet. Washington, DC. Accessed January 12, 2016. www.myHealth.va.gov.
4. Department of Veterans Affairs Home Page. Pharmacy benefits management services. 2013. Washington, DC. Accessed January 12, 2016. http://www.pbm.va.gov/PBM/.
5. Public Law 104-262—Veterans Health Care Eligibility Reform Act of 1996. Accessed March 1, 2014. http://www.govtrack.us/congress/bills/104.
6. Institute of Medicine. Description and analysis of the VA National Formulary. National Academy of Sciences, Washington, DC. June 2000. http://www.nap.edu/catalog/9879/description-and-analysis-of-the-va-national-formulary.
7. General Accounting Office. VA drug formulary: Better oversight is required, but veterans are getting needed drugs (GAO-01-183). January 2001. Accessed March 7, 2014. http://www.gao.gov/new.items/d01183.pdf.
8. General Accounting Office. VA Health Care: VA's management of drugs on its National Formulary (GAO/HEHS-00-34). 1999. Washington, DC. Accessed March 7, 2014. http://www.gao.gov/archive/2000/he00034.pdf.
9. Lavigne JE, Au A, Jiang R, Wang Y, Good CB, Glassman P, Cunningham FE. Utilization of prescription drugs with warnings of suicidal thoughts and behaviors in the USA and US Department of Veterans Affairs. *J Pharm Health Serv Res.* 2012;3(3):157–163.
10. Burk M, Moore V, Glassman PA, Good CB, Emmendorfer T, Leadholm TC, Cunningham FE. Medication-use evaluation with a Web application. *Am J Health Syst Pharm.* 2013;70:2226–2234.
11. Stroupe K, Smith B, Hogan T, St. Andre J, Gellad W, Weiner S, Lee T et al. Medication acquisition across systems of care and patient-provider communication among older veterans. *Am J Health Syst Pharm.* May 2013;70(9):804–813.
12. Aspinall SA, Zhao X, Good CB, Stone RA, Smith KJ, Cunningham FE. FDA warning and removal of Rosiglitazone from VA National Formulary. *Am J Manag Care.* 2013;19(9):748–758.
13. Robb MA, Racoosin JA, Worrall C, Chapman S, Coster T, Cunningham FE. Active surveillance of post market medical product safety in the Federal Partners' Collaboration. *Med Care.* November 2012;50(11):948–953.
14. Aspinall SL, Cunningham FE, Zhao X, Boresi JS, Tonnu-Mihara IQ, Smith KJ, Stone RA, Good CB, ESA Clinic Study Group. Impact of erythropoiesis-stimulating agents clinics for patients with non-dialysis-dependent CKD. *Am J Kidney Dis.* September 2012;60(3):371–379. Epub May 26, 2012.
15. Aspinall SL, Good CB, Cunningham FE. Glycemic control was unchanged in Veterans Health Administration patients converted from glyburide to glipizide. *J Manag Care Pharm.* January–February 2012;18(1):73.
16. Kales HC, Kim HM, Zivin K, Valenstein M, Seyfried LS, Chiang C, Cunningham F, Schneider LS, Blow FC. Risk of mortality among individual antipsychotics in patients with dementia. *Am J Psychiatry.* January 2012;169(1):71–79. Epub October 31, 2011.
17. Kales HC, Zivin K, Kim HM, Valenstein M, Chiang C, Ignacio R, Ganoczy D, Cunningham FE, Schneider LS, Blow FC. Trends in antipsychotic use in dementia 1999–2007. *Arch Gen Psychiatry.* 2011;68(2):190–197.
18. Aspinall SL, Smith KJ, Cunningham FE, Good CB. Incremental cost-effectiveness of various monthly doses of vardenafil. *Value Health.* 2011;14(1):97–101.
19. Maciejewski M, Bryson C, Perkins M, Blough DK, Cunningham FE, Fortney JC, Krein SL, Stroupe KT, Sharp ND, Liu C. Increasing copayments and adherence to diabetes, hypertension, and hyperlipidemic medications. *Am J Manag Care.* 2010;16(1):e20–e34.
20. Hanlon JT, Wang X, Good CB, Rossi MI, Stone RA, Semla TP, Cunningham FE, Handler SM. Racial differences in medication use among older long stay veteran nursing home care unit patients. *Consult Pharm.* 2009;24:439–436.
21. Aspinall SL, Banthin J, Good CB, Miller E, Cunningham F. VA Pharmacy users: How they differ from other veterans. *Am J Manag Care.* 2009;15(10):701–708.
22. Aspinall SL, Good CB, Jiang R, McCarren M, Dong D, Cunningham FE. Severe dysglycemias with the fluoroquinolones: A class effect? *Clin Infect Dis.* 2009;49:402–408.

23. Pugh MJ, Rosen AK, Montez-Rath M, Amuman ME, Fincke BG, Burk M, Bierman A, Cunningham FE, Mortensen EM, Berlowitz DR. Potentially inappropriate prescribing for the elderly: Effects of geriatric care at the patient and health care system level. *Med Care.* 2008;46:167–173.
24. Iqbal SU, Cunningham F, Lee A, Miller DR, Li NC, Cheung R, Kazis L. Persistence with hepatitis C therapy in the Department of Veterans Affairs. *J Clin Pharm Ther.* June 2008;33(3):251–261.
25. Johnson C, Carlson R, Tucker C, Willette C. Using BCMA software to improve patient safety in Veterans Administration Medical Centers. *J Healthc Inf Manag.* 2002;16(1):46–51.
26. The United States Pharmacopeia Convention (USPC). Chapters 797 and 795: Pharmaceutical compounding-sterile preparations (<797>). Pharmaceutical compounding—Nonsterile preparations (⟨795⟩). In: *The United States Pharmacopeia*, 35th ed. and *The National Formulary*, 30th ed. Rockville, MD: USPC; 2013.
27. Subramaniam V, Coggins P, Dang C, Vargas J. USP 797 Monitoring guidelines: Standards for pharmacy practice. *Pharm Pract News.* 2011;38(4):22–23.
28. Lutz E, Carvalho M, Subramaniam V, Davidson G, Pauletti G, Ashworth L, Llambi, F. The role of compounding in closing therapeutic gaps. *Int J Pharm Compd.* 2014;18:1, 6–12.
29. Subramaniam V, Coggins P, Wilkes V, Sehgal S, Dhokai M. Pharmacy design guidance—Update on compliance with USP 797 Standards. May 2008. Accessed March 2, 2014. http://www.pbm.va.gov/PBM/linksotherresources/docs/VAVHAUSP797PharmacyDesignGuidance EnvironmentalandArchitecturalCleanroomDesignDocumentMay2008.doc.
30. Subramaniam V, Huynh T, Jalundhwala Y. Hazardous drugs—Maintaining standards for safe pharmacy practice. *Pharm Pract News.* 2010;37(12):4–6.
31. Subramaniam V, Chasler J. Waste management strategies every pharmacist should know: Tips for disposal of unused and expired medications. *Pharm Pract News.* 2011;38(12):30–33.
32. Purcell JA. Department of Veterans Affairs. Patient safety and usability, experiences in the U.S. Department of Veterans Affairs. *User Experience.* 2007;6(4). Retrieved from http://uxpamagazine.org/patient_safety_usability/. Accessed January 12, 2016.
33. VA Healthcare. Moodle-Based Website. Accessed March 7, 2014. http://vapharmacytraining.remote-learner.net.

Chapter 28

Public Health Service

Robert E. Pittman

Contents

Improving the health of the nation has been the central mission of the U.S. Public Health Service (PHS) for over 200 years. As the health needs of the nation changed, the priorities and activities of the PHS changed to meet those needs. Today, PHS health-care providers including pharmacists provide service in almost all federal health agencies.

U.S. Marine Hospital Service (1798–1902)

The federal government's involvement in public health began soon after the founding of the United States. Much of the commerce of our new nation made its way by ship between ports located along the seacoasts and rivers. Sailors who became sick or injured were often dropped off at the next available town or city. In many cases, these communities did not have the facilities or funding necessary to take care of the sick or injured sailors. Sailors with communicable diseases, such as yellow fever or smallpox, posed a great risk to communities that were unable to provide appropriate care for these patients. To provide care for sick and injured sailors, the Congress passed and

President John Adams signed an act, in 1798, creating Marine Hospital Service (MHS) (which would become the U.S. Public Health Service [PHS] in 1912).[1]

To allow the new MHS to begin to meet the needs of sailors, the Treasury Department imposed a monthly fee on sailor's pay to go into a marine hospital fund. These funds, collected and administered locally, allowed ports to provide some health-care services to sick and injured merchant sailors and Navy officers, sailors, and marines. These funds were used to contract space in local hospitals and construct new hospitals. By 1802, hospitals were operating in Castle Island (in Boston Harbor), in Charleston (a section of Boston), Washington Point (near Norfolk), Newport, and Charlestown (Maryland). Navy personnel received services at the marine hospitals until 1818 when the Navy Hospital Fund was established. As the nation continued to grow, additional hospitals were added to the system.[2]

By the end of the civil war, the marine hospital system had fallen into disrepair. Of the 31 hospitals built since 1800, only 9 were still in operation. In 1870, legislation changed the MHS from a locally managed system to a centrally managed system with a supervising surgeon to lead the MHS. This position would later become the supervising surgeon general and then surgeon general of the United States. In 1871, John Maynard Woodworth, a physician and pharmacist,[3] was appointed as the first supervising surgeon. Dr. Woodworth, who had served in the Union Army during the Civil War, reorganized the MHS improving contract and outpatient care and closing poor facilities. He also instituted examinations for all applicants, and providers were hired by the MHS rather than by the local facilities. The newly reorganized MHS grew rapidly throughout the 1870s. By the mid-1870s, one hundred ports provided care to sailors at either private, municipal, or MHS hospitals.[4]

Pharmacists (also known as stewards) had key responsibilities in the newly reorganized MHS. Procurement and distribution of medications and medical supplies was centralized, and new regulations in 1879 required the medical purveyor (head of the purveying division) to be a pharmacist. In 1879, Dr. Oscar Oldberg was the first pharmacist appointed to this position. Pharmacists serving at the MHS hospitals were also entrusted with great responsibility. While the pharmacist reported to the medical officer in charge, the pharmacist was responsible for most of the administrative duties required to run the hospital.[5]

The role of the MHS was to change in the late 1870s. Up until the development of a centrally controlled MHS, no national health program existed in the United States. State health departments were just starting and the American Public Health Association was created (in 1872). While some leaders advocated for a federal government role in public health since epidemics did not recognize state boarders, many states believed that public health activities should remain at the state and local level. This discussion changed with a cholera epidemic in 1877 and two major yellow fever epidemics in 1877 and 1878.[6] The Quarantine Act of 1878 gave MHS the authority to regulate ships with contagious disease on board or vessels coming from ports where contagious disease existed.[7] The quarantine system was directed largely at yellow fever, smallpox, and cholera. Ships entering port would be boarded and inspected to assure that passengers and crew did not bring in disease. Ships from ports known to be infected were quarantined until the disease incubation period had passed.[8] While all quarantine stations had a MHS physician in charge, only a few of the larger stations had a pharmacist. Early pharmacists in the quarantine service included E.J. Thurston (in 1903) in Gulf Quarantine, Mississippi; M.R. Mason (in 1904) at San Francisco, California; John Archenbach (in 1904) at Port Townsend, Washington; L.C. Spangler (in 1904) at Savannah, Georgia; C.H. Bierman (in 1904) at Tampa Bay, Florida; and W.L. Sterns (in 1905) at Santa Rosa, Florida.[9] A new national quarantine act in 1893 required ships to have both a bill of health signed by a U.S. consul and a certificate from a U.S. quarantine officer before they could land cargo or passengers in the United States. The act also allowed the Secretary of the Treasury to take over quarantine buildings states did not want. These measures, along with mosquito killing campaigns when yellow fever outbreaks occurred, greatly reduced outbreaks of disease. The last large yellow fever outbreak in the United States occurred in New Orleans in 1905.[10]

In 1887, Dr. Joseph Kinyoun established the first bacteriological laboratory in the United States at the MHS hospital in Staten Island, New York, to research infectious diseases. This Hygienic Laboratory (the predecessor of the National Institutes of Health [NIH]) was moved to the headquarters of the MHS in Washington, DC, in 1891. The laboratory continued to grow and moved into a new building in 1904.[11] In August 1904, the first pharmacist, Frank J. Herty, joined the staff at the Hygienic Laboratory.[12]

President Grover Cleveland signed an act creating the Commissioned Corps of the MHS in 1889. The law specified that the Corps was to be established along military lines. Only physicians were allowed to be commissioned at that time. Other employees, including pharmacists, continued to serve as civilian employees.[13]

In 1898, with the outbreak of the Spanish–American War, the MHS was asked to provide health-care and quarantine services for the U.S. military. MHS hospitals were made available to sick and wounded troops returning from the war. The MHS was also assigned the task of preventing the spread of yellow fever by troops returning from Cuba and Puerto Rico. Commissioned Corps physicians were assigned to ports in both countries and to ships returning troops back to the United States.[14] Over 30,000 returning troops were inspected and quarantined by MHS physicians at quarantine stations in Florida and New York before returning home.[15]

Concern about the large numbers of immigrants arriving in the United States, the potential for these immigrants to bring in disease, and the number of immigrants becoming public charges due to physical disabilities led to changes in immigration law in 1891. The new law required MHS physicians to complete a mandatory health inspection of all immigrants. MHS doctors looked for leprosy, ringworm, trachoma, smallpox, plague, typhus, cholera, and yellow fever. They were also screened for disabilities that could lead to the immigrant becoming a public charge. This examination process became critical when a cholera epidemic in Asia and Europe led to an estimated 300,000 deaths in Russia and 80,000 deaths in Persia.[16] Approximately 50 U.S. ports of entry were designated for immigrants. Two of the best known immigration ports were Angel Island near San Francisco and the largest inspection center for immigrants, Ellis Island in New York Harbor. Through the early 1900s, Ellis Island was the only immigration station large enough to require MHS pharmacists. The pharmacists assigned to Ellis Island in the early 1900s were W.F. MacDowell (in 1902) and George Neves (in 1904). Approximately 1% of the 20 million immigrants passing through Ellis Island between 1892 and 1924 were denied entry to the United States.[17]

U.S. Public Health and Marine Hospital Service (1902–1912)

In recognition of the expanded mission of the MHS, the Congress passed legislation in 1902 changing the name of the MHS to Public Health and Marine Hospital Service (PHMHS). The act changed the title of the supervising surgeon general to that of surgeon general. The law defined administrative divisions for the PHMHS, including marine hospitals and relief, domestic quarantine, foreign and insular quarantine, scientific research, sanitary reports and statistics, and personnel and accounts. The law also expanded the number of divisions in the Hygienic Laboratory to include bacteriology and pathology, pharmacology, chemistry, and zoology. The law also authorized the surgeon general to collect standardized statistics from state and territorial health officer on mortality and morbidity.[18]

In July 1902, the Congress expanded the role of the Hygienic Laboratory through the Biologics Control Act. Prior to this time, there were no national controls over the manufacturing of vaccines, serum, and antitoxins. Tragedies such as the deaths of 13 children in St. Louis in 1901, as a result of receiving tetanus-contaminated diphtheria antitoxin, demonstrated the need for national oversight in the manufacture of biologics. The Act mandated that vaccine producers be licensed by the Secretary of the Treasury, that manufacturing facilities be inspected, and that the production process be supervised by qualified personnel and provided labeling requirements for biologic products. Regulatory authority over biologics was further enhanced with the passage of the Food, Drug, and Cosmetics Act in 1938.[19]

While highly infectious diseases such as smallpox received the greatest priority, other infectious diseases were also monitored by PHMHS. In 1901, a prevalence report showed 278 cases of leprosy (Hansen's disease) in the United States with most cases being identified in immigrant communities. It had also been noted by MHS officers that leprosy had spread throughout the Hawaiian Islands. Kalawao on the Makanalua Peninsula of the island of Molokai had been used as a leprosy colony since the 1860s. In 1905, the Congress appropriated funds for a hospital and laboratory on the island of Molokai in Hawaii. The PHMHS station opened in March 1906 with nine patients. PHMHS physicians spent little time at the Kalawao station. Instead they conducted experiments and research at the PHMHS station at Kalihi (close to Honolulu). Pharmacist Frank Leighton Gibson served as the onsite administrator at the hospital in Molokai from 1906 to 1913. The station at Molokai closed a few years later, and PHMHS staff continued their leprosy research at Kalihi.[20] The Congress funded a home for lepers in 1917. The home and a leprosarium opened in 1921 in Carville, Louisiana. The Gillis W. Long Hansen's Disease Center became a world famous center for research, treatment, rehabilitation, and training on Hansen's disease. The first major breakthrough in the treatment of Hansen's disease was developed by Dr. Guy Faget using sodium glucosulfone. Results of his study were published in 1943.[21]

U.S. Public Health Service (1912–2014)

Legislation in 1912 changed the name of the PHMHS to the U.S. PHS. The legislation added broad authority to conduct research and field investigations into public health problems, including infectious and noninfectious diseases, and how disease is spread. The law recognized the importance of poor sanitation, sewage, and water pollution as potential causes of disease and authorized PHS to conduct research and investigation into these areas.[22] In 1913, the Sundry Civil Appropriations Act provided $(USD)200,000 for field investigations, including earmarks for pellagra and trachoma campaigns. Field investigations were also carried out on typhus, hookworm, and water pollution on the Ohio River.[23]

In 1914, the Congress authorized the Secretary of the Treasury to detail PHS physicians and other personnel as needed to revenue cutters (predecessor to the coast guard) as needed and that those cutters with medical personnel aboard to provide medical care to American ships involved in deep sea fishing. While Revenue Cutter Service personnel had been able to receive care at PHS hospitals since 1875, the Act greatly expanded the availability of medical services. In 1915, the Congress established the U.S. Coast Guard formed from the Revenue Cutter Service (formerly the Revenue Marine Service, created in 1790) and the U.S. Life-Saving Service (formed in 1878).[24]

World War I was a time of growth and change for the PHS. In April 1917, President Woodrow Wilson issued an executive order making the PHS part of the military forces of the United States. The order further allowed PHS officers and employees to be detailed to the Army or Navy and opened PHS hospitals and stations to care for sick and wounded sailors and soldiers. There was a great need for PHS officers and employees to prevent and contain disease outbreaks around hastily constructed military training camps. Concern about possible outbreaks of typhoid fever, malaria, and communicable diseases around military bases leads PHS officers and employees to make mosquito control, waste disposal, clean water, clean milk, and controlling venereal disease as their top priorities. To meet the need for additional staffing and resources, the Congress increased PHS funding from $(USD)3 million in 1917 to $(USD)50 million in 1918. Nonofficer personnel increased from approximately 3,000 to 23,000 employees. Due to the war, it was difficult to find additional qualified physicians for the regular corps of the PHS Commissioned Corps. Surgeon General Rupert Blue asked the Congress for the creation of a reserve corps to bring in additional medical officers. Unfortunately, the PHS Reserve Corps legislation did not become law until October 1918. While it came too late to help in the war effort, it did for the first time authorize nonphysicians to serve in the PHS, including dentists, pharmacists, and engineers.[25]

In September 1918, the Spanish influenza pandemic reached New England. In a desire to get information about the Spanish influenza out to the public as quickly as possible, the PHS printed and distributed six million pamphlets detailing what was known about the influenza and methods that might be effective in preventing the spread of the disease. The PHS also sent out a warning article to 10,000 newspapers.[26] Finding additional physicians and nurses to serve during the epidemic proved to be difficult. Appeals to the American Medical Association, the Volunteer Medical Service Corps, and the American Red Cross assisted in this recruitment effort. Between October 1918 and June 1919, the PHS employed 1085 physicians and 703 nurses and nurse aides to provide care to influenza patients. In the last 3 months of 1918, over 4.1 million cases of influenza and pneumonia were reported in the United States. The Census Bureau estimated that over 500,000 influenza deaths occurred in the continental United States between 1918 and 1919.[27]

At the end of World War I, the United States needed to provide compensation for disabilities, medical care and treatment, and reeducation to disabled veterans. In March 1919, the Congress passed a law designating the Bureau of War Risk Insurance in the Treasury Department as the lead for these activities. The Bureau of War Risk Insurance did not have medical or vocational agencies. The medical function was assigned to the PHS, and the vocational training was assigned to an independent federal organization, the Federal Board for Vocational Education. The monumental task of providing health care to disabled veterans was assigned to the PHS Division of Marine Hospitals and Relief (later became the PHS Hospital Division).[28] The need for additional hospitals was accomplished through leasing suitable buildings and converting them to hospitals, taking over buildings no longer needed by other federal agencies, and contracting with civilian hospitals. By the end of June 1919, PHS had added an additional 10 large hospitals and treated over 93,000 patients.[29] One year later, the surgeon general reported that in the fiscal year ending June 1920, the PHS had added an additional 26 hospitals (36 total since March 1919) and served 87,000 hospitalized veterans. The desire to consolidate all veterans' services under one organization leads to the creation of the U.S. Veterans Bureau (VB) (eventually becoming the Department of Veterans Affairs) in August 1921. In April 1922, the president, through the executive order, transferred 57 hospitals, 13,000 patients, 900 physicians and dentists (most were reserve officers), and 1400 nurses from PHS to the U.S. VB.[30]

In November 1921, the Snyder Act was passed by the Congress. It authorized appropriations and expenditures for the administration of Indian affairs for a variety of purposes, including conservation of health. Funding for the Bureau of Indian Affairs and recruitment of competent health professionals were both issues of concern.[31] An agreement between the Secretary of Interior and the Secretary of the Treasury leads to the detail, in March 1926, of physician Marshall C. Guthrie to the Office of Indian Affairs in Washington, DC. Dr. Guthrie served as Director of Health of the Bureau of Indian Affairs. Other PHS officers served on his staff, and several physicians eventually served as medical supervisors for the field service.[32] The first pharmacist assigned to the Bureau of Indian Affairs was Edwin M. Holt on July 18, 1931.[33] Officers continued to be assigned to the Bureau of Indian Affairs until 1955 when all Indian health programs were transferred to the new Division of Indian Health (DIH) in the PHS.

While inspection, quarantine, and fumigation activities for passenger and cargo ships were well established in the United States, an increase in international air travel raised concerns about the need for inspection of international flights. The Air Commerce Act of 1926, along with concerns about yellow fever in some countries led to the beginning of quarantine and immigration inspection of international aircraft by the PHS officers in 1927. PHS conducted studies on insect survival on airline flights and on fumigation agents and application methods. An international agreement for sanitary control of aircraft especially related to plague, cholera, yellow fever, and typhus was signed at the International Sanitary Convention for Aerial Navigation in The Hague in 1933.[34]

The problem of narcotic addiction had long been recognized in the United States. In 1929, legislation mandated the construction of two narcotic facilities to treat and study narcotic addiction. The legislation created a PHS Narcotics Division (which would become the National Institute of Mental Health in 1946) to administer the two hospitals, conduct research into addiction and treatment, and disseminate information on the best treatments and research.[35] While most of the patients would be federal prisoners who were drug addicts, others were probationers from courts who voluntarily submitted for treatment, and ordinary citizens seeking treatment. The first facility, the United States Narcotic Farm, opened in 1935 in Lexington, Kentucky. Dr. Lawrence Kolb, a PHS psychiatrist who had begun studying drug addiction at the Hygienic Laboratory in 1923, was selected to be the director of the first narcotic farm.[36] Clarence H. Bierman helped open the facility as its first pharmacist.[37] The second narcotic farm opened in Fort Worth, Texas, in 1938.

In 1930, two bills were passed by the Congress and signed by President Hoover. The Parker Act authorized dentists, pharmacists, sanitary engineers, and Hygienic Laboratory scientists (at the level of division director) to be commissioned into the regular corps of the PHS.[38] The first two pharmacists commissioned into the regular corps of the PHS, on July 23, 1930, were Edgar B. Scott assigned to the Hospital Division in Washington, DC, and Edwin M. Holt assigned to the Division of Marine Hospitals and Relief in Washington, DC. Scott and Holt had worked as civilian employees for PHS since 1896 and 1900, respectively.[39] The Parker Act also tied the pay for commissioned officers to that of the Army and authorized the surgeon general to assign personnel to other agencies. The other law, the Ransdell Act, changed the name of the Hygienic Laboratory to National Institute of Health (NIH), provided funding for additional physical space, and established a fellowship and private endowment program.[38]

A law, in 1930, created the Federal Bureau of Prisons (BOP) within the Department of Justice. Since the founding of the United States individuals found guilty of federal offenses were held in local or state prisons. The Three Prison Act of 1891 began the process of creating the federal prison system. The first penitentiaries were built in Leavenworth, Kansas; Atlanta, Georgia; and McNeil Island, Washington.[40] Prior to the reorganization in 1930, federal prisons operated more or less independently. The prisons were overcrowded and had few health-care providers. By 1930 the system consisted of 7 federal prisons with 12,000 inmates. The 1930 law included a provision for PHS officers to supervise and provide medical, psychiatric, and other scientific services.[38] By September 1930, PHS had provided physicians, dentists, psychologists, and pharmacists to the U.S. penitentiaries at Atlanta and Leavenworth.[41]

The Social Security Act of 1935 emphasized a shared responsibility for public health between the federal government and states. Title VI of the Social Security Act provided $(USD)8 million annually for matching grants to states to stimulate the development of state and local public health programs. Part of the funding was to be used for training state and local health personnel. Over 4000 professional employees in state and local health departments received professional training by 1940. In addition to administering the grants, PHS provided consultation to state and local health departments on many issues, including laboratory methods, nutrition, and dental hygiene.[42] In 1938, the National Venereal Disease Control Act provided grants to states to combat syphilis and gonorrhea. By 1940, clinics for the diagnosis and treatment of venereal diseases had increased from 1750 to 2900.[43]

With advances in public health, the nation shifted its focus from acute infectious disease to chronic diseases leading to high morbidity and mortality. Most disease research funded by the federal government up until this time was done by the PHS through the NIH. This changed with the National Cancer Act of 1937. The Act established the National Cancer Institute and dedicated funding and an extramural grant program for this disease. Federal funding of research done outside the federal government was to become the model as additional institutes were added to NIH.[44]

Under the Reorganization Act of 1939, the Federal Security Agency (FSA) was established. The new agency incorporated the PHS, the Civilian Conservation Corps, the Office of Education, and the Social Security Board. The new agency brought together all federal programs in the fields of health, education, and social security. In 1940, the Food and Drug Administration (FDA) transferred from the Department of Agriculture to FSA.[45]

As the nation entered World War II, the PHS was once again called upon to work on sanitation, water safety, and communicable disease issues affecting both the military and local communities in the United States. PHS officers worked with Army Service Commands assuring food inspection, sewage disposal, and disease control. Over 660 PHS officers were detailed to the U.S. Coast Guard during the war. Other PHS officers coordinated development of state plans setting up a system of hospitals to receive casualties from the war. PHS dentists researched the use of fluoride to prevent tooth carries (400,000 potential military recruits were rejected due to significant tooth loss).[46] To prevent and control disease, PHS detailed hundreds physicians, nurses, and engineers to communities to improve sanitation and local medical facilities. NIH scientists improved vaccines used for yellow fever and plague, treatments for malaria, and ways to improve the drinking water purification processes in tropical areas. In 1942, the Office of Malaria Control in War Areas (which would become the Communicable Disease Center, then the Center for Disease Control in 1970 and finally the Centers for Disease Control and Prevention [CDC] in 1992) conducted mosquito eradication campaigns protecting 1800 war establishments.[47] The PHS Commissioned Corps was declared a part of the military services by a Wartime Presidential Order in 1945. This status remained in effect until July 1952.[14]

Nurses were in short supply before the start of the war. To create additional nurses for both essential civilian and military duty, the Congress passed the Nurse Training Act in June 1943. This Act creating the Cadet Nurse Corps of the PHS provided scholarships and stipends to students enrolled in accredited schools of nursing. Graduates agreed to work in essential nursing services for the duration of the war. Before the program ended in 1948, more than 124,000 nurses completed their training.[48]

Major legislative changes affected the PHS in 1943 and 1944. A 1943 law reorganized the PHS into four components: The Office of the Surgeon General to manage general administration of the PHS, the NIH to conduct and fund scientific research, the Bureau of State Services to administer and coordinate federal–state health programs, and the Bureau of Medical Services (BMS) to administer the hospitals and provide medical care. The BMS' four divisions included Foreign Quarantine Division, Mental Hygiene Division, Federal Employee Health Division, and the Hospital Division. The PHS Act of 1944 strengthened the administrative authority of the surgeon general and codified all of the authorities of the PHS. It authorized commissioning of nurses, dieticians, physical therapists, and sanitarians. This Act also allowed NIH to conduct a postwar grant program for medical research.[49]

The Hospital Survey and Construction Act (Hill–Burton) of 1946 authorized grants to states to survey hospital and health facility needs, plan for additional facilities, and provide federal funding for up to one-third of the construction costs.[50] To assist in the local planning process, floor plans for pharmacies for small, medium, and large hospitals were developed by the PHS Division of Hospital Facilities and published in the May 1946 issue of the journal *Hospital* and the September 1946 *Journal of the American Pharmaceutical Association*.[51]

The Pharmacy Service in the BMS was established in 1947. The first chief of the Pharmacy Branch, Capt George F. Archambault, served in this position from 1947 to 1965. Capt Archambault also provided advice and consultation on pharmacy issues to the PHS leaders serving as the pharmacy liaison to the surgeon general from 1957 to 1965. A strong advocate for the pharmacist's role in protecting patients, he was appointed the Medicare pharmacy planning consultant in 1965, responsible for developing regulations related on pharmacy's role in the Medicare and Medicaid programs.[52] Capt Archambault served as president of both the American Society of Hospital Pharmacists (now the American Society of Health-System Pharmacists) from 1954 to 1955 and the American Pharmaceutical Association (now the American Pharmacists Association) from 1962 to 1963. He also helped found the American Society of Consultant Pharmacists in 1970.[53]

In 1951, the Epidemic Intelligence Service (EIS) was established in the Communicable Disease Center in Atlanta, Georgia. With the outbreak of the Korean War in 1950, the need to have trained epidemiologists to investigate ordinary public health threats and possible biological attacks was essential. The first class of EIS officers in July 1951 consisted of 22 physicians and 1 sanitarian. When these new EIS officers finished their training, approximately half were assigned to positions at CDC, either in headquarters or in field stations. Other graduates were assigned to state epidemiologists and a small number to consultants in universities. As additional EIS officers were trained and more funding become available, more officers were assigned to state and local health departments. Any officer could be called on a moment's notice to respond to a call for epidemic aid from a state. While the vast majority of EIS officers are physicians, professionals in other categories including veterinarians, statisticians, nurses, and pharmacists have completed the EIS training.[54] The first pharmacist to become an EIS officer was Lt Arthur S. Watanabe in 1979.[55]

By presidential executive order in 1953, the FSA was elevated to cabinet status and became the Department of Health, Education, and Welfare (DHEW). The six components of DHEW were the PHS, the Social Security Administration, the FDA, the Office of Education, the Office of Vocational Rehabilitation, and St. Elizabeth's Hospital. In spring of 1955, polio vaccine became the dominant issue for the department and the administration. In the 1950s, the CDC estimated approximately 35,000 cases of paralysis occurred annually in the United States due to polio.[56] In April 1954, a field trial to test the Salk vaccine began with more than 1.8 million children. One year later, in April 1955, trial results showed the vaccine to be safe and effective. The Salk vaccine was rushed to market in April 1955. Cases of polio were reported in newly vaccinated children within the first 2 weeks of mass inoculations. The source of the iatrogenic polio was traced to one of the six vaccine manufacturers, Cutter Laboratories. Overall, 260 cases of polio were attributed to Cutter vaccine, with 192 cases being paralytic.[57] The DHEW secretary and her special assistant for health and medical affairs resigned.[58]

Despite health-care services provided by the Bureau of Indian Affairs, the health of American Indians remained poor. Several studies of Indian health including the Institute for Government Research (1928), the Hoover Commission (1948), and the American Medical Association (1949) showed high rates of infectious disease, including tuberculosis, infant mortality double that of the general population, and a life expectance 10 years less than the general U.S. population. Public health advocates including the American Public Health Association, the American Medical Association, and the Association of State and Territorial Health Officials campaigned to have the responsibility for Indian health care moved to the PHS. The Transfer Act of 1954 was implemented in 1955, moving the responsibility for Indian health care to the PHS DIH (renamed the Indian Health Service [IHS] in 1968). The transfer included 48 hospitals, 130 health centers and school infirmaries, and 2500 staff.[31] The transfer of Indian health programs from the BIA to the PHS DIH in 1955 included the BIA Pharmacy Program. This program, established in 1953, had six pharmacists focused mainly on assuring adequate medication supplies were available at the 48 hospitals. Allen J. Brands was appointed to lead the DIH Pharmacy Program and served as DIH chief pharmacist from 1955 to 1981. His leadership in DIH pharmacy led to Capt Allen Brands being appointed as pharmacy liaison officer to the surgeon general from 1967 to 1981. The title was changed to chief pharmacist officer in 1979, and the position was elevated to the rank of assistant surgeon general (rear admiral).[59]

The second influenza pandemic of the twentieth century swept the United States in 1957 and 1958. The Communicable Disease Center (CDC) estimated that approximately 25% of the U.S. population became infected with the new influenza virus in the last quarter of 1957. While most cases were mild, almost 70,000 deaths were reported by April 1958.[60] In June 1957, CDC staff realized that data gathered through death reports to the National Office of Vital Statistics were insufficient for planning and response to the influenza crisis. They instituted additional reporting requirements that were the beginning of the reporting system used today.[61] The CDC continued to grow throughout the late 1950s and early 1960s adding the PHS' Venereal Disease Division in 1957 and the Tuberculosis Division in 1960. In 1961, the CDC acquired the *Morbidity and Mortality Weekly Report* (MMWR) turning it into the CDC's primary vehicle for providing public health information and recommendations to health-care providers, scientists, and educators.[62]

Surgeon General Luther Terry propelled the Office of the Surgeon General into the media spotlight in 1964 by releasing the landmark report *Smoking and Health: Report of the Advisory Committee to the Surgeon General*. This was not the first time a surgeon general had spoken out about smoking. In 1957, Surgeon General Leroy E. Burney declared that there was evidence pointing to a causal relationship between smoking and lung cancer. The 1964 report was extensive and well documented and clearly showed some of the health risks of tobacco, including a significant increase in mortality for cigarette smokers. This report eventually led to the introduction of the now-familiar surgeon general's warnings on cigarette packages.[63]

Expansion of the health-care professional workforce was a legislative priority in the mid-1960s. The Health Professions Educational Assistance Act (1963), the Nurse Training Act (1964), and the Allied Health Professions Training Act (1966) provided funding for new schools and expansion of existing schools to increase capacity for training health professionals, including physicians, pharmacists, and nurses. The laws also provided scholarship programs and additional funding for student loans.[64] While these programs dramatically increase the number of physicians and other health professionals in the workforce, many areas of the country, especially rural areas and inner cities, continued to have health professional shortages. The National Health Services Corps (NHSC), created in 1970, used student scholarships and loan repayment for health professionals to encourage service in underserved areas. Over the last 40 years, NHSC has provided support to 45,000 primary health-care practitioners working in communities with limited access to primary care.[65]

Legislation creating Medicare and Medicaid in 1965 had a great impact on millions of Americans, but little immediate impact on PHS. While located in DHEW, these health-care financing programs were not in PHS. Other legislation in 1965 had a much greater impact on PHS. The establishment of the Federal Water Pollution Control Administration moved water pollution issues from PHS to the Department of Interior. In 1970, the PHS programs in air pollution and solid waste moved to the newly created Environmental Protection Agency. With these changes, PHS lost its leadership role in federal environmental management.[44]

Two DHEW agencies transferred to the PHS in 1967 and 1968. In an effort to consolidate mental health services and increase opportunities for research, St. Elizabeth's Hospital became part of the National Institute of Mental Health in 1967. This government managed mental health hospital begun in 1855 in Washington, DC.[66] In 1968, the FDA became the major regulatory agency of the PHS. As part of the transfer, the FDA assumed responsibility for assuring safe milk supplies, safe shellfish, and safe food, water, and good sanitary facilities on public transportation; promoting sanitary practices in restaurants; and providing poison control centers with information needed for emergency treatment. In 1972, the regulation of biological drugs was transferred from the NIH to the FDA. The transfer strengthened control over biological products by applying provisions of the Federal Food, Drug, and Cosmetic Act.[67]

The 1960s were a time of clinical growth for DIH pharmacy practice. While many of the innovations of the DIH Pharmacy Program may seem commonplace today, they were far ahead of general pharmacy practice in the 1960s. The original 6 pharmacists in the DIH Pharmacy Program quickly expanded to 19 pharmacists by the end of 1955. The number of pharmacists continued to slowly grow with 30 hospitals having at least one pharmacist by the 1960. DIH pharmacist Albert Ripley, at Crow Agency, began filling physician outpatient prescriptions using the patient's medical record in 1962. Access to the complete medical record allowed the pharmacist to review the diagnosis, physician notes, allergies, laboratory results, and other medications being prescribed. After reviewing the medical record, the pharmacist could contact the physician with any questions or to make recommendations about alternate medication use. Few pharmacists counseled patients about their medications in the mid-1960s. If a patient had a question about their medication, they were referred to their physician. DIH pharmacists were concerned that patients might not know how to take their medication correctly. To assess if there was a problem, a medication compliance review was conducted by pharmacist Ronald Gilbert at Sacaton, Arizona, in 1965. The review found that a large percentage of outpatients were not taking their medications correctly and 18% were not taking their medications at all. The need to talk to patient about their medications was evident, so DIH pharmacists at some sites began counseling patients about their medications. A problem was quickly noted with the medication counseling. Many patients did not want to talk to the pharmacist about their medications. To determine why, a review of patient counseling practices was done at the Whiteriver Indian Hospital in Whiteriver, Arizona, in 1963. At that time, medications were being dispended through a Dutch door, with the pharmacist on one side and the patient on the other and a line of patients in the hall. When asked why they did not want to discuss their medication use with the pharmacist, patients stated they did not want other patients in line could hear the conversation. These and other reviews led to a redesign of DIH outpatient pharmacies. In 1966, the DIH began including private counseling rooms in each pharmacy. By 1980, every pharmacy had at least one counseling room.[68]

By the late 1968, long wait times to see a physician were occurring because many patients were presenting to physicians with minor complaints. To be able to spend time with more seriously ill patients, physicians at the IHS, Red Lake, Minnesota, outpatient clinic trained pharmacists to quickly assess patients presenting at the pharmacy with minor complaints. The pharmacist would then assess the patient and either refer the patient to the outpatient clinic, if appropriate, or document the assessment in the patient's medical record and provide the patient with nonprescription medications for colds, coughs, upset stomachs, headaches, insect bites, eczema, or diarrhea. This process worked well, and by 1970 the first IHS chronic medication management protocols were being developed for pharmacists to manage drug therapy.

By 1970, the number of pharmacists at IHS hospitals and clinics had grown to 120 pharmacists at 72 hospital and clinic pharmacies. IHS pharmacists had established themselves as members of the health-care team. Pharmacists were using the patient medical record to provide patient medication counseling in all but two IHS areas. The number of pharmacists continued to grow with 303 pharmacists in 103 sites by 1980. Many hospitals and clinics now had multiple pharmacists. The military draft was a major factor in the recruitment of the best pharmacists to PHS and IHS. Health professionals could satisfy their selective service requirement by serving 2 years in the PHS Commissioned Corps. This resulted in many applicants for each position. Physicians also joined PHS and IHS to meet their selective service requirement. Young physicians coming to IHS were impressed by the clinical skills of pharmacists and were generally receptive to supporting new pharmacy practice activities.[69]

By 1971, the Phoenix Indian Medical Center had developed guidelines for the expanded role of pharmacists from therapeutic screening to primary care. Each role was detailed, including required approvals, pharmacist training requirements, and program evaluation. By the mid-1970s, these guidelines had been updated to include management of chronic diseases. The guidelines were eventually used throughout the IHS. Pharmacists in Arizona, New Mexico, and Oklahoma were experimenting with different methods of providing medication monitoring and management of chronic disease therapy. Physicians and pharmacists worked together to develop protocols with disease-based guidelines. This allowed physicians to refer stable patients with chronic disease to the pharmacy clinic with the certainty that the pharmacist would be able to provide routine follow-up care. Should a problem arise, the pharmacist would consult with the physician or if needed refer the patient back to the physician for evaluation. Pharmacists used the patient medical record to document their assessment and orders and to record laboratory tests and physical exam results. These programs were the initial step toward IHS pharmacists providing primary care to stable patients using medical staff–approved protocols.[70] In 1996, the IHS director, Dr. Michael Trujillo, codified pharmacists' role as primary care providers via a special memorandum.[71]

The need for additional primary care providers at IHS hospitals and clinics and the demonstrated results from these initial pharmacy programs led to a research grant from the National Center for Health Services Research and Development (NCHSRD) in 1973. The results were submitted to NCHSRD in 1975, and shortly thereafter the IHS Pharmacist Practitioner Training Program (PPTP) was begun. From 1976 to 1980, 60 pharmacists received PPTP training consisting of 530 h of didactic and clinic experience followed by 240 h of physician monitored on-the-job training over 3 months. The PPTP demonstrated that appropriately trained pharmacists could provide a high level of primary care services.[70] In fiscal year 1983, pharmacist primary care providers were seeing 16% of all patients visiting their clinics, with half of the patients treated for acute conditions and half for chronic conditions. An easing of the primary care provider shortage in 1980 led to the discontinuation of the PPTP.[68]

By 1972, PHS consisted of three agencies: the FDA, the NIH, and the Health Services and Mental Health Administration (HSMHA). HSMHA included the IHS, the CDC, PHS hospitals, the Nation Institute of Mental Health, and many other programs. In 1973, PHS was reorganized into six agencies. These were the FDA, NIH, CDC, Health Services Administration (HSA), Health Resources Administration (HRA), and the Alcohol, Drug Abuse and Mental Health Administration (ADAMHA). The HRA contained the PHS health delivery activities, while the HSA contained training, facilities, and construction programs. The ADAMHA was responsible for community-based treatment and prevention and research.[72]

The global eradication of smallpox was achieved in 1979. The Global Smallpox Eradication Program, begun by the World Health Organization in 1967, was directed by CDC scientist Dr. D.A. Henderson. The program worked with 20 countries in Africa to provide disease surveillance and vaccination in every country. Over 300 CDC staff took part in the eradication effort. On December 9, 1979, 2 years after the last case of smallpox in Merka, Somalia, the World Health Organization officially certified that smallpox had been eradicated.[66]

The first pharmacist appointed as commissioner of the FDA was Jere E. Goyan, PhD, in 1979. Dr. Goyan's tenure involved several high-profile FDA issues, including an attempt to require patient package inserts and the investigation of polychlorinated biphenyl contamination of livestock and feed.[73]

The 1980s were a time of change for the department. A separate department of education was created, taking education activities out of DHEW. The department was renamed the Department of Health and Human Services (HHS). The Omnibus Budget Reconciliation Act of 1981 ended the health program for merchant seamen. The eight remaining BMS hospitals and 27 clinics were closed. While this ended the health-care program for which the PHS had been founded, the PHS still provided health-care services to American Indians and Alaska Natives, federal prisoners, and members of the U.S. Coast Guard and their families.[74] Also in 1981, the CDC's MMWR reported the first diagnosis of the fatal disease known as acquired immunodeficiency syndrome (AIDS). By 1984, the NIH and French scientists had identified the human immunodeficiency virus (HIV) that caused AIDS. The release of *The Surgeon General's Report on Acquired Immune Deficiency Syndrome*, in October 1986, generated a moral and political debate about AIDS. In 1988, the PHS brochure *Understanding AIDS* was sent to all 107 million households in the United States.[75]

In 1982, seven people died after taking cyanide-laced Extra Strength Tylenol capsules. To help prevent future poisonings, the FDA issued tamper-resistant packaging regulations for over-the-counter medications. Two additional deaths in 1991 from cyanide-laced Sudafed capsules led the FDA to strengthen the requirements.[76] In 1983, the Orphan Drug Act was passed to stimulate the development of drugs for rare diseases. The FDA Office of Orphan Products Development managed this program.[77] The dangers of secondhand smoke were detailed in the 1986 release of the surgeon general's report on the dangers of passive smoking.[78] In 1987, the IHS was elevated to an agency in HHS. In 1989, the NIH established the National Center for Human Genome Research to carry out the NIH role in the International Human Genome Project. In 2003, the human genome sequence was completed.[79]

The 1990s saw many changes to the medication dispensing and approval process. The Omnibus Budget Reconciliation Act of 1990 modified the Medicaid Act creating new requirements for state prospective drug use review (DUR) programs. The law also created requirements for pharmacists to complete DURs, maintain a patient medication profile, and offer patient medication counseling.[80] To assure that pharmacists and pharmacy students could provide effective medication counseling, the IHS created a patient consultation video (demonstrating the IHS three prime questions and a show-and-tell technique). This video was distributed to pharmacy schools and professional organizations nationwide.

Several FDA programs saw changes in the 1990s. Legislation in 1992 required the FDA to charge drug and biologics manufacturers fees for product applications and other services. These fees (know as user fees) allowed the FDA to hire additional reviewers to speed the regulatory review process. In 1993, the FDA MedWatch program was created. This program consolidated several adverse reaction report systems and allowed voluntary reporting of medical product problems by health professionals. The 1997, the FDA Modernization Act reauthorized user fees. It also provided accelerated review of devices and regulated advertising for unapproved uses for approved drugs and devices.[77]

The PHS Commissioned Corps learned how to respond to disasters in the 1990s. Physicians, nurses, pharmacists, sanitarians, and other officers deployed to provide health care to victims and rescue workers in several natural and manmade disasters. These included the Northridge earthquake in California (1994), tropical storm Alberto (1994), the Alfred P. Murrah Federal Building, Oklahoma City, bombing (1995), and hurricanes Opal and Marilyn (1995). Identifying a need for essential medical supplies after a disaster or terrorist event, in 1999 the CDC established the National Pharmaceutical Stockpile (NPS). States developed plans to receive and distribute these supplies during an emergency. The NPS is later renamed the Strategic National Stockpile.[81]

Disaster preparedness and response and humanitarian health missions were a priority for HHS and the PHS Commissioned Corps in the first decade of this century. The terrorist attacks of September 11, 2001, affected all Americans. PHS Commissioned Corps officers deployed to assist in the cleanup and recovery operations that started shortly after the attacks at the World Trade Center, Pentagon, and Pennsylvania. PHS officers, including pharmacists, provided health-care services to emergency response workers in New York. In October 2001, CDC investigators and PHS Commissioned Corps officers, including pharmacists, responded to the anthrax letter attacks in Washington, DC, and New York. Hundreds of postal workers, congressional staff, and others potentially affected by letters containing anthrax were interviewed and evaluated for exposure. PHS pharmacists provided those potentially exposed with medications and medication counseling. In total, over 900 Commissioned Corps officers responded to these disasters.[82] In 2002, the HHS created the Office of Public Health Emergency Preparedness to coordinate HHS response to bioterrorism and other emergency health threats.

The 2005 hurricane season devastated the gulf coast. Over 2100 commissioned officers, including approximately 400 pharmacists, were deployed to support the evacuation and recovery efforts from hurricanes Katrina, Rita, Wilma, Ophelia, and Dennis. Working with military personnel, and state and local responders, PHS officers led medical teams, immunization teams, assessment teams, and special needs shelter operations.[83]

The PHS Commissioned Corps was deployed in support of U.S. government health diplomacy missions in 2007, 2008, and 2009. These missions delivered humanitarian assistance, performed public health assessments, and conducted public health infrastructure repairs in the Caribbean, Latin America, the Pacific Rim, and Pacific Islands.[84]

In 2003, the Centers for Medicare and Medicaid Services (CMS) was created, replacing the Health Care Financing Administration. That same year, Medicare expanded to include a prescription drug benefit with the passage of the Medicare Prescription Drug Improvement and Modernization Act. Implemented in January 2006, this program affected every Medicare beneficiary by changing the way the federal government paid for outpatient medications. The Act also required medication therapy management programs to optimize therapeutic outcomes for patients taking multiple medications.[85] The CMS again assumed leadership for a major new health program in 2010. The passage of the Patient Protection and Affordable Care Act put in place comprehensive U.S. health insurance reforms.[86]

In 2012, sterile drug compounding made national news headlines. A fungal meningitis outbreak associated with a compounded sterile drug resulted in over 750 cases of infections and in 64 deaths. By February 2014, a total of 33 firms had conducted recalls overseen by the FDA and 7 firms had conducted recalls overseen by a state. In November 2013, President Obama signed the Drug Quality and Security Act that provides the FDA with additional responsibilities to oversee compounding activities.[87]

HHS and PHS Commissioned Corps Today

In 2014, the HHS had over 77,000 employees and a budget of over $(USD)962 billion.[88] The HHS used its 11 agencies (Table 28.1) and over 300 programs (and $[USD]962 billion budget) to meet its mission "to help provide the building blocks that Americans need to live healthy, successful lives." HHS civilian and PHS Commissioned Corps personnel worked side by side to accomplish this mission.

Over the last 80 years, legislation has mandated that the HHS provide personnel resources to select federal and nonfederal programs (Table 28.2). Generally, these organizations either do not have their own system of health-care professionals, need specific expertise already available in the HHS, or may have difficulty recruiting certain types of health professionals. PHS Commissioned Corps officers are assigned to these organizations, and the HHS receives reimbursement for the salaries of these officers. By increasing the number of officers in outside organizations, the HHS

Table 28.1 Organizational Structure of the Department of Health and Human Services

Administration for Children and Families (ACF)
Administration for Community Living (ACL)
Agency for Healthcare Research and Quality (AHRQ)
Agency for Toxic Substances and Disease Registry (ATSDR)
Centers for Disease Control and Prevention (CDC)
Centers for Medicare and Medicaid Services (CMS)
Food and Drug Administration (FDA)
Health Resources and Services Administration (HRSA)
Indian Health Service (IHS)
National Institutes of Health (NIH)
Substance Abuse and Mental Health Services Administration (SAMHSA)

Table 28.2 Other Departments, Agencies, Bureaus, and Commissions Employing Public Health Service Officers

Department of Agriculture (USDA)
Department of Defense (DOD)[a]
Department of Justice (DOJ)[b]
Department of Homeland Security (DHS)[c]
Department of Interior (DOI)[d]
District of Columbia Commission on Mental Health Services (CMHS)
Environmental Protection Agency (EPA)

Source: U.S. Department of Health and Human Services, Commissioned Corps of the U.S. Public Health Service, Non-HHS Agencies and Programs, http://www.usphs.gov/aboutus/agencies/non-hhs.aspx, Updated November 22, 2011, Accessed March 31, 2014.

[a] Includes TRICARE Management Authority.
[b] Includes the Federal Bureau of Prisons and the U.S. Marshal Service.
[c] Includes the U.S. Immigration and Customs Enforcement Health Service Corps and U.S. Coast Guard.
[d] Includes the National Park Service.

not only helps these organizations meet their own missions, but also the HHS has additional officers they can call upon in the event of a disaster response.

The PHS Commissioned Corps was created in 1889. While established along military lines, it is not one of the military services of the United States (i.e., Air Force, Army, Marine Corps, Navy, and Coast Guard). As one of the seven uniformed services of the United States (Table 28.3),

Table 28.3 Seven Uniformed Services of the United States

Department of Commerce
• Commissioned Corps of the National Oceanic and Atmospheric Administration
Department of Defense
• U.S. Air Force
• U.S. Army
• U.S. Marine Corps
• U.S. Navy
Department of Health and Human Services
• U.S. Public Health Service Commissioned Corps
Department of Homeland Security
• U.S. Coast Guard

the PHS Commissioned Corps can become part of the military, by executive order, during a time of war. The PHS Commissioned Corps' mission is "to protect, promote, and advance the health and safety of our Nation. As America's uniformed service of public health professionals, the Commissioned Corps achieves its mission through: rapid and effective response to public health needs, leadership and excellence in public health practices, and advancement of public health science."[90]

Table 28.4 Total Officers and Pharmacists in the Public Health Service Commissioned Corps

Department, Agency, or Commission	*Officers*	*Pharmacists*
Administration for Children and Families	7	0
Administration for Community Living	0	0
Agency for Healthcare Research and Quality	8	1
Agency for Toxic Substances and Disease Registry	38	0
Centers for Disease Control and Prevention	921	19
Centers for Medicare and Medicaid Services	165	32
Department of Agriculture	20	0
Department of Defense	266	13
Department of Justice	13	0
Department of Homeland Security	498	34
Department of Interior	49	0
District of Columbia Commission on Mental Health Services	19	9
Environmental Protection Agency	63	0
Federal Bureau of Prisons	881	154
Food and Drug Administration	1021	368
Health Resources and Services Administration	194	16
Indian Health Service	2075	572
National Institutes of Health	296	10
Office of the Secretary	173	14
Program Support Center	35	0
Substance Abuse and Mental Health Services Administration	51	7
U.S. Army Medical Reserve Corps	1	0
Total	6794	1240

As of March 31, 2014, Commissioned Corps officers constituted approximately 9% of HHS employees. There were approximately 1640 pharmacists in HHS of which 1240 were PHS Commissioned Corps officers (Table 28.4).[91] There were approximately 400 civil service pharmacists in HHS, most working in the FDA. Most PHS Commissioned Corps pharmacists serve in three organizations: the IHS, the FDA, and the BOP.

Most pharmacists begin their PHS Commissioned Corps career in a clinical care setting (e.g., IHS, BOP, Commission on Mental Health Services [CMHS], Department of Homeland Security [DHS]). Some pharmacists will remain in the clinical setting their entire career, moving up the clinical tract or moving into pharmacy administration at a hospital or clinic. Other pharmacists will decide to move to a different type of health-care practice where they can use their pharmacy knowledge and experience. PHS pharmacists have the ability to specialize in regulatory affairs (e.g., FDA), research (e.g., NIH), health access (e.g., Health Resources and Services Administration [HRSA]), or surveillance/epidemiology/disaster response (e.g., CDC).

Clinical Care (IHS, BOP, CMHS, DHS)

The IHS is the principal federal health-care provider and health advocate for 1.9 million American Indians and Alaska Natives who belong to 566 federally recognized tribes in 35 states. IHS' goal is to raise their health status to the highest possible level. The IHS has approximately 15,000 employees and a fiscal year 2014 budget of $(USD)4.58 billion. Pharmacists in the IHS work in a variety of practice settings from small ambulatory clinics to large hospitals. Pharmacists use the electronic health record to assess the appropriateness of medication therapy. IHS pharmacists at many facilities can become credentialed to provide primary care services.[92]

The BOP mission, as part of the U.S. Department of Justice, is to protect society by confining over 216,000 offenders in 147 prisons and community-based facilities. Commissioned Corps officers work for the Health Services Division and provide and manage a variety of physical and mental health-care services. The BOP has over 39,000 employees and a fiscal year 2014 budget of $(USD)6.9 billion. Pharmacists in the BOP use the electronic health record to assess patient care and provide complete clinical pharmacy services. They are part of a clinical health-care team and have the ability to provide pharmacy managed care clinics.[93]

The District of Columbia CMHS (formerly St. Elizabeth's Hospital) works to establish a community-based system of care for individuals in Washington, DC, who experience mental health problems. St. Elizabeth's Hospital is the district's public psychiatric facility for individuals with serious and persistent mental illness. The new 450,000 square foot, state-of-the-art facility completed in April 2010 provides intensive inpatient care. Commissioned Corps pharmacists working at St. Elizabeth's Hospital provide both general medical and psychiatry pharmacy care.[94]

The U.S. DHS, established in 2002, works to protect the nation and ensure safe and secure borders. Commissioned Corps pharmacists working in DHS serve in either the Immigration and Customs Enforcement (ICE) Health Service Corps or the U.S. Coast Guard. The ICE had a custody operations budget of over $(USD)2 billion in fiscal year 2012. The ICE Health Service Corps staff consists of more than 900 federal and contract support staff (19 are PHS Commissioned Corps pharmacists). ICE Health Service Corps provides direct care to approximately 15,000 detainees housed at 21 designated facilities throughout the nation.[95] ICE Health Service Corps pharmacists provide ambulatory care pharmacy services for detainees. The U.S. Coast Guard has a budget of over $(USD)10 billion of which $(USD)185 million was allocated for health services in fiscal year 2014. The U.S. Coast Guard has over 43,000 active duty members and over 8,800 civilian employees. Among the 15 pharmacist positions, 13 pharmacists assigned to field billets provide pharmaceutical care to coast guard members and their families. These 13 pharmacists oversee 40 coast guard clinics and over 150 independent duty sites. Each pharmacy officer not only is responsible for total pharmacy operations at their assigned clinics but also has the responsibility of collateral sites assigned to their area of responsibility. Pharmacists in the coast guard tend to be individuals with former military experience with good clinical and managerial skills.[96]

Regulatory Affairs (FDA)

The FDA ensures the safety of foods and cosmetics and the safety and efficacy of pharmaceuticals, biological products, and medical devices. The FDA has over 13,000 employees and a fiscal year 2014 budget of over $(USD)4.6 billion. Most FDA employees work in either the Center for Drug Evaluation and Research or the Office of Regulatory Affairs. Most FDA pharmacists review new, generic, and orphan drug applications, work in adverse event reporting, or conduct audits of manufacturing facilities.[87]

Research (NIH)

The NIH is the nation's medical research agency. Composed of 27 institutes and centers, the NIH provides leadership and financial support for 50,000 competitive grants to more than 300,000 researchers at more than 2,500 universities, medical schools, and other research institutions. About 10% of the NIH's budget supports projects conducted by nearly 6000 scientists in its own laboratories. The NIH has over 18,000 employees and a fiscal year 2014 budget over $(USD)30 billion. Most PHS Commissioned Corps pharmacists work in the NIH Clinical Center Hospital inpatient pharmacy. Pharmacists also manufacture medications for drug studies and serve on investigational drug protocol teams.[97]

Health Access (HRSA)

The HRSA directs programs that improve the nation's health by assuring access to comprehensive, quality health care. The HRSA works to improve and extend life for people living with HIV/AIDS, provide primary health care to medically underserved people, serve women and children through state programs, and train a health workforce motivated to work in underserved communities. The HRSA has over 1800 employees and a fiscal year 2014 budget of over $(USD)8 billion. Most HRSA pharmacists work in the Office of Pharmacy Affairs administering the 340B Drug Pricing Program. The 340B Drug Pricing Program requires drug manufacturers to provide outpatient drugs at significantly reduced prices to eligible health-care organizations/covered entities.[98]

Surveillance/Epidemiology/Disaster Response (e.g., CDC)

The CDC serves as the national focus for developing and applying disease prevention and control, environmental health, and health promotion and health education activities designed to improve peoples' health. The CDC also has a major role in protecting the public from chemical or biological terrorism. PHS Commissioned Corps pharmacists manage the Strategic National Stockpile to provide states additional resources during disasters.[99]

Conclusion

The PHS has continued to grow and evolve over the last 200 years. From its humble beginnings as a provider of health-care services to sailors, it has evolved to include research, regulatory affairs, health policy, and disaster response becoming the premiere health organization in the world. PHS pharmacists have also used their knowledge and skills to grow along with the PHS. In the years to come, there will be a continuing need for both PHS and PHS pharmacists to be innovators in advancing and protecting the public health.

Disclaimer

The views and statements expressed in this chapter are solely those of the author and do not necessarily reflect the opinions of the United States Department of Health and Human Services, United States Public Health Service, or other federal agencies.

References

1. Thurm R. *For the Relief of the Sick and Disabled: A History of the First U.S. Public Health Service Hospital*, Pub No. 1729-0010. Washington, DC: U.S. Department of Health, Education, and Welfare, 1970, pp. 19–26.
2. Williams R. *The United States Public Health Service 1798–1950*. Washington, DC: Commissioned Officers Association of the United States Public Health Service, 1951, pp. 29–41.
3. U.S. Department of Health and Human Services, SurgeonGeneral.gov, Previous Surgeons General. John Maynard Woodworth (1871–1879). http://www.surgeongeneral.gov/about/previous/biowoodworth.html. Updated January 4, 2007. Accessed March 28, 2014.
4. Mullan F. *Plagues and Politics: The Story of the United States Public Health Service*. New York: Basic Books, 1989, p. 20.
5. Williams R. *The United States Public Health Service 1798–1950*. Washington, DC: Commissioned Officers Association of the United States Public Health Service, 1951, pp. 530–531.
6. Furman B. *A Profile of the United States Public Health Service: 1798–1948*, Pub No. 73-369. Washington, DC: U.S. Department of Health, Education, and Welfare, 1973, p. 129.
7. Michael JM. The National Board of Health: 1879–1883. *Public Health Reports*. January–February 2011;126(1):123–129.
8. Williams R. *The United States Public Health Service 1798–1950*. Washington, DC: Commissioned Officers Association of the United States Public Health Service, 1951, pp. 80–84.
9. United States Public Health Service. *Official List of Commissioned and Noncommissioned Officers of the Public Health and Marine-Hospital Service of the United States; Also List of U.S. Marine Hospitals, Quarantine Stations, and Quarantine Vessels July 1905. Pub No. 11*. Washington, DC: Government Printing Office, 1905, pp. 24, 25.
10. Furman B. *A Profile of the United States Public Health Service: 1798–1948*, Pub No. 73-369. Washington, DC: U.S. Department of Health, Education, and Welfare, 1973, pp. 208–211, 254.
11. Williams R. *The United States Public Health Service 1798–1950*. Washington, DC: Commissioned Officers Association of the United States Public Health Service, 1951, pp. 176–181.
12. United States Public Health Service. *Official List of Commissioned and Noncommissioned Officers of the Public Health and Marine-Hospital Service of the United States; Also List of U.S. Marine Hospitals, Quarantine Stations, and Quarantine Vessels July 1905*. Pub No. 11. Washington, DC: Government Printing Office, 1905, pp. 17, 22.
13. Mullan F. *Plagues and Politics: The Story of the United States Public Health Service*. New York: Basic Books, 1989, p. 31.

14. Parascandola J. History of the militarization of the PHS Commissioned Corps. *Commissioned Corps Bulletin*. October 2001;15(10):5.
15. Williams R. *The United States Public Health Service 1798–1950*. Washington, DC: Commissioned Officers Association of the United States Public Health Service, 1951, pp. 559–560.
16. Furman B. *A Profile of the United States Public Health Service: 1798–1948*, Pub No. 73-369. Washington, DC: U.S. Department of Health, Education, and Welfare, 1973, pp. 199–215.
17. Kondratas R. *Images from the History of the Public Health Service*. Washington, DC: U.S. Department of Health and Human Services, Public Health Service, 1994, pp. 20–22.
18. Furman B. *A Profile of the United States Public Health Service: 1798–1948*, Pub No. 73-369. Washington, DC: U.S. Department of Health, Education, and Welfare, 1973, pp. 248–250.
19. U.S. Department of Health and Human Services, U.S. Food and Drug Administration. About FDA. The St. Louis Tragedy and Enactment of the 1902 Biologics Control Act. 2009. http://www.fda.gov/AboutFDA/WhatWeDo/History/ProductRegulation/100YearsofBiologicsRegulation/ucm070022.htm. Updated April 9, 2009. Accessed March 31, 2014.
20. Gibson E. *Under the Cliffs of Molokai*. Fresno, CA: Academy Library Guild, 1957, pp. 18–26.
21. Parascandola J. The Gillis W. Long Hansen's Disease Center at Carville. *Public Health Reports*. November–December 1994;109(6):728–730.
22. U.S. Department of Health and Human Services, SurgeonGeneral.gov, Previous Surgeons General. Rupert Blue (1912–1919). http://www.surgeongeneral.gov/about/previous/bioblue.html. Updated January 4, 2007. Accessed March 31, 2014.
23. Furman B. *A Profile of the United States Public Health Service: 1798–1948*, Pub No. 73-369. Washington, DC: U.S. Department of Health, Education, and Welfare, 1973, pp. 288–303.
24. Williams R. *The United States Public Health Service 1798–1950*. Washington, DC: Commissioned Officers Association of the United States Public Health Service, 1951, p. 48.
25. Williams R. *The United States Public Health Service 1798–1950*. Washington, DC: Commissioned Officers Association of the United States Public Health Service, 1951, pp. 560–579.
26. Furman B. *A Profile of the United States Public Health Service: 1798–1948*, Pub No. 73-369. Washington, DC: U.S. Department of Health, Education, and Welfare, 1973, p. 326.
27. Williams R. *The United States Public Health Service 1798–1950*. Washington, DC: Commissioned Officers Association of the United States Public Health Service, 1951, pp. 597–602.
28. Williams R. *The United States Public Health Service 1798–1950*. Washington, DC: Commissioned Officers Association of the United States Public Health Service, 1951, pp. 602–607.
29. Furman B. *A Profile of the United States Public Health Service: 1798–1948*, Pub No. 73-369. Washington, DC: U.S. Department of Health, Education, and Welfare, 1973, p. 331.
30. Williams R. *The United States Public Health Service 1798–1950*. Washington, DC: Commissioned Officers Association of the United States Public Health Service, 1951, pp. 605–611.
31. Johnson E, Rhoades E. The history and organization of Indian health services and systems. In Rhoades E (Ed.), *American Indian Health: Innovations in Health Care, Promotion, and Policy*. Baltimore, MD: The Johns Hopkins University Press, 2000, p. 75–76.
32. Williams R. *The United States Public Health Service 1798–1950*. Washington, DC: Commissioned Officers Association of the United States Public Health Service, 1951, pp. 427–428.
33. United States Public Health Service. *Official List of Commissioned and Noncommissioned Officers of the Public Health and Marine-Hospital Service of the United States; Also List of U.S. Marine Hospitals, Quarantine Stations, and Quarantine Vessels July 1905*. Pub No. 11. Washington, DC: Government Printing Office, 1905, pp. 14,43.
34. Williams R. *The United States Public Health Service 1798–1950*. Washington, DC: Commissioned Officers Association of the United States Public Health Service, 1951, pp. 93–94, 453.
35. Mullan F. *Plagues and Politics: The Story of the United States Public Health Service*. New York: Basic Books, 1989, p. 86.
36. Furman B. *A Profile of the United States Public Health Service: 1798–1948*, Pub No. 73-369. Washington, DC: U.S. Department of Health, Education, and Welfare, 1973, pp. 355, 386.

37. United States Public Health Service. *Official List of Commissioned and Noncommissioned Officers of the Public Health and Marine-Hospital Service of the United States; Also List of U.S. Marine Hospitals, Quarantine Stations, and Quarantine Vessels July 1905*. Pub No. 11. Washington, DC: Government Printing Office, 1905, p. 14.
38. Mullan F. *Plagues and Politics: The Story of the United States Public Health Service*. New York: Basic Books, 1989, p. 90.
39. *Official List of Commissioned and Other Officers of the United States Public Health Service; Also A List of All Stations of the Service January 1, 1933*, Pub No. 11. Washington, DC: Government Printing Office, 1933, pp. 13, 37.
40. Keve P. *Prisons and the American Conscience: A History of U.S. Federal Corrections*. Carbondale, IL: Southern Illinois University Press, 1991, pp. 1–13.
41. *Official List of Commissioned and Other Officers of the United States Public Health Service; Also A List of U.S. Marine Hospitals, Quarantine, Immigration, Relief Stations and Quarantine Vessels October 1, 1930*, Pub No. 11. Washington, DC: Government Printing Office, 1931, p. 65.
42. Mullan F. *Plagues and Politics: The Story of the United States Public Health Service*. New York: Basic Books, 1989, pp. 105–107.
43. Williams R. *The United States Public Health Service 1798–1950*. Washington, DC: Commissioned Officers Association of the United States Public Health Service, 1951, pp. 155–156.
44. Mullan F. *Plagues and Politics: The Story of the United States Public Health Service*. New York: Basic Books, 1989, p. 111.
45. U.S. Department of Health and Human Services, Assistant Secretary for Planning and Evaluation. *A Common Thread of Service. An Historical Guide to HEW*, Excerpt from DHEW Publication No. (OS) 73-45, July 1, 1972. http://aspe.hhs.gov/info/hewhistory.htm. Accessed March 31, 2014.
46. Mullan F. *Plagues and Politics: The Story of the United States Public Health Service*. New York: Basic Books, 1989, pp. 112–116.
47. Mountin J, Kovar E. *Emergency Health and Sanitation Activities of the Public Health Service during World War II*, Public Health Bulletin. No. 302. Washington, DC: Government Printing Office, 1949, pp. 20–38, 46–52, 69–78.
48. Willever H. The Cadet Nurse Corps, 1943–1948. *Public Health Reports*. May–June 1994;109(3): 455–457.
49. Parascandola J. Commissioned Officers Association of the USPHS, Inc. Public Health History. 2012. http://www.coausphs.org/phhistory4.cfm. Updated January 17, 2012. Accessed April 2, 2014.
50. Hoge V. The Hospital Survey and Construction Act. *Social Security Bulletin*. October 1946; 9(10):15–17.
51. Plans for a hospital pharmacy. *Journal of the American Pharmaceutical Association*. 1946;7(9):418–21.
52. Worthen D. George Francis Archambault (1909–2001). *Journal of the American Pharmacists Association*. 2003;43(3):441–442.
53. U.S. Department of Health and Human Services, U.S. Public Health Service Commissioned Corps, USPHS Professional Advisory Committee—Chief Pharmacists, Pharmacy Chief Professional Officers. CAPT George Archambault (August 14, 1959 to May 1, 1967). http://www.usphs.gov/corpslinks/pharmacy/aboutus_phcpos.aspx. Updated March 11, 2013. Accessed March 31, 2014.
54. Langmuir A. The Epidemic Intelligence Service of the Center for Disease Center. *Public Health Reports*. September–October 1980;95(5):470–474.
55. Epidemic Intelligence Service Officer by Class Year, 1951–2005. *American Journal of Epidemiology*. 2011;174(Suppl 11):i–x. http://aje.oxfordjournals.org/content/174/suppl_11/i.full.
56. Centers for Disease Control and Prevention. A polio-free U.S. Thanks to vaccine efforts. 2014. http://www.cdc.gov/features/poliofacts/. Updated February 12, 2014. Accessed March 31, 2014.
57. U.S. Food and Drug Administration, Center for Biologics Evaluation and Research. Science and the regulation of biological products. The story of polio vaccine. 2013. http://www.fda.gov/downloads/aboutfda/whatwedo/history/productregulation/100yearsofbiologicsregulation/ucm070313.pdf. Updated July 3, 2013. Accessed December 5, 2015.
58. Mullan F. *Plagues and Politics: The Story of the United States Public Health Service*. New York: Basic Books, 1989, p. 134.

59. U.S. Department of Health and Human Services, U.S. Public Health Service Commissioned Corps, USPHS Professional Advisory Committee—Chief Pharmacists. RADM Allen J. Brands (May 2, 1967–April 1, 1981). http://www.usphs.gov/corpslinks/pharmacy/aboutus_phcpos.aspx. Updated March 11, 2013. Accessed March 31, 2014.
60. Henederson D, Courtney B, Inglesby TV, Toner E, Nuzzo JB. Public health and medical responses to the 1957–58 influenza pandemic. *Biosecurity and Bioterrorism: Biodefense Strategy, Practice, and Science*. 2009;7(3):265–272.
61. Centers for Disease Control and Prevention, CDC Epidemiology Branch. Alert to possible influenza outbreaks. 1957. http://portaldev.rti.org/10_Midas_Docs/CDCFlu/CDC_Influenza_Report_1957.pdf. Accessed March 31, 2014.
62. Mullan F. *Plagues and Politics: The Story of the United States Public Health Service*. New York: Basic Books, 1989, p. 141.
63. U.S. Department of Health and Human Services, National Institutes of Health, U.S National Library of Medicine. The reports of the Surgeon General. The 1964 report on smoking and health. 1964. http://profiles.nlm.nih.gov/ps/retrieve/Narrative/NN/p-nid/60. Updated December 3, 2013. Accessed March 31, 2014.
64. Mullan F. *Plagues and Politics: The Story of the United States Public Health Service*. New York: Basic Books, 1989, p. 150.
65. Health Resources and Services Administration, National Health Service Corps. https://nhsc.hrsa.gov/corpsexperience/aboutus/missionhistory/index.html. Accessed March 31, 2014.
66. Mullan F. *Plagues and Politics: The Story of the United States Public Health Service*. New York: Basic Books, 1989, pp. 156–157.
67. U.S. Food and Drug Administration. The story of the laws behind the labels. 1981. http://www.fda.gov/AboutFDA/WhatWeDo/History/Overviews/ucm056044.htm. Updated March 11, 2014. Accessed March 31, 2014.
68. Brands AJ. [Presentation]. *Proceedings of the Third Drug Symposium in Saudi Arabia on Role of Pharmacy in Health Care*. College of Pharmacy, King Saud University, Riyadh, Saudi Arabia. November 18–21, 1984.
69. Fisher R, Brands A, Herrier R. History of the Indian Health Service model of pharmacy practice: Innovations in pharmaceutical care. *Pharmacy in History*. 1995;37(2):107–116.
70. Fisher R, Brands A, Herrier R. History of the Indian Health Service model of pharmacy practice: Innovations in pharmaceutical care. *Pharmacy in History*. 1995;37(2):115–122.
71. Indian Health Service, Indian Health Manual. Special General Memorandum 96-2. Designation of pharmacists as primary care providers with prescriptive authority. 1996. http://www.ihs.gov/ihm/index.cfm?module=dsp_ihm_sgm_main&sgm=ihm_sgm_9602. Accessed March 31, 2014.
72. Mullan F. *Plagues and Politics: The Story of the United States Public Health Service*. New York: Basic Books, 1989, p. 177.
73. U.S. Food and Drug Administration. Commissioner's Page. 2009. Jere E. Goyan, Ph.D. http://www.fda.gov/AboutFDA/CommissionersPage/ucm113340.htm. Updated June 4, 2009. Accessed March 31, 2014.
74. Mullan F. *Plagues and Politics: The Story of the United States Public Health Service*. New York: Basic Books, 1989, p. 201.
75. Mullan F. *Plagues and Politics: The Story of the United States Public Health Service*. New York: Basic Books, 1989, p. 204.
76. Pharmaceutical and Medical Packaging News. Sealed two-piece capsules mandatory. 2009. http://www.pmpnews.com/article/sealed-two-piece-capsules-mandatory. Accessed March 31, 2014.
77. U.S. Department of Health and Human Services, U.S. Food and Drug Administration. About FDA. Significant dates in U.S. Food and Drug Law history. 2014. http://www.fda.gov/AboutFDA/WhatWeDo/History/Milestones/ucm128305.htm. Updated March 25, 2014. Accessed March 31, 2014.
78. U.S. Department of Health and Human Services, SurgeonGeneral.gov, Previous Surgeons General. C. Everett Koop (1982–1989). 2007. http://www.surgeongeneral.gov/about/previous/biokoop.html. Updated January 4, 2007. Accessed March 31, 2014.
79. National Institutes of Health, National Human Genome Research Institute. About NHGRI: A brief history and timeline. 2014. http://www.genome.gov/10001763. Updated January 13, 2014. Accessed March 31, 2014.
80. Spector S, Youdelman M. *Analysis of State Pharmacy Laws: Impact of Pharmacy Laws on the Provision of Language Services*. Washington, DC: National Health Law Program, 2010, pp. 7–8.

81. U.S. Department of Health and Human Services, Centers for Disease Control and Prevention, Office of Public Health Preparedness and Response. Strategic National Stockpile (SNS). 2012. http://www.cdc.gov/phpr/stockpile/stockpile.htm. Updated October 15, 2012. Accessed March 31, 2014.
82. Statement of the Commissioned Officers Association of the U.S. Public Health Service (COA) before the military compensation and retirement modernization commission on uniformed services pay and benefits. http://www.coausphs.org/docs/news/COA%20MCRMC%20Testimony%20-%20Statement%20for%20record.pdf. Accessed March 31, 2014.
83. Department of Health and Human Services, Office of the Inspector General. The Commissioned Corps' response to Hurricanes Katrina and Rita. February 2007. http://oig.hhs.gov/oei/reports/oei-09-06-00030.pdf. Accessed March 31, 2014.
84. Galson S. USPHS Commissioned Corps: A global emergency preparedness and response asset. *Public Health Reports*. September–October 2009;124(5):622–623.
85. Academy of Managed Care Pharmacy. Medication Therapy Management (MTM) resources. http://www.amcp.org/MTMResources/. Accessed 2016.
86. Centers for Medicare and Medicaid Services, The Center for Consumer Information & Insurance Oversight. Summary of benefits and coverage and uniform glossary. http://www.cms.gov/CCIIO/Programs-and-Initiatives/Consumer-Support-and-Information/Summary-of-Benefits-and-Coverage-and-Uniform-Glossary.html. Accessed March 31, 2014.
87. U.S. Department of Health and Human Services, Food and Drug Administration. FY 2015 justification for estimates for appropriations committees. http://www.fda.gov/downloads/AboutFDA/ReportsManualsForms/Reports/BudgetReports/UCM388309.pdf. Updated March 7, 2014. Accessed March 31, 2014.
88. U.S. Department of Health and Human Services. HHS FY2015 budget in brief. 2014. http://www.hhs.gov/budget/fy2015-hhs-budget-in-brief/hhs-fy2015budget-in-brief-overview.html. Updated March 27, 2014. Accessed March 31, 2014.
89. U.S. Department of Health and Human Services, Commissioned Corps of the U.S. Public Health Service. Non-HHS agencies and programs. 2011. http://www.usphs.gov/aboutus/agencies/non-hhs.aspx. Updated November 22, 2011. Accessed March 31, 2014.
90. U.S. Department of Health and Human Services, Commissioned Corps of the U.S. Public Health Service. Mission and core values. 2014. http://www.usphs.gov/aboutus/mission.aspx. Updated February 3, 2014. Accessed March 31, 2014.
91. U.S. Department of Health and Human Services, Commissioned Corps of the U.S. Public Health Service, Management Information System, Public Statistical Information. Agency vs category. http://dcp.psc.gov/CCMIS/StatusCharts/Public_Pivot.aspx. Accessed March 31, 2014.
92. U.S. Department of Health and Human Services, Indian Health Service. IHS Year 2014 profile. 2014. http://www.ihs.gov/newsroom/factsheets/ihsyear2014profile/. Updated January 2014. Accessed March 31, 2014.
93. U.S. Department of Health and Human Services, U.S. Public Health Service Commissioned Corps. USPHS Professional Advisory Committee—BOP employment. 2014. http://www.usphs.gov/corpslinks/pharmacy/bop_employment.aspx. Updated February 14, 2014. Accessed March 31, 2014.
94. District of Columbia, Department of Behavioral Health, Saint Elizabeths Hospital. http://dmh.dc.gov/page/saint-elizabeths-hospital. Accessed March 31, 2014.
95. U.S. Department of Homeland Security, ICE. ICE Health Service Corps. http://www.ice.gov/about/offices/enforcement-removal-operations/ihs/. Accessed March 31, 2014.
96. U.S. Department of Homeland Security, U.S. Coast Guard, Human Resources. Pharmacy. 2014. http://www.uscg.mil/hr/cg112/cg1122/pharmacy.asp. Updated March 12, 2014. Accessed March 31, 2014.
97. U.S. Department of Health and Human Services, National Institutes of Health. About NIH. 2014. http://www.nih.gov/about/. Updated February 27, 2014. Accessed March 31, 2014.
98. U.S. Department of Health and Human Services, Health Resources and Services Administration. About HRSA. http://www.hrsa.gov/about/index.html. Accessed March 31, 2014.
99. U.S. Department of Health and Human Services, Centers for Disease Control and Prevention. CDC facts. 2010. http://www.cdc.gov/media/subtopic/factsheet.htm. Updated September 10, 2010. Accessed March 31, 2014.

Index

A

B

H

I

J

K

L

M

N

O

P